Asset Pricing Theory and Tests
Volume II

The International Library of Critical Writings in Financial Economics

Series Editor: Richard Roll

Allstate Professor of Economics
The Anderson School at UCLA, USA

This major series presents by field outstanding selections of the most important articles across the entire spectrum of financial economics – one of the fastest growing areas in business schools and economics departments. Each collection has been prepared by a leading specialist who has written an authoritative introduction to the literature.

1. The Theory of Corporate Finance (Volumes I and II)
    Michael J. Brennan
2. Futures Markets (Volumes I, II and III)
    A.G. Malliaris
3. Market Efficiency: Stock Market Behaviour in Theory and Practice (Volumes I and II)
    Andrew W. Lo
4. Microstructure: The Organization of Trading and Short Term Price Behavior (Volumes I and II)
    Hans R. Stoll
5. The Debt Market (Volumes I, II and III)
    Stephen A. Ross
6. Options Markets (Volumes I, II and III)
    George M. Constantinides and A.G. Malliaris
7. Empirical Corporate Finance (Volumes I, II, III and IV)
    Michael J. Brennan
8. The Foundations of Continuous Time Finance
    Stephen M. Schaefer
9. International Securities (Volumes I and II)
    George C. Philippatos and Gregory Koutmos
10. Behavioral Finance (Volumes I, II and III)
    Hersh Shefrin
11. Asset Pricing Theory and Tests (Volumes I and II)
    Robert R. Grauer

Future titles will include:

Financial Forecasting
Roy Batchelor and Pami Dua

Foreign Exchange Markets
Richard J. Sweeney

Financial Markets and the Real Economy
John H. Cochrane

International Capital Markets
G. Andrew Karolyi and René M. Stulz

Emerging Markets
Geert Bekaert and Campbell R. Harvey

Wherever possible, the articles in these volumes have been reproduced as originally published using facsimile reproduction, inclusive of footnotes and pagination to facilitate ease of reference.

For a list of all Edward Elgar published titles visit our site on the World Wide Web at
http://www.e-elgar.co.uk

Asset Pricing Theory and Tests
Volume II

Edited by

Robert R. Grauer

Endowed University Professor, Faculty of Business Administration
Simon Fraser University, Canada

THE INTERNATIONAL LIBRARY OF CRITICAL WRITINGS IN FINANCIAL ECONOMICS

An Elgar Reference Collection
Cheltenham, UK • Northampton, MA, USA

Published by
Edward Elgar Publishing Limited
Glensanda House
Montpellier Parade
Cheltenham
Glos GL50 1UA
UK

Edward Elgar Publishing, Inc.
136 West Street
Suite 202
Northampton
Massachusetts 01060
USA

A catalogue record for this book is available from the British Library

Library of Congress Cataloguing in Publication Data

Asset pricing theory and tests / edited by Robert R. Grauer.
    p. cm. — (The international library of critical writings in financial economics ; 11)
    Includes bibliographical references and index.
    1. Capital assets pricing model. I. Grauer, Robert R., 1947- II. Series.

HG4636 .A86 2003
332.6—dc21   2002040886

ISBN   1 84064 473 7 (2 volume set)

Printed and bound in Great Britain by MPG Books Ltd, Bodmin, Cornwall

Contents

Acknowledgements

The editor and publishers wish to thank the authors and the following publishers who have kindly given permission for the use of copyright material.

Blackwell Publishing Ltd for articles: Richard Roll and Stephen A. Ross (1980), 'An Empirical Investigation of the Arbitrage Pricing Theory', *Journal of Finance*, **XXXV** (5), December, 1073–103; Jay Shanken (1982), 'The Arbitrage Pricing Theory: Is it Testable?', *Journal of Finance*, **XXXVII** (5), December, 1129–40; Douglas T. Breeden, Michael R. Gibbons and Robert H. Litzenberger (1989), 'Empirical Tests of the Consumption-Oriented CAPM', *Journal of Finance*, **XLIV** (2), June, 231–62; Richard Roll and Stephen A. Ross (1994), 'On the Cross-sectional Relation between Expected Returns and Betas', *Journal of Finance*, **XLIX** (1), March, 101–21; Josef Lakonishok, Andrei Shleifer and Robert W. Vishny (1994), 'Contrarian Investment, Extrapolation, and Risk', *Journal of Finance*, **XLIX** (5), December, 1541–78; Shmuel Kandel and Robert F. Stambaugh (1995), 'Portfolio Inefficiency and the Cross-section of Expected Returns', *Journal of Finance*, **L** (1), March, 157–84; S.P. Kothari, Jay Shanken and Richard G. Sloan (1995), 'Another Look at the Cross-section of Expected Stock Returns', *Journal of Finance*, **L** (1), March, 185–224; Ravi Jagannathan and Zhenyu Wang (1996), 'The Conditional CAPM and the Cross-Section of Expected Returns', *Journal of Finance*, **LI** (1), March, 3–53; Raymond Kan and Chu Zhang (1999), 'Two-Pass Tests of Asset Pricing Models with Useless Factors', *Journal of Finance*, **LIV** (1), February, 203–35; Robert R. Grauer (1999), 'On the Cross-Sectional Relation between Expected Returns, Betas, and Size', *Journal of Finance*, **LIV** (2), April, 773–89; Raymond Kan and Guofu Zhou (1999), 'A Critique of the Stochastic Discount Factor Methodology', *Journal of Finance*, **LIV** (4), August, 1221–48; Wayne E. Ferson and Campbell R. Harvey (1999), 'Conditioning Variables and the Cross Section of Stock Returns', *Journal of Finance*, **LIV** (4), August, 1325–60; John Y. Campbell (2000), 'Asset Pricing at the Millennium', *Journal of Finance*, **LV** (4), August, 1515–67.

Elsevier Science for articles: Robert R. Grauer (1978), 'Generalized Two Parameter Asset Pricing Models: Some Empirical Evidence', *Journal of Financial Economics*, **6**, 11–32; A. Craig MacKinlay (1995), 'Multifactor Models Do Not Explain Deviations from the CAPM', *Journal of Financial Economics*, **38**, 3–28.

Oxford University Press for article: Andrew W. Lo and A. Craig MacKinlay (1990), 'Data-Snooping Biases in Tests of Financial Asset Pricing Models', *Review of Financial Studies*, **3** (3), 431–67.

University of Chicago Press for articles: Nai-Fu Chen, Richard Roll and Stephen A. Ross (1986), 'Economic Forces and the Stock Market', *Journal of Business*, **59** (3), 383–403; John H. Cochrane (1996), 'A Cross-Sectional Test of an Investment-Based Asset Pricing Model', *Journal of Political Economy*, **104** (3), 572–621.

Every effort has been made to trace all the copyright holders but if any have been inadvertently overlooked the publishers will be pleased to make the necessary arrangement at the first opportunity.

In addition the publishers wish to thank the Marshall Library of Economics, Cambridge University and the Library of the University of Warwick for their assistance in obtaining these articles.

Part IV
Post-1990 Tests of the Mean-Variance Capital Asset Pricing Model: Criticisms of Testing Methods together with Behavioral and Conditional Alternatives to the Mean-Variance and Three-Factor Models

[1]

Data-Snooping Biases in Tests of Financial Asset Pricing Models

Andrew W. Lo
Sloan School of Management
Massachusetts Institute of Technology

A. Craig MacKinlay
Wharton School
University of Pennsylvania

Tests of financial asset pricing models may yield misleading inferences when properties of the data are used to construct the test statistics. In particular, such tests are often based on returns to portfolios of common stock, where portfolios are constructed by sorting on some empirically motivated characteristic of the securities such as market value of equity. Analytical calculations, Monte Carlo simulations, and two empirical examples show that the effects of this type of data snooping can be substantial.

The reliance of economic science upon nonexperimental inference is, at once, one of the most challenging and most nettlesome aspects of the discipline. Because of the virtual impossibility of controlled experimentation in economics, the importance of sta-

Research support from the Batterymarch Fellowship (Lo), the Geewax-Terker Research Fund (MacKinlay), the John M. Olin Fellowship at the National Bureau of Economic Research (Lo), and the National Science Foundation (SES-8821583) is gratefully acknowledged. We thank David Aldous, Cliff Ball, Michael Brennan, Herbert David, Mike Gibbons, Jay Shanken, a referee, and seminar participants at the Board of Governors of the Federal Reserve, Boston College, Columbia, Dartmouth, Harvard, M.I.T., Northwestern, Princeton, Stanford, University of Chicago, University of Michigan, University of Wisconsin at Madison, Washington University, and Wharton for useful comments and suggestions. Address reprint requests to Andrew Lo, Sloan School of Management, M.I.T., 50 Memorial Drive, Cambridge, MA 02139.

The Review of Financial Studies 1990 Volume 3, number 3, pp. 431–467
© 1990 The Review of Financial Studies 0893-9454/90/$1.50

The Review of Financial Studies / v 3 n 3 1990

tistical data analysis is now well-established. However, there is a growing concern that the procedures under which formal statistical inference have been developed may not correspond to those followed in practice.[1] For example, the classical statistical approach to selecting a method of estimation generally involves minimizing an expected loss function, irrespective of the actual data. Yet in practice the properties of the realized data almost always influence the choice of estimator.

Of course, ignoring obvious features of the data can lead to nonsensical inferences even when the estimation procedures are optimal in some metric. But the way we incorporate those features into our estimation and testing procedures can affect subsequent inferences considerably. Indeed, by the very nature of empirical innovation in economics, the axioms of classical statistical analysis are violated routinely: future research is often motivated by the successes and failures of past investigations. Consequently, few empirical studies are free of the kind of data-instigated pretest biases discussed in Leamer (1978). Moreover, we can expect the degree of such biases to increase with the number of published studies performed on any single data set—the more scrutiny a collection of data is subjected to, the more likely will interesting (spurious) patterns emerge. Since stock market prices are perhaps the most studied economic quantities to date, tests of financial asset pricing models seem especially susceptible.

In this paper, we attempt to quantify the inferential biases associated with one particular method of testing financial asset pricing models such as the capital asset pricing model (CAPM) and the arbitrage pricing theory (APT). Because there are often many more securities than there are time series observations of stock returns, asset pricing tests are generally performed on the returns of *portfolios* of securities. Besides reducing the cross-sectional dimension of the joint distribution of returns, grouping into portfolios has also been advanced as a method of reducing the impact of measurement error. However, the selection of securities to be included in a given portfolio is almost never at random, but is often based on some of the stocks' empirical characteristics. The formation of size-sorted portfolios, portfolios based on the market value of the companies' equity, is but one example. Conducting classical statistical tests on portfolios formed this way creates potentially significant biases in the test statistics. These are

---

[1] Perhaps the most complete analysis of such issues in economic applications is by Leamer (1978). Recent papers by Lakonishok and Smidt (1988), Merton (1987), and Ross (1987) address data snooping in financial economics. Of course, data snooping has been a concern among probabilists and statisticians for quite some time, and is at least as old as the controversy between Bayesian and classical statisticians. Interested readers should consult Berger and Wolpert (1984, chapter 4.2) and Leamer (1978, chapter 9) for further discussion.

Data-Snooping Biases

examples of "data-snooping statistics," a term used by Aldous (1989, p. 252) to describe the situation "where you have a family of test statistics $T(a)$ whose null distribution is known for fixed a, but where you use the test statistic $T = T(a)$ for some a chosen using the data." In our application the quantity a may be viewed as a vector of zeros and ones that indicates which securities are to be included in or omitted from a given portfolio. If the choice of a is based on the data, then the sampling distribution of the resulting test statistic is generally not the same as the null distribution with a fixed a; hence, the actual size of the test may differ substantially from its nominal value under the null. Under plausible assumptions our calculations show that this kind of data snooping can lead to rejections of the null hypothesis with probability 1 even when the null hypothesis is true!

Although the term "data snooping" may have an unsavory connotation, our usage neither implies nor infers any sort of intentional misrepresentation or dishonesty. That prior empirical research may influence the way current investigations are conducted is often unavoidable, and this very fact results in what we have called data snooping. Moreover, it is not at all apparent that this phenomenon necessarily imparts a "bias" in the sense that it affects inferences in an undesirable way. After all, the primary reason for publishing scientific discoveries is to add to a store of common knowledge on which future research may build.

But when scientific discovery is statistical in nature, we must weigh the significance of newly discovered relations in view of past inferences. This is recognized implicitly in many formal statistical circumstances, as in the theory of sequential hypothesis testing. But it is considerably more difficult to correct for the effects of specification searches in practice since such searches often consist of *sequences* of empirical studies undertaken by many individuals over many years.[2] For example, as a consequence of the many investigations relating the behavior of stock returns to size, Chen, Roll, and Ross (1986, p. 394) write: "It has been facetiously noted that size may be the best theory we now have of expected returns. Unfortunately, this is less of a theory than an empirical observation." Then, as Merton (1987, p. 107) asks in a related context: "Is it reasonable to use the standard t-statistic as a valid measure of significance when the test is conducted on the same data used by many earlier studies whose results influenced the choice of theory to be tested?" We rephrase this question

---

[2] Statisticians have considered a closely related problem, known as the "file drawer problem," in which the overall significance of several published studies must be assessed while accounting for the possibility of unreported insignificant studies languishing in various investigators' file drawers. An excellent review of the file drawer problem and its remedies, which has come to be known as "meta-analysis," is provided by Iyengar and Greenhouse (1988).

The Review of Financial Studies / v 3 n 3 1990

in the following way: Are standard tests of significance valid when the construction of the test statistics is influenced by empirical relations derived from the very same data to be used in the test? Our results show that using prior information only marginally correlated with statistics of interest can distort inferences dramatically.

In Section 1, we quantify the data-snooping biases associated with testing financial asset pricing models with portfolios formed by sorting on some empirically motivated characteristic. Using the theory of induced order statistics, we derive in closed form the asymptotic distribution of a commonly used test statistic before and after sorting. This not only yields a measure of the effect of data snooping, but also provides the appropriate sampling theory when snooping is unavoidable. In Section 2, we report the results of Monte Carlo experiments designed to gauge the accuracy of the asymptotic approximations used in Section 1. In Section 3, two empirical examples are provided that illustrate the potential importance of data-snooping biases in existing tests of asset pricing models, and, in Section 4, we show how these biases can arise naturally from our tendency to focus on the unusual. We conclude in Section 5.

1. Quantifying Data-Snooping Biases With Induced Order Statistics

Many tests of the CAPM and APT have been conducted on returns of groups of securities rather than on individual security returns, where the grouping is often according to some empirical characteristic of the securities. Perhaps the most common attribute by which securities are grouped is market value of equity or "size." The prevalence of size-sorted portfolios in recent tests of asset pricing models has not been precipitated by any economic theory linking size to asset prices. It is a consequence of a series of empirical studies demonstrating the statistical relation between size and the stochastic behavior of stock returns.[3] Therefore, we must allow for our foreknowledge of size-related phenomena in evaluating the actual significance of tests performed on size-sorted portfolios. More generally, grouping securities by some characteristic that is empirically motivated may affect the size of the usual significance tests,[4] particularly when the empirical motivation is derived from the very data set on which the test is based.

---

[3] See Banz (1978, 1981), Brown, Kleidon, and Marsh (1983), and Chan, Chen, and Hsieh (1985), for example. Although Banz's (1978) original investigation may have been motivated by theoretical considerations, virtually all subsequent empirical studies exploiting the size effect do so because of Banz's empirical findings, and not his theory.

[4] Unfortunately the use of "size" to mean both market value of equity and type I error is unavoidable. Readers beware.

We quantify these effects in the following sections by appealing to asymptotic results for induced order statistics, and show that even mild forms of data snooping can change inferences substantially. In Section 1.1, a brief summary of the asymptotic properties of induced order statistics is provided. In Section 1.2, results for tests based on individual securities are presented, and in Section 1.3, corresponding results for portfolios are reported. We provide a more positive interpretation of data-snooping biases as power against deviations from the null hypothesis in Section 1.4.

1.1. Asymptotic properties of induced order statistics

Since the particular form of data snooping we are investigating is most common in empirical tests of financial asset pricing models, our exposition will lie in that context. Suppose for each of N securities we have some consistent estimator $\hat{\alpha}_i$ of a parameter α_i which is to be used in the construction of an aggregate test statistic. For example, in the Sharpe–Lintner CAPM, $\hat{\alpha}_i$ would be the estimated intercept from the following regression:

$$R_{it} - R_{ft} = \hat{\alpha}_i + (R_{mt} - R_{ft})\beta_i + \epsilon_{it} \qquad (1)$$

where R_{it}, R_{mt}, and R_{ft} are the period-t returns on security i, the market portfolio, and a risk-free asset, respectively. A test of the null hypothesis that $\alpha_i = 0$ would then be a proper test of the Sharpe–Lintner version of the CAPM; thus, $\hat{\alpha}_i$ may serve as a test statistic itself. However, more powerful tests may be obtained by combining the $\hat{\alpha}_i$'s for many securities. But how should we combine them?

Suppose for each security i we observe some characteristic X_i, such as its out-of-sample market value of equity or average annual earnings, and we learn that X_i is correlated empirically with $\hat{\alpha}_i$. By this we mean that the relation between X_i and $\hat{\alpha}_i$ is an empirical fact uncovered by "searching" through the data, and not motivated by any a priori theoretical considerations. This search need not be a systematic sifting of the data, but may be interpreted as any one of Leamer's (1978) six specification searches, which even the most meticulous of classical statisticians has conducted at some point. The key feature is that our interest in characteristic X_i is derived from a look at the data, the same data to be used in performing our test. Common intuition suggests that using information contained in the X_i's can yield a more powerful test of economic restrictions on the $\hat{\alpha}_i$'s. But if this characteristic is not a part of the original null hypothesis, and only catches our attention after a look at the data (or after a look at another's look at the data), using it to form our test statistics may lead us to reject those economic restrictions even when they obtain. More formally,

The Review of Financial Studies / v 3 n 3 1990

if we write $\hat{\alpha}_i$ as

$$\hat{\alpha}_i = \alpha_i + \zeta_i, \tag{2}$$

then it is evident that under the null hypothesis where $\alpha_i = 0$, any correlation between X_i and $\hat{\alpha}_i$ must be due to correlation between the characteristic and estimation or measurement error ζ_i. Although measurement error is usually assumed to be independent of all other relevant economic variables, the very process by which the characteristic comes to our attention may induce spurious correlation between X_i and ζ_i. We formalize this intuition in Section 4 and proceed now to show that such spurious correlation has important implications for testing the null hypothesis.

This is most evident in the extreme case where the null hypothesis $\alpha_i = 0$ is tested by performing a standard t-test on the largest of the $\hat{\alpha}_i$'s. Clearly such a test is biased toward rejection unless we account for the fact that the largest $\hat{\alpha}_i$ has been drawn from the set $\{\hat{\alpha}_j\}$. Otherwise, extreme realizations of estimation error will be confused with a violation of the null hypothesis. If, instead of choosing $\hat{\alpha}_i$ by its value relative to other $\hat{\alpha}_j$'s, our choice is based on some characteristic X_i correlated with the estimation errors of $\hat{\alpha}_i$, a similar bias might arise, albeit to a lesser degree.

To formalize the preceding intuition, suppose that only a subset of n securities is used to form the test statistic and these n are chosen by sorting the X_i's. That is, let us reorder the bivariate vectors $[X_i \hat{\alpha}_i]'$ according to their first components, yielding the sequence

$$\begin{pmatrix} X_{1:N} \\ \hat{\alpha}_{[1:N]} \end{pmatrix}, \begin{pmatrix} X_{2:N} \\ \hat{\alpha}_{[2:N]} \end{pmatrix}, \ldots, \begin{pmatrix} X_{N:N} \\ \hat{\alpha}_{[N:N]} \end{pmatrix}, \tag{3}$$

where $X_{1:N} < X_{2:N} < \cdots < X_{N:N}$ and the notation $X_{i:N}$ follows that of the statistics literature in denoting the ith order statistic from the sample of N observations $\{X_i\}$.[5] The notation $\hat{\alpha}_{[i:N]}$ denotes the ith *induced order statistic* corresponding to $X_{i:N}$, or the ith *concomitant* of the order statistic $X_{i:N}$.[6] That is, if the bivariate vectors $[X_i \hat{\alpha}_i]'$ are ordered according to the X_i entries, $\hat{\alpha}_{[i:N]}$ is defined to be the second component of the ith ordered vector. The $\hat{\alpha}_{[i:N]}$'s are not themselves

---

[5] It is implicitly assumed throughout that both $\hat{\alpha}_i$ and X_i have continuous joint and marginal cumulative distribution functions; hence, strict inequalities suffice.

[6] The term *concomitant* of an order statistic was introduced by David (1973), who was perhaps the first to systematically investigate its properties and applications. The term *induced* order statistic was coined by Bhattacharya (1974) at about the same time. Although the former term seems to be more common usage, we use the latter in the interest of brevity. See Bhattacharya (1984) for an excellent review.

Data-Snooping Biases

ordered but correspond to the ordering of the $X_{i:N}$'s.[7] For example, if X_i is firm size and $\hat{\alpha}_i$ is the intercept from a market-model regression of firm i's excess return on the excess market return, then $\hat{\alpha}_{[j:N]}$ is the $\hat{\alpha}$ of the jth smallest of the N firms. We call this procedure *induced ordering* of the $\hat{\alpha}_i$'s.

It is apparent that if we construct a test statistic by choosing n securities according to the ordering (3), the sampling theory cannot be the same as that of n securities selected independently of the data. From the following remarkably simple result by Yang (1977), an asymptotic sampling theory for test statistics based on induced order statistics may be derived analytically:[8]

Theorem 1.1. *Let the vectors $[X_i \hat{\alpha}_i]'$, $i = 1, \ldots, N$, be independently and identically distributed and let $1 < i_1 < i_2 < \cdots < i_n < N$ be sequences of integers such that, as $N \to \infty$, $i_k/N \to \xi_k \in (0, 1)$ ($k = 1, 2, \ldots, n$). Then*

$$\lim_{N \to \infty} \Pr(\hat{\alpha}_{[i_1:N]} < a_1, \ldots, \hat{\alpha}_{[i_n:N]} < a_n)$$

$$= \prod_{k=1}^{n} \Pr(\hat{\alpha}_k < a_k \mid F_x(X_k) = \xi_k), \tag{4}$$

where $F_x(\cdot)$ is the marginal cumulative distribution function of X_i.

Proof. See Yang (1977). ∎

This result gives the large-sample joint distribution of a finite subset of induced order statistics whose identities are determined solely by their relative rankings ξ_k (as ranked according to the order statistics $X_{i:N}$). From (4) it is evident that the $\hat{\alpha}_{[i_k:N]}$'s are mutually independent in large samples. If X_i were the market value of equity of the ith company, Theorem 1.1 shows that the $\hat{\alpha}_i$ of the security with size at, for example, the 27th percentile is asymptotically independent of the $\hat{\alpha}_j$ of the security with size at the 45th percentile.[9] If the characteristics $\{X_i\}$ and $\{\hat{\alpha}_i\}$ are statistically independent, the joint distribution of

---

[7] If the vectors are independently and identically distributed and X_i is perfectly correlated with $\hat{\alpha}_i$, then $\hat{\alpha}_{[i:N]}$ are also order statistics. But as long as the correlation coefficient ρ is strictly between -1 and 1, then, for example, $\hat{\alpha}_{[N:N]}$ will generally not be the largest $\hat{\alpha}_i$.

[8] See also David and Galambos (1974) and Watterson (1959). In fact, Yang (1977) provides the exact finite-sample distribution of any finite collection of induced order statistics, but even assuming bivariate normality does not yield a tractable form of this distribution.

[9] This is a limiting result and implies that the identities of the stocks with 27th and 45th percentile sizes will generally change as N increases.

The Review of Financial Studies / v 3 n 3 1990

the latter clearly cannot be influenced by ordering according to the former. It is tempting to conclude that as long as the correlation between X_i and $\hat{\alpha}_i$ is economically small, induced ordering cannot greatly affect inferences. Using Yang's result we show the fallacy of this argument in Sections 1.2 and 1.3.

1.2 Biases of tests based on individual securities
We evaluate the bias of induced ordering under the following assumption:

(A) The vectors $[X_i \ \hat{\alpha}_i]'$ $(i = 1, 2, \ldots, N)$ are independently and identically distributed bivariate normal random vectors with mean $[\mu_x \ \alpha]'$, variance $[\sigma_x^2 \ \sigma_\alpha^2]'$, and correlation $\rho \in (-1, 1)$.

The null hypothesis H is then

$$H: \alpha = 0.$$

Examples of asset pricing models that yield restrictions of this form are the Sharpe–Lintner CAPM and the exact factor pricing version of Ross's APT.[10] Under this null hypothesis, the $\hat{\alpha}_i$'s deviate from zero solely through estimation error.

Since the sampling theory provided by Theorem 1.1 is asymptotic, we construct our test statistics using a finite subset of n securities where it is assumed that $n \ll N$. If these securities are selected without the prior use of data, then we have the following well-known result:

$$\theta \equiv \frac{1}{\hat{\sigma}_\alpha^2} \sum_{i=1}^{n} \hat{\alpha}_i^2 \overset{a}{\sim} \chi_n^2, \tag{5}$$

where $\hat{\sigma}_\alpha^2$ is any consistent estimator of σ_α^2.[11] Therefore, a 5 percent test of H may be performed by checking whether θ is greater or less than $C_{.05}^n$, where $C_{.05}^n$ is defined by

$$F_{\chi_n^2}(C_{.05}^n) = .95 \tag{6}$$

and $F_{\chi_n^2}(\cdot)$ is the cumulative distribution function of a χ_n^2 variate.

Now suppose we construct θ from the induced order statistics

---

[10] See Chamberlain (1983), Huberman and Kandel (1987), Lehmann and Modest (1988), and Wang (1988) for further discussion of exact factor pricing models. Examples of tests that fit into the framework of H are those in Campbell (1987), Connor and Korajczyk (1988), Gibbons, Ross, and Shanken (1987), Huberman and Kandel (1987), Lehmann and Modest (1988), and MacKinlay (1987).

[11] In most contexts the consistency of $\hat{\sigma}_\alpha^2$ is with respect to the number of time series observations T. In that case something must be said of the relative rates at which T and N increase without bound so as to guarantee convergence of θ. However, under H the parameter σ_α^2 may be estimated cross-sectionally; hence, the relation $\overset{a}{\sim}$ in (5) need only represent N-asymptotics.

$\hat{\alpha}_{[i_k:N]}$, $k = 1, \ldots, n$, instead of the $\hat{\alpha}_i$'s. Specifically, define the following test statistic:

$$\tilde{\theta} \equiv \frac{1}{\hat{\sigma}_\alpha^2} \sum_{k=1}^n \hat{\alpha}_{[i_k:N]}^2. \tag{7}$$

Using Theorem 1.1, the following proposition is easily established:

Proposition 1.1. *Under the null hypothesis H and assumption (A), as N increases without bound the induced order statistics $\hat{\alpha}_{[i_k:N]}$ (k = 1, \ldots, n) converge in distribution to independent gaussian random variables with mean μ_k and variance σ_k^2, where*

$$\mu_k \equiv \rho(\sigma_\alpha/\sigma_x)[F_x^{-1}(\xi_k) - \mu_x] = \rho\sigma_\alpha\Phi^{-1}(\xi_k), \tag{8}$$

$$\sigma_k^2 \equiv \sigma_\alpha^2(1 - \rho^2), \tag{9}$$

which implies

$$\tilde{\theta} \overset{a}{\sim} (1 - \rho^2)\cdot\chi_n^2(\lambda), \tag{10}$$

with noncentrality parameter

$$\lambda = \sum_{k=1}^n \left(\frac{\mu_k}{\sigma_k}\right)^2 = \frac{\rho^2}{1 - \rho^2} \sum_{k=1}^n [\Phi^{-1}(\xi_k)]^2, \tag{11}$$

where $\Phi(\cdot)$ is the standard normal cumulative distribution function.

Proof. This follows directly from the definition of a noncentral chi-squared variate. The second equality in (8) follows from the fact that $\Phi(\xi_k) = F_x(\xi_k\sigma_x + \mu_x)$. ∎

Proposition 1.1 shows that the null hypothesis H is violated by induced ordering since the means of the ordered $\hat{\alpha}_i$'s are no longer zero. Indeed, the mean of $\hat{\alpha}_{[i_k:N]}$ may be positive or negative depending on ρ and the (limiting) relative rank ξ_k. For example, if $\rho = .10$ and $\sigma_\alpha = 1$, the mean of the induced order statistic in the 95th percentile is 0.164.

The simplicity of $\tilde{\theta}$'s asymptotic distribution follows from the fact that the $\hat{\alpha}_{[i_k:N]}$'s become independent as N increases without bound. It follows from the fact that induced order statistics are conditionally independent when conditioned on the order statistics that determine the induced ordering. This seemingly counterintuitive result is easy to see when $[X, \hat{\alpha}_i]$ is bivariate normal, since, in this case

$$\hat{\alpha}_i = \alpha + \rho(\sigma_\alpha/\sigma_x)[X_i - \mu_x] + Z_i,$$

$$Z_i \quad \text{i.i.d.} \quad N(0, \sigma_\alpha^2(1 - \rho^2)), \tag{12}$$

The Review of Financial Studies / v 3 n 3 1990

where X_i and Z_i are independent. Therefore, the induced order statistics may be represented as

$$\hat{\alpha}_{[i_k:N]} = \alpha + \rho(\sigma_\alpha/\sigma_x)[X_{i_k:N} - \mu_x] + Z_{[i_k]},$$

$$Z_{[i_k]} \quad \text{i.i.d.} \quad N(0, \sigma_\alpha^2(1 - \rho^2)), \qquad (13)$$

where the $Z_{[i_k]}$ are independent of the (order) statistics $X_{i_k:N}$. But since $X_{i_k:N}$ is an order statistic, and since the sequence i_k/N converges to ξ_k, $X_{i_k:N}$ converges to the ξ_kth quantile, $F^{-1}(\xi_k)$. Using (13) then shows that $\hat{\alpha}_{[i_k:N]}$ is gaussian, with mean and variance given by (8) and (9), and independent of the other induced order statistics.[12]

To evaluate the size of a 5 percent test based on the statistic $\tilde{\theta}$, we need only evaluate the cumulative distribution function of the noncentral $\chi_n^2(\lambda)$ at the point $C_{.05}^n/(1 - \rho^2)$, where $C_{.05}^n$ is given in (6). Observe that the noncentrality parameter λ is an increasing function of ρ^2. If $\rho^2 = 0$ then the distribution of $\tilde{\theta}$ reduces to a central χ_n^2 which is identical to the distribution of θ in (5)—sorting on a characteristic that is statistically independent of the $\hat{\alpha}_i$'s cannot affect the null distribution of θ. As $\hat{\alpha}_i$ and X_i become more highly correlated, the noncentral χ^2 distribution shifts to the right. However, this does not imply that the actual size of a 5 percent test necessarily increases since the relevant critical value for $\tilde{\theta}$, $C_{.05}^n/(1 - \rho^2)$, also grows with ρ^2.[13]

Numerical values for the size of a 5 percent test based on $\tilde{\theta}$ may be obtained by first specifying choices for the relative ranks $\{\xi_k\}$ of the n securities. We choose three sets of $\{\xi_k\}$, yielding three distinct test statistics $\tilde{\theta}_1$, $\tilde{\theta}_2$, and $\tilde{\theta}_3$:

$$\tilde{\theta}_1 \leftrightarrow \xi_k = \frac{k}{n+1}, \qquad k = 1, 2, \ldots, n; \qquad (14)$$

---

[12] In fact, this shows how our parametric specification may be relaxed. If we replace normality by the assumption that $\hat{\alpha}_i$ and X_i satisfy the linear regression equation,

$$\hat{\alpha}_i = \mu_\alpha + \beta_i(X_i - \mu_x) + Z_n$$

where Z_i is independent of X_n, then our results remain unchanged. Moreover, this specification may allow us to relax the rather strong i.i.d. assumption since David (1981, chapters 2.8 and 5.6) does present some results for order statistics in the nonidentically distributed and the dependent cases separately. However, combining and applying them to the above linear regression relation is a formidable task which we leave to the more industrious.

[13] In fact, if $\rho^2 = 1$, the limiting distribution of $\tilde{\theta}$ is degenerate since the test statistic converges in probability to the following limit:

$$\sum_{k=1}^{n} [\Phi^{-1}(\xi_k)]^2.$$

This limit may be greater or less than $C_{.05}^n$ depending on the values of ξ_k; hence, the size of the test in this case may be either zero or unity.

Data-Snooping Biases

$$\tilde{\theta}_2 \leftrightarrow \xi_k = \begin{cases} \dfrac{k}{(m+1)(n_o+1)}, & \text{for } k=1,2,\dots,n_o, \\[3mm] \dfrac{k+m(n_o+1)-n_o}{(m+1)(n_o+1)}, & \text{for } k=n_o+1,\dots,2n_o; \end{cases} \tag{15}$$

$$\tilde{\theta}_3 \leftrightarrow \xi_k = \begin{cases} \dfrac{k+n_o+1}{(m+1)(n_o+1)}, & \text{for } k=1,2,\dots,n_o, \\[3mm] \dfrac{k+(m-1)(n_o+1)-n_o}{(m+1)(n_o+1)}, & \text{for } k=n_o+1,\dots,2n_o; \end{cases} \tag{16}$$

where $n \equiv 2n_o$ and n_o is an arbitrary positive integer. The first method (14) simply sets the ξ_k's so that they divide the unit interval into n equally spaced increments. The second procedure (15) first divides the unit interval into $m + 1$ equally spaced increments, sets the first half of the ξ_k's to divide the *first* such increment into equally spaced intervals each of width $1/(m + 1)(n_o + 1)$, and then sets the remaining half so as to divide the *last* increment into equally spaced intervals also of width $1/(m + 1)(n_o + 1)$ each. The third procedure is similar to the second, except that the ξ_k's are chosen to divide the second smallest and second largest $m + 1$ increments into equally spaced intervals of width $1/(m + 1)(n_o + 1)$.

These three ways of choosing n securities allow us to see how an attempt to create (or remove) dispersion—as measured by the characteristic X_t—affects the null distribution of the statistics. The first choice for the relative ranks is the most disperse, being evenly distributed on $(0, 1)$. The second yields the opposite extreme: the $\hat{\alpha}_{[i_k:N]}$'s selected are those with characteristics in the lowest and highest $100/(m + 1)$-percentiles. As the parameter m is increased, more extreme outliers are used to compute $\tilde{\theta}_2$. This is also true for $\tilde{\theta}_3$, but to a lesser extent since the statistic is based on $\hat{\alpha}_{[i_k:N]}$'s in the second lowest and second highest $100/(m + 1)$-percentiles.

Table 1 shows the size of the 5 percent test using $\tilde{\theta}_1$, $\tilde{\theta}_2$, and $\tilde{\theta}_3$ for various values of n, ρ^2, and m. For concreteness, observe that ρ^2 is simply the R^2 of the cross-sectional regression of $\hat{\alpha}_i$ on X_i, so that $\rho = \pm.10$ implies that only 1 percent of the variation in $\hat{\alpha}_i$ is explained by X_i. For this value of R^2, the entries in the second panel of Table 1 show that the size of a 5 percent test using $\tilde{\theta}_1$ is 4.9 percent for samples of 10 to 100 securities. However, using securities with extreme characteristics does affect the size, as the entries in the "$\tilde{\theta}_2$-test" and "$\tilde{\theta}_3$-test" columns indicate. Nevertheless the largest deviation is only 8.1 percent. As expected, the size is larger for the test based on $\tilde{\theta}_2$ than for that of $\tilde{\theta}_3$ since the former statistic is based on more extreme induced order statistics than the latter.

441

The Review of Financial Studies / v 3 n 3 1990

Table 1
Theoretical sizes of nominal 5 percent χ^2_n-tests of H: $\alpha_i = 0$ $(i = 1, \ldots, n)$ using the test statistics $\tilde{\theta}_j$

n	$\tilde{\theta}_1$-test	$\tilde{\theta}_2$-test $(m = 4)$	$\tilde{\theta}_3$-test $(m = 4)$	$\tilde{\theta}_2$-test $(m = 9)$	$\tilde{\theta}_3$-test $(m = 9)$	$\tilde{\theta}_2$-test $(m = 19)$	$\tilde{\theta}_3$-test $(m = 19)$
$R^2 = .005$							
10	0.049	0.051	0.049	0.053	0.050	0.054	0.052
20	0.050	0.052	0.049	0.054	0.050	0.056	0.052
50	0.050	0.053	0.048	0.056	0.050	0.060	0.053
100	0.050	0.054	0.047	0.059	0.050	0.064	0.054
$R^2 = .01$							
10	0.049	0.053	0.048	0.056	0.050	0.059	0.053
20	0.049	0.054	0.047	0.058	0.050	0.063	0.054
50	0.049	0.056	0.046	0.063	0.051	0.071	0.057
100	0.049	0.059	0.045	0.069	0.051	0.081	0.059
$R^2 = .05$							
10	0.045	0.063	0.041	0.080	0.051	0.101	0.066
20	0.045	0.070	0.038	0.096	0.052	0.130	0.073
50	0.046	0.086	0.033	0.135	0.053	0.201	0.087
100	0.047	0.107	0.028	0.190	0.054	0.304	0.106
$R^2 = .10$							
10	0.040	0.076	0.032	0.116	0.052	0.166	0.083
20	0.041	0.093	0.028	0.158	0.053	0.244	0.099
50	0.042	0.133	0.020	0.267	0.055	0.442	0.137
100	0.043	0.192	0.014	0.423	0.058	0.680	0.191
$R^2 = .20$							
10	0.030	0.104	0.019	0.202	0.052	0.330	0.121
20	0.032	0.146	0.013	0.318	0.054	0.528	0.163
50	0.034	0.262	0.006	0.599	0.059	0.862	0.272
100	0.036	0.432	0.002	0.857	0.064	0.987	0.429

$\tilde{\theta}_j = \sum_{k=1}^{2n} \hat{\alpha}^2_{\{i_k : j\}} N_j / \hat{\sigma}^2_a$, $j = 1, 2, 3$, for various sample sizes n. The statistic $\tilde{\theta}_1$ is based on induced order statistics with relative ranks evenly spaced in $(0,1)$; $\tilde{\theta}_2$ is constructed from induced order statistics ranked in the lowest and highest $100/(m + 1)$-percent fractiles; and $\tilde{\theta}_3$ is constructed from those ranked in the second lowest and second highest $100/(m + 1)$-percent fractiles. The R^2 is the square of the correlation between $\hat{\alpha}_i$ and the sorting characteristics.

When the R^2 increases to 10 percent the bias becomes more important. Although tests based on a set of securities with evenly spaced characteristics still have sizes approximately equal to their nominal 5 percent value, the size deviates more substantially when securities with extreme characteristics are used. For example, the size of the $\tilde{\theta}_2$ test that uses the 100 securities in the lowest and highest characteristic decile is 42.3 percent! In comparison, the 5 percent test based on the second lowest and second highest deciles exhibits only a 5.8 percent rejection rate. These patterns become even more pronounced for R^2's higher than 10 percent.

The intuition for these results may be found in (8)—the more extreme induced order statistics have means farther away from zero; hence, a statistic based on evenly distributed $\hat{\alpha}_{\{i_k : N\}}$'s will not provide evidence against the null hypothesis $\alpha = 0$. If the relative ranks are extreme, as is the case for $\hat{\theta}_2$ and $\hat{\theta}_3$, the resulting $\hat{\alpha}_{[i_k:N]}$'s may appear to be statistically incompatible with the null.

1.3 Biases of tests based on portfolios of securities

The entries in Table 1 show that as long as the n securities chosen have characteristics evenly distributed in relative rankings, test statistics based on individual securities yield little inferential bias. However, in practice the ordering by characteristics such as market value of equity is used to group securities into *portfolios,* and the portfolio returns are used to construct test statistics. For example, let $n = n_o q$, where n_o and q are arbitrary positive integers, and consider forming q portfolios with n_o securities in each portfolio, where the portfolios are formed randomly. Under the null hypothesis H we have the following:

$$\phi_k \equiv \frac{1}{n_o} \sum_{j=(k-1)n_0+1}^{kn_0} \hat{\alpha}_j \sim N\left(0, \frac{\sigma_\alpha^2}{n_o}\right), \quad k = 1, 2, \ldots, q, \quad (17)$$

$$\theta_p \equiv \frac{n_o}{\hat{\sigma}_\alpha^2} \sum_{k=1}^{q} \phi_k^2 \overset{a}{\sim} \chi_q^2, \quad (18)$$

where ϕ_k is the estimated alpha of portfolio k and θ_p is the aggregate test statistic for the q portfolios. To perform a 5 percent test of H using θ_p, we simply compare it with the critical value $C\%_5$ defined by

$$F_{\chi_q^2}(C\%_5) = .95. \quad (19)$$

Suppose, however, we compute this test statistic using the induced order statistics $\{\hat{\alpha}_{[i_k:N]}\}$ instead of randomly chosen $\{\hat{\alpha}_i\}$. From Theorem 1.1 we have:

Proposition 1.2. *Under the null hypothesis H and assumption (A), as N increases without bound, the statistics $\tilde{\phi}_k$ ($k = 1, 2, \ldots, q$) and $\tilde{\theta}_p$ converge in distribution to the following:*

$$\tilde{\phi}_k \equiv \frac{1}{n_o} \sum_{j=(k-1)n_0+1}^{kn_0} \hat{\alpha}_{[ij:N]} \overset{a}{\sim} N\left(\sum_{j=(k-1)n_0+1}^{kn_0} \frac{\mu_j}{n_o}, \frac{\sigma_\alpha^2(1-\rho^2)}{n_o}\right), \quad (20)$$

$$\tilde{\theta}_p \equiv \frac{n_o}{\hat{\sigma}_\alpha^2} \sum_{k=1}^{q} \tilde{\phi}_k^2 \overset{a}{\sim} (1-\rho^2) \cdot \chi_q^2(\lambda), \quad (21)$$

with noncentrality parameter

$$\lambda = \frac{n_o \rho^2}{1 - \rho^2} \sum_{k=1}^{q} \left(\frac{1}{n_o} \sum_{j=(k-1)n_0+1}^{kn_0} [\Phi^{-1}(\xi_j)]\right)^2. \quad (22)$$

The Review of Financial Studies / v 3 n 3 1990

Proof. Again, this follows directly from the definition of a noncentral chi-squared variate and the asymptotic independence of the induced order statistics. ∎

The noncentrality parameter (22) is similar to that of the statistic based on individual securities—it is increasing in ρ^2 and equals zero when $\rho = 0$. However, it differs in one respect: because of portfolio aggregation, each term of the outer sum (the sum with respect to k) is the average of $\Phi^{-1}(\xi_j)$ over all securities in the kth portfolio. To see the importance of this, consider the case where the relative ranks ξ_j are chosen to be evenly spaced in $(0, 1)$, that is,

$$\xi_j = j/(n_o q + 1). \tag{23}$$

Recall from Table 1 that for individual securities the size of 5 percent tests based on *evenly spaced* ξ_j's was not significantly biased. Table 2 reports the size of 5 percent tests based on the portfolio statistic $\tilde{\theta}_p$, also using evenly spaced relative rankings. The contrast is striking—even for as low an R^2 as 1 percent, which implies a correlation of only ± 10 percent between $\hat{\alpha}_i$ and X_i, a 5 percent test based on 50 portfolios with 50 securities in each rejects 67 percent of the time! We can also see how portfolio grouping affects the size of the test for a fixed number of securities by comparing the $(q = i, n_o = j)$ entry with the $(q = j, n_o = i)$ entry. For example, in a sample of 250 securities a test based on 5 portfolios of 50 securities has size 16.5 percent, whereas a test based on 50 portfolios of 5 securities has only a 7.5 percent rejection rate. Grouping securities into portfolios increases the size considerably. The entries in Table 2 are also monotonically increasing across rows and across columns, implying that the test size increases with the number of securities, regardless of whether the number of portfolios or the number of securities per portfolio is held fixed.

   To understand why forming portfolios yields much higher rejection rates than using individual securities, recall from (8) and (9) that the mean of $\hat{\alpha}_{[i_k:N]}$ is a function of its relative rank i_k/N (in the limit), whereas its variance $\sigma_\alpha^2(1 - \rho^2)$ is fixed. Forming a portfolio of the induced order statistics within a characteristic-fractile amounts to averaging a collection of n_o approximately independent random variables with similar means and identical variances. The result is a statistic $\tilde{\phi}_k$ with a comparable mean but with a variance n_o times smaller than each of the $\hat{\alpha}_{[i_k:N]}$'s. This variance reduction amplifies the importance of the deviation of the $\tilde{\phi}_k$ mean from zero, and is ultimately reflected in the entries of Table 2. A more dramatic illustration is provided in Table 3, which reports the appropriate 5 percent critical values for the tests in Table 2—when $R^2 = .05$, the 5 percent critical

Data-Snooping Biases

Table 2
Theoretical sizes of nominal 5 percent χ_q^2-tests of H: $\alpha_i = 0$ ($i = 1, \ldots, n$) using the test statistic $\hat{\theta}_p$

q	$n_o = 5$	$n_o = 10$	$n_o = 20$	$n_o = 25$	$n_o = 50$
$R^2 = .005$					
5	0.053	0.058	0.068	0.073	0.102
10	0.055	0.062	0.077	0.086	0.134
20	0.057	0.067	0.091	0.105	0.185
25	0.058	0.070	0.097	0.113	0.208
50	0.062	0.079	0.123	0.148	0.311
$R^2 = .01$					
5	0.056	0.066	0.087	0.099	0.165
10	0.060	0.075	0.110	0.130	0.247
20	0.065	0.088	0.146	0.179	0.382
25	0.067	0.093	0.161	0.202	0.440
50	0.075	0.117	0.232	0.302	0.669
$R^2 = .05$					
5	0.080	0.140	0.288	0.368	0.716
10	0.104	0.212	0.477	0.602	0.941
20	0.142	0.333	0.728	0.854	0.998
25	0.159	0.387	0.808	0.914	1.000
50	0.235	0.607	0.971	0.995	1.000
$R^2 = .10$					
5	0.114	0.255	0.568	0.697	0.971
10	0.174	0.434	0.847	0.935	1.000
20	0.276	0.688	0.985	0.998	1.000
25	0.323	0.773	0.996	1.000	1.000
50	0.523	0.960	1.000	1.000	1.000
$R^2 = .20$					
5	0.193	0.514	0.913	0.971	1.000
10	0.348	0.816	0.997	1.000	1.000
20	0.596	0.980	1.000	1.000	1.000
25	0.688	0.994	1.000	1.000	1.000
50	0.926	1.000	1.000	1.000	1.000

$\hat{\theta}_p = n_o \Sigma_{i=1} \hat{\phi}_k^2 / \sigma_k^2$, and $\hat{\phi}_k = (1/n_o) \Sigma_{(k-1)q+1}^{kq} \hat{\alpha}_{[j:N]}$ is constructed from portfolio k, with portfolios formed by sorting on some characteristic correlated with estimates $\hat{\alpha}_i$. This induced ordering alters the null distribution of $\hat{\theta}_p$ from χ_q^2 to $(1 - R^2)/\chi_q^2(\lambda)$, where the noncentrality parameter λ is a function of the number q of portfolios, the number n_o of securities in each portfolio, and the squared correlation coefficient R^2 between $\hat{\alpha}_i$ and the sorting characteristic.

value for the χ^2 test with 50 securities in each of 50 portfolios is 211.67. If induced ordering is unavoidable, these critical values may serve as a method for bounding the effects of data snooping on inferences.

When the R^2 increases to 10 percent, implying a cross-sectional correlation of about ± 32 percent between $\hat{\alpha}_i$ and X_i, the size approaches unity for tests based on 20 or more portfolios with 20 or more securities in each portfolio. These results are especially surprising in view of the sizes reported in Table 1, since the portfolio test statistic is based on evenly spaced induced order statistics

The Review of Financial Studies / v 3 n 3 1990

Table 3
Critical values C_{05} for 5 percent χ^2-tests of H: $\alpha_i = 0$ ($i = 1, \ldots, n$) using the test statistic $\hat{\theta}_p$

q	$C_{05} \cdot \chi_q^2$	$C_{05} \cdot \chi_q^2(\lambda)$ $(n_o = 5)$	$C_{05} \cdot \chi_q^2(\lambda)$ $(n_o = 10)$	$C_{05} \cdot \chi_q^2(\lambda)$ $(n_o = 20)$	$C_{05} \cdot \chi_q^2(\lambda)$ $(n_o = 25)$	$C_{05} \cdot \chi_q^2(\lambda)$ $(n_o = 50)$
$R^2 = .005$						
5	11.07	11.22	11.45	11.93	12.16	13.29
10	18.31	18.60	19.03	19.87	20.28	22.31
20	31.41	31.97	32.72	34.22	34.96	38.58
25	37.65	38.33	39.24	41.05	41.94	46.33
50	67.50	68.78	70.44	73.72	75.35	83.39
$R^2 = .01$						
5	11.07	11.36	11.83	12.74	13.19	15.31
10	18.31	18.89	19.73	21.36	22.16	26.00
20	31.41	32.52	34.01	36.93	38.36	45.31
25	37.65	39.01	40.81	44.34	46.08	54.52
50	67.50	70.05	73.33	79.79	82.98	98.60
$R^2 = .05$						
5	11.07	12.45	14.53	18.39	20.21	28.68
10	18.31	21.09	24.88	32.00	35.41	51.54
20	31.41	36.72	43.62	56.75	63.09	93.59
25	37.65	44.18	52.56	68.59	76.35	113.82
50	67.50	79.85	95.41	125.47	140.16	211.67
$R^2 = .10$						
5	11.07	13.65	17.45	24.37	27.63	42.96
10	18.31	23.58	30.62	43.74	50.02	79.98
20	31.41	41.60	54.63	79.32	91.27	148.98
25	37.65	50.21	66.13	96.44	111.15	182.43
50	67.50	91.49	121.42	179.11	207.33	345.24
$R^2 = .20$						
5	11.07	15.70	22.44	34.82	40.71	68.73
10	18.31	27.98	40.86	65.01	76.65	132.76
20	31.41	50.51	74.89	121.32	143.91	253.93
25	37.65	61.32	91.29	148.61	176.58	313.10
50	67.50	113.43	170.67	281.43	335.83	603.10

$\hat{\theta}_p = n_o \Sigma_{k=1} \hat{\phi}_k^2/\sigma_o^2$, and $\hat{\phi}_k = (1/n_o)\Sigma_{j=1}^{n_o}{}_{(k-1)q+1} \hat{\alpha}_{[i_k:N]}$ is constructed from portfolio k, with portfolios formed by sorting on some characteristic correlated with estimates $\hat{\alpha}_r$. This induced ordering alters the null distribution of $\hat{\theta}_p$ from χ_q^2 to $(1 - R^2)/\chi_q^2(\lambda)$, where the noncentrality parameter λ is a function of the number q of portfolios, the number n_o of securities in each portfolio, and the squared correlation coefficient R^2 between $\hat{\alpha}_t$ and the sorting characteristic. C_{05} is defined implicitly by the relation $\text{Pr}(\hat{\theta}_p > C_{05}) = 1 - F_{\chi^2_{(0)}} (C_{05}/(1 - R^2)) = .05$. For comparison, we also report the 5 percent critical value of the central χ_q^2 distribution in the second column.

$\hat{\alpha}_{[i_k:N]}$. Using 100 securities, Table 1 shows a size of 4.3 percent with evenly spaced $\hat{\alpha}_{[i_k:N]}$'s; Table 2 shows that placing those 100 securities into 5 portfolios with 20 securities in each increases the size to 56.8 percent. Computing $\hat{\theta}_p$ with extreme $\hat{\alpha}_{[i_k:N]}$ would presumably yield even higher rejection rates. The biases reported in Tables 2 and 3 are even more surprising in view of the limited use we have made of the data. The only data-related information impounded in the induced order statistics is the rankings of the characteristics $\{X_i\}$. Nowhere

have we exploited the actual values of the X_i's, which contain considerably more precise information about the $\hat{\alpha}_i$'s.

1.4 Interpreting data-snooping bias as power

We have so far examined the effects of data snooping under the null
hypothesis that $\alpha_i = 0$, for all i. Therefore, the degree to which
induced ordering increases the probability of rejecting this null is
implicitly assumed to be a bias, an increase in type I error. However,
the results of the previous sections may be reinterpreted as describing
the power of tests based on induced ordering against certain alternative hypotheses.

Recall from (2) that $\hat{\alpha}_i$ is the sum of α_i and estimation error ζ_i. Since
all α_i's are zero under H, the induced ordering of the estimates $\hat{\alpha}_i$
creates a spurious incompatibility with the null arising solely from
the sorting of the estimation errors ζ_i. But if the α_i's are nonzero and
vary across i, then sorting by some characteristic X_i related to α_i and
forming portfolios does yield a more powerful test. Forming portfolios
reduces the estimation error through diversification (or the law of
large numbers), and grouping by X_i maintains the dispersion of the
α_i's across portfolios. Therefore what were called biases in Sections
1.1–1.3 may also be viewed as measures of the power of induced
ordering against alternatives in which the α_i's differ from zero and
vary cross-sectionally with X_i. The values in Table 2 show that grouping on a marginally correlated characteristic can increase the power
substantially.[14]

To formalize the above intuition within our framework, suppose
that the α_i's were i.i.d. random variables independent of ζ_i and have
mean μ_α and variance σ_α^2. Then the $\hat{\alpha}_i$'s are still independently and
identically distributed, but the null hypothesis that $\alpha_i = 0$ is now
violated. Suppose the estimation error ζ_i were identically zero, so that
all variation in $\hat{\alpha}_i$ was due to variations in α_i. Then the values in Table
2 would represent the *power* of our test against this alternative, where
the squared correlation is now given by

$$\rho_p^2 = \frac{\mathrm{Cov}^2[X_i, \alpha_i]}{\mathrm{Var}[X_i] \cdot \mathrm{Var}[\alpha_i]}. \tag{24}$$

If, as under our null hypothesis, all α_i's were identically zero, then

---

[14] However, implicit in Table 2 is the assumption that the $\hat{\alpha}_i$'s are cross-sectionally independent,
which may be too restrictive a requirement for interesting alternative hypotheses. For example, if
the null hypothesis $\alpha_i = 0$ corresponds to the Sharpe–Lintner CAPM, then one natural alternative
might be a two-factor APT. In that case, the $\hat{\alpha}_i$'s of assets with similar factor loadings would tend
to be positively cross-sectionally correlated as a result of the omitted factor. This positive correlation
reduces the benefits of grouping. Grouping by induced ordering does tend to cluster $\hat{\alpha}_i$'s with
similar (nonzero) means together, but correlation works against the variance reduction that gives
portfolio-based tests their power. The importance of cross-sectional dependence is evident in
MacKinlay's (1987) power calculations. We provide further discussion in Section 2.3.

The Review of Financial Studies / v 3 n 3 1990

the values in Table 2 must be interpreted as the *size* of our test, where the squared correlation reduces to

$$\rho_s^2 = \frac{\text{Cov}^2[X_i, \zeta_i]}{\text{Var}[X_i] \cdot \text{Var}[\zeta_i]}. \tag{25}$$

More generally, the squared correlation ρ^2 is related to ρ_s^2 and ρ_p^2 in the following way:

$$\rho^2 = \frac{\text{Cov}^2[X_i, \hat{\alpha}_i]}{\text{Var}[X_i] \cdot \text{Var}[\hat{\alpha}_i]} = \frac{(\text{Cov}[X_i, \alpha_i] + \text{Cov}[X_i, \zeta_i])^2}{\text{Var}[X_i] \cdot (\text{Var}[\alpha_i] + \text{Var}[\zeta_i])} \tag{26}$$

$$= \left(\rho_s \sqrt{\pi} + \rho_p \sqrt{1 - \pi} \right)^2, \quad \pi \equiv \frac{\text{Var}[\zeta_i]}{\text{Var}[\hat{\alpha}_i]}. \tag{27}$$

Holding the correlations ρ_s and ρ_p fixed, the importance of the spurious portion of ρ^2, given by ρ_s, increases with π, the fraction of variability in $\hat{\alpha}_i$ due to estimation error. Conversely, if the variability of $\hat{\alpha}_i$ is largely due to fluctuations in α_i, then ρ^2 will reflect mostly ρ_p^2.

Of course, the essence of the problem lies in our inability to identify π except in very special cases. We observe an empirical relation between X_i and $\hat{\alpha}_i$, but we do not know whether the characteristic varies with α_i or with estimation error ζ_i. It is a type of identification problem that is unlikely to be settled by data analysis alone, but must be resolved by providing theoretical motivation for a relation, or no relation, between X_i and α_i. That is, economic considerations must play a dominant role in determining π. We shall return to this issue in the empirical examples of Section 3.

2. Monte Carlo Results

Although the values in Tables 1–3 quantify the magnitude of the biases associated with induced ordering, their practical relevance may be limited in at least three respects. First, the test statistics we have considered are similar in spirit to those used in empirical tests of asset pricing models, but implicitly use the assumption of cross-sectional independence. The more common practice is to estimate the covariance matrix of the N asset returns using a finite number T of time series observations, from which an F-distributed quadratic form may be constructed. Both sampling error from the covariance matrix estimator and cross-sectional dependence will affect the null distribution of $\hat{\theta}$ in finite samples.

Second, the sampling theory of Section 1 is based on asymptotic approximations, and few results on rates of convergence for Theorem

Data-Snooping Biases

1.1 are available.[15] How accurate are such approximations for empirically realistic sample sizes?

Finally, the form of the asymptotics does not correspond exactly to procedures followed in practice. Recall that the limiting result involves a finite number n of securities with relative ranks that converge to fixed constants ξ_i as the number of securities N increases without bound. This implies that as N increases, the number of securities in between any two of our chosen n must also grow without bound. However, in practice characteristic-sorted portfolios are constructed from *all* securities within a fractile, not just from those with particular relative ranks. Although intuition suggests that this may be less problematic when n is large (so that within any given fractile there will be many securities), it is surprisingly difficult to verify.[16]

In this section we report results from Monte Carlo experiments that show the asymptotic approximations of Section 1 to be quite accurate in practice despite these three reservations. In Section 2.1, we evaluate the quality of the asymptotic approximations for the $\tilde{\theta}_p$ test used in calculating Tables 2 and 3. In Section 2.2, we consider the effects of induced ordering on F-tests with fixed N and T when the covariance matrix is estimated and the data-generating process is cross-sectionally independent. In Section 2.3, we consider the effects of relaxing the independence assumption.

2.1 Simulation results for $\tilde{\theta}_p$

The $\chi_q^2(\lambda)$ limiting distribution of $\tilde{\theta}_p$ obtains because any finite collection of induced order statistics, each with a fixed distinct limiting relative rank ξ_i in $(0, 1)$, becomes mutually independent as the total number N of securities increases without bound. This asymptotic approximation implies that between any two of the n chosen securities there will be an increasing number of securities omitted from all portfolios as N increases. In practice, all securities within a particular characteristic fractile are included in the sorted portfolios; hence, the theoretical sizes of Table 2 may not be an adequate approximation to this more empirically relevant situation. To explore this possibility we simulate bivariate normal vectors $(\hat{\alpha}_i, X_i)$ with squared correlation R^2, form portfolios using the induced ordering by the X_i's, compute $\tilde{\theta}_p$ using *all* the $\hat{\alpha}_{[i:N]}$'s (in contrast to the asymptotic

---

[15] However, see Bhattacharya (1984) and Sen (1981).

[16] When n is large relative to a finite N, the asymptotic approximation breaks down. In particular, the dependence between adjacent induced order statistics becomes important for nontrivial n/N. A few elegant asymptotic approximations for sums of induced order statistics are available using functional central limit theory and may allow us to generalize our results to the more empirically relevant case. See, for example, Bhattacharya (1974), Nagaraja (1982a, 1982b, 1984), Sandström (1987), Sen (1976, 1981), and Yang (1981a, 1981b). However, our Monte Carlo results suggest that this generalization may be unnecessary.

The Review of Financial Studies / v 3 n 3 1990

Table 4
Empirical sizes of nominal 5 percent χ^2_q-tests of H: $\alpha_i = 0$ ($i = 1, \ldots, n$) using the test statistic $\hat{\theta}_p$

q	$n_o = 5$	$n_o = 10$	$n_o = 20$	$n_o = 25$	$n_o = 50$
$R^2 = .005$					
5	0.055	0.057	0.067	0.075	0.108
10	0.054	0.063	0.080	0.084	0.139
20	0.056	0.068	0.086	0.106	0.182
25	0.062	0.070	0.104	0.112	0.209
50	0.059	0.077	0.119	0.146	0.314
$R^2 = .01$					
5	0.058	0.064	0.093	0.105	0.174
10	0.059	0.076	0.119	0.130	0.257
20	0.057	0.083	0.140	0.188	0.385
25	0.069	0.100	0.170	0.206	0.445
50	0.083	0.118	0.244	0.300	0.679
$R^2 = .05$					
5	0.091	0.149	0.310	0.392	0.723
10	0.117	0.227	0.493	0.611	0.943
20	0.156	0.351	0.744	0.854	0.999
25	0.163	0.401	0.818	0.916	1.000
50	0.249	0.616	0.971	0.997	1.000
$R^2 = .10$					
5	0.141	0.285	0.601	0.721	0.973
10	0.197	0.473	0.854	0.937	1.000
20	0.308	0.709	0.985	0.998	1.000
25	0.338	0.789	0.995	1.000	1.000
50	0.545	0.961	1.000	1.000	1.000
$R^2 = .20$					
5	0.267	0.577	0.922	0.974	1.000
10	0.405	0.833	0.997	1.000	1.000
20	0.635	0.982	1.000	1.000	1.000
25	0.728	0.996	1.000	1.000	1.000
50	0.933	1.000	1.000	1.000	1.000

$\hat{\theta}_p = n_o \Sigma_{k=1}^q \hat{\phi}_k^2 / \sigma_a^2$, and $\hat{\phi}_k = (1/n_o)\Sigma_{j=(k-1)q+1}^{kn} \hat{a}_{(j:N)}$ is constructed from portfolio k, with portfolios formed by sorting on some characteristic correlated with estimates $\hat{a}_i$. This induced ordering alters the null distribution of $\hat{\theta}_p$ from χ^2_q to $(1 - R^2) \cdot \chi^2_q(\lambda)$, where the noncentrality parameter λ is a function of the number q of portfolios, the number n_o of securities in each portfolio, and the squared correlation coefficient R^2 between $\hat{a}_i$ and the sorting characteristic. Each simulation is based on 5000 replications; asymptotic standard errors for the size estimates may be obtained from the usual binomial approximation, and is 3.08×10^{-3} for the 5 percent test.

experiment where only those induced order statistics of given relative ranks are used), and then repeat this procedure 5,000 times to obtain the finite sample distribution.

Table 3 reports the results of these simulations for the same values of R^2, n_o, and q as in Table 2. Except when both n_o and q are small, the empirical sizes of Table 4 match their asymptotic counterparts in Table 2 closely. Consider, for example, the $R^2 = .05$ panel; with five portfolios each with five securities, the difference between the theoretical and empirical size is 1.1 percentage points, whereas this difference is only 0.2 percentage points for 25 portfolios each with 25 securities. When n_o and q are both small, the theoretical and empirical sizes differ more for larger R^2, by as much as 7.4 percent when $R^2 = .20$. However, for the more relevant values of R^2, the empirical and theoretical sizes of the $\tilde{\theta}_p$ test are virtually identical.

2.2 Effects of induced ordering on *F*-tests

Although the results of Section 2.1 support the accuracy of our asymptotic approximation to the sampling distribution of $\tilde{\theta}_p$, the closely related F-statistic is used more frequently in practice. In this section we consider the finite-sample distribution of the F-statistic after induced ordering. We perform Monte Carlo experiments under the now standard multivariate data-generating process common to virtually all static financial asset pricing models. Let r_{it} denote the return of asset i between dates $t - 1$ and t, where $i = 1, 2, \ldots, N$ and $t = 1, 2, \ldots, T$. We assume that for all assets i and dates t the following obtains:

$$r_{it} = \alpha_i + \sum_{j=1}^{k} \beta_{ij} r_t^j + \epsilon_{it}, \tag{28}$$

where α_i and β_{ij} are fixed parameters, r_t^j is the return on some portfolio j (systematic risk), and ϵ_{it} is mean-zero (idiosyncratic) noise. Depending on the particular application, r_{it} may be taken to be nominal, real, or excess asset returns. The process (28) may be viewed as a factor model where the factors correspond to particular portfolios of traded assets, often called the "mimicking portfolios" of an exact factor pricing model. In matrix notation, we have

$$r_t = \alpha + Br_t^p + \epsilon_t, \quad E[\epsilon_t \mid r_t^p] = 0, \quad E[r_t^p] = \mu_p; \tag{29}$$

$$E[\epsilon_s \epsilon_t'] = \begin{cases} \Sigma, \text{ for } s = t, \\ 0, \text{ otherwise}; \end{cases} \tag{30}$$

$$E[(r_s^p - \mu_p)(r_t^p - \mu_p)'] = \begin{cases} \Omega, \text{ for } s = t, \\ 0, \text{ otherwise}. \end{cases} \tag{31}$$

Here, r_t is the $N \times 1$ vector of asset returns at a time t, B is the $N \times k$ matrix of factor loadings, r_t^p is the $k \times 1$ vector of time-t spanning portfolio returns, and α and ϵ_t are $N \times 1$ vectors of asset return intercepts and disturbances, respectively.

This data-generating process is the starting point of the two most

The Review of Financial Studies / v 3 n 3 1990

popular static models of asset pricing, the CAPM and the APT. Further restrictions are usually imposed by the specific model under consideration, often reducing to the following null hypothesis:

$$H: g(\alpha, B) = 0,$$

where the function g is model dependent.[17] Many tests simply set $g(\alpha, B) = \alpha$ and define r_t as excess returns, such as those of the Sharpe–Lintner CAPM and the exact factor-pricing APT. With the added assumption that r_t and r_t^p are jointly normally distributed, the finite-sample distribution of the following test statistic is well known:

$$\psi = \kappa \cdot \frac{\hat{\alpha}'\hat{\Sigma}^{-1}\hat{\alpha}}{1 + \bar{r}^p\hat{\Omega}^{-1}\bar{r}^p} \sim F_{N,T-k-N}, \quad \kappa \equiv \frac{T - k - N}{N}, \quad (32)$$

where $\hat{\Sigma}$ and $\hat{\Omega}$ are the maximum likelihood estimators of the covariance matrices of the disturbances $\hat{\epsilon}_t$ and the spanning portfolio returns r_t^p, respectively, and $\bar{r}^p$ is the vector of sample means of r_t^p. If the number of available securities N is greater than the number of time series observations T less $k + 1$, the estimator $\hat{\Sigma}$ is singular and the test statistic (32) cannot be computed without additional structure. This problem is most often circumvented in practice by forming portfolios. That is, let r_t be a $q \times 1$ vector of returns of q portfolios of securities where $q \ll N$. Since the return-generating process is linear for each security i, a linear relation also obtains for portfolio returns. However, as the analysis of Section 1 foreshadows, if the portfolios are constructed by sorting on some characteristic correlated with $\hat{\alpha}$ then the null distribution of ψ is altered.

To evaluate the null distribution of ψ under characteristic-sorting data snooping, we design our simulation experiments in the following way. The number of time series observations T is set to 60 for all simulations. With little loss in generality, we set the number of spanning portfolios k to zero so that $\hat{\alpha}_i = \Sigma_{t=1}^{T} r_{it}/T$. To separate the effects of *estimating* the covariance matrix from the effects of cross-sectional dependence, we first assume that the covariance matrix Σ of ϵ_t is equal to the identity matrix I—this assumption is relaxed in Section 2.3. We simulate T observations of the $N \times 1$ gaussian vector r_t (where N takes the values 200, 500, and 1000), and compute $\hat{\alpha}$. We then form q portfolios (where q takes the values 10 and 20) by constructing a characteristic X_i that has correlation ρ with $\hat{\alpha}_i$ (where ρ^2 takes the

---

[17] Examples of tests that fit into this framework are those in Campbell (1987), Connor and Korajczyk (1988), Gibbons (1982), Gibbons and Ferson (1985), Gibbons, Ross, and Shanken (1989), Huberman and Kandel (1987), MacKinlay (1987), Lehmann and Modest (1988), Stambaugh (1982), and Shanken (1985).

values .005, .01, .05, .10, and .20), and then sorting the $\hat{\alpha}_i$'s by this characteristic. To do this, we define

$$X_i \equiv \hat{\alpha}_i + \eta_i, \qquad \eta_i \text{ i.i.d. } N(0, \sigma_\eta^2), \qquad \sigma_\eta^2 = \frac{1 - \rho^2}{T\rho^2}. \qquad (33)$$

Having constructed the X_i's, we order $\{\hat{\alpha}_i\}$ to obtain $\{\hat{\alpha}_{[i:N]}\}$, construct portfolio intercept estimates that we call $\hat{\phi}_k$, $k = 1, \ldots, n$,

$$\hat{\phi}_k = \frac{1}{n_o} \sum_{i=(k-1)n_o+1}^{kn_o} \hat{\alpha}_{[i:N]}, \qquad N \equiv n_o q, \qquad (34)$$

from which we form the F-statistic

$$\psi = \kappa \cdot \hat{\phi}' \hat{\Sigma}^{-1} \hat{\phi} \sim F_{q,T-q}, \qquad \kappa \equiv (T - q)/q, \qquad (35)$$

where $\hat{\phi}$ denotes the $q \times 1$ vector of $\hat{\phi}_k$'s, and $\hat{\Sigma}$ is the maximum likelihood estimator of the $q \times q$ covariance matrix of the q portfolio returns. This procedure is repeated 5000 times, and the mean and standard deviation of the resulting distribution for the statistic ψ are reported in Table 5, as well as the size of 1, 5, and 10 percent F-tests.

Even for as small an R^2 as 1 percent, the empirical size of the 5 percent F-test differs significantly from its nominal value for all values of q and n_o. For the sample of 1000 securities grouped into ten portfolios, the empirical rejection rate of 36.7 percent deviates substantially from 5 percent. When the 1000 securities are grouped into 20 portfolios, the size is somewhat lower—26.8 percent—matching the pattern in Table 2. Also similar is the monotonicity of the size with respect to the number of securities. For 200 securities the empirical size is only 7.1 percent with 10 portfolios, but it is more than quintupled with 1000 securities. When the squared correlation between $\hat{\alpha}_i$ and X_i increases to 10 percent, the size of the F-test is essentially unity for sample sizes of 500 or more. Thus even for finite sample sizes of practical relevance, the importance of data snooping via induced ordering cannot be overemphasized.

2.3 F-tests with cross-sectional dependence

The substantial bias that induced ordering imparts on the size of portfolio-based F-tests comes from the fact that the induced order statistics $\{\hat{\alpha}_{[i:N]}\}$ generally have nonzero means;[18] hence, the averages of these statistics within sorted portfolios also have nonzero means but reduced variances about those means. Alternatively, the bias from portfolio formation is a result of the fact that the $\hat{\alpha}_i$'s of the extreme portfolios do not approach zero as more securities are combined,

---

[18] Only those $\hat{\alpha}_{[i:N]}$ for which $i/N \to \frac{1}{2}$ will have zero expectation under the null hypothesis H.

The Review of Financial Studies / v 3 n 3 1990

Table 5
Empirical size of $F_{q,T-q}$ tests based on q portfolios sorted by a random characteristic whose squared correlation with $\hat{\alpha}_i$ is R^2

q	n_o	n	Mean	Std. Dev.	Size 10%	Size 5%	Size 1%
$R^2 = .005$							
10	20	200	1.111	0.542	0.124	0.041	0.014
20	10	200	1.081	0.424	0.107	0.054	0.009
10	50	500	1.238	0.611	0.177	0.070	0.026
20	25	500	1.147	0.462	0.152	0.079	0.018
10	100	1000	1.406	0.679	0.270	0.118	0.046
20	50	1000	1.240	0.500	0.194	0.114	0.033
$R^2 = .01$							
10	20	200	1.225	0.619	0.181	0.071	0.026
20	10	200	1.148	0.460	0.148	0.079	0.018
10	50	500	1.512	0.728	0.318	0.152	0.070
20	25	500	1.301	0.514	0.240	0.143	0.036
10	100	1000	2.030	0.908	0.576	0.367	0.203
20	50	1000	1.554	0.596	0.405	0.268	0.098
$R^2 = .05$							
10	20	200	1.980	0.883	0.549	0.342	0.189
20	10	200	1.505	0.582	0.369	0.241	0.082
10	50	500	3.501	1.335	0.945	0.846	0.700
20	25	500	2.264	0.801	0.798	0.670	0.382
10	100	1000	5.991	1.976	0.999	0.997	0.986
20	50	1000	3.587	1.169	0.992	0.972	0.879
$R^2 = .10$							
10	20	200	2.961	1.196	0.868	0.713	0.538
20	10	200	1.977	0.727	0.658	0.510	0.257
10	50	500	5.939	1.931	0.999	0.997	0.987
20	25	500	3.526	1.128	0.988	0.968	0.868
10	100	1000	10.888	3.050	1.000	1.000	1.000
20	50	1000	6.123	1.811	1.000	1.000	0.999
$R^2 = .20$							
10	20	200	4.831	1.657	0.997	0.982	0.937
20	10	200	2.895	0.992	0.948	0.882	0.667
10	50	500	10.796	3.022	1.000	1.000	1.000
20	25	500	6.005	1.758	1.000	1.000	0.998
10	100	1000	20.695	5.112	1.000	1.000	1.000
20	50	1000	11.194	2.988	1.000	1.000	1.000

n_o is the number of securities in each portfolio and $n = n_o q$ is the total number of securities. The number of time series observations T is set to 60. The mean and standard deviation of the test statistic over the 5000 replications are reported. The population mean and standard deviation of $F_{10,50}$ are 1.042 and 0.523, respectively; those of the $F_{20,40}$ are 1.053 and 0.423, respectively. Asymptotic standard errors for the size estimates may be obtained from the usual binomial approximation; they are 4.24×10^{-3}, 3.08×10^{-3}, and 1.41×10^{-3} for the 10, 5, and 1 percent tests, respectively.

whereas the residual variances of the portfolios (and consequently the variances of the portfolio $\hat{\alpha}_i$'s) do tend to zero. Of course, our assumption that the disturbances ϵ_t of (29) are cross-sectionally independent implies that the portfolio residual variance approaches zero rather quickly (at rate $1/n_o$). But in many applications (such as the CAPM), cross-sectional independence is counterfactual. Firm size and industry membership are but two factors that might induce cross-sectional correlation in return residuals. In particular, when the residuals are positively cross-sectionally correlated, the bias is likely to be smaller since there is less variance reduction in forming portfolios than in the cross-sectionally independent case.

To see how restrictive the independence assumption is, we simulate a data-generating process in which disturbances are cross-sectionally correlated. The design is identical to that of Section 2.2 except that the residual covariance matrix Σ is no longer diagonal. Instead, we set

$$\Sigma = \delta\delta' + I, \tag{36}$$

where δ is an $N \times 1$ vector of parameters and I is the identity matrix. Such a covariance matrix would arise, for example, from a single common factor model for the $N \times 1$ vector of disturbances ϵ_t:

$$\epsilon_t = \delta\Lambda_t + v_t, \tag{37}$$

where Λ_t is some i.i.d. zero-mean unit-variance common factor independent of v_t, and v_t is N-dimensional vector white noise with covariance matrix I. For our simulations, the parameters δ are chosen to be equally spaced in the interval $[-1, 1]$. With this design the cross-correlation of the disturbances will range from -0.5 to 0.5. The X_i's are constructed as in (33) with

$$\sigma_\eta^2 = \frac{(1 - \rho^2)\sigma^2(\alpha)}{\rho^2}, \qquad \sigma^2(\alpha) \equiv \frac{1}{NT}\sum_{i=1}^{N}(\delta_i^2 + 1), \tag{38}$$

where ρ^2 is fixed at .05.

Under this design, the results of the simulation experiments may be compared to the third panel of Table 5, and are reported in Table 6.[19] Despite the presence of cross-sectional dependence, the impact of induced ordering on the size of the F-test is still significant. For example, with 20 portfolios each containing 25 securities the empirical size of the 5 percent test is 32.3 percent; with 10 portfolios of 50 securities each the empirical size increases to 82.0 percent. As in the cross-sectionally independent case, the bias increases with the number of securities given a fixed number of portfolios, and the bias decreases as the number of portfolios is increased given a fixed number of securities. Not surprisingly, for fixed n_o and q, cross-sectional dependence of the $\hat{\alpha}_i$'s lessens the bias. However, the entries in Table 6 demonstrate that the effects of data snooping may still be substantial even in the presence of cross-sectional dependence.

---

[19] The correspondence between the two tables is not exact because the dependency introduced in (36) induces cross-sectional heteroskedasticity in the $\hat{\alpha}_i$'s; hence, $\rho^2 = .05$ yields an R^2 of .05 only approximately.

The Review of Financial Studies / v 3 n 3 1990

Table 6
Empirical size of $F_{\hat{a},r-q}$ tests based on q portfolios sorted by a random characteristic whose squared correlation with $\hat{a}_i$ is approximately .05

q	n_o	n	Mean	Std. Dev.	Size 10%	Size 5%	Size 1%
$R^2 \approx .05$							
10	20	200	1.700	0.763	0.422	0.216	0.100
20	10	200	1.372	0.528	0.270	0.167	0.047
10	50	500	2.520	1.041	0.765	0.565	0.367
20	25	500	1.867	0.693	0.593	0.322	0.205
10	100	1000	3.624	1.605	0.925	0.820	0.682
20	50	1000	2.516	0.966	0.844	0.743	0.501

n_o is the number of securities in each portfolio and $n = n_o q$ is the total number of securities. The $\hat{a}_i$'s of the portfolios are cross-sectionally correlated, where the source of correlation is an i.i.d. zero-mean common factor in the returns. The number of time series observations T is set to 60. The mean and standard deviation of the test statistic over the 5000 replications are reported. The population mean and standard deviation of $F_{10,50}$ are 1.042 and 0.523, respectively; those of the $F_{20,40}$ are 1.053 and 0.423, respectively. Asymptotic standard errors for the size estimates may be obtained from the usual binomial approximation; they are 4.24×10^{-3}, 3.08×10^{-3}, and 1.41×10^{-3} for the 10, 5, and 1 percent tests, respectively.

3. Two Empirical Examples

To illustrate the potential relevance of data-snooping biases associated with induced ordering, we provide two examples drawn from the empirical literature. The first example is taken from the early tests of the Sharpe–Lintner CAPM, where portfolios were formed by sorting on out-of-sample betas. We show that such tests can be biased towards falsely rejecting the CAPM if in-sample betas are used instead, underscoring the importance of the elaborate sorting procedures used by Black, Jensen, and Scholes (1972) and Fama and MacBeth (1973). Our second example concerns tests of the APT that reject the zero-intercept null hypothesis when applied to portfolio returns sorted by market value of equity. We show that data-snooping biases can account for much the same results, and that only additional economic restrictions will determine the ultimate source of the rejections.

3.1 Sorting by beta
Although tests of the Sharpe–Lintner CAPM may be conducted on individual securities, the potential benefits of using multiple securities are well known. One common approach for allocating securities to portfolios has been to rank them by their betas and then group the sorted securities. Beta-sorted portfolios will exhibit more risk dispersion than portfolios of randomly chosen securities, and may therefore yield more information about the CAPM's risk–return relation. Ideally, portfolios would be formed according to their true betas. However, since the population betas are unobservable, in practice

portfolios have grouped securities by their estimated betas. For example, both Black, Jensen, and Scholes (1972) and Fama and MacBeth (1973) use portfolios formed by sorting on estimated betas, where the betas are estimated with a *prior* sample of stock returns. Their motivation for this more complicated procedure was to avoid grouping common estimation or measurement error since, within the sample, securities with high estimated betas will tend to have positive realizations of estimation error, and vice versa for securities with low estimated betas.

Suppose, instead, that securities are grouped by betas estimated *in sample*. Can grouping common estimation error change inferences substantially? To answer this question within our framework, suppose the Sharpe–Lintner CAPM obtains so that

$$r_{it} = \beta_i r_{mt} + \epsilon_{it}, \qquad E[\epsilon_t \mid r_{mt}] = 0, \qquad E[\epsilon_t \epsilon_t'] = \sigma_\epsilon^2 I, \qquad (39)$$

where r_{it} denotes the excess return of security i, r_{mt} is the excess market return, and ϵ_t is the $N \times 1$ vector of disturbances. To assess the impact of sorting on in-sample betas, we require the squared correlation of $\hat{\alpha}_i$ and $\hat{\beta}_i$. However, since our framework requires that both $\hat{\alpha}_i$ and $\hat{\beta}_i$ be independently and identically distributed, and since $\hat{\beta}_i$ is the sum of β_i and estimation error ζ_i, we assume β_i to be random to allow for cross-sectional variation in the betas. Therefore, let

$$\beta_i \text{ i.i.d. } N(\mu_\beta, \sigma_\beta^2), \qquad i = 1, 2, \ldots, N,$$

where each β_i is independent of all ϵ_{jt} in (39). The squared correlation between $\hat{\alpha}_i$ and $\hat{\beta}_i$ may then be explicitly calculated as

$$\rho^2(\hat{\alpha}_i, \hat{\beta}_i) = \frac{\text{Cov}^2[\hat{\alpha}_i, \hat{\beta}_i]}{\text{Var}[\hat{\alpha}_i]\,\text{Var}[\hat{\beta}_i]} = \frac{\hat{S}_m^2}{1 + \hat{S}_m^2} \cdot \frac{1}{1 + (\sigma_\beta^2 \hat{\sigma}_m^2/\sigma_\epsilon^2)T}, \qquad (40)$$

where $\hat{\mu}_m$ and $\hat{\sigma}_m$ are the sample mean and standard deviation of the excess market return, respectively, $S_m \equiv \hat{\mu}_m/\hat{\sigma}_m$ is the ex post Sharpe measure, and T is the number of time series observations used to estimate the α_i's and β_i's.

The term $\sigma_\beta^2 \hat{\sigma}_m^2 T/\sigma_\epsilon^2$ in (40) captures the essence of the errors-in-variables problem for in-sample beta sorting. This is simply the ratio of the cross-sectional variance in betas, σ_β^2, to the variance of the beta estimation error, $\sigma_\epsilon^2/(\hat{\sigma}_m^2 T)$. When the cross-sectional dispersion of the betas is much larger than the variance of the estimation errors, this ratio is large, implying a small value for ρ^2 and little data-snooping bias. In fact, since the estimation error of the betas declines with the number of observations T, as the time period lengthens, in-sample beta sorting becomes less problematic. However, when the variance of the estimation error is large relative to the cross-sectional variance

The Review of Financial Studies / v 3 n 3 1990

Table 7
Theoretical sizes of nominal 5 percent χ_q^2-tests under the null hypothesis of the Sharpe-Lintner CAPM using q in-sample beta-sorted portfolios with n_o securities per portfolio

Sample period	$\hat{R}^2$	$q = 10$ $n_o = 250$	$q = 20$ $n_o = 125$	$q = 50$ $n_o = 50$
January 1954–December 1958	.044	1.000	1.000	1.000
January 1959–December 1963	.007	0.790	0.656	0.435
January 1964–December 1968	.048	1.000	1.000	1.000
January 1969–December 1973	.008	0.869	0.756	0.529
January 1974–December 1978	.001	0.183	0.139	0.100
January 1979–December 1983	.023	1.000	1.000	0.991
January 1984–December 1988	.002	0.248	0.183	0.123

$\hat{R}^2$ is the estimated squared correlation between $\hat{\beta}_i$ and $\hat{\alpha}_i$ under the null hypothesis that $\alpha_i = 0$ and that the β_i's are i.i.d. normal random variables with mean and variance μ_β and σ_β^2, respectively. Within each subsample, the estimate $\hat{R}^2$ is based on the first 200 stocks in the CRSP monthly returns files with complete return histories over the five-year subperiod, and the CRSP equal-weighted index. For illustrative purposes, the theoretical size is computed under the assumption that the total number of securities $n = n_o q$ is fixed at 2500.

of the betas, then ρ^2 is large and grouping common estimation errors becomes a more serious problem.

To show just how serious this might be in practice, we report in Table 7 the estimated ρ^2 between $\hat{\alpha}_i$ and $\hat{\beta}_i$ for five-year subperiods from January 1954 to December 1988, where each estimate is based on the first 200 securities listed in the CRSP monthly returns files with complete return histories within the particular five-year subsample, and the CRSP equal-weighted index. Also reported is the probability of rejecting the null hypothesis $\alpha_i = 0$ when it is true using a 5 percent test, assuming a sample of 2500 securities, where the number of portfolios q is 10, 20, or 50 and the number of securities per portfolio n_o is defined accordingly.[20]

The entries in Table 7 show that the null hypothesis is quite likely to be rejected even when it is true. For many of the subperiods, the probability of rejecting the null is unity, and when only 10 beta-sorted portfolios are used, the smallest size of a nominal 5 percent test is still 18.3 percent. We conclude, somewhat belatedly, that the elaborate out-of-sampling sorting procedures used by Black, Jensen, and Scholes (1972) and Fama and MacBeth (1973) were indispensable to the original tests of the Sharpe–Lintner CAPM.

3.2 Sorting by size

As a second example of the practical relevance of data-snooping biases, we consider Lehmann and Modest's (1988) multivariate test of a 15-

---

[20] Our analysis is limited by the counterfactual assumption that the market model disturbances are cross-sectionally uncorrelated. But the simulation results presented in Section 2.3 indicate that biases are still substantial even in the presence of cross-sectional dependence. A more involved application would require a deeper analysis of cross-sectional dependence in the ϵ_{it}'s.

Data-Snooping Biases

factor APT model, in which they reject the zero-intercept null hypothesis using five portfolios formed by grouping securities ordered by market value of equity.[21] We focus on this particular study because of the large number of factors employed—our framework requires the disturbances ϵ_t of (29) to be cross-sectionally independent, and since 15 factors are included in Lehmann and Modest's cross-sectional regressions, a diagonal covariance matrix for ϵ_t is not implausible.

It is well-known that the estimated intercept $\hat{\alpha}_t$ from the single-period CAPM regression (excess individual security returns regressed on an intercept and the market risk premium) is negatively cross-sectionally correlated with log size.[22] Since this $\hat{\alpha}_t$ will in general be correlated with the estimated intercept from a 15-factor APT regression, it is likely that the estimated APT intercept and log size will also be empirically correlated.[23] Unfortunately, we do not have a direct measure of the correlation of the APT intercept and log size which is necessary to derive the appropriate null distribution after induced ordering.[24] As an alternative, we estimate the cross-sectional R^2 of the estimated CAPM alpha with the logarithm of size, and we use this R^2 as well as $\frac{1}{2}R^2$ and $\frac{1}{4}R^2$ to estimate the bias attributable to induced ordering.

Following Lehmann and Modest (1988), we consider four five-year time periods from January 1963 to December 1982. X_t is defined to be the logarithm of beginning-of-period market values of equity. The $\hat{\alpha}_t$'s are the intercepts from regressions of excess returns on the market risk premium as measured by the difference between an equal-weighted NYSE index and monthly Treasury bill returns, where the NYSE index is obtained from the Center for Research in Security Prices (CRSP) database. The R^2's of these regressions are reported in the second column of Table 8. One cross-sectional regression of $\hat{\alpha}_t$ on log size X_t is run for each five-year time period using monthly NYSE-AMEX data from CRSP. We run regressions only for those stocks having complete return histories within the relevant five-year period.

Table 8 contains the test statistics for a 15-factor APT framework using five size-sorted portfolios. The first four rows contain results

---

[21] See Lehmann and Modest (1988, table 1, last row). Connor and Korajczyk (1988) report similar findings.

[22] See, for example, Banz (1981) and Brown, Kleidon, and Marsh (1983).

[23] We recognize that correlation is not transitive, so if X is correlated with Y and Y with Z, X need not be correlated with Z. However, since the intercepts from the two regressions will be functions of some common random variables, situations in which they are independent are the exception rather than the rule.

[24] Nor did Lehmann and Modest prior to their extensive investigations. If they are subject to any data-snooping biases it is only from their awareness of size-related empirical results for the single-period CAPM, and of corresponding results for the APT as in Chan, Chen, and Hsieh (1985).

Asset Pricing Theory and Tests II

The Review of Financial Studies / v 3 n 3 1990

Table 8
Comparison of *p*-values for Lehmann and Modest's (1988) tests of the APT with and without correcting for the effects of induced ordering

Sample	N	$\hat{R}^2$	$\hat{\theta}_p$	χ^2 p-value	$\chi^2(\lambda_1)$ p-value	$\chi^2(\lambda_2)$ p-value	$\chi^2(\lambda_3)$ p-value
6301–6712	1001	0.015	13.70	0.018	0.687	0.315	0.131
6801–7212	1359	0.040	15.50	0.008	1.000	0.919	0.520
7301–7712	1346	0.033	10.20	0.070	1.000	0.963	0.720
7801–8212	1281	0.004	12.05	0.034	0.272	0.134	0.078
Aggregate	—	—	51.45	0.00014	1.000	0.917	0.298

In the absence of data snooping, the appropriate test statistics and their p-values (using the central χ^2 distribution) are given in Lehmann and Modest (1988, table 1) and reported below in columns 4 and 5 (we transform their F-statistics into χ^2 variates for purposes of comparison). Corresponding p-values that account for induced ordering are calculated in columns labeled "$\chi^2(\lambda_i)$ p-value" (i = 1, 2, 3) (using the noncentral χ^2 distribution), where λ_1, λ_2, and λ_3 are noncentrality parameters computed with $\hat{R}^2$, $\frac{2}{3}\hat{R}^2$, and $\frac{1}{2}\hat{R}^2$, respectively. In all cases, five portfolios are formed from the total number of securities; this yields five degrees of freedom for the χ^2 statistics in the first four rows, and 20 degrees of freedom for the aggregate χ^2 statistics.

for each of the four subperiods and the last row contains aggregate test statistics. To apply the results of Sections 1 and 2 we transform Lehmann and Modest's (1988) F-statistics into (asymptotic) χ^2 variates.[25] The total number of available securities ranges from a minimum of 1001 for the first five-year subperiod to a maximum of 1359 for the second subperiod. For each test statistic in Table 8 we report four different p-values: the first is with respect to the null distribution that ignores data snooping, and the next three are with respect to null distributions that account for induced ordering to various degrees.

The entries in Table 8 show that the potential biases from sorting by characteristics that have been empirically selected can be immense. The p-values range from 0.008 to 0.070 in the four subperiods according to the standard theoretical null distribution, yielding an aggregate p-value of 0.00014, considerable evidence against the null. When we adjust for the fact that the sorting characteristic is selected empirically (using the $\hat{R}^2$ from the cross-sectional regression of $\hat{\alpha}_i$ on X_i), the p-values for these same four subperiods range from 0.272 to 1.000, yielding an aggregate p-value of 1.000! Therefore, whether or not induced ordering is allowed for can change inferences dramatically.

The appropriate R^2 in the preceding analysis is the squared correlation between log size and the intercept from a 15-factor APT regression, and not the one used in Table 8. To see how this may affect our conclusions, recall from (2) that the cross-sectional correlation between $\hat{\alpha}_i$ and log size can arise from two sources: the

---

[25] Since Lehmann and Modest (1988) use weekly data, the null distribution of their test statistics is $F_{5,240}$. In practice the inferences are virtually identical using the χ^2_5 distribution after multiplying the test statistic by 5.

estimation error ζ_i in $\hat{\alpha}_i$, and the cross-sectional dispersion in the "true" CAPM α_i (which is zero under the null hypothesis). Correlation between X_i and ζ_i will be partially reflected in correlation between the estimated APT intercept and log size. The second source of correlation will not be relevant *under the APT null hypothesis* since under that scenario we assume that the 15-factor APT obtains and therefore the intercept vanishes for all securities. As a conservative estimate for the appropriate R^2 to be used in Table 8, we set the squared correlation equal to $\frac{1}{2}\hat{R}^2$ and $\frac{1}{4}\hat{R}^2$, yielding the p-values reported in the last two columns of Table 8. Even when the squared correlation is only $\frac{1}{4}\hat{R}^2$, the inferences change markedly after induced ordering, with p-values ranging from 0.078 to 0.720 in the four sub-periods and 0.298 in the aggregate. This simple example illustrates the severity with which even a mild form of data snooping can bias our inferences in practice.

Nevertheless, it should not be inferred from Table 8 that all size-related phenomena are spurious. After all, the correlation between X_i and $\hat{\alpha}_i$ may be the result of cross-sectional variations in the population α_i's, and not estimation error. Even so, tests using size-sorted portfolios are still biased if based on the same data from which the size effect was previously observed. A procedure that is free from such biases is to decide today that size is an interesting characteristic, collect ten years of new data, and then perform tests on size-sorted portfolios from this fresh sample. Provided that the old and new samples are statistically independent, this will yield a perfectly valid test of the null hypothesis H, since the only possible source of correlation between the X_i's and the $\hat{\alpha}_i$'s in the new sample is from the α_i's (presumably the result of some underlying economic relation between the two), and not from the estimation errors. In such cases, induced ordering cannot affect the distribution of the test statistics under the null hypothesis, and will yield a considerably more powerful test against many alternatives.

4. How the Data Get Snooped

Whether the probabilities of rejection in Table 2 are to be interpreted as size or power depends, of course, on the particular null and alternative hypotheses at hand, the key distinction being the source of correlation between $\hat{\alpha}_i$ and the characteristic X_i. Since our starting point in Section 1 was the assertion that this correlation is "spurious," we view the values of Table 2 as probabilities of falsely rejecting the null hypothesis. We suggested in Section 1 that the source of this spurious correlation is correlation between the characteristic and the estimation errors in $\hat{\alpha}_i$, since such errors are the only source of vari-

461

The Review of Financial Studies / v 3 n 3 1990

ation in $\hat{\alpha}_i$ under the null. But how does this correlation arise? One possibility is the very mechanism by which characteristics are selected. Without any economic theories for motivation, a plausible behavioral model of how we determine characteristics to be particularly "interesting" is that we tend to focus on those that have unusually large squared sample correlations or R^2's with the $\hat{\alpha}_i$'s. In the spirit of Ross (1987), economists study "interesting" events, as well as events that are interesting from a theoretical perspective. If so, then even in a collection of K characteristics all of which are independent of the $\hat{\alpha}_i$'s, correlation between the $\hat{\alpha}_i$'s and the most "interesting" characteristic is artificially induced.

More formally, suppose for each of N securities we have a collection of K distinct and mutually independent characteristics Y_{ik}, $k = 1, 2, \ldots, K$, where Y_{ik} is the kth characteristic of the ith security. Let the null hypothesis obtain so that $\alpha_i = 0$, for all i, and assume that all characteristics are independent of $\{\hat{\alpha}_i\}$. This last assumption implies that the distribution of a test statistic based on grouped $\hat{\alpha}_i$'s is unaffected by sorting on any of the characteristics. For simplicity let each of the characteristics and the $\hat{\alpha}_i$'s be normally distributed with zero mean and unit variance, and consider the sample correlation coefficients:

$$\hat{\rho}_k = \frac{\sum_{i=1}^{N}(Y_{ik} - \bar{Y}_k)(\hat{\alpha}_i - \bar{\hat{\alpha}})}{\sqrt{\sum_{i=1}^{N}(Y_{ik} - \bar{Y}_k)^2} \cdot \sqrt{\sum_{i=1}^{N}(\hat{\alpha}_i - \bar{\hat{\alpha}})^2}}, \quad k = 1, 2, \ldots, K, \quad (41)$$

where $\bar{Y}_k$ and $\bar{\hat{\alpha}}$ are the sample means of characteristic k and the $\hat{\alpha}_i$'s, respectively. Suppose we choose as our sorting characteristic the one that has the largest squared correlation with the $\hat{\alpha}_i$'s, and call this characteristic X_i. That is, $X_i \equiv Y_{ik^*}$, where the index k^* is defined by

$$\hat{\rho}_{k^*}^2 = \underset{1 \leq k \leq K}{\text{Max}} \; \hat{\rho}_k^2 . \qquad (42)$$

This X_i is a new characteristic in the statistical sense, in that its distribution is no longer the same as that of the Y_{ik}'s.[26] It is apparent that X_i and $\hat{\alpha}_i$ are not mutually independent since the $\hat{\alpha}_i$'s were used in selecting this characteristic. By construction, extreme realizations of the random variables $\{X_i\}$ tend to occur when extreme realizations of $\{\hat{\alpha}_i\}$ occur.

To estimate the magnitude of correlation spuriously induced between X_i and $\hat{\alpha}_i$, first observe that although the correlation between Y_{ik} and $\hat{\alpha}_i$ is zero for all k, $E[\hat{\rho}_k^2] = 1/(N - 1)$ under our normality assumption. Therefore, $1/(N - 1)$ should be our benchmark in assessing the degree of spurious correlation between X_i and $\hat{\alpha}_i$. Since the $\hat{\rho}_k^2$'s are well-known to be independently and identically distributed

Beta$(\frac{1}{2}, \frac{1}{2}(N-2))$ variates, the distribution and density functions of $\hat{\rho}_{k^*}^2$, denoted by $F_*(v)$ and $f_*(v)$, respectively, may be readily derived as[27]

$$F_*(v) = [F_\beta(v)]^K, \quad v \in (0, 1), \tag{43}$$

$$f_*(v) = K[F_\beta(v)]^{K-1} f_\beta(v), \quad v \in (0, 1), \tag{44}$$

where F_β and f_β are the cumulative distribution function and probability density function of the Beta distribution with parameters $\frac{1}{2}$ and $\frac{1}{2}(N-2)$. A measure of that portion of squared correlation between X_t with $\hat{\alpha}_t$ due to sorting on $\hat{\rho}_k^2$ is then given by

$$\gamma \equiv E[\hat{\rho}_{k^*}^2] - E[\hat{\rho}_k^2] = \int_0^1 vf_*(v) \, dv - \frac{1}{N-1}. \tag{45}$$

For 25 securities and 50 characteristics, γ is 20.5 percent![28] With 100 securities, γ is still 5.4 percent and only declines to 1.1 percent for 500 securities. With only 25 characteristics, the values of γ for 25, 100, and 500 securities fall to 16.4, 4.2, and 0.8 percent, respectively. However, these smaller values of γ can still yield misleading inferences for tests based on few portfolios, each containing many securities. This is seen in Table 9, in which the theoretical sizes of 5 percent tests with R^2's equal to the appropriate γ for each cell are displayed. For example, the first entry in the first row of Table 9, 0.163, is the size of the 5 percent portfolio-based test with five portfolios and five securities in each, where the R^2 used to perform the calculation is the γ corresponding to 25 securities and 25 characteristics, or 16.4 percent. As the number of securities per portfolio grows, γ declines but the bias worsens—with 50 securities in each of 5 portfolios, γ is only 1.7 percent but the actual size of a 5 percent test is 26.4 percent. Although there is in fact no statistical relation between

---

[26] In fact, if we denote by Y_k the $N \times 1$ vector containing values of characteristic k for each of the N securities, then the vector most highly correlated with $\hat{\alpha}$ (which we have called X) may be viewed as the concomitant $Y_{[K\ n]}$ of the Kth order statistic $\hat{\rho}_{[K\ K]}^2 = \hat{\rho}_k^{2*}$. As in the scalar case, induced ordering does change the distribution of the vector concomitants.

[27] That the squared correlation coefficients are i.i.d. Beta random variables follows from our assumptions of normality and the mutual independence of the characteristics and the $\hat{\alpha}_t$'s [see Stuart and Ord (1987, chapter 16.28) for example]. The distribution and density functions of the maximum follow directly from this.

[28] Note that γ is only an approximation to the squared population correlation:

$$\left[\frac{E(X_t - E[X])(\hat{\alpha}_t - E[\hat{\alpha}])}{\sqrt{E(X_t - E[X])^2} \cdot \sqrt{E(\hat{\alpha}_t - E[\hat{\alpha}])^2}} \right]^2.$$

However, Monte Carlo simulations with 10,000 replications show that this approximation is excellent even for small sample sizes. For example, fixing K at 50, the correlation from the simulations is 22.82 percent for $N = 25$, whereas (45) yields $\gamma = 20.47$ percent; for $N = 100$ the simulations yield a correlation of 6.25 percent, compared to a γ of 5.39 percent.

The Review of Financial Studies / v 3 n 3 1990

Table 9
Theoretical sizes of nominal 5 percent χ_q^2-tests of H: $\alpha_i = 0$ ($i = 1, \ldots, n$) using the test statistic $\hat{\theta}_p$

q	$n_o = 5$	$n_o = 10$	$n_o = 20$	$n_o = 25$	$n_o = 50$
$K = 25$					
5	0.163	0.216	0.246	0.253	0.264
10	0.150	0.182	0.200	0.202	0.210
20	0.125	0.144	0.153	0.155	0.159
25	0.117	0.132	0.140	0.142	0.145
50	0.096	0.104	0.109	0.110	0.112
$K = 50$					
5	0.197	0.270	0.311	0.319	0.337
10	0.183	0.228	0.254	0.259	0.270
20	0.151	0.178	0.192	0.195	0.201
25	0.141	0.163	0.175	0.177	0.182
50	0.112	0.125	0.131	0.133	0.136

$\hat{\theta}_p = n_o \sum_{i=1}^L \hat{\phi}_i^2 / \sigma_a^2$, and $\hat{\phi}_k = (1/n_o)\sum_{j=1}^{n_o}{}_{(k-1)q+1} \hat{\alpha}_{ij \cdot N|}$ is constructed from portfolio k, with portfolios formed by sorting on some characteristic correlated with estimates $\hat{\alpha}_r$. This induced ordering alters the null distribution of $\hat{\theta}_p$ from χ_q^2 to $(1 - R^2) \cdot \chi_q^2(\lambda)$, where the noncentrality parameter λ is a function of the number q of portfolios, the number n_o of securities in each portfolio, and the squared correlation coefficient R^2 between $\hat{\alpha}_i$ and the sorting characteristic. The values of R^2 used for the size calculations vary with the total number of securities $n_o q$ and with K, the total number of independent characteristics from which the most "interesting" is selected.

any of the characteristics and the $\hat{\alpha}_i$'s, a procedure that focuses on the most striking characteristic can *create* spurious statistical dependence.

As the number of securities N increases, this particular source of dependence becomes less important since all the sample correlation coefficients $\hat{\rho}_k$ converge almost surely to zero, as does γ. However, recall from Table 2 that as the sample size grows the bias increases if the number of portfolios is held fixed; hence, as Table 9 illustrates, a larger N and thus a smaller γ need not imply a smaller bias. Moreover, since γ is increasing in the number of characteristics K, we cannot find refuge in the law of large numbers without weighing the number of securities against the number of characteristics and portfolios in some fashion. Table 9 provides one informal measure of this trade-off.

Perhaps even the most unscrupulous investigator might hesitate at the kind of data snooping we have just considered. However, the very review process that published research undergoes can have much the same effect, since competition for limited journal space tilts the balance in favor of the most striking and dissonant of empirical results. Indeed, the "Anomalies" section of the *Journal of Economic Perspectives* is the most obvious example of our deliberate search for the unusual in economics. As a consequence, interest may be created in otherwise theoretically irrelevant characteristics. In the absence of an economic paradigm, such data-snooping biases are not easily distinguishable from violations of the null hypothesis. This inability to separate pretest bias from alternative hypotheses is the most compelling criticism of "measurement without theory."

5. Conclusion

Although the size effect may signal important differences between the economic structure of small and large corporations, how these differences are manifested in the stochastic properties of their equity returns cannot be reliably determined through data analysis alone. Much more convincing would be the empirical significance of size, or any other quantity, that is based on a model of economic equilibrium in which the characteristic is related to the behavior of asset returns endogenously. Our findings show that tests using securities grouped according to theoretically motivated correlations between X_i and $\hat{\alpha}_i$ can be powerful indeed—interestingly, tests of the APT with portfolios sorted by such characteristics (own-variance and dividend yield) no longer reject the null hypothesis [see Lehmann and Modest (1988)]. Sorting on size yields rejections whereas sorting on theoretically relevant characteristics such as own-variance and dividend yield does not. This suggests that data-instigated grouping procedures should be employed cautiously.

It is widely acknowledged that incorrect conclusions may be drawn from procedures violating the assumptions of classical statistical inference, but the nature of these violations is often as subtle as it is profound. In observing that economists (as well as those in the natural sciences) tend to seek out anomalies, Merton (1987, p. 104) writes: "All this fits well with what the cognitive psychologists tell us is our natural individual predilection to focus, often disproportionately so, on the unusual. . . . This focus, both individually and institutionally, together with little control over the number of tests performed, creates a fertile environment for both unintended selection bias and for attaching greater significance to otherwise unbiased estimates than is justified." The recognition of this possibility is a first step in guarding against it. The results of our paper provide a more concrete remedy for such biases in the particular case of portfolio formation via induced ordering on data-instigated characteristics. However, nonexperimental inference may never be completely free from data-snooping biases since the attention given to empirical anomalies, incongruities, and unusual correlations is also the modus operandi for genuine discovery and progress in the social sciences. Formal statistical analyses such as ours may serve as primitive guides to a better understanding of economic phenomena, but the ability to distinguish between the spurious and the substantive is likely to remain a cherished art.

The Review of Financial Studies / v 3 n 3 1990

References

Aldous, D., 1989, *Probability Approximations via the Poisson Clumping Heuristic*, Springer, New York.

Banz, R. W., 1978, "Limited Diversification and Market Equilibrium: An Empirical Analysis," Ph.D. dissertation, University of Chicago.

Banz, R. W., 1981, "The Relationship Between Return and Market Value of Common Stocks," *Journal of Financial Economics*, 9, 3–18.

Berger, J., and R. Wolpert, 1984, *The Likelihood Principle*, Lecture Notes—Monograph Series Volume 6, Institute of Mathematical Statistics, Hayward, Cal.

Bhattacharya, P. K., 1974, "Convergence of Sample Paths of Normalized Sums of Induced Order Statistics," *Annals of Statistics*, 2, 1034–1039.

Bhattacharya, P. K., 1984, "Induced Order Statistics: Theory and Applications," in P. R. Krishnaiah and P. K. Sen (eds.), *Handbook of Statistics 4: Nonparametric Methods*, North-Holland, Amsterdam.

Black, F., M. Jensen, and M. Scholes, 1972, "The Capital Asset Pricing Model: Some Empirical Tests," in M. Jensen (ed.), *Studies in the Theory of Capital Markets*, Praeger, New York.

Brown, P., A. Kleidon, and T. Marsh, 1983, "New Evidence on the Nature of Size Related Anomalies in Stock Prices," *Journal of Financial Economics*, 12, 33–56.

Campbell, J. Y., 1987, "Stock Returns and the Term Structure," *Journal of Financial Economics*, 18, 373–400.

Chamberlain, G., 1983, "Funds, Factors, and Diversification in Arbitrage Pricing Models," *Econometrica*, 51, 1305–1323.

Chan, K., N. Chen, and D. Hsieh, 1985, "An Exploratory Investigation of the Firm Size Effect," *Journal of Financial Economics*, 14, 451–471.

Chen, N., R. Roll, and S. Ross, 1986, "Economic Forces and the Stock Market," *Journal of Business*, 59, 383–403.

Connor, G., and R. Korajczyk, 1988, "Risk and Return in an Equilibrium APT: Application of a New Test Methodology," *Journal of Financial Economics*, 21, 255–290.

David, H. A., 1973, "Concomitants of Order Statistics," *Bulletin of the International Statistical Institute*, 45, 295–300.

David, H. A., 1981, *Order Statistics* (2nd ed.), Wiley, New York.

David, H. A., and J. Galambos, 1974, "The Asymptotic Theory of Concomitants of Order Statistics," *Journal of Applied Probability*, 11, 762–770.

Fama, E., and J. MacBeth, 1973, "Risk, Return, and Equilibrium: Empirical Tests," *Journal of Political Economy*, 71, 607–636.

Gibbons, M. R., 1982, "Multivariate Tests of Financial Models: A New Approach," *Journal of Financial Economics*, 10, 3–27.

Gibbons, M. R., and W. Ferson, 1985, "Testing Asset Pricing Models with Changing Expectations and an Unobservable Market Portfolio," *Journal of Financial Economics*, 14, 217–236.

Gibbons, M. R., S. A. Ross, and J. Shanken, 1989, "A Test of the Efficiency of a Given Portfolio," *Econometrica*, 57, 1121–1152.

Huberman, G., and S. Kandel, 1987, "Mean Variance Spanning," *Journal of Finance*, 42, 873–888.

Iyengar, S., and J. Greenhouse, 1988, "Selection Models and the File Drawer Problem," *Statistical Science*, 3, 109–135.

Data-Snooping Biases

Lakonishok, J., and S. Smidt, 1988, "Are Seasonal Anomalies Real? A Ninety-Year Perspective," *Review of Financial Studies*, 1, 403–426.

Leamer, E., 1978, *Specification Searches*, Wiley, New York.

Lehmann, B. N., and D. Modest, 1988, "The Empirical Foundations of the Arbitrage Pricing Theory," *Journal of Financial Economics*, 21, 213–254.

MacKinlay, A. C., 1987, "On Multivariate Tests of the CAPM," *Journal of Financial Economics*, 18, 341–372.

Merton, R., 1987, "On the Current State of the Stock Market Rationality Hypothesis," in R. Dornbusch, S. Fischer, and J. Bossons (eds.), *Macroeconomics and Finance: Essays in Honor of Franco Modigliani*, M.I.T. Press, Cambridge, Mass.

Nagaraja, H. N., 1982a, "Some Asymptotic Results for the Induced Selection Differential," *Journal of Applied Probability*, 19, 233–239.

Nagaraja, H. N., 1982b, "Some Nondegenerate Limit Laws for the Selection Differential," *Annals of Statistics*, 10, 1306–1310.

Nagaraja, H. N., 1984, "Some Nondegenerate Limit Laws for Sample Selection Differential and Selection Differential," *Sankhyā*, 46, Series A, 355–369.

Ross, S., 1987, "Regression to the Max," Working Paper, Yale School of Organization and Management.

Sandström, A., 1987, "Asymptotic Normality of Linear Functions of Concomitants of Order Statistics," *Metrika*, 34, 129–142.

Sen, P. K., 1976, "A Note on Invariance Principles for Induced Order Statistics," *Annals of Probability*, 4, 474–479.

Sen, P. K., 1981, "Some Invariance Principles for Mixed Rank Statistics and Induced Order Statistics and Some Applications," *Communications in Statistics*, A10, 1691–1718.

Shanken, J., 1985, "Multivariate Tests of the Zero-Beta CAPM," *Journal of Financial Economics*, 14, 327–348.

Stambaugh, R. F., 1982, "On the Exclusion of Assets from Tests of the Two Parameter Model," *Journal of Financial Economics*, 10, 235–268.

Stuart, A., and J. Ord, 1987, *Kendall's Advanced Theory of Statistics*, Oxford U.P., New York.

Wang, T., 1988, *Essays on the Theory of Arbitrage Pricing*, unpublished doctoral dissertation, Wharton School, University of Pennsylvania.

Watterson, G. A., 1959, "Linear Estimation in Censored Samples from Multivariate Normal Populations," *Annals of Mathematical Statistics*, 30, 814–824.

Yang, S. S., 1977, "General Distribution Theory of the Concomitants of Order Statistics," *Annals of Statistics*, 5, 996–1002.

Yang, S. S., 1981a, "Linear Functions of Concomitants of Order Statistics with Application to Nonparametric Estimation of a Regression Function," *Journal of the American Statistical Association*, 76, 658–662.

Yang, S. S., 1981b, "Linear Combinations of Concomitants of Order Statistics with Application to Testing and Estimation," *Annals of the Institute of Statistical Mathematics*, 33 (Part A), 463–470.

[2]

ELSEVIER   Journal of Financial Economics 38 (1995) 3–28

Multifactor models do not explain deviations from the CAPM

A. Craig MacKinlay

The Wharton School, University of Pennsylvania, Philadelphia, PA 19104-6367, USA

(Received July 1993; final version received June 1994)

Abstract

A number of studies have presented evidence rejecting the validity of the Sharpe–Lintner capital asset pricing model (CAPM). Possible alternatives include risk-based models, such as multifactor asset pricing models, or nonrisk-based models which address biases in empirical methodology, the existence of market frictions, or the presence of irrational investors. Distinguishing between the alternatives is important for applications such as cost of capital estimation. This paper develops a framework which shows that, ex ante, CAPM deviations due to missing risk factors will be very difficult to detect empirically, whereas deviations resulting from nonrisk-based sources are easily detectable. The results suggest that multifactor pricing models alone do not entirely resolve CAPM deviations.

Key words: Capital asset pricing model; Data snooping; Market frictions; Multifactor models
JEL classification: G12; C52

1. Introduction

One of the important problems of modern financial economics is the quantification of the tradeoff between risk and expected return. Although common sense

I thank Fischer Black, Kent Daniel, Eugene Fama, Bruce Grundy, John Heaton, Ravi Jagannathan, Shmuel Kandel, Krishna Ramaswamy, Jay Shanken, Robert Whitelaw, and especially Andrew Lo, Bill Schwert, Robert Stambaugh, and an anonymous referee for helpful comments. A preliminary draft was completed while I was a summer visitor at the University of British Columbia in July 1991; thanks to the UBC finance faculty for constructive suggestions. An early draft circulated under the title 'Distinguishing Among Asset Pricing Theories'. I am grateful to seminar participants at Indiana University, MIT, NBER Asset Pricing Conference, Princeton, Rutgers University, Stanford, University of California at Berkeley, University of Chicago, University of Illinois, University of Rochester, Vanderbilt, and Wharton for helpful comments. Research support from the Batterymarch Fellowship and the Geewax-Terker Research Fund is gratefully acknowledged.

4 *A.C. MacKinlay/Journal of Financial Economics 38 (1995) 3–28*

suggests that investments free of risk will generally yield lower returns than riskier investments such as the stock market, it was only with the development of the Sharpe–Lintner capital asset pricing model (CAPM) that economists were able to quantify these differences in returns. In particular, the CAPM shows that the cross-section of expected excess returns of financial assets must be linearly related to the market betas, with an intercept of zero. Because of the practical importance of this risk–return relation, it has been empirically examined in numerous studies. Over the past fifteen years, a number of studies have presented evidence that contradict the CAPM, statistically rejecting the hypothesis that the intercept of a regression of excess returns on the excess return of the market is zero.

The apparent violations of the CAPM have spawned research into possible explanations. In this paper, the explanations will be divided into two categories: risk-based alternatives and nonrisk-based alternatives. The risk-based category includes multifactor asset pricing models developed under the assumptions of investor rationality and perfect capital markets. For this category, the source of deviations from the CAPM is either missing risk factors or the misidentification of the market portfolio as in Roll (1977).

The nonrisk-based category includes biases introduced in the empirical methodology, the existence of market frictions, or explanations arising from the presence of irrational investors. Examples are data-snooping biases, biases in computing returns, transaction costs and liquidity effects, and market inefficiencies. Although some of these explanations contain elements of risk, the elements of risk are different than those associated with perfect capital markets.

The empirical finding that the intercepts of the CAPM deviate statistically from zero has naturally led to the empirical examination of multifactor asset pricing models motivated by the arbitrage pricing theory (APT) developed by Ross (1976) and the intertemporal capital asset pricing model (ICAPM) developed by Merton (1973) (see Fama, 1993, for a detailed discussion of these multifactor model theories). The basic approach has been to introduce additional factors in the form of excess returns on traded portfolios and then reexamine the zero-intercept hypothesis. Fama and French (1993) use this approach and document that the estimates of the CAPM intercepts deviate from zero for portfolios formed on the basis of the ratio of book value to market value of equity as well as for portfolios formed based on market capitalization.[1] On finding that the intercepts for these portfolios with a three-factor model are closer to zero, they conclude that missing risk factors in the CAPM are the source of the deviations. They go on to advocate the use of a multifactor model,

---

[1] Fama and French are also concerned with the observation that the relation between average returns and market betas is weak. Although not addressed here, this point has been addressed in a number of recent papers, including Chan and Lakonishok (1993), Kandel and Stambaugh (1994), Kothari, Shanken, and Sloan (1994), and Roll and Ross (1994).

A.C. MacKinlay/Journal of Financial Economics 38 (1995) 3–28   5

stating that, with respect to the use of the Sharpe–Lintner CAPM, their results 'should help to break this common habit' (p. 44).

However, the conclusion that additional risk factors are required may be premature. One of several explanations consistent with the presence of deviations is data-snooping, as presented in Lo and MacKinlay (1990). The argument is that on an *ex post* basis one will always be able to find deviations from the CAPM. Such deviations considered in a group will appear statistically significant. However, they are merely a result of grouping assets with common disturbance terms. Since in financial economics our empirical analysis is *ex post* in nature, this problem is difficult to control. Direct adjustments for potential snooping are difficult to implement and, when implemented, make it very difficult to find real deviations.

While it is generally difficult to quantify and adjust for the effects of data-snooping biases, there are some related biases that can be examined. One such case pursued by Kothari, Shanken, and Sloan (1994) is sample selection bias. The authors show that significant biases can arise in academic research when the analysis is conditioned on the assets appearing in both the Center for Research in Security prices (CRSP) database and the Compustat database. Their analysis suggests that deviations from the CAPM such as those documented by Fama and French (1993) can be explained by sample selection biases. Breen and Korajczyk (1993) provide further evidence on selection biases that supports the Kothari, Shanken, and Sloan conclusion.

Other researchers interpret the deviations from the CAPM as indications of the presence of irrational behavior by market participants (e.g., DeBondt and Thaler, 1985). A number of theories have been developed that are consistent with this line of thought. A recent example is the work of Lakonishok, Shleifer, and Vishny (1993) who argue that the deviations arise from investors following naive strategies, such as extrapolating past growth rates too far into the future, assuming a trend in stock prices, overreacting to good or bad news, or preferring to invest in firms with a high level of profitability. With this alternative the possibility of nonzero intercepts arises not only from missing risk factors but also from specific firm characteristics.

Conrad and Kaul (1993) consider the possibility that biases in computed returns explain the deviations. They find that the implicit portfolio rebalancing in most analyses biases measured returns upwards, leading to overstated returns and CAPM deviations. This problem will be most severe for tests using frequently rebalanced portfolios and short observation intervals.

Finally, market frictions and liquidity effects could induce a nonzero intercept in the CAPM tests. Since the model is developed in a perfect market, such effects are not accommodated. Amihud and Mendelson (1986) present some evidence of returns containing effects from market frictions and demands for liquidity.

The controversy over whether or not the CAPM deviations are due to missing risk factors flourishes because empirically it is hard to distinguish between the

6   *A.C. MacKinlay/Journal of Financial Economics 38 (1995) 3–28*

various hypotheses. On an *ex post* basis, one can always find a set of risk factors that will make the asset pricing model intercept zero. Without a specific theory identifying the risk factors, one will always be able to explain the cross-section of expected returns with a multifactor asset pricing model, even if the real explanation lies in one of the nonrisk-based categories.

Although it is difficult to distinguish between the risk-based and nonrisk-based categories, the practical implications of the distinction are important. For example, if the risk-based explanation is correct, then cost of capital calculations using the CAPM can be badly misspecified. A better approach would be to use a multifactor model that captures the missing risk factors. On the other hand, if the deviations are a result of the nonrisk-based explanations, then disposing of the CAPM in favor of a multifactor model may lead to serious errors. The cost of capital estimate from a multifactor model can be very different than the estimate from the CAPM.

In this paper, I discriminate between the risk-based and the nonrisk-based explanations using *ex ante* analysis. The objective is to evaluate the plausibility of the argument that the deviations from the CAPM can be explained by additional risk factors. I argue that one should expect *ex ante* that CAPM deviations due to missing risk factors will be very difficult to detect because the deviation in expected return is also accompanied by increased variance. I formally analyze the issue using mean–variance efficient set mathematics in conjunction with the zero-intercept F-test presented in Gibbons, Ross, and Shanken (1989) and MacKinlay (1987). The difficulty exists because when deviations from the CAPM or other multifactor pricing models are the result of omitted risk factors, there is an upper limit on the distance between the null distribution of the test statistic and the alternative distribution. With the nonrisk-based alternatives, for which the source of the deviations is something other than missing factors, no such limit exists because the deviations need not be linked to the variances and covariances.

The paper also draws on a related distinction between the two categories, namely the difference in the behavior of the maximum squared Sharpe measure as the cross-section of securities is increased. (The Sharpe measure is the ratio of the mean excess return to the standard deviation of the excess return.) For the risk-based alternatives the maximum squared Sharpe measure is bounded, and for the nonrisk-based alternatives the maximum squared Sharpe measure is a less useful construct and can, in principle, be unbounded.

The results of the paper underscore the important role that economic analysis plays in distinguishing among different pricing models for the relation between risk and return. In the absence of specific alternative theories, and without very long time series of data, one is limited in what can be said about risk/return relations among financial securities.

The paper proceeds as follows. In Section 2 the framework for the analysis is presented and the *optimal orthogonal portfolio* is defined. This portfolio will play

A.C. MacKinlay/Journal of Financial Economics 38 (1995) 3–28   7

a key role in the arguments of the paper. Many of the results in the paper can be related to the values of the squared Sharpe measure for relevant portfolios. In Section 3 the relations between the parameters of the returns and the Sharpe measures are presented. Section 4 develops the implications relating to the controversy over missing risk factors. Theoretically, the framework used to distinguish between risk-based and nonrisk-based explanations assumes a large number of assets. Section 5 illustrates that the usefulness of the framework does not depend on this assumption. The paper concludes with Section 6.

2. Linear pricing models, mean–variance analysis, and the optimal orthogonal portfolio

I begin by specifying the distributional properties of excess returns for $\bar{N}$ primary assets in the economy. Let z_t represent the $\bar{N} \times 1$ vector of excess returns for period t. Assume z_t is stationary and ergodic with mean μ and a covariance matrix V that is full rank. Given these assumptions for any set of factor portfolios, a linear relation between the excess returns and the portfolios' excess returns results. The relation can be expressed as

$$z_t = \alpha + B z_{pt} + \varepsilon_t ,$$ (1)

$$E[\varepsilon_t] = 0 ,$$ (2)

$$E[\varepsilon_t \varepsilon_t'] = \Sigma ,$$ (3)

$$E[z_{pt}] = \mu_p , \qquad E[(z_{pt} - \mu_p)(z_{pt} - \mu_p)'] = \Omega_p ,$$ (4)

$$\text{cov}[z_{pt}, \varepsilon_t] = 0 .$$ (5)

B is the $\bar{N} \times K$ matrix of factor loadings, z_{pt} is the $K \times 1$ vector of time-t factor portfolio excess returns, and α and ε_t are $\bar{N} \times 1$ vectors of asset return intercepts and disturbances, respectively. The values of α, B, and Σ will depend on the factor portfolios. This dependence is suppressed for notational convenience.

It is well-known that all of the elements of the vector α will be zero if a linear combination of the factor portfolios form the tangency portfolio (i.e., the mean–variance efficient portfolio of risky assets given the presence of a risk-free asset). Let z_{qt} be the excess return of the (*ex ante*) tangency portfolio and let x_q be the $\bar{N} \times 1$ vector of portfolio weights. Here, and throughout the paper, let ι represent a conforming vector of ones. From mean–variance analysis:

$$x_q = (\iota' V^{-1} \mu)^{-1} V^{-1} \mu .$$ (6)

In the context of our previous discussion, the asset pricing model will be considered well-specified when the tangency portfolio can be formed from a linear combination of the K-factor portfolios.

8   A.C. MacKinlay/Journal of Financial Economics 38 (1995) 3–28

Our interest is in formally developing the relation between the deviations from the asset pricing model, α, and the residual covariance matrix Σ when a linear combination of the factor portfolios do not form the tangency portfolio. To facilitate this I define the *optimal orthogonal portfolio*,[2] which is the unique portfolio given $\bar{N}$ assets that can be combined with the factor portfolios to form the tangency portfolio and is orthogonal to the factor portfolios.

Take as given K-factor portfolios which cannot be combined to form the tangency portfolio or the global minimum variance portfolio. A portfolio h will be defined as the optimal orthogonal portfolio with respect to these K-factor portfolios if

$$x_q = X_p \omega + x_h (1 - \iota' \omega), \tag{7}$$

$$x_h' V X_p = 0, \tag{8}$$

for a $K \times 1$ vector ω, where X_p is the $\bar{N} \times K$ matrix of asset weights for the factor portfolios, x_h is the $\bar{N} \times 1$ vector of asset weights for the optimal orthogonal portfolio, and x_q is the $\bar{N} \times 1$ vector of asset weights for the tangency portfolio. If one considers a model without any factor portfolios ($K = 0$), then the optimal orthogonal portfolio will be the tangency portfolio.

The weights of portfolio h can be expressed in terms of the parameters of the K-factor model. For the vector of weights,

$$x_h = (\iota' V^{-1} \alpha)^{-1} V^{-1} \alpha = (\iota' \Sigma^\dagger \alpha)^{-1} \Sigma^\dagger \alpha, \tag{9}$$

where the $\dagger$ superscript indicates the generalized inverse. The usefulness of this portfolio comes from the fact that when added to (1) the intercept will vanish and the factor-loading matrix B will not be altered. The optimality restriction in (7) leads to the intercept vanishing, and the orthogonality condition in (8) leads to B being unchanged. Adding in z_{ht}:

$$z_t = B z_{pt} + \beta_h z_{ht} + u_t, \tag{10}$$

$$E[u_t] = 0, \tag{11}$$

$$E[u_t u_t'] = \Phi, \tag{12}$$

$$E[z_{ht}] = \mu_h, \qquad E[(z_{ht} - \mu_h)^2] = \sigma_h^2, \tag{13}$$

$$\text{cov}[z_{pt}, u_t] = 0, \tag{14}$$

$$\text{cov}[z_{ht}, u_t] = 0. \tag{15}$$

---

[2]See Roll (1980) for properties of orthogonal portfolios in a general context and Lehmann (1987, 1988, 1992) for discussions of the role of orthogonal portfolios in asset pricing tests. Also related is the orthogonal factor employed in MacKinlay (1987), the active portfolio considered by Gibbons, Ross, and Shanken (1989), and the modifying payoff used in Hansen and Jagannathan (1994).

A.C. MacKinlay/Journal of Financial Economics 38 (1995) 3–28   9

The link results from comparing (1) and (10). Taking the unconditional expectations of both sides,

$$\alpha = \beta_h \mu_h,$$
(16)

and by equating the variance of ε_t with the variance of $\beta_h z_{ht} + u_t$:

$$\Sigma = \beta_h \beta_h' \sigma_h^2 + \Phi = \alpha \alpha' \frac{\sigma_h^2}{\mu_h^2} + \Phi.$$
(17)

The key link between the model deviations and the residual variances and covariances emerges from (17). The intuition for the link is straightforward. Deviations from the model must be accompanied by a common component in the residual variance to prevent the formation of a portfolio with a positive deviation and a residual variance that decreases to zero as the number of securities in the portfolio grows. When the link is not present (i.e., the link is undone by Φ), asymptotic arbitrage opportunities will exist.

3. Squared Sharpe measures

The squared Sharpe measure is a useful construct for interpreting much of the ensuing analysis. The Sharpe measure for a given portfolio is calculated by dividing the mean excess return by the standard deviation of return. It is well-known that the tangency portfolio q will have the maximum squared Sharpe measure of all portfolios.[3] The squared Sharpe measure of q, s_q^2, is

$$s_q^2 = \mu' V^{-1} \mu.$$
(18)

Since the K-factor portfolios p and the optimal orthogonal portfolio h can be combined to form the tangency portfolio, it follows that the maximum squared Sharpe measure of these $K + 1$ portfolios will be s_q^2. Since h is orthogonal to the portfolios p, one can express s_q^2 as the sum of the squared Sharpe measure of the orthogonal portfolio and the squared maximum Sharpe measure of the factor portfolios,

$$s_q^2 = s_h^2 + s_p^2,$$
(19)

where $s_h^2 = \mu_h^2/\sigma_h^2$ and $s_p^2 = \mu_p' \Omega_p^{-1} \mu_p$.

---

[3]See Jobson and Korkie (1982) for a development of this point and a performance measurement application. The existence of a maximum Sharpe measure as the number of assets becomes large is central to the arbitrage pricing theory. For further discussion see Chamberlain and Rothschild (1983) and Ingersoll (1984).

10   A.C. MacKinlay/Journal of Financial Economics 38 (1995) 3–28

In applications I will be employing subsets of the $\bar{N}$ assets. The factor portfolios need not be linear combinations of the subset of assets. Results similar to those above will hold within a subset of N assets. For the subset analysis when considering the tangency portfolio (of the subset), the maximum squared Sharpe measure of the assets and factor portfolios, and the optimal orthogonal portfolio for the subset, it is necessary to augment the N assets with the factor portfolios p. Defining $z_{t_s}^*$ as the $N + K \times 1$ vector $[z_t'\ z_{pt}']'$ with mean $\mu_s^{*\prime}$ and covariance matrix V_s^*, for the tangency portfolio of these $N + K$ assets:

$$s_{q_s}^2 = \mu_s^{*\prime} V_s^{*-1} \mu_s^* . \tag{20}$$

The subscript s indicates that a subset of the assets is being considered. If any combination of the factor portfolios is a linear combination of the N assets, it will be necessary to use the generalized inverse in (20).

As we shall see, the analysis (with a subset of assets) will involve the quadratic $\alpha' \Sigma^{-1} \alpha$ computed using the parameters for the N assets. Gibbons, Ross, and Shanken (1989) and Lehmann (1988, 1992) provide interpretations of this quadratic term in terms of Sharpe measures. Assuming Σ is of full rank (if Σ is singular then one must use the generalized inverse), they show

$$\alpha_s' \Sigma_s^{-1} \alpha_s = s_{q_s}^2 - s_p^2 . \tag{21}$$

Consistent with (19), for the subset of assets $\alpha' \Sigma^{-1} \alpha$ will be the squared Sharpe measure of the subset's optimal orthogonal portfolio h_s. Therefore, for a given subset of assets:

$$s_{h_s}^2 = \alpha_s' \Sigma_s^{-1} \alpha_s , \tag{22}$$

$$s_{q_s}^2 = s_{h_s}^2 + s_p^2 . \tag{23}$$

Also note that the squared Sharpe measure of the subset's optimal orthogonal portfolio is less than or equal to that of the population optimal orthogonal portfolio:

$$s_{h_s}^2 \leqslant s_h^2 . \tag{24}$$

Next I use the optimal orthogonal portfolio and the Sharpe measure results together with the model deviation residual variance link to develop implications for distinguishing among asset pricing models. Hereafter I will suppress the s subscript. No ambiguity will result since, in the subsequent analysis, I will be working only with subsets of the assets.

4. Implications for risk-based versus nonrisk-based alternatives

Many asset pricing model tests involve testing the null hypothesis that the model intercept is zero using tests in the spirit of the zero-intercept

A.C. MacKinlay/Journal of Financial Economics 38 (1995) 3–28   11

F-test.[4] A common conclusion is that rejection of this hypothesis using one- or more-factor portfolios shows that more risk factors are required to explain the risk–return relation, leading to the inclusion of additional factors so that the null hypothesis will be accepted (Fama and French, 1993, adopt this approach). A shortcoming of this approach is that there are multiple potential interpretations of why the hypothesis is accepted. One view is that genuine progress in terms of identifying the 'right' asset pricing model has been made. However, the apparent success in identifying a better model may also have come from finding a good within-sample fit through data-snooping. The likelihood of this possibility is increased by the fact that the additional factors lack theoretical motivation.

This section integrates the link between the pricing model intercept and the residual covariance matrix of (17) and the squared Sharpe measure results with the distribution theory for the zero-intercept F-test to discriminate between the two interpretations. I consider two approaches. The first approach is a testing approach that compares the null hypothesis test statistic distribution with the distribution under each of the alternatives. The second approach is estimation-based, drawing on the squared Sharpe measure analysis to develop estimators for the squared Sharpe measure of the optimal orthgonal portfolio. Before presenting the two approaches, the zero-intercept F-test is summarized.

4.1. Zero intercept F-test

To implement the F-test, the additional assumption that excess asset returns are jointly normal and temporally independently and identically distributed is added. This assumption, though restrictive, buys us exact finite-sample distributional results, thereby simplifying the analysis. However, it is important to note that this assumption is not central to the point; similar results will hold under much weaker assumptions. Using a generalized method of moments approach, MacKinlay and Richardson (1991) present a more general test statistic that has asymptotically a chi-square distribution. Analysis similar to that presented for the F-test holds for this general statistic.

I begin with a summary of the zero-intercept F-test of the null hypothesis that the intercept vector α from (1) is zero. Let H_0 be the null hypothesis and H_a be the alternative:

$$H_0: \quad \alpha = 0, \tag{25}$$

$$H_a: \quad \alpha \neq 0. \tag{26}$$

---

[4]Examples of tests of this type include Campbell (1987), Connor and Korajczyk (1988), Fama and French (1993), Gibbons, Ross, and Shanken (1989), Huberman, Kandel, and Stambaugh (1987), Kandel and Stambaugh (1990), Lehmann and Modest (1988), and MacKinlay (1987). The arguments in the paper can also be related to the zero-beta CAPM tests in Gibbons (1982), Shanken (1985), and Stambaugh (1982).

H_0 can be tested using the following test statistic:

$$\theta_1 = [(T - N - K)/N][1 + \hat{\mu}_p'\hat{\Omega}_p^{-1}\hat{\mu}_p]^{-1}\hat{\alpha}'\hat{\Sigma}^{-1}\hat{\alpha}, \tag{27}$$

where T is the number of time series observations, N is the number of assets or portfolios of assets included, and K is the number of factor portfolios. The hat superscripts indicate the maximum likelihood estimators. Under the null hypothesis, θ_1 is unconditionally distributed central F with N degrees of freedom in the numerator and $T - N - K$ degrees of freedom in the denominator.

. The distribution of θ_1 can also be characterized in general. Conditional on the factor portfolio excess returns, the distribution of θ_1 is

$$\theta_1 \sim F_{N, T-N-K}(\lambda), \tag{28}$$

$$\lambda = T[1 + \hat{\mu}_p'\hat{\Omega}_p^{-1}\hat{\mu}_p]^{-1}\alpha'\Sigma^{-1}\alpha, \tag{29}$$

where λ is the noncentrality parameter of the F distribution. If $K = 0$, then the term $[1 + \hat{\mu}_p'\hat{\Omega}_p^{-1}\hat{\mu}_p]^{-1}$ will not appear in (27) or in (29) and θ_1 will be unconditionally distributed noncentral F.

4.2. Testing approach

In this approach I consider the distribution of θ_1 under two different alternatives. The alternatives can be separated by their implications for the maximum value of the squared Sharpe measure. With the risk-based multifactor alternative there will be an upper bound on the squared Sharpe measure, whereas with the nonrisk-based alternatives the maximum squared Sharpe measure can be unbounded (as the number of assets increases).

First I consider the distribution of θ_1 under the alternative hypothesis when deviations are due to missing factors. Drawing on the results for the squared Sharpe measures, the noncentrality parameter of the F distribution is

$$\lambda = T[1 + \hat{\mu}_p'\hat{\Omega}_p^{-1}\hat{\mu}_p]^{-1}s_{h_s}^2. \tag{30}$$

From (24), the third term in (30) is positive and bounded above by s_h^2. The second term is bounded between zero and one. Thus there is an upper bound for λ,

$$\lambda < Ts_h^2 \leqslant Ts_q^2. \tag{31}$$

The second inequality follows from the fact that the tangency portfolio q has the maximum Sharpe measure of any asset or portfolio.[5]

---

[5]The first half of this bound appears in MacKinlay (1987) for the case of the Sharpe–Lintner CAPM. Related results appear in Kandel and Stambaugh (1987), Shanken (1987), and Hansen and Jagannathan (1991).

A.C. MacKinlay/Journal of Financial Economics 38 (1995) 3–28   13

Given a maximum value for the squared Sharpe measure, the upper bound on the noncentrality parameter can be important. With this bound, independent of how one arranges the assets to be included as dependent variables in the pricing model regression and for any value of N, there is a limit on the distance between the null distribution and the distribution when the alternative is missing factors. (In practice, when using the F-test it will be necessary for N to be less than $T - K$ so that $\hat{\Sigma}$ will be of full rank.) All the assets can be mispriced and yet the bound will still apply. As a consequence, one should be cautious in interpreting rejections of the zero intercept as evidence in favor of a model with more risk factors.

In contrast, when the source of nonzero intercepts is nonrisk-based, such as data-snooping, market frictions, or market irrationalities, the notion of a maximum squared Sharpe measure is not useful. The squared Sharpe measure (and the noncentrality parameter) are in principle unbounded because the argument linking the deviations and the residual variances and covariances does not apply. When comparing alternatives with the intercepts of about the same magnitude, in general, one would expect to see larger test statistics in this nonrisk-based case.

One can examine the potential usefulness of the above analysis by considering alternatives with realistic parameter values. I construct the distribution of the test statistic for three cases: the null hypothesis, the missing risk factors alternative, and the nonrisk-based alternative. For the risk-based alternative, I draw on a framework designed to be similar to that in Fama and French (1993). For the nonrisk-based alternative I use a setup that is consistent with the analysis of Lo and MacKinlay (1990) and the work of Lakonishok, Shleifer, and Vishny (1993).

Consider a one-factor asset pricing model using a time series of the excess returns for 32 portfolios for the dependent variable. The one factor (independent variable) is the excess return of the market so that the zero-intercept null hypothesis is the CAPM. The length of the time series is 342 months. This setup corresponds to that of Fama and French (1993, Table 9, regression ii). The null distribution of the test statistic θ_1 is

$$\theta_1 \sim F_{32,309}(0). \tag{32}$$

To define the distribution of θ_1 under the risk-based and nonrisk-based alternatives one needs to specify the parameters necessary to calculate the noncentrality parameter. For the risk-based alternative, given a value for the squared Sharpe measure of the optimal orthogonal portfolio, the distribution corresponding to the upper bound of the noncentrality parameter from (31) can be considered. The Sharpe measure of the optimal orthogonal portfolio can be obtained using (19) given the squared Sharpe measures of the tangency portfolio and of the included factor portfolio. My view is that in a perfect capital markets setting, a reasonable value for the squared Sharpe measure of the tangency portfolio for an observation interval of one month is 0.031 (or approximately 0.6

for the Sharpe measure on an annualized basis). This value, for example, corresponds to a portfolio with an annual expected excess return of 10% and a standard deviation of 16%. If the maximum squared Sharpe measure of the included factor portfolios is the *ex post* squared Sharpe measure of the CRSP value-weighted index, the implied maximum squared Sharpe measure for the optimal orthogonal portfolio is 0.021. This monthly value of 0.021 would be consistent with a portfolio which has an annualized mean excess return of 8% and annualized standard deviation of 16%.

The selection of the above Sharpe measure can be rationalized both theoretically and empirically. For theoretical justification I consider Sharpe measures of equity returns in the literature examining the equity risk premium puzzle (see Mehra and Prescott, 1985). While the focus of this research does not concern the Sharpe measure, that measure can be calculated from the analysis provided by Cecchetti and Mark (1990) and Kandel and Stambaugh (1991). Both papers are informative for the question at hand since they do not assume any imperfections in the asset markets. If their models, with reasonable parameters, imply Sharpe measures that are higher than the value selected for use in this paper, the value selected here should perhaps be reconsidered. However, one should not completely rely on the measures from these papers for justification. In the presented models the aggregate equity portfolio generally will not be mean–variance efficient and therefore need not have the highest Sharpe measure of all equity portfolios.

Common to the papers is the use of a representative agent framework and a Markov switching model for the consumption process. The parameters of the consumption process are chosen to match estimates from the data. Cecchetti and Mark, using the standard time-separable constant relative risk aversion utility function, specify a range of values for the time preference parameter and the risk aversion coefficient. For each pair of values they generate the implied theoretical unconditional mean and standard deviation of the equity risk premium from which the Sharpe measures can be calculated. The annualized Sharpe measures range from 0.08 to 0.16, substantially below the value of 0.60 suggested above.

Kandel and Stambaugh allow for more general preferences. For the representative agent, a class is used that allows separation of the effects of risk aversion and intertemporal substitution. The standard time-separable model is a special case with the elasticity of intertemporal substitution equal to the inverse of the risk aversion coefficient. They set the monthly rate of time preference at 0.9978 and consider 16 pairs of the risk aversion coefficient and the intertemporal substitution parameter. The risk aversion coefficient varies from $\frac{1}{2}$ to 29 and the intertemporal substitution parameter varies from $\frac{1}{29}$ to 2. For thirteen of the sixteen cases the annual Sharpe measure of equity is less than 0.6. The three cases where the Sharpe measure is greater than 0.6 seem implausible since they imply the equity risk premium and the interest rate have almost the same

A.C. MacKinlay/Journal of Financial Economics 38 (1995) 3–28   15

Table 1
Historical Sharpe measures for selected stock indices, where the Sharpe measure is defined as the
ratio of the mean excess return to the standard deviation of the excess return

$\hat{s}_p^2$ is the monthly *ex post* squared Sharpe measure and $\hat{s}_p(ann)$ is the positive square root of this
measure annualized. $\tilde{s}_p^2$ is an unbiased estimate of the monthly squared Sharpe measure and $\tilde{s}_p(ann)$
is the positive square root of this measure annualized. The CRSP value-weighted index is a value-
weighted portfolio of all NYSE and Amex stocks. The CRSP small-stock portfolio is the value-
weighted portfolio of stocks in the lowest joint NYSE-Amex market value decile. The portfolio of
four indices is the portfolio with the maximum *ex post* squared Sharpe measure. The four indices are
the CRSP value-weighted index, the CRSP small-stock decile, the CRSP long-term government
bond index, and the CRSP corporate bond index. The bond indices are from the CRSP SBBI file.
The S&P 500 index is a value-weighted index of 500 stocks. The S&P–Barra value index is an index
of stocks within the S&P 500 universe with low ratios of price per share to book value per share.
Every six months a breakpoint price-to-book-value ratio is determined so that approximately half
the market capitalization of the S&P 500 is below the breakpoint and the other half is above. The
value index is a value-weighted index of those stocks in the group of low price-to-book-value ratios.
The S&P 500–Barra growth index is a index of stocks within the S&P 500 universe with high
price-to-book-value ratios. The growth index is a value-weighted index of those S&P 500 stocks in
the group of high price-to-book-value ratios.

Time period	Index	$\hat{s}_p^2$	$\hat{s}_p(ann)$	$\tilde{s}_p^2$	$\tilde{s}_p(ann)$
6307–9112	CRSP value-weighted index	0.0091	0.33	0.0061	0.27
6307–9112	CRSP small-stock portfolio	0.0142	0.40	0.0100	0.35
6307–9112	Portfolio of four indices	0.0145	0.41	0.0021	0.16
8101–9206	S&P 500 index	0.0161	0.44	0.0085	0.32
8101–9206	S&P–Barra value index	0.0208	0.50	0.0130	0.40
8101–9206	S&P–Barra growth index	0.0108	0.36	0.0033	0.20

variance, an impliciation which is strongly contradicted by historical data.
These are the cases with high values for both the risk aversion parameter and the
intertemporal substitution parameter. In aggregate, the results in these papers
are consistent with the value specified for the maximum squared Sharpe
measure in the context of frictionless asset markets.

One can also ask what Sharpe measure is empirically reasonable. To do this,
I present historical Sharpe measures for a number of broad-based indices. These
measures, some of which represent portfolios actually held, are reported in
Table 1. For each index, the *ex post* measure (based on maximum likelihood
estimates) and an unbiased squared Sharpe measure estimate are presented. For
the July 1963 through December 1991 period the squared Sharpe measures are
presented for the CRSP value-weighted index, the CRSP small-stock (10th
decile) portfolio, and the *ex post* optimal portfolio of these two indices plus the
long-term government index and the corporate bond index distributed by CRSP
in the stock, bonds, bills, and inflation file. The small-stock portfolio has
a monthly squared Sharpe measure of 0.014 (or 0.010 using the unbiased

estimate), substantially below the value I use for the tangency portfolio. The *ex post* optimal four-index portfolio's measure is only slightly higher at 0.015.

Table 1 also contains results for the period from January 1981 through June 1992 for the S&P 500 Index, a value index, and a growth index. The value index contains the S&P 500 stocks with low price-to-book-value ratios and the growth index is constructed from stocks with high price-to-book-value ratios. The source of the index return statistics used to calculate the measures is Capaul, Rowley, and Sharpe (1993). These results provide a useful perspective on the maximum magnitudes of Sharpe measures since it is generally acknowledged that the 1980's was a period of strong stock market performance, especially for value-based investment strategies. Given this characterization, one would expect these results to provide a high estimate of possible Sharpe measures. The Sharpe measures from this period are in line with (and lower than) the value used in the analysis of the risk-based alternative. The highest *ex post* estimate is 0.021 for the value index. Generally, I interpret the evidence in this table as supporting the measure selected to calibrate the analysis for the risk-based alternative.

Proceeding using a squared Sharpe measure of 0.021 for the optimal orthogonal portfolio to calculate λ, the distribution of θ_1 is

$$\theta_1 \sim F_{32,309}(7.1). \tag{33}$$

This distribution will be used to characterize the risk-based alternative.

I specify the distribution for two nonrisk-based alternatives by specifying values of α, Σ, and $\hat{\mu}_p' \hat{\Omega}_p^{-1} \hat{\mu}_p$, and then calculating λ from (29). To specify the intercepts I assume that the elements of α are normally distributed with a mean of zero. I consider two values for the standard deviation, 0.0007 and 0.001. When the standard deviation of the elements of α is 0.001 about 95% of the alphas will lie between -0.002 and $+0.002$, an annualized spread of about 4.8%. A standard deviation of 0.0007 for the alphas would correspond to an annual spread of about 3.4%. These spreads are consistent with spreads that could arise from data-snooping[6] and are also plausible and even somewhat conservative given the contrarian strategy returns presented in Lakonishok, Shleifer, and Vishny. For Σ I use a sample estimate based on portfolios sorted by market capitalization for the period 1963 to 1991 (inclusive). The effect of $\hat{\mu}_p' \hat{\Omega}_p^{-1} \hat{\mu}_p$ on λ will typically be small, so I set it to zero. To get an idea of a reasonable value for the noncentrality parameter given this alternative, I calculate the expected value of λ given the distributional assumption for the elements of α conditional upon $\Sigma = \hat{\Sigma}$. The expected value of the noncentrality parameter is 39.4 for a standard

---

[6]With data-snooping the distribution of θ_1 is not exactly a noncentral F (see Lo and MacKinlay, 1990), but for the purposes of this paper, the noncentral F will be a good approximation.

A.C. MacKinlay/Journal of Financial Economics 38 (1995) 3–28   17

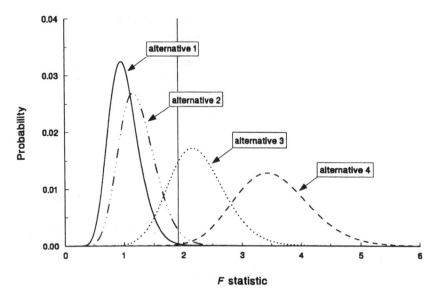

Fig. 1. Distributions for the CAPM zero-intercept test statistic for four alternatives.

Alternative 1 is the CAPM (null hypothesis); alternative 2 is the risk-based alternative (deviations from the CAPM are from missing risk factors); alternatives 3 and 4 are the nonrisk-based alternative (deviations from the CAPM are unrelated to risk). The distributions are $F_{32,309}(0)$, $F_{32,309}(7.1)$, $F_{32,309}(39.4)$, and $F_{32,309}(80.3)$ for alternatives 1, 2, 3, and 4, respectively. The degrees of freedom are set to correspond to monthly observations from July 1963 to December 1991 (342 observations). Using 25 stock portfolios and 7 bond portfolios, and the CRSP value-weighted index as proxy for the market portfolio, the test statistic is 1.91, represented by the vertical line. The probability is calculated using an interval width of 0.02.

deviation of 0.0007 and 80.3 for a standard deviation of 0.001. Using these values for the noncentrality parameter, the distribution of θ_1 is

$$\theta_1 \sim F_{32,309}(39.4) \quad \text{when} \quad \sigma_z = 0.0007, \tag{34}$$

$$\theta_1 \sim F_{32,309}(80.3) \quad \text{when} \quad \sigma_z = 0.001. \tag{35}$$

A plot of the four distributions from (32), (33), (34), and (35) is in Fig. 1. The vertical bar on the plot represents the value 1.91 which Fama and French calculate for the test statistic. From this figure notice that the null hypothesis distribution and the risk-based alternative distribution are quite close together, reflecting the impact of the upper bound on the noncentrality parameter (see MacKinlay, 1987, for detailed analysis of this alternative). In contrast, the nonrisk-based alternatives' distributions are far to the right of the other two distributions, consistent with the noncentrality parameter being unbounded for these alternatives.

What do we learn from this plot? First, if the objective is to distinguish among risk-based linear asset pricing models, the zero-intercept test is not particularly useful because the null distribution and the alternative distribution have substantial overlap. Second, if the goal is to compare a risk-based pricing model with a nonrisk-based alternative, the zero-intercept test can be very useful since the distributions of the test statistic for these alternatives have little overlap. Likelihood analysis provides another interpretation of the plot. Specifically, one can compare the values of the densities for the four alternatives at $\theta_1 = 1.91$. Such a comparison leads to the conclusion that the first nonrisk-based alternative is much more likely than the other three.

This analysis can be related to the Fama and French (1993) finding that a model with three factors does a good job in explaining the cross-section of expected returns. For a given finite cross-section under any alternative, the inclusion of the optimal orthogonal portfolio will lead to their result. As a consequence, their result on its own does not support the risk-based category. Indeed, the Fama and French approach to building the extra factors will tend to create a portfolio like the optimal orthogonal portfolio independent of the explanation for the CAPM deviations. Their extra factors essentially assign positive weights to the high positive alpha stocks and negative weights to the large negative alpha stocks. This procedure is likely to lead to a portfolio similar to the optimal orthogonal portfolio because the extreme alpha assets are likely to have the largest (in magnitude) weights in the optimal orthogonal portfolio [since its weights are proportional to $\Sigma^\dagger \alpha$; see (9)]. Further, the fact that when Fama and French increase the number of factors to three the significance of the test statistic only decreases marginally is also consistent with the argument that missing risk factors is not the whole story.

More evidence of the potential importance of nonrisk explanations can be constructed using weekly data. To see why the analysis of weekly data can be informative, consider the biases introduced with market frictions such as the bid–ask spread. Blume and Stambaugh (1983) show that in the presence of the bid–ask bounce, there is an upward bias in observed returns. For asset i and time period t, Blume and Stambaugh show the following approximation for the relation between expected observed returns and expected true returns:

$$\mathrm{E}(R_{it}^o) = \mathrm{E}(R_{it}) + \vartheta_i, \tag{36}$$

where the superscript 'o' distinguishes the returns observed with bid–ask bounce contamination from the true returns; ϑ_t is the bias which is equal to one-fourth of the proportional bid–ask spread squared. The bias will carry over into the intercept of any factor model. Consider a one-factor model in which the factor is *ex ante* the tangency portfolio. In this model the intercept for all true asset returns will be zero. However, the intercepts for the observed returns and the

A.C. MacKinlay/Journal of Financial Economics 38 (1995) 3–28   19

squared Sharpe measure of the optimal orthogonal portfolio will be nonzero. If the bias of the observed factor return is zero and if the factor return is uncorrelated with the bid–ask bounce process, then the intercept of the observed returns is

$$\alpha_i^o = \vartheta_i , \tag{37}$$

since α_i of the true return will be zero. Then, the squared Sharpe measure of the optimal orthogonal portfolio is

$$s_h^2 = \vartheta' \Sigma^{o(-1)} \vartheta , \tag{38}$$

where Σ^o is the residual covariance matrix for the weekly observed returns and ϑ is the vector of biases for the included portfolios.[7] When the null hypothesis that the intercepts are zero is examined using observed returns, violations exist solely due to the presence of the bid–ask spread.

Bias of the type induced by the bid–ask spread is interesting because its magnitude does not depend on the length of the observation interval. As a consequence its effect will statistically be more pronounced with shorter observation intervals when the variance of the true returns is smaller. To examine the potential relevance of the above example, the F-test statistic is calculated using a sample of weekly returns for 32 portfolios. The data extends from July 1962 through December 1992 (1,591 weeks). NYSE and Amex stocks are allocated to the portfolios based on beginning-of-year market capitalization. Each portfolio is allocated an equal number of stocks and the portfolios are equal-weighted with rebalancing each week. For these portfolios, using the CRSP value-weighted index as the one factor, the F-test statistic is 2.82. Under the null hypothesis, this statistic has a central F distribution with 32 degrees of freedom in the numerator and 1,558 degrees of freedom in the denominator. (Diagnostics reveal some serial correlation in the residuals of the weekly one-factor model, in which case the null distribution will not be exactly central F.) This statistic can be cast in terms of the alternatives presented in Fig. 1 since the noncentrality parameter of the F distribution will be approximately invariant to the observation interval and hence only the degrees of freedom need to be adjusted. Fig. 2 presents the results that correspond to the weekly observation interval. Basically, these results reinforce the monthly observation results in that the observed statistic is most consistent with the nonrisk-based category.

In summary, the results suggest that the risk-based missing risk factors argument is not the whole story. Figs. 1 and 2 show that the test statistic is still in

---

[7]The bias of a portfolio will be a weighted average of the bias of the member assets if the weights are independent of the returns process, as when the portfolio is rebalanced period by period versus when the portfolio is weighted to represent a buy and hold strategy (as in a value-weighted portfolio). In the latter case the bias at the portfolio level will be minimal.

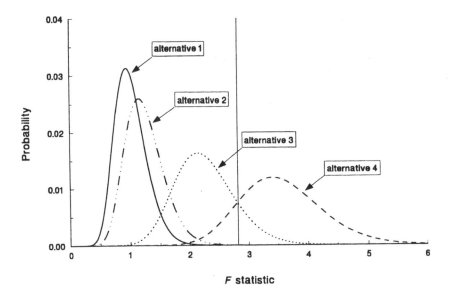

Fig. 2. Distributions for the CAPM zero-intercept test statistic for four alternatives.

Alternative 1 is the CAPM (null hypothesis); alternative 2 is the risk-based alternative (deviations from the CAPM are from missing risk factors); alternatives 3 and 4 are the nonrisk-based alternative (deviations from the CAPM are unrelated to risk). The distributions are $F_{32,1558}(0)$, $F_{32,1558}(7.1)$, $F_{32,1558}(39.4)$, and $F_{32,1558}(80.3)$ for alternatives 1, 2, 3, and 4, respectively. The degrees of freedom are set to correspond to weekly observations from July 1962 to December 1992 (1,591 observations). Using 32 stock portfolios and the CRSP value-weighted index as a proxy for the market portfolio, the test statistic is 2.82, represented by the vertical line. The probability is calculated using an interval width of 0.02.

the upper tail when the distribution of θ_1 in the presence of missing risk factors is tabulated. The *p*-value using this distribution is 0.03 for the monthly data and less than 0.001 for weekly data. Hence there is a lack of support for the view that missing factors completely explain the deviations.

On the other hand, given the parametrizations considered, there is some support for the nonrisk-based alternative views. The test statistic falls almost in the middle of the nonrisk-based alternative with the lower standard deviation of the elements of alpha. Several of the nonrisk-based alternatives could equally well explain the results. Different nonrisk-based views can give the same noncentrality parameter and test statistic distribution. The results are consistent with the data-snooping alternative of Lo and MacKinlay (1990), the related sample selection biases discussed by Kothari, Shanken, and Sloan (1994) and Breen and Korajczyk (1993), and the presence of market inefficiencies. The analysis suggests that missing risk factors alone cannot explain the empirical results.

A.C. MacKinlay/Journal of Financial Economics 38 (1995) 3–28   21

4.3. Estimation approach

In this section I present an estimation approach to make inferences about possible values for Sharpe measures. An estimator for the squared Sharpe measure of the optimal orthogonal portfolio for a given subset of assets is employed. Using this estimator and its variance, confidence intervals for the squared Sharpe measure can be constructed, facilitating judgements on the question of the value implied by the data and reasonable alternatives given this value. An unbiased estimator of the squared Sharpe measure is presented. This estimator corrects for the bias that is introduced by searching over N assets to find the maximum and is derived using the fact that θ_1 from (28) is distributed as a noncentral F variate. Its moments follow from the moments of the noncentral F distribution. The estimator is

$$
\tilde{s}_{h_s}^2 = \left[\theta_1 - \frac{(T-N-K)}{(T-N-K-2)} \right] \left[\frac{N(T-N-K-2)}{T(T-N-K)} \right] [1 + \hat{\mu}_p' \hat{\Omega}_p^{-1} \hat{\mu}_p],
$$

(39)

$$
\mathrm{var}\,(\tilde{s}_{h_s}^2 \mid \hat{\mu}_p' \hat{\Omega}_p^{-1} \hat{\mu}_p)
$$

$$
= \left[\frac{2(1 + \hat{\mu}_p' \hat{\Omega}_p^{-1} \hat{\mu}_p)^2}{T^2} \right]
$$

$$
\times \left[\frac{(N + T[1 + \hat{\mu}_p' \hat{\Omega}_p^{-1} \hat{\mu}_p]^{-1} s_{h_s}^2)^2 + (N + 2T[1 + \hat{\mu}_p' \hat{\Omega}_p^{-1} \hat{\mu}_p]^{-1} s_{h_s}^2)(T-N-K-2)}{(T-N-K-4)} \right].
$$

(40)

Conditional on the factor portfolio excess returns, the estimator of $s_{h_s}^2$ in (39) is unbiased, that is

$$
E[\tilde{s}_{h_s}^2 \mid \hat{\mu}_p' \hat{\Omega}_p^{-1} \hat{\mu}_p] = s_{h_s}^2 .
$$

(41)

Recall that when $K = 0$ the optimal orthogonal portfolio is the tangency portfolio and hence $s_{h_s}^2 = s_{q_s}^2$. The estimator can be applied when $K = 0$ by setting $\hat{\mu}_p' \hat{\Omega}_p^{-1} \hat{\mu}_p = 0$. Jobson and Korkie (1980) contains results for the $K = 0$ case.

The estimation approach is illustrated using the above estimator for the Fama and French (1993) portfolios. I consider the case of $K = 0$ and therefore the maximum squared Sharpe measure from 33 assets: the value-weighted CRSP index, 25 stock portfolios, and 7 bond portfolios is being estimated. (Recall that, with $K = 0$, $s_{h_s}^2 = s_{q_s}^2$.) The estimator of $s_{h_s}^2$ can be readily calculated, but the variance of $\tilde{s}_{h_s}^2$ cannot since it depends on $s_{h_s}^2$. To calculate the variance I use a consistent estimator, $\tilde{s}_{h_s}^2$, and then asymptotically (as T increases):

$$\tilde{s}_{h_s}^2 \sim N(s_{h_s}^2, \widehat{\text{var}}(\tilde{s}_{h_s}^2)) . \tag{42}$$

Using monthly data from July 1963 through December 1991, the estimate of $s_{h_s}^2$ is 0.092 and the asymptotic standard error is 0.044. Using this data set, a two-sided centered 90% confidence interval is thus (0.020, 0.163) and a one-sided 90% confidence interval is (0.036, ∞). It is worth noting the upward bias of the *ex post* maximum squared Sharpe measure as an estimator. For the above case the *ex post* maximum is 0.209, substantially higher than the unbiased estimate of 0.092. The bias is particular severe when N is large (relative to T).

In terms of an annualized Sharpe measure, the two-sided interval corresponds to a lower value of 0.49 and an upper value of 1.40, and the one-sided interval corresponds to a lower value of 0.65. Given that the tangency portfolio and the optimal orthogonal portfolio are the same, this interval can be used to provide an indication of the magnitude of the maximum Sharpe measure needed for a set of factor portfolios to explain the cross-section of excess returns of portfolios based on market-to-book-value ratios. Consistent with the CRSP value-weighted index being unable to explain the cross-section of returns, its *ex post* Sharpe measure lies well outside the intervals, with an annualized value of 0.33. In general, one can use the confidence intervals to decide on promising alternatives. For example, if one believes that *ex ante* Sharpe measures in the 90% confidence interval are unlikely in a risk-based world, then the nonrisk-based alternatives provide an attractive area for future study.

5. Asymptotic arbitrage in finite economies

In the absence of the link between the model deviation and the residual variance expressed in (17), asymptotic arbitrage opportunities can exist. However, the analysis of this paper is based on the importance of the link in a finite economy. To illustrate this importance I use a simple comparison of two economies, economy A in which the link is present and economy B in which the link is absent. The absence of the link is the only distinguishing feature of economy B. For each economy, the behavior of the maximum squared Sharpe measure as a function of the number of securities is examined.

Specification of the mean excess return vector and the covariance matrix is necessary. I draw on the previously introduced notation. In addition to the risk-free asset, assume there exist N risky assets with mean excess return μ and nonsingular covariance matrix V, and a risky factor portfolio with mean excess return μ_p and variance σ_p^2. The factor portfolio is not a linear combination of the N assets. If necessary this criterion can be met by eliminating one of the assets included in the factor portfolio. For both economies A and B,

$$\mu = \alpha + \beta\mu_p, \tag{43}$$

$$V = \beta\beta'\sigma_p^2 + \delta\delta'\sigma_h^2 + I\sigma_\varepsilon^2. \tag{44}$$

Given the above mean and covariance matrix and the assumption that the factor portfolio p is a holdable asset, the maximum squared Sharpe measure for economy I is

$$s_I^2 = s_p^2 + \alpha'(\delta\delta'\sigma_h^2 + I\sigma_\varepsilon^2)^{-1}\alpha. \tag{45}$$

Analytically inverting $(\delta\delta'\sigma_h^2 + I\sigma_\varepsilon^2)$ and simplifying, (46) can be expressed as

$$s_I^2 = s_p^2 + \frac{1}{\sigma_\varepsilon^2}\left[\alpha'\alpha + \frac{\sigma_h^2(\alpha'\delta)^2}{(\sigma_\varepsilon^2 + \sigma_h^2\delta'\delta)}\right]. \tag{46}$$

To complete the specification, the cross-sectional properties of the elements of α and δ are required. I assume that the elements of α are cross-sectionally independent and identically distributed,

$$\alpha_i \sim \text{IID}(0, \sigma_\alpha^2), \qquad i = 1, \ldots, N. \tag{47}$$

The specification of the distribution of the elements of δ conditional on α differentiates economies A and B. For economy A,

$$\delta_i|\alpha \sim \text{IID}(\alpha_i, 0), \qquad i = 1, \ldots, N, \tag{48}$$

and for economy B,

$$\delta_i|\alpha \sim \text{IID}(0, \sigma_\alpha^2), \qquad i = 1, \ldots, N. \tag{49}$$

Unconditionally, the cross-sectional distribution of δ will be the same for both economies, but for economy A conditional on α, δ is fixed. This incorporates the link between the deviation and the residual variance. Because δ is independent of α in economy B, the link is absent.

Using (46) and the cross-sectional distributional properties of the elements of α and δ, an approximation for the maximum squared Sharpe measure for each economy can be derived. For both economies, $(1/N)\alpha'\alpha$ converges to σ_α^2 and $(1/N)\delta'\delta$ converges to σ_α^2. For economy A, $(1/N^2)(\alpha'\delta)^2$ converges to σ_α^4 and, for economy B, $(1/N)(\alpha'\delta)^2$ converges to σ_α^4. Substituting these limits into (46) gives approximations of the maximum squared Sharpe measures squared for each economy. Substitution into (46) gives

$$s_A^2 = s_p^2 + \frac{N\sigma_\alpha^2}{\sigma_\varepsilon^2 + N\sigma_h^2\sigma_\alpha^2}, \tag{50}$$

$$s_B^2 = s_p^2 + N\frac{\sigma_\alpha^2}{\sigma_\varepsilon^2}\left[1 - \frac{\sigma_h^2\sigma_\alpha^2}{\sigma_\varepsilon^2 + N\sigma_h^2\sigma_\alpha^2}\right], \tag{51}$$

for economies A and B, respectively. The accuracy of these approximations for values of N equal to 100 and higher is examined. Simulations show that these approximations are very precise.

The importance of the link asymptotically can be confirmed by considering the values of s_q^2 in (50) and (51) for large N. For economy A and large N,

$$s_q^2 = s_p^2 + \frac{1}{\sigma_h^2}, \tag{52}$$

and for economy B,

$$s_q^2 = s_p^2 + N\left[\frac{\sigma_\alpha^2}{\sigma_\varepsilon^2}\right]. \tag{53}$$

The maximum squared Sharpe measure is bounded as N increases for economy A and unbounded for economy B. Using the correspondence between boundedness of the maximum squared Sharpe measure and the absence of asymptotic opportunities (see Ingersoll, 1984, Theorem I) there will be asymptotic arbitrage opportunities only in economy B.

However, my interest here is to examine the importance of the link between the deviation and the residual variance given a finite number of assets. I do this by considering the value of the maximum Sharpe measures for various values of N. The values of N considered are 100, 500, 1,000, and 5,000. For completeness, I also report the maximum squared Sharpe measure for $N = \infty$. Shanken (1992) presents related results for an economy similar to B with δ restricted to be zero for $N = 3,000$ and $N = 3,000,000$. He notes (p. 1574) that for $N = 3,000,000$ 'something close to a 'pure' arbitrage is possible'. Given (50) and (51), to complete the calculations, s_p^2, σ_h^2, σ_ε^2, and σ_α^2 must be specified. The parameters are selected so that μ and V are realistic for stock returns measures at a monthly observation interval. The selected parameter values are $s_p^2 = 0.01$, $\sigma_h = 2.66$, and $\sigma_\varepsilon = 0.05$. Two values are considered for σ_α, 0.001 and 0.002. The results are reported in Table 2. The difference in the behavior of the maximum squared Sharpe measures between economies A and B is dramatic. For economy A, the boundedness is apparent as the maximum squared Sharpe measure ranges from 0.023 to 0.030 as N increases from 100 to infinity. For economy A the impact of increasing the cross-sectional variation in the mean return is minimal. Comparing $\sigma_\alpha = 0.001$ to $\sigma_\alpha = 0.002$ reveals few differences, with the exception of differences for the $N = 100$ case. For economy B it is a different story. The maximum squared Sharpe measure is very sensitive to both increases in the number of securities and increases in the cross-sectional variation in the mean return. For $\sigma_\alpha = 0.002$, the maximum squared Sharpe measure increases from 0.169 to 1.608 as N increases from 100 to 1,000. When σ_α increases from 0.001 to 0.002, the maximum squared Sharpe measure increases from 0.21 to 0.80 for N equal to 500.

A.C. MacKinlay/Journal of Financial Economics 38 (1995) 3–28   25

Table 2
A comparison of the maximum squared Sharpe measure for two economies denoted A and B, where
the Sharpe measure is the ratio of the mean excess return to the standard deviation of the excess
return

The excess return covariance matrix for the two economies is identical and the cross-sectional
dispersion in mean excess returns is identical. The economies differ in that economy A displays
stronger dependence between the mean excess returns and the covariance matrix of excess returns.
The mean and covariance matrix parameters for the economies are calibrated to correspond roughly
to monthly returns (see the text for details). N is the number of securities, s_I^2 is the maximum squared
Sharpe measure for economy I, $I = A, B$, and $p(z_I < 0)$ is the approximate probability for economy
I that the annual return of the portfolio with the maximum Sharpe measure squared will be less than
the risk-free return assuming that monthly returns are jointly normally distributed and that the
mean excess return is positive. σ_z is the cross-sectional standard deviation of the component of the
mean return that is explained by a second factor in economy A and that is not explained by
a common factor in economy B.

N	s_A^2	$p(z_A < 0)$	s_B^2	$p(z_B < 0)$
$\sigma_z = 0.001$				
100	0.023	0.298	0.050	0.220
500	0.028	0.280	0.210	0.056
1000	0.029	0.277	0.410	0.013
5000	0.030	0.275	2.010	_[a]
∞	0.030	0.274	∞	_[a]
$\sigma_z = 0.002$				
100	0.028	0.282	0.169	0.077
500	0.030	0.276	0.808	_[a]
1000	0.030	0.275	1.608	_[a]
5000	0.030	0.274	8.008	_[a]
∞	0.030	0.274	∞	_[a]

[a]Less than 0.001.

In addition to the maximum squared Sharpe measures, Table 2 reports the
approximate probability that the annual excess return of the portfolio with the
maximum squared Sharpe measure is negative. For this probability calculation,
it is assumed that returns are jointly normally distributed and that the mean
excess return of the portfolio with the maximum squared Sharpe measure is
nonnegative. The mean and variance are annualized by multiplying the monthly
values by 12. This probability allows for an economic interpretation of the size
of the Sharpe measure. Since the excess return represents a payoff on a zero
investment position, if the probability of a negative outcome is zero then there is
an arbitrage opportunity. For economy A this probability is about 28% and
stable as N increases. However, for economy B the probability of a negative
annual excess return quickly approaches zero. For example, for the case of

26 *A.C. MacKinlay/Journal of Financial Economics 38 (1995) 3–28*

σ_α equal to 0.002 and N equal to 500 the probability of a negative outcome is less than 0.001. (For the 67 years from 1926 through 1992 the excess return of the S&P index has been negative 37.3% of the years and the excess return of the CRSP small-stock index has been negative 34.3% of the years; over the 30-year period from 1963 through 1992 the S&P Index has been negative 36.7% of the time and the small-stock index has been negative 30.0% of the time.) Since negative outcomes can occur, the excess return distributions cannot be completely ruled out on economic grounds. However, in aggregate it appears that, given the above model for economy B, unrealistic investment opportunities can be constructed with a relatively small number of stocks. This is not the case for economy A. The bottom line is that in a perfect capital markets environment, the link between the model deviations and the residual variance is important even with a limited number of securities. Analysis which does not recognize this link is unlikely to shed light on the potential for omitted risk factors to explain the deviations.

6. Conclusion

Empirical work in economics in general and in finance in particular is *ex post* in nature, making it sometimes difficult to discriminate among various explanations for observed phenomena. A partial solution to this difficulty is to examine the alternatives and make judgements from an *ex ante* point of view. The current explanations of the empirical results on asset pricing are particularly well-suited to *ex ante* analysis. This paper presents a framework based on the economics of mean–variance analysis to address and reinterpret prior empirical results.

Multifactor asset pricing models have been proposed as an alternative to the Sharpe–Lintner CAPM. However, the results in this paper suggest that looking at other alternatives will be fruitful. The evidence against the CAPM can also be interpreted as evidence that multifactor models on their own cannot explain the deviations from the CAPM. Generally, the results suggest that more can be learned by considering the likelihood of various existing empirical results under differing specific economic models.

References

Amihud, Yakov and Haim Mendelson, 1986, Asset pricing and the bid–ask spread, Journal of Financial Economics 17, 223–250.

Blume, Marshall and Robert Stambaugh, 1983, Biases in computed returns: An application to the size effect, Journal of Financial Economics 12, 387–404.

Breen, William and Robert Korajczyk, 1993, On selection biases in book-to-market based tests of asset pricing models, Working paper no. 167 (Northwestern University, Evanston, IL).

Campbell, John, 1987, Stock returns and the term structure, Journal of Financial Economics 18, 373–399.

A.C. MacKinlay/*Journal of Financial Economics* 38 (1995) 3–28   27

Capaul, Carlo, Ian Rowley, and William Sharpe, 1993, International value and growth stock returns, Financial Analysts Journal 49, 27–36.

Cecchetti, Stephen and Nelson Mark, 1990, Evaluating empirical tests of asset pricing models, American Economic Review 80, 48–51.

Chamberlain, Gary and Michael Rothschild, 1983, Arbitrage, factor structure, and mean–variance analysis on large asset markets, Econometrica 51, 1281–1304.

Chan, Louis K.C. and Josef Lakonishok, 1993, Are reports of beta's death premature?, Journal of Portfolio Management 19, 51–62.

Connor, Gregory and Robert Korajczyk, 1988, Risk and return in an equilibrium APT: Application of a new test methodology, Journal of Financial Economics 21, 255–290.

Conrad, Jennifer and Gautam Kaul, 1993, Long-term market overreaction or biases in computed returns?, Journal of Finance 48, 39–63.

DeBondt, Werner and Richard Thaler, 1985, Does the stock market overreact?, Journal of Finance 40, 793–805.

Fama, Eugene, 1993, Multifactor portfolio efficiency and multifactor asset pricing models, CRSP working paper (University of Chicago, Chicago, IL).

Fama, Eugene and Kenneth French, 1993, Common risk factors in the returns on stocks and bonds, Journal of Financial Economics 33, 3–56.

Gibbons, Michael, 1982, Multivariate tests of financial models: A new approach, Journal of Financial Economics 10, 3–27.

Gibbons, Michael, Stephen Ross, and Jay Shanken, 1989, A test of the efficiency of a given portfolio, Econometrica 57, 1121–1152.

Hansen, Lars and Ravi Jagannathan, 1991, Implications of security market data for models of dynamic economies, Journal of Political Economy 99, 225–262.

Hansen, Lars and Ravi Jagannathan, 1994, Assessing specification errors in stochastic discount factor models, Working paper (University of Minnesota, Minneapolis, MN).

Huberman, Gur, Shmuel Kandel, and Robert Stambaugh, 1987, Mimicking portfolios and exact arbitrage pricing, Journal of Finance 42, 1–10.

Ingersoll, Jonathan, 1984, Some results in the theory of arbitrage pricing, Journal of Finance 39, 1021–1039.

Jobson, J.D. and Bob Korkie, 1980, Estimation for Markowitz efficient portfolios, Journal of the American Statistical Association 75, 544–554.

Jobson, J.D. and Bob Korkie, 1982, Potential performance and tests of portfolio efficiency, Journal of Financial Economics 10, 433–466.

Kandel, Shmuel and Robert Stambaugh, 1987, On correlations and inferences about mean–variance efficiency, Journal of Financial Economics 18, 61–90.

Kandel, Shmuel and Robert Stambaugh, 1990, A mean–variance framework for tests of asset pricing models, Review of Financial Studies 2, 125–156.

Kandel, Shmuel and Robert Stambaugh, 1991, Asset returns and intertemporal preferences, Journal of Monetary Economics 27, 39–71.

Kandel, Shmuel and Robert Stambaugh, 1994, Portfolio inefficiency and the cross-section of mean returns, Rodney White Center for Financial Research paper (Wharton School, University of Pennsylvania, Philadelphia, PA).

Kothari, S.P., Jay Shanken, and Richard Sloan, 1994, Another look at the cross-section of expected returns, Working paper (Wharton School, University of Pennsylvania, Philadelphia, PA).

Lakonishok, Josef, Andrei Shleifer, and Robert Vishny, 1993, Contrarian investment, extrapolation, and risk, Working paper (University of Illinois, Champaign, IL).

Lehmann, Bruce, 1987, Orthogonal frontiers and alternative mean variance efficiency tests, Journal of Finance 42, 601–619.

Lehmann, Bruce, 1988, Mean–variance efficiency tests in large cross-sections, Working paper (National Bureau of Economic Research, Cambridge, MA).

Lehmann, Bruce, 1992, Empirical testing of asset pricing models, in: Peter Newman, Murray Milgate, and John Eatwell, eds., The new Palgrave dictionary of money and finance (Stockton Press, New York, NY) 749–759.

Lehmann, Bruce and David Modest, 1988, The empirical foundations of the arbitrage pricing theory, Journal of Financial Economics 21, 213–254.

Lo, Andrew and A. Craig MacKinlay, 1990, Data-snooping biases in tests of financial asset pricing models, Review of Financial Studies 3, 431–467.

MacKinlay, A. Craig, 1987, On multivariate tests of the CAPM, Journal of Financial Economics 18, 341–372.

MacKinlay, A. Craig and Matthew Richardson, 1991, Using generalized methods of moments to test mean–variance efficiency, Journal of Finance 46, 511–527.

Mehra, Rajnish and Edward Prescott, 1985, The equity premium: A puzzle, Journal of Monetary Economics 15, 145–162.

Merton, Robert, 1973, An intertemporal capital asset pricing model, Econometrica 41, 867–887.

Roll, Richard, 1977, A critique of the asset pricing theory's tests: Part I, Journal of Financial Economics 4, 129–176.

Roll, Richard, 1980, Orthogonal portfolios, Journal of Financial and Quantitative Analysis 15, 1005–1023.

Roll, Richard and Stephen Ross, 1994, On the cross-sectional relation between expected returns and betas, Journal of Finance 49, 101–122.

Ross, Stephen, 1976, The arbitrage theory of capital asset pricing, Journal of Economic Theory 13, 341–360.

Shanken, Jay, 1985, Multivariate tests of the zero-beta CAPM, Journal of Financial Economics 14, 327–348.

Shanken, Jay, 1987, Multivariate proxies and asset pricing relations: Living with the Roll critique, Journal of Financial Economics 18, 91–110.

Shanken, Jay, 1992, The current state of the arbitrage pricing theory, Journal of Finance 47, 1569–1574.

Stambaugh, Robert, 1982, On the exclusion of assets from tests of the two parameter model, Journal of Financial Economics 10, 235–268.

THE JOURNAL OF FINANCE • VOL. L, NO. 1 • MARCH 1995

Another Look at the Cross-section of Expected Stock Returns

S. P. KOTHARI, JAY SHANKEN, and RICHARD G. SLOAN*

ABSTRACT

Our examination of the cross-section of expected returns reveals economically and statistically significant compensation (about 6 to 9 percent per annum) for beta risk when betas are estimated from time-series regressions of annual portfolio returns on the annual return on the equally weighted market index. The relation between book-to-market equity and returns is weaker and less consistent than that in Fama and French (1992). We conjecture that past book-to-market results using COMPUSTAT data are affected by a selection bias and provide indirect evidence.

AN EXTENSIVE BODY OF empirical research over the past 10 to 15 years has provided evidence contradicting the prediction of the Sharpe (1964), Lintner (1965), and Black (1972) capital asset pricing model (CAPM) that the cross-section of expected returns is linear in beta. This research documents that deviations from the linear CAPM risk-return trade-off are related to, among other variables, firm size (e.g., Banz (1981)), earnings yield (e.g., Basu (1977, 1983)), leverage (e.g., Bhandari (1988)), and the ratio of a firm's book value of equity to its market value (e.g., Stattman (1980), Rosenberg, Reid, and Lanstein (1985), and Chan, Hamao, and Lakonishok (1991)). After carefully reexamining this research, a recent article by Fama and French (FF; 1992) draws two main conclusions about the cross-section of average stock returns. First, there is only a weak positive relation between average return and beta over the period 1941 to 1990, and virtually no relation over the shorter period 1963 to 1990. Second, firm size and book-to-market equity (B/M) do a good

* Kothari and Shanken are from the William E. Simon Graduate School of Business Administration, University of Rochester. Sloan is from the Wharton School, University of Pennsylvania. We acknowledge the excellent research assistance of Roger Edelen and Sharmila Hardi. Barr Rosenberg has been particularly helpful on Compustat-related issues in the paper. We thank Ray Ball, Sudipta Basu, Jonathan Berk, Eugene Fama, Kenneth French, Narsimhan Jegadeesh, Jeff Pontiff, Rick Ruback, René Stulz, Dennis Sheehan, two anonymous referees, Dave Mayers (the editor), and seminar participants at the City University Business School at London, Harvard University, the Institute of Quantitative Investment Research Conference in Cambridge, London Business School, Pennsylvania State University, the National Bureau of Economic Research, Southern Methodist University, University of Southern California, SUNY at Buffalo, Wharton, and the Accounting and Economics Conference at Washington University, for useful comments. S. P. Kothari and Jay Shanken acknowledge financial support from the Bradley Policy Center at the Simon School, University of Rochester and the John M. Olin Foundation.

job of capturing the cross-sectional variation in average returns over the 1963 to 1990 period.

This article reexamines whether beta explains cross-sectional variation in average returns over the post-1940 period as well as the longer post-1926 period, and whether B/M captures cross-sectional variation in average returns over a longer 1947 to 1987 period using a somewhat different data set. We draw the following conclusions:

(1) Given the low power of the tests for a positive market risk premium, the FF evidence provides little basis for rejecting the null hypothesis of a nontrivial 6 percent per annum risk premium over the post-1940 period.

(2) When annual returns are employed in the estimation of beta, there is substantial ex post compensation for beta risk over the 1941 to 1990 period and even more over the 1927 to 1990 period. This result is robust to various ways of forming portfolios.

(3) It is likely that the FF results are influenced by a combination of survivorship bias in the COMPUSTAT database affecting the high B/M stocks' performance and period-specific performance of both low B/M, past "winner" stocks, and high B/M, past "loser" stocks.

(4) Using an alternative data source, Standard & Poor's (S&P) industry-level data from 1947 to 1987, we find that B/M is at best weakly related to average stock return. Since 1963, the relation is statistically significant using the 500 largest COMPUSTAT firms each year, but the estimated effect is about 40 percent lower than that obtained using all COMPUSTAT firms.

When we examine the average return-beta relation using annual rather than monthly data, estimates of the annual compensation for beta risk over the 1927 to 1990 period range from 8.9 to 11.7 percent for the equally weighted index and 6.2 to 8.9 percent for the value-weighted index, depending on how we form portfolios. In particular, even when we rank portfolios first on size and then on beta, as in FF, the estimated risk premia are 10.1 percent (equally weighted) and 7.3 percent (value-weighted). While all estimates are significantly positive at the 10 percent level using one-sided tests, far greater statistical significance is observed (*t*-statistics greater than 3) when relating *monthly* expected returns to the annual betas.

Consistent with evidence in FF and elsewhere in the literature, estimated risk premia for the 1941 to 1990 subperiod are smaller, and there is virtually no relation between beta and average return over the relatively short post-1962 period. In contrast, though, our estimates for post-1940 remain economically substantial and statistically significant as well. Although the post-1940 results are included for comparison with FF, we know of no compelling reason for emphasizing this period (or the post-1962 subperiod) over the longer 1927 to 1990 period. The significant results for a variety of portfolio groupings when betas are computed from annual data extend similar findings by Handa, Kothari, and Wasley (1989) for size portfolios.[1] However, the alternative grouping procedures used here provide stronger evidence that size, as well as beta, is needed to account for the cross-section of expected returns.

Section II examines the relation between B/M and stock returns and explores the possibility of selection biases. We suggest that the returns on the high B/M portfolios formed using the COMPUSTAT data may be spuriously inflated for at least two reasons. First, several years of the surviving firms' historical data were included when COMPUSTAT added firms to the database. Second, even in recent years, there are many firms with stock returns on the Center for Research in Securities Prices (CRSP) tapes, but financial data missing on COMPUSTAT. Evidence suggests that the frequency of such firms' experiencing financial distress is relatively high.

To explore the survivorship-bias problem in the COMPUSTAT data, we separately analyze data for firms on CRSP, firms on COMPUSTAT, and those on CRSP but not on COMPUSTAT (hereafter, the CRSP − COMPUSTAT sample). The CRSP sample does not suffer from a survivorship bias problem. Therefore, if the COMPUSTAT sample exhibits survivorship bias, we expect the CRSP − COMPUSTAT sample to include a preponderance of failing stocks. Consistent with the survivorship-bias concern, the returns for small firms on COMPUSTAT are 9 to 10 percentage points higher than those for CRSP − COMPUSTAT small firms.

In thinking about size and B/M effects, it is important to remember that these variables have emerged as the winners in a sequential process of examining and eliminating many other variables. These include the variables explicitly analyzed by FF, taken from past studies, as well as other ex post insignificant variables that never made it into the literature. Under these circumstances, classical measures of statistical significance will likely overstate the true economic significance of the variables that provide the best fit (see Lo and MacKinlay (1990b) for an interesting analysis of related issues). This is of particular concern for the B/M ratio which, unlike size, has only been examined over the relatively short 1963 to 1990 period for which data are available in machine-readable form on the COMPUSTAT tapes.[2]

Related to this concern about "data-snooping," there is good reason to doubt that findings of a positive relation between B/M and stock returns in recent decades would be robust to longer periods. The low B/M portfolios include relatively large market-capitalization "winner" stocks that have experienced above-average stock-price performance prior to their ranking on the B/M

---

[1] Annual betas have also been used by Jagannathan and Wang (1995) in examining the relation between average return and beta, and by Ball and Kothari (1989), Chopra, Lakonishok, and Ritter (1992), and Ball, Kothari, and Shanken (1995) in evaluating the apparent profitability of the contrarian investment strategy (see e.g., DeBondt and Thaler (1985, 1987)). In particular, Ball, Kothari, and Shanken (1995) show that there are no significant abnormal returns for a June-end initiated strategy after adjusting for beta risk.

[2] Davis (1994) is an exception that came to our attention in the final stages of this work. See footnote 13.

ratio. Although we cannot directly study the behavior of low B/M stocks before 1963, we can examine the performance of winners (see the stock-market overreaction literature including DeBondt and Thaler (1985, 1987), Chan (1988), Ball and Kothari (1989), Chopra, Lakonishok, and Ritter (1992), and Ball, Kothari, and Shanken (1995)). Winners outperformed the market prior to 1963, but underperformed over the post-1962 period. Therefore, the negative performance of low B/M stocks since 1963 may be a period-specific phenomenon. Similar remarks apply to the high B/M "loser" stocks.

Given these considerations, we believe it is useful to explore an alternative data set over a longer time period. Using industry data from the *S&P Analyst's Handbook*, we find no evidence of a monotonic relation between B/M and average return over the period 1947 to 1987 or, surprisingly, the FF post-1962 period. Our failure to find a significant positive relation is not due simply to the use of value-weighted *industry-level* data. For example, variation in the B/M ratios of the S&P industry portfolios is comparable to that of the FF B/M portfolios employing COMPUSTAT data. Moreover, the positive relation between B/M and average return is obtained even using value-weighted industry portfolios from COMPUSTAT data.

Overall, we conjecture that the B/M results are influenced by a combination of survivorship bias affecting the high B/M stocks' performance and period-specific performance of both low and high B/M, past winner and loser stocks. We recognize, however, that there are valid economic arguments for ratios like B/M and dividend or earnings yield to be positively related to expected return beyond beta (see Ball (1978) and Sharathchandra and Thompson (1993)). Indeed, when we restrict our attention to the largest 500 COMPUSTAT firms, for which survivorship biases should be relatively minor, the t-statistic on B/M is close to two. Consistent with biases in the larger COMPUSTAT universe, however, the coefficient on B/M is reduced by 40 percent. Therefore, we are not suggesting that all B/M findings are attributable to selection biases but, rather, that the current empirical case for this ratio is weaker than the previous literature would suggest.[3]

Section I provides results of testing the CAPM risk-return relation employing betas estimated using annual returns. Section II examines the effect of COMPUSTAT selection biases on the relation between B/M and stock returns. This section also explores the period-specific nature of both low and high B/M, past winner and loser stocks. Section III offers conclusions and implications for other research.

I. Beta Results

This section begins with a brief review of the FF finding that a flat relation between average return and beta over the 1941 to 1990 period cannot be rejected. We then briefly outline the rationale for employing annual returns

---

[3] Work in progress indicates that B/M tracks significant *time-series* variation in expected market returns.

in the estimation of beta and reexamine the return-beta relation over the post-1926 and post-1940 periods. Results are presented for cross-sectional regressions of average monthly returns on annual betas. In these regressions, portfolios are formed using a variety of aggregation procedures, including the FF approach of ranking stocks first on size and then on beta. Regardless of the portfolio-formation procedure and choice of index (i.e., equally- or value-weighted), the coefficient on beta is economically significant and, with few exceptions, the estimates are more than three standard errors above zero for the post-1940 as well as the post-1926 period.

Before proceeding, we offer a few observations on the choice of an appropriate proxy for the market portfolio. The CAPM implies that the value-weighted portfolio of *all* assets should be mean-variance efficient. It is sometimes suggested, therefore, that the value-weighted *stock* index is preferred as a market proxy over the equally weighted index. This is by no means obvious, however. If we limit our attention to the equity universe, the CAPM implies that the portfolio of stocks that has maximum correlation with the true market portfolio is efficient (see Breeden, Gibbons, and Litzenberger (1989) and related analysis by Kandel and Stambaugh (1987) and Shanken (1987)). Whether the value- or equally weighted index is a better proxy for this benchmark portfolio depends largely on whether the returns on assets other than stocks are more closely related to small- or large-firm stock returns. This is an interesting empirical question, but its examination is beyond the scope of this article. As a practical matter, though, we find that while the level of the market risk premium is lower for the lower volatility value-weighted index, inferences about the risk premium are not at all sensitive to the index employed.

A. Review of Fama and French (1992)

FF present several cross-sectional regression estimates of the risk premium associated with beta. All risk premia are based on betas estimated using monthly returns. A value-weighted market index is employed, although they state (p. 431) that estimating betas using the equally-weighted market index produces "inferences on the role of β in average returns like those reported below." When stocks are grouped on firm size alone (Table AI), their coefficient on beta for the 1941 to 1990 period is a hefty 1.45 percent per month, more than 3 standard errors above zero. However, when stocks are ranked first on size and then on beta to form 100 portfolios, the estimate is only 0.24 percent with a standard error of 0.23 percent for the same period (Table AIII). Thus, they conclude (p. 458) that "... allowing for variation in β that is unrelated to size flattens the relation between average return and β, to the point where it is indistinguishable from no relation at all."

We emphasize that, although the hypothesis that the true coefficient is zero cannot always be rejected, a range of economically significant positive values cannot be rejected either, given the large standard error. In other words, the power of the tests is very low (also see Chan and Lakonishok

(1993)). For example, the t-statistic for a null hypothesis of 50 basis points per month (6 percent per annum) would only be $(0.24 - 0.50)/0.23 = -1.13$, as compared to the t-statistic of 1.07 for the null hypothesis of zero. Alternatively, focusing on the likelihood function, since each parameter value (i.e., zero risk premium and a risk premium of 50 basis points per month) is roughly the same distance from the point estimate obtained by FF, the hypotheses are about equally likely. In a Bayesian framework, the odds for or against a 6 percent risk premium per annum, as compared to no risk premium, would thus be close to one's prior odds.[4] Insofar as the insights of modern portfolio theory are compelling a priori, these prior odds would place more weight on 6 percent, and there would be little reason to modify this weight in light of the FF evidence.

B. *Return-Measurement Interval and Beta*

Previous research has generally examined the risk-return relation using monthly return data (e.g., Fama and MacBeth (1973), Black, Jensen, and Scholes (1972), and FF). There are at least three reasons for reexamining the risk-return relation using longer measurement-interval returns. First, the CAPM does not provide explicit guidance on the choice of horizon in assessing whether beta explains cross-sectional variation in average returns. Since the choice of monthly returns is largely a consequence of data availability, it is of interest to explore the robustness of results to an alternative horizon. Inferences from cross-sectional regressions of average returns on beta can be sensitive to the return-measurement interval used to estimate betas because true betas themselves vary systematically and nonlinearly with the length of the interval used to measure returns (see, for example, Levhari and Levy (1977) and Handa, Kothari, and Wasley (1989)).

Second, beta estimates are biased due to trading frictions and non-synchronous trading (e.g., Ball (1977), Scholes and Williams (1977), and Cohen *et al.* (1983)), or other phenomena inducing systematic cross-temporal covariances in short-interval returns (e.g., Lo and MacKinlay (1990a) and Mech (1993)). These biases are mitigated by using longer interval return observations. An alternative approach to reduce biases in beta estimates, adopted by FF, is to estimate beta as the sum of the slopes in the regression of a portfolio's monthly return on the current and prior month's market return (Dimson (1979) and Fowler and Rorke (1983)).

Third, although it is not fully understood, there appears to be a significant seasonal component to monthly returns (see, for example, Rozeff and Kinney (1976) and Keim (1983)).[5] Using annual returns is one way, although not necessarily the best, of sidestepping the statistical complications that arise from seasonality in returns.

---

[4] In general, the posterior odds ratio equals the product of the prior odds ratio and the likelihood ratio when considering two simple hypotheses. More complicated analyses with composite hypotheses are, of course, possible.

[5] This goes beyond the well-known seasonal in mean returns. Shanken (1990) provides evidence of shifting variances and betas in January.

Empirically, Handa, Kothari, and Wasley (1989) have shown that the betas of small firms increase and those of large firms decrease with the return-measurement interval, substantially reducing the size effect when annual returns are employed. Moreover, the annual estimates of beta are strongly statistically correlated with both monthly and annual average returns. They document this only for size portfolios, however. Thus, their evidence is not inconsistent with that of FF. As discussed earlier, FF find support for beta using size portfolios but not alternatives such as ranking on beta alone, or first on size and then on beta. The important question that remains, therefore, is whether annual betas will continue to produce significant results when alternative portfolio grouping procedures are used. We explore this issue below.[6]

C. Relation between Average Return, Beta, and Firm Size Using Annual Betas

We present cross-sectional regression results based on annual betas for a variety of portfolio aggregation procedures: (i) grouping on beta alone; (ii) grouping on size alone; (iii) taking intersections of independent beta or size groupings; (iv) ranking first on beta and then on size within each beta group; and (v) ranking first on size and then on beta as in FF. When portfolios are formed on beta or size alone, 20 equally weighted portfolios are formed every year. For the remaining three grouping procedures, we form 100 ($= 10 \times 10$) portfolios. Size is measured as the natural logarithm of market value of equity in millions of dollars on June 30 of each calendar year. Annual returns are measured from July 1 to June 30 of the following year, consistent with FF. Use of July of calendar year t as the first month of the annual return-measurement interval makes it very likely that book values are publicly available for most firms of all fiscal-year ends that are assigned calendar year $t - 1$ by COMPUSTAT, and thus there is very little hindsight bias (see Alford, Jones, and Zmijewski (1994)). Using the July-to-June period also mitigates biases in measured returns due to the turn-of-the-year seasonality in bid prices (see Lakonishok and Smidt (1984), Keim (1989), Bhardwaj and Brooks (1992), and Ball, Kothari, and Shanken (1995)).

The betas used to form portfolios are estimated using at least two and, when available, five years of past monthly return data regressed on the CRSP equally weighted index. Any New York Stock Exchange (NYSE) and American Stock Exchange (AMEX) firm with a beta estimate available as of July 1 of a calendar year is included in the analysis. The annual time series of postranking July-to-June returns on the beta-size-ranked "mutual funds" are then used to reestimate full-period postranking betas for use in the cross-sectional regressions, as in FF and many earlier studies going back to Black, Jensen, and Scholes (1972). All returns data taken from the CRSP

---

[6] Jegadeesh (1992) makes a point similar to that of FF using monthly as well as annual return data. However, his results appear to be driven by a portfolio formation procedure that yields relatively little dispersion in beta, while maximizing dispersion in size. Thus, his failure to document a positively sloped average return-beta relation may be due to a combination of low power and the errors-in-variables problem. This impression is strengthened by our results below.

tape are included. This mitigates the survivorship-bias problem affecting average returns on the portfolios. Postranking betas are estimated for each portfolio by regressing portfolio returns on an equally- or value-weighted market average of annual returns on all the stocks included in a given year.

C.1. Descriptive Statistics on Beta, Firm size, and Average Return

Table I reports the ranking betas, postranking betas estimated using the equally and value-weighted market indices, natural logarithm of portfolio firm size, and average annual return over the postranking year for the 20 beta-ranked portfolios for the entire period from 1927 to 1990 and for the post-1940 period. Consistent with the findings in previous research, ranking stocks on past beta also generates considerable spread in both equally- and value-weighted index postranking betas. Over the entire period, the post-ranking period equally-weighted betas range from 0.44 for Portfolio 1 to 1.51 for Portfolio 19. A similar dispersion is observed in the post-1940 betas. The value-weighted index betas range from 0.73 for Portfolio 1 to 2.24 for Portfolio 19. As expected, the portfolios' value-weighted betas are larger than the respective equally-weighted betas because the value-weighted index is dominated by relatively low volatility, large market-capitalization stocks. The greater spread in the value-weighted betas, together with the fact that the two sets of betas are almost perfectly correlated (correlation exceeds 0.99), explains the lower level of the value-weighted risk premia and the robustness of inferences to the choice of market index alluded to earlier.

As in earlier studies, firm size is inversely related to beta. The portfolios' postranking returns are increasing in beta, consistent with a positive risk-return trade-off. Over the entire period, the lowest average return of 12.4 percent is earned by Portfolio 1 with the lowest postranking beta, whereas the highest return of 21.9 percent is earned by Portfolio 17 that has the second highest postranking beta of 1.41. Thus, the spread in average returns across the 20 portfolios is about 9 percent, while the spread is a little over 1 for the equally-weighted betas and 1.51 for the value-weighted betas. Similar remarks apply to the portfolio betas and average returns over the post-1940 period. Detailed information for the remaining portfolio-grouping procedures is available on request.

C.2. Cross-sectional Regression Results with Annual Betas

We have looked at cross-sectional regressions of both monthly and annual returns on the annual betas. The monthly regression (annualized) estimates are generally comparable to, but a bit smaller than, the annual regression estimates. The (annualized) monthly standard errors are much smaller, however, and so we focus on these results.[7] This also facilitates comparison

---

[7] A formal test of the efficiency of the market index over an annual horizon would, of course, consider the linearity of expected return in annual betas. This hypothesis is rejected by the finding (not reported) of a significant risk-adjusted size effect. Insofar as the annual beta estimates are viewed as better estimates of the true monthly betas, our monthly results could be interpreted as tests of efficiency over the monthly horizon. See Roll and Ross (1994) and Kandel and Stambaugh (1995) for analyses of the relation between cross-sectional studies and tests of mean-variance efficiency.

with earlier studies that use monthly returns as the dependent variable. The considerable increase in statistical significance achieved in the monthly regressions is likewise observed for the mean market return. The average monthly return on the equally-weighted index is 1.30 percent (t-statistic 4.55) for the 1927 to 1990 period and 1.28 percent (t-statistic 5.76) for the 1941 to 1990 subperiod. The corresponding numbers for the annual measurement interval are 17.9 percent (t-statistic 3.08) and 17.2 percent (t-statistic 4.38).

Each month, we estimate the following cross-sectional regression of portfolio returns on beta, size, or beta and size:

$$R_{pt} = \gamma_{0t} + \gamma_{1t}\beta_p + \gamma_{2t}\text{Size}_{pt-1} + \varepsilon_{pt} \tag{1}$$

where R_{pt} is the equally-weighted buy-and-hold return on portfolio p for month t; β_p is the full-period postranking beta of portfolio p;[8] $Size_{pt-1}$ is the natural log of the average market capitalization on June 30 of year t of the stocks in portfolio p; γ_{0t}, γ_{1t}, and γ_{2t} are regression parameters; and ε_{pt} is the regression error. We obtain similar results for value-weighted portfolio returns.

The cross-sectional regression results using the equally-weighted index betas are presented in Table II for the five different portfolio aggregation procedures.[9] Results based on the value-weighted index betas are similar and available on request. The average estimated coefficients and associated t-statistics are reported in Panel A of Table II for the period 1927 to 1990, and Panel B for the 1941 to 1990 subperiod. The tenor of the results is unaffected when we make Newey-West adjustments for serial correlation in the time series of estimated coefficients. The t-statistics under the γ_0 estimates test for the difference between the intercept and the average risk-free rate of return. The risk-free T-bill rates are taken from Ibbotson and Sinquefield (1989). The average adjusted R^2s of the annual cross-sectional regressions reflect correlation between the independent variables and both the expected and surprise components of returns, and are reported only as descriptive statistics.

Looking at the results for beta alone in Panel A, the highest risk premium, 1.02 percent (per month), is indeed obtained using size portfolios, whereas the lowest estimate, 0.54 percent, is derived by sorting solely on past beta. Although somewhat surprising at first glance, the relatively weaker results based on beta sorting begin to make sense when we note that the spread in post-ranking beta is greater when portfolios are formed on size (1.07 using beta-sorted portfolios as compared to 1.35 using size-sorted portfolios). Rankings that involve size appear to capture current information about firms that

---

[8] We also use postranking period beta estimates from the 1927 to 1990 period in the post-1940 cross-sectional regressions. Using postranking betas from the post-1940 period yields similar results. The point estimates of the risk premium are generally slightly greater using the post-1940 period betas. Results are also similar when we use betas estimated with just the year of the given cross-sectional regression excluded.

[9] Portfolio rankings for 1927 are based on 18-month estimates of beta from January 1926 through June 1927.

Table I

Preranking and Postranking Betas, Firm Size, and Average Returns on 20 Beta-ranked Portfolios over the Periods 1927 to 1990 and 1941 to 1990.

In Panel A, portfolios are formed each year on June 30 from 1927 to 1989 by ranking all stocks for which a beta estimate, preranking beta, can be obtained using the Center for Research in Securities Prices (CRSP) monthly return data on New York Stock Exchange and American Stock Exchange stocks. The preranking beta for an individual stock is estimated by regressing 24 to 60 monthly portfolio returns ending in June of each year on the CRSP equally-weighted portfolio. Each year 20 equally weighted portfolios are constructed. Portfolio 1 in each year consists of the smallest 5 percent preranking beta stocks, whereas Portfolio 20 consists of the largest 5 percent preranking beta stocks. Portfolios are rebalanced every year. An annual, equally-weighted buy-and-hold return on each portfolio over the period July 1 of year t to June 30 of year $t + 1$ is calculated. If a firm did not survive the 12-month July-to-June period, then the return until the delisting month plus any liquidating dividend as reported on the CRSP tape are used as the return for that stock for the year. A time series of 64 postranking-year returns for each portfolio from year 1927 to 1990 is constructed. Postranking beta for each portfolio is the slope coefficient from a time-series regression of annual postranking returns on an equally weighted market portfolio consisting of the 20 preranking-beta portfolios. Size is the natural logarithm of the average market value of equity in millions of dollars on June 30 of each year, of the stocks in a portfolio. The simple average of size over the 64 years is reported in the table as Ln(Size). The postranking return for each portfolio is a simple average of the time series of 64 annual returns from 1927 to 1990. The above procedures are repeated for the 1941 to 1990 period in Panel B.

Portfolio	Preranking Beta	Postranking Beta		Ln(Size)	Postranking Return
		Eq. Wt.	V. Wt.		
Panel A. 1927 to 1990					
1	0.20	0.44	0.73	5.45	12.4
2	0.38	0.59	0.96	5.75	13.4
3	0.48	0.75	1.17	5.72	15.0
4	0.56	0.68	1.09	5.69	15.3
5	0.63	0.72	1.15	5.59	15.3
6	0.70	0.75	1.20	5.31	16.1
7	0.76	0.80	1.28	5.26	17.1
8	0.81	1.05	1.62	5.15	18.3
9	0.87	0.82	1.30	5.10	16.9
10	0.93	0.91	1.43	4.92	18.0
11	0.99	0.97	1.51	4.82	18.1
12	1.04	1.14	1.72	4.72	19.0
13	1.10	1.19	1.82	4.49	20.9
14	1.17	1.10	1.70	4.47	18.4
15	1.24	1.39	2.09	4.30	21.6
16	1.32	1.28	1.92	4.12	20.4
17	1.42	1.41	2.12	3.93	21.9
18	1.54	1.30	1.96	3.80	20.4
19	1.71	1.51	2.24	3.55	20.7
20	2.17	1.19	1.81	3.27	18.1

continued overleaf...

Cross-section of Expected Stock Returns   195

Table I—Continued

Portfolio	Preranking Beta	Postranking Beta		Ln(Size)	Postranking Return
		Eq. Wt.	V. Wt.		
		Panel B. 1941 to 1990			
1	0.20	0.48	0.71	5.86	13.0
2	0.38	0.54	0.80	6.08	13.8
3	0.48	0.61	0.88	6.06	14.7
4	0.56	0.68	0.99	6.02	16.0
5	0.63	0.76	1.05	5.91	15.9
6	0.70	0.80	1.11	5.62	15.4
7	0.76	0.81	1.15	5.58	17.5
8	0.81	0.89	1.24	5.47	16.7
9	0.87	0.92	1.25	5.37	17.4
10	0.93	1.01	1.36	5.24	17.8
11	0.99	1.01	1.36	5.17	17.2
12	1.04	0.99	1.31	5.00	17.1
13	1.10	1.11	1.47	4.83	19.2
14	1.17	1.08	1.47	4.79	17.6
15	1.24	1.22	1.61	4.63	18.4
16	1.32	1.25	1.63	4.46	19.1
17	1.42	1.46	1.86	4.26	19.6
18	1.54	1.33	1.72	4.19	18.5
19	1.71	1.47	1.86	3.95	19.4
20	2.17	1.58	1.97	3.63	18.5

is missed by the "stale" (and noisy) historical betas used in forming beta-ranked portfolios. The important point, however, is that regardless of the portfolio formation procedure, the point estimates of risk premia are substantial in magnitude and fairly consistent across grouping methods. The t-statistic for the beta rankings is close to 2, while all others exceed 3.[10]

Panel B of Table II presents similar results for the 1941 to 1990 period. The risk-premium estimates range from 0.36 percent using the beta-size independently ranked portfolios to 0.76 percent employing the size-ranked portfolios. Thus, the estimated risk premia for the post-1940 subperiod are quite a bit lower, but still economically important in magnitude. Again, all but one t-statistic exceeds 3, in part reflecting the lower volatility of the 1941 to 1990 period. Even the size-then-beta rankings of FF produce a substantial risk premium of 0.5 percent (t-statistic 3.12) for this period. As in earlier studies, the γ_0 estimates are positive and often reliably greater than the average risk-free rate, which was 3.7 percent for the full period and 4.4 percent for the post-1940 period.

Consistent with the results in previous research, when size alone is included in the cross-sectional regression (1), the γ_2 coefficient on size is

[10] Chan and Lakonishok (1993) and Jagannathan and Wang (1995) also report a reliably positive coefficient on beta over comparable time periods.

Table II

Cross-sectional Regressions of Monthly Returns on Beta and Firm Size: Equally-weighted Market Index

Time-series averages of estimated coefficients from the following monthly cross-sectional regressions from 1927 to 1990 (Panel A) and from 1941 to 1990 (Panel B), associated t-statistics, and adjusted R^2s are reported (with and without Size being included in the regressions).

$$R_{pt} = \gamma_{0t} + \gamma_{1t}\beta_p + \gamma_{2t}Size_{pt-1} + \varepsilon_{pt}$$

where R_{pt} is the buy-and-hold return on portfolio p for one month during the year beginning from July 1 of year t to June 30 of year $t + 1$; β_p is the full-period postranking beta of portfolio p and is the slope coefficient from a time-series regression of annual buy-and-hold postranking portfolio returns on the returns on an equally-weighted portfolio of all the beta-size portfolios; $Size_{pt-1}$ is the natural log of the average market capitalization in millions of dollars on June 30 of year t of the stocks in portfolio p; γ_{0t}, γ_{1t}, and γ_{2t} are regression parameters; and ε_{pt} is the regression error. Portfolios are formed in five different ways: (i) 20 portfolios by grouping on beta alone; (ii) 20 portfolios by grouping on size alone; (iii) taking intersections of 10 independent beta or size groupings to obtain 100 portfolios; (iv) ranking stocks first on beta into 10 portfolios and then on size within each beta group into 10 portfolios; and (v) ranking stocks first on size into 10 portfolios and then on beta within each size group into 10 portfolios. When ranking on beta, the beta for an individual stock is estimated by regressing 24 to 60 monthly portfolio returns ending in June of each year on the CRSP equally-weighted portfolio. The t-statistic below the average γ_0 value is for the difference between the average γ_0 and the average risk-free rate of return over the 1927 to 1990 or 1941 to 1990 period. The t-statistics below γ_1 and γ_2 are for their average values from zero.

Portfolios	γ_0 t-statistic	γ_1 t-statistic	γ_2 t-statistic	Adj. R^2
Panel A. 1927 to 1990				
20, beta ranked	0.76	0.54		0.32
	3.25	1.94		
	1.76		−0.16	0.27
	2.48		−2.03	
	1.68	0.09	−0.14	0.35
	3.82	0.41	−2.57	
20, size ranked	0.30	1.02		0.32
	−0.18	3.91		
	1.73		−0.18	0.33
	3.70		−3.50	
	−0.05	1.15	0.03	0.40
	−0.85	4.61	0.76	
100, beta and	0.63	0.66		0.07
size ranked	1.67	3.65		
independently	1.72		−0.17	0.09
	3.92		−3.71	
	1.21	0.40	−0.11	0.12
	3.74	2.63	−2.83	
100, first beta,	0.57	0.73		0.12
then size ranked	1.43	3.49		
	1.73		−0.18	0.12
	3.70		−3.48	
	1.12	0.45	−0.10	0.16
	3.43	2.83	−2.65	

continued overleaf...

Cross-section of Expected Stock Returns   197

Table II—*Continued*

Portfolios	γ_0 t-statistic	γ_1 t-statistic	γ_2 t-statistic	Adj. R^2
Panel A. 1927 to 1990				
100, first size,	0.58	0.71		0.12
then beta ranked	1.54	3.39		
	1.72		−0.18	0.12
	3.66		−3.43	
	1.14	0.43	−0.10	0.16
	3.78	2.58	−2.87	
Panel B. 1941 to 1990				
20, beta ranked	0.95	0.36		0.33
	4.69	1.63		
	1.61		−0.10	0.28
	2.31		−1.49	
	1.70	−0.03	−0.10	0.36
	3.49	−0.18	−2.00	
20, size ranked	0.54	0.76		0.32
	0.82	3.69		
	1.73		−0.14	0.34
	4.03		−3.28	
	0.32	0.85	0.02	0.44
	−0.15	4.35	0.56	
100, beta and	0.87	0.42		0.07
size ranked	2.95	3.33		
independently	1.70		−0.13	0.10
	4.29		−3.40	
	1.43	0.20	−0.10	0.13
	4.63	2.12	−2.89	
100, first beta,	0.82	0.49		0.12
then size ranked	2.76	3.07		
	1.73		−0.14	0.13
	3.99		−3.22	
	1.35	0.26	−0.09	0.17
	4.35	2.20	−2.78	
100, first size	0.81	0.49		0.12
then beta ranked	2.75	3.12		
	1.71		−0.13	0.13
	3.96		−3.17	
	1.32	0.27	−0.09	0.17
	4.39	2.38	−2.77	

generally reliably negative. Alternative grouping procedures have relatively little effect on the size coefficient. Not surprisingly, given the strong correlation between size and beta, the significance of beta and size is reduced over the 1927 to 1990 and 1941 to 1990 periods when both are included as independent variables in the cross-sectional regressions. As in Handa, Kothari, and Wasley (1989), beta continues to dominate size for size-ranked portfolios. Most t-statistics still exceed 2 in magnitude, however, for both beta and size.[11,12] Note that since beta is measured with error and is fixed over the full period, size could in part be proxying for variation in the true beta that is missed by the estimate. In any event, the main point to take away from Table II is that there is indeed evidence of a positive simple relation between beta and average monthly return for a variety of asset portfolios. Risk premium estimates (not reported) from cross-sectional regressions of annual returns on beta are typically somewhat greater than 12 times the monthly estimates, and all are significant at the 10 percent level in one-sided tests. These results are available on request.

In assessing the economic significance of the size effect, it is important to remember that the implied deviations from the "beta-only" model are *not* equal to the multiple regression γ_2 times (log) size. Rather, these deviations equal γ_2 times the residuals from an auxiliary cross-sectional regression of size on beta and a constant. Since beta and size are strongly negatively correlated, these residuals are relatively small. As a result, the estimated deviations never exceed 3 percent and average less than 1 percent across all of our portfolios, whose average returns range from 8.1 to 38.2 percent per annum. Alternatively, the cross-sectional correlations between the expected returns predicted by the beta-only and beta-size models range from 0.96 to 1.00 for the five grouping procedures. These measures indicate that the *incremental* contribution of size, while not unimportant, is not large either.

D. Summary

FF regress monthly returns on betas estimated using monthly returns. They fail to reject the null hypothesis of zero risk premium. Following previous research documenting the sensitivity of Fama-MacBeth regression results to return-measurement interval employed for estimating betas, we report results using annual betas. Results based on annual betas for a variety of portfolio aggregation procedures reveal economically and statistically significant compensation for beta risk. These findings are robust to: full post-1927 period or 1941 to 1990 subperiod analysis; the use of equally- and value-

---

[11] As demonstrated in Shanken (1992), provided that the true coefficient on beta in nonzero, "t-statistics" for the null hypothesis of no size effect are biased upward due to measurement error in the betas. T-statistics for the null hypothesis of no risk-premium remain asymptotically valid, however.

[12] Some differences in experimental design between our study and Handa, Kothari, and Wasley (1989) should be noted. The time period examined in Handa, Kothari, and Wasley (1989) is 1941 to 1982; they reestimate beta every year using data over the past 15 years and they use January-to-December returns.

weighted index betas; the use of equally- and value-weighted portfolios; and forming portfolios by ranking on beta or size alone, or independently ranking on beta and size, or ranking on beta then size, or size then beta.

II. Selection Biases and Book-to-Market

This section begins by replicating some of the FF analysis using B/M equity. The main objective is to demonstrate that although we use slightly different variable definitions and sample selection procedures, there is still a near-monotonic relation between B/M and average returns over the 1963 to 1989 period using COMPUSTAT data. We then explore the possibility of selection biases affecting the B/M results. This is done using the COMPUSTAT data and S&P industry-level data.

A. B/M Equity and Average Returns: COMPUSTAT Data

To provide some continuity with the FF (1992, 1993) studies, we begin this subsection by presenting results for 13 equally weighted B/M portfolios. Each year, from 1963 to 1989, all NYSE-AMEX firms with returns on the CRSP monthly tapes and COMPUSTAT book value of equity data are ranked on the ratio of book equity to the market value of equity. As in FF, returns are measured beginning on July 1 to ensure that the accounting data for the previous fiscal year are publicly available for most of the firms. Book equity is measured at the end of a firm's fiscal year. Market equity in the denominator of the B/M ratio is also measured at the end of the fiscal year, although similar results are obtained using the prior December-end market equity. We neither include firms from the CRSP National Association of Securities Dealers Automated Quotation system (NASDAQ) tape, nor exclude financial firms. FF exclude financial firms since they also examine leverage variables, which might have different interpretations for financial and nonfinancial firms.

Companies with negative values of book equity are grouped together in Portfolio −1. Portfolios 1A and 1B contain firms in the lowest and next-lowest 5 percent of the (positive) B/M rankings, while Portfolios 10B and 10A consist of the highest and next-highest 5 percent. Of course, the set of firms in any given portfolio can change from year to year. Table III presents, for each portfolio, the mean and standard deviation of B/M equity and return, average market capitalization, as well as Jensen alphas, betas, and adjusted R^2s of excess-return time-series regressions of annual buy-and-hold portfolio returns on the equally-weighted market index.

The average B/M ratios in Table III range from 0.18 to 2.80 for the positive B/M portfolios, similar to the range in FF (Table IV, Panel A). Market capitalization is inversely related to B/M, but even the highest B/M portfolio's average size, $155 million, corresponds to that of the median NYSE-AMEX firm over the post-1962 period. As in FF, average return increases monotonically with B/M, except for the negative B/M portfolio, which has

Table III

Average Return, Size, Alpha, Beta, and Adjusted R^2 from Excess-return Time-series Regressions for Portfolios Constructed by Ranking COMPUSTAT Stocks on Book-to-Market Equity; 1963 to 1989

Each year, from 1963 to 1989, all New York Stock Exchange and American Stock Exchange firms with returns on the CRSP monthly tapes and book value of equity data on COMPUSTAT are ranked on the ratio of book equity to the market value of equity (B/M). The market equity in the denominator of the B/M ratio is measured at the end of the fiscal year. Companies with negative values of book equity are grouped together in Portfolio 0. Portfolios 1A and 1B contain firms in the lowest and next lowest 5 percent of the B/M rankings, while Portfolios 10B and 10A consist of the highest and next highest 5 percent. The composition of each portfolio changes from year to year. Equally-weighted buy-and-hold annual returns on the portfolios are calculated from July 1 of year t to June 30 of year $t + 1$ when the B/M equity is calculated using data at the end of fiscal year $t - 1$. If a firm is delisted over the 12-month period beginning on July 1, then return until the delisting month plus any liquidating dividend reported on the CRSP tape are used as the return on that stock for the year. To calculate the past return, first the average annual return over a 5-year period ending in June of year t for each security is calculated (if returns over the past 5 years are not available, then average annual return is calculated using a minimum of the past 2 years' returns). Then, for each year t and for each portfolio, an equally-weighted portfolio average past return is calculated. Finally, portfolio returns are averaged across the years to obtain the past return as reported below. Average size is market capitalization in millions of dollars on December 31 of year t of the stocks in each portfolio, averaged over the years 1963 to 1989. Alpha, Beta, and Adjusted R^2 are from time-series regressions of annual buy-and-hold portfolio returns, in excess of the risk-free rate, on the excess returns on the equally-weighted market index from 1963 to 1989.

Portfolio	Book-to-Market Std. Dvn.	Return Std. Dvn.	Past Return	Avg. Size	Alpha	Alpha t-Statistic	Beta	Beta t-Statistic	Adj. R^2
-1	-1.39	0.29	0.07	69	0.102	1.52	1.47	6.21	61.0
	1.43	0.51							
1A	0.18	0.10	0.29	1328	-0.060	-2.62	1.05	12.70	86.0
	0.06	0.30							
1B	0.30	0.11	0.28	1159	-0.047	-2.83	0.99	16.47	91.2
	0.10	0.28							

continued overleaf...

Table III—*Continued*

Portfolio	Book-to-Market Std. Dvn.	Return Std. Dvn.	Past Return	Avg. Size	Alpha t-Statistic	Beta t-statistic	Adj. R^2
2	0.41 0.15	0.12 0.26	0.25	852	-0.033 -2.28	0.93 18.18	92.7
3	0.54 0.21	0.13 0.28	0.22	987	-0.027 -1.54	1.00 16.28	91.0
4	0.66 0.25	0.14 0.26	0.20	664	-0.016 -1.25	0.94 20.04	93.9
5	0.77 0.30	0.15 0.28	0.18	719	-0.009 -0.64	1.02 20.93	94.3
6	0.89 0.34	0.16 0.25	0.16	695	0.005 0.52	0.93 26.78	96.5
7	1.03 0.40	0.18 0.27	0.16	550	0.019 1.72	0.99 25.49	96.2
8	1.21 0.47	0.18 0.24	0.14	435	0.032 2.77	0.85 20.97	94.4
9	1.49 0.60	0.20 0.26	0.12	283	0.039 3.21	0.96 21.72	94.8
10A	1.87 0.77	0.22 0.32	0.10	195	0.051 2.40	1.13 14.89	89.5
10B	2.80 1.20	0.23 0.35	0.07	155	0.051 1.80	1.22 12.05	84.7

The Journal of Finance

Table IV
Average Return, Beta, and Size of 12 Market-value-ranked Portfolios: CRSP, COMPUSTAT, and CRSP – COMPUSTAT Samples from 1963 to 1989

The CRSP, COMPUSTAT, and CRSP – COMPUSTAT samples consist of 63,581 firm-year observations on CRSP, 46,021 on COMPUSTAT, and 17,568 that appear on CRSP, but not COMPUSTAT, from 1963 to 1989. The number of firms in the COMPUSTAT sample ranges from 352 in 1963 to between 1900 and 2200 during 1971 to 1989. The number of firms in the CRSP – COMPUSTAT sample ranges from 1694 in 1963 to between 500 and 300 from 1971 to 1989. The CRSP sample represents the sum of the COMPUSTAT and CRSP – COMPUSTAT samples. Average portfolio market values, means and standard deviations of return, and market betas for 12 portfolios formed on size rankings of individual securities are reported below. The rankings are done separately in each year for the CRSP, COMPUSTAT, and CRSP – COMPUSTAT samples. Portfolios 1A and 1B represent the smallest 5 percent and next smallest 5 percent market capitalization stocks. Similarly, Portfolios 10B and 10A represent the largest 5 percent and next largest 5 percent stocks. Portfolios are equally-weighted. Betas are estimated by regressing the time series of annual buy-and-hold portfolio returns from 1963 to 1989 on the equally-weighted market return.

Portfolio	Size	Return Avg.	Return Std. Dvn.	Beta
Panel A. CRSP				
1A	3.5	0.22	0.44	1.51
1B	7.2	0.20	0.38	1.36
2	13.0	0.17	0.34	1.23
3	23.8	0.17	0.32	1.17
4	39.3	0.17	0.29	1.07
5	62.9	0.15	0.27	1.01
6	104.3	0.16	0.27	1.02
7	182.9	0.16	0.25	0.92
8	339.1	0.14	0.23	0.84
9	715.8	0.14	0.21	0.73
10A	1445.1	0.12	0.19	0.64
10B	6435.0	0.11	0.17	0.50
Panel B. COMPUSTAT				
1A	5.8	0.23	0.42	1.44
1B	11.5	0.22	0.39	1.40
2	19.8	0.18	0.33	1.22
3	35.5	0.17	0.32	1.18
4	57.2	0.16	0.30	1.08
5	93.1	0.16	0.27	1.00
6	153.4	0.16	0.28	1.03
7	262.4	0.16	0.25	0.88
8	461.7	0.13	0.23	0.80
9	913.0	0.13	0.21	0.68
10A	1750.4	0.12	0.19	0.62
10B	7832.2	0.11	0.17	0.50

continued overleaf...

Table IV—*Continued*

Portfolio	Size	Return		Beta
		Avg.	Std. Dvn.	
Panel C. CRSP – COMPUSTAT				
1A	3.3	0.14	0.44	1.42
1B	7.0	0.12	0.40	1.32
2	13.0	0.14	0.35	1.23
3	22.4	0.17	0.31	1.12
4	34.6	0.14	0.25	0.89
5	50.6	0.13	0.24	0.88
6	76.1	0.12	0.26	0.94
7	119.2	0.14	0.25	0.91
8	205.2	0.13	0.22	0.81
9	406.8	0.12	0.21	0.75
10A	807.8	0.13	0.21	0.69
10B	3606.1	0.12	0.18	0.53

the highest return; nearly 30 percent per year, with a standard deviation in excess of 50 percent and a beta of 1.47. Since there is little cross-sectional variation in beta for Portfolios 1A through 10B, the Jensen alpha abnormal return estimates are also closely related to the B/M ratio.

B. Exploring Selection Biases

In this section we first discuss how COMPUSTAT has included firms on its tapes over the years. This discussion suggests potential sample selection or survivorship biases in COMPUSTAT data.[13] To further explore these biases, we report results of separately analyzing the samples of firms on the CRSP tape, on COMPUSTAT, and on CRSP but not on COMPUSTAT (the CRSP – COMPUSTAT sample). If the COMPUSTAT sample exhibits a survivorship bias, we expect the CRSP – COMPUSTAT sample to include a preponderance of failing stocks. This provides indirect evidence consistent with an upward bias in the average returns for the high B/M portfolios. Finally, we present some indirect evidence that the positive relation between B/M and returns is period specific.

---

[13] Banz and Breen (1986) explore selection biases in COMPUSTAT data in examining the anomalous performance of extreme earnings-yield portfolios. In a different context, Chari, Jagannathan, and Ofer (1988) control for survivorship by restricting the sample of firms in their study to only those firms that were on a COMPUSTAT tape dated prior to their analysis period. Several recent studies have followed up on our arguments and obtained results consistent with survivorship bias. Breen and Korajczyk (1993) conclude that more than half of the B/M effect documented in FF is due to survivorship bias. La Porta (1993) finds that the B/M effect is weakened after partially controlling for survivorship bias. While the remaining effect is significant, we doubt that all bias has been eliminated. A recent study by Davis (1994) that is free of survivorship bias finds a statistically significant B/M effect over the period 1940 to 1963. The estimated effect and *t*-statistic are only about half that obtained by FF, however.

B.1. COMPUSTAT Selection Procedures

There are at least two aspects of COMPUSTAT selection procedures that appear to impart a survivorship bias in COMPUSTAT data. First, based on our conversations with COMPUSTAT officials, it appears that prior to 1978 COMPUSTAT routinely included *historical* financial statement information for as many years as available going back to 1946 on firms added to their database in a given year. In 1978 COMPUSTAT launched a major database expansion project from about 2700 NYSE-AMEX and high-profile NASDAQ companies to about 6000 companies. Five years of annual data, i.e., data going back to 1973, were added for most of these firms. Consider a firm in 1973, with substantial assets but relatively poor earnings prospects, considerable uncertainty, and correspondingly low market value. Suppose this high B/M firm performed poorly over the next five years, with earnings even lower than expected and negative stock returns. If this company was not on COMPUSTAT to begin with, it might not be added to the database in 1978, either because of delisting or failure to meet minimum asset or market value requirements. On the other hand, if this high B/M company performed unexpectedly well over the next five years, it could very well be included in 1978.[14] The high ex post returns over this period and the high initial B/M ratio could give the appearance of a positive relation between B/M and *expected* returns even when no such relation existed.

Second, even in recent years, COMPUSTAT's procedures for inclusion of financial data on firms favor surviving firms. This is important because we would expect that the survivorship-bias story just told (i.e., the first reason) is more relevant in the early start-up years of COMPUSTAT. Yet, FF report significant B/M results in both the 1963 to 1976 and 1977 to 1990 subperiods. An additional source of survivorship bias may help explain this finding.

Alford, Jones, and Zmijewski (1994) report that firms experiencing unfavorable economic conditions have a high propensity to delay the filing of their financial statements to the Securities and Exchange Commission (SEC) and the stock exchanges. Eventually some of these firms' stocks are delisted from the exchanges because of failure to comply with disclosure requirements, thin trading activity, or financial distress. Financial statement information for these firms during the distress period is less likely to be obtainable and included in the COMPUSTAT database. Indeed, of the 6433 CRSP firm-year observations on firms that were on COMPUSTAT for some earlier period but were removed from COMPUSTAT or do not have book value data on COMPUSTAT, 2009 (i.e., 31 percent of 6433) were subsequently delisted from the stock exchanges because of financial distress, exchange-forced delistings, and SEC-forced delistings. The 31 percent financial-distress frequency in this sample is more than ten times as much as that for a typical firm on CRSP. The median market capitalization of the 2009 firms, at the beginning of the

---

[14] Banz and Breen's (1986, p. 792) assessment of COMPUSTAT's selection procedures is similar: "For example, among all firms that begin public trading in a year, only the successful ones will be added to the current COMPUSTAT at some time in the future."

year in which they are delisted for financial-distress reasons, is only $12 million.

Some of the firms that delay filing of financial statements due to financial distress subsequently improve their performance. They then file their previously delayed financial statements and COMPUSTAT incorporates data on these firms. Thus, COMPUSTAT's selection procedures may induce an upward bias in the average return on COMPUSTAT firms, particularly the high B/M firms, even in the later period.[15]

B.2. CRSP, COMPUSTAT, and CRSP – COMPUSTAT Samples: Descriptive Results

Ideally, we would like to examine the relation between B/M and average returns separately for firms on and not on COMPUSTAT. Since accounting data for the latter firms are not readily available, this is not feasible. We can provide some indirect evidence on the potential impact of the selection bias, however, by analyzing returns for the CRSP, COMPUSTAT, and CRSP – COMPUSTAT samples. Over the 1963 to 1989 period, there are 63,581 NYSE-AMEX firm-year observations on CRSP. Of these, 46,021 appear on COMPUSTAT, leaving 17,568 in the CRSP – COMPUSTAT sample.[16] The COMPUSTAT sample is assembled by combining data on the COMPUSTAT Expanded Annual Industrial and Full Coverage file and the COMPUSTAT Research Annual Industrial file. The former contains historical data on firms that are currently traded on the NYSE, AMEX, or NASDAQ over the counter (OTC) exchanges. The COMPUSTAT Research tape contains historical data on firms until they either were delisted or did not survive due to bankruptcies or corporate control transactions. The number of NYSE-AMEX firms on COMPUSTAT is low in the initial few years since 1963, but it increases rapidly from 1967. The number increases from 352 in 1963 to between 1900 and 2200 from 1971 to 1989. As expected, the number of NYSE-AMEX firms in the CRSP – COMPUSTAT sample declines, from 1694 in 1963 to between 500 and 300 from 1971 to 1989.

Consistent with the survivorship bias (or COMPUSTAT selection bias) stories, we find that the average annual return on the COMPUSTAT sample, 15.8 percent, exceeds that on the CRSP – COMPUSTAT sample, 13.9 percent, by 1.9 percent. The t-statistic, 1.45, for the difference is significant at the 10 percent level using a one-sided test. The difference in average returns

---

[15] Although we provide no direct evidence, the low B/M stocks' poor performance might be related to merger-and-takeover activity. While B/M data on failed takeover targets are available on COMPUSTAT, the database does not always include financial data on the successfully acquired firms for the most recent year. The failed targets experience abnormal price declines when the takeover bids fail (e.g., Bradley, Desai, and Kim (1983)). Since the B/M ratio of takeover targets is low due to the price run-up that they initially experience, the tendency to include failed targets on COMPUSTAT, but not the successful ones, downward biases the low B/M stocks' performance.

[16] Book value of equity data is not available on COMPUSTAT prior to 1963, even though data on earnings and a few other selected variables are available since 1946.

is about the same over two subperiods: 1.75 percent over 1963 to 1975 and 2.04 percent over 1976 to 1989. It cannot be explained by differences in beta, which are small. The higher average return for COMPUSTAT firms is particularly interesting considering that the average annual market capitalization of equity of the COMPUSTAT sample, $657 million, is about twice that of the CRSP − COMPUSTAT sample, $317 million. Absent a survivorship bias in the COMPUSTAT sample, one expects the smaller sized CRSP − COMPUSTAT firms to earn larger raw returns, on average, than the COMPUSTAT sample firms.

The survivorship bias story predicts that distressed firms on COMPUSTAT with low market value (and high volatility) will have higher subsequent returns than similar-sized firms that are on CRSP but not on COMPUSTAT. Table IV presents market values, means and standard deviations of return, and market betas for 12 portfolios formed on size rankings of individual securities. The rankings are done separately for the entire CRSP universe as well as the COMPUSTAT and CRSP − COMPUSTAT subsets. Portfolios 1A and 1B represent the smallest 5 percent and next smallest 5 percent market-capitalization stocks. Similarly, Portfolios 10B and 10A represent the largest 5 percent and next largest 5 percent stocks. Since we do not isolate the distressed firms from other more healthy firms of a given size, the return differences observed between the COMPUSTAT and CRSP − COMPUSTAT samples probably understate any survivorship bias that may be present. We expect the proportion of distressed firms to be higher within extremely small firm portfolios, however, and thus there should be both more signal (bias) and less noise (dilution by healthy firms) in this case.

Although the measures of risk are quite similar, average returns for the smallest COMPUSTAT size portfolios are indeed much higher than the corresponding CRSP − COMPUSTAT portfolio returns. This is true despite the fact that the smallest COMPUSTAT firms are somewhat larger in market value than the corresponding CRSP − COMPUSTAT portfolio. For example, average returns on portfolios 1A and 1B are 23 and 22 percent, respectively, for firms on COMPUSTAT, as compared to 14 and 12 percent, respectively, for the corresponding CRSP − COMPUSTAT portfolios. The average returns on Portfolios 1A and 1B for firms on COMPUSTAT are reliably greater than those on the corresponding CRSP − COMPUSTAT portfolios. Differences in returns for the larger size portfolios are less dramatic, but still nontrivial. For example, average annual return on the COMPUSTAT firm-size deciles 4 to 7 is 16 percent, whereas CRSP − COMPUSTAT deciles 4 to 8, which consist of marginally smaller size firms, earn 12 to 14 percent annual return. There is thus a 2 to 4 percent difference in average annual returns between these low-to-medium-capitalization stocks of the COMPUSTAT and CRSP − COMPUSTAT samples. The potential for a survivorship bias affecting COMPUSTAT stocks therefore does not appear limited to the extremely small firms. Overall, results in Table IV are consistent with a selection bias or survivorship bias affecting average returns on the COMPUSTAT high B/M stocks.

It is conceivable that the lower average return on the CRSP –
COMPUSTAT sample is due to COMPUSTAT systematically excluding certain kinds of securities that are included by CRSP. We therefore repeated the
analysis in this section, excluding all securities other than "Ordinary Common Shares." The excluded securities are Certificates, American Depository
Receipts (ADRs), Share Beneficial Interests (SBIs), Voting Trust Shares,
Capital Shares, and Units that include Depository units, Units of Beneficial
Interests, Units of Limited Partnership Interest, and Depository Receipts,
etc. These results are very similar to those reported in the article and are
available upon request. For example, the small capitalization stocks in the
CRSP – COMPUSTAT sample continue to earn about 10 percent less on
average than those in the COMPUSTAT sample.

B.3. B/M and Size Factor Results

This section examines whether the differences in small-firm returns noted
above are explained by systematic differences in the B/M ratios for small
firms on and off of COMPUSTAT. Although we cannot test this directly due
to lack of B/M data for the CRSP – COMPUSTAT sample, we consider an
indirect test. Fama and French (1993) show that the cross-sectional explanatory power of B/M equity and size is also captured by multiple regression
coefficients on B/M and size "factors." We construct similar factors and
include these along with the market index in three-factor (annual) excess-return time-series regressions for the size portfolios.

To construct size and B/M equity factors, we independently rank all the
COMPUSTAT stocks into five size portfolios and five B/M portfolios each
year. Since we do not have B/M data on the CRSP – COMPUSTAT sample,
we cannot use the CRSP sample to construct the size and B/M factors. We
exclude the negative B/M equity stocks in forming the quintile portfolios.
The size factor is the difference, each year, between the simple average
return on the five portfolios within the smallest market-capitalization quintile (i.e., the smallest firm quintile that is split into five portfolios on the basis
of low to high B/M) minus the simple average return on the five portfolios
within the largest market-capitalization quintile.[17] The B/M factor is constructed similarly as the difference between the average return on the five
portfolios within the highest B/M quintile minus the average return on the
five portfolios within the lowest B/M quintile. As in Fama and French (1993),
the B/M and size factors are only weakly correlated (correlation −0.20). The
size factor has a correlation coefficient of 0.69 with the equally-weighted
market, whereas the B/M factor has a correlation of −0.26 with the market.

Results for excess return time-series regressions of 12 size-portfolio returns
on the equally weighted market and the size and B/M equity factors are
reported in Table V. The intercepts for the COMPUSTAT size portfolios are

---

[17] Since stocks are ranked *independently* on size and B/M, the five B/M portfolios within the
smallest market capitalization quintile are unbalanced. Hence, the average of the returns on
these five portfolios within the smallest size quintile would be different from the equally
weighted return on the smallest size quintile portfolio.

Table V

Results for Excess-Return Time-series Regressions of 12 Size-portfolio Returns on the Equally-weighted Market and the Size and Book-to-Market-Equity Factors: 1963 to 1989

Estimated coefficients from the following excess-return time-series regressions using annual-return data from 1963 to 1989, associated t-statistics below the parameter estimates, and adjusted R^2s are reported for the CRSP, COMPUSTAT, and CRSP – COMPUSTAT samples:

$$R_{pt} = \alpha_0 + \beta_1 R_{mt} + \beta_2 R_{B/Mt} + \beta_3 R_{Sizet} + \varepsilon_{pt}$$

where R_{pt} is the equally-weighted excess return on size portfolio p calculated from July of year t to June of year $t + 1$ where size is measured as of June-end of year t and returns are in excess of the T-bill rate; R_{mt} is the annual excess return on the equally weighted market portfolio; $R_{B/Mt}$ is the return on the book-to-market equity (B/M) factor; R_{Sizet} is the return on the size factor; α_0, β_1, β_2, and β_3 are regression parameters; and ε_{pt} is the regression error. The CRSP, COMPUSTAT, and CRSP – COMPUSTAT samples consist of 63,581 firm-year observations on CRSP, 46,021 on COMPU-STAT, and 17,568 that appear on CRSP but not COMPUSTAT from 1963 to 1989. Portfolios are formed on size rankings of individual securities done separately in respective samples each year. Portfolios 1A and 1B represent the smallest 5 percent and next smallest 5 percent market-capitalization stocks. Similarly, Portfolios 10B and 10A represent the largest 5 percent and next largest 5 percent stocks. Portfolios are equally weighted.

The size and B/M equity factors are constructed by independently ranking all the COMPUSTAT stocks into five size portfolios and five B/M portfolios each year. The negative B/M stocks are excluded in forming the quintile portfolios. The size factor is the difference, each year, between the simple average return on the five portfolios within the smallest market-capitalization quintile (i.e., the smallest firm quintile that is split into five portfolios on the basis of low to high B/M) minus the simple average return on the five portfolios within the largest market-capitalization quintile. The B/M factor is constructed similarly as the difference between the average return on the five portfolios within the highest B/M quintile minus the average return on the five portfolios within the lowest B/M quintile.

continued overleaf...

Table V—Continued

Portfolio	α_0 t-statistic	β_1 t-statistic	β_2 t-statistic	β_3 t-statistic	Adj. R^2
			Panel A. CRSP		
1A	−0.025	1.00	0.54	0.82	95.8
	−1.14	10.59	3.44	8.93	
1B	−0.009	1.00	0.20	0.55	98.2
	−0.73	18.66	2.26	10.56	
2	−0.019	1.03	0.15	0.32	98.7
	−2.00	26.01	2.28	8.16	
3	−0.005	1.03	0.04	0.21	98.0
	−0.48	22.00	0.45	4.64	
4	−0.004	0.99	0.09	0.14	98.4
	−0.43	26.22	1.41	3.71	
5	−0.001	0.99	−0.10	0.02	99.0
	−0.01	35.99	−2.12	0.79	
6	0.005	1.07	−0.05	−0.08	98.6
	0.61	31.87	−0.86	−2.37	
7	0.018	1.04	−0.11	−0.18	97.4
	1.79	24.69	−1.56	−4.47	
8	0.006	1.00	−0.13	−0.26	98.7
	0.88	37.10	−2.94	−9.73	
9	0.012	0.99	−0.15	−0.39	97.5
	1.51	28.57	−2.53	−11.54	
10A	−0.002	0.93	−0.06	−0.43	96.6
	−0.23	25.50	−1.03	−12.01	
10B	0.005	0.80	−0.15	−0.46	84.8
	0.31	11.52	−1.29	−6.74	

Table V—*Continued*

Panel B. COMPUSTAT

Portfolio	α_0 t-statistic	β_1 t-statistic	β_2 t-statistic	β_3 t-statistic	Adj. R^2
1A	-0.015	1.06	0.64	0.65	95.1
	-0.66	11.02	3.99	6.94	
1B	0.015	1.04	0.13	0.53	98.4
	1.21	20.14	1.50	10.53	
2	-0.018	1.03	0.24	0.31	97.6
	-1.39	19.25	1.91	2.71	
3	-0.020	1.09	0.16	0.14	97.4
	-1.62	20.74	1.81	2.78	
4	-0.022	1.15	0.17	-0.08	94.0
	-1.22	15.37	1.35	-1.05	
5	-0.004	1.07	0.04	-0.10	96.4
	-0.29	20.21	0.46	-1.85	
6	0.002	1.14	-0.02	-0.16	95.7
	0.16	18.93	-0.24	-2.76	
7	0.005	1.08	0.03	-0.28	97.6
	0.58	27.70	0.49	-7.43	
8	-0.006	1.05	-0.08	-0.37	96.0
	-0.52	22.02	-1.01	-7.94	
9	-0.002	1.10	-0.02	-0.48	97.0
	-0.20	27.28	-0.37	-13.19	
10A	-0.003	0.94	-0.02	-0.46	94.7
	-0.23	20.54	-0.23	-10.25	
10B	0.006	0.80	-0.15	-0.45	80.3
	0.31	9.89	-0.09	-5.74	

continued overleaf....

Table V—*Continued*

Portfolio	α_0 t-statistic	β_1 t-statistic	β_2 t-statistic	β_3 t-statistic	Adj. R^2
		Panel C. CRSP – COMPUSTAT			
1A	-0.068	0.89	0.22	0.80	85.4
	-1.65	5.15	0.74	4.70	
1B	-0.071	0.82	0.11	0.73	88.9
	-2.18	5.96	0.48	5.46	
2	-0.043	1.00	0.08	0.35	90.4
	-1.64	8.92	0.43	3.19	
3	0.014	0.96	-0.20	0.20	93.2
	0.70	11.46	-1.42	2.42	
4	-0.003	0.84	0.02	0.08	87.6
	-0.16	9.12	0.11	0.92	
5	-0.008	0.76	-0.04	0.17	92.3
	-0.47	10.78	-0.30	2.43	
6	-0.015	0.89	-0.20	0.04	91.2
	-0.82	11.15	-1.48	0.45	
7	0.007	0.96	-0.27	-0.12	96.1
	0.63	18.87	-3.16	-2.33	
8	0.001	0.92	-0.19	-0.19	94.2
	0.04	16.50	-2.07	-3.55	
9	0.008	0.88	-0.25	-0.23	91.8
	0.53	13.91	-2.35	-3.70	
10A	0.013	0.95	-0.21	-0.40	94.4
	1.12	18.78	-2.52	-8.04	
10B	0.015	0.82	-0.19	-0.45	90.2
	1.12	14.55	-2.04	-8.21	

small and not significantly different from zero, consistent with the hypothesis that the size and B/M factors capture the relevant components of systematic risk as in Fama and French (1993). The extremely small firms have a nontrivial coefficient on the B/M factor as well as the size factor in the CRSP and COMPUSTAT samples (Panels A and B). Apart from this, the B/M factor betas are small and generally statistically insignificant. This remains true even when the size factor is excluded (results available on request).

Results for the small firm portfolios of the CRSP – COMPUSTAT sample are still at odds with those for the CRSP and COMPUSTAT samples. Intercepts for the CRSP – COMPUSTAT small-firm Portfolios 1A and 1B are about -7 percent. The intercept for Portfolio 1B is reliably negative at the 5 percent level, whereas intercepts for Portfolios 1A and 2 are marginally significantly below zero. These portfolios have very small and statistically insignificant coefficients on the B/M equity factor. Thus, whether because of a selection bias or some alternative explanation, the COMPUSTAT size and B/M equity factors are not able to account for the low returns on the CRSP – COMPUSTAT small-firm portfolios.

Overall, the results of this subsection are supportive of the COMPUSTAT selection-bias stories. Although we do not find evidence of a bias for relatively large distressed firms, this is not surprising given the "dilution" effect of healthy firms referred to earlier; in other words, the power of the test is likely to be low in this case.

C. Period-Specific Results

We now consider another aspect of the B/M puzzle. We analyze the COMPUSTAT B/M portfolios' returns over the 12-month *preranking* period ending on June 30. The results in Table III indicate that the low B/M Portfolios 1A and 1B earn average returns of 29 and 28 percent, respectively, over this one-year period. More generally, prior one-year returns monotonically decline with B/M, with Portfolio 10B averaging only a 7.3 percent return.

The above-average stock-price performance over the preranking period accords low (high) B/M stocks the "winner-stock" ("loser-stock") status from the stock-market overreaction literature revived by DeBondt and Thaler (1985, 1987). This is interesting because it provides the basis for an "educated guess" as to whether the positive relation between average returns and book-to-market is a period-specific phenomenon or indicative of a more general relation. Ball, Kothari, and Shanken (1995) examine the performance of 50 winner and loser stock portfolios over two periods. Like the low B/M stocks, winners *underperform* the losers in the post-1957 period, but the reverse is true in the pre-1958 period.

While Ball, Kothari, and Shanken (1995) examine winner stocks' performance over a five-year period, as is often done in the stock-market overreaction literature, more relevant to this study is the winner stocks' performance in the first postranking year. Using their method, we estimate winner stocks' one-year postranking abnormal returns over the pre-1963 and post-1962 subperiods. Over the pre-1963 period, winner stocks earn 3.6 percent average annual abnormal return (Jensen alpha), whereas they earn −4.2 percent abnormal return over the post-1962 period. On the other hand, the losers outperform the market by 2.3 percent in the post-1962 period, but underperform by 3.3 percent in the pre-1963 period. Thus, a positive relation between returns and B/M, even after adjusting for the survivorship biases discussed above, may be period-specific as well. Given the difficulty of satisfactorily quantifying the statistical impact of data snooping over the more recent period, definitive conclusions about B/M as a predictor of the expected rate of return beyond beta are not feasible.

D. B/M and Average Returns: S&P Data

We now turn to an alternative data set—B/M ratios obtained from the *S&P Analyst's Handbook* for industries represented in the S&P 500 and monthly share prices for these industries reported in the *S&P Stock Price Guide*. This data set has the advantage of permitting us to examine the relation between B/M and stock returns back to 1947. The *S&P Analyst's Handbook* reports selected accounting data on a per share basis that corresponds to S&P's industry stock price indexes. S&P selects stocks to be included in each industry on the basis of "their industry representation and adequacy of their market activity" (*S&P Analyst's Handbook*, 1989, in the Description of Methodology section). The number of industries and their composition thus changes over time, but the year-to-year changes in a given industry are generally not dramatic. The share-price index and the per share accounting data are adjusted for stock splits and the index itself is value weighted. The accounting data are reported for calendar years, although data for the individual firms included in an industry are on a fiscal year basis. S&P places accounting data in the calendar year in which the most months of a company's fiscal year fall. COMPUSTAT follows the same procedure, which is hardly surprising because S&P sells the COMPUSTAT tapes.

For consistency with FF, we calculate B/M ratios by taking the ratio of the (industry) book-value per share at the end of the previous calendar year to the share-price index for the month of June of the next year. S&P's definition of book value is: "Total of common stock, capital surplus, and retained earnings less treasury stock, intangibles, and the difference between the carrying value and liquidating value of preferred stock." Annual July-to-June returns are calculated using the monthly share-price indexes and adding the (annual cash) dividend per share as reported in the *S&P Analyst's Handbook*. We obtain similar results using December-end returns.

Since firms that do not survive or become less attractive on S&P's criteria are excluded from the S&P industry indexes, the S&P industry data suffers from a survivorship bias. Insofar as the composition of the industry indices changes from the year in which we obtain B/M ratios to the following year in which we compute returns, there could be a bias against finding a B/M effect.[18] Although we can not rule out this possibility, it seems at least equally plausible that there is actually a bias in favor of the B/M effect. High B/M industries that consist of one or more poorly performing stocks are more likely to lose some firms that do not survive. Since these failing stocks are not included in the industry index in the future, the return on the industry may be biased upward. The degree of bias is probably small, however, because the S&P industry portfolios are value weighted and include the (primarily) large market-capitalization S&P 500 stocks that fail relatively infrequently.

Each year from 1947 to 1987, we form 10 B/M portfolios as with the COMPUSTAT data, except that the portfolios are now equally-weighted combinations of industries rather than individual firms. The number of industries in a given year ranges from 45 to 75. Unlike the COMPUSTAT data, none of the industries has a negative book value, so there is no separate negative B/M portfolio. Summary data are provided in Table VI and Figure 1 for the entire period, 1947 to 1988, as well as two subperiods split at 1963.

As expected, working with industry data reduces the range of B/M relative to that in Table III using the COMPUSTAT data. The B/M ratio ranges from 0.27 for Portfolio 1 to 1.65 for Portfolio 10. The spread is still considerable, however, and corresponds roughly to the range for Portfolios 1B through 10A based on the COMPUSTAT data. Absence of an S&P-based B/M portfolio that corresponds to Portfolio 10B using the COMPUSTAT data should not, however, be a serious deficiency. The return on the COMPUSTAT Portfolio 10B, 23 percent, is only slightly higher than that of Portfolio 10A, 22 percent, in Table III (and it is actually *lower* in the FF sample), despite Portfolio 10B's much higher B/M ratio relative to Portfolio 10A. Thus, the S&P industry data retains most of the range over which average return has been observed to be positively related to B/M in the COMPUSTAT data.

Looking at the entire-period results in Panel A of Table VI, we see that, apart from the lowest B/M portfolio 1, average returns remain essentially flat as B/M increases. While the lowest return of 13 percent is indeed earned by Portfolio 1, average returns for Portfolios 2 through 10 range only between 15 and 18 percent per annum and are not monotonically related to the B/M ratios. From Panel B, it is apparent that the low return on Portfolio 1 is due to the pre-1963 data. Moreover, the highest return over this fairly short subperiod is achieved by the low B/M Portfolio 2. Most surprising is the fact that average return is flat for the post-1962 period as well, in sharp contrast to the monotonic relation in Table III and in FF using the COMPUSTAT data. In this subperiod, Portfolio 1's average return is 15 percent compared to 16 percent for Portfolio 10. Other portfolios earn between 13 and 18 percent per year. Figure 1 vividly conveys these patterns.

Another perspective is provided in Table VII, via cross-sectional regressions of average return on the natural logarithm of B/M equity. Regression

---

[18] It is encouraging to note that a significant relation between annual returns and the following year's earnings growth is observed both in time series and cross-section for the S&P industry indices. See Collins *et al.* (1994).

results using the S&P data for the entire, pre-1963, and post-1962 periods, are given in Panel A of Table VII. The results using the industry portfolios are virtually identical to those based on 10 B/M portfolios. The pre-1963 coefficients on B/M are about 1.6 standard errors above zero, although the relation appears in Figure 1 to be nonlinear and driven entirely by the lowest B/M portfolio. The t-statistics are only slightly above one for the entire period. The t-statistic on B/M for the post-1962 period using the industry-level data is only 0.15, and it is 0.31 using 10 B/M portfolios.

Panel B presents COMPUSTAT cross-sectional regression results for the 1963 to 1989 period. To facilitate comparison with the S&P industry data analysis, results are first presented for COMPUSTAT industry portfolios and then for ten B/M-portfolios formed by ranking industries on their average B/M. Results using both equally and value-weighted portfolios are reported. We use the 3-digit Standard Industrial Classification (SIC) code for industry portfolios.

As seen from Panel B of Table VII, in each case there is a reliably positive relation between B/M and average return, the lowest t-statistic being 2.63. Most of the increase in statistical significance comes from the estimated coefficients, as the standard errors (not shown) are only slightly smaller than those obtained using the S&P data. Similar strong results are still obtained with the COMPUSTAT data even if we leave firms with negative B/M equity in the industry portfolios, as is the case with the S&P data. Finally, we report results using 10 equally and value-weighted portfolios formed each year by ranking all the available COMPUSTAT firms on their B/M ratios (i.e., without regard to their industry membership). Once again, the evidence indicates a strong positive relation between average return and B/M ratios that is robust to equally and value-weighted portfolio formation.[19] In summary, the evidence in Table VII suggests that the startling differences between our S&P results and the earlier findings of FF are not attributable to value weighting or to our ranking at the industry, rather than individual security, level.[20]

The finding of a significant B/M effect for the value-weighted COMPUS-TAT portfolios, but not the S&P portfolios, is puzzling in that it is not likely due to the survivorship biases discussed earlier. To explore this further, we redo the cross-sectional analysis restricted to the 500 largest market-capitali-

---

[19] Even stronger evidence is obtained using individual securities or 20 book-to-market portfolios based on individual security book-to-market-rankings. These results are available upon request.

[20] Since expected return is known to be negatively related to firm size, flat returns for the S&P B/M-portfolios might conceivably be the result of offsetting effects due to a strong positive association between B/M and size. This seems unlikely, though, given the strong negative relation between size and B/M for COMPUSTAT data in Table III. Unfortunately, information on market capitalization is not available for the S&P portfolios to provide direct evidence on the relation between B/M and size for the S&P data. However, when we regress the S&P portfolios on the market index and a size factor (returns on the smallest firm-size quintile minus returns on the largest firm-size quintile) there is no systematic pattern to the coefficients on size. Therefore, it is unlikely that the flat returns are driven by a size effect.

Table VI

Returns on Book-to-market Equity Portfolios Using the S&P Industry Data

Book-to-market equity (B/M) ratios are calculated using S&P industry book values per share and industry price indexes. Book values are from the *Standard and Poor Analyst's Handbook* and price indexes are from *Standard and Poor's Stock Price Guide*. Each year from 1947 to 1987 industries are ranked on their B/M ratios and 10 portfolios are formed. The average and standard deviation of the B/M ratios over the 1946 to 1986 period for each portfolio is reported. An equally-weighted annual return on the industries in each B/M portfolio is calculated from July of year t to June of year $t + 1$ where B/M is for year $t - 1$. The average return, standard deviation, minimum, and maximum return for each portfolio over the period 1947 to 1987 are reported. The same procedures are repeated for the 1947 to 1962 and 1963 to 1987 subperiods.

Portfolio	B/M		Return			
	Average	Std. Dvn.	Average	Std. Deviation	Minimum	Maximum
			Panel A. 1947 to 1987			
1	0.27	0.10	0.13	0.26	−0.27	1.11
2	0.38	0.13	0.27	0.24	−0.32	0.60
3	0.48	0.14	0.15	0.24	−0.32	0.60
4	0.57	0.16	0.16	0.27	−0.27	1.06
5	0.65	0.17	0.15	0.20	−0.24	0.72
6	0.75	0.19	0.17	0.22	−0.19	0.77
7	0.87	0.20	0.15	0.20	−0.30	0.68
8	1.01	0.25	0.15	0.22	−0.33	0.74
9	1.19	0.30	0.17	0.21	−0.18	0.68
10	1.65	0.35	0.18	0.22	−0.16	0.98

continued overleaf....

Table VI—Continued

Portfolio	B/M		Return			
	Average	Std. Dvn.	Average	Std. Deviation	Minimum	Maximum
			Panel B. Pre-1963			
1	0.33	0.09	0.11	0.19	−0.27	0.38
2	0.47	0.12	0.22	0.20	−0.15	0.60
3	0.57	0.13	0.17	0.19	−0.19	0.64
4	0.66	0.15	0.16	0.20	−0.14	0.56
5	0.73	0.16	0.17	0.17	−0.16	0.44
6	0.81	0.18	0.15	0.20	−0.19	0.56
7	0.92	0.20	0.16	0.16	−0.12	0.44
8	1.10	0.25	0.16	0.22	−0.29	0.55
9	1.34	0.33	0.20	0.24	−0.18	0.50
10	1.77	0.35	0.21	0.20	−0.14	0.53
			Panel C. Post-1962			
1	0.22	0.09	0.15	0.30	−0.26	1.11
2	0.32	0.10	0.13	0.26	−0.32	0.58
3	0.41	0.11	0.13	0.28	−0.33	0.82
4	0.50	0.13	0.16	0.32	−0.27	1.06
5	0.60	0.16	0.14	0.23	−0.24	0.72
6	0.72	0.19	0.18	0.24	−0.16	0.77
7	0.83	0.20	0.14	0.22	−0.30	0.68
8	0.94	0.22	0.15	0.24	−0.33	0.74
9	1.09	0.25	0.16	0.20	−0.18	0.68
10	1.58	0.33	0.16	0.24	−0.16	0.98

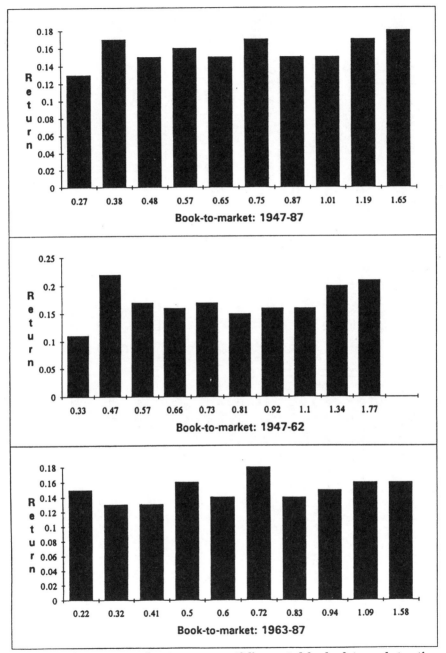

Figure 1. Average annual returns on portfolios sorted by book-to-market ratios.
Data are from 1947 to 1987 on S&P industry portfolios.

Table VII

Cross-sectional Regressions of Average Return on the Natural Logarithm of the Book-to-market Equity

Time-series averages of estimated coefficients from the following annual cross-sectional regressions, associated t-statistics in parentheses, and adjusted R^2s are reported:

$$R_{pt} = \gamma_{0t} + \gamma_{1t} B/M_{pt-1} + \varepsilon_{pt}$$

where R_{pt} is the return on the industry or book-to-market equity (B/M) portfolio p, calculated from July of year t to June of year $t + 1$, B/M_{pt-1} is the natural logarithm of the average B/M of the industries in portfolio p (or simply industry p's B/M ratio) at the end of calendar year $t - 1$; γ_{0t} and γ_{1t} are regression parameters; and ε_{pt} is the regression error. Average return and B/M ratios for the portfolios are calculated using S&P industry book values of equity per share, dividends per share, and industry price indexes. Book values are from the *Standard and Poor Analyst's Handbook* and price indexes are from *Standard and Poor's Stock Price Guide*. For the analysis using 10 B/M portfolios, each year from 1947 to 1987 industries are ranked on their B/M ratios, and 10 portfolios are formed.

Portfolio	Period	γ_0 (%)	t-Statistic	γ_1 (%)	t-Statistic	Adj. R^2 (%)
Panel A. S&P data						
Industry	Entire	16.3	5.40	1.41	1.02	4.0
Industry	Pre-1963	17.9	4.40	2.99	1.59	2.4
Industry	Post-1962	15.2	3.64	0.29	0.15	5.1
10 portfolios	Entire	16.4	5.38	1.59	1.17	11.6
10 portfolios	Pre-1963	17.9	4.06	2.99	1.61	7.1
10 portfolios	Post-1962	15.3	3.62	0.59	0.31	14.7
Panel B. COMPUSTAT data						
Industry, equally-weighted	Post-1962	16.5	2.73	5.18	2.96	1.3
10 portfolios, from equally-weighted industry portfolios	Post-1962	16.5	2.72	5.35	2.86	9.4
Industry, value-weighted	Post-1962	16.9	2.85	5.07	2.63	1.2
10 portfolios, from value-weighted industry portfolios	Post-1962	17.0	2.85	5.39	2.64	12.0
10 equally-weighted portfolios from firm-level data	Post-1962	17.1	3.42	5.29	3.85	46.9
10 value-weighted portfolios from firm-level data	Post-1962	14.8	2.21	5.23	4.26	28.7

zation COMPUSTAT stocks each year. We expect considerable overlap between these stocks and those included in S&P industry portfolios. Comparison of the S&P 500 stocks and the 500 largest market-capitalization stocks in one year (1988) reveals a 69 percent overlap. We find that S&P includes many midsize stocks in constructing the industry portfolios. This is perhaps because S&P attempts to include only those firms in the industry portfolios that have a relatively high fraction of their business activity in one industry. Also, foreign stocks are excluded, but some of those are included by COMPUSTAT and CRSP.

We form 10 B/M portfolios using 3-digit SIC codes of the 500 largest market capitalization stocks. These portfolios are value weighted. The average returns on these portfolios are not monotonically related to B/M. The average coefficient on B/M from annual cross-sectional regressions is 2.55, with a *t*-statistic of 1.38. This is only about half as large as the average coefficient reported in Panel B of Table VII (comparable standard error) and, although statistically insignificant, it is larger than that using the S&P industry data. Precision is improved by using firm-level data in the cross-sectional regressions. The average estimated slope coefficient is 3.12 with a *t*-statistic of 1.96. The coefficient is approximately 40 percent smaller than that using all COMPUSTAT stocks. Although we cannot fully explain the difference between the results using the S&P and COMPUSTAT data, the substantial reduction in the B/M coefficient is consistent with the survivorship bias stories discussed earlier.

III. Conclusions and Implications for Research

We have presented evidence that average returns do indeed reflect substantial compensation for beta risk, provided that betas are measured at the annual interval. Of course, this does not mean that beta alone accounts for all the cross-sectional variation in expected returns, as implied by the capital asset pricing model. While doubt has been cast on the explanatory power of B/M equity, we do see evidence of a size effect. Although a more complete examination of the pantheon of past anomalies is beyond the scope of this article, such an analysis may well suggest other expected return deviations, even with annual betas. Whether these deviations reflect the imperfect nature of our proxies for the market portfolio, the limitations of unconditional time-series estimates of beta or more fundamental inadequacies of the asset pricing theory are issues that are difficult to sort out.[21] In this regard, the analytical framework developed recently by Kandel and Stambaugh (1987) and Shanken (1987, 1992) provides a useful perspective that has yet to be fully exploited. In the meantime, we find it comforting to know that a simple measure of nondiversifiable risk does help account for the actual differences in average returns over the past sixty years or so.

[21] Of course, conversely, evidence consistent with efficiency of the proxy certainly does not guarantee that the true market portfolio is efficient (see Roll (1977)).

While this article has employed full-period annual betas in addressing the question of whether there is compensation for beta risk, the important issue of how best to estimate an ex ante beta in a given empirical application needs to be considered. Given the observed sensitivity of asset pricing empirical results to the return interval employed, a deeper understanding of the source of these differences is clearly called for and may prove relevant to other research questions as well. Two of the current prime suspects are trading frictions and associated risk estimation issues on the one hand, and more theoretical concerns involving investment horizon on the other.

Our analysis of the explanatory power of B/M, in particular the related investigation of selection biases associated with the COMPUSTAT tapes, has implications for other research. Fairfield and Harris (1993), Ou and Penman (1989a, 1989b) and Lev and Thiagarajan (1993) have reported abnormal returns to a trading strategy that exploits information in financial statements (i.e., fundamental analysis). Since these studies rely on the COMPUS-TAT samples to document abnormal returns and market inefficiency, selection biases in the COMPUSTAT data are likely to have a bearing on their findings as well (also see Holthausen and Larcker (1992) on this issue).

The finance and accounting literature has extensively documented the tendency of stock prices to drift upwards following extreme earnings increases and drift downwards following extreme earnings declines (see Jones and Litzenberger (1970) for an early example and Bernard and Thomas (1989) for a recent example). The evidence on B/M equity and sample-selection biases in the COMPUSTAT data could be relevant for this "postearnings-announcement drift" anomaly. Firms reporting extreme earnings increases (decreases) are more likely to be high (low) B/M stocks and studies documenting the drift have relied on COMPUSTAT data. Our evidence suggests that a small portion of the drift may be attributable to the COMPUSTAT survivorship bias.

Finally, we emphasize that the failure of a significant relation between B/M and return to emerge from the S&P industry portfolios, insofar as it is not driven by low power, poses a serious challenge to the B/M "empirical asset pricing model." This is true regardless of the extent of the COMPUSTAT selection bias. A useful pricing model must be trusted to work under a wide variety of conditions and not just for a limited set of portfolios.

REFERENCES

Alford, Andrew W., Jennifer J. Jones, and Mark E. Zmijewski, 1994, Extension and violation of the statutory SEC Form 10-K filing requirements, *Journal of Accounting & Economics* 17, 229–254.

Ball, Ray, 1977, A note on errors in variables and estimates of systematic risk, *Australian Journal of Management* 2, 79–84.

———, 1978, Anomalies in relationships between securities' yields and yield-surrogates, *Journal of Financial Economics* 6, 103–126.

———, and S. P. Kothari, 1989, Nonstationary expected returns: Implications for tests of market efficiency and serial correlation in returns, *Journal of Financial Economics* 25, 51–74.

Ball, Ray, S. P. Kothari, and Jay Shanken, 1995, Problems in measuring portfolio performance: An application to contrarian investment strategies, *Journal of Financial Economics*, Forthcoming.

Banz, Rolf W., 1981, The relationship between return and market value of common stocks, *Journal of Financial Economics* 9, 3–18.

———, and William J. Breen, 1986, Sample dependent results using accounting and market data: Some evidence, *Journal of Finance* 41, 779–793.

Basu, Sanjoy, 1977, Investment performance of common stocks in relation to their price-earnings ratios: A test of the efficient market hypothesis, *Journal of Finance* 32, 663–682.

———, 1983, The relationship between earnings yield, market value, and return for NYSE common stocks: Further evidence, *Journal of Financial Economics* 12, 129–156.

Bernard, Victor L., and Jacob K. Thomas, 1989, Post-earnings announcement drift: Delayed price response or risk premium, *Journal of Accounting Research* (Supplement) 27, 1–36.

Bhandari, Lakshmi Chand, 1988, Debt/equity ratio and expected common stock returns: Empirical evidence, *Journal of Finance* 43, 507–528.

Bhardwaj, Ravinder K., and Leroy D. Brooks, 1992, The January anomaly: Effects of low share price, transaction costs, and bid-ask bias, *Journal of Finance* 47, 553–575.

Black, Fischer, 1972, Capital market equilibrium with restricted borrowing, *Journal of Business* 45, 444–455.

———, Michael C. Jensen, and Myron Scholes, 1972, The capital asset pricing model: Some empirical tests, in Michael C. Jensen, Ed.: *Studies in the Theory of Capital Markets* (Praeger, New York).

Bradley, Michael, Anand Desai, and E. Han Kim, 1983, The rationale behind interfirm tender offers: Information or synergy, *Journal of Financial Economics* 11, 183–206.

Breeden, Douglas T., Michael R. Gibbons, and Robert H. Litzenberger, 1989, Empirical tests of the consumption-oriented CAPM, *Journal of Finance* 44, 231–262.

Breen, William J., and Robert A. Korajczyk, 1993, On selection biases in book-to-market based tests of asset pricing models, Working paper no. 167, Northwestern University.

Chan, K. C., 1988, On the contrarian investment strategy, *Journal of Business* 61, 147–163.

———, and Nai-fu Chen, 1988, An unconditional asset-pricing test and the role of firm size as an instrumental variable for risk, *Journal of Finance* 43, 309–325.

Chan, Louis K. C., Yasushi Hamao, and Josef Lakonishok, 1991, Fundamentals and stock returns in Japan, *Journal of Finance* 46, 1739–1764.

Chan, Louis K. C., and Josef Lakonishok, 1993, Are the reports of beta's death premature? *Journal of Portfolio Management* 19, 51–62.

Chari, V. V., Ravi Jagannathan, and Aharon R. Ofer, 1988, Seasonalities in security returns: The case of earnings announcements, *Journal of Financial Economics* 21, 101–121.

Chopra, Navin, Josef Lakonishok, and Jay R. Ritter, 1992, Measuring abnormal performance: Do stocks overreact, *Journal of Financial Economics* 31, 235–268.

Cohen, Kalman J., Gabriel A. Hawawini, Steven F. Maier, Robert A. Schwartz, and David K. Whitcomb, 1983, Friction in trading process and the estimation of systematic risk, *Journal of Financial Economics* 12, 263–278.

Collins, Daniel W., S. P. Kothari, Jay Shanken, and Richard G. Sloan, 1994, Lack of timeliness and noise as explanations for the low contemporaneous return-earnings association, *Journal of Accounting and Economics* 18, 289–324.

Davis, James L., 1994, The cross-section of realized stock returns: The pre-COMPUSTAT evidence, *Journal of Finance* 49, 1579–1593.

DeBondt, Werner, and Richard Thaler, 1985, Does the stock market overreact? *Journal of Finance* 40, 793–805.

———, 1987, Further evidence on investor overreaction and stock market seasonality, *Journal of Finance* 42, 557–581.

Dimson, Elroy, 1979, Risk measurement when shares are subject to infrequent trading, *Journal of Financial Economics* 7, 197–226.

Fairfield, Patricia M., and Trevor S. Harris, 1993, Price-earnings and price-to-book anomalies: Tests of intrinsic value explanation, *Contemporary Accounting Research* 9, 590–611.

Fama, Eugene F., and Kenneth R. French, 1992, The cross-section of expected returns, *Journal of Finance* 47, 427–465.

———, 1993, Common risk factors in the returns on bonds and stocks, *Journal of Financial Economics* 33, 3–56.

Fama Eugene F., and James MacBeth, 1973, Risk, return, and equilibrium: Empirical tests, *Journal of Political Economy* 81, 607–636.

Fowler, David J., and C. Harvey Rorke, 1983, Risk measurement when shares are subject to infrequent trading: Comment, *Journal of Financial Economics* 12, 279–283.

Handa, Puneet, S. P. Kothari, and Charles E. Wasley, 1989, The relation between the return interval and betas: Implications for the size effect, *Journal of Financial Economics* 23, 79–100.

Holthausen, Robert W., and David F. Larcker, 1992, The prediction of stock returns using financial statement information, *Journal of Accounting & Economics* 15, 373–411.

Ibbotson Roger C., and Rex Sinquefield, 1989, *Stocks, Bonds, Bills, and Inflation: Historical Returns*, (The Research Foundation of The Institute of Chartered Financial Analysts, Charlottesville, Va.)

Jagannathan, Ravi, and Zhenyu Wang, 1995, The conditional CAPM and the cross-section of expected returns, Working paper, University of Minnesota.

Jegadeesh, Narasimhan, 1992, Does market risk really explain the size effect, *Journal of Financial and Quantitative Analysis* 27, 337–351.

Jones, C. P., and Robert H. Litzenberger, 1970, Quarterly earnings reports and intermediate stock price trends, *Journal of Finance* 25, 143–148.

Kandel, Shmuel, and Robert F. Stambaugh, 1987, On correlations and inferences about mean-variance efficiency, *Journal of Financial Economics* 18, 61–90.

———, 1995, Portfolio inefficiency and the cross-section of expected returns, *Journal of Finance* 50, 157–184.

Keim, Donald B., 1983, Size-related anomalies and stock return seasonality: Further empirical evidence, *Journal of Financial Economics* 12, 13–32.

———, 1989, Trading patterns, bid-ask spreads, and estimated security returns: The case of common stocks at calendar turning points, *Journal of Financial Economics* 25, 75–98.

Lakonishok, Josef, and Seymour Smidt, 1984, Volume and turn-of-the-year behavior, *Journal of Financial Economics* 13, 435–455.

La Porta, Rafael, 1993, Survivorship bias and the predictability of stock returns in the COMPUSTAT sample, Working paper, Harvard University.

Lev, Baruch, and S. Ramu Thiagarajan, 1993, Fundamental information analysis, *Journal of Accounting Research* 31, 190–215.

Levhari, David, and Haim Levy, 1977, The capital asset pricing model and the investment horizon, *Review of Economics and Statistics* 59, 92–104.

Lintner, John, 1965, The valuation of risk assets and the selection of risky investments in stock portfolios and capital budgets, *Review of Economics and Statistics* 47, 13–37.

Lo, Andrew W., and A. Craig MacKinlay, 1990a, When are contrarian profits due to stock market overreaction? *Review of Financial Studies* 3, 175–205.

———, 1990b, Data-snooping biases in tests of financial asset pricing models, *Review of Financial Studies* 3, 431–467.

Mech, Timothy, 1993, Portfolio return autocorrelation, *Journal of Financial Economics* 34, 307–344.

Ou, Jane A. and Stephen H. Penman, 1989a, Financial statement analysis and the prediction of stock returns, *Journal of Accounting & Economics* 11, 295–329.

———, 1989b, Accounting measurement, P/E ratios and the information content of security prices, *Journal of Accounting Research* (Supplement) 27, 111–144.

Roll, Richard, 1977, A critique of the asset pricing theory's test–Part 1: On past and potential testability of the theory, *Journal of Financial Economics* 4, 129–176.

———, and Stephen A. Ross, 1994, On the cross-sectional relation between expected returns and betas, *Journal of Finance* 49, 101–121.

Rosenberg, Barr, Kenneth Reid, and Ronald Lanstein, 1985, Persuasive evidence of market inefficiency, *Journal of Portfolio Management* 11, 9–17.

Rozeff, Michael S., and William R. Kinney, Jr., 1976, Capital market seasonality: The case of stock returns, *Journal of Financial Economics* 3, 379–402.

Scholes, Myron S., and John Williams, 1977, Estimating betas from nonsynchronous data, *Journal of Financial Economics* 14, 327–348.

Shanken, Jay, 1987, Multivariate proxies and asset pricing relations: Living with the Roll critique, *Journal of Financial Economics* 45, 99–120.

———, 1990, Intertemporal asset pricing: An empirical investigation, *Journal of Econometrics* 45, 99–120.

———, 1992, On the estimation of beta-pricing models, *Review of Financial Studies* 5, 1–33.

Sharpe, William F., 1964, Capital asset prices: A theory of market equilibrium under conditions of risk, *Journal of Finance* 19, 425–442.

Sharathchandra, G., and Rex Thompson, 1993, Book-to-market as a surrogate for priced risk when risk is time varying, Working paper, Southern Methodist University.

Stattman, Dennis, 1980, Book values and stock returns, *The Chicago MBA: A Journal of Selected Papers* 4, 25–45.

[4]

THE JOURNAL OF FINANCE • VOL. XLIX, NO. 1 • MARCH 1994

On the Cross-sectional Relation
between Expected Returns and Betas

RICHARD ROLL and STEPHEN A. ROSS[*]

ABSTRACT

There is an *exact* linear relation between expected returns and true "betas" when the market portfolio is on the ex ante mean-variance efficient frontier, but empirical research has found little relation between sample mean returns and estimated betas. A possible explanation is that market portfolio proxies are mean-variance inefficient. We categorize proxies that produce particular relations between expected returns and true betas. For the special case of a zero relation, a market portfolio proxy must lie inside the efficient frontier, but it may be close to the frontier.

CONTRARY TO THE PREDICTIONS of the Sharpe, Lintner, and Black Capital Asset Pricing Model (hereafter the SLB CAPM or SLB Model; see Sharpe (1964), Lintner (1965), and Black (1972)), a decade of empirical studies has reported little evidence of a significant cross-sectional relation between average returns and betas. Yet it is well known (Roll (1977), Ross (1977)) that a positive and *exact* cross-sectional relation between ex ante expected returns and betas *must* hold if the market index against which betas are computed lies on the positively sloped segment of the mean-variance efficient frontier. Not finding a positive cross-sectional relation suggests that the index proxies used in empirical testing are not ex ante mean-variance efficient.

Some of the empirical studies have uncovered variables other than beta that have power in explaining the sample cross-sectional variation in mean returns. But the true cross-sectional expected return-beta relation is exact when the index is efficient, so *no* variable other than beta can explain any part of the true cross-section of expected returns. Conversely, if the index is not efficient, the ex ante cross-sectional relation does not hold exactly and other variables can have explanatory power. Indeed, any variable that happens to be cross-sectionally related to expected returns could have discernible empirical power when the index proxy is ex ante *in*efficient. Again, the empirical evidence supports an inference that market index proxies used in testing are not on the ex ante efficient frontier.

But the puzzle in the empirical work is not so much that the cross-sectional mean return-beta relation is imperfect nor that other variables have empiri-

[*] Roll is from the Anderson School of Management, University of California, Los Angeles, and Ross is from the Yale School of Management, Yale University. We are grateful for comments from T. Daniel Coggin, Mark Grinblatt, John E. Hunter, Chi-Cheng Hsia, Andrew Lo, Simon Wheatley, three referees, the coeditor of the *Journal*, David Mayers, and the editor, René Stulz.

102   *The Journal of Finance*

cal power. This is to be expected given that direct tests reject mean-variance efficiency for many market index proxies.[1] Instead, the surprising thing is that the cross-sectional mean-beta relation appears to be virtually zero. Intuitively, it would seem that there should be *some* nonzero cross-sectional relation if the index is not too far inside the ex ante efficient frontier, even if it is statistically reliably inside. Why should we not anticipate at least a modest connection between expected returns and betas even on indices that are unmistakably inefficient?[2]

Yet the recent paper by Fama and French (1992) forcefully resurrects an old finding that there is virtually no detectable cross-sectional beta-mean return relation. They state, "...the relation between market β and average return is flat, even when β is the only explanatory variable" (Abstract). Earlier papers report the same result. For instance, Reinganum (1981), using two different indices, concludes, "...cross-sectional differences in portfolio betas estimated with common market indices are not reliably related to differences in average portfolio returns" (p. 460). Lakonishok and Shapiro (1986), after an extensive series of empirical tests, conclude, "...neither the traditional measure of risk (beta) nor the alternative measures (variance or residual standard deviation), can explain—again, at standard levels of significance—the cross-sectional variation in returns; only size appears to matter" (p. 131).[3]

Fama and French find no cross-sectional mean-beta relation after controlling for size and the ratio of book-to-market value, variables which *do* play statistically significant roles. Similar findings are reported by others, for a variety of different explanatory variables. For instance, Chen, Roll, and Ross (1986) conclude, "Although stock market indices 'explain' much of the intertemporal movements in other stock portfolios, their estimated exposures (their betas) do not explain cross-sectional differences in average returns after the betas of the economic state variables have been included" (p. 399).[4]

---

[1] Among the papers that reject efficiency for various market index proxies are Ross (1980), Gibbons (1982), Jobson and Korkie (1982), Shanken (1985), Kandel and Stambaugh (1987) and (1989, pp. 134, 135), Gibbons, Ross, and Shanken (1989), Zhou (1991), and MacKinlay and Richardson (1991).

[2] Note that the puzzle has no bearing on *market* efficiency. It is purely a mathematical and statistical problem. Whatever the distribution of returns, however well or poorly the market is operating, there exists an ex ante efficient frontier of portfolios. Any market index is located somewhere, either on the frontier or inside. The cross-sectional relation between expected return and beta, whether it is exact, imperfect, or zero, is completely determined by the position of the index.

[3] Coggin and Hunter (1985) find a negative relation between beta and mean return for large firms.

[4] Unlike Fama and French (1992), however, Chen, Roll, and Ross (1986) *do* find a nonzero cross-sectional mean return-beta relation in a univariate test. They use the value-weighted and the equally weighted New York Stock Exchange–listed indices. Similarly, Lakonishok and Shapiro find that "the coefficient of beta generally has the correct sign" (p. 131) across various subperiods, though it is not statistically significant.

The Fama and French paper made us wonder where an index would have to be located to produce a set of *true* betas that had no relation whatever to true expected returns. We soon discovered that such indices exist and that they lie within a set whose boundaries can be directly calculated from basic parameters (expected returns and covariances of returns). More generally, for *any* arbitrary cross-sectional linear slope coefficient between betas and expected returns, there is a bounded set of possible indices.

In Section I of this paper, we derive the analytic characterization of indices that produce an arbitrary cross-sectional relation between expected return and beta. Section II presents some "back-of-the-envelope" calculations of plausible locations for widely used market index proxies, i.e., how far inside the ex ante efficient frontier do such proxies lie? This section also discusses the implications of the empirical findings for the CAPM both as a scientific theory and as a practical tool for financial analysis. Sampling error, the other major possible explanation of the empirical findings, is analyzed briefly. Section III provides a summary and conclusion.

I. Indices That Produce a Given Ordinary Least Squares Slope Coefficient in the Cross-sectional Relation between Expected Return and Beta

To characterize market index proxies that produce particular cross-sectional mean-beta relations, we derive the boundary of the set of possible indices by finding members of the set with minimum return variance. This involves minimizing portfolio return variance subject to three constraints: (1) that the index portfolio's expected return is a given value, (2) that the index portfolio's investment proportions (weights) sum to unity, and (3) that a cross-sectional regression of expected returns on betas computed against the resulting index portfolio has a particular slope. Our derivation applies to any universe or subuniverse of assets provided that the index portfolio is composed only of stocks in the same group.

We employ the following notation:[5]

$\mathbf{R}$ = Expected returns vector for N individual assets in the universe,
$\mathbf{V}$ = $N \times N$ Covariance matrix of returns,
$\mathbf{1}$ = Unit vector,
$\mathbf{q}$ = Portfolio weights vector,
r = Scalar expected portfolio return, $\mathbf{q'R}$,
σ^2 = Scalar portfolio return variance, $\mathbf{q'Vq}$,
σ_j^2 = Cross-sectional or time series variance of j,
μ = Cross-sectional mean of expected returns, $\mathbf{R'1}/N$,
π = Vector of scaled expected return deviations from the cross-sectional mean, $(\mathbf{R} - \mu\mathbf{1})/N$,
β = Beta vector, $\beta \equiv \mathbf{Vq}/\mathbf{q'Vq}$,

---

[5] Vectors and matrices are denoted in boldface.

The Journal of Finance

k = The cross-sectional covariance of **R** and β; i.e., the numerator of the ordinary least squares (OLS) slope from regressing individual expected returns on betas computed with an index-portfolio having weights **q**.[6]

The appendix proves that any portfolio that is a solution to this problem must lie within a mean-variance region whose boundary is given by the equation

$$B\sigma^4 + Cr\sigma^2 + Dr^2 + F\sigma^2 + Gr + H = 0, \tag{1}$$

where the upper case constants are, $B = k^2(ac - b^2)$, $C = -2dkc$, $D = gc$, $F = 2dkb - g(ac - b^2) + cd^2$, $G = -2gb$, and $H = ag - d^2$, and where the lower case constants and parameters are as follows: three of these scalar elements, $a \equiv \mathbf{R'V^{-1}R}$, $b \equiv \mathbf{R'V^{-1}1}$, $c \equiv \mathbf{1'V^{-1}1}$, are the efficient frontier information constants (cf. Roll (1977), appendix). The two elements new in this paper are, $d \equiv \mathbf{R'R}/N - \mu^2$, which is the *cross-sectional variance of expected returns*, $(d \equiv \sigma_R^2)$, and $g \equiv \mu^2\sigma_{R-1}^2$, where σ_{R-1}^2 denotes the time series variance of the *difference* in returns between two portfolios, one weighted proportionately to the vector of expected returns and the second one equally weighted.

Equation (1) is the general form of a second-degree equation in r/σ^2 space. It is a parabola, a circle, an ellipse, or a hyperbola, depending on the value of $C^2 - 4BD$. The Appendix shows that $C^2 - 4BD$ is either zero (for $k = 0$) or negative. For $k \neq 0$, equation (1) is an *ellipse* in r/σ^2 space. The axes of the ellipse are oblique, i.e., not parallel to the r/σ^2 axes. In the special case $k = 0$ (a zero cross-sectional slope between expected returns and betas), equation (1) describes a parabola with an axis parallel to the σ^2 axis. Figures 1 and 2 illustrate these two cases, Figure 1 for $k = 0$ and Figure 2 for $k \neq 0$.

Portfolios that produce a zero cross-sectional slope, $\text{Cov}(\mathbf{R}, \beta) = k = 0$, lie within a parabola that is tangent to the efficient frontier at the global minimum variance point. It has long been known that the global minimum variance portfolio used as an index produces $\beta = 1$ for *every* asset, and, of course, $\text{Cov}(\mathbf{R}, \mathbf{1}) = 0$. No other mean-variance efficient portfolio produces $k = 0$.

The minimum distance between the efficient frontier and a market index proxy with $\text{Cov}(\mathbf{R}, \beta) = 0$, measured along the return dimension at a given portfolio variance σ^2, is

$$M \equiv r^* - r$$

$$= \left\{[(c\sigma^2 - 1)(ac - b^2)]^{1/2} - [(c\sigma^2 - 1)(ac - b^2 - cd^2/g)]^{1/2}\right\}/c, \tag{2}$$

where r is the expected return on the market proxy and r^* is the return on an efficient portfolio with the same variance as the proxy. In Figure 1, M is

---

[6] The parameter k is one measure of the relation between expected returns and β's. In the cross-sectional OLS regression, $\mathbf{R} = \gamma_0 + \gamma_1\beta + \varepsilon$, (with ε the residual), the slope coefficient is $\gamma_1 = k/\sigma_\beta^2$, where σ_β^2 is the cross-sectional variance of β.

Cross-sectional Relation between Expected Returns and Betas   105

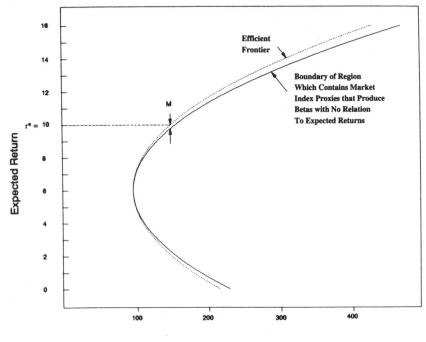

Variance of Returns

Figure 1. Market index proxies that produce betas having no relation to expected returns. These proxies are located within a restricted region of the mean-variance space, a region bounded by a parabola that lies inside the efficient frontier except for a tangency at the global minimum variance point. The distance, M, between the bounded region and the efficient frontier is proportional to the cross-sectional standard deviation of expected returns, σ_R. The M depicted is for $\sigma_R = 3\%$/annum and a market index proxy with expected return 9.78%/annum. The proxy is located on the boundary at a distance of $M = 22$ basis points below the efficient frontier. While betas against this market proxy have zero cross-sectional correlation with expected returns, a market proxy on the efficient frontier just 22 basis points above it would produce betas that are perfectly positively collinear with expected returns.

plotted for the case $\sigma_R = 3$, $\sigma_{R-1} = 5$, $\mu = 10$, and a proxy corresponding to an efficient portfolio with $r^* = 10\%$.

A useful and particularly tractable variant of (2) can be obtained by dividing both sides by $r^* - r_0$ where $r_0 = b/c$ is the expected return of the global minimum variance portfolio. The result is

$$M = (r^* - r_0)\left[1 - \left[1 - \frac{cd^2}{g(ac - b^2)}\right]^{1/2}\right], \qquad (3)$$

i.e., the return distance of the proxy from the efficient frontier is a *constant* multiple (the term in large brackets) of the excess return $r^* - r_0$ of the efficient portfolio over the global minimum variance portfolio return, r_0. The

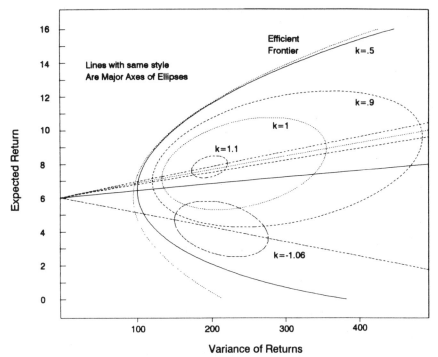

Figure 2. Market index proxies that produce betas having particular cross-sectional relations with expected returns. To produce a particular nonzero cross-sectional relation between betas and expected returns, a market index proxy must lie within a closed region of the mean-variance space. The regions are bounded by ellipses that may or may not have a tangency with the efficient frontier. If there is no tangency, then no mean-variance efficient market proxy can produce that particular relation. The major axes of the ellipses have positive (or negative) slopes when the resulting betas are positively (or negatively) related to expected returns. Ellipses are depicted for several values of k, the cross-sectional covariance between beta and expected return. The bounded region becomes smaller as this covariance increases. There is a maximum value of k beyond which the region vanishes; i.e., *no* market index proxy can produce a larger k.

term in large brackets in (3) is invariant with respect to the cross-sectional dispersion of expected returns.[7]

Index proxies that happen to lie within the sliver of space between the upper branch of the efficient frontier and the upper branch of the parabola,

---

[7] To see this, use the concept of a "mean-preserving spread" in the cross-sectional distribution of expected returns; i.e., $\mathbf{R} \equiv \sigma_R \mathbf{Z} + \mu \mathbf{1}$, where $\mathbf{Z}$ is a standardized vector of expected returns (mean zero and cross-sectional standard deviation of unity). Define standardized counterparts to the efficient set parameters (a and b) as $a^* \equiv \mathbf{Z}'\mathbf{V}^{-1}\mathbf{Z}$ and $b^* \equiv \mathbf{Z}'\mathbf{V}^{-1}\mathbf{1}$. It is straightforward to show that $ac - b^2 = \sigma_R^2(a^*c - b^{*2})$, $d = (\sigma_R^2/N)\mathbf{Z}'\mathbf{Z}$, and $g = (\sigma_R^2/N^2)\mathbf{Z}'\mathbf{VZ}$. Thus, the expression in (3), $cd^2/[g(ac - b^2)] = c(\mathbf{Z}'\mathbf{Z})^2/[\mathbf{Z}'\mathbf{VZ}(a^*c - b^{*2})]$, which is independent of σ_R. A similar development shows that $M = r^* - r$ in (2) is proportional to σ_R; thus, the standardized difference, $(r^* - r)/\sigma_R$, between the efficient frontier and the inner $k = 0$ parabola is invariant with respect to the cross-sectional dispersion of expected returns.

produce positive cross-sectional slopes. To prove this, note that if some index within the upper sliver had a negative slope, then by choosing appropriate weights the index could be combined with the corresponding efficient portfolio having the same mean such that the resulting combination had a zero slope. But, such a combined portfolio must lie under the $k = 0$ parabola of minimum variance portfolios with zero cross-sectional slopes, a contradiction.

The situation of $k \neq 0$ is more complex. The Appendix shows that the set of indices producing $\mathrm{Cov}(\mathbf{R}, \boldsymbol{\beta}) = k$, is bounded by an ellipse which may or may not be tangent to the efficient frontier. For any k greater in absolute value than formula (A9) in the Appendix, there is no tangency between the efficient frontier and the ellipse bounding the set of all index proxies that produce a cross-sectional covariance of k.

In Figure 2, ellipses have been plotted for several choices of the cross-sectional covariance k. The major axes of the ellipses have slopes in r/σ^2 space with the same sign as their associated k and they all intersect the return axis at r_0, the expected return of the global minimum variance portfolio. Notice that as k becomes larger, the ellipse becomes more concentrated about its center (which, incidentally, lies at the point $\sigma^2 = \frac{1}{2}g/k^2$, $r = r_0 + \frac{1}{2}d/k$). The collapse becomes complete at $k = \pm \frac{1}{2}\sqrt{cg}$. For larger absolute values of k, the ellipse becomes imaginary; i.e., there are *no* market index proxies that produce a larger cross-sectional covariance between $\mathbf{R}$ and $\boldsymbol{\beta}$.

Our results are reminiscent of those in two papers by Kandel and Stambaugh (1987, 1989) and in a paper by Shanken (1987). In their first paper, Kandel and Stambaugh derive the correlation between an arbitrary portfolio and a portfolio on the efficient frontier. They prove that this correlation is maximized when the two portfolios have the same expected return and they use this result to derive tests for the efficiency of an unknown market proxy that has a given correlation with the observed proxy. The idea is that an observed proxy may not be the true market index whose mean-variance efficiency is required by CAPM theory, but if one is willing to assume that the unobservable true market index has a given level of correlation with the observable proxy, an unambiguous test of the CAPM can still be conducted (conditional on the assumed correlation).[8]

A section of their paper deduces the boundary of the set of all portfolios that possess a particular minimum correlation with any given index. These sets may be closed. As the minimum correlation approaches 1.0, the set collapses to the single point coincidental with the index. At low correlations, however, the sets may be unbounded. For instance, when the index is inefficient, zero-beta portfolios (portfolios possessing zero correlation with the index) exist at all levels of expected return, a result derived by Roll (1980). Kandel and Stambaugh show that intermediate correlations can produce

---

[8] Using a similar approach, Shanken (1987) presents evidence that the SLB Model is invalid unless each of the several market proxies he employs is only weakly correlated (multiple correlation less than 0.7) with the true market portfolio.

bounded but open sets, e.g., with a minimum or maximum expected return but no limit on variance.

These Kandel-Stambaugh (1987) sets contain portfolios with a given minimum correlation to the original index proxy, whereas the sets we derive here contain index proxies that produce a given cross-sectional relation between expected return and beta. Thus, they are formally distinct, but they do possess some common properties. Perhaps the most important to emphasize is that the sets (the regions are graphed in our Figures 1 and 2 and in Kandel and Stambaugh's Figure 1) are not *exclusive*. There are other portfolios lying within these regions which do *not* produce the same result. Within the Kandel-Stambaugh regions are portfolios with *higher* correlations to the index proxy than the specified minimum correlation. Within our regions are portfolios that produce other values of the cross-sectional mean-beta relation. For both types of regions, no portfolio lying outside can produce the given relation, but an infinite number of portfolios *inside* can produce some other relation.

Figure 2 provides an intuitive depiction of nonexclusivity. Notice that some ellipses plotted there fall entirely within others. Thus, within the $k = 1$ ellipse, $[k = \text{Cov}(\mathbf{R}, \boldsymbol{\beta})]$, are market proxies producing $k = 0.9$, $k = 0.5$, etc., although there are no market proxies producing $k = 1.1$ or $k = -1.06$ unless they lie also within their respective ellipses.

In contrast, the later paper by Kandel and Stambaugh (1989) derives exclusive regions of mean-variance space, but for a different purpose. Kandel and Stambaugh (1989) develop likelihood ratio tests for the ex ante mean-variance efficiency of a given index proxy. They show that the rejection region (or a given significance level) is bounded by a "critical hyperbola" in *sample* mean-variance space. Portfolios that lie away from the sample efficient frontier beyond this critical hyperbola should be judged inefficient. One only needs to plot the position of proxy being tested in order to conduct the test.

It is instructive to understand intuitively why a statistical test for proxy efficiency might lead to an exclusive rejection region while correlation sets and mean-beta relation sets would not be exclusive. In the first case, the further a proxy lies below the sample efficient frontier, the less likely it lies on the *true* ex ante frontier, provided that one is willing to assume stationarity of the expected return vector and the covariance matrix. However, there is only an indirect connection between the position of the proxy in mean-variance space and either its correlation with other portfolios or its cross-sectional mean-beta relation. For example, take correlation: if the covariance matrix is nonsingular and the number of assets is finite, there is no other portfolio *perfectly* positively correlated with the index proxy. Thus, a correlation of 1.0 implies a single position in mean-variance space. But if the index proxy is inefficient enough, there are other distinct portfolios *with the same mean and variance* having *zero* correlation with the proxy! Thus, two uncorrelated portfolios can lie at exactly the same point in mean-variance space. Clearly, there are an infinite number of portfolios, all lying at exactly the same mean-variance position, yet possessing an infinite number of different correlations with the index proxy.

The nonexclusivity of our sets makes it impossible to determine the cross-sectional mean-beta relation simply by plotting the position of the proxy in the mean-variance space. We wish this were possible. It is not. We know only that particular cross-sectional mean-beta relations *cannot* be produced by index proxies that lie outside the boundaries of the sets we derive here. Each set places an upper or a lower bound on the cross-sectional covariance between $\mathbf{R}$ and $\boldsymbol{\beta}$.

II. The Cross-sectional Return-Beta Relation and Tests of the CAPM

A. *The Plausibility of Test Sensitivity to the Choice of a Market Proxy*

The SLB Model implies mean-variance efficiency of the market index; this efficiency is equivalent to a perfect cross-sectional relation between expected returns and betas computed against the market index. But, when the market index is proxied by an *in*efficient portfolio, these two representations of the same theory are no longer strongly related. We have shown that the cross-sectional slope can have any absolute value below a certain maximum (including zero) depending on the index proxy's position inside the ex ante mean-variance efficient frontier. This implies that an index proxy can conceivably be substantially inefficient and still produce a strong cross-sectional regression between expected returns and betas or it can conceivably be close to the efficient frontier and yet produce a zero cross-sectional relation. What actually *is* produced in the empirical cross-sectional regression depends on the ensemble of expected returns, variances, and covariances.

This suggests that the slope of the cross-sectional return-beta relation may be of little direct use in assessing the distance of the index proxy from the ex ante efficient frontier and, therefore, it may not be useful for determining how inefficient is the true market index. An inefficient proxy with a zero cross-sectional slope may be quite close to the true market portfolio and the true market portfolio may be efficient.

The plausibility of such possibilities can be examined with back-of-the-envelope calculations using reasonable guesses of parameter values. For instance, given current levels of inflation, it seems reasonable to assume an expected return on the global minimum variance portfolio of 6 percent (per annum) and a minimum standard deviation of 10 percent; $r_0 = 6\%$, and $\sigma_0 = 10\%$. Similarly, an expected return of, say, 11 percent, seems reasonable for the efficient portfolio located where a ray from the origin through the global minimum variance position intercepts the efficient frontier, $r_1 = 11\%$. These values are sufficient to determine the equation of the efficient frontier. We also need to guess the values of three other parameters: μ, the average expected return on risky assets; σ_R, the cross-sectional dispersion of expected returns; and σ_{R-1}, the time series standard deviation of the difference between an expected return-weighted portfolio and an equally weighted portfolio. Reasonable values might be: $\mu = 10\%$, $\sigma_R = 3\%$, and $\sigma_{R-1} = 5\%$.

Notice that the last value is relatively small, but this is appropriate given that two well-diversified portfolios are likely to be significantly correlated.[9]

Using these parameter values in equation (3) gives $M = 0.055542(r^* - r_0)$ as the expected return distance of a market index proxy from the efficient frontier. If we happened to select a proxy whose corresponding mean-variance efficient portfolio with equal variance had the same mean as the global average mean, $r^* = 10\%$ and since $r_0 = 6\%$, $M = 0.2222\%$. Thus, given these parameter values, the mean return of an index proxy that produces a cross-sectional mean-beta relation of *zero* could lie only about 22 basis points below the efficient frontier; its expected return would be 9.78 percent while the efficient portfolio with the same variance would have an expected return of 10 percent. These positions are plotted in Figure 1; see the arrows below "M." Thus, the index proxy could produce a zero cross-sectional mean-beta slope while the corresponding efficient portfolio, if used as a proxy, would produce a *perfect* cross-sectional relation with a positive slope.

The presence of sampling error only strengths the caution with which we must approach cross-sectional empirical tests. If expected returns and betas could be measured with little or no error, then we could reject index mean-variance efficiency by finding a flat cross-sectional relation. But, with measurement error we can only say that we cannot reject a flat relation. For that matter, we probably also cannot reject that the slope is, say, 3 percent. With 60 years of observations on an index with an annual standard deviation of 20 percent, the standard error of the *sample* mean would be $20\% / \sqrt{60} = 2.6\%$.

With a standard error of, say, 3 percent in the measurement of index expected returns, the power of cross-sectional tests is suspect. If the true market portfolio is, in fact, efficient, index proxies that produce a flat *sample* cross-sectional relation may be positioned well within a 3 percent interval of the ex post efficient frontier. Thus, the probability of not rejecting a flat slope when the slope is actually not flat, may be quite high.[10]

It is perplexing, then, that some authors relate the absence of a detectable cross-sectional slope for a particular market index proxy to a general condemnation of the SLB CAPM model. Fama and French (1992) include a section entitled "Can the SLB Model be Saved?" (p. 459), where they state, "We are forced to conclude that the SLB model does not describe the last 50 years of average stock returns" (p. 464). We would add, "for this particular market index proxy."

---

[9] The assumed value of σ_{R-1}^2 is one-half the standard deviation of the global minimum variance portfolio; larger values of σ_{R-1}^2 would cause the index proxy to lie closer to the efficient frontier.

[10] Cross-sectional mean-beta tests are different from direct tests of the mean-variance efficiency of a given index (cf. Gibbons, Ross, and Shanken (1989)). The null hypothesis of cross-sectional tests is that the theory is *not* true. In contrast, the null hypothesis of direct tests is that the index is efficient. The power of cross-sectional tests is the probability of accepting a cross-sectional relation when there really is one. The power of direct tests is the probability of rejecting index efficiency when the index really is not on the efficient frontier. Thus, these two index efficiency tests have the null and alternative hypotheses reversed.

An alternative interpretation of their results is that the SLB Model may be of little use in explaining cross-sectional returns no matter how close the index is to the efficient frontier unless it is *exactly* on the frontier. Since such exactitude can never be verified empirically, we would endorse (again, as we have in the past when we first asserted the proposition; see, e.g., Roll (1977), and Chen, Roll, and Ross (1986)), that the SLB is of little practical use in explaining stock returns.

In a different section of their paper, Fama and French argue that

> different approaches to the tests are not likely to revive the Sharpe-Lintner-Black model. Resuscitation of the SLB model requires that a better proxy for the market portfolio (a) overturns our evidence that the simple relation between β and average stock returns is flat and (b) leaves β as the only variable relevant for explaining average returns. Such results seem unlikely, given Stambaugh's (1982) evidence that tests of the SLB model do not seem to be sensitive to the choice of a market proxy. Thus, if there is a role for β in average returns, it is likely to be found in a multi-factor model that transforms the flat simple relation between average return and β into a positively sloped conditional relation (p. 449).

This essentially alleges that *no* reasonable market proxy can produce a nonzero cross-sectional expected return/beta relation in which beta is the sole relevant explanatory variable.

But, viewed in the context of our analysis, such a statement seems at least questionable. It appears that a proxy can be quite close to the ex ante frontier and still produce a cross-sectional beta-return relation with a slope near zero, and a proxy that is far from the frontier can still have a significant cross-sectional relation. In particular, another proxy can be close to the ones used now and have a positive cross-sectional relation or a zero one. An empirical slope near zero tells us little, if anything, about whether the SLB Model describes "average stock returns," but it does tell us something about the market index proxies we are using. As for whether an inefficient proxy can be found with betas that alone explain average returns, there is no a priori reason to reject such a possibility.[11]

B. Plausibility and Short Positions

Several readers of a previous version of this paper speculated that the central results may be driven by short positions in market index proxies that produce a particular mean-beta cross-sectional slope. Indices with short positions have not been used in the empirical tests. Yet the indices we

---

[11] This can be true notwithstanding the observation that size, for example, appears to be a significant explanatory variable in cross-sectional studies. Given the hundreds of parameters that have been used in such studies, it would be astonishing if the best performing of them were not significant by chance alone.

characterize in Section I have no restrictions against short positions and thus may not be empirically relevant.

We have not yet been able to assess this objection in a completely general context, but a limited assessment is possible given a few more assumptions about the process generating asset returns. The objection is valid for some relatively simple asset return structures including the example represented by a limited version of the single-factor arbitrage pricing theory (APT) model. If there is just one priced APT factor *and every asset has positive sensitivity to that factor*, any well-diversified market index proxy without short positions will produce a positive cross-sectional expected return–CAPM beta relation if the market risk premium is positive.[12]

However, this simple example fails to generalize into a more complicated world. For instance, there need be no necessary relation between expected return and beta, even when there is only a single generating factor, when the APT is not true. Suppose there is cross-sectional variability in expected returns that is unrelated to the asset's factor sensitivity. Although this would admit the potential for arbitrage cash flows (with virtually no risk and no investment),[13] it permits any variety of cross-sectional relation between expected return and CAPM beta even when the market index proxy has nonnegative weights on all assets.

In the absence of arbitrage opportunities but with a multiple factor asset return structure, totally positive well-diversified market index proxies may produce an insignificant cross-sectional mean-beta relation. A simple numerical example is provided by the two-factor hypothetical economy described in Table I. In this economy, the APT holds exactly but some positively weighted portfolios produce betas that have no cross-sectional relation to expected returns; even an *equally* weighted market index proxy produces a slightly negative but statistically insignificant cross-sectional slope.[14] The hypothetical economy in Table I represents a counterexample to the objection that our results are driven by short positions. There are, of course, other possible asset

---

[12] In a single-factor APT model, every asset j has returns in time t given by $\rho_{jt} = r_j + b_j \delta_t + \varepsilon_{jt}$ where r_j is the asset's expected return, δ_t is the mean-zero single factor, b_j (> 0 by assumption) is the asset's factor sensitivity, and ε_{jt} is an idiosyncratic white noise disturbance. If the APT holds perfectly, there exist constants γ_0 and γ_1 such that $r_j = \gamma_0 + \gamma_1 b_j$. A well-diversified market proxy M is simply a portfolio with negligible idiosyncratic disturbance, i.e., $\rho_{Mt} \approx r_M + b_M \delta_t$. If M has nonnegative investment proportions in all individual assets, then since $b_j > 0\ \forall j$, $b_M > 0$. In this situation, the CAPM beta is approximately $\beta_j = b_j/b_M$. Thus, the cross-sectional slope coefficient between individual asset expected returns and CAPM betas is $\mathrm{Cov}(r_j, \beta_j)/\mathrm{Var}(\beta_j) = \gamma_1 b_M$, which is positive if the market price of risk, γ_1, is positive.

[13] Pure arbitrage cash flows, *zero* risk and no investment, would technically be feasible only with an infinite number of assets.

[14] Note that an equally weighted index is *not* likely to be on the boundary of one of our sets. The equally weighted index is 200 basis points below the frontier but there are positively weighted proxies closer to the efficient frontier that produce roughly the same cross-sectional mean return-beta relation.

Table I

A Simulated Two-Factor APT Economy

Number of Assets: 25
Every asset j has return ρ_{jt} in time t generated by a two-factor model,

$$\rho_{jt} = r_j + b_{1j}\delta_{1t} + b_{2j}\delta_{2t} + \varepsilon_{jt},$$

where r_j is j's expected return, the b's are factor sensitivities, the δ's are mean-zero factors, and ε is a disturbance independently distributed across assets and over time.

The APT holds exactly: $r_j = \gamma_0 + \gamma_1 b_{1j} + \gamma_2 b_{2j}$.

In the simulated economy, $\gamma_0 = 5\%$ and $\gamma_1 = \gamma_2 = 8\%$ per period. Each of the two factors is independently and normally distributed over time with a standard deviation of 13% per period. The 25 values of b_1 are randomly selected from a normal distribution with mean 1.0 and standard deviation 0.4. Twenty-three of the 25 values of b_2 are zero, but $b_{21} = -b_{22} = 3.34$. Finally, each asset's generating equation is fully specified by selecting a random R-square from a uniform distribution between 0.15 and 0.30 (this conforms roughly to actual stock returns).

Once the R-square is selected, the asset's total return variance is readily calculated from the generating equation. It is also possible to calculate the exact composition of the Markowitz efficient frontier, to determine the mean-variance position of any potential market index proxy, and to calculate true values of each asset's CAPM betas. Here are the resulting calculations when the market index proxy is an *equally* weighted portfolio.

	True Parameters	
	Mean Return (%)	Std. Dev. (%)
Equally weighted portfolio	13.0	14.8
Efficient portfolio, same mean	13.0	12.0
Efficient portfolio, same standard deviation	15.0	14.8
Global minimum variance portfolio	8.74	8.77

The cross-sectional OLS regression of true expected returns on CAPM betas computed with the equally weighted portfolio as a market index proxy is (t-statistics in parentheses):

$$r_j = 13.1 - 0.215\beta_j$$
$$(4.12) \quad (-0.0761)$$

The adjusted R-square of the cross-sectional regression is -0.0432.

structures that would bring about our results, but one counterexample is sufficient to dispel the notion that the objection is valid in general.

C. The Potential Sensitivity of CAPM Tests to the Econometric Method

Although the superiority of generalized least squares (GLS) to OLS is well-recognized by finance empiricists, our results above depend on the cross-sectional regressions being OLS. Most of the existing literature relies on this technique. There are, however, some exceptions. A recent paper by Amihud, Christensen, and Mendelson (1992), for instance, replicates the Fama and French tests while employing the more advanced econometric techniques of GLS and pooled time series–cross-section analysis. Although Amihud *et al.* find the same results as Fama and French using OLS, their results are reversed when using either pooled time series–cross-section methods or when using GLS; the estimated impact of beta on expected return is particularly strong when both methods are employed.[15] They conclude that "beta is still alive and well" (p. 1).

One might be tempted to conclude that more powerful econometric techniques and better estimation reveal that the market index proxy is not too far from the efficient frontier after all. But our analysis above is based on true expected returns, variances, and covariances; estimation problems are assumed away. We show above that the OLS definition of the cross-sectional mean-beta coefficient can be *truly* zero if the market index is sufficiently mean-variance inefficient. This result does not depend on statistical misestimation of any relevant parameter, but it does assume that the cross-sectional mean-beta regression coefficient is calculated with the OLS formula.

Thanks to a private communication from Simon Wheatley in 1992, we learned that using a GLS calculation rather than OLS can have a significant effect on the resulting true cross-sectional coefficient. GLS produces a *positive* cross-sectional relation between true expected returns and true betas regardless of the inefficiency of the market index proxy so long as its expected return exceeds the expected return, r_0, of the global minimum variance portfolio![16]

Intuitively, the GLS method diagonalizes the covariance matrix of regression residuals. It is equivalent to using OLS when the covariance matrix of returns, V, is proportional to the identity matrix. But if V is proportional to the identity matrix I, $\beta = Iq/q'q$. Thus, to obtain a portfolio with expected return $r = R'q$ and with $Cov(R, \beta) = 0$, we must have $R'\beta - \mu 1'\beta = 0$, which implies $r = \mu$. There is no solution to the problem $k = 0$ unless the portfolio's expected return, r, is the cross-sectional mean of the expected returns of all assets, μ. And when $V \propto I$, the expected return, r_0, of the global minimum variance portfolio is also the cross-sectional mean expected return, μ.

The use of GLS is likely to overturn the Fama and French empirical result of a zero cross-sectional slope. Unless the index proxy is grossly inefficient, with expected return less than or equal to r_0, a GLS regression would almost certainly find a significant and positive mean-beta relation in large samples. But what would this really imply about the validity of the CAPM, about whether the true market portfolio of all assets is ex ante mean-variance efficient? If the mean return-beta relation is positive for *every possible* market proxy whose mean return exceeds r_0, what conceivable set of empirical results would cause us to *reject* the CAPM?

Kandel and Stambaugh (1993) derive a goodness-of-fit statistic, expressed as an R-square, for the true cross-sectional GLS relation between expected returns and betas. They show that R-square decreases (or increases) as the index proxy lies farther (or closer) to the efficient frontier. Thus, if the true

---

[15] However, the strength of beta as an explanatory factor is much greater in the 1953 to 1971 sample period than in the 1972 to 1990 sample period. In the later period, beta is *not* significant.

[16] A formal proof is in the GLS section of the Appendix. Kandel and Stambaugh (1993) derive and elaborate the same result.

parameters were known, the Kandel and Stambaugh R-square is a metric of the index proxy's degree of inefficiency. The problem is that the true parameters are *not* known; thus, any observed empirical GLS R-square consists both of sampling error and (possibly) true ex ante scatter. It is not immediately clear how an empirical investigator can tell the difference. Perhaps it will prove best to employ a direct test of the index proxy's efficiency, such as the Kandel and Stambaugh (1989) likelihood ratio test which depends only on the proxy's location relative to the *sample* efficient frontier.

We don't want to leave the impression that the Wheatley–Kandel and Stambaugh result fully explains the differences between the findings of Fama and French and of Amihud, Christensen, and Mendelson. The GLS proof assumes knowledge of all true parameters in the spirit of this paper. The empirical researchers have only estimates. Also, the GLS method used by Amihud *et al.* is somewhat different than that assumed by Wheatley and Kandel and Stambaugh. Nonetheless, we think it is appropriate to bring attention to the bizarre idea that the very range of *possible* findings can be affected by the econometric technique. Shanken (1992) provides a thoughtful analysis of the different inferences that might be obtained with various econometric techniques. He investigates not only OLS versus GLS but also the impact of errors in the variables on familiar two-pass tests of beta pricing models. In the context of factor models, he also shows that autocorrelation in the underlying factors can lead to problems of inference.

III. Summary and Conclusion

The empirical absence of a detectable relation between average returns and betas is an indictment of the SLB Model, at least for use with the most widely employed market index proxies. If the SLB Model cannot tell us about average returns, then it is not of practical value for a variety of applications including the computation of the cost of capital and the construction of investment portfolios.

As we have seen, though, the empirical findings are not by themselves sufficient cause for rejection of the theory. The cross-sectional OLS relation is very sensitive to the choice of an index and indices can be quite close to each other and to the mean-variance frontier and yet still produce significantly different cross-sectional slopes, positive, negative, or zero. The finding that a market index proxy does not explain cross-sectional returns is consistent with even a very close, but unobserved, true market index being efficient.

The almost pathological knife-edged nature of the expected return-beta OLS cross-sectional relation, even without measurement error, is a shaky base for modern finance. Surely the idea of a tradeoff between risk and expected return is valid and meaningful. Whatever model is eventually used to measure and apply that basic idea will have to be considerably more robust.

As proved by Wheatley (1992) and Kandel and Stambaugh (1993), using a GLS cross-sectional fit between true expected returns and betas renders the relation less subject to these knife-edged properties. The GLS slope is positive so long as the expected return on the index proxy exceeds the expected return of the global minimum variance portfolio. This implies that virtually *any* proxy for the market index that is not grossly inefficient will produce a positive cross-sectional relation between mean returns and betas in large samples. But since every conceivable proxy candidate produces a positive relation, an empirical finding of a positive slope by itself implies very little about whether the proxy is ex ante efficient. Such a finding must be abetted by other direct tests of efficiency.

Sampling error makes these problems all the more troublesome. Since estimates of the efficient frontier and of the index proxy's mean and variance are subject to serious sampling error, the proxy itself may have a true positive cross-sectional expected return-beta OLS relation that cannot be detected in the sample mean return–estimated beta relation. For the GLS version, one is obliged to detect the difference between sampling scatter and ex ante scatter about the true cross-sectional relation. Again, it seems likely that cross-sectional tests of the mean-beta relation will take a back seat to direct tests of portfolio efficiency.

Despite these problems with the SLB Model, market value weighted index proxies are of considerable interest in their own right because they reflect averages of investor holdings. Whether or not such indices produce betas that are cross-sectionally related to average returns, their own returns serve as a benchmark for investment comparisons. Beating or trailing a value-weighted index has become the most widely accepted criterion of investment performance. It is an appropriate criterion relative to the wealth-weighted average returns of other investors.

Appendix: Derivation of Index Proxies That Produce a Given Cross-sectional Slope between Expected Returns and Betas

Notation:[17]

$\mathbf{R}$ = Expected returns vector for N individual assets,

$\mathbf{V}$ = $N \times N$ Covariance matrix of returns,

$\mathbf{1}$ = Unit vector,

$\mathbf{q}$ = Portfolio weights vector,

r = Scalar expected portfolio return, $\mathbf{q'R}$,

σ^2 = Scalar portfolio return variance, $\mathbf{q'Vq}$,

σ_j^2 = Cross-sectional or time series variance of j,

μ = Cross-sectional mean of expected returns, $\mathbf{R'1}/N$,

π = Vector of scaled expected return deviations from the cross-sectional mean, $(\mathbf{R} - \mu\mathbf{1})/N$,

k = Scalar slope from cross-sectionally regressing $\mathbf{R}$ on betas computed for individual assets against portfolio $\mathbf{q}$.

---

[17] Vectors and matrices are denoted in boldface.

The mathematical problem is to find a *minimum variance* portfolio-index proxy that satisfies three conditions: (1) that the portfolio's expected return is a fixed value r, (2) that its weights $\mathbf{q}$ sum to unity, and (3) that a cross-sectional regression of expected returns $\mathbf{R}$ on betas $\boldsymbol{\beta} \equiv \mathbf{Vq}/\mathbf{q'Vq}$ has a given slope.

Formally,

$$\text{minimize } \mathbf{q'Vq} \text{ with respect to } \mathbf{q},$$

subject to

$$\mathbf{q'R} = r$$
$$\mathbf{q'1} = 1$$
$$\mathbf{q'V\pi} = k\mathbf{q'Vq}.$$

The parameter k in the last constraint fixes the cross-sectional relation between expected returns and β's. In the cross-sectional regression, $\mathbf{R} = \gamma_0 + \gamma_1\boldsymbol{\beta} + \boldsymbol{\varepsilon}$, the slope coefficient is $\gamma_1 = k/\sigma_\beta^2$, where σ_β^2 is the cross-sectional variance of $\boldsymbol{\beta}$.[18]

The first-order condition for a minimum is

$$\mathbf{Vq} - \lambda_1\mathbf{R} - \lambda_2\mathbf{1} - \lambda_3(\mathbf{V\pi} - 2k\mathbf{Vq}) = 0,$$

where the λ's are Lagrange multipliers.

To eliminate the Lagrange multipliers, define the 3×3 matrix

$$\mathbf{A} \equiv [\mathbf{R} \quad \mathbf{1} \quad \mathbf{V\pi}]'\mathbf{V}^{-1}[\mathbf{R} \quad \mathbf{1} \quad \mathbf{V\pi}], \tag{A1}$$

collect terms and simplify the first-order condition to

$$\mathbf{q} = \mathbf{V}^{-1}[\mathbf{R} \quad \mathbf{1} \quad \mathbf{V\pi}]\mathbf{A}^{-1}[r \quad 1 \quad k\sigma^2]' \tag{A2}$$

The equation of the boundary of the set of permissible indices in the r/σ^2 space can be obtained by using $\mathbf{q}$ from (A2) in the definition $\sigma^2 = \mathbf{q'Vq}$ and then simplifying to obtain,

$$\sigma^2 = [r \quad 1 \quad k\sigma^2]\mathbf{A}^{-1}[r \quad 1 \quad k\sigma^2]'. \tag{A3}$$

Note that (A3) is not yet a functional relation since σ^2 appears on both sides.

To reduce the solution further, we are obliged to pay some attention to the structure of $\mathbf{A}^{-1}$. From (A1), the matrix $\mathbf{A}$ is a quadratic form in $\mathbf{V}$ and thus positive definite if $\mathbf{V}$ is positive definite (which we will assume); thus $|\mathbf{A}| > 0$. However, since (A3) is nonlinear in σ^2, $\mathbf{A}$ being positive definite does not guarantee that every solution to the first-order conditions is a minimum. Inspection of the cross-sectional beta constraint,

$$\mathbf{q'V\pi} = k\mathbf{q'Vq},$$

---

[18] The constraint may be slightly confusing because only the expected return is de-meaned (while beta is not de-meaned). But when calculating a covariance, it is necessary to de-mean only one of the two random variables; i.e., $\text{Cov}(x, y) = E\{x[y - E(y)]\} = E(xy) - E(x)E(y)$.

reveals that $\mathbf{q}$ is bounded from above; this implies that the constraint will provide both a maximum and a minimum. For our problem the appropriate second-order condition is the definiteness of

$$(1 + 2k\lambda_3)\mathbf{V},$$

which depends on the sign of $(1 + 2k\lambda_3)$ since $\mathbf{V}$ is positive definite. The first-order equation (A3) is a quadratic and has two roots corresponding to the minimum when the above expression is positive and the maximum when it is negative.

$\mathbf{A}$ can be written

$$\mathbf{A} = \begin{bmatrix} a & b & d \\ b & c & e \\ d & e & g \end{bmatrix}$$

where three of the scalar elements, $a = \mathbf{R'V^{-1}R}$, $b = \mathbf{R'V^{-1}1}$, $c = \mathbf{1'V^{-1}1}$, are the familiar efficient frontier information constants (cf. Roll (1977), appendix). The other three elements can be expanded and interpreted as follows:

$$d = \mathbf{R'\pi} = \mathbf{R'(R - \mu 1)}/N = \mathbf{R'R}/N - \mu^2. \tag{A4}$$

Thus, d can be recognized as the *cross-sectional variance of expected returns*, $d = \sigma_R^2$. Similarly,

$$e = \mathbf{1'\pi} = \mathbf{1'(R - \mu 1)}/N = 0.$$

Finally,

$$g = \mathbf{\pi'V\pi} = [\mathbf{R'VR} - 2\mu\mathbf{R'V1} + \mu^2\mathbf{1'V1}]/N^2, \tag{A5}$$

and since $\mu = \mathbf{R'1}/N$,

$$g = \mu^2\sigma_{R-1}^2,$$

where σ_{R-1}^2 denotes the time series variance of the *difference* in returns between two portfolios, one weighted proportionately to the vector of expected returns and the second one equally weighted.

Since the scalar element e is zero, the matrix inversion is simplified slightly and

$$\mathbf{A}^{-1} = \begin{bmatrix} cg & -bg & -cd \\ -bg & ag - d^2 & bd \\ -cd & bd & ac - b^2 \end{bmatrix} \frac{1}{|\mathbf{A}|}$$

where $|\mathbf{A}| = g(ac - b^2) - cd^2$. Using this expression for $\mathbf{A}^{-1}$, the formula describing the boundary of possible indices, equation (A3), can be written as

$$B\sigma^4 + C r\sigma^2 + Dr^2 + F\sigma^2 + Gr + H = 0 \tag{A6}$$

where

$$B = k^2(ac - b^2), \quad C = -2dkc, \quad D = gc,$$

$$F = 2dkb - g(ac - b^2) + cd^2, \quad G = -2gb, \quad \text{and} \quad H = ag - d^2.$$

Cross-sectional Relation between Expected Returns and Betas 119

Equation (A6) can be recognized as the general form of a second-degree equation in r/σ^2 space. From analytic geometry, it is a parabola, a circle, an ellipse, or a hyperbola, depending on the value of $C^2 - 4BD$. Examining this expression,

$$C^2 - 4BD = 4d^2k^2c^2 - 4k^2(ac - b^2)gc = -4k^2c|A|,$$

and since c and $|A|$ are positive, $C^2 - 4BD$ is either zero (for $k = 0$) or negative. For $k \neq 0$, equation (A6) is an *ellipse* in r/σ^2 space. The axes of the ellipse are oblique, i.e., not parallel to the r/σ^2 axes. In the special case $k = 0$, (a zero cross-sectional slope between expected returns and betas), equation (A6) describes a parabola with an axis parallel to the σ^2 axis.

The situation for $k \neq 0$ is complex; the set of k-slope-producing indices is bounded by an ellipse that may or may not have a tangency point to the efficient frontier, depending on the value of k. To prove this assertion, note that the cross-sectional slope between expected returns and betas computed against a mean-variance efficient portfolio has the value $\Delta \equiv r^* - r_z$, where r^* is the portfolio's expected return and r_z is the return on its companion "zero-beta" portfolio. It is straightforward to show[19] that $r_z = (br^* - a)/(cr^* - b)$. Thus,

$$\partial\Delta/\partial r^* = 1 - \left[(ac - b^2)/(cr^* - b)^2\right]$$

$$= 0 \Rightarrow r^* = r_0 \pm (ac - b^2)^{1/2}/c, \quad (A7)$$

where $r_0 = b/c$ is the return on the global minimum variance portfolio. Equation (A7) indicates the presence of two local extrema. Checking the second-order conditions,

$$\partial^2\Delta/\partial r^{*2} > 0 \Rightarrow r^* > r_0.$$

Thus, the positive root of (A7) is a local minimum above which $\Delta > 0$ while the negative root is a local maximum below which $\Delta < 0$. There is a discontinuity at r_0, at which point Δ is undefined. There is no efficient portfolio with a "risk premium," Δ, between the two extrema. By direct substitution, the values of Δ at the extrema are,

$$\Delta_{max} = -\Delta_{min} = 2(ac - b^2)^{1/2}/c. \quad (A8)$$

For a mean-variance efficient portfolio, there is an exact cross-sectional linear relation between expected returns and betas,

$$R = r_z 1 + (r^* - r_z)\beta.$$

Thus, $\sigma_R^2 = (r^* - r_z)^2\sigma_\beta^2$, and since $k = \sigma_\beta^2(r^* - r_z) \Rightarrow k = \sigma_R^2/(r^* - r_z)$. This implies that $|k|$ has a *maximum* determined by the two extrema in (A8),

$$|k| \leq \frac{1}{2} \frac{\sigma_R^2/\sigma_0^2}{(ac - b^2)^{1/2}} \quad (A9)$$

[19] Cf. Roll (1977), appendix.

where $\sigma_0^2 = 1/c$ is the global minimum variance. For any value of k greater in absolute value than the expression above, there is no tangency between the efficient frontier and the ellipse bounding the set of all index proxies that produce a cross-sectional slope of k.

Notice, too, that since σ_β^2 is endogenous to the problem, constraining k is not the same as constraining $\gamma_1 = k/\sigma_\beta^2$, the cross-sectional slope coefficient, in the case where $k \neq 0$. This more complex problem introduces nonlinearities that will change the shapes of our boundaries but will not alter the qualitative properties we report.

A. Using GLS in the Cross-sectional Mean-Beta Regression

Begin with the familiar cross-sectional model, $\mathbf{R} = \gamma_0 \mathbf{1} + \gamma_1 \boldsymbol{\beta} \equiv \mathbf{B}\boldsymbol{\Gamma}$, where $\mathbf{B} \equiv [\mathbf{1} \quad \boldsymbol{\beta}]$ and $\boldsymbol{\Gamma} = (\gamma_0 \quad \gamma_1)'$. Since $\mathbf{V}$ is the covariance matrix of returns, it is natural to consider a GLS estimator based on the sample mean returns and a consistent estimator of $\mathbf{V}$. In large samples, the maximum likelihood consistent GLS estimator of $\boldsymbol{\Gamma}$ will be

$$[\mathbf{B}'\mathbf{V}^{-1}\mathbf{B}]^{-1}\mathbf{B}'\mathbf{V}^{-1}\mathbf{R}.$$

By expanding this expression, it is straightforward to show that the sign of the resulting estimator of γ_1 depends on the sign of

$$(\boldsymbol{\beta}'\mathbf{V}^{-1}\mathbf{R})(\mathbf{1}'\mathbf{V}^{-1}\mathbf{1}) - (\mathbf{1}'\mathbf{V}^{-1}\boldsymbol{\beta})(\mathbf{1}'\mathbf{V}^{-1}\mathbf{R}).$$

But since $\boldsymbol{\beta} = \mathbf{Vq}/\mathbf{q}'\mathbf{Vq}$, where $\mathbf{q}$ is the vector of investment proportions of the market index proxy, the above expression is proportional to

$$\mathbf{q}'\mathbf{R} - (\mathbf{1}'\mathbf{V}^{-1}\mathbf{R})/(\mathbf{1}'\mathbf{V}^{-1}\mathbf{1}) = r - r_0.$$

Thus, regardless of the position of the market index proxy, as the sample size grows larger, the sign of this particular GLS estimator of γ_1 will converge to a positive (or negative) value when the proxy's expected return, r, is greater (or less) than the expected return, r_0, of the global minimum variance portfolio.[20]

REFERENCES

Amihud, Yakov, Bent Jesper Christensen, and Haim Mendelson, 1992, Further evidence on the risk-return relationship, Working paper, Graduate School of Business, Stanford University.
Black, Fischer, 1972, Capital market equilibrium with restricted borrowing, *Journal of Business* 45, 444–455.
Chen, Nai-fu, Richard Roll, and Stephen A. Ross, 1986, Economic forces and the stock market, *Journal of Business* 59, 383–403.
Coggin, T. Daniel, and John E. Hunter, 1985, Are high-beta, large-capitalization stocks overpriced? *Financial Analysts Journal* 41, 70–71.
Fama, Eugene F., and Kenneth R. French, 1992, The cross-section of expected stock returns, *Journal of Finance* 67, 427–465.

[20] We are indebted to Simon Wheatley for pointing out these results.

Cross-sectional Relation between Expected Returns and Betas   121

Gibbons, Michael R., 1982, Multivariate tests of financial models: A new approach, *Journal of Financial Economics* 10, 3–27.

———, Stephen A. Ross, and Jay Shanken, 1989, A test of the efficiency of a given portfolio, *Econometrica* 57, 1121–1152.

Jobson, J. D., and Bob Korkie, 1982, Potential performance and tests of portfolio efficiency, *Journal of Financial Economics* 10, 433–466.

Kandel, Shmuel, and Robert F. Stambaugh, 1987, On correlations and inferences about mean-variance efficiency, *Journal of Financial Economics* 18, 61–90.

———, 1989, A mean-variance framework for tests of asset pricing models, *Review of Financial Studies* 2, 125–156.

———, 1993, Portfolio inefficiency and the cross-section of mean returns, Working paper.

Lakonishok, Josef, and Alan C. Shapiro, 1986, Systematic risk, total risk and size as determinants of stock market returns, *Journal of Banking and Finance* 10, 115–132.

Lintner, John, 1965, The valuation of risk assets and the selection of risky investments in stock portfolios and capital budgets, *Review of Economics and Statistics* 47, 13–37.

MacKinlay, A. Craig, and Matthew P. Richardson, 1991, Using generalized method of moments to test mean-variance efficiency, *Journal of Finance* 46, 511–527.

Reinganum, Marc R., 1981, A new empirical perspective on the CAPM, *Journal of Financial and Quantitative Analysis* 16, 439–462.

Roll, Richard, 1977, A critique of the asset pricing theory's tests, *Journal of Financial Economics* 4, 129–176.

———, 1980, Orthogonal portfolios, *Journal of Financial and Quantitative Analysis* 15, 1005–1023.

Ross, Stephen A., 1977, The capital asset pricing model (CAPM), short-scale restrictions and related issues, *Journal of Finance* 32, 177–183.

Shanken, Jay, 1985, Multivariate tests of the zero-beta CAPM, *Journal of Financial Economics* 14, 327–348.

———, 1987, Multivariate proxies and asset pricing relations, *Journal of Financial Economics* 18, 91–110.

———, 1992, On the estimation of beta-pricing models, *Review of Financial Studies* 5, 1–33.

Sharpe, William F., 1964, Capital asset prices: A theory of market equilibrium under conditions of risk, *Journal of Finance* 19, 425–442.

Stambaugh, Robert F., 1982, On the exclusion of assets from tests of the two-parameter model: A sensitivity analysis, *Journal of Financial Economics* 10, 237–268.

Wheatly, Simon, 1992, Private communication.

Zhou, Guofu, 1991, Small sample tests of portfolio efficiency, *Journal of Financial Economics* 30, 165–191.

[5]

THE JOURNAL OF FINANCE • VOL. L, NO. 1 • MARCH 1995

Portfolio Inefficiency and the Cross-section of Expected Returns

SHMUEL KANDEL and ROBERT F. STAMBAUGH*

ABSTRACT

The Capital Asset Pricing Model implies that (i) the market portfolio is efficient and (ii) expected returns are linearly related to betas. Many do not view these implications as separate, since either implies the other, but we demonstrate that either can hold nearly perfectly while the other fails grossly. If the index portfolio is inefficient, then the coefficients and R^2 from an ordinary least squares regression of expected returns on betas can equal essentially any values and bear no relation to the index portfolio's mean-variance location. That location does determine the outcome of a mean-beta regression fitted by generalized least squares.

EXPECTED RETURNS ON A set of risky assets obey an exact linear relation to betas computed against an index portfolio that lies on the minimum-variance boundary of those assets. If the betas are computed instead against an index portfolio that lies inside the minimum-variance boundary, then expected returns must deviate to some degree from any fitted cross-sectional linear relation.[1] These properties are well known, but they leave open the question of whether, in the latter case, the extent to which expected returns are approximated by a linear function of beta is at all related to the mean-variance location of the index portfolio. For example, one might ask whether, with only negligible inefficiency in the index portfolio, a plot of expected returns versus betas would display a near perfect linear relation.

In fact, the mean-variance location of an inefficient index portfolio bears essentially no relation to the plot of expected returns versus betas. For example, expected returns can display essentially no correlation with betas computed against an index portfolio that has an expected return arbitrarily close to that of the efficient portfolio with the same variance. Alternatively, expected returns can display a nearly perfect linear relation to betas computed against an index portfolio that is grossly inefficient. Such plots of expected returns versus betas can be summarized by ordinary least squares (OLS) regression. We show that, if the index portfolio is inefficient, the OLS regression coefficients and R^2 can equal essentially any values desired. This

---

* Kandel is from the Recanati Graduate School of Business Administration, Tel-Aviv University, and the Wharton School, University of Pennsylvania. Stambaugh is from the Wharton School, University of Pennsylvania. The authors are grateful for comments by Yakov Amihud, Eugene Fama, Gur Huberman, Ravi Jagannathan, Craig MacKinlay, Richard Roll, René Stulz, Simon Wheatley, an anonymous referee, and workshop participants at Tel-Aviv University, Temple University, and the University of Pennsylvania.

[1] See Fama (1976), Roll (1977), and Ross (1977).

157

general result, as well as the two examples noted, can be demonstrated by repackaging a given set of risky assets into alternative sets that generate the same portfolio opportunities. Such repackagings change neither the index portfolio nor the minimum-variance boundary, but they can change the cross-sectional mean-beta relation in virtually any manner desired.

This study shows that generalized least squares (GLS) regression provides a framework wherein the *exact* linear mean-beta relation implied by strict efficiency of the index portfolio can be generalized to an *approximate* linear relation when the index is inefficient. The GLS regression uses the covariance matrix of the asset returns, and much of the information in that matrix is omitted in a plot of expected return versus beta. An index portfolio's location in mean-variance space is unaffected by repackaging the individual assets, and we define a measure of relative efficiency that is determined by a portfolio's mean-variance location. This relative efficiency measure approaches its maximum value of unity as the index portfolio moves closer to the upper portion of the minimum-variance boundary. We find that this measure provides a simple link between the index portfolio's mean-variance location and the properties of the fitted GLS mean-beta relation. As the index portfolio's relative efficiency moves closer to unity, the fitted GLS mean-beta relation moves closer to the exact linear relation corresponding to an efficient portfolio with the same variance as the index. A slope coefficient of zero occurs only when the mean return on the index is equal to that of the global minimum-variance portfolio. Moreover, the goodness-of-fit measure for the GLS cross-sectional regression is simply the squared relative efficiency of the index portfolio.

In the absence of an exact linear relation between expected returns and betas, a variety of criteria could be used to fit a line and judge its goodness-of-fit. Developing such criteria is difficult without an economic context in which to view a fitted linear mean-beta relation. We consider a context in which such a relation is judged by its ability to provide fitted expected returns that are useful substitutes for true expected returns as inputs to a standard one-period portfolio optimization. For a given set of cross-sectional independent variables, including but not limited to beta, using the expected returns fitted from a GLS regression produces a portfolio with a higher expected return than using any other linear function of the independent variables. The squared relative efficiency of that portfolio is simply the goodness-of-fit for the GLS regression.

The remainder of the article is organized as follows. Section I shows that the cross-sectional mean-beta relation fitted by OLS bears essentially no relation to the mean-variance location of an inefficient index portfolio. Section II defines a portfolio's relative efficiency, using a measure that can be stated in terms of either expected returns or variances. Section III provides simple relations between the index portfolio's relative efficiency and a GLS regression of expected returns on betas. Section IV offers a portfolio-optimization setting in which to compare GLS to other methods for fitting and judging cross-sectional relations for expected returns. Although this study deals almost exclusively with population moments, Section V presents a brief discussion of issues related to estimation and inference. Conclusions are then presented in Section VI. The Appendix contains proofs of all propositions.

I. Inefficiency and Deviations from Mean-Beta Linearity

For a universe of n risky assets, define

R: n-vector of returns realized in a given period,
E: n-vector of expected returns,
V: $n \times n$ covariance matrix of returns, assumed to be nonsingular.

For a given portfolio p, a combination of the n assets, define

w_p : n-vector of weights in portfolio p,
μ_p : mean return on portfolio p $(= w_p' E)$,
σ_p^2 : variance of return on portfolio p $(= w_p' V w_p)$,
β : n-vector of betas with respect to p $[= (1/\sigma_p^2) V w_p]$.

Let ι denote an n-vector of ones, and define

$$X = [\iota \quad \beta]. \tag{1}$$

Assume that neither E nor β are proportional to ι.

The mean-variance location of portfolio p has virtually no bearing on the degree to which the elements of E and β conform to a linear relation, when goodness-of-fit is measured by the standard Euclidean norm. That is, portfolio p can lie arbitrarily close to the minimum-variance boundary and yet produce an OLS slope and R^2 that are arbitrarily close to zero. Similarly, portfolio p can lie far from the minimum-variance boundary (by whatever metric desired) and yet still produce an OLS fit between expected returns and betas that is arbitrarily close to exact linearity.

We verify the above statements by considering "repackagings" of assets. The portfolio opportunities generated by one set of n assets are identical to those generated by an alternative set of n assets that simply repackage the original set, provided that returns on the new assets also have a nonsingular covariance matrix. Such a repackaging does not change the minimum-variance boundary or the location of portfolio p in mean-variance space, but it can change the relation between the n assets' expected returns and their betas with respect to portfolio p.

A given repackaging of assets can be represented by a nonsingular $n \times n$ matrix A, where $A\iota = \iota$. The returns on the repackaged assets are constructed as $R^* = AR$, so the means and betas of the repackaged assets are given by $E^* = AE$ and $\beta^* = A\beta$. For a given repackaging of the n assets, let γ^* denote the vector of coefficients in an OLS regression of expected returns on betas with respect to portfolio p. That is,

$$\gamma^* = (X^{*\prime} X^*)^{-1} X^{*\prime} E^*, \tag{2}$$

where

$$X^* = [\iota \quad \beta^*] = AX. \tag{3}$$

The goodness-of-fit in this regression is given by

$$R^2_{OLS} = 1 - \frac{(E^* - X^*\gamma^*)'(E^* - X^*\gamma^*)}{\left(E^* - \frac{\iota'E^*}{n}\iota\right)'\left(E^* - \frac{\iota'E^*}{n}\iota\right)}. \tag{4}$$

If portfolio p is inefficient, the following proposition states that one can always find a repackaging such that expected returns on the new set of n assets obey essentially any desired OLS regression outcome.

PROPOSITION 1: *If portfolio p is inefficient, then for any $\omega \in (0,1)$, $\varepsilon > 0$, and two-element vector θ, there exists a nonsingular $n \times n$ matrix A, with $A\iota = \iota$, such that*[2]

$$\|\gamma^* - \theta\| < \varepsilon, \quad and \tag{5}$$

$$R^2_{OLS} = \omega. \tag{6}$$

The results of an OLS regression correspond closely, of course, to what one would infer visually from a simple plot of expected returns versus betas. Proposition 1 implies that such a plot could in fact appear to contradict standard theory, since small degrees of portfolio inefficiency or deviations from perfect mean-beta linearity may not be visible in a plot. Two such examples are presented in Figure 1. The minimum-variance boundaries in Figures 1a and 1c are identical, and they are generated using sample means and covariances of monthly returns on ten portfolios of common stocks sorted by equity capitalization (firm size) for the period from 1926 to 1992.[3]

The ten points plotted in Figure 1a as solid dots represent means and variances on ten assets that simply repackage the ten size portfolios. Portfolio p, shown as a small circle, is inefficient, having a monthly expected return that is 88 basis points less than the expected return on the efficient portfolio with the same variance. Figure 1b plots the expected returns on the ten assets versus the assets' betas with respect to portfolio p. The mean-beta relation is not exactly linear, although the violations of exact linearity are too slight to be visible on the graph. The OLS regression line on which all of the points appear to lie has an intercept of 30 basis points, close to the average monthly interest rate for the 1926 to 1992 period, and the slope of the line is 76 basis points, the average excess return on portfolio p. In other words, shown only Figure 1b, one would be inclined to conclude that portfolio p is the Sharpe-Lintner tangent portfolio of the ten assets.

---

[2] The Euclidean norm of an n-vector v is defined as $\|v\| = (v'v)^{1/2}$.

[3] The portfolios include all stocks on the New York Stock Exchange, and the returns within a portfolio are value-weighted. Portfolio returns were obtained from the Index File supplied by the Center for Research in Security Prices.

Portfolio Inefficiency and Cross-section of Expected Returns 161

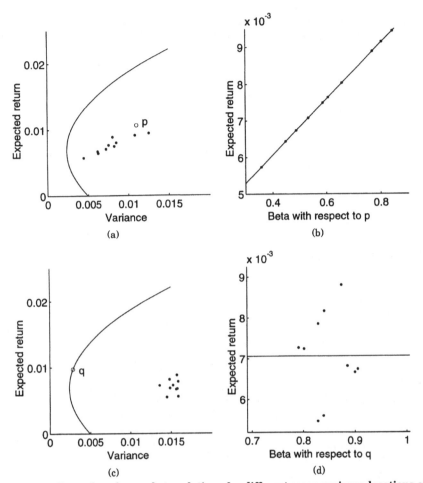

Figure 1. Examples of mean-beta relations for different mean-variance locations of the index portfolio. Figure 1*a* plots ten assets (*solid dots*), their minimum-variance boundary, and a portfolio *p* of those ten assets (*circle*). Figure 1*b* plots the expected returns and betas of those assets with respect to portfolio *p* as well as the OLS regression line through those points. Figures 1*c* and 1*d* display a similar case, except that the ten assets are a "repackaging" of those in the first case. The points in Figure 1*b* do not lie *exactly* on the regression line, and portfolio *q* in Figure 1*c* does not lie *exactly* on the minimum-variance boundary.

The ten assets whose means and variances are plotted in Figure 1*c* are obtained as a different repackaging of the ten size portfolios. Portfolio *q* is inefficient, although it lies too close to the minimum-variance boundary for the inefficiency to be visible on the graph. For the ten assets, a least squares regression of expected returns on betas with respect to portfolio *q* produces an R^2_{OLS} less than 0.0001, and the corresponding plot is shown in Figure 1*d*.

Shown only that plot, one would be inclined to conclude that portfolio q is inefficient. Such a conclusion must be correct, of course, but the degree of inefficiency can be of no economic significance.

Although we focus in this study on the cross-sectional relation between expected returns and betas with respect to a single portfolio, we should note that an extension of Proposition 1 to multifactor models is straightforward. That is, suppose X has instead $k + 1$ columns, where columns 2 through $k + 1$ contain the assets' sensitivities to a set of k factors—or betas with respect to k portfolios that mimic the factors. Then, unless expected returns conform exactly to some linear combination of the columns of X, the n assets can again be repackaged to produce essentially any desired OLS coefficients and R^2_{OLS}. In other words, if no portfolio of the mimicking portfolios is *exactly* mean-variance efficient, then a multifactor model faces the same problems associated with the single-beta model.[4]

Issues related to OLS regressions of expected returns on betas are discussed in several recent studies. Roll and Ross (1994) derive the region in mean-variance space containing the portfolios that produce a mean-beta relation whose OLS slope is exactly zero (and thus R^2_{OLS} is zero). Our observation that inefficient portfolios can also give arbitrarily good fits to any given linear mean-beta relation goes beyond the analysis of Roll and Ross, who do not consider goodness-of-fit measures.[5] Jagannathan and Wang (1994) construct a four-asset example in which repackaging changes R^2_{OLS} from 0.95 to 0.0, although those authors do not address the generality of the example or its relation to the mean-variance location of the index portfolio. Grauer (1994) constructs a number of examples illustrating that the difference between the OLS intercept and the riskless rate does not correspond to the proximity of the index portfolio to the Sharpe-Linter tangent portfolio.

Roll and Ross (1994) show that the distance between the minimum-variance boundary and the zero-slope-producing region is increasing in the cross-sectional variance of expected returns on the n assets, holding constant the product of the cross-sectional mean of the expected returns and the variance of the payoff on a specific zero-investment position.[6] As shown here, repackaging the n assets allows the goodness-of-fit to become arbitrarily close to zero for *any* inefficient index portfolio. Moreover, the following proposition states that such a repackaging can be constructed to produce expected returns and betas exhibiting any desired cross-sectional mean and variance.[7]

---

[4] Huberman, Kandel, and Stambaugh (1987) define mimicking portfolios and analyze their relation to the minimum-variance boundary under exact k-factor pricing.

[5] Roll and Ross derive mean-variance regions for portfolios that produce a given positive OLS slope for the mean-beta relation, but, other than in the case where the slope is zero, the value for the slope does not provide information about the goodness-of-fit.

[6] The zero-investment position goes long \$1 in the portfolio with weights $(1/\iota' E)E$ and short \$1 in the equally weighted portfolio of the n assets.

[7] This repackaging would not necessarily satisfy additional constraints involving the covariance matrix of returns, such as an upper bound on the variance of the zero-investment position defined by Roll and Ross (1994).

Portfolio Inefficiency and Cross-section of Expected Returns   163

PROPOSITION 2: *If portfolio p is inefficient, then for any scalars $\bar{\beta}^*$, $\bar{E}^*$, $\sigma_{\beta^*} > 0$, $\sigma_{E^*} > 0$, and $\omega \in (0,1)$, there exists a nonsingular $n \times n$ matrix A, with $A\iota = \iota$, such that*

$$\frac{1}{n}\iota' A\beta = \bar{\beta}^*, \tag{7}$$

$$\frac{1}{n}\iota' AE = \bar{E}^*, \tag{8}$$

$$\frac{1}{n}(A\beta - \bar{\beta}^*\iota)'(A\beta - \bar{\beta}^*\iota) = \sigma_{\beta^*}^2, \tag{9}$$

$$\frac{1}{n}(AE - \bar{E}^*\iota)'(AE - \bar{E}^*\iota) = \sigma_{E^*}^2, \quad and \tag{10}$$

$$R_{OLS}^2 = \omega. \tag{11}$$

Numerous empirical investigations of asset pricing have tested the hypothesis that the OLS slope in the cross-sectional mean-beta relation is equal to zero. (A recent example can be found in Fama and French (1992).) Failure to reject this null hypothesis with a finite number of time-series observations does not, of course, translate into a rejection of the hypothesis of mean-variance efficiency. In an infinite sample, failure to reject a zero OLS slope must reject *exact* efficiency of the index. Roll and Ross show that such a result could occur with an index portfolio that is close to efficient, so, following Roll (1977), inferences about the pricing theory could be sensitive to construction of the index.

Some readers might interpret the Roll-Ross analysis as implying that the outcome of a zero slope with a near-efficient index portfolio requires low dispersion in expected returns. If that were indeed the case, then the above criticism might not be very relevant to many empirical studies. That is, such investigations often select assets so as to create substantial dispersion in expected returns. Given Proposition 2, however, an outcome of a near-zero slope with a near-efficient index portfolio can occur with large dispersions in both expected returns and betas. In other words, it seems difficult to argue that simply selecting assets with disperse expected returns or betas necessarily endows the zero-slope test with power against an alternative hypothesis of near efficiency in the index portfolio.

A reasonable reaction to the examples in Figure 1 could be that the sets of ten assets are unusual, so that, although these special cases illustrate theoretical possibilities, one could simply avoid using such assets in empirical investigations. Although the assets selected in the examples are no doubt unusual by some criteria, the relevant question is how one would develop such criteria. We employ repackaging as an expositional and analytical device. Our use of this device might lead one to suggest that assets constructed using extreme values in the matrix *A* could be ruled out, but such a suggestion misses the point. Any given set of assets can be viewed as an extreme repackaging of one set but a modest repackaging of another. In other words, the assets selected by an empirical researcher do not come with a well-defined A matrix. So if one seeks to admit only modest repackagings, or even no repackagings, the question arises, "Repackagings of what?".

One source of information about how "unusual" a set of assets might be is the covariance matrix of their returns. The plots in Figure 1 omit much information about the covariance matrix. For example, the covariance matrix of the assets plotted in Figure 1*a*, although nonsingular, has one very small eigenvalue. We consider below a framework that uses this additional information to measure the relation between expected returns and betas with quantities that correspond directly to portfolio p's position in mean-variance space. A portfolio's position in mean-variance space will be characterized by a simple measure of relative mean-variance efficiency.

II. A Measure of Relative Portfolio Efficiency

For a given portfolio p, let x denote the efficient portfolio with the same variance as p, and let y denote the minimum-variance portfolio with the same mean as p. Define

μ_x : mean return on portfolio x,
μ_{x0}: mean return on portfolios uncorrelated with portfolio x,
σ_y^2 : variance of portfolio y,
μ_g : mean of the global minimum-variance portfolio,
σ_g^2 : global minimum variance.

The *relative efficiency* of portfolio p is defined as

$$\psi_p \equiv \frac{\mu_p - \mu_g}{\mu_x - \mu_g}. \tag{12}$$

The relative efficiency measure defined in equation (12) has a range from -1 to 1, with the latter value corresponding to exact efficiency. Relative efficiency is undefined for the global minimum-variance portfolio. When portfolio p lies on the minimum-variance boundary but has the *lowest* expected return for its variance, then $\psi_p = -1$. The square of this efficiency measure can also be expressed in terms of variances, as given by the following proposition.

PROPOSITION 3:

$$\psi_p^2 = \frac{\sigma_y^2 - \sigma_g^2}{\sigma_p^2 - \sigma_g^2}. \tag{13}$$

Both equations (12) and (13) are represented graphically in Figure 2. Figure 3 displays the locations in mean-variance space of portfolios with given values of ψ_p. The minimum-variance boundary is the same as that constructed in Figures 1*a* and 1*c*.

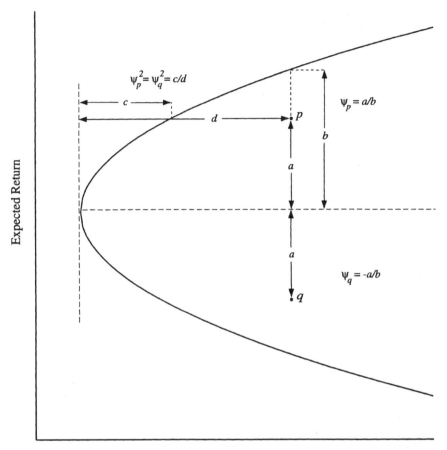

Variance of Return

Figure 2. The relative efficiency measure ψ in mean-variance space. The *solid curve* represents the minimum-variance boundary of portfolio opportunities. The relative efficiencies of portfolios p and q are denoted by ψ_p and ψ_q.

A portfolio's inefficiency can also be characterized in terms of correlation. Kandel and Stambaugh (1987) and Shanken (1987) show that ρ_p, the maximum correlation between the return on portfolio p and the return on any minimum-variance portfolio, is given by

$$\rho_p = \frac{\sigma_y}{\sigma_p}. \qquad (14)$$

This measure, like ψ_p, approaches unity as portfolio p approaches the minimum-variance boundary, but it is bounded below by zero. Combining

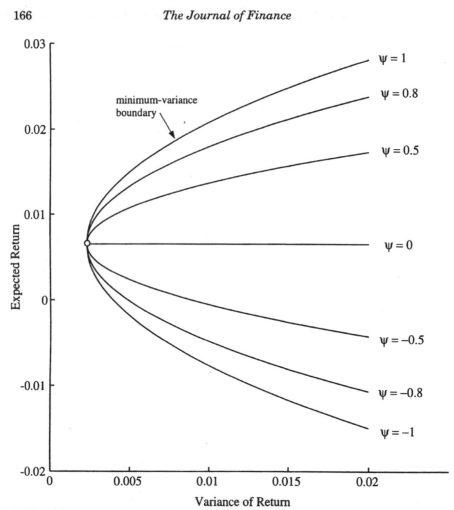

Figure 3. Mean-variance locations of portfolios with various levels of relative efficiency. Each *curve* displays the locus of portfolios with a given measure of relative efficiency, ψ. Relative efficiency is undefined for the global minimum-variance portfolio (denoted by the *small circle*).

equations (13) and (14) gives

$$1 - \rho_p^2 = \left(1 - \frac{\sigma_g^2}{\sigma_p^2}\right)(1 - \psi_p^2), \tag{15}$$

which implies that

$$\psi_p < \rho_p \tag{16}$$

if portfolio p is inefficient.

III. The Mean-Beta Relation and the Covariance Matrix

Consider a cross-sectional regression of E on β, where the covariance matrix V is used to perform GLS. That is, the coefficient vector in the regression is given by

$$\phi = \begin{bmatrix} \phi_1 \\ \phi_2 \end{bmatrix} = (X'V^{-1}X)^{-1}X'V^{-1}E. \tag{17}$$

PROPOSITION 4: *The slope coefficient ϕ_2 is given by*

$$\phi_2 = \psi_p(\mu_x - \mu_{x0}) \tag{18}$$

and the intercept ϕ_1 is given by $\phi_1 = \mu_p - \phi_2$ or

$$\phi_1 = \mu_{x0} + (1 - \psi_p)(\mu_g - \mu_{x0}). \tag{19}$$

If p is efficient, so $\psi_p = 1$, then ϕ_1 must equal μ_{x0} and ϕ_2 must be the portfolio's premium over that zero-beta rate, $\mu_x - \mu_{x0}$. The above proposition reveals that, if p is inefficient, then $\phi_1 > \mu_{x0}$ and $\phi_2 < \mu_x - \mu_{x0}$. As ψ_p gets closer to 1, ϕ_1 approaches μ_{x0} and ϕ_2 approaches its maximum value, $\mu_x - \mu_{x0}$. A negative slope occurs for $\mu_p < \mu_g$, and a zero slope occurs if and only if $\psi_p = 0$, or when $\mu_p = \mu_g$.[8]

The standard measure for the GLS regression's goodness-of-fit is

$$R^2_{GLS} = 1 - \frac{(E - X\phi)'V^{-1}(E - X\phi)}{(E - \iota\bar{\mu})'V^{-1}(E - \iota\bar{\mu})}, \tag{20}$$

where

$$\bar{\mu} = (E'V^{-1}\iota)/(\iota'V^{-1}\iota), \tag{21}$$

which is the coefficient in a GLS regression of E on ι. Note that exact linearity gives $R^2_{GLS} = 1$, a slope of zero gives $R^2_{GLS} = 0$, and $0 \le R^2_{GLS} \le 1$.

PROPOSITION 5:

$$R^2_{GLS} = \psi_p^2. \tag{22}$$

We see that, unlike the OLS regression, the outcome of a GLS regression of expected returns on betas is determined completely by portfolio p's location in mean-variance space, as summarized by ψ_p. In Figure 1a, $\psi_p = 0.3$, so the goodness-of-fit in a GLS regression of means on betas with respect to portfolio p is 0.09. In Figure 1c, ψ_q is nearly 1, and so is the goodness-of-fit in the GLS mean-beta regression. Although it can be shown algebraically that the coefficient vector ϕ and the goodness-of-fit measure R^2_{GLS} are invariant to repackaging the n assets, this result follows immediately from the fact that portfolio p's location in mean-variance space is unaffected by repackaging the assets used to generate the set of portfolio opportunities.

---

[8] This last point is made independently by Roll and Ross (1994), who attribute private correspondence with Simon Wheatley.

The GLS regression constructs a least squares fit between means and betas that are transformed using the factored inverse of the covariance matrix, and, as is obvious from Figure 1, the outcome of that regression need bear no resemblance to a plot of the "raw" expected returns versus betas. To decide whether fitted lines and goodness-of-fit measures are more relevant when computed with the raw means and betas than with their transformed counterparts, it may be useful to have a context in which fitted cross-sectional relations for expected returns would be used. The next section considers the use of such relations in providing expected returns as inputs to portfolio optimization. It is shown that the fitted GLS regression provides the optimal inputs for the optimization, and the regression's goodness-of-fit provides the squared relative efficiency of the resulting portfolio. If, in other contexts, the goodness-of-fit of the raw means and betas is a more relevant metric, however, then one must simply recognize that such a metric need bear no relation to the relative mean-variance efficiency of portfolio p.

IV. Using Fitted Mean Returns: An Optimization Setting

In the absence of an exact linear relation between expected returns and betas, it seems useful to have an economic context in which one might, at a theoretical level, fit a linear relation and judge its goodness-of-fit. We consider here the simple context of mean-variance portfolio optimization, where the expected returns fitted from a linear cross-sectional relation are used as inputs to the problem of maximizing a portfolio's expected return for a given variance. The extent to which the portfolio constructed in the optimization differs from the efficient portfolio depends only on the differences between true and fitted expected returns.

Because the cross-section of mean returns can possibly be explained better by variables used in addition to, or even in place of, betas computed against an inefficient portfolio, we allow such variables to be included in the analysis. For $k < n$, let Z denote an $n \times k$ matrix of full column rank, where one column is ι. The matrix Z can simply be the $n \times 2$ matrix X defined previously, so that the results below include fitting the mean-beta relation as a special case. We consider linear cross-sectional relations that fit expected returns as

$$\hat{E} = Za, \tag{23}$$

for some $k \times 1$ vector a.

The quality of the approximation to expected returns in equation (23) is characterized by the results of a portfolio optimization that uses $\hat{E}$ instead of E as inputs. Let $w(\hat{E}; \sigma^2)$ denote the solution to the portfolio maximization problem,

$$\max_{w} w'\hat{E} \tag{24}$$

Portfolio Inefficiency and Cross-section of Expected Returns   169

subject to the constraints

$$w'Vw = \sigma^2 \quad \text{and} \tag{25}$$

$$w'\iota = 1, \tag{26}$$

for a given $\sigma^2 > \sigma_g^2$.

Let δ denote the coefficient vector in a GLS regression of E on Z,

$$\delta = (Z'V^{-1}Z)^{-1}Z'V^{-1}E. \tag{27}$$

The fitted mean returns from the GLS regression are given by

$$E^{\dagger} = Z\delta. \tag{28}$$

Note that $E^{\dagger}$ is a special case of $\hat{E}$ in equation (23) with $a = \delta$. We see that this choice of a is best in the following sense.

PROPOSITION 6:

$$[w(E^{\dagger}; \sigma^2)]'E \geq [w(\hat{E}; \sigma^2)]'E \tag{29}$$

for all a.

In other words, the *true* expected return of the portfolio constructed using the GLS inputs is greater than or equal to the true expected return of a portfolio constructed using any other inputs of the form in equation (23).

As before, the goodness-of-fit for the GLS regression is given by

$$R_{GLS}^2 = 1 - \frac{(E - Z\delta)'V^{-1}(E - Z\delta)}{(E - \iota\bar{\mu})'V^{-1}(E - \iota\bar{\mu})}, \tag{30}$$

where $\bar{\mu}$ is defined as in equation (21). This goodness-of-fit is also the squared relative efficiency of the portfolio constructed using GLS inputs.

PROPOSITION 7: *For any $\sigma^2 > \sigma_g^2$, let q denote the portfolio with weights $w(E^{\dagger}; \sigma^2)$. Then*

$$R_{GLS}^2 = \psi_q^2. \tag{31}$$

In other words, the portfolio constructed using the fitted expected returns from the GLS regression has a squared relative efficiency equal to that regression's goodness-of-fit. Note that R_{GLS}^2, and thus ψ_q^2, do not depend on the value for σ^2 specified in the portfolio optimization. In the special case where $Z = X$, it follows from Propositions 5 and 7 that the portfolio constructed with the GLS inputs has the same (squared) relative efficiency as portfolio p. In fact, it can also be shown in that case that the weights in portfolio p are equal to $w(E^{\dagger}; \sigma_p^2)$.

V. Estimation and Inference

In many empirical investigations of asset pricing, cross-sectional regressions are typically estimated using sample estimates of expected returns, betas, and, in the case of GLS, the covariance matrix. Recent examples include Fama and French (1992) in the case of OLS and Amihud, Christensen, and Mendelson (1992) in the case of GLS. It is straightforward to show that the probability limits of these regression estimators equal their population counterparts, γ^* in the case of OLS (equation (2)) and ϕ in the case of GLS (equation (17)).

When portfolio p is exactly mean-variance efficient, then $\gamma^* = \phi$ for any repackaging of the assets, so the OLS and GLS estimators then have the same probability limits. In that case, Shanken (1992) shows that the GLS estimator is asymptotically efficient, even though the betas used as independent variables are first estimated in OLS regressions.[9] As Shanken cautions, however, one might be concerned about the GLS estimator in finite samples. Amsler and Schmidt (1985) conduct a Monte Carlo investigation and find that, with six years of monthly returns on fifteen or fewer assets, the GLS estimator of the zero-beta rate generally outperforms the OLS estimator in terms of variance, mean square error, and mean absolute error, but not in terms of bias.

When portfolio p is inefficient, there can be substantial divergence between the probability limits of the OLS and GLS estimators, given the possible differences between γ^* and ϕ demonstrated in this study. This potential divergence in probability limits complicates a comparison of these estimators in small samples. On one hand, OLS may very well perform better as an estimator of γ^* than does GLS as an estimator of ϕ. On the other hand, γ^* may be a less interesting quantity to estimate, since it need bear essentially no relation to the degree of inefficiency in portfolio p.

Propositions 4 and 5 also hold with the population moments replaced by their sample counterparts, which implies that the outcome of the GLS estimation is determined by the location of the index portfolio in sample mean-variance space. In other words, the GLS estimation summarizes the information in the sample covariance matrix by the index portfolio's sample mean-variance location. A portfolio's sample mean-variance location has been used in a variety of approaches to estimation and inference. Shanken (1985) shows that the outcome of a cross-sectional GLS regression of means on betas can be used to test mean-variance efficiency in the absence of a riskless asset, and Roll (1985) provides a geometric mean-variance interpretation of this test. Kandel and Stambaugh (1989) show that likelihood-ratio tests of mean-variance efficiency, with or without a riskless asset, can also be computed using the index portfolio's sample mean-variance location.[10] Inferences about the degree of inefficiency in a portfolio, formulated as a composite hypothesis instead of a point hypothesis of exact efficiency, have also been based on a portfolio's sample mean-variance location. Kandel and Stambaugh (1987) and

---

[9] Shanken's GLS estimator is defined using the covariance matrix of the residuals from the first-pass market-model regressions, but he shows in earlier work (Shanken (1985, footnote 16)) that the same estimator is obtained using the covariance matrix of returns.

[10] The mean-variance characterization for the likelihood-ratio test in the riskless-asset case is due to Gibbons, Ross, and Shanken (1989).

Shanken (1987) conduct such tests in a frequentist setting, while Kandel, McCulloch, and Stambaugh (1995) investigate a portfolio's degree of inefficiency in a Bayesian setting.

In contrast to all of the alternative approaches noted above, the outcome of an OLS regression of sample means on betas is essentially unrelated to the index portfolio's sample mean-variance location. This statement follows from the observation that Propositions 1 and 2 also hold with sample moments in place of population moments. Although it seems sensible that inferences about a portfolio's *population* mean-variance location should be based on its *sample* mean-variance location, perhaps finite-sample statistical considerations should temper such logic. Further investigation of these issues would no doubt be useful.

VI. Conclusions

As is well known, an exact linear relation between expected returns and betas with respect to a given portfolio p occurs if and only if portfolio p lies exactly on the minimum-variance boundary. If portfolio p is at all inefficient, however, a plot of expected returns versus betas bears essentially no relation to the position of portfolio p in mean-variance space. An OLS slope and R^2 arbitrarily close to zero can occur when portfolio p is arbitrarily close to the minimum-variance boundary. A near-perfect linear relation can occur, with any desired intercept and slope, if portfolio p is grossly inefficient.

Although OLS is inadequate to the task, the *exact* linear mean-beta relation implied by the efficiency of portfolio p can indeed be generalized to an *approximate* linear relation in the presence of inefficiency in portfolio p. If the linear relation is fitted as a GLS regression of expected returns on betas, using the variance-covariance matrix of returns, then that relation's coefficients and goodness-of-fit measure bear simple relations to the location of portfolio p in mean-variance space. If portfolio p is close to efficient, based on a relative efficiency measure that can be stated in terms of either means or variances, then the fitted relation will be close to the exact linear relation corresponding to an efficient portfolio whose mean and variance are close to those of portfolio p.

When portfolio p is inefficient, it may be useful to adopt an economic context in which to fit a linear relation between expected return and beta and characterize, at a theoretical level, that relation's goodness-of-fit. We consider a context in which the quality of the linear relation is judged by its ability to provide fitted expected returns that are useful substitutes for true expected returns as inputs to a standard one-period portfolio optimization. For a given set of cross-sectional independent variables, including but not limited to beta, using the expected returns fitted from a GLS regression produces a portfolio with a higher expected return than using any other linear combination of the independent variables. The (squared) relative efficiency of that portfolio is simply the goodness-of-fit for the GLS regression.

The absence of a relation between the index portfolio's relative efficiency and a plot of expected returns versus betas illustrates the difficulty in using and assessing any model that delivers multiple implications. For example, the Capital Asset Pricing Model of Sharpe (1964), Lintner (1965), and Black (1972) delivers two major implications: (i) the market portfolio is mean-variance efficient, and (ii) the relation between expected returns and betas is linear. Many finance academics prefer not to view these implications as separate, since either one implies the other, but such a strict view does not easily accommodate the fact that any financial model is at best a convenient and useful abstraction rather than an exact representation of reality.[11] That is, the strict view does not easily entertain the possibility that, for practical purposes, one implication can hold while the other fails. This study demonstrates that either implication can hold nearly perfectly while the other is grossly violated.

In some applications, the implication of interest may be that the market portfolio is mean-variance efficient or, in practical terms, very nearly so. This implication might lead, for example, to an "index fund" portfolio strategy or to the use of a market index as a performance benchmark against which to compare other portfolios of similar volatility. If the model's implication of interest is instead the cross-sectional mean-beta relation, then we see that the relative efficiency of the index portfolio offers little guidance as to the properties of such a relation. An additional problem with the mean-beta implication arises, however. Even if a linear mean-beta relation fits arbitrarily well (but not perfectly) for a given set of n assets that generate all portfolio opportunities, the same relation can still provide a poor approximation for the expected return on another asset (a repackaging of the n assets). Many applications of the model are likely to use a relation fitted with one set of assets to approximate the expected return on another asset, such as a project in a capital budgeting problem or a managed portfolio in a performance evaluation. Thus, unless one takes seriously the possibility that the linear mean-beta relation holds perfectly, this implication of the model seems to offer limited applicability.

Appendix

Proof of Proposition 1: Let F be a nonsingular $n \times n$ matrix whose first three columns are

$$f_1 = \iota, \qquad \text{(A1)}$$

$$f_2 = \beta, \qquad \text{(A2)}$$

and

$$f_3 = E - X\theta, \qquad \text{(A3)}$$

---

[11] Such a view of modeling is advanced, for example, by Fama (1976).

Portfolio Inefficiency and Cross-section of Expected Returns   173

respectively. Note that when portfolio p is inefficient, the above three vectors are linearly independent. Define the OLS coefficient vector

$$\gamma = (X'X)^{-1}X'E. \tag{A4}$$

Let Q be an $n \times n$ diagonal matrix whose diagonal elements are all ones except for the $(3,3)$ element, which satisfies

$$q_{(3,3)} < \frac{\varepsilon}{\left(f_3'X(X'X)^{-2}X'f_3\right)^{1/2}} \tag{A5}$$

when $\theta \neq \gamma$ and $q_{(3,3)} = 1$ when $\theta = \gamma$. In the latter case, note that $f_3'X = 0$. Define the nonsingular matrix $B \equiv FQF^{-1}$. It is easy to verify that the columns of F are eigenvectors of B, and that the diagonal elements of Q are the corresponding eigenvalues. Hence,

$$B\iota = Bf_1 = f_1 q_{(1,1)} = \iota, \tag{A6}$$

$$B\beta = Bf_2 = f_2 q_{(2,2)} = \beta, \tag{A7}$$

and

$$Bf_3 = f_3 q_{(3,3)}. \tag{A8}$$

Equations (A6) and (A7) can be rewritten as:

$$BX = X. \tag{A9}$$

Let G be a nonsingular $n \times n$ matrix whose columns are orthogonal to each other and whose first three columns are

$$g_1 = \iota, \tag{A10}$$

$$g_2 = \beta - \frac{(\iota'\beta)}{n}\iota, \tag{A11}$$

and

$$g_3 = BE - X(X'X)^{-1}X'BE. \tag{A12}$$

Note that g_3 is the vector of residuals from the regression of BE on BX ($= X$). When portfolio p is inefficient, the vector E is not spanned by the columns of X, and, therefore, the above three columns of G are linearly independent and orthogonal to each other. Let $\Lambda \equiv (G'G)^{-1}$. Since the columns of G are orthogonal to each other, Λ is a diagonal matrix. Let H be an $n \times n$ diagonal matrix whose diagonal elements are all ones except for the $(3,3)$ element, which is given by

$$h_{(3,3)} = \left(\frac{(v'v)(1-\omega)}{(g_3'g_3)\omega}\right)^{1/2}, \tag{A13}$$

where

$$v \equiv X(X'X)^{-1}X'BE - \frac{(\iota'BE)}{n}\iota. \tag{A14}$$

Define the nonsingular matrix $C \equiv GH\Lambda G'$. It is easy to verify that the columns of G are eigenvectors of C as well as C', and the diagonal elements of H are the corresponding eigenvalues of both C and C'. Hence,

$$C'\iota = C\iota = Cg_1 = g_1 h_{(1,1)} = \iota, \qquad (A15)$$

$$C'\beta = C\beta = C\left(g_2 + \frac{(\iota'\beta)}{n}g_1\right) = \beta, \qquad (A16)$$

$$C'X = CX = X, \qquad (A17)$$

and

$$Cg_3 = h_{(3,3)}g_3. \qquad (A18)$$

Now let $A \equiv CB$, which is nonsingular. Equations (A9) and (A17) imply that

$$AX = CBX = CX = X, \qquad (A19)$$

so $A\iota = \iota$. Substituting (A19) into the definition of γ^* in equation (2) and simplifying by using equations (A3), (A8), (A9), and (A17) gives:

$$\gamma^* = (X'A'AX)^{-1}X'A'AE = (X'X)^{-1}X'CBE$$
$$= (X'X)^{-1}X'BE = (X'X)^{-1}X'B(X\theta + f_3)$$
$$= \theta + (X'X)^{-1}X'Bf_3$$
$$= \theta + q_{(3,3)}(X'X)^{-1}X'f_3. \qquad (A20)$$

If $\gamma = \theta$, then $\gamma^* = \theta$, since in that case $q_{(3,3)} = 1$ and $X'f_3 = 0$. When $\gamma \neq \theta$, inequality (5) is obtained by combining equation (A20) with equation (A5):

$$\|\gamma^* - \theta\| = \left(q_{(3,3)}^2 f_3' X(X'X)^{-2}X'f_3\right)^{1/2} < \varepsilon. \qquad (A21)$$

Using equations (2), (3), (A17), and (A19) we get:

$$(E^* - X^*\gamma^*) = AE - AX(X'A'AX)^{-1}X'A'AE$$
$$= AE - X(X'X)^{-1}X'BE$$
$$= C(BE - X(X'X)^{-1}X'BE)$$
$$= Cg_3 = g_3 h_{(3,3)}, \qquad (A22)$$

which implies that

$$AE = g_3 h_{(3,3)} + X(X'X)^{-1}X'BE. \qquad (A23)$$

Using equations (A17), (A23), and the definition of v in (A14) we get:

$$E^* - \frac{(\iota'E^*)}{n}\iota = AE - \frac{(\iota'AE)}{n}\iota$$
$$= g_3 h_{(3,3)} + X(X'X)^{-1}X'BE - \frac{(\iota'BE)}{n}\iota$$
$$= g_3 h_{(3,3)} + v. \qquad (A24)$$

Equation (6) is obtained by substituting equations (A22) and (A24) into equation (4), observing that $(v'g_3) = 0$, and using the definition of $h_{(3,3)}$ in equation (A13):

$$R_{OLS}^2 = 1 - \frac{(E^* - X^*\gamma^*)'(E^* - X^*\gamma^*)}{\left(E^* - \frac{(\iota'E^*)}{n}\iota\right)'\left(E^* - \frac{(\iota'E^*)}{n}\iota\right)}$$

$$= 1 - \frac{(g_3'g_3)h_{(3,3)}^2}{(g_3'g_3)h_{(3,3)}^2 + v'v}$$

$$= \frac{v'v}{(g_3'g_3)h_{(3,3)}^2 + v'v}$$

$$= \omega. \tag{A25}$$

Proof of Proposition 2: In this proof we use matrix notation similar to that employed in the proof of Proposition 1, although the matrices are redefined here and may be different from those in that proof. Proposition 1 implies that there exists a nonsingular $n \times n$ matrix C, with $C\iota = \iota$, such that $R_{OLS}^2 = \omega$ in the regression of CE on $C\beta$. Here we construct an additional repackaging, using a nonsingular matrix B, and then consider the regression of BCE on $BC\beta$. Define

$$\bar{\beta} = \frac{1}{n}\iota'C\beta, \tag{A26}$$

$$\bar{E} = \frac{1}{n}\iota'CE, \tag{A27}$$

$$\sigma_\beta^2 = \frac{1}{n}(C\beta - \bar{\beta}\iota)'(C\beta - \bar{\beta}\iota), \quad \text{and} \tag{A28}$$

$$\sigma_E^2 = \frac{1}{n}(CE - \bar{E}\iota)'(CE - \bar{E}\iota). \tag{A29}$$

The following construction of the matrix B applies to the case where

$$\sigma_\beta^2 \neq \sigma_{\beta^*}^2 \quad \text{and} \quad \sigma_E^2 \neq \sigma_{E^*}^2. \tag{A30}$$

The special cases where one of these inequalities does not hold will be discussed later. Define

$$k_\beta = \frac{\bar{\beta}^*\sigma_\beta - \bar{\beta}\sigma_{\beta^*}}{\sigma_\beta - \sigma_{\beta^*}} \tag{A31}$$

and

$$k_E = \frac{\bar{E}^* \sigma_E - \bar{E}\sigma_{E^*}}{\sigma_E - \sigma_{E^*}}. \tag{A32}$$

Let F be a nonsingular $n \times n$ matrix whose first three columns are

$$f_1 = \iota, \tag{A33}$$

$$f_2 = C\beta - k_\beta \iota, \tag{A34}$$

and

$$f_3 = CE - k_E \iota. \tag{A35}$$

Note that when portfolio p is inefficient, the above three vectors are linearly independent. Let Q be an $n \times n$ diagonal matrix whose diagonal elements are all ones except for the $(2, 2)$ and $(3, 3)$ elements, which are given by

$$q_{(2,2)} = \frac{\sigma_{\beta^*}}{\sigma_\beta} \quad \text{and} \tag{A36}$$

$$q_{(3,3)} = \frac{\sigma_{E^*}}{\sigma_E}. \tag{A37}$$

Define the nonsingular matrix B,

$$B \equiv FQF^{-1}. \tag{A38}$$

It is easy to verify that the columns of F are eigenvectors of B and that the diagonal elements of Q are the corresponding eigenvalues. Hence,

$$B\iota = \iota, \tag{A39}$$

$$Bf_2 = f_2 q_{(2,2)}, \tag{A40}$$

and

$$Bf_3 = f_3 q_{(3,3)}. \tag{A41}$$

Equations (A40) and (A41) can be rewritten as:

$$BC\beta = q_{(2,2)}C\beta + k_\beta(1 - q_{(2,2)})\iota$$
$$= \frac{1}{\sigma_\beta}\left[\sigma_\beta . C\beta + \left(\beta^* \sigma_\beta - \bar{\beta}\sigma_{\beta^*}\right)\iota\right], \tag{A42}$$

and

$$BCE = q_{(3,3)}CE + k_E(1 - q_{(3,3)})\iota$$
$$= \frac{1}{\sigma_E}\left[\sigma_E . CE + \left(E^* \sigma_E - \bar{E}\sigma_{E^*}\right)\iota\right]. \tag{A43}$$

Portfolio Inefficiency and Cross-section of Expected Returns   177

Now let $A \equiv BC$, which is nonsingular. Using equations (A31), (A32), (A36), (A37), (A42), and (A43), we can verify equations (7) and (8):

$$\frac{1}{n}\iota' A\beta = \frac{1}{n}\iota' BC\beta$$

$$= \frac{1}{\sigma_\beta}\left[\sigma_{\beta\cdot}n\bar\beta + \left(\beta^*\sigma_\beta - \bar\beta\sigma_{\beta\cdot}\right)n\right]$$

$$= \bar\beta^*, \tag{A44}$$

$$\frac{1}{n}\iota' AE = \frac{1}{n}\iota' BCE$$

$$= \frac{1}{\sigma_E}\left[\sigma_{E\cdot}n\bar E + \left(E^*\sigma_E - \bar E\sigma_{E\cdot}\right)n\right]$$

$$= \bar E^*. \tag{A45}$$

From equations (A42) and (A43) observe that

$$BC\beta - \bar\beta\iota = \frac{\sigma_{\beta\cdot}}{\sigma_\beta}(C\beta - \bar\beta\iota) \quad \text{and} \tag{A46}$$

$$BCE - \bar E\iota = \frac{\sigma_{E\cdot}}{\sigma_E}(CE - \bar E\iota), \tag{A47}$$

which, combined with (A28) and (A29), can be used to verify equations (9) and (10):

$$\frac{1}{n}(A\beta - \bar\beta^*\iota)'(A\beta - \bar\beta^*\iota) = \frac{1}{n}(BC\beta - \bar\beta^*\iota)'(BC\beta - \bar\beta^*\iota)$$

$$= \frac{1}{n}\frac{\sigma_{\beta\cdot}^2}{\sigma_\beta^2}(C\beta - \bar\beta\iota)'(C\beta - \bar\beta\iota)$$

$$= \sigma_{\beta\cdot}^2, \tag{A48}$$

$$\frac{1}{n}(AE - \bar E^*\iota)'(AE - \bar E^*\iota) = \frac{1}{n}(BCE - \bar E^*\iota)'(BCE - \bar E^*\iota)$$

$$= \frac{1}{n}\frac{\sigma_{E\cdot}^2}{\sigma_E^2}(CE - \bar E\iota)'(CE - \bar E\iota)$$

$$= \sigma_{E\cdot}^2. \tag{A49}$$

To prove equation (11), note from equations (A42) and (A43) that the vector BCE is obtained from the vector CE by adding a constant to each element of the product of CE and a constant. Similarly, the vector $BC\beta$ is obtained from the vector $C\beta$ by adding a constant to each element of the product of $C\beta$ and a constant. The value of R^2_{OLS} is invariant with respect to such linear transformations of the dependent and independent regression variables, so

The Journal of Finance

we conclude that the value of R^2_{OLS} in the regression of BCE on $BC\beta$ is ω, the same as the value of R^2_{OLS} in the regression of CE on $C\beta$.

In the special case where one of the inequalities in equation (A30) does not hold, one can construct the matrix B as a product of two repackaging matrices, $B = B_2 B_1$. Consider, for example, the case where $\sigma_{\beta\bullet} = \sigma_\beta$. Construct B_1 using equations (A31) to (A38) but with $\sigma_{\beta\bullet}$ changed to $\sigma_\beta \cdot c$ for some $c > 1$. The resulting vector of betas, $B_1 C\beta$, will have the desired mean $\bar{\beta}^*$. For the construction of the second matrix, B_2, use the vector $B_1 C\beta$ instead of $C\beta$ in equations (A26) and (A28), change $\sigma_{\beta\bullet}$ to $\sigma_\beta \cdot (1/c)$, and then again follow equations (A31) to (A38). After this second repackaging, the cross-sectional variance of the betas is the desired value $\sigma_{\beta\bullet}$. The value of R^2_{OLS} does not change in either of these repackagings.

Proof of Proposition 3: We first define the 2×2 matrix,

$$\begin{bmatrix} L & M \\ M & N \end{bmatrix} = \begin{bmatrix} \iota'V^{-1}\iota & \iota'V^{-1}E \\ \iota'V^{-1}E & E'V^{-1}E \end{bmatrix} \tag{A50}$$

and its determinant,

$$D = LN - M^2. \tag{A51}$$

As is well known (Roll (1977)),

$$\mu_g = \frac{M}{L}, \tag{A52}$$

$$\sigma_g^2 = \frac{1}{L}, \tag{A53}$$

and if (μ, σ^2) is a point on the minimum variance boundary, then

$$\sigma^2 = \frac{(L\mu^2 - 2M\mu + N)}{D}. \tag{A54}$$

Equation (A54) can then be rewritten as:

$$\sigma^2 - \frac{1}{L} = \frac{L}{D}\left(\mu - \frac{M}{L}\right)^2. \tag{A55}$$

By construction, (μ_p, σ_y^2) and (μ_x, σ_p^2) are on the minimum variance boundary. Using equations (A52), (A53), and (A55) we get

$$\sigma_y^2 - \sigma_g^2 = \frac{L}{D}(\mu_p - \mu_g)^2 \quad \text{and} \tag{A56}$$

$$\sigma_p^2 - \sigma_g^2 = \frac{L}{D}(\mu_x - \mu_g)^2. \tag{A57}$$

Dividing equation (A56) by (A57) gives

$$\left(\frac{\mu_p - \mu_g}{\mu_x - \mu_g}\right)^2 = \left(\frac{\sigma_y^2 - \sigma_g^2}{\sigma_p^2 - \sigma_g^2}\right). \tag{A58}$$

Equation (13) follows from (A58) and the definition of ψ in equation (12).

Proof of Proposition 4: The geometric analysis of the GLS coefficients in Roll (1985) may be used as a starting point for this proof. For the sake of clarity, we provide a complete proof. Observe that

$$X = \left[\iota \quad \frac{1}{w_p' V w_p} V w_p \right],$$
(A59)

so

$$X'V^{-1}X = \begin{bmatrix} \iota'V^{-1}\iota & \dfrac{1}{w_p' V w_p} \\ \dfrac{1}{w_p' V w_p} & \dfrac{1}{w_p' V w_p} \end{bmatrix} = \frac{1}{\sigma_p^2}\begin{bmatrix} L\sigma_p^2 & 1 \\ 1 & 1 \end{bmatrix},$$
(A60)

$$(X'V^{-1}X)^{-1} = \frac{\sigma_p^2}{L\sigma_p^2 - 1}\begin{bmatrix} 1 & -1 \\ -1 & L\sigma_p^2 \end{bmatrix},$$
(A61)

and

$$X'V^{-1}E = \begin{bmatrix} \iota'V^{-1}E \\ w_p' E \\ w_p' V w_p \end{bmatrix} = \begin{bmatrix} M \\ \mu_p \\ \sigma_p^2 \end{bmatrix}.$$
(A62)

Multiplying equations (A61) and (A62) gives

$$\phi = \frac{\sigma_p^2}{L\sigma_p^2 - 1}\begin{bmatrix} M - \dfrac{\mu_p}{\sigma_p^2} \\ L\mu_p - M \end{bmatrix}.$$
(A63)

Using equations (A52) and (A53), the second element of ϕ in equation (A63) can be written as

$$\phi_2 = \left(\frac{\sigma_p^2}{\sigma_p^2 - \sigma_g^2} \right)(\mu_p - \mu_g).$$
(A64)

This expression for ϕ_2 is presented also by Roll (1985). The expression in equation (18) is obtained by observing that, since portfolio x is on the minimum-variance boundary, we can write μ_g as

$$\mu_g = \mu_{x0} + (\mu_x - \mu_{x0})\frac{\text{cov}\{r_g, r_x\}}{\sigma_x^2}$$

$$= \mu_{x0} + (\mu_x - \mu_{x0})\frac{\sigma_g^2}{\sigma_p^2},$$
(A65)

where the second line follows by substituting σ_p^2 for σ_x^2 (equal by construction) and from the property that every asset has covariance σ_g^2 with the global minimum-variance portfolio (Roll (1977)). Equation (A65) can be rewritten as

$$\sigma_p^2 = \sigma_g^2 \frac{(\mu_x - \mu_{x0})}{(\mu_g - \mu_{x0})} \qquad (A66)$$

Substituting equation (A66) for σ_p^2 in (A64), simplifying, and using the definition of ψ_p in equation (12) gives equation (18). The expression for ϕ_1 in equation (19) follows directly by substituting equations (A52), (A53), and (A65) into the first element of ϕ in equation (A63) and simplifying.

Proof of Proposition 5: Equation (20) can be rewritten as:

$$1 - R_{GLS}^2 = \frac{(E - X\phi)'V^{-1}(E - X\phi)}{(E - \iota\bar{\mu})'V^{-1}(E - \iota\bar{\mu})}, \qquad (A67)$$

Through straightforward algebra, using equations (A50) to (A63), one can express the numerator of $(1 - R_{GLS}^2)$ in equation (A67) as

$$(E - X\phi)'V^{-1}(E - X\phi) = \frac{L\mu_p^2 - 2M\mu_p + N - D\sigma_p^2}{1 - L\sigma_p^2}$$

$$= \frac{D\left(\sigma_p^2 - \sigma_y^2\right)}{L\left(\sigma_p^2 - \sigma_g^2\right)} \qquad (A68)$$

where the second line makes use of the equation for the minimum-variance boundary in equation (A54),

$$\sigma_y^2 = \left(L\mu_p^2 - 2M\mu_p + N\right)/D. \qquad (A69)$$

The denominator of $(1 - R_{GLS}^2)$ can be expressed, using equations (21), (A50), and (A51), as

$$(E - \iota\bar{\mu})'V^{-1}(E - \iota\bar{\mu}) = \frac{D}{L}. \qquad (A70)$$

Taking one minus the ratio of (A68) to (A70) gives

$$R_{GLS}^2 = \frac{\left(\sigma_y^2 - \sigma_g^2\right)}{\left(\sigma_p^2 - \sigma_g^2\right)}, \qquad (A71)$$

which is equal to ψ_p^2 using Proposition 3.

Proof of Proposition 6: Since $w(\hat{E}; \sigma^2)$ is the solution to the portfolio maximization problem in equations (24) to (26), there exist scalars $\zeta_1 > 0$ and ζ_2 such that the following first-order condition is satisfied:

$$w(\hat{E}; \sigma^2) = \zeta_1 V^{-1}\hat{E} + \zeta_2 V^{-1}\iota$$

$$= \zeta_1 V^{-1}Za + \zeta_2 V^{-1}\iota, \qquad (A72)$$

where the second line uses equation (23). The maximization problem's constraints imply that

$$\zeta_2 = \frac{1}{L}(1 - \zeta_1 \iota' V^{-1} Za), \quad \text{and} \tag{A73}$$

$$\zeta_1 = \left(\frac{L\sigma^2 - 1}{La' Z' V^{-1} Za - (\iota' V^{-1} Za)^2} \right)^{1/2}. \tag{A74}$$

Using equations (A50), (A73), and (A74), the expected return $[\,w(\hat{E};\sigma^2)]'E$ can be written as

$$[w(\hat{E};\sigma^2)]'E = \frac{M}{L} + \zeta_1 \left[(E'V^{-1}Za) - \frac{M}{L}(\iota'V^{-1}Za) \right]. \tag{A75}$$

Recall that $\delta = (Z'V^{-1}Z)^{-1}Z'V^{-1}E$. Let d_1 be an n-vector with 1 in the first element and 0 elsewhere. Noting that the first column of Z is ι, it is easily verified that

$$Zd_1 = \iota, \tag{A76}$$

$$d_1 = (Z'V^{-1}Z)^{-1}Z'V^{-1}\iota, \tag{A77}$$

$$\delta'Z'V^{-1}\iota = E'V^{-1}Zd_1 = E'V^{-1}\iota = M, \quad \text{and} \tag{A78}$$

$$\iota'V^{-1}Zd_1 = d_1'Z'V^{-1}Zd_1 = \iota'V^{-1}\iota = L. \tag{A79}$$

Define

$$K \equiv E'V^{-1}Z\delta = (E'V^{-1}Z)(Z'V^{-1}Z)^{-1}(Z'V^{-1}E), \tag{A80}$$

and note that $K \geq (M^2/L)$, using equations (A76) to (A79) and the Cauchy-Schwarz inequality. For any n-vector a there exist scalars c_1 and c_2 and an n-vector u such that

$$a = c_1\delta + c_2 d_1 + u, \tag{A81}$$

$$u'(Z'V^{-1}Z)d_1 = u'Z'V^{-1}\iota = 0, \quad \text{and} \tag{A82}$$

$$u'(Z'V^{-1}Z)\delta = u'Z'V^{-1}E = 0. \tag{A83}$$

Maximizing the expected return $[w(\hat{E};\sigma^2)]'E$ with respect to a is, therefore, equivalent to maximizing the expected return with respect to c_1, c_2, and an n-vector u that satisfies equations (A82) and (A83). Using equations (A78), (A79), (A82), and (A83), we get

$$\iota'V^{-1}Za = c_1(\iota'V^{-1}Z\delta) + c_2(\iota'V^{-1}Zd_1) + (\iota'V^{-1}Zu)$$
$$= c_1 M + c_2 L, \tag{A84}$$

$$E'V^{-1}Za = c_1(E'V^{-1}Z\delta) + c_2(E'V^{-1}Zd_1) + (E'V^{-1}Zu)$$
$$= c_1 K + c_2 M, \quad \text{and} \tag{A85}$$

$$a'Z'V^{-1}Za = c_1^2 K + c_2^2 L + 2c_1 c_2 M + u'Z'V^{-1}Zu. \tag{A86}$$

Substituting equations (A84) to (A86) into equations (A74) and (A75) gives

$$[w(\hat{E}; \sigma^2)]'E = \frac{M}{L} + \frac{(L\sigma^2 - 1)^{1/2} c_1(KL - M^2)}{[c_1^2(KL - M^2) + (u'Z'V^{-1}Zu)]^{1/2} L}. \quad (A87)$$

Let $c_2 = 0$, since equation (A87) does not depend on c_2. The maximum must occur with $c_1 > 0$, since the denominator and the other factors in the numerator are positive. For any $c_1 > 0$, the maximum occurs at $u = 0$ and does not depend on c_1. Thus, let $c_1 = 1$, which implies the maximum occurs at $a = \delta$ or $\hat{E} = Z\delta = E^\dagger$.

Proof of Proposition 7: We first observe that $(E - Z\delta)$ can be written as

$$(E - Z\delta) = [I - Z(Z'V^{-1}Z)^{-1}Z'V^{-1}]E, \quad (A88)$$

which, when substituted into the numerator of $(1 - R_{GLS}^2)$, using equation (30), provides

$$(E - Z\delta)'V^{-1}(E - Z\delta) \quad (A89)$$
$$= E'[I - Z(Z'V^{-1}Z)^{-1}Z'V^{-1}]'V^{-1}[I - Z(Z'V^{-1}Z)^{-1}Z'V^{-1}]E$$
$$= E'V^{-1}E - E'V^{-1}Z(Z'V^{-1}Z)^{-1}Z'V^{-1}E$$
$$= N - K \quad (A90)$$

where the last line uses equations (A50) and (A80). The denominator of $1 - R_{GLS}^2$ can be expressed, using equations (21), (A50), and (A51), as

$$(E - \iota\bar{\mu})'V^{-1}(E - \iota\bar{\mu}) = \frac{D}{L}. \quad (A91)$$

Taking one minus the ratio of equations (A90) to (A91) and using equation (A51) gives

$$R_{GLS}^2 = \frac{(KL - M^2)}{D}. \quad (A92)$$

Let μ_q and σ_q^2 denote the mean and variance of the return on the portfolio q, respectively. By Proposition 3,

$$\psi_q^2 = \frac{\sigma_y^2 - \sigma_g^2}{\sigma_q^2 - \sigma_g^2}, \quad (A93)$$

where σ_y^2 denotes here the variance of the minimum-variance portfolio with mean return μ_q. Equation (A56) implies that the numerator of equation

Portfolio Inefficiency and Cross-section of Expected Returns   183

(A93) can be written as

$$\sigma_y^2 - \sigma_g^2 = \frac{L}{D}(\mu_q - \mu_g)^2. \tag{A94}$$

Rewriting the maximized value of equation (A87) in terms of μ_q, σ_q^2, and μ_g gives:

$$(\mu_q - \mu_g)^2 = \frac{(\sigma_q^2 - \sigma_g^2)(KL - M^2)}{L}, \tag{A95}$$

which implies that the denominator of equation (A93) can be written as:

$$\sigma_q^2 - \sigma_g^2 = \frac{L(\mu_q - \mu_g)^2}{KL - M^2}. \tag{A96}$$

Dividing equation (A94) by (A96) yields

$$\psi_q^2 = \frac{(KL - M^2)}{D} = R_{GLS}^2, \tag{A97}$$

where the second equality is based on equation (A92).

REFERENCES

Amihud, Yakov, Bent Jesper Christensen, and Haim Mendelson, 1992, Further evidence on the risk-return relationship, Working paper, New York University and Stanford University.

Amsler, Christine E., and Peter Schmidt, 1985, A Monte Carlo investigation of the accuracy of multivariate CAPM tests, *Journal of Financial Economics* 14, 359–375.

Black, Fischer, 1972, Capital market equilibrium with restricted borrowing, *Journal of Business* 45, 444–455.

Fama, Eugene F., 1976, *Foundations of Finance* (Basic Books, New York).

——, and Kenneth R. French, 1992, The cross-section of expected stock returns, *Journal of Finance* 47, 427–465.

Gibbons, Michael R., Stephen A. Ross, and Jay Shanken, 1989, A test of the efficiency of a given portfolio, *Econometrica* 57, 1121–1152.

Grauer, Robert R., 1994, Tests of the capital asset pricing model based on the cross-section of expected returns, Working paper, Simon Fraser University.

Huberman, Gur, Shmuel Kandel, and Robert F. Stambaugh, 1987, Mimicking portfolios and exact arbitrage pricing, *Journal of Finance* 42, 1–9.

Jagannathan, Ravi, and Zhenyu Wang, 1994, The conditional CAPM and the cross section of average stock returns, Working paper, University of Minnesota.

Kandel, Shmuel, and Robert F. Stambaugh, 1987, On correlations and inferences about mean-variance efficiency, *Journal of Financial Economics* 18, 61–90.

——, 1989, A mean-variance framework for tests of asset pricing models, *Review of Financial Studies* 2, 125–156.

Kandel, Shmuel, Robert McCulloch, and Robert F. Stambaugh, 1995, Bayesian inference and portfolio efficiency, *Review of Financial Studies*, Forthcoming.

Lintner, John, 1965, The valuation of risk assets and the selection of risky investments in stock portfolios and capital budgets, *Review of Economics and Statistics* 47, 13–37.

Roll, Richard, 1977, A critique of the asset pricing theory's tests; Part 1: On past and potential testability of the theory, *Journal of Financial Economics* 4, 129–176.

———, 1985, A note on the geometry of Shanken's CSR T^2 test for mean/variance efficiency, *Journal of Financial Economics* 14, 349–357.

———, and Stephen A. Ross, 1994, On the cross-sectional relation between expected returns and betas, *Journal of Finance*, 49, 101–121.

Ross, Stephen A., 1977, The capital asset pricing model (CAPM), short-sale restrictions and related issues, *Journal of Finance* 32, 177–183.

Shanken, Jay, 1985, Multivariate tests of the zero-beta CAPM, *Journal of Financial Economics* 14, 327–348.

———, 1987, Multivariate proxies and asset pricing relations: Living with the Roll critique, *Journal of Financial Economics* 18, 91–110.

———, 1992, On the estimation of beta-pricing models, *The Review of Financial Studies* 5, 1–33.

Sharpe, William F., 1964, Capital asset prices: A theory of market equilibrium under conditions of risk, *Journal of Finance* 19, 425–442.

[6]

THE JOURNAL OF FINANCE • VOL. LIV, NO. 2 • APRIL 1999

On the Cross-Sectional Relation between Expected Returns, Betas, and Size

ROBERT R. GRAUER*

ABSTRACT

In this paper, I set up scenarios where the mean-variance capital asset pricing model is true and where it is false. Then I investigate whether the coefficients from regressions of population expected excess returns on population betas, and expected excess returns on betas and size, allow us to distinguish between the scenarios. I show that the coefficients from either ordinary least squares or generalized least squares regressions do not allow us to tell whether the model is true or false.

EACH OF THE FOLLOWING FIVE statements has implications for how we might judge whether the Sharpe (1964)–Lintner (1965) mean-variance capital asset pricing model (MV CAPM) is true or false. First, the market portfolio is MV efficient. Second, there is at least one positively weighted efficient portfolio. Third, in the riskless asset version of the model, the market portfolio is the tangency portfolio—it is the point of tangency between a ray emanating from the riskless interest rate and the minimum-variance frontier of risky assets. Fourth, there is a linear relation between the expected returns and market betas of securities, that is, securities plot on the security market line (SML). Fifth, market betas are the only measures of risk needed to explain the cross section of expected returns. If the riskless asset version of the model holds exactly, the fourth and fifth statements have two implications. Either an ordinary least squares (OLS) or a generalized least squares (GLS) regression of population expected excess rates of return on population market portfolio betas will have a zero intercept and a slope equal to the expected excess return on the market.[1] Furthermore, either an OLS or a

* Department of Economics, Faculty of Business Administration, Simon Fraser University. Financial support from the Social Sciences and Humanities Research Council of Canada is greatly appreciated as is the capable assistance of Maciek Kon, John Janmaat, and William Ting. I thank Reo Audette, Avi Bick, George Blazenko, Peter Clarkson, Wayne Ferson, John Heaney, Burton Hollifield, Avi Kamara, Peter Klein, Andy Siegel, Simon Wheatley, and especially John Herzog, Ray Koopman, John Janmaat, two anonymous referees, and the editor René Stulz for extremely helpful comments. But, naturally, I am responsible for both interpretation and errors. The paper was presented at Simon Fraser University, the Pacific Northwest Finance Conference in Seattle, and the Northern Finance Association Meetings in Vancouver. It was originally titled: "Tests of the Capital Asset Pricing Model Based on the Cross-Section of Expected Returns."

[1] An expected excess rate of return is defined as an expected rate of return less the riskless interest rate.

GLS regression of expected excess returns on market portfolio betas and size will have the same intercept and slope for the beta variable as the previous regression and a zero slope for the size variable.

In this paper, I set up scenarios where the CAPM is true and where it is false. When the CAPM is true, all five statements hold exactly. When the CAPM is false, all the statements are almost true—in some scenarios. In other scenarios, some of the statements are almost true—others are grossly violated. I then investigate whether the coefficients from regressions of population expected excess returns on population betas, and expected excess returns on betas and size, allow us to distinguish between the scenarios. I show that the OLS and GLS regression coefficients do not allow us to distinguish between the true and false scenarios.

In the early 1970s, Black, Jensen, and Scholes (1972), Blume and Friend (1973), and Fama and MacBeth (1973) produced the first extensive tests of the model. They focus on the cross-sectional expected return-beta trade-off and the special prediction of the Sharpe–Lintner version of the model that the returns on "zero-beta" or "orthogonal" portfolios (portfolios whose returns are uncorrelated with the returns on the market portfolio) have expected returns equal to the riskless rate of interest. Their findings are well known. The average return-beta plot is almost linear, but the estimated slope of the SML is too flat and the intercept too high. The evidence is interpreted as providing grounds for rejection of the Sharpe–Lintner model and as being consistent with Black's (1972) zero-beta version.

However, two types of difficulties with the tests have been identified. First, there are serious doubts regarding the validity of the tests that focus on either financial or logical rather than statistical or empirical considerations. Roll's (1977) critique is the best known. He argues that the theory is equivalent to the assertion that the market portfolio is MV efficient. Insofar as proxies—that include only a subset of assets—are used for the market portfolio, the CAPM is not being tested. Second, there are several empirical contradictions of the model that have been highlighted in a recent article by Fama and French (1992). They report that size and book-to-market equity combine to capture the cross-sectional variation in average stock returns associated with market beta, size, leverage, book-to-market equity, and earnings-to-price ratios. Arguably the size effect, first documented by Banz (1981) and Reinganum (1981), is the most important, and, therefore, I focus on it exclusively. Fama and French run OLS regressions of: (1) means on betas, calculated relative to a number of proxies for the market portfolio, (2) means on betas and size, and (3) means on size. In the regression of means on betas, the slope is small, positive, and statistically insignificant. In the regression of means on betas and size, the beta coefficient is negative and statistically insignificant, and the size coefficient is negative and statistically significant. In the regression of means on size, the slope is negative and statistically significant. Together these results are taken to be strong evidence against the CAPM.

Papers closely related to this study (Roll and Ross (1994) and Kandel and Stambaugh (1995)), highlight the danger of focusing exclusively on mean-beta space.[2] Roll and Ross derive the set of all possible portfolios that produce a given value for the cross-sectional slope in an OLS regression of population expected returns on population betas. More specifically, they show a market proxy can be nearly MV efficient in mean-variance space and produce a zero slope in an OLS regression of means on that portfolio's betas. Kandel and Stambaugh, also working with population parameters, demonstrate that a market proxy can be almost MV efficient and produce no relationship between means and betas using OLS. Conversely, when the set of securities is repackaged into an alternative set that generates the same portfolio opportunities, there can be a near perfect OLS fit between means and betas calculated relative to a proxy that is grossly inefficient in mean-variance space. See, for example, Figure 1 in Kandel and Stambaugh (1995). More importantly, they show that, in a GLS regression of mean returns on betas, the slope and R^2 are determined uniquely by the mean-variance location of the market index relative to the minimum-variance boundary. In contrast to OLS, GLS gives a zero slope only if the mean return on the market index equals that of the global minimum-variance portfolio. This latter result was derived earlier by Roll (1985)—see his Figure 1. Finally, Kandel and Stambaugh report that their results may be extended to a multi-factor model. Once again, repackaging the assets can produce essentially any desired OLS coefficients and R^2.

This paper is similar in spirit to the papers by Roll (1977), Roll and Ross (1994), and Kandel and Stambaugh (1995). However, it differs from the later two in three significant ways. First, the MV CAPM predicts that prices will adjust until the market portfolio is MV efficient. Or, to put it another way, a precondition for the CAPM to hold is that there is at least one positively weighted efficient portfolio. Somewhat surprisingly, neither Roll and Ross nor Kandel and Stambaugh verify whether the minimum-variance frontier contains a positively weighted portfolio. Thus, we cannot be sure whether their results hold if the CAPM is true, that is, if the positively weighted market portfolio is MV efficient. Second, any reasonable proxy portfolio should contain positive weights. Roll and Ross, for example, note that readers of an earlier version of their paper speculated that the central results may be driven by short positions in the market proxies. (See Roll and Ross (1994), Sec. II.B, Plausibility and Short Positions, pp. 111–113.) Roll and Ross are able to construct one example where a proxy portfolio contains positive weights, but the proxies in Stambaugh and Kandel's (1995) Figure 1 do not contain positive weights.[3]

---

[2] The first version of this paper was completed before I was aware of these papers.

[3] It is clear that the proxy portfolios p and q in Kandel and Stambaugh's (1995) Figure 1 are not positively weighted. First, p and q have higher expected returns than the 10 size portfolios. Second, all the betas with respect to both p and q are less than one. The only way this can happen is if p and q have (some) negative weights.

By way of contrast, I (like Roll) examine two scenarios: one where the CAPM is true, the other where it is false. In the first scenario, the Sharpe–Lintner model holds exactly. In mean-standard deviation space, the positively weighted market portfolio is the MV efficient tangency portfolio. In mean-beta space, securities plot on the SML. In the second scenario, the CAPM is false. In mean-standard deviation space, the position of the now inefficient market portfolio and the tangency portfolio differ—sometimes dramatically—and no positively weighted portfolios plot on the minimum-variance frontier of risky assets. In mean-beta space, securities do not plot on the SML. Second, my examples are consistent with a size effect; that is, low (high) mean assets have high (low) weights in the market portfolio. Third, with one exception, I only employ the apparently innocuous equal-weighted portfolio as a positively weighted proxy for the market portfolio—a proxy commonly employed in empirical work[4] (see, for example, Black et al. (1972), Fama and MacBeth (1973), or Fama and French (1992)).

In these scenarios, I show two main results. First, when the CAPM is true, coefficients of OLS and GLS regressions employing proxy portfolios—that are almost efficient—can incorrectly indicate that the model is false. Second, and perhaps more important, when the CAPM is false, coefficients of OLS, GLS, or both OLS and GLS regressions employing the market portfolio can incorrectly indicate that the model is true.

The paper proceeds as follows. Section I presents the details of the experimental design. Section II records and interprets the results. Section III summarizes the paper.

I. The Experimental Design

A. Examples where the CAPM is True

The data set employed in the examples consists of 10 size portfolios compiled from all New York Stock Exchange and American Stock Exchange stocks contained in the Center for Research in Security Prices database. Returns from the 1926 to 1989 period are employed. The covariance matrix is calculated from the historical return data. It serves as the population covariance matrix for the examples. Then, following Best and Grauer (1985), a set of (Σ, x_m)-compatible means—or equivalently SML means—is calculated from

$$\mu = \theta_1 \iota + \theta_2 \beta_m, \tag{1}$$

---

[4] An equal-weighted portfolio is apparently innocuous in two senses. First, equal-weighted portfolios have positive weights and have been employed extensively in empirical work. Second, the weights in an equal-weighted portfolio are not chosen to produce a specific result, for example, a zero slope in an OLS regression of means on betas. On the other hand, it has never been entirely clear why anyone would choose an equal-weighted portfolio as a proxy for the value-weighted market portfolio.

Relation between Expected Returns, Betas, and Size   777

where μ, ι, and $\mathbf{x}_m$ are n-vectors containing the expected rates of return on the n-assets, ones, and the weights in the market portfolio, respectively; Σ is an $n \times n$ positive-definite covariance matrix of asset returns; θ_1 and θ_2 are (positive) scalar constants; and $\boldsymbol{\beta}_m = (\Sigma\mathbf{x}_m)/(\mathbf{x}_m'\Sigma\mathbf{x}_m)$ is an n-vector of market portfolio betas; for example, the jth element of $\boldsymbol{\beta}_m$ is the covariance of the return on security j with the return on the market portfolio divided by the variance of the return on the market portfolio.

The parameters θ_1 and θ_2 are chosen so that the Sharpe–Lintner version of the CAPM holds exactly. θ_1 is chosen so that the zero-beta rate is equal to the risk-free rate of 0.5 percent per month (6 percent per annum), and θ_2 is chosen so that the expected excess return on the MV efficient market portfolio is 0.75 percent per month. This latter value corresponds to the excess return of the Standard & Poor's 500 Index over Treasury bills during the last half century. Thus, the population expected returns in percentage per month are

$$\mu = 0.5\iota + 0.75\boldsymbol{\beta}_m \tag{2}$$

when the hypothesis "the market portfolio is MV efficient" is true.

The CAPM makes no predictions about the magnitude of the weights in the market portfolio, but in order to examine the size effect I assign the market portfolio weights to be consistent with the empirical observation that large (small) firms have low (high) expected returns. I take the average capitalization weights of the decile portfolios over the 1926 to 1992 period to be the weights in the market portfolio. The weights range from 62.29 percent (86.24 percent) in the largest (largest three) capitalization decile(s) to 0.23 percent (1.64 percent) in the smallest (smallest three) capitalization decile(s).[5]

Having set up a world where the Sharpe–Lintner version of the CAPM holds exactly, I then run the following OLS and GLS regressions

$$\mu_j - r = b_0 + b_1\,\text{beta}_j + \epsilon_j \tag{3}$$

$$\mu_j - r = b_0 + b_1\,\text{beta}_j + b_2\,\text{size}_j + \epsilon_j \tag{4}$$

$$\mu_j - r = b_0 + b_1\,\text{size}_j + \epsilon_j \tag{5}$$

---

[5] Given a covariance matrix, it is easy to make any portfolio MV efficient. However, in general, the SML means from equation (1) will not be consistent with the scenario of the low-mean asset having the largest weight in the market portfolio. Nonetheless, in the 10 size portfolios universe, the average capitalization weights and the means from equation (1) are exactly consistent with the low-mean, high-weight scenario.

where the size variable is defined to be the market portfolio weights[6] and both market portfolio betas and proxy portfolio betas are employed. (The betas are calculated directly from the covariance matrix and the portfolio weights; that is, $\boldsymbol{\beta}_x = (\Sigma \mathbf{x})/(\mathbf{x}'\Sigma \mathbf{x})$, where the portfolio $\mathbf{x}$ may be either the market portfolio or a proxy portfolio.) With market portfolio betas in equation (3), $b_0 = 0$, and $b_1 = \mu_m - r$. In addition, size will have no effect whatsoever. That is, in equation (4) $b_0 = 0$, $b_1 = \mu_m - r$, and $b_2 = 0$. With proxy portfolio betas, it appears to be an open question what the slope and intercept—as well as the interpretation of them—should be. On the one hand, Roll (1977) argues that we can conclude nothing about the CAPM, unless we observe the true market portfolio. On the other hand, Fama (1991) and Fama and French (1992), among others—citing Stambaugh's (1982) empirical evidence that the tests are not sensitive to the proxy for the market—suggest that Roll's critique is overstated. But, in the examples in this paper, we know that the market portfolio is MV efficient. Therefore, any size effect will simply be an artifact arising from the use of proxy portfolio betas. The last regression (5) documents the strength of the relation between expected excess returns and size.

To summarize, in asset universes where the riskless asset version of the CAPM is true, I run OLS and GLS regressions of population expected excess returns on population betas (market portfolio betas and proxy portfolio betas), expected excess returns on betas and size, and expected excess returns on size. In mean-beta space, I plot the data, the OLS regression line, and the SML. (Note that when I use proxy portfolio betas, I still call the line passing through the riskless interest rate and the proxy portfolio the SML. This is a misnomer, but it is consistent with the nomenclature employed in the empirical literature.) In mean-standard deviation space, I plot the data, the minimum-variance frontier of risky assets, and the tangency portfolio. I also keep track of positively weighted minimum-variance portfolios.

B. Examples where the CAPM is False

If the CAPM is true, there is an exact linear trade-off between expected returns and market portfolio betas. If the CAPM is false, securities do not plot on the SML. Therefore, I construct examples where the CAPM is false by perturbing the SML means. But I do so in ways that make the CAPM appear to be true according to the coefficients of the cross-sectional regressions (3) and (4). Roughly speaking, I make the CAPM false by finding a set of perturbations in the SML means that is orthogonal to the betas, the market weights, and a vector of ones.

More specifically, consider the general linear regression model

$$\mathbf{y} = \mathbf{XB} + \boldsymbol{\epsilon},$$

---

[6] In most empirical studies the size of a firm is defined as the natural log of its equity where equity is equal to the number of shares times the price per share.

where $\mathbf{y}$ is an n-vector containing n-observations on the dependent variable, $\mathbf{X}$ is an $n \times k$ matrix containing n-observations on the k-independent variables, $\mathbf{B}$ is a k-vector of parameters, and ϵ is an n-vector of random errors. In an OLS regression, it is assumed that the error terms are independently and identically distributed (i.i.d.) with zero means and covariance matrix $\Sigma = \sigma^2 \mathbf{I}$, where $\mathbf{I}$ is an $n \times n$ identity matrix. The OLS estimated coefficients are calculated as

$$\mathbf{b}^{\text{ols}} = (\mathbf{X}'\mathbf{X})^{-1}\mathbf{X}'\mathbf{y}. \tag{6}$$

In a regression of expected excess returns on betas, $\mathbf{y}$ contains the expected excess returns, and $\mathbf{X} = [\boldsymbol{\iota} : \boldsymbol{\beta}]$ is an $n \times 2$ matrix, containing ones in the first column, and either market portfolio betas or proxy portfolio betas in the second column. In the regression of expected excess returns on betas and size, $\mathbf{y}$ again contains the expected excess returns, and $\mathbf{X} = [\boldsymbol{\iota} : \boldsymbol{\beta} : \mathbf{x}_m]$ is an $n \times 3$ matrix of ones, betas, and size—market-portfolio weights.

If the Sharpe–Lintner version of the model is true, there is an exact linear relation between expected returns and market portfolio betas. If the CAPM is false, the relation between expected returns and market betas is not linear. However, regressions of population expected excess returns on population market portfolio betas (or proxy portfolio betas) and population expected excess returns on population betas and size can yield exactly the same intercepts and slopes as in the case where the model is true—or the intercepts and slopes can be made to have practically any other values one might wish. To see this, let

$$\mathbf{y} = \boldsymbol{\mu} + \mathbf{e},$$

where $\mathbf{e}$ is an n-vector containing deviations from the security market line means $\boldsymbol{\mu}$; for example, $\mathbf{e} = \Delta\boldsymbol{\mu}$. In this case, the coefficients are

$$\mathbf{b}^{\text{ols}} = (\mathbf{X}'\mathbf{X})^{-1}\mathbf{X}'\boldsymbol{\mu} + (\mathbf{X}'\mathbf{X})^{-1}\mathbf{X}'\mathbf{e} = \mathbf{b}_0^{\text{ols}} + \Delta\mathbf{b}^{\text{ols}}. \tag{7}$$

Clearly, $\mathbf{b}_0^{\text{ols}} = (\mathbf{X}'\mathbf{X})^{-1}\mathbf{X}'\boldsymbol{\mu}$ gives the coefficients when the CAPM is true, and $\Delta\mathbf{b}^{\text{ols}} = (\mathbf{X}'\mathbf{X})^{-1}\mathbf{X}'\mathbf{e}$ represents the change in the coefficients. If we set

$$\Delta\mathbf{b}^{\text{ols}} = (\mathbf{X}'\mathbf{X})^{-1}\mathbf{X}'\mathbf{e} = \mathbf{0}, \tag{8}$$

where $\mathbf{0}$ is a k-vector of zeros, we have exactly the same OLS coefficients as when the CAPM is true. On the other hand, if we set $\Delta\mathbf{b}^{\text{ols}}$ equal to a vector of values other than zeros, we can generate practically any values for the intercept and slope—or intercept and slopes if we include size in the regression.

Instead of restricting the coefficients in equation (8), however, we can simply set $\mathbf{X}'\mathbf{e} = \mathbf{0}$. In the case of an OLS regression of expected excess returns on betas and size the restrictions are

$$\boldsymbol{\iota}'\mathbf{e} = 0, \qquad \boldsymbol{\beta}'\mathbf{e} = 0, \quad \text{and} \quad \mathbf{x}_m'\mathbf{e} = 0. \tag{9}$$

The advantage of writing the restrictions in this manner is that they provide insights about other variables in addition to the slopes and intercepts of the cross-sectional regressions. For example, the first and third restrictions say that the means of an equal-weighted proxy portfolio and the value-weighted market portfolio are unchanged from their original values.

In a GLS regression, the assumption that the error terms are i.i.d. is relaxed. In this case, the error terms are assumed to have zero means and covariance matrix $\mathbf{\Sigma}$. The GLS coefficients are

$$\mathbf{b}^{\mathbf{gls}} = (\mathbf{X}'\mathbf{\Sigma}^{-1}\mathbf{X})^{-1}\mathbf{X}'\mathbf{\Sigma}^{-1}\mathbf{y}.$$

If the CAPM is false, the GLS regressions of population expected excess returns on population betas and expected excess returns on betas and size can again yield exactly the same intercepts and slopes as in the case where the model is true. But the conditions for this to occur are slightly different than in the case of the OLS regressions. To see this, again let $\mathbf{y} = \mathbf{\mu} + \mathbf{e}$. Then, the GLS coefficients are

$$\mathbf{b}^{\mathbf{gls}} = (\mathbf{X}'\mathbf{\Sigma}^{-1}\mathbf{X})^{-1}\mathbf{X}'\mathbf{\Sigma}^{-1}\mathbf{\mu} + (\mathbf{X}'\mathbf{\Sigma}^{-1}\mathbf{X})^{-1}\mathbf{X}'\mathbf{\Sigma}^{-1}\mathbf{e} = \mathbf{b}_0^{\mathbf{gls}} + \mathbf{\Delta b}^{\mathbf{gls}}.$$

As in the case of OLS, $\mathbf{b}_0^{\mathbf{gls}} = (\mathbf{X}'\mathbf{\Sigma}^{-1}\mathbf{X})^{-1}\mathbf{X}'\mathbf{\Sigma}^{-1}\mathbf{\mu}$ gives the coefficients when the CAPM is true, and $\mathbf{\Delta b}^{\mathbf{gls}} = (\mathbf{X}'\mathbf{\Sigma}^{-1}\mathbf{X})^{-1}\mathbf{X}'\mathbf{\Sigma}^{-1}\mathbf{e}$ represents the change in the coefficients. As before, if we set

$$\mathbf{\Delta b}^{\mathbf{gls}} = (\mathbf{X}'\mathbf{\Sigma}^{-1}\mathbf{X})^{-1}\mathbf{X}'\mathbf{\Sigma}^{-1}\mathbf{e} = \mathbf{0}, \tag{10}$$

we have exactly the same GLS coefficients as when the CAPM is true. Or, more simply, in the case of a regression of expected excess returns on betas and size, we can set $\mathbf{X}'\mathbf{\Sigma}^{-1}\mathbf{e} = \mathbf{0}$ to yield

$$\mathbf{\iota}'\mathbf{\Sigma}^{-1}\mathbf{e} = 0, \quad \mathbf{\beta}'\mathbf{\Sigma}^{-1}\mathbf{e} = 0, \quad \text{and} \quad \mathbf{x}_m'\mathbf{\Sigma}^{-1}\mathbf{e} = 0. \tag{11}$$

Again, two of the three restrictions provide insights about other variables in addition to the coefficients of the cross-sectional regressions. The first restriction says that the mean of the global minimum-variance portfolio of risky assets remains unchanged. The second says that if the equal-weighted proxy portfolio is used to calculate the betas then $\mathbf{\beta} = n\mathbf{\Sigma}\mathbf{\iota}/(\mathbf{\iota}'\mathbf{\Sigma}\mathbf{\iota})$ and the GLS restriction $\mathbf{\beta}'\mathbf{\Sigma}^{-1}\mathbf{e} = 0$ reduces to the OLS restriction $\mathbf{\iota}'\mathbf{e} = 0$. Similarly, if the market portfolio is used to calculate the betas, $\mathbf{\beta} = \mathbf{\Sigma}\mathbf{x}_m/(\mathbf{x}_m'\mathbf{\Sigma}\mathbf{x}_m)$, and the GLS restriction $\mathbf{\beta}'\mathbf{\Sigma}^{-1}\mathbf{e} = 0$ reduces to the OLS restriction $\mathbf{x}_m'\mathbf{e} = 0$.

To summarize, I make the CAPM false by solving for a set of perturbations in the SML means that satisfy some subset of the restrictions in equations (8)–(11)—and, in one case, change the intercept and slope of a regression of expected excess returns on equal-weighted proxy portfolio betas. I then run the OLS and GLS regressions of expected excess returns on population

Relation between Expected Returns, Betas, and Size   781

betas, expected excess returns on betas and size, and expected excess returns on size, given in equations (3)–(5). Next, in mean-beta space, I plot the
data, the regression line, and the SML. In mean-standard deviation space, I
plot the data, the minimum-variance frontier of risky assets, and keep track
of the tangency portfolio and positively weighted minimum-variance portfolios.

II. The Results

Space limitations dictate that only a subset of the examples can be reported here. Therefore, I limit discussion to: (1) a 10 size-ranked portfolios
universe; (2) market portfolio betas and three instances of proxy portfolio
betas; and (3) examples where, with one exception, the tangency portfolio
deviates rather dramatically from the market portfolio—when the CAPM is
false. However, similar results are generated in 10, 20, and 50 asset universes as well as in a 20 beta-ranked portfolios universe.

The main results are reported in Table I and in Figures 1 to 5. Table I
contains the results for OLS and GLS regressions of population expected
excess returns on population betas and population expected excess returns
on population betas and size. The first panel of Table I and Figures 1 and 2
depict scenarios where the CAPM is true. The final five panels of Table I
and Figures 3–5 portray scenarios where the CAPM is false.

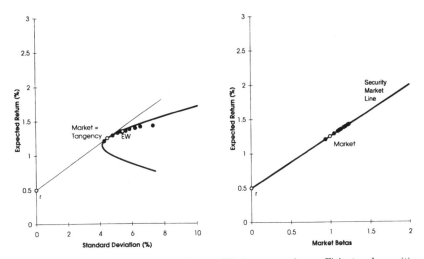

Figure 1. The CAPM is true. The market portfolio is mean-variance efficient and securities
plot on the security market line. Coefficients of ordinary least squares and generalized least
squares regressions of expected excess returns on market portfolio betas, and expected excess
returns on market portfolio betas and size, correctly indicate that the CAPM is true. See
Table I, Panel A.

Table I

Results for the Cross-Sectional Regressions

$$\mu_j - r = b_0 + b_1 \, beta_j + \epsilon_j$$

$$\mu_j - r = b_0 + b_1 \, beta_j + b_2 \, size_j + \epsilon_j.$$

In each panel, the risk-free rate is 0.5 percent and the expected return on the market portfolio is 1.25 percent. Thus, when the mean-variance capital asset pricing model (CAPM) is true, $b_0 = 0$ and $b_1 = \mu_m - r = 0.75$ percent in the first regression, and $b_0 = 0$, $b_1 = 0.75$ percent, and $b_2 = 0$ in the second. The first two rows in each panel employ market portfolio betas. Rows three and four in Panels A and F employ equal-weighted proxy portfolio betas. Rows six and seven in Panel A employ a Roll and Ross (1994) proxy portfolio that generates a zero slope in an ordinary least squares (OLS) regression of means on betas. The odd rows in each panel contain the results for OLS and the even rows contain the generalized least squares (GLS) results. In Panel A, the CAPM is true (see Figures 1 and 2). The Roll–Ross proxy portfolio (not shown in the figures) contains negative weights. Its mean equals that of the market portfolio and its standard deviation is only 27 basis points larger. In the remaining panels, the CAPM is false. In Panel B, the tangency portfolio's expected return is 1.35 percent (see Figure 3). In Panel C, the tangency portfolio's expected return is 2.5 percent (see Figure 4). In Panel D, the tangency portfolio's expected return is 26,654 percent. In Panel E, the tangency portfolio's expected return is −21,572 percent (see Figure 5). In Panel F, the tangency portfolio's expected return is 418 percent.

		b_0	b_1	R^2	b_0	b_1	b_2	R^2
				Panel A				
Value-weighted	OLS	0.00	0.75	1.00	0.00	0.75	0.00	1.00
Market portfolio	GLS	0.00	0.75	1.00	0.00	0.75	0.00	1.00
Equal-weighted	OLS	0.46	0.39	0.98	0.53	0.32	−0.07	0.98
Proxy portfolio	GLS	0.36	0.48	0.85	0.42	0.43	−0.04	0.87
Roll–Ross	OLS	0.85	0.00	0.00	1.38	−0.54	−0.35	0.89
Proxy portfolio	GLS	0.30	0.45	0.53	0.48	0.30	−0.09	0.64
				Panel B				
Value-weighted	OLS	0.77	0.00	0.00	1.42	−0.55	−0.29	0.48
Market portfolio	GLS	0.00	0.75	0.51	0.00	0.75	0.00	0.51
				Panel C				
Value-weighted	OLS	0.00	0.75	0.54	0.00	0.75	0.00	0.54
Market portfolio	GLS	0.00	0.75	0.08	0.00	0.75	0.00	0.08
				Panel D				
Value-weighted	OLS	0.00	0.75	0.01	0.00	0.75	0.00	0.01
Market portfolio	GLS	−4.71	5.46	0.05	−11.73	11.44	2.46	0.11
				Panel E				
Value-weighted	OLS	0.00	0.75	0.01	0.00	0.75	0.00	0.01
Market portfolio	GLS	−4.75	5.50	0.05	−11.84	11.54	2.48	0.11
				Panel F				
Value-weighted	OLS	0.00	0.75	0.00	0.00	0.75	0.00	0.00
Market portfolio	GLS	−1.10	1.85	0.00	−1.88	2.52	0.27	0.00
Equal-weighted	OLS	0.59	0.26	0.00	0.97	−0.08	−0.36	0.00
Proxy portfolio	GLS	0.00	0.85	0.00	0.00	0.85	−0.00	0.00

Relation between Expected Returns, Betas, and Size   783

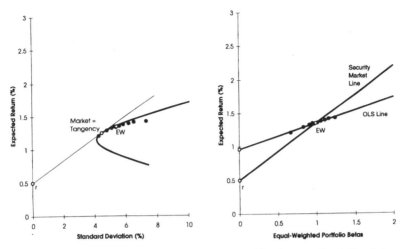

Figure 2. The CAPM is true. The equal-weighted proxy portfolio plots very close to the minimum-variance frontier of risky assets. But, coefficients of ordinary least squares regressions of expected excess returns on equal-weighted proxy portfolio betas, and expected excess returns on equal-weighted proxy portfolio betas and size, incorrectly indicate that the CAPM is false. See Table I, Panel A. Note that, consistent with the empirical literature, the line from the riskless asset through the equal-weighted proxy portfolio is called the security market line. A more accurate label might be the empirical security market line. Also note the difference in the magnitudes of the equal-weighted proxy portfolio betas in this figure and the market portfolio betas in Figure 1.

A. The CAPM Is True

The CAPM is true in a 10 size-ranked portfolios universe shown in Table I, Panel A, and in Figures 1 and 2. The first two rows of Panel A show that with market portfolio betas the coefficients of OLS and GLS regressions are exactly as predicted. That is, in the regression of population expected excess returns on population market portfolio betas, $b_0 = 0$, and $b_1 = \mu_m - r = 0.75$. And, in the regression of expected excess returns on market betas and size, $b_0 = 0$, $b_1 = \mu_m - r = 0.75$, and $b_2 = 0$.[7] Figure 1 contains the corresponding mean-standard deviation and mean-beta plots. The plots are the classic ones envisioned in theory: the market portfolio coincides with the tangency portfolio and securities plot on the SML.

When the CAPM is true, the only way the regression coefficients can lead us to believe that the model is false is if we employ a proxy for the market portfolio. The next two examples illustrate this possibility—one with a pos-

---

[7] In an OLS (GLS) regression of expected excess returns on size, not reported in Table I, the size coefficient is -0.30 (-0.15). When the CAPM is false, the size coefficient is unchanged if the coefficients in the regression of means on betas and means on betas and size are unchanged, as in, for example, Panels C through F for OLS, and in Panels B and C for GLS. In Panel B, the OLS size coefficient is -0.07. In Panels D and E, the GLS size coefficient is 0.19, and, in Panel F, it is -0.23.

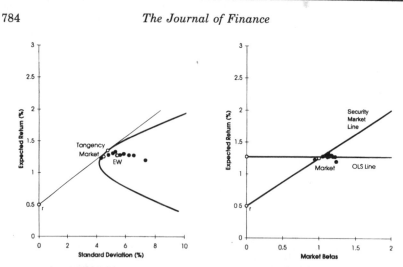

Figure 3. The CAPM is false. Although there are no positively weighted minimum variance portfolios, the market portfolio is almost mean-variance efficient. Yet, in an ordinary least squares (OLS) regression of expected excess returns on market portfolio betas, the slope is zero. And, in an OLS regression of expected excess returns on market portfolio betas and size, both slope coefficients are negative. Thus, the model appears to be dead wrong. On the other hand, coefficients of generalized least squares regressions of expected excess returns on market betas, and expected excess returns on market betas and size, incorrectly indicate that the CAPM is true. See Table I, Panel B.

itively weighted proxy, one without. First, Figure 2 shows that an equal-weighted proxy portfolio plots very close to the minimum-variance frontier of risky assets. Second, Figure 2 and rows three and four of Table I, Panel A, show that OLS and GLS regressions of expected excess returns on equal-weighted proxy portfolio betas are consistent with the well-known result found in Black et al. (1972): the intercept is too large and the slope is too flat. Third, in an OLS and a GLS regression of expected excess returns on equal-weighted portfolio betas and size, the size coefficient is negative. But the size effect is simply an artifact caused by using equal-weighted proxy portfolio betas instead of market portfolio betas.

The noteworthy aspect of this example is that both the MV-efficient market portfolio and the inefficient equal-weighted proxy portfolio contain all positive weights. In the 10 size-ranked portfolios universe, there are no positively weighted portfolios that produce zero slopes in OLS regressions of means on betas.[8] However, if we relax the requirement that the proxy portfolio should contain all positive weights, then a portfolio—with the same mean as the market portfolio and a standard deviation only 27 basis points

---

[8] In 10, 20, and 50 asset examples not reported in the paper, a weaker statement holds. There are no positively weighted portfolios on the minimum-variance frontier of portfolios that produce a zero slope in an OLS regression of means on betas. I verified this using the method described in Best and Grauer (1992).

Relation between Expected Returns, Betas, and Size   785

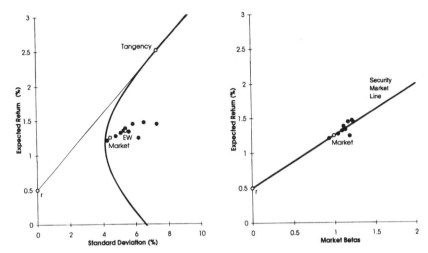

Figure 4. The CAPM is false. The CAPM is clearly false in mean-standard deviation space. The market portfolio is not mean-variance efficient and tangency portfolio's mean is 2.5 percent. However, coefficients of ordinary least squares and generalized least squares regressions of expected excess returns on market portfolio betas, and expected excess returns on market portfolio betas and size, incorrectly indicate that the CAPM is true. See Table I, Panel C.

larger—yields a zero slope in an OLS regression of means on betas. See the fifth and sixth rows of Table I, Panel A. The GLS slope is also too flat. Moreover, in an OLS and a GLS regression of means on betas and size, the size coefficient is negative.

B. The CAPM Is False

In the examples where the CAPM is false, there are no positively weighted minimum-variance portfolios. Nor are there any positively weighted portfolios on the minimum-variance frontier of portfolios that produce zero slopes in OLS regressions of means on betas. In light of this fact and the fact that there are no positively weighted portfolios that produce a zero slope in an OLS regression of means on betas when the CAPM is true, it is surprising to see that the positively weighted market portfolio produces a zero slope in an OLS regression of means on betas in the example shown in Figure 3 and in Table I, Panel B. The model does not look all that bad in mean-standard deviation space. The market portfolio plots very close to the minimum-variance frontier of risky assets and its expected return is only 10 basis less than that of the tangency portfolio. By way of contrast, the OLS and GLS regression coefficients support wildly divergent conclusions. In an OLS regression of expected excess return on market portfolio betas, the slope is zero, and in an OLS regression of expected excess return on market betas and size, both slope coefficients are negative. In other words, the model

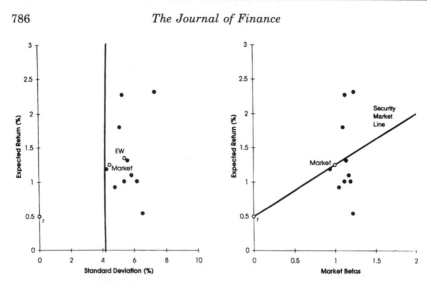

Figure 5. The CAPM is false. The CAPM is clearly false in mean-standard deviation space. The minimum-variance frontier appears to be a vertical line. The tangency portfolio has an expected return of $-21,572$ percent and standard deviation of $10,157$ percent. Yet, coefficients of ordinary least squares regressions of expected excess returns on market portfolio betas, and expected excess returns on market portfolio betas and size, incorrectly indicate that the CAPM is true. See Table I, Panel E.

appears to be dead wrong. On the other hand, the GLS coefficients indicate that the model holds exactly. It is ironic that, although the OLS coefficients may arguably overstate "how wrong the model is," it is the GLS coefficients with market portfolio betas that incorrectly indicate the CAPM is true.

In Figure 4 and in Table I, Panel C, the model is more obviously false in mean-standard deviation space. The tangency portfolio has a 2.5 percent expected rate of return—which is double the inefficient market portfolio's expected rate of return—and the minimum-variance frontier looks appreciably different than it does when the CAPM is true. This occurs even though the expected returns of the 10 size portfolios are little changed, ranging from 1.21 percent to 1.47 percent—compared to a range of 1.21 percent to 1.43 percent when the CAPM is true. On the other hand, all the regression coefficients in Table I, Panel C, are identical to the coefficients in Table I, Panel A, when the CAPM is true. Thus, OLS and GLS regression coefficients with market portfolio betas incorrectly indicate that the CAPM is true.

This is not an isolated case. In examples not recorded in the table or figures, the OLS and GLS regression coefficients are identical to those when the CAPM is true—whether the tangency portfolio's expected rate of return is as low as 1.26 or 1.28 percent or as high as 6.25, 12.5, or even 62.5 percent. Only the R^2 and the 10 size portfolios' expected rates of return differ. In the case where the tangency portfolio's expected rate of return is 1.26 (1.28) percent, two (four) of the tangency weights are negative. But the ex-

Relation between Expected Returns, Betas, and Size   787

pected rates of return for the 10 size portfolios are virtually unchanged from the case where the CAPM is true. Furthermore, when the tangency portfolio's expected rate of return is 6.25, 12.5, and 62.5 percent—5, 10, and 50 times the market portfolio's expected rate of return—the 10 size portfolios' expected rates of return are again relatively unchanged (ranging from 1.10 to 1.52 percent, from 0.95 to 1.58 percent, and from 0.35 to 1.85 percent, respectively).

The examples in Table I, Panels D and E, and in Figure 5 are more extreme. The minimum-variance frontier appears to be a vertical line rather than a hyperbola as in Figures 1–4. In Table I, Panel D, the tangency portfolio plots near plus infinity—with an expected rate of return in excess of +26,000 percent and a standard deviation in excess of 12,000 percent. In Table I, Panel E, and in Figure 5, the tangency portfolio plots near minus infinity—with an expected return well below −21,000 percent and a standard deviation in excess of 10,000 percent. (By way of contrast, the expected returns of the 10 size portfolios only range from 0.55 percent to 2.31 percent in both cases.) Yet the coefficients of the OLS regressions of expected excess returns on market portfolio betas, and expected excess returns on market portfolio betas and size, take on exactly the same values as when the CAPM is true. Once more the Sharpe–Lintner version of the CAPM appears to be true when, in fact, in these cases it is again dead wrong. Furthermore, the GLS regression coefficients are almost the same in the two panels even though the tangency portfolio's expected return is +26,654 percent in one case and −21,572 percent in the other.

Table I, Panel F, muddies the waters even further. The CAPM is clearly false—the tangency portfolio's expected return is 418 percent and the expected returns of the 10 size portfolios range from 0.5 percent to 3.72 percent. However, the model appears to be exactly true according to the coefficients of OLS regressions coupled with market portfolio betas, as well as to be almost true in GLS regressions coupled with equal-weighted proxy portfolio betas. This conformity in the regression results employing the market and equal-weighted portfolios in this case is surprising given the complete lack of agreement between the results for the market and equal-weighted portfolios when the CAPM is true.

Clearly, then, the OLS and GLS regression coefficients themselves do not allow us to distinguish between scenarios where the CAPM is true and where it is false. Still, in light of Kandel and Stambaugh's (1995) demonstration that in a GLS regression of means on betas the slope and R^2 are uniquely determined by the mean-variance location of the market index relative to the minimum-variance boundary, a remaining question is: How much better is GLS? The answer is not clear cut. While it provides more information, the GLS R^2 is a somewhat ambiguous measure of efficiency in the presence of a riskless asset. More specifically, the GLS R^2 implicitly compares the positions of the market index, the minimum-variance portfolio with either the same expected return or variance as the market, and the global minimum-variance portfolio. (See Kandel and Stambaugh (1995), pp. 164–167.) However, when there is a riskless asset, we usually compare the positions of the market and tangency portfolios.

The results reported in Table I show that the two measures may give quite different impressions of how inefficient a portfolio is. In the examples, the riskless asset (with a yield of 0.5 percent) and the market portfolio (with an expected return of 1.25 percent and a standard deviation of 4.48 percent) are fixed points. In the GLS regressions of expected excess returns on market portfolio betas, reported in Panels B through F, the R^2 are 0.51, 0.08, 0.05, 0.05, and 0.00, respectively. However, the relative magnitudes of the R^2 are somewhat difficult to reconcile with the expected return of the tangency portfolio, which takes on values of 1.35, 2.5, 26,654, $-21,572$, and 418 percent in Panels B through F.

III. Summary

For more than 30 years the MV CAPM has formed one of the central paradigms of financial economics, and, for a quarter of a century, the model has been subjected to extensive testing. Yet, for more than 20 years, the tests have been called into question. Roll (1977) shows that the use of a proxy for the market portfolio—that includes only a subset of assets—can make the model appear to be true when it is false, or to be false when it is true. In universes where all the assets are observed, Roll and Ross (1994) demonstrate that a market proxy can be almost MV efficient and produce no relationship between means and betas using OLS. Moreover, Kandel and Stambaugh (1995) show that there can be a near perfect OLS fit between means and betas calculated relative to a proxy that is grossly inefficient. More importantly, they show that, in a GLS regression of mean returns on betas, the slope and R^2 are determined uniquely by the mean-variance location of the market index relative to the minimum-variance boundary. However, neither Roll and Ross nor Kandel and Stambaugh verify whether the minimum-variance frontier contains a positively weighted portfolio. Thus, we cannot be sure whether their results hold if the CAPM is true, that is, if the positively weighted market portfolio is MV efficient. Furthermore, any reasonable proxy portfolio should contain positive weights. Roll and Ross are able to construct one example where a proxy portfolio contains positive weights, but the proxies in Stambaugh and Kandel do not contain positive weights.

My method of analysis differs from that of Roll and Ross (1994) and Kandel and Stambaugh (1995) in two fundamental ways. First, I set up scenarios where the MV CAPM is true and where it is false. When the CAPM is true, all the implications of the model mentioned in the first paragraph of the paper hold exactly. When the model is false, there are no positively weighted minimum-variance portfolios. Nonetheless, the implications of the model are almost true in some scenarios. In other scenarios, some of the implications are almost true but others are not. For example, the positions of the market and tangency portfolios differ dramatically in some cases. Second, in most cases, I do not even employ a proxy for the market. When I do, with one exception I employ a positively weighted proxy.

I then investigate whether the coefficients from OLS and GLS regressions of population expected excess returns on population betas, and expected excess returns on betas and size, allow us to distinguish between the true and false scenarios. I show two main results. First, when the CAPM is true, coefficients of OLS and GLS regressions employing proxy portfolios—that are almost efficient—can incorrectly indicate that the model is false. However, when the CAPM is true in a 10 size portfolios universe, no positively weighted portfolio produces a zero slope in an OLS regression of means on betas. Second, and perhaps more important, when the CAPM is false, coefficients of OLS, GLS, or both OLS and GLS regressions employing market portfolio betas can incorrectly indicate that the model is true even when the market is grossly inefficient. The lack of any clear-cut agreement among the different implications of the CAPM, when it is false, is particularly disturbing. It does not bode well for those seeking to design an unambiguous test of the model.

REFERENCES

Banz, Rolf W., 1981, The relationship between return and market value of common stocks, *Journal of Financial Economics* 9, 3–18.

Best, Michael J., and Robert R. Grauer, 1985, Capital asset pricing compatible with observed market value weights, *Journal of Finance* 40, 85–103.

Best, Michael J., and Robert R. Grauer, 1992, Positively weighted minimum-variance portfolios and the structure of asset expected returns, *Journal of Financial and Quantitative Analysis* 27, 513–537.

Black, Fischer, 1972, Capital market equilibrium with restricted borrowing, *Journal of Business* 45, 444–455.

Black, Fischer, Michael C. Jensen, and Myron Scholes, 1972, The capital asset pricing model: Some empirical evidence; in Michael C. Jensen, ed.: *Studies in the Theory of Capital Markets* (Praeger Publishers, New York, N.Y.).

Blume, Marshall E., and Irwin Friend, 1973, A new look at the capital asset pricing model, *Journal of Finance* 28, 19–33.

Fama, Eugene F., 1991, Efficient capital markets: II, *Journal of Finance* 46, 1575–1617.

Fama, Eugene F., and Kenneth R. French, 1992, The cross-section of expected returns, *Journal of Finance* 47, 427–465.

Fama, Eugene F., and James MacBeth, 1973, Risk, return and equilibrium: Empirical tests, *Journal of Political Economy* 81, 607–636.

Kandel, Shmuel, and Robert F. Stambaugh, 1995, Portfolio inefficiency and the cross-section of mean returns, *Journal of Finance* 50, 157–184.

Lintner, John, 1965, The valuation of risk assets and the selection of risky investments in stock portfolios and capital budgets, *Review of Economics and Statistics* 47, 13–47.

Reinganum, Marc R., 1981, Misspecification of capital asset pricing: Empirical anomalies based on earnings' yields and market values, *Journal of Financial Economics* 9, 19–46.

Roll, Richard, 1977, A critique of asset pricing theory's tests; Part 1: On past and potential testability of the theory, *Journal of Financial Economics* 4, 129–176.

Roll, Richard, 1985, A note on the geometry of Shanken's CSR T^2 test for mean/variance efficiency, *Journal of Financial Economics* 14, 349–357.

Roll, Richard, and Stephen A. Ross, 1994, On the cross-sectional relation between expected returns and betas, *Journal of Finance* 49, 101–121.

Sharpe, William F., 1964, Capital asset prices: A theory of market equilibrium under conditions of risk, *Journal of Finance* 19, 425–442.

Stambaugh, Robert F., 1982, On the exclusion of assets from tests of the two-parameter model: A sensitivity analysis, *Journal of Financial Economics* 10, 237–268.

[7]

THE JOURNAL OF FINANCE • VOL. LIV, NO. 1 • FEBRUARY 1999

Two-Pass Tests of Asset Pricing Models with Useless Factors

RAYMOND KAN and CHU ZHANG*

ABSTRACT

In this paper we investigate the properties of the standard two-pass methodology of testing beta pricing models with misspecified factors. In a setting where a factor is useless, defined as being independent of all the asset returns, we provide theoretical results and simulation evidence that the second-pass cross-sectional regression tends to find the beta risk of the useless factor priced more often than it should. More surprisingly, this misspecification bias exacerbates when the number of time series observations increases. Possible ways of detecting useless factors are also examined.

WHEN TESTING ASSET PRICING MODELS relating risk premiums on assets to their betas, the primary question of interest is whether the beta risk of a particular factor is priced (i.e., whether the estimated risk premium associated with a given factor is significantly different from zero). Black, Jensen, and Scholes (1972) and Fama and MacBeth (1973) develop a two-pass methodology in which the beta of each asset with respect to a factor is estimated in a first-pass time series regression, and estimated betas are then used in second-pass cross-sectional regressions (CSRs) to estimate the risk premium of the factor. This two-pass methodology is very intuitive and has been widely used in the literature. The properties of the test statistics and goodness-of-fit measures under the two-pass methodology are usually developed under the assumptions that the asset pricing model is correctly specified and that the factors are correctly identified. Shanken (1992) provides an excellent discussion of this two-pass methodology, especially the large sample proper-

* Kan is at the University of Toronto, Zhang is at the Hong Kong University of Science and Technology and the University of Alberta. We thank K. C. Chan, Sean Cleary, Jin-Chuan Duan, Wayne Ferson, René Garcia, Mark Huson, Vijay Jog, Youngsoo Kim, George Kirikos, Peter Klein, Bob Korkie, Anthony Lynch, Vikas Mehrotra, Angelo Melino, Randall Morck, Sergei Sarkissian, Ken Shah, Tim Simin, Robert Stambaugh, René Stulz (the editor), Mike Vetsuypens, Zhenyu Wang, John Wei, Min-Teh Yu, Guofu Zhou, Xiaodong Zhu, seminar participants at the Hong Kong University of Science and Technology, National Central University (Taiwan), Queen's University, Southern Methodist University, University of Alberta, University of California at Irvine, University of Toronto, participants at the 1996 Northern Finance Meetings in Quebec City and the 1997 Western Finance Meetings in San Diego, and particularly Naifu Chen and Ravi Jagannathan for their helpful comments and discussions. We would also like to thank Ravi Jagannathan and Zhenyu Wang for sharing their data set with us, and Teresa Chan and Martin Forest for their research assistance. All remaining errors are ours.

ties of the two-pass CSR for the correctly specified model under the assumption that returns are conditionally homoskedastic. Jagannathan and Wang (1998) generalize Shanken's large sample results to the case of conditionally heteroskedastic returns. However, little is known about how these test statistics and goodness-of-fit measures behave if the model is misspecified.

In this paper, we study the properties of the two-pass CSR when the asset pricing model is misspecified. Misspecification of an asset pricing model can take various forms; here we focus on the extreme case in which the proposed factor is independent of all the asset returns used in the test. We call such a factor a *useless factor*. One might expect that when a useless factor is used in testing an asset pricing model, the hypothesis that its risk premium is zero would only be rejected with a low probability as indicated by the size of the test. We show that this view cannot be justified. Analytical and simulation results indicate that in a finite sample, the beta risk associated with a useless factor is found to be priced more often than the size of the test. A more surprising result is its large sample property. Since the problem arises because the betas are unobservable and estimated with errors, one might expect that as the number of the time series observations increases, the estimates of the betas will become more accurate and the above-mentioned problem will diminish. We show that this is not the case. In fact, as the number of time series observations goes to infinity, the probability of rejecting the null hypothesis that the risk premium of a useless factor equals zero goes to one.

The reason this problem arises is that the true betas of the assets with respect to the useless factor are all zeros, so the "true" risk premium with respect to the useless factor is in fact undefined. Therefore, as the estimated betas approach zero, the absolute value of the estimated risk premium needs to go to infinity, instead of zero, in order to "explain" the cross-sectional difference in the expected returns.

Although the misspecification bias in the case of a useless factor is due to the estimation errors of betas in the first-pass time series regression, traditional errors-in-variables (EIV) adjustments as suggested by Shanken (1992) and Kim (1995) cannot be used to correct for this bias. This is because such adjustments are derived under the assumption that the model tested is the correct one, and, therefore, they are not applicable to the case of misspecified models. We show that even with the EIV adjustments of Shanken (1992), the asymptotic probability of rejecting the null hypothesis that the risk premium of a useless factor equals zero is still much greater than the size of the test. Since the "true" risk premium of a useless factor is undefined, it is not possible to come up with an EIV adjustment that is appropriate for a useless factor, as well as for the true factor.

Our results present a significant complication regarding the interpretation of many empirical tests of asset pricing models. This investigation has particular relevance to the models of the Arbitrage Pricing Theory (APT) of Ross (1976) and the Intertemporal Capital Asset Pricing Model of Merton

(1973), in which factors and state variables are unidentified. These factors or state variables are chosen for empirical analysis based on economic intuition. We have no way of determining ex ante whether an asset pricing model to be tested is correct and whether the factors used are the correct ones. There is always a possibility that some proposed factors are in fact useless. Even for the well-known Capital Asset Pricing Model (CAPM) of Sharpe (1964), Lintner (1965), and Black (1972), in which the market portfolio is the sole factor, the problem still exists because the true market portfolio is unobservable (Roll (1977)).

Given the importance of the two-pass methodology in testing asset pricing models and the potential problem of misspecifying factors, a relevant question is how we can detect useless factors in the two-pass methodology. We suggest several tests that can serve as diagnostic tools and we also provide simulation results about their effectiveness.

The rest of the paper is organized as follows. Section I discusses the properties of the test statistics in the two-pass methodology under both correct specification and incorrect specifications. Section II provides simulation evidence that illustrates the magnitude of the bias caused by misspecification. The final section provides our conclusions and the Appendix contains proofs of all propositions.

I. Analytic Results on the Misspecification Bias

A. The Two-pass Regression under Correct Specification

For illustrative purposes the raw returns on N assets at time t, R_t, are assumed to be independently drawn across t from $N(\mu,V)$ where μ is its unconditional mean and V is its unconditional variance-covariance matrix. We also assume R_t are generated from the following one-factor model:[1]

$$R_t = \mu + \beta f_t + \varepsilon_t, \qquad t = 1,\ldots,T, \tag{1}$$

where f_t is the realization of the common factor at time t, and $\beta = \text{Cov}[R_t, f_t]/\text{Var}[f_t]$ is a vector of the betas of the N assets with respect to the common factor f_t which is assumed to be constant over time. The term factor is used in a weak sense, so conditioned on $f = [f_1, f_2, \ldots, f_T]$ we assume the error term ε_t to have mean zero but it can be a cross-sectionally correlated random vector (see Chamberlain and Rothschild (1983)).

Under an exact static one-factor beta pricing model, for some constants γ_0 and γ_1,

$$\mu = \gamma_0 1_N + \gamma_1 \beta, \tag{2}$$

---

[1] We thank Naifu Chen for suggesting this simple example to illustrate the problem. However, the subsequent results do not depend on the structure of one-factor models.

where 1_N is the N-vector of ones. When testing equation (2), the main interest is focused on the hypothesis $H_0: \gamma_1 = 0$. If a researcher can observe β, then an Ordinary Least Squares (OLS) CSR of R_t on β can be run for each period. By letting $X = [1_N, \beta]$ and $\gamma = [\gamma_0, \gamma_1]'$, the OLS estimate of γ at time t is

$$\hat{\gamma}_t^{OLS} = \begin{bmatrix} \hat{\gamma}_{0t}^{OLS} \\ \hat{\gamma}_{1t}^{OLS} \end{bmatrix} = (X'X)^{-1}(X'R_t). \tag{3}$$

Since $\mu = X\gamma$, under the assumption that returns are independently and identically distributed (i.i.d.) $N(\mu, V)$, it is easy to verify that

$$\hat{\gamma}_t^{OLS} \sim N(\gamma, (X'X)^{-1}(X'VX)(X'X)^{-1}). \tag{4}$$

In particular,

$$\hat{\gamma}_{1t}^{OLS} \sim N\left(\gamma_1, \frac{\beta'MVM\beta}{(\beta'M\beta)^2}\right), \tag{5}$$

where $M = I_N - (1_N 1_N')/(1_N' 1_N)$ and $\{\hat{\gamma}_{1t}^{OLS}\}$ is a sequence of i.i.d. unbiased estimators of γ_1. We can test $H_0: \gamma_1 = 0$ using a t-test on the time series of $\hat{\gamma}_{1t}^{OLS}$. The test statistic is given by

$$t_{OLS} = \frac{\bar{\hat{\gamma}}_1^{OLS}}{s(\hat{\gamma}_1^{OLS})/\sqrt{T}}, \tag{6}$$

where $\bar{\hat{\gamma}}_1^{OLS}$ and $s(\hat{\gamma}_1^{OLS})$ are the sample average and standard deviation of $\hat{\gamma}_{1t}^{OLS}$, respectively.

Under the null hypothesis, t_{OLS} has a central t-distribution with $T - 1$ degrees of freedom. But when $\gamma_1 \neq 0$, t_{OLS} has a noncentral t-distribution with the square of its noncentrality parameter given by[2]

$$\delta_{OLS}^2(\beta) = \frac{T(\beta'M\mu)^2}{(\beta'MVM\ \beta)} = \frac{T(\mu'M\mu)^2}{(\mu'MVM\mu)} = \delta_{OLS}^2(\mu). \tag{7}$$

It is well known that if a random variable t_δ has a noncentral t-distribution with noncentrality parameter δ, then $P[|t_\delta| > d]$ for $d > 0$ is an increasing function of δ^2. Therefore, if μ is not constant across assets, then $\delta_{OLS}(\beta) \neq 0$ and the probability of rejecting the null hypothesis using a two-tailed t-test will be

---

[2] See, for example, Johnson, Kotz, and Balakrishnan (1995, Chap. 31). The square of the noncentrality parameter is invariant to rescaling of the factor, or rescaling of β, hence, it only depends on μ but not on γ_1.

Two-Pass Tests of Asset Pricing Models with Useless Factors   207

higher than the size of the test obtained from a central t-distribution. In the parlance of asset pricing theory, one is likely to find β priced when using the t-test if $\gamma_1 \neq 0$.

The CSR can also be run by generalized least squares (GLS). The GLS estimate of γ at time t is

$$\hat{\gamma}_t^{GLS} = \begin{bmatrix} \hat{\gamma}_{0t}^{GLS} \\ \hat{\gamma}_{1t}^{GLS} \end{bmatrix} = (X'V^{-1}X)^{-1}(X'V^{-1}R_t). \tag{8}$$

It is easy to verify that

$$\hat{\gamma}_t^{GLS} \sim N(\gamma, (X'V^{-1}X)^{-1}), \tag{9}$$

and in particular, we have

$$\hat{\gamma}_{1t}^{GLS} \sim N\left(\gamma_1, \frac{1}{\tilde{\beta}'\tilde{M}\tilde{\beta}}\right), \tag{10}$$

where $\tilde{M} = I_N - (\tilde{1}_N\tilde{1}_N')/(\tilde{1}_N'\tilde{1}_N)$, $\tilde{1}_N = V^{-1/2}1_N$ and $\tilde{\beta} = V^{-1/2}\beta$. Therefore, $\{\hat{\gamma}_{1t}^{GLS}\}$ is also a sequence of i.i.d. unbiased estimators of γ_1 and similarly we can test $H_0 : \gamma_1 = 0$ using the t-test given by

$$t_{GLS} = \frac{\bar{\hat{\gamma}}_1^{GLS}}{s(\hat{\gamma}_1^{GLS})/\sqrt{T}}, \tag{11}$$

where $\bar{\hat{\gamma}}_1^{GLS}$ and $s(\hat{\gamma}_1^{GLS})$ are the sample average and standard deviation of $\hat{\gamma}_{1t}^{GLS}$, respectively. Under the null hypothesis, t_{GLS} has a central t-distribution with $T - 1$ degrees of freedom. But when $\gamma_1 \neq 0$, t_{GLS} has a noncentral t-distribution with the square of its noncentrality parameter given by

$$\delta_{GLS}^2(\beta) = \frac{T(\tilde{\beta}'\tilde{M}\tilde{\mu})^2}{(\tilde{\beta}'\tilde{M}\tilde{\beta})} = T(\tilde{\mu}'\tilde{M}\tilde{\mu}) = \delta_{GLS}^2(\mu), \tag{12}$$

where $\tilde{\mu} = V^{-1/2}\mu$. It is well known that $\delta_{GLS}^2(\beta) \geq \delta_{OLS}^2(\beta)$. Therefore, if β and V are observable, GLS CSR is more powerful than OLS CSR under the correct model.[3]

---

[3] Due to this inequality, Amihud, Christensen, and Mendelson (1992) suggest the CSR should be run using GLS instead of OLS.

In practice, betas are not observable and have to be estimated. The popular two-pass CSR methodology involves first estimating betas in a first-pass time series OLS regression of R_t on f_t. The estimated betas, $\hat{\beta}$, are then used to run the CSR of equations (3) or (8) by replacing X with $\hat{X} = [1_N, \hat{\beta}]$. When estimated betas instead of true betas are used in the second-pass CSR, the estimators $\bar{\tilde{\gamma}}^{OLS}$ and $\bar{\tilde{\gamma}}^{GLS}$ are biased but as the estimation period is lengthened, the estimation errors of $\hat{\beta}$ diminish and $\bar{\tilde{\gamma}}^{OLS}$ and $\bar{\tilde{\gamma}}^{GLS}$ are still consistent. Nevertheless, as discussed in Shanken (1992) and Jagannathan and Wang (1998), EIV adjustments are still required to obtain asymptotically correct standard errors of $\bar{\tilde{\gamma}}^{OLS}$ and $\bar{\tilde{\gamma}}^{GLS}$, where $\gamma_1 \neq 0$. For the case $\gamma_1 = 0$, such an EIV adjustment is not required and the t-tests of equations (6) and (11) are valid asymptotically.

When the same estimated betas, $\hat{\beta}$, are used to run CSR every period, the estimated risk premium ($\bar{\tilde{\gamma}}_1^{OLS}$ or $\bar{\tilde{\gamma}}_1^{GLS}$) described above is numerically equivalent to that in the single CSR of $\bar{R}$ on $\hat{\beta}$, where $\bar{R}$ is the time series average of R_t. However, it is important to distinguish the conventional t-ratio of the slope coefficient in this single CSR from the t-ratio in the two-pass CSR. As recognized by Black et al. (1972) and Miller and Scholes (1972), error terms in this single CSR are heteroskedastic and cross-sectionally (positively) correlated and hence the conventional t-ratio in this single OLS CSR tends to overstate the actual significance of the estimated risk premium. Therefore, researchers do not use this conventional t-ratio in the single OLS CSR to test $H_0: \gamma_1 = 0$.

From the single CSR of $\bar{R}$ on estimated β, R^2s are often reported as a measure of the goodness-of-fit of the model. For OLS CSR, the sample R^2_{OLS} is given by

$$R^2_{OLS}(\hat{\beta}) = \frac{(\bar{R}'M\hat{\beta})^2}{(\bar{R}'M\bar{R})(\hat{\beta}'M\hat{\beta})}. \tag{13}$$

For GLS CSR, the sample R^2_{GLS} is given by

$$R^2_{GLS}(\hat{\beta}) = \frac{(\tilde{\bar{R}}'\widetilde{M}\tilde{\beta})^2}{(\tilde{\bar{R}}'\widetilde{M}\tilde{\bar{R}})(\tilde{\beta}'\widetilde{M}\tilde{\beta})}, \tag{14}$$

where $\tilde{\beta} = V^{-1/2}\hat{\beta}$, and $\tilde{\bar{R}} = V^{-1/2}\bar{R}$. Under the correct specification, as $T \to \infty$, $\hat{\beta} \to \beta$, and $\bar{R} \to \mu$. Therefore, both the sample R^2_{OLS} and R^2_{GLS} tend to one as T tends to infinity. However, for us to use R^2_{OLS} and R^2_{GLS} as measures of goodness-of-fit, we need to understand their properties under incorrect specifications. It turns out that when the average returns are cross-sectionally correlated, the sample R^2_{OLS} in the single CSR, as an increasing function of the square of the conventional OLS t-ratio, also tends to overstate the goodness-of-fit.

Two-Pass Tests of Asset Pricing Models with Useless Factors   209

B. Misspecification Bias under Incorrect Specifications

Although misspecification may take various forms, we consider the extreme case where the chosen factor, g_t, is a useless factor in the sense that $\{R_1, R_2, \ldots, R_T\}$ are conditionally independent of $g = \{g_1, g_2, \ldots, g_T\}$. Without knowing g is useless, the researcher estimates the betas of the N assets with respect to the useless factor in the first-pass time series regression. Conditioned on g and under the assumption that $R_t \sim N(\mu, V)$, the estimated betas of the N assets, b, have a distribution given by

$$b \sim N(0, V/s_{gg}), \tag{15}$$

where $s_{gg} = \sum_{t=1}^{T}(g_t - \bar{g})^2$ and $\bar{g} = \sum_{t=1}^{T} g_t / T$. Since the distributions of the t-ratio and sample R^2 do not depend on s_{gg}, the unconditional distributions of the t-ratio and R^2 are identical to the ones conditioned on g. Therefore, we do not need to place any restrictions on the joint distribution of g. g_t could be correlated over time and it could even have time-varying distributions. Without knowing that b is the estimated betas with respect to a useless factor, the risk premium γ_1 is estimated in the second-pass CSR of R_t on b for each period and the hypothesis $H_0: \gamma_1 = 0$ is tested using the t-test described in the last subsection. Although the mean of b is zero for all assets, realizations are nonzero and may provide some explanatory power for expected returns. In this subsection, we address the following questions for a fixed number of time series observations, T:

1. For a given realization of b, what is the probability of rejecting $H_0: \gamma_1 = 0$ using the t-test? And what is the probability of rejecting $H_0: \gamma_1 = 0$, unconditioned on the realization of b, using the t-test to test if a useless factor is priced?
2. How do the goodness-of-fit measures, $R^2_{OLS}(b)$ and $R^2_{GLS}(b)$, of the CSR of $\bar{R}$ on b behave? Will the R^2s be inflated?

Running the CSR of R_t on $[1_N, b]$ using OLS and GLS, we obtain the OLS and GLS estimates of γ_1 for each period as

$$\hat{\gamma}_{1t}^{OLS}(b) = \frac{b'MR_t}{b'Mb}, \tag{16}$$

$$\hat{\gamma}_{1t}^{GLS}(b) = \frac{\tilde{b}'\tilde{M}\tilde{R}_t}{\tilde{b}'\tilde{M}\tilde{b}}, \tag{17}$$

where $\tilde{R}_t = V^{-1/2}R_t$ and $\tilde{b} = V^{-1/2}b$, and we can compute the OLS and GLS t-ratios in equations (6) and (11) to test $H_0: \gamma_1 = 0$. Researchers often treat $\hat{\gamma}_{1t}^{OLS}(b)$ and $\hat{\gamma}_{1t}^{GLS}(b)$ as i.i.d. normal conditioned on b, and compute the p-values of the OLS and GLS t-ratios based on a central t-distribution with $T - 1$ degrees of freedom. However, when we use the same period to estimate b as well as to run the OLS CSR, then $\hat{\gamma}_{1t}^{OLS}(b)$ and $\hat{\gamma}_{1t}^{GLS}(b)$ are no longer i.i.d. conditioned on b. We are able to derive the exact distribution of the t-ratios but due to its length and complexity, we choose to present the approximate distribution of the t-ratios by ignoring the dependence of $\hat{\gamma}_{1t}^{OLS}(b)$ and $\hat{\gamma}_{1t}^{GLS}(b)$ for simplicity.[4]

PROPOSITION 1: *If $\mu \neq k 1_N$ for any scalar k, then, conditioned on b, the OLS and GLS t-ratios of testing $H_0: \gamma_1 = 0$ have an approximate noncentral t-distribution with noncentrality parameters*

$$\delta_{OLS}(b) = \frac{\sqrt{T}(b'M\mu)}{(b'MVMb)^{1/2}},$$ (18)

$$\delta_{GLS}(b) = \frac{\sqrt{T}(\tilde{b}'\widetilde{M}\tilde{\mu})}{(\tilde{b}'\widetilde{M}\tilde{b})^{1/2}},$$ (19)

and $T - 1$ degrees of freedom. Except for a set of b with a zero measure, $\delta_{OLS}(b) \neq 0$ and $\delta_{GLS}(b) \neq 0$. Unconditioned on b, the expected value and the variance of the OLS and GLS t-ratios are given by

$$E[t_{OLS}(b)] = 0,$$ (20)

$$\text{Var}[t_{OLS}(b)] = \left(\frac{T-1}{T-3}\right) + \left(\frac{T-1}{T-3}\right) E[\delta_{OLS}^2(b)],$$ (21)

$$E[t_{GLS}(b)] = 0,$$ (22)

$$\text{Var}[t_{GLS}(b)] = \left(\frac{T-1}{T-3}\right) + \left(\frac{T-1}{T-3}\right) E[\delta_{GLS}^2(b)].$$ (23)

Therefore, conditioned on b, the probability of rejecting the null hypothesis using a two-tailed t-test will be higher than the size of the test obtained from a central t-distribution. In other words, one is likely to find b priced when using the t-test. Although conditioned on almost every b, the t-ratio does not have a mean equal to zero, the unconditional mean of the t-ratio is equal to zero and therefore we do not expect the estimated risk premium to take a particular sign. However, the unconditional variance of the t-ratio is higher than the variance of a central t-distribution, so we expect the two-tailed t-test to overreject the null hypothesis unconditionally. It should be emphasized that the results in Proposition 1 are just approximations. The

---

[4] The derivation of the exact distribution of the t-ratio is available upon request. The approximate distribution is very close to the exact distribution when T is reasonably large.

Two-Pass Tests of Asset Pricing Models with Useless Factors   211

results based on the exact distribution of the t-ratios suggest it is possible that we can underreject the null hypothesis unconditionally when the factor is useless. This could happen when T is small or when μ is close to $k1_N$.

We now have the answer to the first question: In most of the cases, the null hypothesis $H_0 : \gamma_1 = 0$ will be rejected with a higher probability than the size of the test, due to the misspecification bias in the t-test. This indicates the serious problem in using this t-test to determine whether a beta risk is priced under incorrect specifications.

Note that since b is a random variable, both $\delta_{OLS}^2(b)$ and $\delta_{GLS}^2(b)$ are random variables. Though the misspecification bias applies to both the OLS and GLS t-tests, it is desirable to compare $E[\delta_{OLS}^2(b)]$ and $E[\delta_{GLS}^2(b)]$ because they reveal whether the OLS t-test or the GLS t-test is more susceptible to misspecification bias when T is finite. However, whether $E[\delta_{OLS}^2(b) - \delta_{GLS}^2(b)]$ is positive or negative depends on both μ and V, so one cannot make a general statement about relative superiority of OLS or GLS in detecting useless factors. The following proposition gives an analytical expression for $E[\delta_{OLS}^2(b)]$ and $E[\delta_{GLS}^2(b)]$. By eigenvalue decomposition, we have $V^{1/2}MV^{1/2} = H\Lambda H'$, where H is an $N \times (N-1)$ orthonormal matrix and $\Lambda = \text{Diag}(\lambda_1, \ldots, \lambda_{N-1})$ where $0 < \lambda_1 \leq \cdots \leq \lambda_{N-1}$ are the $N - 1$ nonzero eigenvalues of $V^{1/2}MV^{1/2}$.

PROPOSITION 2

$$E[\delta_{OLS}^2(b)] = E\left[\frac{T(Z'\Lambda\eta)^2}{Z'\Lambda^2 Z}\right] \leq \delta_{OLS}^2(\beta), \tag{24}$$

$$E[\delta_{GLS}^2(b)] = \frac{\delta_{GLS}^2(\beta)}{N-1} = \frac{T(\tilde{\mu}'\tilde{M}\tilde{\mu})}{N-1}, \tag{25}$$

where $\eta = H'V^{-1/2}\mu$ and $Z \sim N(0, I_{N-1})$. The exact analytical expression of $E[\delta_{OLS}^2(b)]$ is given in the Appendix.

Proposition 2 suggests that for the GLS t-test when b is the estimated beta with respect to a useless factor, the unconditional expectation of the square of the noncentrality parameter is $1/(N-1)$ of that for the true beta. For the OLS t-test, even though b is the estimated beta with respect to a useless factor, the unconditional expectation of the square of the noncentrality parameter can be as high as that for the true beta. The equality can be attained when the returns have an exact one-factor structure without noise.[5] This is because when returns follow an exact one-factor structure without noise, we have

$$R_t = \mu + \beta f_t, \tag{26}$$

[5] We thank Naifu Chen for pointing this out to us.

212   The Journal of Finance

and the estimated betas of the returns with respect to a useless factor g_t are given by

$$b = \frac{\sum_{t=1}^{T} R_t(g_t - \bar{g})}{\sum_{t=1}^{T} (g_t - \bar{g})^2}$$

$$= \frac{\sum_{t=1}^{T} \beta f_t(g_t - \bar{g})}{\sum_{t=1}^{T} (g_t - \bar{g})^2}$$

$$= c_{fg} \beta, \tag{27}$$

where $\bar{g} = \sum_{t=1}^{T} g_t/T$ and c_{fg} is the slope coefficient of regressing f_t on g_t. Although $E[c_{fg}] = 0$, its realization is not equal to zero with probability 1. Therefore, b is always a linear function of β and it is virtually impossible to distinguish betas estimated with respect to a useless factor from the betas with respect to a true factor.

Proposition 2 also suggests that, generally, the misspecification bias does not necessarily diminish as $N \to \infty$. For example, when $V = I_N$ (i.e., when there is no difference between OLS and GLS), we have

$$E[\delta_{GLS}^2(b)] = E[\delta_{OLS}^2(b)] = \frac{T(\mu'M\mu)}{N-1} = T\left[\frac{\sum_{i=1}^{N}(\mu_i - \bar{\mu})^2}{N-1}\right], \tag{28}$$

where $\bar{\mu} = (\mu'1_N)/N$. The term in the last brackets is the cross-sectional variance of the expected returns of the N assets. To the extent that test assets are randomly drawn from a universe of firms, the cross-sectional variance does not decrease as the number of assets increases. Therefore, using more test assets may not reduce the misspecification bias.

For two independent random variables, it is well known that if one of these two variables has a spherical distribution, then the sample R^2 in the OLS regression of one variable on the other is distributed as a Beta$(\frac{1}{2},(N-2)/2)$ where N is the number of observations, and the sample OLS R^2 has an expected value of $1/(N-1)$. However, in the OLS CSR of $\bar{R}$ on b, the distribution of R_{OLS}^2 is difficult to derive because the N observations of b are correlated and the N observations of $\bar{R}$ are correlated and have different means. Although, under the normality assumption, $\bar{R}$ is independent of b, the OLS CSR R^2 does not have a Beta distribution except in some special cases, and its expected value is equal to (proof available upon request)

$$E[R_{OLS}^2(b)] = \sum_{i=1}^{N-1} E\left[\frac{\lambda_i Y_i^2}{\left(\sum_{j=1}^{N-1} \lambda_j Y_j^2\right)}\right] E\left[\frac{\lambda_i Z_i^2}{\left(\sum_{j=1}^{N-1} \lambda_j Z_j^2\right)}\right], \qquad (29)$$

where $Y \sim N(\sqrt{T}\eta, I_{N-1})$ and $Z \sim N(0, I_{N-1})$ with η and λ_i as defined in Proposition 2. From this expression, we can see that when λ_{N-1} is very large compared with λ_1 to λ_{N-2} (for example, when returns are close to having an exact one-factor structure), $E[R_{OLS}^2(b)] \approx 1$ even if b is estimated with respect to a useless factor.

PROPOSITION 3: *In the cross-sectional regression of $\bar{R}$ on b, $R_{GLS}^2(b)$ is distributed as* Beta$(\frac{1}{2}, (N-2)/2)$. *$R_{OLS}^2(b)$ will be distributed as* Beta$(\frac{1}{2}, (N-2)/2)$ *if MVM $= cM$ for some constant $c > 0$.*

Therefore, a partial answer to the second question is that $R_{GLS}^2(b)$ of the CSR behaves like that of two independent variables with i.i.d. observations. Since its distribution is known and independent of T, R_{GLS}^2 can be easily used to test whether the proposed factor is useless. However, since returns are cross-sectionally correlated, $R_{OLS}^2(b)$ of the CSR will typically not behave like the one between two independent variables with i.i.d. observations. Even though the factor is useless, the expected value of $R_{OLS}^2(b)$ can be much higher than $1/(N-1)$. This result should not be confused with those in Roll and Ross (1994), Grauer (1994), and Kandel and Stambaugh (1995). Their studies suggest that when betas are computed based on an inefficient portfolio, R_{OLS}^2 and the risk premium could assume almost any value, having no relationship as to how close the inefficient portfolio is to the efficient frontier. Our results differ from theirs in two ways. First, we do not require the factor to be a portfolio of the N assets. Second, we deal with issues of sampling distribution, whereas they deal mainly with issues of population moments. If we can observe the population moments of useless factors and the returns of the assets (whose betas are all zero), we would not have any misspecification bias because the population R^2 should always be equal to zero. Although the problem we discuss here is related to theirs (i.e., misspecification), the results we obtain cannot be easily foreshadowed from their studies, which do not study the sampling distribution of R^2 or t-ratio.

C. Large Sample Properties

In this subsection, we discuss the properties of t-tests and R^2s when the number of time series observations, T, increases, assuming the first-pass time series regression and the second-pass CSR are performed using returns of the same period.[6] Since the bias problem with a useless factor arises from the errors of the estimated betas, and the variances of such estimated betas go down with T, one might expect that the misspecification bias in the t-test will diminish as T increases, and the t-test will work at least asymptotically. Unfortunately, this is not the case. In fact, the following proposition suggests that when T increases, the bias is even larger for the t-tests.

PROPOSITION 4: *Suppose $\mu \neq k1_N$ for any scalar k. As $T \to \infty$, $|t_{OLS}(b)| \to \infty$ and $|t_{GLS}(b)| \to \infty$ with probability one. As a result, the probability of rejecting the null hypothesis, $H_0: \gamma_1 = 0$, tends to one.*

This proposition illustrates the seriousness of misspecification bias in the two-pass methodology. The bias problem cannot be alleviated by increasing the number of time series observations. Intuitively, the reason for this result is that although the estimated betas become more accurate and tend to zero stochastically, the estimate of γ_1 does not. Since the expected returns, μ, are not constant across assets, the intercept term of the CSR cannot fully explain the variation in μ and it leaves something for the estimated betas to explain. As the estimates b tend to zero, the calculated OLS slope coefficient needs to go to infinity to explain the variation in μ,[7] so the numerator of the OLS t-ratio tends to infinity. However, the time series estimate of the standard error remains finite. That is, the denominator of the OLS t-ratio remains finite. As a result, when $T \to \infty$, $t_{OLS}(b)$ explodes. The same is true for $t_{GLS}(b)$.

One might suspect that this result comes from multicollinearity because, in the limit, the regressors of the CSR are an N-vector of ones and an N-vector of zeros. That this is not true can be shown in two ways. First, if one runs a CSR using excess returns without the intercept term, there will not be multicollinearity, but it can be easily shown that the problem remains. Second, suppose it is true that $\mu = k1_N$ for some scalar k. Then the multicollinearity is present, but it can be shown that the t-ratio has an asymptotic standard normal distribution and it will not explode. These two points make it clear that the problem comes from misspecification, rather than multicollinearity.

The following proposition describes the limit of R^2_{OLS} and R^2_{GLS} as T increases.

PROPOSITION 5: *Suppose $\mu \neq k1_N$ for any scalar k. Let $Z \sim N(0, I_{N-1})$. Denote*

$$h = \frac{(Z'\Lambda\eta)^2}{Z'\Lambda Z},$$ (30)

---

[6] It is easy to show that Proposition 4 holds as long as the number of time series observations in performing the CSR goes to infinity. Therefore, the asymptotic results of Proposition 4 hold even when the betas of the useless factor are estimated using a different period from the one in which the CSR is performed.

[7] From the expression, $\tilde{\gamma}_1^{OLS}(b) = b'M\bar{R}/b'Mb$, it is easy to see that $|\tilde{\gamma}_1^{OLS}(b)| \to \infty$ as $b \to 0$, because $M\bar{R} \to M\mu \neq 0$ if $\mu \neq k1_N$ for any k, so the denominator tends to zero at a faster rate than the numerator.

where η and Λ are defined in Proposition 2. As $T \to \infty$,

$$R_{OLS}^2 \xrightarrow{D} \frac{h}{\mu' M \mu}, \tag{31}$$

$$R_{GLS}^2 \xrightarrow{D} \text{Beta}\left(\frac{1}{2}, \frac{N-1}{2}\right). \tag{32}$$

This proposition says that both R_{OLS}^2 and R_{GLS}^2 converge in distribution to some random variables. They do not converge to zero, even though the betas of a useless factor all converge to zeros. The result for R_{GLS}^2 is anticipated from Proposition 3, which states that the distribution of R_{GLS}^2 is Beta$(\frac{1}{2}, (N-2)/2)$ and does not depend on T.

Since the t-tests are not reliable, and from Proposition 4 even more unreliable for larger T, the fact that R_{GLS}^2 has a Beta distribution for the case of useless factors provides us with a diagnostic test to detect useless factors. In theory, one can also use R_{OLS}^2 to detect useless factors if one knows the distribution of sample R_{OLS}^2. However, the distribution of sample R_{OLS}^2 for the useless factor case depends on T, μ, and V. Since information on μ and V is generally not available to the researcher, it is difficult to assess the distribution of sample R_{OLS}^2 even through simulations. Although sample R_{GLS}^2 is superior to sample R_{OLS}^2 in testing whether the factor is useless, one should not interpret our results as suggesting that R_{GLS}^2 is superior to R_{OLS}^2 in every situation. If R^2 is not used for detecting useless factors but is meant to provide a measure of goodness-of-fit to compare models, then to the extent that the test assets are economically meaningful, Jagannathan and Wang (1996) argue that R_{OLS}^2 could be a better metric than R_{GLS}^2.

D. EIV Adjustment

Since the misspecification bias is partly due to the fact that we estimate betas with errors in the first-pass time series regression, one may think that we can correct the problem using the EIV adjustment proposed by Shanken (1992). Instead of computing OLS and GLS t-ratios as in equations (6) and (11), Shanken (1992) suggests that when the betas are estimated with errors, we should compute the EIV-adjusted OLS and GLS t-ratios as:

$$t_{OLS}^* = \frac{\tilde{\gamma}_1^{OLS}}{\left[\frac{s^2(\hat{\gamma}_1^{OLS})}{T} + \left(\frac{\tilde{\gamma}_1^{OLS}}{\hat{\sigma}_g}\right)^2 \left(\frac{s^2(\hat{\gamma}_1^{OLS})}{T} - \frac{\hat{\sigma}_g^2}{T}\right)\right]^{1/2}}, \tag{33}$$

$$t_{GLS}^* = \frac{\tilde{\gamma}_1^{GLS}}{\left[\frac{s^2(\hat{\gamma}_1^{GLS})}{T} + \left(\frac{\tilde{\gamma}_1^{GLS}}{\hat{\sigma}_g}\right)^2 \left(\frac{s^2(\hat{\gamma}_1^{GLS})}{T} - \frac{\hat{\sigma}_g^2}{T}\right)\right]^{1/2}}, \tag{34}$$

where $\hat{\sigma}_g^2 = s_{gg}/T$. The second term in the denominator is designed to take into account the measurement errors in the estimated betas. Shanken (1992) states that such an adjustment is not needed when testing $H_0: \gamma_1 = 0$. But this is true only if the model is correctly specified under the null hypothesis, i.e., $\mu = \gamma_0 1_N$ and expected returns are constant across assets. Here, we are interested in the properties of adjusted t-tests in the case of useless factors.

Since $s^2(\hat{\gamma}_1^{OLS}) > \hat{\sigma}_g^2$ and $s^2(\hat{\gamma}_1^{GLS}) > \hat{\sigma}_g^2$, we have $|t_{OLS}^*| < |t_{OLS}|$ and $|t_{GLS}^*| < |t_{GLS}|$ in any sample, so the rejection rate of the null hypothesis using the adjusted t-ratio will always be lower than the rejection rate of using the unadjusted t-ratio. Therefore, the adjusted t-ratio can help to reduce the misspecification bias even though it is incorrect for the case of useless factor.

Unlike the unadjusted t-ratios, the limits of adjusted t-ratios as the sample size T goes to infinity are finite (though unbounded) random variables. The properties of the asymptotic distributions are given in the following proposition. For convenience, they are stated in terms of t_{OLS}^{*2} and t_{GLS}^{*2}. Let $F_{\lim t_{OLS}^{*2}}(u)$ be the limiting distribution function of t_{OLS}^{*2} and let $F_{\chi_k^2}(u)$ be the distribution function of a χ_k^2 variable.

PROPOSITION 6: *As T goes to infinity,*

$$t_{OLS}^{*2} \xrightarrow{D} \frac{(Z'\Lambda Z)^2}{Z'\Lambda^2 Z} \tag{35}$$

$$t_{GLS}^{*2} \xrightarrow{D} \chi_{N-1}^2, \tag{36}$$

where $Z \sim N(0, I_{N-1})$ and Λ is defined in Proposition 2, and

$$F_{\chi_1^2}(u) > F_{\lim t_{OLS}^{*2}}(u) \geq F_{\chi_{N-1}^2}(u) \quad \text{for } u > 0. \tag{37}$$

Under the correctly specified model, t_{OLS}^{*2} and t_{GLS}^{*2} both should have limiting distribution of χ_1^2, so the acceptance/rejection decision is based on the distribution of χ_1^2. However, when the factor is useless, t_{OLS}^{*2} and t_{GLS}^{*2} no longer have limiting distribution of χ_1^2. When $N > 2$, overrejection occurs asymptotically if we use the EIV-adjusted GLS t-ratio. For the case of OLS, the overrejection also occurs asymptotically, but the severity depends on the relative magnitude of the nonzero eigenvalues of $V^{1/2}MV^{1/2}$. If the nonzero eigenvalues are equal, the limiting distribution of the t_{OLS}^{*2} is χ_{N-1}^2 and the overrejection is severe. If the nonzero eigenvalues are unequal, the limiting distribution of t_{OLS}^{*2} is closer to that of χ_1^2 and the overrejection is less severe.

E. Discussion

To understand why the misspecification bias occurs, we examine the null and the alternative hypotheses of the test. When the asset pricing model is correctly specified and the factor is correctly identified, the alternative hypothesis says that the expected returns are a linear function of the betas with respect to the true factor, but the null says the expected returns are constant across all assets. Such a null should be rejected in favor of the alternative when the true beta risk is priced. However, when the asset pricing model is incorrectly specified, then the alternative hypothesis, which says that the beta risk of a useless factor is priced, and the null, which says that the expected returns are constant across assets, are both wrong. As a result, there will be a good chance for the null hypothesis to be rejected in favor of the alternative. Rejection simply means that the alternative (that the useless factor is priced) is better than the null (that expected returns are constant across assets), which is not a very interesting benchmark. As the number of time series observations increases, the problem gets even worse, as we explain in the previous subsection.

The two-pass methodology has its advantage when the model is correctly specified, but our analysis indicates that the methodology is inadequate in the case of useless factors. A natural question is how one can detect a useless factor. We offer some suggestions.

The first suggestion is to test whether the betas of the assets with respect to a particular factor are significantly different from zero in the first-pass time series regression before we run the second-pass CSR.[8] If we cannot reject the hypothesis that the betas are jointly equal to zero, then we should be concerned about whether the factor is useless. Chen, Roll, and Ross (1986) and Ferson and Harvey (1993) performed such a test in their studies, but unfortunately this procedure has been largely ignored by many researchers.

The second suggestion pertains to the use of R^2_{OLS} and R^2_{GLS} in detecting useless factors. Since R^2_{OLS} can be highly inflated for useless factors and its distribution is in general unknown, simulations are required to find out its distribution in order to determine whether the factor is useless. From Proposition 3, R^2_{GLS} is not inflated much by the misspecification and its distribution for a useless factor is known. Therefore, in the CSR of the returns on the betas with respect to a common factor, it is more convenient to use R^2_{GLS} to check if the factor is useless. However, as a goodness-of-fit measure to compare models, Jagannathan and Wang (1996) suggests that R^2_{GLS} is inferior to R^2_{OLS} because the latter measure applies to the transformed returns and betas.

The third suggestion is to use Shanken's EIV-adjusted t-ratio for testing the null hypothesis in the case of conditional homoskedastic returns. Such an adjustment is far from being perfect, but it helps reduce the overrejection rate as compared with the unadjusted t-ratio. More generally, one can use the EIV-adjusted t-ratio of Jagannathan and Wang (1997), which allows for conditional heteroskedasticity in the returns.

---

[8] In theory, a variable could be a legitimate factor even though it has very low (but not zero) correlations with returns, because if we add pure measurement errors to a true factor, the betas with respect to this new factor still explain the cross-sectional differences of expected returns perfectly. Empirically, a very noisy factor is not very useful because there will be large errors in the estimated betas.

If there are two or more independent sets of samples available, it is always beneficial to perform the test on all the samples separately and draw inference upon the joint results. But for a given sample, a fourth way to detect useless factors is to utilize the fact that the t-ratios of a useless factor have an unconditional mean equal to zero. The difference between a true factor and a useless factor is that the beta estimates are stable for a true factor, but unstable for a useless factor. Thus, we can split the whole sample period into several subperiods, estimate betas of the assets for each subperiod, perform CSR for each subperiod using estimated betas from the respective subperiod, and reject the hypothesis $\gamma_1 = 0$ if the hypothesis is rejected in all subperiods in the same direction.[9] One empirical question is the trade-off between detecting useless factors and maintaining the power of the test under the correct model. In the next section, we illustrate this with simulation and report the performance of such a test.

II. Simulation Results

A. The Data

To evaluate the magnitude of the misspecification bias discussed in the previous section, we rely on simulation evidence. We use both actual and simulated returns. For actual returns, we choose two sets of portfolios which are commonly used in the empirical literature. The first set is 10 size-ranked equally weighted portfolios of the combined NYSE and AMEX stocks, sorted by market value at the end of June in each year. The second set of portfolios is 100 size-and-beta-ranked portfolios that are obtained by ranking the stocks within each size portfolio by their value-weighted betas estimated using 24 to 60 months of past return data and subdividing them into 10 beta portfolios. The portfolios are equally weighted and are rebalanced on a monthly basis. The monthly return series for both sets covers from July 1963 to December 1990.[10]

While actual portfolio returns are relevant in evaluating the impact of misspecification bias in actual empirical studies, actual returns alone are not sufficient for us to gauge its impact. The problem is that we do not know the data generating process of actual returns, and because we have only one realization of actual returns, the analysis is bound to be a conditional analysis and may not be generalizable to other realizations of returns. Moreover, actual returns could be nonnormal, conditionally heteroskedastic, and serially correlated. All these features may bias the t-test, thus we cannot attribute the overrejection of $H_0: \gamma_1 = 0$ for useless factors entirely to the problem we

[9] That is, all the γ_1s are significantly positive, or all are significantly negative, with the size appropriately adjusted. In practice, the subperiod joint test has an additional advantage when the betas are time varying.

[10] Monthly returns on the 100 size-beta portfolios are kindly provided to us by Jagannathan and Wang. Monthly returns on the 10 size portfolios are constructed based on these 100 size-beta portfolios.

discuss in the previous section. For this reason, we use simulated returns to demonstrate the magnitude of the misspecification bias due to useless factors only. To this end, we simulate i.i.d. returns from $N(\mu,V)$ where μ and V are set equal to the average and estimated variance-covariance matrix of the actual returns. To facilitate comparison with the results of using actual portfolio returns, we generate two sets of parameters for the simulated returns. One set corresponds to the 10 size portfolios and the other corresponds to the 100 size-beta portfolios. If we observe a bias of similar magnitude in both actual returns and simulated returns, we then have more confidence that the observed magnitude of the bias in the actual returns is not driven by the other violations of the assumptions for the t-test and that the bias is not unique to a particular realization of returns.

B. Simulation Results for Fixed T

In this subsection, we report simulation results with a fixed number of time series observations: $T = 330$, which corresponds to the number of time series observations used by Fama and French (1992) and Jagannathan and Wang (1996). The purpose of the simulations is to find out the magnitude of the misspecification bias that we can expect to observe in real world data. The number of replications in all our simulations is 10,000.

First, we take the actual returns as given, and for each simulation a useless factor is generated as an independent $N(0,1)$ variate. (The mean and standard deviation of the useless factor are irrelevant.[11]) Using the two-pass procedure, the betas with respect to this useless factor are estimated in the first-pass time series regression and γ_1 is estimated in the second-pass CSR. The purpose of this exercise is to determine how often the betas of useless factors will be found priced. Table I reports the results of this experiment. The left half of Table I reports the simulation results of CSR using only the betas of the useless factor. In the case of 10 size portfolios, rejection rates are quite different between OLS and GLS t-tests. For OLS CSR, the two-tailed t-test slightly underrejects the null hypothesis for significance levels at 1 percent and 5 percent, but grossly overrejects the null at the 10 percent level. For GLS CSR, the two-tailed t-test overrejects the null at all three significance levels but the rejection rates are not as bad as OLS CSR at the 10 percent level. One possible explanation for the difference between OLS and GLS results is that actual returns are fraught with problems of conditional heteroskedasticity, nonnormality, and a time-varying factor structure and these problems have different impacts on the OLS t-test and GLS t-test. Whatever the reason for the overrejection, the simulation results indicate

---

[11] If R_t is i.i.d. $N(\mu,V)$, then the distribution and time series properties of the useless factor are irrelevant. However, when we condition on actual returns, the choice of the distribution and time series properties of the useless factor could matter. We generate the useless factor as an independent $N(0,1)$ variate here just to illustrate the typical magnitude of the misspecification bias. Conditioned on the actual data, the misspecification bias could be higher or lower than what we report if the useless factor is not normally distributed or autocorrelated.

Table I

Probability of Rejecting $H_0: \gamma_1 = 0$ and Empirical Distribution of R^2 Using Actual Returns and Estimated Betas of a Random Factor

The table presents the probability of rejecting $H_0: \gamma_1 = 0$ in 10,000 simulations using the two-tailed t-test at various significance levels. N is the number of assets. For $N = 10$, the assets are 10 size portfolios and for $N = 100$, the assets are 100 size-beta portfolios. In both cases, the returns are equally weighted monthly returns constructed using the combined NYSE-AMEX monthly file over the period July 1963 to December 1990 ($T = 330$). In each simulation, a useless factor of 330 observations is randomly drawn from $N(0,1)$ and the beta with respect to this factor, b, is estimated for each asset. Monthly returns, R_t are regressed on b with and without β^{vw}, where β^{vw} is the beta of the returns with respect to the value-weighted NYSE-AMEX market index:

$$R_t = \gamma_0 1_N + \gamma_1 b + \varepsilon_t,$$

$$R_t = \gamma_0 1_N + \gamma_1 b + \gamma_2 \beta^{vw} + \varepsilon_t,$$

using ordinary least squares (OLS) and generalized least squares (GLS). A two-tailed t-test is performed to test $H_0: \gamma_1 = 0$ using the time series of the estimated slope coefficients. The table also presents the empirical distribution of the OLS and GLS R^2 between the average returns and the fitted expected returns in the 10,000 simulations.

	Without β^{vw}				With β^{vw}			
	$N = 10$		$N = 100$		$N = 10$		$N = 100$	
Panel A: Probability of Rejecting $H_0: \gamma_1 = 0$								
Significance Level	OLS	GLS	OLS	GLS	OLS	GLS	OLS	GLS
0.01	0.001	0.029	0.033	0.031	0.008	0.038	0.082	0.036
0.05	0.045	0.127	0.142	0.104	0.090	0.143	0.413	0.108
0.10	0.692	0.206	0.232	0.168	0.294	0.238	0.595	0.176
Panel B: Distribution of R^2								
Percentile	OLS	GLS	OLS	GLS	OLS	GLS	OLS	GLS
0.010	0.058	0.002	0.002	0.000	68.059	0.047	1.349	0.664
0.025	0.366	0.012	0.012	0.001	68.093	0.059	1.365	0.665
0.050	1.433	0.051	0.045	0.005	68.205	0.102	1.425	0.668
0.100	5.088	0.207	0.182	0.018	68.704	0.280	1.635	0.682
0.200	17.308	0.840	0.727	0.067	70.469	1.033	2.521	0.734
0.300	31.457	1.991	1.591	0.152	73.012	2.288	3.921	0.823
0.400	46.251	3.641	2.842	0.282	75.977	4.109	5.995	0.952
0.500	57.768	5.971	4.557	0.457	78.810	6.699	8.637	1.134
0.600	67.457	9.052	6.921	0.716	81.452	10.149	11.871	1.400
0.700	75.449	13.384	9.989	1.070	84.256	15.065	15.975	1.781
0.800	81.584	19.480	13.982	1.626	86.919	21.877	21.171	2.329
0.900	86.914	30.547	20.887	2.735	89.993	32.655	28.276	3.464
0.950	89.992	40.264	26.111	3.871	92.042	43.547	33.981	4.658
0.975	92.075	48.438	31.128	5.042	93.555	52.817	38.349	5.809
0.990	93.979	59.573	35.981	6.664	95.057	62.065	43.282	7.424
Average	51.547	11.178	7.813	1.002	79.080	12.259	12.119	1.698

that the t-tests are not reliable when the model is misspecified. As for the case of 100 size-beta portfolios, the overrejection rates are in general lower than the 10 size portfolios case but they are still very significant.

The bias of the t-test on the risk premium of the useless factor exists because the model is misspecified. Some may think that including more factors may help to alleviate this problem. This is not necessarily the case if the additional factors included are also not the correct factors. To illustrate this, we add the betas of the portfolios with respect to the value-weighted NYSE-AMEX market index in the CSR along with the betas of the useless factor. The betas of both the useless factor and the value-weighted NYSE-AMEX market index are simple regression betas, so the set of value-weighted NYSE-AMEX betas stays the same on every simulation.[12] The right half of Table I reports the simulation results. Compared with the results without the value-weighted NYSE-AMEX betas, we find that in most cases the overrejection rates of $H_0: \gamma_1 = 0$ for the useless factor are substantially increased. Therefore, including more factors in the model does not always help to exclude useless factors. It could even exacerbate the misspecification bias if the other factors included in the model do not nest the true data generating process.

The sample R^2s for OLS regressions of $\bar{R}$ on b appear to be very high. The sample R^2_{GLS}, by Proposition 3, should follow a Beta distribution with mean $1/(N-1)$. Although the GLS is run with an estimated V matrix, the distribution of sample R^2_{GLS} in Table I is still quite similar to a Beta distribution.

Though the results in Table I show that the bias in the t-test is quite severe, one could attribute the bias to many possible sources. In Table II, we repeat the same experiment except that in every replication we simulate both the returns from $N(\mu, V)$ and the useless factor from $N(0,1)$. By simulating also the returns in every replication, we can isolate the magnitude of the misspecification bias from other sources of bias in the t-test.

For GLS CSR, we report both the true GLS (using the actual V) and the estimated GLS (using the estimated $\hat{V}$). For the t-ratios, we can see that the rejection rates are mostly higher than the ones reported in Table I, indicating that the misspecification bias is one of the main reasons causing overrejection of $H_0: \gamma_1 = 0$. In the 10 assets case, we find that the estimated GLS has roughly the same properties as the true GLS since with 330 observations, the variance-covariance matrix of the returns on the 10 assets can be estimated quite accurately. However, in the case of 100 assets, the variance-covariance matrix of their returns cannot be estimated very accurately with only 330 observations and it introduces another source of bias in the GLS CSR t-ratio. The effect of this bias is to further increase the rejection rate. Therefore, although true GLS is less likely to reject $H_0: \gamma_1 = 0$ for the useless factors given our choice of parameters, the estimated GLS turns out to be worse than the OLS in the case of 100 assets because the estimation errors of the variance-covariance matrix of the returns further contaminate the t-ratios.

---

[12] We have also performed simulations using multiple regression betas and the results are qualitatively similar.

Table II

Probability of Rejecting $H_0: \gamma_1 = 0$ and Empirical Distribution of R^2 Using Simulated Returns and Estimated Betas of a Random Factor

The table presents the probability of rejecting $H_0: \gamma_1 = 0$ in 10,000 simulations using the two-tailed t-test at various significance levels. In each simulation, 330 observations of a useless factor are randomly drawn from $N(0,1)$ and 330 observations of returns on N assets are independently drawn from $N(\mu,V)$, where μ and V are chosen based on the sample estimates over the period July 1963 to December 1990. The parameters are estimated from 10 size portfolios for $N = 10$, and from 100 size-beta portfolios for $N = 100$. The simulated monthly returns, R_t, are regressed on their betas (b) estimated with respect to the useless factor:

$$R_t = \gamma_0 1_N + \gamma_1 b + \varepsilon_t,$$

using ordinary least squares (OLS), true generalized least squares (GLS) (using true V) and estimated GLS (using $\hat{V}$ estimated from the simulated returns). A two-tailed t-test is performed to test $H_0: \gamma_1 = 0$ using the time series of the estimated slope coefficients. The table also presents the empirical distribution of OLS, true GLS, and estimated GLS R^2 between the average returns and the fitted expected returns in the 10,000 simulations.

	$N = 10$			$N = 100$		
	\multicolumn{6}{c}{Panel A: Probability of Rejecting $H_0: \gamma_1 = 0$}
Significance level	OLS	GLS(V)	GLS($\hat{V}$)	OLS	GLS(V)	GLS($\hat{V}$)
0.01	0.188	0.107	0.114	0.111	0.061	0.172
0.05	0.386	0.231	0.242	0.236	0.154	0.297
0.10	0.502	0.318	0.332	0.320	0.238	0.384
	\multicolumn{6}{c}{Panel B: Distribution of R^2}
Percentile	OLS	GLS(V)	GLS($\hat{V}$)	OLS	GLS(V)	GLS($\hat{V}$)
0.010	0.033	0.002	0.003	0.002	0.000	0.000
0.025	0.168	0.011	0.012	0.012	0.001	0.001
0.050	0.722	0.047	0.048	0.045	0.004	0.004
0.100	2.864	0.211	0.214	0.160	0.016	0.016
0.200	10.957	0.898	0.883	0.634	0.064	0.065
0.300	22.090	2.054	1.987	1.426	0.157	0.152
0.400	34.139	3.735	3.670	2.594	0.284	0.283
0.500	44.963	6.055	6.030	4.233	0.474	0.465
0.600	56.651	9.295	9.200	6.454	0.736	0.728
0.700	66.416	13.628	13.695	9.593	1.108	1.108
0.800	75.161	20.064	19.985	13.863	1.680	1.690
0.900	83.745	30.129	30.518	21.045	2.765	2.758
0.950	88.624	39.908	40.099	28.023	3.941	3.881
0.975	91.477	48.553	48.804	33.729	5.045	5.120
0.990	93.796	58.373	58.458	39.392	6.536	6.355
Average	44.333	11.281	11.273	7.846	1.013	1.011

For the R^2, we observe the same pattern as in Table I. The R^2_{OLS} is highly inflated, but R^2_{GLS} (for both true GLS and estimated GLS) behaves quite like a Beta distribution with a mean approximately equal to $1/(N - 1)$.

In summary, our simulation experiment shows that the misspecification bias could lead to overrejection of the null hypothesis using the central

t-distribution. The magnitude of this bias is significant for the typical return data used in empirical research and should not be ignored. The results suggest that one should not jump to the conclusion that a factor is "priced" whenever one finds its estimated risk premium has a significant t-ratio. Furthermore, we find that the R^2_{OLS} is inflated by a large amount and renders it inappropriate to detect useless factors. On the other hand, R^2_{GLS} is not subject to this problem and can serve as a useful measure to detect useless factors.

C. The Rejection Rate as T Increases

In Table III, we report simulation results for different numbers of time series observations used in OLS and GLS CSR in the cases of 10 assets and 100 assets. The parameters of the two sets of returns are chosen in exactly the same way as in Table II, but we increase the length of time series observations of the simulated returns from $T = 120$ to $T = 1200$ by an increment of 120. By looking at time series of different lengths, we can better understand the magnitude of misspecification biases for different samples. Table III shows that the unconditional means of the computed OLS and GLS t-ratios are very close to zero, but their variances go up roughly linearly with T. It is obvious that they can get much higher than that of a central t-distribution. As a result, the rejection rates using the central t-distribution are much higher than the one suggested by the size of the test. Even for $T = 120$, we find that the rejection rates are often more than twice the size of the test. When $T = 1200$, we find that a useless factor is priced at the 10 percent level with a probability of more than 0.5, and can be as high as 0.892 (for OLS CSR when $N = 10$). This experiment shows how fast the rejection rate increases and how the misspecification bias becomes more severe as the length of time series increases.

In Table IV, we report the simulation results of using the EIV-adjusted t-ratios instead of using the unadjusted t-ratios. Similar to the unadjusted t-ratios, we find the rejection rate of the null hypothesis $H_0: \gamma_1 = 0$ to be an increasing function of the length of time series observations. The unconditional means of the EIV-adjusted OLS and GLS t-ratios are very close to zero, and their variances go up with T. However, unlike the unadjusted t-ratios, the variances of the adjusted t-ratios do not explode but instead converge to some limits. The rejection rates of using the EIV-adjusted t-ratios are in general less than the numbers in Table III for the unadjusted t-ratios. However, for $N = 100$, the rejection rates of using the EIV-adjusted t-ratio are still very close to the ones using the unadjusted t-ratio. For $T = 360$, the EIV-adjusted t-ratio rejects the null hypothesis with a probability of more than twice the size of the test. The only case where the EIV-adjusted t-ratio does not create significant overrejection of the null hypothesis is the OLS case for $N = 10$. Therefore, although EIV-adjusted t-ratios are better behaved than the unadjusted ones, we still find useless factors to be priced when T or N are large.

The Journal of Finance

Table III

Probability of Rejecting $H_0 : \gamma_1 = 0$ and Unconditional Mean and Variance of OLS and GLS t-ratios of the Risk Premium Associated with the Betas of a Random Factor for Different Lengths of Time Series

The table presents the probability of rejecting $H_0 : \gamma_1 = 0$ in 10,000 simulations using the two-tailed t-test at various significance levels and the mean and variance of the t-ratios for different lengths of time series (T). In each simulation, T observations of a useless factor are randomly drawn from $N(0,1)$ and T observations of returns on N assets are independently drawn from $N(\mu, V)$, where μ and V are chosen based on the sample estimates over the period July 1963 to December 1990. The parameters are estimated from 10 size portfolios for $N = 10$, and from 100 size-beta portfolios for $N = 100$. The simulated monthly returns, R_t, are regressed on their betas (b) estimated with respect to the useless factor:

$$R_t = \gamma_0 1_N + \gamma_1 b + \varepsilon_t,$$

using ordinary least squares (OLS) and estimated generalized least squares (GLS). A two-tailed t-test is performed to test $H_0 : \gamma_1 = 0$ using the time series of the estimated slope coefficients. The table also presents the mean and the variance of the OLS and GLS t-ratios in the 10,000 simulations.

| | OLS | | | | | GLS | | | | |
| | t-ratio | | Prob. of Rejecting $H_0 : \gamma_1 = 0$ | | | t-ratio | | Prob. of Rejecting $H_0 : \gamma_1 = 0$ | | |
T	Mean	Var.	1%	5%	10%	Mean	Var.	1%	5%	10%
					Panel A: $N = 10$					
120	0.031	1.998	0.055	0.166	0.258	0.003	1.686	0.044	0.128	0.202
240	−0.004	3.031	0.121	0.289	0.405	−0.001	2.286	0.083	0.191	0.277
360	0.004	4.047	0.202	0.405	0.525	−0.003	2.799	0.126	0.247	0.336
480	−0.002	5.066	0.285	0.504	0.622	0.008	3.333	0.161	0.290	0.378
600	0.021	6.142	0.374	0.600	0.707	0.007	3.993	0.204	0.343	0.427
720	0.002	7.083	0.449	0.672	0.767	0.012	4.539	0.237	0.379	0.461
840	0.015	8.041	0.516	0.729	0.810	0.018	5.077	0.270	0.402	0.484
960	0.034	9.126	0.587	0.774	0.841	0.025	5.708	0.300	0.432	0.513
1080	0.041	10.098	0.642	0.810	0.868	0.017	6.233	0.322	0.455	0.534
1200	0.031	11.165	0.696	0.841	0.892	0.021	6.842	0.343	0.482	0.559
					Panel B: $N = 100$					
120	0.017	1.487	0.032	0.102	0.176	−0.072	9.817	0.390	0.506	0.579
240	0.017	2.164	0.077	0.184	0.265	−0.022	3.569	0.169	0.297	0.378
360	−0.003	2.788	0.120	0.254	0.338	−0.044	3.535	0.171	0.302	0.383
480	−0.022	3.392	0.169	0.303	0.389	−0.041	3.886	0.189	0.325	0.410
600	−0.034	3.974	0.209	0.343	0.428	−0.048	4.361	0.217	0.344	0.431
720	−0.027	4.654	0.248	0.385	0.469	−0.065	4.870	0.243	0.376	0.454
840	−0.025	5.277	0.280	0.414	0.502	−0.081	5.325	0.266	0.398	0.482
960	−0.014	5.832	0.301	0.442	0.517	−0.072	5.774	0.285	0.422	0.501
1080	−0.020	6.489	0.331	0.466	0.544	−0.074	6.298	0.309	0.438	0.514
1200	−0.014	7.178	0.356	0.488	0.563	−0.068	6.853	0.326	0.458	0.535

Table IV

Probability of Rejecting $H_0 : \gamma_1 = 0$ and Unconditional Mean and Variance of OLS and GLS EIV-adjusted t-ratios of the Risk Premium Associated with the Betas of a Random Factor for Different Lengths of Time Series

The table presents the probability of rejecting $H_0 : \gamma_1 = 0$ in 10,000 simulations using the two-tailed errors-in-variables (EIV) adjusted t-test at various significance levels and the mean and variance of the t-ratios for different lengths of time series (T) as well as for the limiting distribution. In each simulation, T observations of a useless factor are randomly drawn from $N(0,1)$ and T observations of returns on N assets are independently drawn from $N(\mu,V)$, where μ and V are chosen based on the sample estimates over the period July 1963 to December 1990. The parameters are estimated from 10 size portfolios for $N = 10$, and from 100 size-beta portfolios for $N = 100$. The simulated monthly returns, R_t, are regressed on their betas (b) estimated with respect to the useless factor:

$$R_t = \gamma_0 1_N + \gamma_1 b + \varepsilon_t,$$

using ordinary least squares (OLS) and estimated generalized least squares (GLS). A two-tailed EIV-adjusted t-test is performed to test $H_0 : \gamma_1 = 0$ using the time series of the estimated slope coefficients.

	OLS					GLS				
	EIV-adjusted t-ratio		Prob. of Rejecting $H_0 : \gamma_1 = 0$			EIV-adjusted t-ratio		Prob. of Rejecting $H_0 : \gamma_1 = 0$		
T	Mean	Var.	1%	5%	10%	Mean	Var.	1%	5%	10%
					Panel A: $N = 10$					
120	0.017	0.696	0.000	0.002	0.012	0.002	1.144	0.002	0.044	0.115
240	0.000	0.895	0.000	0.004	0.024	0.004	1.403	0.006	0.073	0.167
360	0.003	1.037	0.000	0.006	0.034	−0.002	1.608	0.009	0.102	0.216
480	−0.003	1.156	0.000	0.010	0.049	0.003	1.798	0.018	0.130	0.253
600	0.011	1.255	0.000	0.013	0.061	0.002	2.014	0.024	0.164	0.302
720	0.003	1.335	0.000	0.016	0.072	0.006	2.183	0.035	0.194	0.334
840	0.008	1.409	0.000	0.020	0.086	0.010	2.331	0.044	0.222	0.365
960	0.017	1.476	0.001	0.026	0.104	0.013	2.484	0.052	0.246	0.393
1080	0.015	1.514	0.001	0.031	0.108	0.010	2.604	0.060	0.264	0.415
1200	0.017	1.554	0.001	0.034	0.120	0.010	2.734	0.069	0.282	0.438
Limit	0.000	2.335	0.039	0.153	0.286	0.000	9.000	0.675	0.922	0.975
					Panel B: $N = 100$					
120	0.014	1.140	0.005	0.050	0.116	−0.069	9.309	0.388	0.506	0.578
240	0.010	1.553	0.021	0.103	0.199	−0.020	3.362	0.159	0.292	0.374
360	−0.003	1.894	0.036	0.157	0.268	−0.043	3.289	0.160	0.295	0.378
480	−0.018	2.193	0.058	0.202	0.317	−0.040	3.568	0.176	0.318	0.404
600	−0.023	2.455	0.081	0.235	0.353	−0.046	3.945	0.202	0.337	0.425
720	−0.019	2.743	0.101	0.275	0.390	−0.061	4.354	0.229	0.370	0.450
840	−0.015	2.989	0.121	0.304	0.423	−0.077	4.710	0.252	0.390	0.476
960	−0.009	3.153	0.140	0.324	0.444	−0.068	5.051	0.271	0.415	0.496
1080	−0.009	3.378	0.157	0.350	0.469	−0.069	5.442	0.295	0.429	0.507
1200	−0.008	3.576	0.178	0.370	0.488	−0.066	5.840	0.310	0.449	0.529
Limit	0.000	14.029	0.881	1.000	1.000	0.000	99.000	1.000	1.000	1.000

D. Subperiod Joint Test

As we have suggested, one way to mitigate the misspecification bias caused by a useless factor is to run CSR for different subperiods and reject the hypothesis $H_0: \gamma_1 = 0$ if and only if the t-ratios have the same sign and are significant in all subperiods. Let α be the significance level for such a test. Denote $t_n(\alpha)$ as the upper 100α percentage points of the central t-distribution with n degrees of freedom. For an entire period of T observations, let t_1 and t_2 be the t-ratios for two subperiods of $T/2$ observations. The subperiod joint test is to reject $H_0: \gamma_1 = 0$ at a significance level of α if and only if

$$t_1 > t_{\frac{T}{2}-1}\left(\sqrt{\frac{\alpha}{2}}\right) \quad \text{and} \quad t_2 > t_{\frac{T}{2}-1}\left(\sqrt{\frac{\alpha}{2}}\right) \tag{38}$$

or

$$t_1 < -t_{\frac{T}{2}-1}\left(\sqrt{\frac{\alpha}{2}}\right) \quad \text{and} \quad t_2 < -t_{\frac{T}{2}-1}\left(\sqrt{\frac{\alpha}{2}}\right). \tag{39}$$

Now, under the assumption that returns are uncorrelated over time, such a test has a significance level α if the null hypothesis is correct. To see how such a test behaves for a useless factor, we again rely on simulation with both returns and useless factors simulated.

Table V reports the results of the rejection rates for both the true beta and the beta of a useless factor using the t-test over the entire period and the joint t-test over two subperiods. The true beta used in simulation is simply the vector μ for generating returns. For the true beta, the rejection rates from the joint t-test over two subperiods are still quite high as compared with the rejection rates from the t-test over the entire period. They are only slightly smaller for the OLS and the true GLS, indicating the small loss of the power of the joint t-test. For estimated GLS with $N = 10$, the power is even higher. This means that the subperiod joint test still maintains relatively high power in rejecting the null hypothesis under the correctly specified model. For the beta of a useless factor, although the subperiod joint test still overrejects the null hypothesis, the rejection rates are substantially reduced compared to those of the full period test. On average, the rejection rates are reduced by more than half. We conclude that the subperiod joint test is fairly effective in detecting useless factors without sacrificing too much the ability to reject the null hypothesis under the correctly specified model.

III. Concluding Remarks

In this paper, we argue that there is a problem of misspecification bias in the two-pass methodology of testing beta pricing models when the factor is misspecified. This problem renders the t-test inadequate. Simulation evi-

Table V

Probability of Rejecting $H_0: \gamma_1 = 0$ Using the t-test over the Entire Period and the Joint t-test over Two Subperiods

The table presents the probability of rejecting $H_0: \gamma_1 = 0$ in 10,000 simulations using a two-tailed t-test over the entire period and a joint t-test over two subperiods at various significance levels. In each simulation, 330 observations of a useless factor are randomly drawn from $N(0,1)$ and 330 observations of returns on N assets are independently drawn from $N(\mu, V)$, where μ and V are chosen based on the sample estimates over the period July 1963 to December 1990. The parameters are estimated from 10 size portfolios for $N = 10$, and from 100 size-beta portfolios for $N = 100$. The simulated monthly returns, R_t, are regressed on their betas (b) estimated with respect to the useless factor:

$$R_t = \gamma_0 1_N + \gamma_1 b + \varepsilon_t,$$

using ordinary least squares (OLS), true generalized least squares (GLS) (using true V) and estimated GLS (using $\hat{V}$ estimated from the simulated returns) with the entire period and two subperiods. Let α be the significance level for the test. Denote $t_n(\alpha)$ as the upper 100α percentage points of the central t-distribution with n degrees of freedom. Let t_1 and t_2 be the t-ratios of two subperiods. The hypothesis $H_0: \gamma_1 = 0$ is rejected by the joint t-test if and only if

$$t_1 > t_{\frac{T}{2}-1}\left(\sqrt{\frac{\alpha}{2}}\right) \quad \text{and} \quad t_2 > t_{\frac{T}{2}-1}\left(\sqrt{\frac{\alpha}{2}}\right)$$

or

$$t_1 < -t_{\frac{T}{2}-1}\left(\sqrt{\frac{\alpha}{2}}\right) \quad \text{and} \quad t_2 < -t_{\frac{T}{2}-1}\left(\sqrt{\frac{\alpha}{2}}\right)$$

where T is the number of time series observations.

	Probability of Rejecting $H_0: \gamma_1 = 0$							
	N = 10				N = 100			
	True β		Useless b		True β		Useless b	
Significance Level	Full	Joint	Full	Joint	Full	Joint	Full	Joint
OLS								
0.01	0.256	0.206	0.188	0.074	0.949	0.873	0.111	0.038
0.05	0.487	0.414	0.386	0.165	0.988	0.957	0.236	0.103
0.10	0.615	0.531	0.502	0.234	0.996	0.975	0.320	0.162
GLS(V)								
0.01	0.886	0.795	0.107	0.035	1.000	1.000	0.061	0.021
0.05	0.966	0.910	0.231	0.102	1.000	1.000	0.154	0.074
0.10	0.982	0.949	0.318	0.166	1.000	1.000	0.238	0.129
GLS($\hat{V}$)								
0.01	0.596	0.778	0.114	0.038	1.000	1.000	0.172	0.046
0.05	0.815	0.906	0.242	0.108	1.000	1.000	0.297	0.121
0.10	0.897	0.945	0.332	0.169	1.000	1.000	0.384	0.182

dence suggests that the *t*-test rejects the zero risk premium for a useless factor with a probability more than twice the size of the test for a typical length of time series used in empirical studies. The problem is exacerbated when the number of time series observations increases. This type of misspecification bias may provide misleading results.

Since the two-pass methodology does have some merits that other testing methodologies do not possess,[13] and some of the factors used in empirical studies could be useless, the relevant question here is how one can detect the problem. The diagnostics we suggest are as follows.

1. The hypothesis that all the betas with respect to a factor are zero should be tested before the second-pass CSR is run.
2. In the second-pass CSR, the OLS R^2 can be used as a measure of goodness of fit, but to test whether the factor is useless, simulations are needed to find its distribution. The GLS R^2 can be used to detect useless factors because its distribution is readily available, but GLS R^2 is inappropriate as a goodness-of-fit measure because it applies to transformed data (as reasoned in Jagannathan and Wang (1996)).
3. Shanken's EIV adjustment can be used to reduce the overrejection rates for useless factors when the returns are conditionally homoskedastic. But in the presence of conditional heteroskedasticity in returns, the EIV adjustment developed in Jagannathan and Wang (1997) should be used.
4. As a trade-off between detecting useless factors and maintaining the power of the test, a subperiod joint test can be performed. A more effective way, when possible, is to use another independent sample to examine the significance of the risk premium associated with a proposed factor.

These suggested diagnostic methods are not perfect, and they should be combined, contrasted, and used with care.[14]

As opposed to the traditional treatment, which assumes the proposed model is the correct model, we assume the proposed factor is useless in this paper. Both assumptions are extreme cases, and therefore both are unlikely to be true. In practice, probably all models suffer from some sort of misspecification and probably all proposed factors are not strictly useless. Between the

---

[13] The methodologies developed by Gibbons (1982) and Gibbons, Ross, and Shanken (1989) are one-pass regressions, but they can only be applied to the cases where only asset returns are used as factors.

[14] In an earlier version of this paper, we question whether the growth rate of labor income used in Jagannathan and Wang (1996) is a useless factor. Although we cannot reject the hypothesis that the labor betas are jointly equal to zero, simulation evidence of various test statistics as well as evidence from Japan (Jagannathan, Kubota, and Takehara (1997)) suggest that it is inappropriate to claim that the growth rate of labor income is a useless factor simply based on the insignificance of the labor betas. Moreover, the labor beta of the value-weighted market portfolio is negative and statistically significant, which further indicates that the growth rate of labor income is unlikely to be a useless factor.

true factor and useless factors, there are many misspecified models. Existing empirical asset pricing models probably all fall into this category of misspecified models. Testing whether these models are right or wrong is not very interesting by itself; a more interesting and challenging question is how we compare the performance of these models. Hansen and Jagannathan (1997) address this question from a certain perspective, and we hope future research will continue to address this important question.

Appendix

Proof of Proposition 1: Conditioned on b, and assuming $\hat{\gamma}_{1t}^{OLS}$ and $\hat{\gamma}_{1t}^{GLS}$ are i.i.d. normal, the OLS and GLS t-ratios for testing $H_0 : \gamma_1 = 0$ are given by

$$t_{OLS}(b) = \frac{\bar{\hat{\gamma}}_1^{OLS}(b)}{s(\hat{\gamma}_1^{OLS}(b))/\sqrt{T}} \tag{A1}$$

and

$$t_{GLS}(b) = \frac{\bar{\hat{\gamma}}_1^{GLS}(b)}{s(\hat{\gamma}_1^{GLS}(b))/\sqrt{T}}. \tag{A2}$$

Using equations (16) and (17), it is easy to verify their noncentrality parameters. Note that if $\mu = k 1_N$ for some scalar k, then $\delta_{OLS}(b) = \delta_{GLS}(b) = 0$ for every realization of b and both the OLS and GLS t-tests are properly specified. If $\mu \neq k 1_N$ for any scalar k, then $\delta_{OLS}(b) = 0$ if and only if $b'M\mu = 0$ and $\delta_{GLS}(b) = 0$ if and only if $\tilde{b}'\tilde{M}\tilde{\mu} = 0$. If b has a continuous distribution, then both sets of b have measure zero.

Unconditionally, $t_{OLS}(b)$ has a compound noncentral t-distribution that depends on the distribution of $\delta_{OLS}(b)$. Its expected value and variance are given by

$$E[t_{OLS}(b)] = \left(\frac{T-1}{2}\right)^{1/2} \frac{\Gamma\left(\dfrac{T-2}{2}\right)}{\Gamma\left(\dfrac{T-1}{2}\right)} E[\delta_{OLS}(b)], \tag{A3}$$

$$\mathrm{Var}[t_{OLS}(b)] = \left(\frac{T-1}{T-3}\right) + \left[\left(\frac{T-1}{T-3}\right) - \left(\frac{T-1}{2}\right)\frac{\Gamma\left(\dfrac{T-2}{2}\right)^2}{\Gamma\left(\dfrac{T-1}{2}\right)^2}\right] E[\delta_{OLS}^2(b)]$$

$$+ \left[\left(\frac{T-1}{2}\right)\frac{\Gamma\left(\dfrac{T-2}{2}\right)^2}{\Gamma\left(\dfrac{T-1}{2}\right)^2}\right] \mathrm{Var}[\delta_{OLS}(b)]. \tag{A4}$$

Since $\delta_{OLS}(b)$ is an odd function of b and the normal density function of b is an even function of b, it follows that $E[\delta_{OLS}(b)] = 0$ and $\text{Var}[\delta_{OLS}(b)] = E[\delta_{OLS}^2(b)]$, and we have

$$E[t_{OLS}(b)] = 0, \tag{A5}$$

$$\text{Var}[t_{OLS}(b)] = \left(\frac{T-1}{T-3}\right) + \left(\frac{T-1}{T-3}\right) E[\delta_{OLS}^2(b)]. \tag{A6}$$

Therefore, although the t-ratio has an unconditional mean of zero, its variance is higher than that of the central t-distribution. The unconditional expected value and variance of $t_{GLS}(b)$ are similarly obtained by replacing $\delta_{OLS}(b)$ by $\delta_{GLS}(b)$ in (A3) and (A4).   Q.E.D.

Proof of Proposition 2: For $E[\delta_{OLS}^2(b)]$, define $Z = \sqrt{s_{gg}}H'V^{-1/2}b \sim N(0, I_{N-1})$ and we can write

$$E[\delta_{OLS}^2(b)] = E\left[\frac{T(Z'\Lambda\eta)^2}{Z'\Lambda^2 Z}\right] = T\sum_{i=1}^{N-1} E\left[\frac{\lambda_i^2 Z_i^2}{\sum_{j=1}^{N-1}\lambda_j^2 Z_j^2}\right]\eta_i^2. \tag{A7}$$

The off-diagonal elements do not matter because, by symmetry, $E[Z_i Z_j/(Z'\Lambda^2 Z)]$ vanishes when $i \neq j$. For analytical expression of $E[\delta_{OLS}^2]$, we apply the results of Sawa (1978) and obtain

$$E[\delta_{OLS}^2(b)] = T\int_0^\infty \frac{1}{\prod_{j=1}^{N-1}(1+2t\lambda_j^2)^{1/2}} \sum_{i=1}^{N-1}\frac{\lambda_i^2 \eta_i^2}{(1+2t\lambda_i^2)}\, dt. \tag{A8}$$

The numerical integration of this expression can be facilitated by a change of variable with $u = 1/(1 + 2t\lambda_1^2)$ and the integral can be evaluated over u from 0 to 1.

Similarly, we can write

$$\delta_{OLS}^2(\beta) = \frac{T(\mu'M\mu)^2}{\mu'MVM\mu} = \frac{T(\eta'\Lambda\eta)^2}{\eta'\Lambda^2\eta} = \frac{T\left(\sum_{i=1}^{N-1}\lambda_i\eta_i^2\right)^2}{\sum_{i=1}^{N-1}\lambda_i^2\eta_i^2}. \tag{A9}$$

To prove the inequality, it suffices to show the following

$$\left(\sum_{i=1}^{N-1} E\left[\frac{\lambda_i^2 Z_i^2}{\sum_{j=1}^{N-1} \lambda_j^2 Z_j^2} \right] \eta_i^2 \right) \left(\sum_{i=1}^{N-1} \lambda_i^2 \eta_i^2 \right)$$

$$\leq \left(\sum_{i=1}^{N-1} E\left[\frac{\lambda_i^2 Z_i^2}{\lambda_i^2 Z_i^2 + \lambda_{N-1}^2 Z_{N-1}^2} \right] \eta_i^2 \right) \lambda_{N-1} \left(\sum_{i=1}^{N-1} \lambda_i \eta_i^2 \right)$$

$$= \left(\sum_{i=1}^{N-1} \lambda_{N-1} E\left[\frac{Z_i^2}{Z_i^2 + \frac{\lambda_{N-1}^2}{\lambda_i^2} Z_{N-1}^2} \right] \eta_i^2 \right) \left(\sum_{i=1}^{N-1} \lambda_i \eta_i^2 \right)$$

$$= \left(\sum_{i=1}^{N-1} \left[\frac{\lambda_{N-1}}{1 + \frac{\lambda_{N-1}}{\lambda_i}} \right] \eta_i^2 \right) \left(\sum_{i=1}^{N-1} \lambda_i \eta_i^2 \right)$$

$$\leq \left(\sum_{i=1}^{N-1} \lambda_i \eta_i^2 \right)^2. \tag{A10}$$

The last equality follows because for $c \geq 0$,

$$E\left[\frac{Z_i^2}{Z_i^2 + c^2 Z_{N-1}^2} \right] = \frac{1}{1+c}. \tag{A11}$$

For $E[\delta_{GLS}^2]$, since $\tilde{M}$ is idempotent, there exists an $N \times (N-1)$ orthonormal matrix Q (the columns of Q are simply the $N-1$ eigenvectors of $\tilde{M}$ associated with the $N-1$ eigenvalues of 1) such that $Q'Q = I_{N-1}$ and $QQ' = \tilde{M}$. Define $a = Q'\tilde{\mu}$ and $Z = \sqrt{s_{gg}} Q'\tilde{b}$, then we have $Z \sim N(0, I_{N-1})$ and

$$E[\delta_{GLS}^2(b)] = T(\tilde{\mu}'\tilde{M}\tilde{\mu})E\left[\frac{(\tilde{b}'\tilde{M}\tilde{\mu})^2}{(\tilde{\mu}'\tilde{M}\tilde{\mu})(\tilde{b}'\tilde{M}\tilde{b})} \right]$$

$$= \delta_{GLS}^2(\beta)E\left[\frac{(a'Z)^2}{(a'a)(Z'Z)} \right]$$

$$= \delta_{GLS}^2(\beta)E\left[\frac{Z'BZ}{Z'Z} \right] \tag{A12}$$

by writing $B = (aa')/(a'a)$. It is easy to verify that B is an $(N-1) \times (N-1)$ symmetric idempotent matrix of rank 1. Since Z has a spherical distribution, using Theorem 1.5.7 in Muirhead (1982), $(Z'BZ)/(Z'Z)$ is distributed as $\text{Beta}(\frac{1}{2}, (N-2)/2)$ and its expected value is $1/(N-1)$. Q.E.D.

Proof of Proposition 3: That $R_{GLS}^2(b)$ follows a Beta$(\frac{1}{2},(N-2)/2)$ distribution when $b \sim N(0,V/s_{gg})$ follows directly from the proof of Muirhead (1982), Theorem 5.1.1, which states that in order for the squared sample correlation between two variables to follow the Beta distribution, only the observations of one variable need to be spherical. Define $U = Q'\tilde{R}$ and $Z = \sqrt{s_{gg}}Q'\tilde{b}$, where Q is defined in the proof of Proposition 2, then we have

$$R_{GLS}^2(b) = \frac{(\tilde{\tilde{R}}'\tilde{M}\tilde{b})^2}{(\tilde{\tilde{R}}'\tilde{M}\tilde{\tilde{R}})(\tilde{b}'\tilde{M}\tilde{b})}$$

$$= \frac{(U'Z)^2}{(U'U)(Z'Z)}. \tag{A13}$$

Since $Z \sim N(0,I_{N-1})$ and it has a spherical distribution, the proof of Theorem 5.1.1 in Muirhead (1982) goes through.

That $R_{OLS}^2(b)$ follows a Beta$(\frac{1}{2},(N-2)/2)$ distribution when $MVM = cM$ for some constant $c > 0$ can be shown as follows. Define H and Λ as in Proposition 2, then we premultiply and postmultiply $MVM = cM$ by $V^{1/2}$, and we have $\Lambda = cI_{N-1}$ and $V^{1/2}MV^{1/2} = cHH'$ or $H' = (1/c)H'V^{1/2}MV^{1/2}$. Since $H'\tilde{1}_N = 0$, we have $\tilde{M} = HH'$. Therefore, $V^{-1/2}\tilde{M}V^{-1/2} = V^{-1/2}HH'V^{-1/2} = (1/c)M$, and hence GLS R^2 and OLS R^2 are the same.   Q.E.D.

Proof of Proposition 4: Since the case of GLS is almost identical to the case of OLS, we will only prove the case of OLS here. In the literature of probability theory (see, e.g., Amemiya (1985) or Davidson (1994)), the notation $z_T = O_p(T^a)$ for a sequence of random variables z_T means that, for any $\varepsilon > 0$, there exists an M_ε such that $P[|z_T/T^a| < M_\varepsilon] > 1 - \varepsilon$; that is, z_T is at most of order T^a. There is also a notation $z_T = o_p(T^a)$ that means plim $z_T/T^a = 0$; that is, z_T is of an order less than T^a. In the following we will use $z_T = O_p(T^a)$ in a narrower sense, that it is $O_p(T^a)$ but not $o_p(T^a)$; in other words, z_T is exactly of order T^a.

From large sample theory of regression analysis, $b \to 0$ with probability one and, according to the central limit theorem, the rate of convergence is $T^{-1/2}$. That is, $b = O_p(T^{-1/2})$.

As $T \to \infty$, if $\mu \neq k1_N$ for any scalar k, $M\bar{R} \to M\mu \neq 0$. Hence,

$$\bar{\hat{\gamma}}_1^{OLS} = \frac{1}{T}\sum_{t=1}^T \hat{\gamma}_{1t}^{OLS} = \frac{1}{T}\sum_{t=1}^T \frac{b'MR_t}{b'Mb} = \frac{b'M\bar{R}}{b'Mb} = O_p(T^{1/2}). \tag{A14}$$

That is, $\bar{\hat{\gamma}}_1^{OLS} \to \infty$ in probability at an order $\sqrt{T}$. Let

$$\hat{V} = \frac{1}{T-1}\sum_{t=1}^T (R_t - \bar{R})(R_t - \bar{R})'. \tag{A15}$$

Then $\hat{V} \to V$ with probability one, and

$$s^2(\hat{\gamma}_1^{OLS}) = \frac{1}{T-1} \sum_{t=1}^{T} (\hat{\gamma}_{1t}^{OLS} - \bar{\hat{\gamma}}_1^{OLS})^2 = \frac{b'M\hat{V}Mb}{(b'Mb)^2} = O_p(T). \tag{A16}$$

Therefore, both $s^2(\hat{\gamma}_1^{OLS})/T$ and $s(\hat{\gamma}_1^{OLS})/\sqrt{T}$ are $O_p(1)$. As a result,

$$t_{OLS}(b) = \frac{\bar{\hat{\gamma}}_1^{OLS}}{s(\hat{\gamma}_1^{OLS})/\sqrt{T}} = O_p(T^{1/2}). \tag{A17}$$

By definition, for any $M > 0$,

$$P[|t_{OLS}(b)| > M] \to 1, \quad \text{as } T \to \infty. \tag{A18}$$

The probability of the hypothesis $H_0: \gamma_1 = 0$ to be rejected using $t_{OLS}(b)$ tends to one.   Q.E.D.

Proof of Proposition 5: Since $H'V^{-1/2}\bar{R} \xrightarrow{P} \eta$ and $Z = \sqrt{s_{gg}}H'V^{-1/2}b \sim N(0, I_{N-1})$, by using the Cramer–Slutsky theorem (see Amemiya (1985, p. 89) or Davidson (1994, p. 355)),

$$R_{OLS}^2 = \frac{(\bar{R}'Mb)^2}{(\bar{R}'M\bar{R})(b'Mb)} \xrightarrow{D} \frac{h}{(\mu'M\mu)}. \tag{A19}$$

For $h = (Z'\Lambda\eta)^2/(Z'\Lambda Z)$ defined in (30), its distribution is bounded. To see this, note the lowest value for h is 0 when the realization of b is orthogonal to $M\mu$. The highest value for h is $\mu'M\mu$, using the result $R_{OLS}^2 \leq 1$, which happens when the realization of b is a linear function of 1_N and μ. Therefore h has a continuous distribution over $[0, \mu'M\mu]$ and $\text{Var}[h] > 0$. The proof for R_{GLS}^2 follows directly from Proposition 3.   Q.E.D.

Proof of Proposition 6: t_{OLS}^{*2} can be written as

$$t_{OLS}^{*2} = \frac{(\bar{\hat{\gamma}}_1^{OLS})^2}{\frac{s^2(\hat{\gamma}_1^{OLS})}{T} + \left(\frac{\bar{\hat{\gamma}}_1^{OLS}}{\hat{\sigma}_g}\right)^2 \left[\frac{s^2(\hat{\gamma}_1^{OLS})}{T} - \frac{\hat{\sigma}_g^2}{T}\right]}. \tag{A20}$$

Since $s^2(\hat{\gamma}_1^{OLS})/T = O_p(1)$ and $\bar{\hat{\gamma}}_1^{OLS} = O_p(T^{1/2})$, it follows that

$$t_{OLS}^{*2} - \frac{s_{gg}}{s^2(\hat{\gamma}_1^{OLS})} \xrightarrow{P} 0. \tag{A21}$$

From the Cramer–Slutsky theorem, the limiting distribution of t_{OLS}^{*2} is the same as that of

$$\frac{s_{gg}}{s^2(\hat{\gamma}_1^{OLS})} = \frac{s_{gg}(b'Mb)^2}{b'M\hat{V}Mb}, \tag{A22}$$

which, in turn, has the same limiting distribution as $s_{gg}(b'Mb)^2/(b'MVMb)$ since $\hat{V} \to V$. Define $Z = \sqrt{s_{gg}}H'V^{-1/2}b \sim N(0, I_{N-1})$, where H is defined in Proposition 2, we have

$$\frac{s_{gg}(b'Mb)^2}{b'MVMb} = \frac{(Z'\Lambda Z)^2}{Z'\Lambda^2 Z} = \frac{\left(\sum\limits_{i=1}^{N-1} \lambda_i Z_i^2\right)^2}{\sum\limits_{i=1}^{N-1} \lambda_i^2 Z_i^2}. \tag{A23}$$

To show the first inequality, we note that

$$\left(\sum_{i=1}^{N-1} \lambda_i Z_i^2\right)^2 > \lambda_{N-1} Z_{N-1}^2 \left(\sum_{i=1}^{N-1} \lambda_i Z_i^2\right) \ge Z_{N-1}^2 \left(\sum_{i=1}^{N-1} \lambda_i^2 Z_i^2\right). \tag{A24}$$

Therefore $\lim t_{OLS}^{*2} > Z_{N-1}^2$, or $F_{\chi_1^2}(u) > F_{\lim t_{OLS}^{*2}}(u)$. To show the other inequality, note from the Cauchy–Schwarz inequality,

$$\left[\sum_{i=1}^{N-1} (\lambda_i Z_i)Z_i\right]^2 \le \sum_{i=1}^{N-1} (\lambda_i Z_i)^2 \sum_{i=1}^{N-1} Z_i^2. \tag{A25}$$

So that $\lim t_{OLS}^{*2} \le \sum_{i=1}^{N-1} Z_i^2$, or $F_{\lim t_{OLS}^{*2}}(u) \ge F_{\chi_{N-1}^2}(u)$.

For GLS, the limiting distribution of t_{GLS}^{*2} is simply $s_{gg}(\tilde{b}'\tilde{M}\tilde{b})$. Define $Z = \sqrt{s_{gg}}Q'\tilde{b}$, where Q is defined in the proof of Proposition 2, then we have $Z \sim N(0, I_{N-1})$ and

$$s_{gg}(\tilde{b}'\tilde{M}\tilde{b}) = Z'Z, \tag{A26}$$

which is a χ_{N-1}^2 random variable.   Q.E.D.

REFERENCES

Amemiya, Takeshi, 1985, *Advanced Econometrics* (Harvard University Press, Boston, Massachusetts).

Amihud, Yakov, Bent Jesper Christensen, and Haim Mendelson, 1992, Further evidence on the risk-return relationship, Working paper, New York University.

Black, Fischer, 1972, Capital market equilibrium with restricted borrowing, *Journal of Business* 45, 444–454.

Black, Fischer, Michael C. Jensen, and Myron Scholes, 1972, The capital asset pricing model: Some empirical findings; in Michael C. Jensen, ed.: *Studies in the Theory of Capital Markets* (Praeger, New York).

Chamberlain, Gary, and Michael Rothschild, 1983, Arbitrage, factor structure and mean-variance analysis on large asset markets, *Econometrica* 51, 1281–1304.

Chen, Naifu, Richard R. Roll, and Stephen A. Ross, 1986, Economic forces and the stock market, *Journal of Business* 59, 383–403.

Davidson, James, 1994, *Stochastic Limit Theory: An Introduction to Econometricians* (Oxford University Press, New York).

Fama, Eugene F., and Kenneth R. French, 1992, The cross-section of expected stock returns, *Journal of Finance* 47, 427–465.

Fama, Eugene F., and James D. MacBeth, 1973, Risk, return and equilibrium: Empirical tests, *Journal of Political Economy* 81, 607–636.

Ferson, Wayne E., and Campbell Harvey, 1993, The risk and predictability of international equity returns, *Review of Financial Studies* 6, 527–566.

Gibbons, Michael R., 1982, Multivariate tests of financial models: A new approach, *Journal of Financial Economics* 10, 3–28.

Gibbons, Michael R., Stephen A. Ross, and Jay Shanken, 1989, A test of the efficiency of a given portfolio, *Econometrica* 57, 1121–1152.

Grauer, Robert R., 1994, Tests of the capital asset pricing model based on the cross-section of expected returns, Working paper, Simon Fraser University.

Hansen, Lars Peter, and Ravi Jagannathan, 1997, Assessing specification errors in stochastic discount factor models, *Journal of Finance* 52, 557–590.

Jagannathan, Ravi, Keiichi Kubota, and Hitoshi Takehara, 1997, Relationship between labor-income risk and average return: Empirical evidence from the Japanese stock market, Discussion paper 117, Institute for Empirical Macroeconomics, Federal Reserve Bank of Minneapolis.

Jagannathan, Ravi, and Zhenyu Wang, 1996, The conditional CAPM and the cross-section of expected returns, *Journal of Finance* 51, 3–53.

Jagannathan, Ravi, and Zhenyu Wang, 1998, An asymptotic theory for estimating beta-pricing models using cross-sectional regression, *Journal of Finance* 53, 1285–1309.

Johnson, Norman L., Samuel Kotz, and N. Balakrishnan, 1995, *Continuous Univariate Distributions, Vol. 2* (Wiley, New York).

Kandel, Shmuel, and Robert F. Stambaugh, 1995, Portfolio inefficiency and the cross-section of expected returns, *Journal of Finance* 50, 157–184.

Kim, Dongcheol, 1995, The errors in the variables problem in the cross-section of expected stock returns, *Journal of Finance* 50, 1605–1634.

Lintner, John, 1965, The valuation of risky assets and the selection of risky investments in the portfolios and capital budgets, *Review of Economics and Statistics* 47, 13–37.

Merton, Robert C., 1973, An intertemporal capital asset pricing model, *Econometrica* 41, 867–887.

Miller, Merton H., and Myron Scholes, 1972, Rates of return in relation to risk: A reexamination of some recent findings; in Michael C. Jensen, ed.: *Studies in the Theory of Capital Markets* (Praeger, New York).

Muirhead, Robb J., 1982, *Aspects of Multivariate Statistical Theory* (Wiley, New York).

Roll, Richard, 1977, A critique of the asset pricing theory's tests; Part I: On past and potential testability of theory, *Journal of Financial Economics* 4, 129–176.

Roll, Richard, and Stephen A. Ross, 1994, On the cross-sectional relation between expected returns and betas, *Journal of Finance* 49, 101–121.

Ross, Stephen A., 1976, The arbitrage theory of capital asset pricing, *Journal of Economic Theory* 13, 341–360.

Sawa, Takamitsu, 1978, The exact moments of the least squares estimator for the autoregressive model, *Journal of Econometrics* 8, 159–172.

Shanken, Jay, 1992, On the estimation of beta-pricing models, *Review of Financial Studies* 5, 1–33.

Sharpe, William F., 1964, Capital asset prices: A theory of market equilibrium under conditions of risk, *Journal of Finance* 19, 425–442.

[8]

THE JOURNAL OF FINANCE • VOL. XLIX, NO. 5 • DECEMBER 1994

Contrarian Investment, Extrapolation, and Risk

JOSEF LAKONISHOK, ANDREI SHLEIFER, and
ROBERT W. VISHNY*

ABSTRACT

For many years, scholars and investment professionals have argued that value strategies outperform the market. These value strategies call for buying stocks that have low prices relative to earnings, dividends, book assets, or other measures of fundamental value. While there is some agreement that value strategies produce higher returns, the interpretation of why they do so is more controversial. This article provides evidence that value strategies yield higher returns because these strategies exploit the suboptimal behavior of the typical investor and not because these strategies are fundamentally riskier.

FOR MANY YEARS, SCHOLARS and investment professionals have argued that value strategies outperform the market (Graham and Dodd (1934) and Dreman (1977)). These value strategies call for buying stocks that have low prices relative to earnings, dividends, historical prices, book assets, or other measures of value. In recent years, value strategies have attracted academic attention as well. Basu (1977), Jaffe, Keim, and Westerfield (1989), Chan, Hamao, and Lakonishok (1991), and Fama and French (1992) show that stocks with high earnings/price ratios earn higher returns. De Bondt and Thaler (1985, 1987) argue that extreme losers outperform the market over the subsequent several years. Despite considerable criticism (Chan (1988) and Ball and Kothari (1989)), their analysis has generally stood up to the tests (Chopra, Lakonishok, and Ritter (1992)). Rosenberg, Reid, and Lanstein (1984) show that stocks with high book relative to market values of equity outperform the market. Further work (Chan, Hamao, and Lakonishok (1991)

* Lakonishok is from the University of Illinois, Shleifer is from Harvard University, and Vishny is from the University of Chicago. We are indebted to Gil Beebower, Fischer Black, Stephen Brown, K. C. Chan, Louis Chan, Eugene Fama, Kenneth French, Bob Haugen, Jay Ritter, René Stulz, and two anonymous referees for helpful comments and to Han Qu for outstanding research assistance. This article has been presented at the Berkeley Program in Finance, University of California (Berkeley), the Center for Research in Securities Prices Conference, the University of Chicago, the University of Illinois, the Massachusetts Institute of Technology, the National Bureau of Economic Research (Asset Pricing and Behavioral Finance Groups), New York University, Pensions and Investments Conference, the Institute for Quantitative Research in Finance (United States and Europe), Society of Quantitative Analysts, Stanford University, the University of Toronto, and Tel Aviv University. The research was supported by the National Science Foundation, Bradley Foundation, Russell Sage Foundation, the National Bureau of Economic Research Asset Management Research Advisory Group, and the National Center for Supercomputing Applications, University of Illinois.

and Fama and French (1992)) has both extended and refined these results. Finally, Chan, Hamao, and Lakonishok (1991) show that a high ratio of cash flow to price also predicts higher returns. Interestingly, many of these results have been obtained for both the United States and Japan. Certain types of value strategies, then, appear to have beaten the market.

While there is some agreement that value strategies have produced superior returns, the interpretation of why they have done so is more controversial. Value strategies might produce higher returns because they are *contrarian* to "naive"[1] strategies followed by other investors. These naive strategies might range from extrapolating past earnings growth too far into the future, to assuming a trend in stock prices, to overreacting to good or bad news, or to simply equating a good investment with a well-run company irrespective of price. Regardless of the reason, some investors tend to get overly excited about stocks that have done very well in the past and buy them up, so that these "glamour" stocks become overpriced. Similarly, they overreact to stocks that have done very badly, oversell them, and these out-of-favor "value" stocks become underpriced. Contrarian investors bet against such naive investors. Because contrarian strategies invest disproportionately in stocks that are underpriced and underinvest in stocks that are overpriced, they outperform the market (see De Bondt and Thaler (1985) and Haugen (1994)).

An alternative explanation of why value strategies have produced superior returns, argued most forcefully by Fama and French (1992), is that they are *fundamentally riskier*. That is, investors in value stocks, such as high book-to-market stocks, tend to bear higher fundamental risk of some sort, and their higher average returns are simply compensation for this risk. This argument is also used by critics of De Bondt and Thaler (Chan (1988) and Ball and Kothari (1989)) to dismiss their overreaction story. Whether value strategies have produced higher returns because they are contrarian to naive strategies or because they are fundamentally riskier remains an open question.

In this article, we try to shed further light on the two potential explanations for why value strategies work. We do so along two dimensions. First, we examine more closely the predictions of the contrarian model. In particular, one natural version of the contrarian model argues that the overpriced *glamour stocks* are those which, first, have performed well in the past, and second, are expected by the market to perform well in the future. Similarly, the underpriced out-of-favor or *value stocks* are those that have performed poorly in the past and are expected to continue to perform poorly. Value strategies that bet against those investors who extrapolate past performance too far into the future produce superior returns. In principle, this version of the contrarian model is testable because past performance and expectation of future performance are two distinct and separately measurable characteristics of glamour and value. In this article, past performance is measured using

---

[1] What we call "naive strategies" are also sometimes referred to as "popular models" (Shiller (1984)) and "noise" (Black (1986)).

information on past growth in sales, earnings, and cash flow, and expected performance is measured by multiples of price to current earnings and cash flow.

We examine the most obvious implication of the contrarian model, namely that value stocks outperform glamour stocks. We start with simple one-variable classifications of glamour and value stocks that rely in most cases on measures of either past growth or expected future growth. We then move on to classifications in which glamour and value are defined using both past growth and expected future growth. In addition, we compare past, expected, and future growth rates of glamour and value stocks. Our version of the contrarian model predicts that differences in expected future growth rates are linked to past growth and overestimate actual future growth differences between glamour and value firms. We find that a wide range of value strategies have produced higher returns, and that the pattern of past, expected, and actual future growth rates is consistent with the contrarian model.

The second question we ask is whether value stocks are indeed fundamentally riskier than glamour stocks. To be fundamentally riskier, value stocks must underperform glamour stocks with some frequency, and particularly in the states of the world when the marginal utility of wealth is high. This view of risk motivates our tests. We look at the frequency of superior (and inferior) performance of value strategies, as well as at their performance in bad states of the world, such as extreme down markets and economic recessions. We also look at the betas and standard deviations of value and glamour strategies. We find little, if any, support for the view that value strategies are fundamentally riskier.

Our results raise the obvious question of how the higher expected returns on value strategies could have continued if such strategies are not fundamentally riskier? We present some possible explanations that rely both on behavioral strategies favored by individual investors and on agency problems plaguing institutional investors.

The next section of the article briefly discusses our methodology. Section II examines a variety of simple classification schemes for glamour and value stocks based on the book-to-market ratio, the cash flow-to-price ratio, the earnings-to-price ratio, and past growth in sales. Section II shows that all of these simple value strategies have produced superior returns and motivates our subsequent use of combinations of measures of past and expected growth. Section III then examines the performance of value strategies that are defined using both past growth and current multiples. These two-dimensional value strategies outperform glamour strategies by approximately 10 to 11 percent per year. Moreover, the superior performance of value stocks relative to glamour stocks persists when we restrict our attention to the largest 50 percent or largest 20 percent of stocks by market capitalization. Section IV provides evidence that contrarian strategies work because they exploit expectational errors implicit in stock prices. Specifically, the differences in expected growth rates between glamour and value stocks implicit in their relative valuation multiples significantly overestimate actual future growth rate differences. Section V examines risk characteristics of value strategies and provides evidence that, over longer horizons, value strategies have outperformed glamour strategies quite consistently and have done particularly well in "bad" states of the world. This evidence provides no support for the hypothesis that value strategies are fundamentally riskier. Finally, Section VI attempts to interpret our findings.

I. Methodology

The sample period covered in this study is from the end of April 1963 to the end of April 1990. Some of our formation strategies require 5 years of past accounting data. Consequently, we look at portfolios formed every year starting at the end of April 1968.[2] We examine subsequent performance and other characteristics of these portfolios for up to 5 years after formation using returns data from the Center for Research in Security Prices (CRSP) and accounting data from COMPUSTAT (including the research file). The universe of stocks is the New York Stock Exchange (NYSE) and the American Stock Exchange (AMEX).

A key question about this sample is whether results for stock returns are contaminated by significant look-ahead or survivorship bias (Banz and Breen (1986) and Kothari, Shanken, and Sloan (1992)). The potentially most serious bias is due to COMPUSTAT's major expansion of its database in 1978, which increased its coverage from 2,700 NYSE/AMEX firms and large National Association of Securities Dealers Automated Quotation (NASDAQ) firms to about 6,000 firms. Up to 5 years of data were added retroactively for many of these firms. As Kothari, Shanken, and Sloan (1992) point out, this raises the prospect of a look-ahead bias. Particularly among the firms that start out small or low priced, only those that perform well are added to the database. Hence, as one goes to lower and lower market valuation firms on COMPUSTAT, one finds that the population is increasingly selected from firms having good 5-year past performance records. This could potentially explain the positive association between low initial valuation and future returns. The potential bias toward high returns among low valuation firms is driven by data for the first 5 or so years that the firm appears on COMPUSTAT.

Our results potentially suffer from the same bias. However, our methodology differs from those in other recent studies in ways that should mitigate this bias. First, many of the strategies we focus on require 5 years of past data to classify firms before we start measuring returns. This means that we do not use returns for the first 5 years that the firm appears on COMPUSTAT to evaluate our strategies. But these first 5 years of returns is where the look-ahead bias in returns is found. Second, we study only NYSE and AMEX firms. The major expansion of COMPUSTAT largely involved adding

---

[2] We form portfolios in April to ensure that the previous year's accounting numbers were available at the time of formation.

(successful) NASDAQ firms. Finally, we also report results for the largest 50 percent of firms on the NYSE and AMEX. The selection bias is less serious among these larger firms (La Porta (1993)).

Within each of our portfolios, we equally weight all the stocks and compute returns using an annual buy-and-hold strategy for Years $+1, +2, \ldots, +5$ relative to the time of formation. If a stock disappears from CRSP during a year, its return is replaced until the end of the year with the return on a corresponding size decile portfolio. At the end of each year, the portfolio is rebalanced and each surviving stock gets the same weight.

For most of our results, we present size-adjusted returns as well as raw returns. To adjust portfolio returns for size, we first identify, for every stock in the sample, its market capitalization decile at the end of the previous year. We then construct a size benchmark return for each portfolio as follows. For each stock in the portfolio, replace its return in each year with an annual buy-and-hold return on an equally weighted portfolio of all stocks in its size decile for that year. Then equally weight these returns across all stocks in the original portfolio. The annual size-adjusted return on the original portfolio is then computed as the return on that portfolio minus the return on that year's size benchmark portfolio.

In addition to returns for the various portfolios, we compute growth rates and multiples for accounting measures such as sales, earnings, and cash flow. All accounting variables are taken from COMPUSTAT. Earnings are measured before extraordinary items, and cash flow is defined as earnings plus depreciation.

Let us illustrate our procedure for computing growth rates using the case of earnings growth from Year -4 to Year -3 relative to portfolio formation. We consider the portfolio that invests \$1 in each stock at the end of Year -4. This fixes the proportion of each firm owned at $1/$(market capitalization), where market capitalization is calculated at the end of Year -4. We then calculate the earnings per dollar invested that are generated by this portfolio in each of Years -4 and -3 as follows. For each stock in the portfolio, we multiply total firm earnings by the proportion of the firm owned. We then sum these numbers across all stocks in the portfolio for that year and divide by the number of stocks in the portfolio. Computing growth rates from these numbers is complicated by the fact that the earnings (and cash flows) are negative for some entire portfolios for some years.[3] This makes it impossible to compute the average earnings growth rate from period -4 to period -3 as the average of the $(-4, -3)$ growth rates across all 22 formation periods since, for some formation periods, the base Year -4 earnings is negative. Even without the negative earnings years, these year-to-year growth rates are highly volatile because the base year's earnings were sometimes very close to zero. This makes year-by-year averaging of growth rates unreliable. To deal with these problems, we average Year -4 and Year -3 portfolio

---

[3] Obviously, there is no such problem for sales. However, for symmetry we use the same methodology to compute growth rates of sales, earnings, and cash flow.

earnings across all 22 formation periods *before* computing growth rates. Hence, the earnings growth rate from Year -4 to Year -3 is computed as $(AE_{(-3)} - AE_{(-4)})/AE_{(-4)}$ where $AE_{(-3)}$ and $AE_{(-4)}$ are just the averages across all formation periods of the portfolio earnings in Years -3 and -4. In this fashion, we compute the growth rate in earnings, cash flow, and sales for each portfolio and for each year prior and postformation.

Finally, we compute several accounting ratios, such as cash-flow-to-price and earnings-to-price. These ratios are also used to sort individual stocks into portfolios. For these classifications, we consider only stocks with positive ratios of cash flow-to-price or earnings-to-price because negative ratios cannot be interpreted in terms of expected growth rates.[4] For purposes other than classifying individual stocks into portfolios, these ratios are computed for the entire equally weighted portfolios (and then averaged across all formation periods) without eliminating individual stocks in the portfolio that have negative values for the variable. For example, we compute the cash flow-to-price ratio for each stock and then take the average over all stocks in the portfolio. This gives us the cash flow per \$1 invested in the portfolio where each stock receives the same dollar investment.

II. Simple Glamour and Value Strategies

Table I, Panel A presents the returns on a strategy that has received a lot of attention recently (Fama and French (1992)), namely the book-to-market strategy. We divide the universe of stocks annually into book-to-market (B/M) deciles, where book value is taken from COMPUSTAT for the end of the previous fiscal year, and market value is taken from CRSP as the market value of equity at portfolio formation time. In general, we focus on long-horizon returns (of up to 5 years) on various strategies. The reason for looking at such long horizons is that we are interested in performance of alternative investment strategies over horizons suitable for long-term investors. Moreover, we assume annual buy and hold periods in contrast to monthly buy and hold periods assumed in most previous studies. Because of various market microstructure issues as well as execution costs, our procedure produces returns that are closer to those that investors can actually capture. We defer statistical testing of return differences across value and glamour portfolios to

---

[4] While we would ultimately like to say something about the future returns of firms with negative earnings, not including them here should not be viewed as a source of bias. As long as our strategy is feasible, in the sense that it constructs portfolios based on characteristics that were observable at the time of portfolio formation (see our discussion on look-ahead biases), the estimated differences in returns should be viewed as an unbiased measure of actual return differences *between subsets of firms that are all part of the set of firms with positive earnings.* While a strategy that incorporates the negative earnings firms may produce different returns, this is quite a different strategy from the one that we are studying. In our regression in Table IV, we do include firms with negative earnings or cash flow by separately including a dummy variable for negative earnings or cash flow along with the actual E/P ratio or C/P ratio if the numerator is positive.

Table VI where year-by-year return differences are reported starting in April 1968 and ending in April 1990.

In Panel A of Table I, we present the returns for Years 1 through 5 after the formation (R_1 through R_5), the average annual 5-year return (AR), the cumulative 5-year return (CR_5), and the size-adjusted average annual 5-year return ($SAAR$). The numbers presented are the averages across all formation periods in the sample. The results confirm and extend the results established by Rosenberg, Reid, and Lanstein (1984), Chan, Hamao, and Lakonishok (1991), and Fama and French (1992). On average over the postformation years, the low B/M (glamour) stocks have an average annual return of 9.3 percent and the high B/M (value) stocks have an average annual return of 19.8 percent, for a difference of 10.5 percent per year. If portfolios are held with the limited rebalancing described above, then cumulatively value stocks outperform glamour stocks by 90 percent over Years 1 through 5. Adjusting for size reduces the estimated return differences between value and glamour stocks somewhat, but the differences are still quite large. The size-adjusted average annual return is -4.3 percent for glamour stocks and 3.5 percent for value stocks, for a difference of 7.8 percent.

The natural question is: what is the B/M ratio really capturing? Unfortunately, many different factors are reflected in this ratio. A low B/M may describe a company with a lot of intangible assets, such as research and development (R & D) capital, that are not reflected in the accounting book value because R & D is expensed. A low B/M can also describe a company with attractive growth opportunities that do not enter the computation of book value but do enter the market price. Also, a natural resource company, such as an oil producer without good growth opportunities but with high temporary profits, might have a low B/M after an increase in oil prices. A stock whose risk is low and future cash flows are discounted at a low rate would have a low B/M as well. Finally, a low B/M may describe an overvalued glamour stock. The point here is simple: although the returns to the B/M strategy are impressive, B/M is not a "clean" variable uniquely associated with economically interpretable characteristics of the firms.

Arguably, the most important of such economically interpretable characteristics are the market's expectations of future growth and the past growth of these firms. To proxy for expected growth, we use ratios of various measures of profitability to price, so that firms with lower ratios have *higher* expected growth. The idea behind this is Gordon's formula, which states that $P = D(+1)/(r - g)$, where $D(+1)$ is next period's dividend, P is the current stock price, r is the required rate of return on the stock, and g is the expected growth rate of dividends (Gordon and Shapiro (1956)). A similar formula applies to cash flow and earnings. For example, to get an expression in terms of cash flow, we write $D(+1) = \rho C(+1)$, where $C(+1)$ is next period's cash flow and ρ, the payout ratio, is the constant fraction of cash flow paid out as dividends. We can then write $P = \rho C(+1)/(r - g)$ where the growth rate g for dividends is also the growth rate for cash flow on the assumption that dividends are proportional to cash flow. A similar formula

Table I

Returns for Decile Portfolios Based on One-Dimensional Classifications by Various Measures of Value

At the end of each April between 1968 and 1989, 10-decile portfolios are formed in ascending order based on B/M, C/P, E/P, and GS. B/M is the ratio of book value of equity to market value of equity; C/P is the ratio of cash flow to market value of equity; E/P is the ratio of earnings to market value of equity, and GS refers to preformation 5-year average growth rate of sales. The returns presented in the table are averages over all formation periods. R_t is the average return in year t after formation, $t = 1, \ldots, 5$. AR is the average annual return over 5 postformation years. CR_5 is the compounded 5-year return assuming annual rebalancing. $SAAR$ is the average annual size-adjusted return computed over 5 postformation years. The glamour portfolio refers to the decile portfolio containing stocks ranking lowest on B/M, C/P, or E/P, or highest on GS. The value portfolio refers to the decile portfolio containing stocks ranking highest on B/M, C/P, or E/P, or lowest on GS.

	Glamour									Value
	1	2	3	4	5	6	7	8	9	10
					Panel A: B/M					
R_1	0.110	0.117	0.135	0.123	0.131	0.154	0.154	0.170	0.183	0.173
R_2	0.079	0.107	0.140	0.145	0.153	0.156	0.169	0.164	0.182	0.188
R_3	0.107	0.132	0.155	0.167	0.165	0.172	0.191	0.207	0.196	0.204
R_4	0.081	0.133	0.136	0.160	0.170	0.169	0.188	0.204	0.213	0.207
R_5	0.088	0.137	0.163	0.175	0.171	0.176	0.216	0.201	0.206	0.215
AR	0.093	0.125	0.146	0.154	0.158	0.166	0.184	0.189	0.196	0.198
CR_5	0.560	0.802	0.973	1.045	1.082	1.152	1.320	1.375	1.449	1.462
$SAAR$	-0.043	-0.020	-0.003	0.004	0.006	0.012	0.024	0.028	0.033	0.035
					Panel B: C/P					
R_1	0.084	0.124	0.140	0.140	0.153	0.148	0.157	0.178	0.183	0.183
R_2	0.067	0.108	0.126	0.153	0.156	0.170	0.177	0.180	0.183	0.190
R_3	0.096	0.133	0.153	0.172	0.170	0.191	0.191	0.202	0.193	0.204
R_4	0.098	0.111	0.146	0.159	0.166	0.172	0.182	0.192	0.223	0.218
R_5	0.108	0.134	0.161	0.162	0.187	0.177	0.191	0.209	0.212	0.208
AR	0.091	0.122	0.145	0.157	0.166	0.171	0.180	0.192	0.199	0.201
CR_5	0.543	0.779	0.969	1.074	1.158	1.206	1.283	1.406	1.476	1.494
$SAAR$	-0.049	-0.025	-0.006	0.005	0.013	0.019	0.025	0.034	0.037	0.039

would apply to earnings but with a different payout ratio. According to these expressions, *holding discount rates and payout ratios constant*,[5] a high cash flow-to-price (C/P) firm has a low expected growth rate of cash flow, while a low C/P firm has a high expected growth rate of cash flow, and similarly for the ratio of earnings-to-price (E/P).[6] While the assumption of a constant

---

[5] In Section V, we compare risk characteristics, and hence appropriate discount rates, of the various portfolios.

[6] An alternative approach is to use analysts' forecasts to proxy for expectations of future growth. This approach is used by La Porta (1993).

Contrarian Investment, Extrapolation, and Risk   1549

Table I—*Continued*

	Glamour									Value
	1	2	3	4	5	6	7	8	9	10

Panel C: E/P

R_1	0.123	0.125	0.140	0.130	0.135	0.156	0.170	0.180	0.193	0.162
R_2	0.101	0.113	0.124	0.143	0.167	0.164	0.180	0.185	0.183	0.174
R_3	0.118	0.138	0.157	0.171	0.171	0.191	0.198	0.188	0.188	0.195
R_4	0.111	0.124	0.145	0.151	0.157	0.159	0.198	0.199	0.205	0.214
R_5	0.119	0.129	0.151	0.167	0.171	0.168	0.196	0.201	0.211	0.207
AR	0.114	0.126	0.143	0.152	0.160	0.167	0.188	0.191	0.196	0.190
CR_5	0.717	0.808	0.953	1.031	1.102	1.168	1.370	1.393	1.446	1.388
$SAAR$	−0.035	−0.024	−0.009	−0.001	0.005	0.013	0.026	0.026	0.029	0.019

Panel D: GS

	Value									Glamour
	1	2	3	4	5	6	7	8	9	10
R_1	0.187	0.183	0.164	0.169	0.162	0.157	0.159	0.164	0.142	0.114
R_2	0.181	0.180	0.186	0.169	0.166	0.162	0.152	0.157	0.147	0.131
R_3	0.204	0.206	0.194	0.186	0.181	0.180	0.168	0.178	0.157	0.138
R_4	0.205	0.193	0.201	0.190	0.181	0.174	0.160	0.153	0.167	0.126
R_5	0.197	0.213	0.194	0.199	0.168	0.184	0.185	0.168	0.163	0.125
AR	0.195	0.195	0.188	0.183	0.171	0.171	0.165	0.164	0.155	0.127
CR_5	1.434	1.435	1.364	1.314	1.205	1.206	1.144	1.136	1.057	0.818
$SAAR$	0.022	0.027	0.025	0.024	0.015	0.015	0.008	0.008	0.000	−0.024

growth rate for dividends and strict proportionality between cash flow (or earnings) and dividends are restrictive, the intuition behind Gordon's formula is quite general. Differences in C/P or E/P ratios across stocks should proxy for differences in expected growth rates.[7]

Panel B of Table I presents the results of sorting on the ratio of C/P. High C/P stocks are identified with value stocks because their growth rate of cash flow is expected to be low, or, alternatively, their prices are low per dollar of cash flow. Conversely, low C/P stocks are glamour stocks. On average, over the 5 postformation years, first-decile C/P stocks have a return of 9.1 percent per annum, whereas the tenth-decile C/P stocks have an average return of 20.1 percent per annum, for a difference of 11 percent. The 5-year cumulative returns are 54.3 percent and 149.4 percent, respectively, for a difference of 95.1 percent. On a size-adjusted basis, the difference in returns is 8.8 percent per annum. Sorting on C/P thus appears to produce somewhat

---

[7] We use current cash flow and earnings rather than one-period-ahead numbers because we require our investment strategies to be functions of observable variables only.

bigger differences in returns than sorting on B/M ratios. This is consistent with the idea that measuring the market's expectations of future growth more directly gives rise to better value strategies.[8]

Another popular multiple, studied by Basu (1977), is the E/P. Table I, Panel C presents our results for E/P. On average, over the 5 postformation years, first-decile E/P stocks have an average annual return of 11.4 percent and tenth-decile E/P stocks have an average annual return of 19.0 percent, for a difference of 7.6 percent. On a size-adjusted basis, the difference in returns is 5.4 percent per annum. Low E/P stocks underperform high E/P stocks by a fairly wide margin, although the difference is not as large as that between extreme B/M or C/P deciles. One possible reason for this is that stocks with temporarily depressed earnings are lumped together with well-performing glamour stocks in the high expected growth/low E/P category. These stocks with depressed earnings do not experience the same degree of poor future stock performance as the glamour stocks, perhaps because they are less overpriced by the market.

An alternative way to operationalize the notions of glamour and value is to classify stocks based on past growth rather than by expectations of future growth. We measure past growth by growth in sales (GS) since sales is less volatile than either cash flow or earnings, particularly for stocks in the extreme portfolios that we are most interested in. Specifically, for each company for each of Years $-1, -2, \ldots, -5$ prior to formation, we calculate the GS in that year. Then, for each year, we rank all firms by GS for that year. We then compute each firm's weighted average rank, giving the weight of 5 to its growth rank in Year -1, the weight of 4 to its growth rank in Year -2, etc. Finally, we form deciles based on each stock's weighted average sales growth rank. This procedure is a crude way to both pick out stocks with consistently high past GS, and to give greater weight to more recent sales growth in ranking stocks.[9]

Table I, Panel D presents the results for the GS strategy. On average, over the 5 postformation years, the portfolio of firms in the lowest decile of past sales growth earns an average return of 19.5 percent per annum and the portfolio of firms in the highest decile earns an average return of 12.7 percent per annum. On a size-adjusted basis the average annual abnormal returns are 2.2 percent for the low GS strategy and -2.4 percent for the high GS strategy. These magnitudes are not as dramatic as those for the B/M and C/P strategies, nevertheless the spread in returns is sizeable.

In this section, we have largely confirmed and extended the results of others. A wide variety of simple value strategies based on classification of firms by a single fundamental variable produce very large returns over the 22-year period April 1968 to April 1990. In contrast to previous work, our

---

[8] La Porta (1993) shows that contrarian strategies based directly on analysts' forecasts of future growth can produce even larger returns than those based on financial ratios.

[9] We have also tried a procedure in which we equally weight the ranks for all 5 years of past sales growth and obtain very similar results.

strategies involve classifying firms based on fundamentals and then buying and holding for 5 years. In the next section, we explore more sophisticated two-dimensional versions of these strategies that are designed to correct some of the misclassification of firms inherent in a one-variable approach. For example, low E/P stocks, which are supposedly glamour stocks, include many stocks with temporarily depressed earnings that are expected to recover. The two-dimensional strategies of the next section are formulated with an eye toward more directly exploiting the possible mistakes made by naive investors.

III. Anatomy of a Contrarian Strategy

A. *Performance of Contrarian Strategies*

Much psychological evidence indicates that individuals form their predictions of the future without a full appreciation of mean reversion. That is, individuals tend to base their expectations on past data for the individual case they are considering without properly weighting data on what psychologists call the "base rate," or the class average. Kahneman and Tversky (1982, p. 417) explain:

> One of the basic principles of statistical prediction, which is also one of the least intuitive, is that the extremeness of predictions must be moderated by considerations of predictability ... Predictions are allowed to match impressions only in the case of perfect predictability. In intermediate situations, which are of course the most common, the prediction should be regressive; that is, it should fall between the class average and the value that best represents one's impression of the case at hand. The lower the predictability the closer the prediction should be to the class average. Intuitive predictions are typically nonregressive: people often make extreme predictions on the basis of information whose reliability and predictive validity are known to be low ...

To exploit this flaw of intuitive forecasts, contrarian investors should sell stocks with high past growth as well as high expected future growth and buy stocks with low past growth as well as low expected future growth. Prices of these stocks are most likely to reflect the failure of investors to impose mean reversion on growth forecasts. Accordingly, we define a glamour stock to be a stock with high growth in the past and high expected future growth. A value stock must have had low growth in the past and be expected by the market to continue growing slowly. In this section, we continue to use high ratios of C/P (E/P) as a proxy for a low expected growth rate.

Table II, Panel A presents the results for the strategy that sorts on both GS and C/P. Since we are sorting on two variables, sorting stocks into deciles on each variable is impractical. Accordingly, we independently sort stocks into three groups ((1) bottom 30 percent, (2) middle 40 percent, and (3) top 30 percent) by GS and by C/P, and then take intersections resulting

Table II

Returns for Portfolios Based on Two-Dimensional Classifications by Various Measures of Value

At the end of each April between 1968 and 1989, 9 groups of stocks are formed. The stocks are independently sorted in ascending order into 3 groups ((1) bottom 30 percent, (2) middle 40 percent, and (3) top 30 percent) based on each of two variables. The sorts are for 5 pairs of variables: C/P and GS, B/M and GS, E/P and GS, E/P and B/M, and B/M and C/P. C/P is the ratio of cash flow to market value of equity; B/M is the ratio of book value of equity to market value of equity; E/P is the ratio of earnings to market value of equity; and GS refers to preformation 5-year average growth rate of sales. The returns presented in the table are averages over all formation periods. R_t is the average return in year t after formation, $t = 1, \ldots, 5$. AR is the average annual return over 5 postformation years. CR_5 is the compounded 5-year return assuming annual rebalancing. $SAAR$ is the average annual size-adjusted return computed over 5 postformation years. Depending on the two variables being used for classification, the value portfolio either refers to the portfolio containing stocks ranked in the top group (3) on both variables from among C/P, E/P, or B/M, or else the portfolio containing stocks ranking in the top group on one of those variables and in the bottom group (1) on GS. The glamour portfolio contains stocks with precisely the opposite set of rankings.

Panel A: C/P and GS									
			Glamour				Value		
C/P	1	1	1	2	2	2	3	3	3
GS	1	2	3	1	2	3	1	2	3
R_1	0.157	0.131	0.113	0.181	0.156	0.139	0.215	0.202	0.137
R_2	0.147	0.120	0.100	0.191	0.165	0.167	0.213	0.188	0.165
R_3	0.165	0.140	0.121	0.197	0.190	0.165	0.227	0.195	0.172
R_4	0.164	0.124	0.114	0.198	0.169	0.166	0.231	0.204	0.177
R_5	0.179	0.135	0.121	0.200	0.173	0.151	0.218	0.216	0.184
AR	0.162	0.130	0.114	0.193	0.171	0.157	0.221	0.201	0.167
CR_5	1.122	0.843	0.712	1.419	1.200	1.076	1.711	1.497	1.163
$SAAR$	-0.006	-0.020	-0.033	0.030	0.014	0.003	0.054	0.036	0.008
Panel B: E/P and GS									
			Glamour				Value		
E/P	1	1	1	2	2	2	3	3	3
GS	1	2	3	1	2	3	1	2	3
R_1	0.184	0.148	0.118	0.188	0.153	0.139	0.224	0.205	0.174
R_2	0.167	0.134	0.100	0.204	0.174	0.154	0.214	0.187	0.190
R_3	0.185	0.153	0.119	0.222	0.189	0.169	0.221	0.198	0.189
R_4	0.190	0.138	0.103	0.205	0.175	0.160	0.232	0.217	0.188
R_5	0.189	0.163	0.104	0.201	0.180	0.157	0.215	0.210	0.199
AR	0.183	0.147	0.109	0.204	0.174	0.156	0.221	0.203	0.188
CR_5	1.315	0.986	0.674	1.533	1.230	1.063	1.716	1.523	1.365
$SAAR$	0.005	-0.011	-0.037	0.033	0.013	0.002	0.040	0.034	0.017

Contrarian Investment, Extrapolation, and Risk   1553

Table II—*Continued*

Panel C: B/M and GS

	Glamour						Value		
B/M	1	1	1	2	2	2	3	3	3
GS	1	2	3	1	2	3	1	2	3
R_1	0.147	0.141	0.132	0.160	0.159	0.121	0.204	0.185	0.135
R_2	0.127	0.138	0.127	0.175	0.166	0.150	0.200	0.172	0.163
R_3	0.149	0.149	0.137	0.190	0.186	0.152	0.221	0.192	0.182
R_4	0.147	0.130	0.130	0.191	0.176	0.154	0.222	0.190	0.195
R_5	0.158	0.140	0.124	0.203	0.180	0.165	0.216	0.211	0.164
AR	0.146	0.140	0.130	0.184	0.173	0.148	0.212	0.190	0.168
CR_5	0.974	0.925	0.842	1.325	1.224	0.996	1.618	1.387	1.171
$SAAR$	−0.009	−0.012	−0.021	0.022	0.015	−0.009	0.039	0.030	0.017

Panel D: E/P and B/M

	Glamour								Value
E/P	1	1	1	2	2	2	3	3	3
B/M	1	2	3	1	2	3	1	2	3
R_1	0.116	0.118	0.186	0.142	0.143	0.174	0.135	0.174	0.189
R_2	0.086	0.120	0.194	0.146	0.163	0.192	0.173	0.178	0.185
R_3	0.114	0.154	0.201	0.157	0.184	0.220	0.177	0.178	0.204
R_4	0.093	0.151	0.218	0.150	0.166	0.193	0.188	0.200	0.214
R_5	0.093	0.188	0.218	0.168	0.169	0.209	0.241	0.205	0.204
AR	0.100	0.146	0.203	0.152	0.165	0.198	0.183	0.187	0.199
CR_5	0.613	0.976	1.521	1.032	1.146	1.464	1.311	1.354	1.479
$SAAR$	−0.039	−0.009	0.022	0.002	0.009	0.033	0.003	0.023	0.030

Panel E: B/M and C/P

	Glamour								Value
B/M	1	1	1	2	2	2	3	3	3
C/P	1	2	3	1	2	3	1	2	3
R_1	0.111	0.153	0.141	0.101	0.144	0.171	0.170	0.161	0.194
R_2	0.085	0.164	0.172	0.111	0.160	0.181	0.174	0.173	0.189
R_3	0.111	0.172	0.179	0.147	0.177	0.191	0.192	0.206	0.207
R_4	0.101	0.153	0.187	0.155	0.168	0.200	0.177	0.195	0.219
R_5	0.108	0.162	0.250	0.184	0.178	0.208	0.233	0.201	0.209
AR	0.103	0.161	0.186	0.139	0.165	0.190	0.189	0.187	0.203
CR_5	0.633	1.108	1.339	0.917	1.148	1.387	1.378	1.355	1.524
$SAAR$	−0.037	0.007	0.018	−0.021	0.011	0.026	0.006	0.020	0.037

from the two classifications. Because the classifications are done independently, extreme glamour (high GS, low C/P) and value portfolios (low GS, high C/P) contain greater than average numbers of stocks, since GS and C/P are negatively correlated.

In an average postformation year in this sample, the glamour portfolio had a return of 11.4 percent, and the value portfolio had a return of 22.1 percent, for a difference of 10.7 percent per year. Over the 5 postformation years, the cumulative difference in returns is 100 percent. On a size-adjusted basis, the difference in returns is 8.7 percent per year. As Figure 1 illustrates, both C/P and GS contribute a great deal of explanatory power in these bivariate classifications. For example, low C/P stocks with low past sales growth, which we don't define as glamour stocks, have an average annual future return of 16.2 percent, but low C/P stocks with a high past sales growth, which we do define as glamour stocks, have an average annual future return of only 11.4 percent.

Table II, Panel B presents the return results for a classification scheme using both past GS and the E/P ratio. The average annual difference in returns over the 5-year period between the two extreme portfolios is 11.2 percent per year, which cumulatively amounts to 104.2 percent over 5 years. As with C/P and GS, the $(E/P, GS)$ strategy produces substantially higher returns than either the E/P or the GS strategy alone. For example, among firms with the lowest E/P ratios, the average annual future return varies from 10.9 percent for firms with the highest past sales growth to 18.3 percent for those with the lowest past sales growth. Even more so than for C/P, using an E/P strategy seems to require differentiating between the stocks

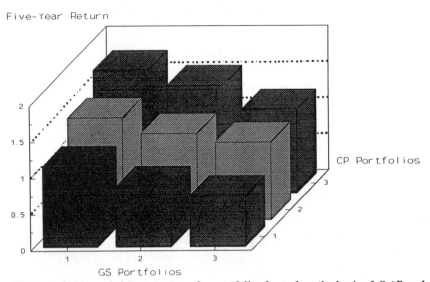

Figure 1. Compounded 5-year return for portfolios formed on the basis of C/P and GS. At the end of each April between 1968 and 1989, 9 groups of stocks are formed. The stocks are independently sorted in ascending order into 3 groups ((1) bottom 30 percent, (2) middle 40 percent, and (3) top 30 percent) based on each of two variables: cash-flow-to-price (C/P) and growth-in-sales (GS). Returns presented are compounded 5-year postformation returns assuming annual rebalancing for these 9 portfolios.

with depressed earnings expected to recover and the true glamour firms.[10] Once this finer classification scheme is used, the two-dimensional strategy based on E/P generates returns as high as those produced by the two-dimensional strategy based on C/P.

Table II, Panel C presents results for portfolios classified by B/M and GS. The results show that GS has significant explanatory power for returns even after sorting by B/M. For example, within the set of firms whose B/M ratios are the highest, the average difference in returns between the low sales growth and high sales growth subgroups is over 4 percent per year (21.2 versus 16.8 percent). A similar result holds for the other two groups sorted by B/M. Note that these results do not appear to be driven by the role of the superimposed GS classification in creating a more precise partition of the firms by B/M. The B/M ratios across GS subgroups are not very different.

Panels D and E of Table II present results for $(B/M, E/P)$ and $(B/M, C/P)$, respectively. Once again, the results confirm the usefulness of more precise classification schemes. For example, among firms with the lowest C/P ratios, future returns vary substantially according to B/M ratios. Future returns vary from 10.3 percent per year for the true glamour firms, to 18.6 percent per year for firms with low ratios of C/P but high B/M ratios. Most likely, the B/M ratio adds information here because it proxies for past growth, which is useful in conjunction with a measure of expected future growth.

The results of this subsection can be summarized and interpreted as follows. First, two-dimensional value strategies, in which firms are independently classified into 3 subgroups according to each of two fundamental variables, produce returns on the order of 10 to 11 percent per year higher than those on similarly constructed glamour strategies over the April 1968 to April 1990 period. Second, the results suggest that value strategies based jointly on past performance and expected future performance produce higher returns than more ad hoc strategies such as that based exclusively on the B/M ratio.

B. Do These Results Apply As Well to Large Stocks?

Even though we have shown that the superior returns to value strategies persist even after adjusting for size, the returns on such strategies might still be driven by the smaller stocks. Larger firms are of greater interest for implementable trading strategies, especially for institutional investors. Larger firms are also more closely monitored, and hence might be more efficiently priced. Finally, the look-ahead and survivorship biases discussed by Banz and Breen (1986) and Kothari, Shanken, and Sloan (1992) should be less important for the larger stocks.

Table III presents a summary version of Table II for the subsample consisting of the largest 50 percent of our NYSE/AMEX firms. The results

---

[10] This probably results from the greater year-to-year percentage swings for earnings than for cash flows.

are similar to those obtained for the whole sample. For example, using the $(C/P, GS)$ classification scheme, the difference in average annual size-adjusted returns between the value and glamour portfolios is 8.7 percent, exactly the same as for the entire sample. Using the $(E/P, GS)$ classification

Table III
Returns for Portfolios Based on Two-Dimensional Classifications for the Largest 50 Percent of Stocks

At the end of each April between 1968 and 1989, 9 subgroups of the largest 50 percent of stocks by market capitalization are formed. The stocks are independently sorted in ascending order into 3 groups ((1) bottom 30 percent, (2) middle 40 percent, and (3) top 30 percent) based on each of two variables. The sorts are for 5 pairs of variables: C/P and GS, B/M and GS, E/P and GS, E/P and B/M, and B/M and C/P. C/P is the ratio of cash flow to market value of equity; B/M is the ratio of book value of equity to market value of equity; E/P is the ratio of earnings to market value of equity; and GS refers to preformation 5-year average growth rate of sales. The returns presented in the table are averages over all formation periods. AR is the average annual return over 5 postformation years. CR_5 is the compounded 5-year return assuming annual rebalancing. $SAAR$ is the average annual size-adjusted abnormal return computed over 5 postformation years. Depending on the two variables being used for classification, the value portfolio either refers to the portfolio containing stocks ranked in the top group (3) on both variables from among C/P, E/P, or B/M, or else the portfolio containing stocks ranking in the top group on one of those variables and in the bottom group (1) on GS. The glamour portfolio contains stocks with precisely the opposite set of rankings.

Panel A: C/P and GS

	Glamour						Value		
C/P	1	1	1	2	2	2	3	3	3
GS	1	2	3	1	2	3	1	2	3
AR	0.159	0.125	0.106	0.178	0.161	0.153	0.184	0.174	0.141
CR_5	1.094	0.799	0.654	1.270	1.106	1.040	1.328	1.226	0.934
$SAAR$	0.001	−0.020	−0.039	0.030	0.010	0.001	0.048	0.021	−0.010

Panel B: E/P and GS

	Glamour						Value		
E/P	1	1	1	2	2	2	3	3	3
GS	1	2	3	1	2	3	1	2	3
AR	0.168	0.136	0.103	0.182	0.163	0.148	0.186	0.181	0.163
CR_5	1.176	0.894	0.631	1.307	1.126	0.997	1.344	1.301	1.124
$SAAR$	0.012	−0.011	−0.037	0.034	0.012	−0.002	0.046	0.031	0.007

Panel C: B/M and GS

	Glamour						Value		
B/M	1	1	1	2	2	2	3	3	3
GS	1	2	3	1	2	3	1	2	3
AR	0.149	0.140	0.124	0.176	0.158	0.131	0.186	0.172	0.153
CR_5	1.001	0.922	0.793	1.248	1.080	0.849	1.347	1.211	1.039
$SAAR$	0.000	−0.008	−0.025	0.027	0.006	−0.020	0.043	0.022	0.005

Table III—*Continued*

Panel D: E/P and B/M

	Glamour								Value
E/P	1	1	1	2	2	2	3	3	3
B/M	1	2	3	1	2	3	1	2	3
AR	0.104	0.146	0.185	0.156	0.155	0.178	0.184	0.170	0.175
CR_5	0.636	0.979	1.335	1.063	1.054	1.265	1.318	1.190	1.244
SAAR	−0.035	0.000	0.028	0.006	0.006	0.037	0.014	0.021	0.031

Panel E: B/M and C/P

	Glamour								Value
B/M	1	1	1	2	2	2	3	3	3
C/P	1	2	3	1	2	3	1	2	3
AR	0.109	0.166	0.148	0.139	0.157	0.168	0.182	0.173	0.178
CR_5	0.675	1.152	0.991	0.909	1.074	1.175	1.301	1.222	1.264
SAAR	−0.031	0.015	−0.007	−0.011	0.010	0.019	0.028	0.029	0.037

scheme, this difference is 8.3 percent per year, compared to 7.7 percent per year for the entire sample. Raw return differences between value and glamour portfolios are slightly lower for the large-firm subsample because the extra return to value firms from their smaller average size is not present in that subsample. Value and glamour firms are essentially the same size in the large firm subsample. We have also done the analysis for the largest 20 percent of the stocks, which effectively mimics the S&P 500, and get a very similar spread of returns between glamour and value stocks. The conclusion is clear: our results apply to the largest stocks as well.

C. Regression Analysis

Previous analysis has identified a variety of variables that can define glamour and value portfolios. In this section, we ask which of these variables are significant in a multiple regression. Table IV presents the results of regressions of raw returns for each stock on the characteristics of stocks that we have identified. Recall that in our analysis we have 22 portfolio formation periods. We run regressions separately for each postformation year, starting with +1 and ending with +5. Thus, for postformation Year +1, we run 22 separate cross-sectional regressions in which the dependent variable is the annual return on stock i and the independent variables are characteristics of stock i observed at the beginning of the year. Then, using the Fama-MacBeth (1973) procedure, the coefficients for these 22 cross-sectional regressions are averaged and the t-statistics are computed. We applied the same procedure for Years +2, +3, +4, and +5 after the formation. The results presented in Table IV are for the Year +1.

Table IV

Regression of Returns on Characteristics for All Firms

At the end of each April between 1968 and 1989, we compute for every firm in the sample the 1-year holding-period return starting at the end of April. We then run 22 cross-sectional regressions with these returns for each formation period as dependent variables. The independent variables are (1) GS, the preformation 5-year weighted average rank of sales growth; (2) B/M, the ratio of end of previous year's book value of equity to market value of equity; (3) $SIZE$, the end of April natural logarithm of market value of equity (in millions); (4) $E/P+$, equal to E/P—the ratio of previous year's earnings to end-of-April market value of equity—if E/P is positive—and to zero if E/P is negative; (5) DE/P, equal to 1 if E/P is negative, and zero if E/P is positive; (6) $C/P+$, equal to C/P—the ratio of previous-year's cash flow to end-of-April market value of equity—if C/P is positive—and zero if C/P is negative; (7) DC/P, equal to 1 if C/P is negative, and zero if C/P is positive. The reported coefficients are averages over the 22 formation periods. The reported t-statistics are based on the time-series variation of the 22 coefficients.

	Int.	GS	B/M	SIZE	E/P+	DE/P	C/P+	DC/P
Mean	0.180	-0.061						
t-statistic	3.251	-2.200						
Mean	0.108		0.039					
t-statistic	2.167		2.132					
Mean	0.185			-0.009				
t-statistic	2.140			-1.095				
Mean	0.110				0.526			
t-statistic	2.029				2.541			
Mean	0.099						0.356	
t-statistic	1.873						4.240	
Mean	0.129	-0.058	0.006				0.301	-0.029
t-statistic	2.584	-2.832	0.330				3.697	-1.222
Mean	0.143		0.009	-0.009			0.280	-0.032
t-statistic	1.562		0.565	-1.148			4.223	-1.625
Mean	0.169	-0.044	0.000	-0.009			0.296	-0.036
t-statistic	1.947	-2.125	0.005	-1.062			4.553	-1.625
Mean	0.172	-0.051	0.016	-0.009	0.394	-0.032		
t-statistic	1.961	-2.527	1.036	-1.065	2.008	-1.940		

We use the ratios of C/P and of E/P in the regression analysis. However, for some stocks these ratios are negative, and hence cannot be plausibly interpreted as expected growth rates. We deal with this problem in the same way as Fama and French (1992). Specifically, we define variables $C/P+$ and $E/P+$, which are equal to zero when C/P and E/P are negative, and are equal to C/P and E/P when they are positive. We also include in the regressions dummy variables, called DC/P and DE/P, which take the value of 1 when C/P or E/P are negative, respectively, and zero otherwise. This approach enables us to treat observations with negative E/P and C/P differently from observations with positive E/P and C/P.

The first result emerging from Table IV is that, taken separately, each of *GS*, *B/M*, *E/P*, and *C/P*, although not *SIZE*, have statistically significant predictive power for returns. These results are in line with Fama and French (1992), although on a stand-alone basis *C/P* and not *B/M* is the most significant variable. When we use the dependent variables in combination, the weakness of *B/M* relative to *C/P*, *E/P*, and *GS* begins to emerge, and its coefficient drops significantly. For example, when *GS*, *C/P*, and *B/M* are included in the same regression, the first two are significant, but *B/M* is not. In fact, the coefficient on *B/M* is essentially zero. Similarly, when *GS*, *E/P*, and *B/M* are included in the same regression, *E/P* and *GS* are significant, but *B/M* is not. The variables that stand out in the multiple regressions are *GS* and *C/P*.

IV. A Test of the Extrapolation Model

So far we have shown that strategies contrarian to extrapolation earn high abnormal returns relative to the market and to extrapolation strategies. We have not, however, provided any direct evidence that excessive extrapolation and expectational errors are indeed what characterizes glamour and value stocks.[11] In this section, we provide such evidence. The essence of extrapolation is that investors are excessively optimistic about glamour stocks and excessively pessimistic about value stocks because they tie their expectations of future growth to past growth. But if investors make mistakes, these mistakes can presumably be detected in the data. A direct test of extrapolation, then, is to look directly at *actual* future growth rates and compare them to *past* growth rates and to *expected* growth rates as implied by the multiples.

Table V presents some descriptive characteristics for our glamour and value portfolios regarding their valuation multiples, past growth rates, and future growth rates. Panel A reveals that the value portfolios had much higher ratios of fundamentals to price.[12] We interpret these ratios in terms of lower expected growth rates for value stocks. Panel B shows that, using several measures of past growth, including earnings, cash flow, sales, and stock return, glamour stocks grew substantially faster than value stocks over the 5 years before portfolio formation. Finally, Panel C shows that over the 5 postformation years the relative growth of fundamentals for glamour stocks was much less impressive. Indeed, over Years +2 to +5 relative to formation the growth rates of fundamentals for the value portfolio were often higher. This deterioration of relative growth rates of glamour stocks compared to

---

[11] In their study of contrarian strategies based on past stock returns, De Bondt and Thaler (1987) provide some evidence for the expectational errors view.

[12] The one exception is for the *E/P* ratio using the *B/M* classification scheme. Apparently, because of the large number of stocks with temporarily depressed earnings in the highest *B/M* decile, the *E/P* ratio for this group is extremely low. This result goes away when looking at the top two deciles together or when looking at the top decile within the largest 50 percent of our firms.

The Journal of Finance

Table V

Fundamental Variables, Past Performance, and Future Performance of Glamour and Value Stocks

Panel 1: At the end of each April between 1968 and 1989, 10-decile portfolios are formed based on the ratio of end-of-previous-year's book value of equity to end-of-April market value of equity. Numbers are presented for the first (lowest B/M) and tenth (highest B/M) deciles. These portfolios are denoted Glamour and Value, respectively.

Panel 2: At the end of each April between 1968 and 1989, 9 groups of stocks are formed. The stocks are independently sorted in ascending order into 3 groups ((1) bottom 30 percent, (2) middle 40 percent, (3) top 30 percent) based on C/P, the ratio of cash flow to market value of equity, and GS, the preformation 5-year weighted average sales growth rank. Numbers are presented for $(C/P_1, GS_3)$, the bottom 30 percent by C/P and the top 30 percent by GS, and for $(C/P_3, GS_1)$ the top 30 percent by C/P and the bottom 30 percent by GS. These portfolios are denoted Glamour and Value, respectively.

All numbers in the table are averages over all formation periods.

E/P, C/P, S/P, D/P, B/M, and $SIZE$, defined below, use the end-of-April market value of equity and preformation year accounting numbers. E/P is the ratio of earnings to market value of equity. S/P is the ratio of sales to market value of equity. D/P is the ratio of dividends to market value of equity. B/M is the ratio of book value to market value of equity. $SIZE$ is the total dollar value of equity (in millions). $AEG_{(i,j)}$ is the geometric average growth rate of earnings for the portfolio from year i to year j. $ACG_{(i,j)}$ and $ASG_{(i,j)}$ are defined analogously for cash flow and sales, respectively. $RETURN_{(-3,0)}$ is the cumulative stock return on the portfolio over the 3 years prior to formation.

	Panel 1		Panel 2	
	Glamour B/M_1	Value B/M_{10}	Glamour $C/P_1, GS_3$	Value $C/P_3, GS_1$
Panel A: Fundamental Variables				
E/P	0.029	0.004	0.054	0.114
C/P	0.059	0.172	0.080	0.279
S/P	0.993	6.849	1.115	5.279
D/P	0.012	0.032	0.014	0.039
B/M	0.225	1.998	0.385	1.414
$SIZE$	663	120	681	390
Panel B: Past Performance—Growth Rates and Past Returns				
$AEG_{(-5,0)}$	0.309	−0.274	0.142	0.082
$ACG_{(-5,0)}$	0.217	−0.013	0.210	0.078
$ASG_{(-5,0)}$	0.091	0.030	0.112	0.013
$RETURN_{(-3,0)}$	1.455	−0.119	1.390	0.225
Panel C: Future Performance				
$AEG_{(0,5)}$	0.050	0.436	0.089	0.086
$ACG_{(0,5)}$	0.127	0.070	0.112	0.052
$ASG_{(0,5)}$	0.062	0.020	0.100	0.037
$AEG_{(2,5)}$	0.070	0.215	0.084	0.147
$ACG_{(2,5)}$	0.086	0.111	0.095	0.088
$ASG_{(2,5)}$	0.059	0.023	0.082	0.038

Contrarian Investment, Extrapolation, and Risk   1561

past relative growth and expected future relative growth is explored more systematically below.

To interpret differences in financial ratios such as C/P and E/P in terms of expected growth rates, we come back to Gordon's formula (Gordon and Shapiro (1956)). Recall that for cash flow, this formula can be rewritten as $\rho C(+1)/P = r - g$, where $C(+1)$ is one period ahead cash flow, P is the current stock price, r is the required rate of return on the stock, g is the expected growth rate of cash flow, and ρ, the payout ratio for cash flows, is the constant fraction of cash flows received as dividends. An identical formula applies for earnings, under the assumption that dividends are also some fixed fraction of earnings. Taken literally, these formulas imply that, holding discount rates and payout ratios constant, we can directly calculate differences in expected growth rates based on differences in C/P or E/P ratios. Because the assumptions behind these simple formulas are restrictive (e.g., constant growth rates, strict proportionality of dividends, cash flows and earnings, identical payout ratios across stocks, etc.), we do not calculate exact estimates of differences in expected growth rates between value and glamour portfolios. Instead, we choose to analyze differences in past growth, valuation multiples and future growth rates in a way that is more robust with respect to departures from these assumptions. However, the idea behind this analysis is the same. We ask whether the large differences in C/P and E/P ratios between value and glamour stocks can be justified by differences in future growth rates.

We start with the data for portfolios classified according to $(C/P, GS)$. As we know already, the past growth of glamour stocks by any measure was much faster than that of value stocks. For example, over the 5 years before portfolio formation, the annual growth rate of cash flow for the glamour portfolio was 21.0 percent compared to 7.8 percent for the value portfolio. The difference in cash flow multiples between the value and glamour portfolios suggests that the market was expecting these growth differences to persist for many years. A dollar invested in the value portfolio was a claim to 27.9 cents in a current cash flow while a dollar invested in the glamour portfolio was a claim to only 8 cents of current cash flow. Ignoring any differences in required rates of return (this possibility is examined in Section V), these large differences in C/P would have to be justified either by big differences in payout ratios between value and glamour firms or else by an expectation of very different growth rates over a long period of time. A quick look at the respective dividend yields on the value and glamour portfolios suggests that the difference was not due to differences in payout ratios. A dollar invested in the value portfolio was a claim to 3.9 cents in current dividends, while a dollar invested in the glamour portfolio brought in only 1.4 cents in dividends. These differ by roughly the same factor of 3 as for C/P. While the cash flow payout ratios were slightly higher for glamour stocks (0.175 versus 0.140),[13] this does not account for most of the difference in C/P.

---

[13] We estimate these payout ratios by dividing D/P by C/P.

Under the assumption that payout ratios and discount rates were approximately equal, at some future date the expected cash flows per current dollar invested must have been higher for the glamour portfolio than for the value portfolio. Accordingly, we can ask how many years it would take for the cash flows per dollar invested in the glamour portfolio (0.080) to equal the cash flows of the value portfolio (0.279), assuming that the differences in past cash flow growth rates persisted (i.e., 21.0 versus 7.8 percent). The answer turns out to be approximately 11 years. If we do the same calculations using D/P ratios to take account of differences in payout ratios, it would have taken approximately 9 years for dividends per dollar invested in the glamour portfolio (currently 0.014) to catch up to those of the value portfolio (currently 0.039), assuming that past growth rate differences persisted. Note that this equality is on a flow basis not on a present-value basis. Equality on a present-value basis would require an even longer time period over which glamour firms should experience superior growth.

We can now compare these implied growth expectations to the actual cash flow growth experienced by the glamour and value portfolios. Over the first 5 years after formation, the cash flows of the glamour portfolio grew by 11.2 percent per year versus 5.2 percent for the value portfolio. Hence, cash flow per dollar invested grew from 0.080 initially to 0.136 at the end of Year 5, while for the value portfolio cash flow per dollar invested grew from 0.279 to 0.360, still leaving a large gap in cash flow returns between the two portfolios in Year 5. More importantly, the superior postformation growth is driven almost entirely by higher growth in the first 1 to 2 postformation years. From Year +2 to +5 postformation, the annual cash flow growth rates were 9.5 and 8.8 percent for glamour and value, respectively. While the market correctly anticipated higher growth in the very short-term, the persistence of these higher growth rates seems to have been grossly overestimated.[14] If growth rates after Year 5 were comparable to growth rates observed over Years +2 to +5, then, after 10 years, cash flows per dollar on the glamour portfolio would be only 0.214 compared to 0.549 for value. These data are consistent with the idea that the market was too optimistic about the future growth of glamour firms relative to value firms.

A similar conclusion emerges from an analysis of earnings numbers. Over the 5 years before portfolio formation, the growth rate of earnings per dollar invested for the glamour portfolio was 14.2 percent versus 8.2 percent for the value portfolio. At formation, the E/P ratio for glamour was 0.054 compared to 0.114 for value. This difference in E/P ratios does not appear to be driven by differences in earnings payout ratios since the payout ratio for value was actually somewhat higher than for glamour (0.34 versus 0.26). Once again, we can examine the postformation growth rates to see whether higher postformation growth for glamour could justify its lower initial E/P ratio. Here the numbers are even more dramatic than for cash flow. Over the 5 postforma-

---

[14] The result that growth rates of earnings are highly mean reverting is not new. Little (1962) shows this quite clearly in his pathbreaking article.

tion years, cumulative growth in earnings per dollar of initial investment was almost identical for the two portfolios. Earnings growth averaged 8.9 percent per year for glamour versus 8.6 percent per year for value. While growth in the first 1 to 2 years was higher for glamour, this was reversed over the following 3 years. If investors expected the superior growth of glamour firms to persist (as suggested by the differences in E/P ratios), the data indicate that they significantly overestimated future growth rate differences between glamour and value stocks.

Analogous results for portfolios classified according to B/M are also presented in Table V. We focus only on the numbers for cash flow because the E/P ratios for the extreme decile portfolios are so low as to make an expected growth computation somewhat questionable. For example, the E/P ratio for decile 10 (value) was only 0.004, indicating a high proportion of firms with temporarily depressed earnings. Because cash flows are less volatile and less often negative, the C/P ratios are much better behaved. For the glamour portfolio (B/M_1), C/P was equal to 0.059 versus 0.172 for the value portfolio (B/M_{10}). These numbers are quite similar to those for the $(C/P, GS)$ portfolios.

Presumably, this difference in C/P reflects, at least in part, the market's expectation that the superior growth of glamour firms would continue. Over the previous 5 years cash flow for the glamour portfolio had grown at 21.7 percent per year while cash flow growth for the value portfolio had been -1.3 percent per year. Estimated cash flow payout ratios for glamour and value firms were quite similar (0.203 and 0.186, respectively). Hence, differential payout ratios alone could not justify much of the difference in C/P ratios.

Postformation cash flow numbers indicate that glamour stocks indeed outgrew value stocks over the 5 years after formation, but that this is due to much higher growth at the beginning of the postformation period. In the last 3 years of the postformation period, cash flows for the value portfolio actually grew faster (11.1 percent per year versus 8.6 percent per year). In sum, at the end of 5 years cash flow per initial dollar invested rose from 0.059 to 0.107 for the glamour portfolio and from 0.172 to 0.241 for the value portfolio. If cash flow growth rates over Years $+2$ to $+5$ postformation were any indication of growth rates after Year 5, the cash flow return on glamour stocks did not get any closer to that for value stocks. These results mirror those for the $(C/P, GS)$ classification. They are consistent with the view that the superior postformation return on value stocks are explained by upward revisions in expectations about the relative growth rates of value versus glamour stocks.

Contrary to the assertions of Fama and French (1993, Section V), the market was likely to learn about its mistake only slowly over time since its expectation of higher relative growth for individual glamour firms was often confirmed in the short-run but then disconfirmed only in the longer run. Hence, we do not necessarily expect to see a clear spike in returns or E/P ratios. In this respect, the motivation behind the contrarian strategies explored in this article is quite different from that for the strategies explored by Jegadeesh and Titman (1993), Bernard and Thomas (1989), and Givoly and

Lakonishok (1979). The momentum-based strategies of those articles rely on the market's short-term failure to recognize a trend. In contrast, the superior returns to value strategies documented here seem to be driven by the market's unwarranted belief in the continuation of a long-term trend and its gradual abandonment of that belief.

In summary, the evidence in Table V is consistent with the extrapolation model. Glamour stocks have historically grown fast in sales, earnings, and cash flow relative to value stocks. According to most of our measures, the market expected the superior growth of glamour firms to continue for many years. In the very short-run, the expectations of continued superior growth of glamour stocks were on average born out. However, beyond the first couple years, growth rates of glamour stocks and value stocks were essentially the same. The evidence suggests that forecasts were tied to past growth rates and were too optimistic for glamour stocks relative to value stocks. This is precisely what the extrapolation model would predict. In this respect, the evidence in Table V goes beyond the customary evidence on returns in that it shows a relationship between the past, the forecasted, and the actual future growth rates that is largely consistent with the predictions of the extrapolation model.

V. Are Contrarian Strategies Riskier?

Two alternative theories have been proposed to explain why value strategies have produced higher returns in the past. The first theory says that they have done so because they exploit the mistakes of naive investors. The previous section showed that investors appear to be extrapolating the past too far into the future, even though the future does not warrant such extrapolation. The second explanation of the superior returns to value strategies is that they expose investors to greater systematic risk. In this section, we examine this explanation directly.

Value stocks would be fundamentally riskier than glamour stocks if, first, they underperform glamour stocks in some states of the world, and second, those are on average "bad" states, in which the marginal utility of wealth is high, making value stocks unattractive to risk-averse investors. This simple theory motivates our empirical approach.

To begin, we look at the consistency of performance of the value and glamour strategies over time and ask how often value underperforms glamour. We then check whether the times when value underperforms are recessions, times of severe market declines, or otherwise "bad" states of the world in which the marginal utility of consumption is high. These tests do not provide much support for the view that value strategies are fundamentally riskier. Finally, we look at some traditional measures of risk, such as beta and the standard deviation of returns, to compare value and glamour strategies.

Table VI and Figure 2 present the year-by-year performance of the value strategy *relative* to the glamour strategy over the April 1968 to April 1990

Table VI
Year-by-Year Returns: Value—Glamour

Panel 1: At the end of each April between 1968 and 1989, 10-decile portfolios are formed based on the ratio of previous-year's cash flow to end-of-April market-value of equity (C/P). For each portfolio, 1-, 3-, and 5-year holding-period returns are computed. For each formation period, Panel 1 reports the difference in the 1-, 3-, and 5-year return between the 2 highest C/P (value) and 2 lowest C/P (glamour) portfolios.

Panel 2: At the end of each April between 1968 and 1989, 9 groups of stocks are formed as follows. All stocks are independently sorted into 3 groups ((1) bottom 30 percent, (2) middle 40 percent, and (3) top 30 percent) by the ratio of previous-year's cash flow to end-of-April market-value of equity (C/P) and by the preformation 5-year weighted average rank-of-sales growth (GS). The 9 portfolios are intersections resulting from these 2 independent classifications. For each portfolio, 1-, 3-, and 5-year holding period returns are computed. For each formation period, Panel 2 reports the difference in the 1-, 3-, and 5-year return between the lowest GS, highest C/P (value) and the highest GS, lowest C/P (glamour) portfolios.

Panel 3: At the end of each April between 1968 and 1989, 10-decile portfolios are formed based on the ratio of the end-of-previous-year's book value of equity to end-of-April market value of equity (B/M). For each portfolio, 1-, 3-, and 5-year-holding-period returns are computed. For each formation period, Panel 3 reports the difference in the 1-, 3-, and 5-year return between the highest B/M (value) and lowest B/M (glamour) decile portfolios.

The last two rows respectively report the arithmetic mean across periods and the t-statistic for the test of the hypothesis that the difference in returns between value and glamour is equal to zero. These t-statistics are based on standard errors computed according to Hansen and Hodrick (1980).

	Panel 1			Panel 2			Panel 3		
	(C/P: 9, 10 − 1, 2)			(C/P-GS: 3, 1 − 1, 3)			(B/M: 9, 10 − 1, 2)		
	1-Year	3-Year	5-Year	1-Year	3-Year	5-Year	1-Year	3-Year	5-Year
1968	0.022	0.287	0.474	0.144	0.153	0.267	0.098	0.201	0.344
1969	0.123	0.195	0.410	0.065	−0.143	0.283	0.074	0.070	0.303
1970	0.135	0.246	0.428	0.002	0.160	0.356	0.023	0.032	0.279
1971	−0.078	0.231	0.478	−0.144	0.196	0.531	−0.108	0.156	0.463
1972	0.155	0.319	0.693	0.134	0.362	0.932	0.098	0.328	0.784
1973	0.021	0.382	0.846	0.152	0.702	1.416	0.042	0.450	0.925
1974	−0.007	0.496	1.343	0.069	0.650	1.597	0.050	0.642	1.726
1975	0.262	0.816	1.310	0.379	1.115	1.229	0.418	1.034	1.182
1976	0.174	0.673	1.468	0.217	0.715	1.235	0.132	0.727	0.993
1977	0.193	0.247	0.764	0.219	0.149	0.844	0.195	0.181	0.614
1978	0.048	−0.106	0.272	0.039	−0.072	0.581	0.037	−0.264	0.286
1979	−0.168	−0.102	0.274	−0.176	0.098	0.757	−0.207	−0.123	0.569
1980	0.039	0.745	1.225	0.110	1.246	2.000	−0.034	1.066	1.676
1981	0.203	0.650	1.584	0.236	0.940	2.134	0.185	0.810	1.955
1982	−0.032	0.338	1.253	0.118	0.539	1.886	0.240	0.589	1.477
1983	0.204	0.332	0.851	0.252	0.578	1.470	0.221	0.256	0.648
1984	0.192	0.552	0.888	0.052	0.641	1.092	0.043	0.324	0.640
1985	0.014	0.322	0.576	−0.032	0.531	0.708	−0.007	0.237	0.299
1986	0.108	0.339		0.196	0.427		0.051	0.149	
1987	0.093	0.170		0.111	0.290		0.078	0.015	
1988	0.092			0.089			−0.037		
1989	−0.063			0.010			−0.207		
Average	0.079	0.357	0.841	0.102	0.464	1.073	0.063	0.344	0.842
t-statistic	3.379	6.164	7.630	3.746	4.524	5.939	2.076	3.475	7.104

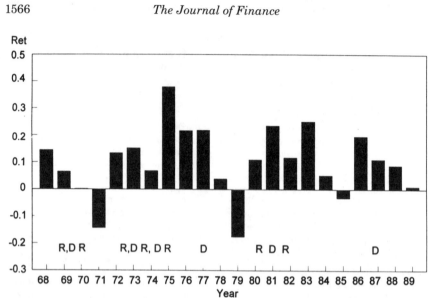

Figure 2. Year-by-year returns: Value minus glamour. At the end of each April between 1968 and 1989, 9 groups of stocks are formed. The stocks are independently sorted in ascending order into 3 groups ((1) bottom 30 percent, (2) middle 40 percent, and (3) top 30 percent) based on each of two variables: cash-flow-to-price (C/P) and growth-in-sales (GS). The value portfolio consists of those stocks in the highest C/P groups and the lowest GS group. The glamour portfolio consists of those stocks in the lowest C/P group and the highest GS group. The numbers presented are annual buy-and-hold returns for the value portfolio minus returns for the glamour portfolio. Annual buy-and-hold returns are calculated beginning at the end of April for the given year. R indicates NBER recession years, and D indicates years in which the CRSP equally weighted index declined in nominal terms.

period. We consider differences in cumulative returns between deciles $(9, 10)$ and $(1, 2)$ for C/P and B/M, and between groups $(3, 1)$ and $(1, 3)$ for $(C/P, GS)$ over 1-, 3-, and 5-year holding horizons starting each year in the sample (1968, 1969, etc.). The arithmetic mean across years for each horizon is reported at the bottom of each column along with t-statistics for the test of the hypothesis that the difference in returns between value and glamour portfolios is equal to zero. Standard errors for t-tests involving overlapping 3- and 5-year horizons are computed using the method of Hansen-Hodrick (1980), assuming annual $MA_{(2)}$ and $MA_{(4)}$ processes, respectively.

The results show that value strategies have consistently outperformed glamour strategies. Using a 1-year horizon, value outperformed glamour in 17 out of 22 years using C/P to classify stocks, in 19 out of 22 years using C/P and GS, and in 17 out of 22 years using the B/M ratio. As we move to longer horizons, the consistency of performance of the value strategy relative to the glamour strategy increases. For all three classification schemes, the value portfolio outperforms the glamour portfolio over every 5-year horizon in the sample period.

Contrarian Investment, Extrapolation, and Risk 1567

These numbers pose a stiff challenge to any risk-based explanation for the higher returns on value stocks. Consider the $(C/P, GS)$ classification. Over a 3-year horizon, the value strategy underperformed the glamour strategy in only two instances. In those instances, the magnitude of the value strategy's underperformance was small relative to its mean outperformance of 46.4 percent. Over any 5-year horizon in the sample, the value strategy was a sure winner. Even for a one-year horizon, the downside of this strategy was fairly low. To explain these numbers with a multifactor risk model would require that the relatively few instances of underperformance of the value portfolio are tightly associated with very bad states of the world as defined by some payoff relevant factor. Put another way, the covariance between the negative realizations of the value minus glamour return and this payoff-relevant factor should be high and the risk-premium associated with that factor should also be quite high.

While it is difficult to reject a risk-based explanation which relies on an unspecified multifactor model, we can examine a set of important payoff-relevant factors that are likely to be associated with large risk premia. If, after examining the association between the negative relative returns to value and this set of factors, we are unable to make sense of the higher average returns on value strategies, we can conclude that a risk-based explanation is unlikely to work except by appealing to large risk premia on factors that are a priori of lesser payoff relevance.

In examining the payoff relevant factors, we do not restrict ourselves to tightly parameterized models such as the Sharpe-Lintner model or the consumption Capital Asset Pricing Model (using consumption data) which are too likely to lead to rejection of risk-based explanations. For example, we do not assume that beta is the appropriate measure of exposure to the market factor. Instead, we proceed nonparametrically and examine the performance of value strategies in extreme down markets. Moreover, we allow for the possibility that the distribution of stock returns does not provide a complete characterization of good and bad states of the world. Barro (1990) and others find that, while the stock market is useful in predicting economic aggregates such as GNP growth, the R^2 is only around 0.4 in the post-war subperiod.

Some evidence on the performance of value and glamour strategies in bad states of the world can be gleaned from Table VI and Figure 2. According to the National Bureau of Economic Research, there were four recessions during our sample period: a mild one from December 1969 to November 1970, a very deep one from November 1973 to March 1975, and also significant ones from January 1980 to July 1980 and July 1981 to November 1982. An examination of Table VI shows that the value strategy did about the same or somewhat better than glamour just before and during the 1970 recession, did much better around the severe recession of 1973 to 1975, did somewhat worse in 1979 to 1980, and did significantly better in 1981 to 1982.[15] It is implausible

---

[15] Recall that returns are computed starting at the end of April of the year listed through April of the following year.

to conclude from this that value strategies did particularly badly in recessions, when the marginal utility of consumption is especially high.

A second approach is to compare the performance of value and glamour portfolios in the worst months for the stock market as a whole. Table VII, Panel 1 presents the performance of our portfolios in each of 4 states of the world; the 25 worst stock return months in the sample based on the equally weighted index, the remaining 88 negative months other than the 25 worst, the 122 positive months other than the 25 best, and the 25 best months in the sample. The average difference in returns between value and glamour portfolios for each state is also reported along with t-statistics for the test that the difference of returns is equal to zero. The results in this table are fairly clear. Using both the B/M and $(C/P, GS)$ classification schemes, the value portfolio outperformed the glamour portfolio in the market's worst 25 months. For example, using the $(C/P, GS)$ classification, the value portfolio lost an average of 8.6 percent of its value in the worst 25 months, whereas the glamour portfolio lost 10.3 percent of its value. Similarly, using both classification schemes, the value portfolio on average outperformed the glamour portfolio and the index in the next worst 88 months in which the index declined. Using the $(C/P, GS)$ classification, the value portfolio lost 1.5 percent in these months when the index experiences a mild decline, compared to 2.9 percent for the glamour portfolio and 2.3 percent for the index itself. So the value strategy did better when the market fell. The value strategy performed most closely to the glamour strategy in the 122 positive months other than the best 25. In the very best months, the value strategy substantially outperformed the glamour strategy and the index, but not by as much as it does when the market fell sharply. Some care should be taken in interpreting these mean differences for the positive market return months, however, given the low t-statistics. Overall, the value strategy performed somewhat better than the glamour strategy in all states and significantly better in some states. If anything, the superior performance of the value strategy was skewed toward negative market return months rather than positive market return months. The evidence in Table VII, Panel 1 thus indicates that the value strategy did not expose investors to greater downside risk.

Table VII, Panel 2 provides numbers analogous to those in Panel 1 except now the states of the world are realizations of real GNP growth.[16] The data are quarterly, so that we have 88 quarters in the sample. These quarters are classified into 4 states of the world; the worst 10 quarters, the next worst 34 quarters, the best 10 quarters, and the next best 34 quarters. The quarterly returns on the various glamour and value portfolios are then matched up with the changes in real GNP for one quarter ahead, since evidence indicates that the stock market leads GNP by approximately one quarter. Average quarterly returns for each portfolio are then computed for each state.

---

[16] In an earlier draft of this article we included results using the change in the unemployment rate. The results are quite similar to those for GNP growth.

The results in Panel 2 mirror the basic conclusions from Panel 1; namely, the value strategy has not been fundamentally riskier than the glamour strategy. For both classification schemes, the value strategy performed at least as well as the glamour strategy *in each of the 4 states* and substantially better in most states. Unlike the results in Panel 1, there was some tendency for the relative returns on value to be higher in good states than in bad states, especially for extreme good states. Roughly speaking, value stocks could be described as having higher up-market betas and lower down-market betas than glamour stocks with respect to economic conditions. Importantly, while the value strategy did disproportionately well in extreme good times, its performance in extreme bad times was also quite impressive. Performance in extreme bad states is often the last refuge of those claiming that a high return strategy *must* be riskier, even when conventional measures of risk such as beta and standard deviation do not show it. The evidence indicates some positive relation between relative performance of the value strategy and measures of prosperity, but there are no significant traces of a conventional asset pricing equilibrium in which the higher returns on the value strategy are compensation for higher systematic risk.

Finally, for completeness, Table VIII presents some more traditional risk measures for portfolios using our classification schemes. These risk measures are calculated using annual measurement intervals over the postformation period, because of the problems associated with use of preformation period data (Ball and Kothari (1989)). For each of our portfolios, we have 22 annual observations on its return in the year following the formation, and hence can compute the standard deviation of returns. We also have corresponding returns on the value-weighted CRSP index and the risk-free asset, and hence can calculate a beta for each portfolio.

First, the betas of value portfolios with respect to the value-weighted index tend to be about 0.1 higher than the betas of the glamour portfolios. As we have seen earlier, the high betas probably come from value stocks having higher "up-market" betas,[17] and that, if anything, the superior performance of the value strategy occurs disproportionally during "bad" realizations of the stock market. Even if one takes a very strong pro-beta position, the difference in betas of 0.1 can explain a difference in returns of only up to 1 percent per year (assuming a market risk premium of 8 percent per year) and surely not the 10 to 11 percent difference in returns that we find.

Table VIII also presents average annual standard deviations of the various portfolio returns. The results show that value portfolios have somewhat higher standard deviations of returns than glamour portfolios. Using the $(C/P, GS)$ classification, the value portfolio has an average standard deviation of returns of 24.1 percent relative to 21.6 percent for the glamour portfolio. Three remarks about these numbers are in order. First, we have already shown that, because of its much higher mean return, the value

---

[17] De Bondt and Thaler (1987) obtain a similar result for their contrarian strategy based on buying stocks with low past returns.

Table VII
Performance of Portfolios in Best and Worst Times

Panel 1: All months in the sample are divided into 25 worst stock return months based on the equally weighted index (W_{25}), the remaining 88 negative months other than the 25 worst (N_{88}), the 122 positive months other than the 25 best (P_{122}), and the 25 best months (B_{25}) in the sample.

Panel 1A: At the end of each April between 1968 and 1989, 9 groups of stocks are independently sorted into 3 groups ((1) bottom 30 percent, (2) middle 40 percent, and (3) top 30 percent) by the ratio of previous year's cash flow to end-of-April market value of equity (CP) and by the preformation 5-year weighted average rank of sales growth (GS). The 9 portfolios are intersections resulting from these 2 independent classifications. For each portfolio (changing every April), Panel 1A presents its average return over the W_{25}, N_{88}, P_{122}, and B_{25} months.

Panel 1B: At the end of each April between 1968 and 1989, 10-decile portfolios are formed based on the ratio of end-of-previous-year's book value of equity to end-of-April market value of equity (B/M). For each portfolio (changing every April), Panel 1B presents its average return over the W_{25}, N_{88}, P_{122}, and B_{25} months.

Panels 2A and 2B have the same structure, but the states are defined in terms of the best and worst quarters for GNP growth. All quarters in the sample are divided into 4 sets: 10 quarters of the lowest real GNP growth during the sample period, 34 next lowest real GNP growth quarters, 34 next worst growth quarters, and 10 highest real GNP growth quarters.

In Panel 2A, the value portfolio contains stocks ranking in the top group on C/P and in the bottom group on GS. The Glamour portfolio contains stocks ranking in the top group on GS. In Panel 2B, the Value portfolio contains stocks ranking in the top two deciles on B/M. The Glamour portfolio contains stocks ranking in the bottom two deciles on B/M. The right-most column contains the t-statistic for testing the hypothesis that the difference in returns between the Value and Glamour portfolios is equal to zero.

Panel 1: Portfolio Returns across Best and Worst Stock Market Months

Panel 1A

	Glamour				Value						Value-Glamour	
C/P	1	1	1	2	2	2	3	3	3	Index	(1,3 − 3,1)	t-Statistic
GS	1	2	3	1	2	3	1	2	3			
W_{25}	−0.114	−0.103	−0.103	−0.090	−0.091	−0.100	−0.086	−0.080	−0.105	−0.102	0.018	3.040
N_{88}	−0.023	−0.025	−0.029	−0.016	−0.020	−0.025	−0.015	−0.016	−0.022	−0.023	0.014	4.511
P_{122}	0.039	0.039	0.038	0.040	0.038	0.039	0.040	0.038	0.038	0.037	0.002	0.759
B_{25}	0.131	0.111	0.110	0.110	0.104	0.115	0.124	0.113	0.124	0.121	0.014	1.021

Panel 1B

	Glamour								Value			Value-Glamour	
B/M	1	2	3	4	5	6	7	8	9	10	Index	(9,10 − 1,2)	t-Statistic
W_{25}	−0.112	−0.110	−0.104	−0.100	−0.097	−0.091	−0.093	−0.092	−0.098	−0.102	−0.102	0.011	1.802
N_{88}	−0.029	−0.028	−0.026	−0.025	−0.023	−0.020	−0.021	−0.020	−0.018	−0.022	−0.023	0.008	2.988
P_{122}	0.038	0.040	0.039	0.037	0.036	0.037	0.038	0.037	0.038	0.039	0.037	−0.001	−0.168
B_{25}	0.114	0.114	0.119	0.113	0.112	0.113	0.117	0.126	0.133	0.148	0.121	0.026	1.729

Table VII—Continued

Panel 2: Portfolio Returns across Best and Worst GNP Growth Quarters

Panel 2A

| | Glamour | | | | | | Value | | | | Value-Glamour | |
| C/P | 1 | 1 | 1 | 2 | 2 | 2 | 3 | 3 | 3 | GNP | (1, 3 − 3, 1) | t-Statistic |
GS	1	2	3	1	2	3	1	2	3			
Worst 10	0.032	0.014	−0.009	0.037	0.016	0.013	0.041	0.020	0.008	−0.017	0.050	2.485
Next worst 34	0.021	0.010	0.011	0.018	0.014	0.011	0.027	0.023	0.012	0.000	0.016	1.473
Next best 34	0.026	0.029	0.026	0.040	0.033	0.029	0.046	0.046	0.034	0.012	0.020	2.176
Best 10	0.122	0.107	0.103	0.140	0.123	0.123	0.139	0.133	0.136	0.031	0.036	1.786

Panel 2B

| | Glamour | | | | | | | | Value | | | Value-Glamour | |
B/M	1	2	3	4	5	6	7	8	9	10	GNP	(9, 10 − 1, 2)	t-Statistic
Worst 10	−0.004	0.001	0.012	0.018	0.009	0.016	0.017	0.028	0.021	0.015	−0.017	0.020	0.983
Next worst 34	0.011	0.008	0.011	0.009	0.008	0.010	0.010	0.016	0.017	0.012	0.000	0.005	0.494
Next best 34	0.022	0.028	0.027	0.025	0.030	0.035	0.036	0.035	0.041	0.039	0.012	0.015	1.555
Best 10	0.092	0.102	0.118	0.117	0.117	0.135	0.132	0.141	0.145	0.151	0.031	0.051	2.685

Table VIII
Traditional Risk Measures for Portfolios

For each portfolio described below, we compute, using 22 year-after-the-formation returns as observations, its beta with respect to the value-weighted index. Using the 22 formation periods, we also compute the standard deviation of returns and the standard deviation of size-adjusted returns in the year after formation.

Panel 1: At the end of each April between 1968 and 1989, 10-decile portfolios are formed based on the ratio of previous-year's cash flow to end-of-April market value of equity (C/P). For each decile portfolio, Panel 1 presents its beta, standard deviation of returns, and standard deviation of size-adjusted returns defined above.

Panel 2: At the end of each April between 1968 and 1989, 9 groups of stocks are formed as follows. All stocks are independently sorted into 3 groups ((1) bottom 30 percent, (2) middle 40 percent, and (3) top 30 percent) by the ratio of previous-year's cash flow to end-of-April market value of equity (C/P) and by the preformation 5-year weighted-average rank of sales growth (GS). The 9 portfolios are intersections resulting from these 2 independent classifications. For each group of stocks, Panel 2 presents its beta, standard deviation of returns, and standard deviation of size-adjusted returns defined above.

Panel 3: At the end of each April between 1968 and 1989, 10-decile portfolios are formed based on the ratio of end-of-previous year's book value of equity to end-of-April market value of equity (B/M). For each decile portfolio, Panel 3 presents its beta, standard deviation of returns, and standard deviation of size-adjusted returns defined above.

Panel 1

C/P	1	2	3	4	5	6	7	8	9	10	Equally Weighted Index
β	1.268	1.293	1.321	1.333	1.318	1.237	1.182	1.247	1.224	1.384	1.304
Standard deviation	0.224	0.227	0.239	0.237	0.232	0.221	0.212	0.223	0.224	0.252	0.250
Standard deviation of size-adjusted return	0.037	0.044	0.049	0.036	0.033	0.034	0.042	0.036	0.048	0.058	—

Table VIII—*Continued*

Panel 2

C/P	1	2	3	1	2	3	1	2	3	Equally Weighted Index
GS	3	3	3	2	2	2	1	1	1	
β	1.249	1.296	1.293	1.239	1.184	1.214	1.330	1.258	1.322	1.304
Standard deviation	0.216	0.232	0.241	0.215	0.207	0.213	0.242	0.224	0.241	0.250
Standard deviation of size-adjusted return	0.061	0.040	0.066	0.049	0.033	0.047	0.066	0.047	0.065	—

Panel 3

B/M	1	2	3	4	5	6	7	8	9	10	Equally Weighted Index
β	1.248	1.268	1.337	1.268	1.252	1.214	1.267	1.275	1.299	1.443	1.304
Standard deviation	0.223	0.223	0.236	0.225	0.221	0.214	0.225	0.233	0.248	0.276	0.250
Standard deviation of size-adjusted return	0.076	0.050	0.040	0.035	0.031	0.040	0.035	0.043	0.046	0.071	—

strategy's higher standard deviation does not translate into greater downside risk. Second, the higher standard deviation of value stocks appears to be due largely to their smaller average size, since the standard deviation of size-adjusted returns is virtually the same for value and glamour portfolios. But the results in Table III suggest that, by focusing on larger value stocks, investors could still get most of the extra return from value stocks without this higher standard deviation. The extra return on a portfolio of large value stocks cannot therefore be explained by appealing to its higher standard deviation. Finally, the difference in standard deviation of returns between value and glamour portfolios (24.1 versus 21.6 percent per year) is quite small in comparison to the difference in average return (10 percent per year). For example, over the 1926 to 1988 period the extra return on the S & P 500 over T-bills was approximately 8 percent per year, while the average standard deviation on the S & P 500 was 21 percent compared to 3 percent for T-bills. In comparison to the reward-to-risk ratio for stocks vis-à-vis T-bills, the reward-to-risk ratio for investing in value stocks is extremely high. A risk model based on differences in standard deviation cannot explain the superior returns on value stocks.

VI. Summary and Interpretation of the Findings

The results in this article establish (in varying degrees of detail) three propositions. First, a variety of investment strategies that involve buying out-of-favor (value) stocks have outperformed glamour strategies over the April 1968 to April 1990 period. Second, a likely reason that these value strategies have worked so well relative to the glamour strategies is the fact that the actual future growth rates of earnings, cash flow, etc. of glamour stocks relative to value stocks turned out to be much lower than they were in the past, or as the multiples on those stocks indicate the market expected them to be. That is, market participants appear to have consistently overestimated future growth rates of glamour stocks relative to value stocks. Third, using conventional approaches to fundamental risk, value strategies appear to be no riskier than glamour strategies. Reward for bearing fundamental risk does not seem to explain higher average returns on value stocks than on glamour stocks.

While one can never reject the "metaphysical" version of the risk story, in which securities that earn higher returns must *by definition* be fundamentally riskier, the weight of evidence suggests a more straightforward model. In this model, out-of-favor (or value) stocks have been underpriced relative to their risk and return characteristics, and investing in them has indeed earned abnormal returns.

This conclusion raises the obvious question: how can the 10 to 11 percent per year in extra returns on value stocks over glamour stocks have persisted for so long? One possible explanation is that investors simply did not know about them. This explanation has some plausibility in that quantitative portfolio selection and evaluation are relatively recent activities. Most investors might not have been able, until recently, to perform the analysis done in this article. Of course, advocacy of value strategies is decades old, going back at least to Graham and Dodd (1934). But such advocacy is usually not accompanied by defensible statistical work and hence might not be entirely persuasive, especially since many other strategies are advocated as well.

Another possible explanation is that we have engaged in data snooping (Lo and MacKinlay (1990)) and have merely identified an ex post pattern in the data. Clearly, these data have been mined in the sense that others have looked at much of these same data before us. On the other hand, we think there is good reason to believe that the cross-sectional return differences reported here reflect an important economic regularity rather than sampling error. First, similar findings on the superior returns of value strategies have been obtained for several different time series. Davis (1994) finds similar results on a subsample of large U.S. firms over the period 1931 to 1960. Chan, Hamao and Lakonishok (1991) find similar results for Japan. Capaul, Rowley, and Sharpe (1993) find similar results for France, Germany, Switzerland, and the United Kingdom, as well as for the United States and Japan.

Second, we have documented more than just a cross-sectional pattern of returns. The evidence suggests a systematic pattern of expectational errors on the part of investors that is capable of explaining the differential stock returns across value and glamour stocks. Investor expectations of future growth appear to have been excessively tied to past growth despite the fact that future growth rates are highly mean reverting. In particular, investors expected glamour firms to continue growing faster than value firms, but they were systematically disappointed. La Porta (1993) shows that a similar pattern of expectational errors and returns on value strategies obtains when growth expectations are measured by analysts' 5-year earnings growth forecasts rather than by financial ratios such as E/P or C/P. The evidence on expectational errors supports the view that the cross-sectional differences in returns reflect a genuine economic phenomenon.

We conjecture that the results in this article can best be explained by the preference of both individual and institutional investors for glamour strategies and by their avoidance of value strategies. Below we suggest some reasons for this preference that might potentially explain the observed returns anomaly.

Individual investors might focus on glamour strategies for a variety of reasons. First, they may make judgment errors and extrapolate past growth rates of glamour stocks, such as Walmart or Microsoft, even when such growth rates are highly unlikely to persist in the future. Putting excessive weight on recent past history, as opposed to a rational prior, is a common judgment error in psychological experiments and not just in the stock market. Alternatively, individuals might just equate well-run firms with good investments, regardless of price. After all, how can you lose money on Microsoft or Walmart? Indeed, brokers typically recommend "good" companies with "steady" earnings and dividend growth.

Presumably, institutional investors should be somewhat more free from judgment biases and excitement about "good companies" than individuals, and so should flock to value strategies.[18] But institutional investors may have reasons of their own for gravitating toward glamour stocks. Lakonishok, Shleifer, and Vishny (1992b) focus on the agency context of institutional money management. Institutions might prefer glamour stocks because they appear to be "prudent" investments, and hence are easy to justify to sponsors. Glamour stocks have done well in the past and are unlikely to become financially distressed in the near future, as opposed to value stocks, which have previously done poorly and are more likely to run into financial problems. Many institutions actually screen out stocks of financially distressed firms, many of which are value stocks, from the universe of stocks they pick. Indeed, sponsors may mistakenly believe glamour stocks to be safer than value stocks, even though, as we have seen, a portfolio of value stocks is no more risky. The strategy of investing in glamour stocks, while appearing "prudent," is not prudent at all in that it earns a lower expected return and is not fundamentally less risky. Nonetheless, the career concerns of money managers and employees of their institutional clients may cause money managers to tilt towards "glamour" stocks.

Another important factor is that most investors have shorter time horizons than are required for value strategies to consistently pay off (De Long *et al.* (1990) and Shleifer and Vishny (1990)). Many individuals look for stocks that will earn them high abnormal returns within a few months, rather than 4 percent per year over the next 5 years. Institutional money managers often have even shorter time horizons. They often cannot afford to underperform the index or their peers for any nontrivial period of time, for if they do, their sponsors will withdraw the funds. A value strategy that takes 3 to 5 years to pay off but may underperform the market in the meantime (i.e., have a large tracking error) might simply be too risky for money managers from the viewpoint of career concerns, especially if the strategy itself is more difficult to justify to sponsors. If a money manager fears getting fired before a value strategy pays off, he will avoid using such a strategy. Importantly, while tracking error can explain why a money manager would not want too strong a tilt toward *either* value or growth, it does not explain why he would not tilt slightly toward value given its apparently superior risk/return profile. Hence, these horizon and tracking error issues *can* explain why money managers do not more aggressively "arbitrage" the differences in returns across value and glamour stocks, but they *cannot* explain why such differences are there in the first place. In our view, such return differences are ultimately explained by the tendency of investors to make judgmental errors and perhaps also by a tendency for institutional investors to actively tilt toward glamour to make their lives easier.

---

[18] According to Dreman (1977), professional money managers are also quite likely to suffer from these biases.

Contrarian Investment, Extrapolation, and Risk 1577

Are the anomalous excess returns on value stocks likely to persist? It is possible that over time more investors will become convinced of the value of being a contrarian with a long horizon and the returns to value strategies will fall. Perhaps the recent move into disciplined quantitative investment strategies, evaluated based only on performance and not on individual stock picks, will increase the demand for value stocks and reduce the agency problems that result in picking glamour stocks. Such sea changes rarely occur overnight, however. The time-series and cross-country evidence support the idea that the behavioral and institutional factors underlying the higher returns to value stocks have been pervasive and enduring features of equity markets.

Perhaps the most interesting implication of the conjecture that institutional investors gravitate toward glamour stocks is that this may explain their inferior performance. In an earlier article, we focused on the striking underperformance of pension fund money managers relative to the market index (Lakonishok, Shleifer, and Vishny (1992b)). The large difference in returns on glamour and value stocks can, at least in principle, explain why money managers have underperformed the market by over 100 basis points per year before accounting for management fees. By looking at the actual portfolios of institutional money managers, one can find out whether they have been overinvested in glamour stocks and underinvested in value stocks. We plan to do that in a follow-up article.

REFERENCES

Ball, R., and S. Kothari, 1989, Non-stationary expected returns: Implications for tests of market efficiency and serial correlation of returns, *Journal of Financial Economics* 25, 51–74.

Banz, R., and W. Breen, 1986, Sample dependent results using accounting and market data: Some evidence, *Journal of Finance* 41, 779–793.

Barro, R., 1990, The stock market and investment, *Review of Financial Studies* 3, 115–131.

Basu, S., 1977, Investment performance of common stocks in relation to their price earnings ratios: A test of the efficient market hypothesis, *Journal of Finance* 32, 663–682.

Bernard, V., and J. Thomas, 1989, Post-earnings announcement drift: Delayed price response or risk premium, *Journal of Accounting Research* 27 (Supplement), 1–36.

Black, F., 1986, Noise, *Journal of Finance* 41, 529–543.

Brown, S., W. Goetzmann, and S. Ross, 1993, Survivorship bias in autocorrelation and long-term memory studies, Mimeo, New York University, Columbia University and Yale University, September.

Capaul, C., I. Rowley, and W. Sharpe, 1993, International value and growth stock returns, *Financial Analysts Journal*, January/February, 27–36.

Chan, K., 1988, On the contrarian investment strategy, *Journal of Business* 61, 147–163.

Chan, L., Y. Hamao, and J. Lakonishok, 1991, Fundamentals and stock returns in Japan, *Journal of Finance* 46, 1739–1764.

Chopra, N., J. Lakonishok, and J. Ritter, 1992, Measuring abnormal performance: Do stocks overreact?, *Journal of Financial Economics* 31, 235–268.

Davis, James, 1994, The cross-section of realized stock returns: The pre-COMPUSTAT evidence, *Journal of Finance* 49, 1579–1593.

De Bondt, W., and R. Thaler, 1985, Does the stock market overreact?, *Journal of Finance* 40, 793–805.

————, 1987, Further evidence on investor overreaction and stock market seasonality, *Journal of Finance* 42, 557–581.

De Long, J. B., A. Shleifer, L. Summers, and R. Waldmann, 1990, Noise trader risk in financial markets, *Journal of Political Economy* 98, 703–738.

Dreman, D., 1977, *Psychology and the Stock Market: Why the Pros Go Wrong and How to Profit* (Warner Books, New York).

Fama, E., and K. French, 1992, The cross-section of expected stock returns, *Journal of Finance* 46, 427–466.

————, 1993, Size and book-to-market factors in earnings and returns, Mimeo, University of Chicago.

Fama, E., and J. MacBeth, 1973, Risk, return and equilibrium: Empirical tests, *Journal of Political Economy* 81, 607–636.

Givoly, D., and J. Lakonishok, 1979, The information content of financial analysts' forecasts of earnings: Some evidence on semi-strong inefficiency, *Journal of Accounting and Economics* 1, 165–185.

Gordon, M., and E. Shapiro, 1956, Capital equipment analysis: the required rate of profit, *Management Science* 3, 102–110.

Graham, B., and D. Dodd, 1934, *Security Analysis*, (McGraw-Hill, New York).

Hansen, L. P., and R. Hodrick, 1980, Forward exchange rates as optimal predictors of future spot rates; An econometric analysis, *Journal of Political Economy* 88, 829–53.

Haugen, R., 1994, *The New Finance: The Case Against Efficient Markets*, (Prentice-Hall, Englewood Cliffs, N.J.).

Jaffe, J., D. B. Keim, and R. Westerfield, 1989, Earnings yields, market values, and stock returns, *Journal of Finance* 44, 135–148.

Jegadeesh, N., and S. Titman, 1993, Returns to buying winners and selling losers: Implications for market efficiency, *Journal of Finance* 48, 65–92.

Kahneman, D., and A. Tversky, 1982, Intuitive prediction: Biases and corrective procedures, in D. Kahneman, P. Slovic, and A. Tversky, Eds.: *Judgment under Uncertainty: Heuristics and Biases* (Cambridge University Press, Cambridge, England).

Kothari, S. P., J. Shanken, and R. Sloan, 1992, Another look at the cross-section of expected stock returns, Mimeo, University of Rochester.

La Porta, R., 1993, Expectations and the cross-section of stock returns, Mimeo, Harvard University.

Lakonishok, J., A. Shleifer, R. Thaler, and R. Vishny, 1991, Window dressing by pension fund managers, *American Economic Review Papers and Proceedings* 81, 227–231.

Lakonishok, J. A. Shleifer, and R. Vishny, 1992a, The impact of institutional trading on stock prices, *Journal of Financial Economics* 32, 23–43.

————, 1992b, The structure and performance of the money management industry, *Brookings Papers on Economic Activity: Microeconomics*, 339–391.

Little, I. M. D., 1962, Higgledy piggledy growth, *Bulletin of the Oxford University Institute of Economics and Statistics* 24, November.

Lo, A., and C. MacKinlay, 1990, Data-snooping biases in tests of financial asset pricing models, *Review of Financial Studies* 3, 431–467.

Rosenberg, B., K. Reid, and R. Lanstein, 1984, Persuasive evidence of market inefficiency, *Journal of Portfolio Management* 11, 9–17.

Shiller, R., 1984, Stock prices and social dynamics, *Brookings Papers on Economic Activity*, 457–498.

Shleifer, A., and R. Vishny, 1990, Equilibrium short horizons of investors and firms, *American Economic Review Papers and Proceedings* 80, 148–153.

The Conditional CAPM and the Cross-Section of Expected Returns

RAVI JAGANNATHAN and ZHENYU WANG*

ABSTRACT

Most empirical studies of the static CAPM assume that betas remain constant over time and that the return on the value-weighted portfolio of all stocks is a proxy for the return on aggregate wealth. The general consensus is that the static CAPM is unable to explain satisfactorily the cross-section of average returns on stocks. We assume that the CAPM holds in a conditional sense, i.e., betas and the market risk premium vary over time. We include the return on human capital when measuring the return on aggregate wealth. Our specification performs well in explaining the cross-section of average returns.

A SUBSTANTIAL PART OF the research effort in finance is directed toward improving our understanding of how investors value risky cash flows. It is generally agreed that investors demand a higher expected return for investment in riskier projects, or securities. However, we still do not fully understand how investors assess the risk of the cash flow on a project and how they determine what risk premium to demand. Several capital asset-pricing models have been suggested in the literature that describe how investors assess risk and value risky cash flows. Among them, the Sharpe-Lintner-Black Capital Asset Pricing Model (CAPM)[1] is the one that financial managers use most often for assessing the risk of the cash flow from a project and for arriving at the appropriate

* Jagannathan is from the Carlson School of Management, University of Minnesota; Hong Kong University of Science and Technology; and the Federal Reserve Bank of Minneapolis. Wang is from Columbia University. The authors benefited from discussions with S. Rao Aiyagari, Gordon Alexander, Michael Brennan, Charlie Calomiris, Mark Carhart, Eugene Fama, Wayne Ferson, Murray Frank, John Geweke, Lars Peter Hansen, Campbell Harvey, Pat Hess, Allan Kleidon, Peter Knez, Robert Korajczyk, Bruce Lehmann, Steve LeRoy, David Modest, Edward Prescott, Judy Rayburn, Richard Roll, Jay Shanken, Michael Sher, Stephen D. Smith, and Robert Stambaugh, as well as with participants at numerous finance workshops in the United States, Canada, and East Asia. Special thanks go to the anonymous referee and the managing editor of the journal for valuable comments. We are grateful to Eugene Fama for providing us with the Fama-French factors and Raymond A. Dragan for editorial assistance. All errors in this paper are the authors' responsibility. The views expressed herein are those of the authors and not necessarily those of the Federal Reserve Bank of Minneapolis or the Federal Reserve System. Ravi Jagannathan gratefully acknowledges financial support from the National Science Foundation (grant SBR-9409824). Zhenyu Wang gratefully acknowledges financial support from the Alfred P. Sloan Foundation (doctoral dissertation fellowship, grant DD-518). An earlier version of the paper appeared under the title, "The CAPM Is Alive and Well." The compressed archive of the data and the FORTRAN programs used for this paper can be obtained via anonymous FTP at ftp.socsci.umn.edu. The path is outgoing/wang/capm.tar.Z.

[1] See Sharpe (1964), Lintner (1965), and Black (1972).

4   *The Journal of Finance*

discount rate to use in valuing the project. According to the CAPM, (a) the risk
of a project is measured by the beta of the cash flow with respect to the return
on the market portfolio of all assets in the economy, and (b) the relation
between required expected return and beta is linear.

Over the past two decades a number of studies have empirically examined
the performance of the static version of the CAPM in explaining the cross-
section of realized average returns. The results reported in these studies
support the view that it is possible to construct a set of portfolios such that the
static CAPM is unable to explain the cross-sectional variation in average
returns among them.[2] In particular, portfolios containing stocks with relatively small capitalization appear to earn higher returns on average than those
predicted by the CAPM.[3]

In spite of the lack of empirical support, the CAPM is still the preferred
model for classroom use in MBA and other managerial finance courses. In a
way it reminds us of cartoon characters like Wile E. Coyote who have the
ability to come back to original shape after being blown to pieces or hammered
out of shape. Maybe the CAPM survives because (a) the empirical support for
other asset-pricing models is no better,[4] (b) the theory behind the CAPM has
an intuitive appeal that other models lack, and (c) the economic importance of
the empirical evidence against the CAPM reported in empirical studies is
ambiguous.

In their widely cited study, Fama and French (1992) present evidence
suggesting that the inability of the static CAPM to explain the cross-section of
average returns that has been reported in the literature may be economically
important. Using return data on a large collection of assets, they examine the
static version of the CAPM and find that the "relation between market beta
and average return is flat."[5] The CAPM is widely viewed as one of the two or
three major contributions of academic research to financial managers during
the postwar era. As Fama and French point out, the robustness of the size
effect and the absence of a relation between beta and average return are so
contrary to the CAPM that they shake the foundations on which MBA and
other managerial course materials in finance are built.

The CAPM was derived by examining the behavior of investors in a hypothetical model-economy in which they live for only one period. In the real world
investors live for many periods. Therefore, in the empirical examination of the
CAPM, using data from the real world, it is necessary to make certain assumptions. One of the commonly made assumptions is that the betas of the assets
remain constant over time. In our view, this is not a particularly reasonable
assumption since the relative risk of a firm's cash flow is likely to vary over the

---

[2] See Banz (1981), Reinganum (1981), Gibbons (1982), Basu (1983), Chan, Chen, and Hsieh
(1985), Shanken (1985), and Bhandari (1988).

[3] Hansen and Jagannathan (1994) find that this is true even after controlling for systematic
risk using a variety of other measures.

[4] See Hansen and Singleton (1982), Connor and Korajczyk (1988a and 1988b), Lehmann and
Modest (1988), and Hansen and Jagannathan (1991 and 1994).

[5] Also see Jegadeesh (1992), who obtains results similar to Fama and French.

The Conditional CAPM and the Cross-Section of Expected Returns   5

business cycle. During a recession, for example, financial leverage of firms in relatively poor shape may increase sharply relative to other firms, causing their stock betas to rise. Also, to the extent that the business cycle is induced by technology or taste shocks, the relative share of different sectors in the economy fluctuates, inducing fluctuations in the betas of firms in these sectors. Hence, betas and expected returns will in general depend on the nature of the information available at any given point in time and vary over time. In this study, therefore, we assume that the conditional version of the CAPM holds, i.e., the expected return on an asset based on the information available at any given point in time is linear in its conditional beta.

Though several researchers have empirically examined the conditional version of the CAPM, no one to our knowledge has directly studied the ability of the conditional CAPM to explain the cross-sectional variation in average returns on a large collection of stock portfolios. The focus of our paper is to fill this gap in the literature. For this purpose, we first derive the unconditional model implied by the conditional CAPM. We show that when the conditional version of the CAPM holds (i.e., when betas and expected returns are allowed to vary over the business cycle), a two-factor model obtains unconditionally. Average returns are jointly linear in the average beta and in a measure of "beta instability," which we show how to calculate. The fact that the implied unconditional model nests the static CAPM facilitates direct comparison of their relative performance.

Using the value-weighted index from CRSP as the market portfolio, we find that the unconditional model implied by the conditional CAPM explains nearly 30 percent of the cross-sectional variation in average returns of 100 stock portfolios similar to those used in Fama and French (1992). This is a substantial improvement when compared to the 1 percent explained by the static CAPM. The rejection by the data and the size effect are much weaker than those for the static CAPM.

In order to implement the CAPM, for practical purposes, it is commonly assumed that the return on the value-weighted portfolio of all stocks listed on the New York Stock Exchange (NYSE) and the American Stock Exchange (AMEX) (as well as those traded on Nasdaq) is a reasonable proxy for the return on the market portfolio of all assets. In view of this, another possible interpretation of the evidence is that the particular proxy Fama and French (1992) use for the return on the market portfolio of all assets is a major cause for the unsatisfactory performance of the CAPM. Hence, in measuring the return on aggregate wealth, we follow Mayers (1972) and include a measure of return on human capital. We find that when human capital is also included in measuring wealth, the unconditional model implied by the conditional CAPM is able to explain over 50 percent of the cross-sectional variation in average returns, and the data fail to reject the model. More importantly, size and book-to-market variables have little ability to explain what is left unexplained.

The rest of the paper is organized as follows: In Section I, we show that when the CAPM holds in a conditional sense (i.e., expected returns and betas vary over time in a systematic stochastic manner), unconditional expected returns

6   *The Journal of Finance*

on assets will be linear in (a) the average beta and (b) a measure of beta instability over time. When betas remain constant over time, this model collapses to the familiar static CAPM. In Section II, we show how to examine this model empirically. Section III describes the data and presents the empirical results. We draw our conclusions in Section IV.

I. Models for the Expected Stock Returns

A. *The Sharpe-Lintner-Black (Static) CAPM*

Let R_i denote the return on any asset i and R_m be the return on the market portfolio of all assets in the economy. The Black (1972) version of the CAPM is

$$E[R_i] = \gamma_0 + \gamma_1 \beta_i, \tag{1}$$

where β_i is defined as

$$\beta_i = \mathrm{Cov}(R_i, R_m)/\mathrm{Var}[R_m],$$

and $E[\cdot]$ denotes the expectation, $\mathrm{Cov}(\cdot)$ denotes the covariance, and $\mathrm{Var}[\cdot]$ denotes the variance.

In their widely cited study, Fama and French (1992) empirically examine the CAPM given above and find that the estimated value of γ_1 is close to zero. They interpret the "flat" relation between average return and beta as strong evidence against the CAPM.

While a "flat" relation between average return (the sample analog of the unconditional expected return) and beta may be evidence against the static CAPM, it is not necessarily evidence against the conditional CAPM. The CAPM was developed within the framework of a hypothetical single-period model economy. The real world, however, is dynamic and hence, as pointed out earlier, expected returns and betas are likely to vary over time. Even when expected returns are linear in betas for every time period, based on the information available at the time, the relation between the unconditional expected return and the unconditional beta could be "flat."[6] The following example illustrates this point.

Consider a hypothetical economy in which the CAPM holds period by period. Suppose that the econometrician considers only two stocks and that there are only two possible types of dates in the world. The betas of the first stock in the two date-types are, respectively, 0.5 and 1.25 (corresponding to an average beta of 0.875). The corresponding betas of the second stock are 1.5 and 0.75 (corresponding to an average beta of 1.125). Suppose that the expected risk premium on the market is 10 percent on the first date and 20 percent on the second date. Then, if the CAPM holds in each period, the expected risk premium on the first stock will be 5 percent on the first date and 25 percent on the second date. The expected risk premium on the second stock will be 15

---

[6] This is because an asset that is on the conditional mean-variance frontier need not be on the unconditional frontier, as Dybvig and Ross (1985) and Hansen and Richard (1987) point out.

The Conditional CAPM and the Cross-Section of Expected Returns 7

percent on both dates. Hence, an econometrician who ignores the fact that betas and risk premiums vary over time will mistakenly conclude that the CAPM does not hold, since the two stocks earn an average risk premium of 15 percent, but their average betas differ. While the numbers we use in this example are rather extreme and unrealistic, they do illustrate the pitfalls involved in any empirical study of the CAPM that ignores time variation in betas.

The need to take time variation in betas into account is also demonstrated by the commercial success of firms like BARRA, which provide beta estimates for risk management and valuation purposes, using elaborate time-series models. Several empirical studies of beta-pricing models reported in the literature find that betas exhibit statistically significant variability over time.[7] Moreover, in empirical studies that examine the reaction of stock prices to certain events (referred to as "event studies" in the financial economics literature), it has become common practice to allow for time variations in betas, following Mandelker (1974). Hence, the inconclusive nature of the empirical evidence for the static CAPM may well be due to systematic stochastic changes affecting the environment that generates returns, as pointed out by Black (1993) and Chan and Lakonishok (1993).

In the next section, we will therefore assume that the CAPM holds in a conditional sense, i.e., it holds at every point in time, based on whatever information is available at that instant. We will then derive an unconditional asset-pricing model starting from the conditional version of the CAPM.

B. The Conditional CAPM

We use the subscript t to indicate the relevant time period. For example, R_{it} denotes the gross (one plus the rate of) return on asset i in period t, and R_{mt} the gross return on the aggregate wealth portfolio of all assets in the economy in period t. We refer to R_{mt} as the market return. Let I_{t-1} denote the common information set of the investors at the end of period $t - 1$. We assume that all the time series in this paper are covariance stationary and that all the conditional and unconditional moments that we use in the paper exist.

Risk-averse rational investors living in a dynamic economy will typically anticipate and hedge against the possibility that investment opportunities in the future may change adversely. Because of this hedging need that arises in a dynamic economy, the conditionally expected return on an asset will typically be jointly linear in the conditional market beta and "hedge portfolio betas."[8] However, following Merton (1980), we will assume that the hedging motives are not sufficiently important, and hence the CAPM will hold in a conditional sense as given below.

---

[7] See Bollerslev, Engle, and Wooldridge (1988), Harvey (1989), Ferson and Harvey (1991, 1993), and Ferson and Korajczyk (1993).

[8] See Merton (1973) and Long (1974).

8   *The Journal of Finance*

THE CONDITIONAL CAPM. *For each asset i and in each period t,*

$$E[R_{it}|I_{t-1}] = \gamma_{0t-1} + \gamma_{1t-1}\beta_{it-1}, \tag{2}$$

where β_{it-1} is the conditional beta of asset i defined as

$$\beta_{it-1} = Cov(R_{it}, R_{mt}|I_{t-1})/Var(R_{mt}|I_{t-1}), \tag{3}$$

γ_{0t-1} *is the conditional expected return on a "zero-beta" portfolio, and γ_{1t-1} is the conditional market risk premium.*

Since our aim is to explain the cross-sectional variations in the unconditional expected return on different assets, we take the unconditional expectation of both sides of equation (2) to get

$$E[R_{it}] = \gamma_0 + \gamma_1\bar{\beta}_i + Cov(\gamma_{1t-1}, \beta_{it-1}), \tag{4}$$

where

$$\gamma_0 = E[\gamma_{0t-1}] \qquad \gamma_1 = E[\gamma_{1t-1}] \qquad \bar{\beta}_i = E[\beta_{it-1}].$$

Here, γ_1 is the expected market risk premium, and $\bar{\beta}_i$ is the expected beta.[9] If the covariance between the conditional beta of asset i and the conditional market risk premium is zero (or a linear function of the expected beta) for every arbitrarily chosen asset i, then equation (4) resembles the static CAPM, i.e., the expected return is a linear function of the expected beta. However, in general, the conditional risk premium on the market and conditional betas are correlated. During bad economic times when the expected market risk premium is relatively high, firms on the "fringe" and more leveraged firms are more likely to face financial difficulties and thus have higher conditional betas. If the uncertainty associated with future growth opportunities is the cause for the higher beta of firms on the "fringe," then their conditional betas will be relatively low during bad economic times, resulting in natural perverse market timing. This is because during bad times the uncertainty as well as the value of future growth opportunities is reduced, and this effect may more than offset the effect of increased leverage.

In fact, we know from earlier studies that the expected risk premium on the market as well as conditional betas are not constant (Keim and Stambaugh (1986), Breen, Glosten, and Jagannathan (1989)), and vary over the business cycle (Fama and French (1989), Chen (1991), and Ferson and Harvey (1991)). Therefore, in general the last term in equation (4) is not zero, and the unconditional expected return is not a linear function of the expected beta alone.

Notice that the last term in equation (4) depends only on the part of the conditional beta that is in the linear span of the market risk premium. This motivates us to decompose the conditional beta of any asset i into two orthogonal components by projecting the conditional beta on the market risk pre-

---

[9] Note that expected betas are not the same as unconditional betas, but we will relate the two in the next subsection.

The Conditional CAPM and the Cross-Section of Expected Returns   9

mium. For each asset i, we define the *beta-prem sensitivity* (denoted by ϑ_i) and *residual beta* (denoted by η_{it-1}) as follows:

$$\vartheta_i = \text{Cov}(\beta_{it-1}, \gamma_{1t-1})/\text{Var}(\gamma_{1t-1}) \tag{5}$$

$$\eta_{it-1} = \beta_{it-1} - \bar{\beta}_i - \vartheta_i(\gamma_{1t-1} - \gamma_1). \tag{6}$$

In the above expression, beta-prem sensitivity, ϑ_i, measures the sensitivity of conditional beta to the market risk premium. It can be verified that, for each asset i, we have

$$\beta_{it-1} = \bar{\beta}_i + \vartheta_i(\gamma_{1t-1} - \gamma_1) + \eta_{it-1}, \tag{7}$$

$$E[\eta_{it-1}] = 0, \tag{8}$$

$$E[\eta_{it-1}\gamma_{it-1}] = 0. \tag{9}$$

Equation (7) decomposes each conditional beta (which is a random variable) into three orthogonal parts. The first part is the expected beta, which is a constant. The second part is a random variable that is perfectly correlated with the market risk premium. The last part is on average zero and uncorrelated with the market risk premium.

C. Implications for Unconditional Expected Returns

Substituting (7) into (4) gives

$$E[R_{it}] = \gamma_0 + \gamma_1\bar{\beta}_i + \text{Var}(\gamma_{1t-1})\vartheta_i. \tag{10}$$

Hence, cross-sectionally, the unconditional expected return on any asset i is a linear function of its expected beta and its beta-prem sensitivity. The larger this sensitivity, the larger is the variability of the above second part of the conditional beta. In this sense, the beta-prem sensitivity of an asset measures the instability of the asset's beta over the business cycle. Stocks with higher expected betas have higher unconditional expected returns. Likewise, stocks with betas that are prone to vary with the market risk premium and hence are less stable over the business cycle also have higher unconditional expected returns. Hence, the one-factor conditional CAPM leads to a two-factor model for unconditional expected returns.

A complete test of the conditional CAPM specification given in (2) requires estimation of expected beta, $\bar{\beta}_i$, and beta-prem sensitivity, ϑ_i, given in (10) as well as other parameters. This requires additional restrictive assumptions regarding the nature of the stochastic process governing the joint temporal evolution of conditional market betas and the conditional market risk premium.[10] However, our objective is to examine whether the unconditional expected

---

[10] See Bodurtha and Mark (1991) for an empirical examination of the conditional CAPM specification under more restrictive assumptions.

returns are consistent with the conditional CAPM. Because of the limited scope of our study, we can get by with somewhat less restrictive assumptions.

It can be seen from equation (10) that the residual betas do not affect the unconditional expected return. So, when considering unconditional returns, we can ignore η_{it-1} and concentrate on the first two parts of each conditional beta. Since we cannot estimate ϑ_i and $\tilde{\beta}_i$, we look directly at how the stock returns react to the market return on average and how they respond to the changes of the market risk premium. This leads us to define the following two types of unconditional betas:

$$\beta_i \equiv \mathrm{Cov}(R_{it}, R_{mt})/\mathrm{Var}(R_{mt}), \tag{11}$$

$$\beta_i^{\gamma} \equiv \mathrm{Cov}(R_{it}, \gamma_{1t-1})/\mathrm{Var}(\gamma_{1t-1}). \tag{12}$$

We refer to the first unconditional beta as the *market beta* and the second as the *premium beta*. They measure the *average market risk* and *beta-instability risk*, respectively.

In Appendix A, we show that under rather mild assumptions, the unconditional expected return is a linear function of the above two unconditional betas. This is summarized as the following theorem:

THEOREM 1. *If β_i^{γ} is not a linear function of β_i, then there are some constants a_0, a_1, and a_2 such that the equation*

$$E[R_{it}] = a_0 + a_1\beta_i + a_2\beta_i^{\gamma} \tag{13}$$

holds for every asset i.

The two-beta model presented here is not a special case of the multi-beta capital asset-pricing models commonly seen in finance literature. For example, according to the general equilibrium multi-beta model of Merton (1973), the conditionally expected return is linear in several conditional betas, one of which is the market beta. In contrast, we assume that the conditionally expected return is linear in the conditional market beta alone. From this, we show that the unconditional expected return is linear in the market beta and the premium beta. Also, there are several important differences between the two-beta model given above and the two-beta version of the linear factor models that owe their origins to the model first proposed by Ross (1976). First, we do not assume that returns have a linear factor structure as is commonly assumed in linear factor models. Second, γ_{1t-1} is a predetermined variable and is not a factor in the sense commonly understood.

II. Econometric Specifications and Tests

A. Empirical Specifications

The model given in equation (13) forms the basis for our empirical work. In order to empirically examine whether equation (13) can explain the cross-section of expected returns on stocks, we need some further assumptions to

The Conditional CAPM and the Cross-Section of Expected Returns 11

estimate the model using time-series data. First, we need observations on the conditional market risk premium γ_{1t-1} for computing β_i^γ. Since the conditional market risk premium depends on the nature of the information available to the investors and how they make use of it, we have to take a stand on the information set for investors. Second, the return on the aggregate wealth portfolio of all assets in the economy is not observable. Hence, we need to use a proxy for R_{mt} as well. We discuss these issues in the rest of this subsection.

A.1. The Proxy for the Conditional Market Risk Premium, γ_{1t-1}

There is a general agreement in the literature that stock prices vary over the business cycle. Hence, one may suspect that the market risk premium will also vary over the business cycle.[11] This observation suggests making use of the same variables that help predict the business cycle for forecasting the market risk premium as well.

While a number of variables may help predict future economic conditions, we need to restrict attention to a small number of such variables in order to ensure that we are able to estimate the parameters of interest with some degree of precision. For convenience, we have decided to restrict our attention in this study to only one forecasting variable. To determine which variable we should pick, we examined the literature on business-cycle forecasting. Our reading of this literature suggests that, in general, interest-rate variables are likely to be most helpful in predicting future business conditions. Stock and Watson (1989) examine several variables and find that the spread between six-month commercial paper and six-month Treasury bill rates and the spread between ten- and one-year Treasury bond rates both outperform nearly every other variable as a forecaster of the business cycle. Bernanke (1990), who runs "a horse race" between a number of interest-rate variables, finds that the best single variable is the spread between the commercial paper rate and Treasury bill rate first used by Stock and Watson.

Based on these findings, we choose the yield spread between BAA- and AAA-rated bonds, denoted by R_{t-1}^{prem}, as a proxy for the market risk premium. The variable R_{t-1}^{prem} is similar to the spread between commercial paper and the Treasury bill rates, but it has been used extensively in finance. In addition, we also assume that the market risk premium is a linear function of R_{t-1}^{prem}, i.e.,

ASSUMPTION 1. *There are some constants κ_0, κ_1 such that*

$$\gamma_{1t-1} = \kappa_0 + \kappa_1 R_{t-1}^{\text{prem}}. \tag{14}$$

For each asset i, we define *prem-beta* as

$$\beta_i^{\text{prem}} = \text{Cov}(R_{it}, R_{t-1}^{\text{prem}})/\text{Var}(R_{t-1}^{\text{prem}}). \tag{15}$$

---

[11] Keim and Stambaugh (1986), Fama and French (1989), and Chen (1991) provide empirical evidence that supports this view.

Under Assumption 1, the expected return is linear in its prem-beta and its market beta. To see this, we can substitute (14) into (12) and make use of (15) and Theorem 1 to obtain the following corollary:

COROLLARY 1. *Suppose that β_i^γ is not a linear function of β_i and that Assumption 1 holds, then there are some constants c_0, c_m, and c_{prem} such that the equation*

$$E[R_{it}] = c_0 + c_m\beta_i + c_{\text{prem}}\beta_i^{\text{prem}} \tag{16}$$

holds for every asset i.

A.2. The Proxy for the Return on the Wealth Portfolio, R_{mt}

In empirical studies of the CAPM it is commonly assumed that the return on the value-weighted portfolio of all stocks traded in the United States is a good proxy for the return on the portfolio of the aggregate wealth. Let R_t^{vw} denote the return on the value-weighted *stock index* portfolio. The implicit assumption is that the market return is a linear function of the stock index, i.e., there are some constants ϕ_0 and ϕ_{vw} such that

$$R_{mt} = \phi_0 + \phi_{\text{vw}}R_t^{\text{vw}}. \tag{17}$$

Let us define the *vw-beta* as

$$\beta_i^{\text{vw}} = \text{Cov}(R_{it}, R_t^{\text{vw}})/\text{Var}(R_t^{\text{vw}}). \tag{18}$$

Suppose that the static CAPM in equation (1) holds unconditionally as well. In this case, we can substitute (17) into equation (11) and use equation (18) and the static CAPM to obtain the following linear relation between the unconditional expected return and the vw-beta:

$$E[R_{it}] = c_0 + c_{\text{vw}}\beta_i^{\text{vw}}, \tag{19}$$

where c_0 and c_{vw} are some constants.

This is the specification that is commonly used in empirical studies of the static CAPM. Hence, tests of the CAPM based on this specification can be interpreted as a joint test of two hypotheses: (i) the static CAPM holds, and (ii) the market return is a linear function of the stock index return. Consequently, the results of these investigations are open to various interpretations. In particular, the reason for the empirical rejections of equation (19) may be that the static CAPM does not hold. Alternatively, it may also be the case that the static CAPM holds, but the return on the stock index portfolio is a poor proxy for the return on the aggregate wealth. Roll (1977) makes a related observation that the market portfolio is not observable. It is possible that the value-weighted index of stocks is a poor proxy for the portfolio of the aggregate wealth; hence, this might be the reason for the poor performance of the CAPM under empirical examination. In fact, Mayers (1972) points out that human capital forms a substantial part of the total capital in the economy. Following

The Conditional CAPM and the Cross-Section of Expected Returns   13

Mayers' suggestion, we therefore consider extending the proxy for the market return to include a measure of return on human capital.

To appreciate the need for examining other proxies for systematic risk, note that stocks form only a small part of the aggregate wealth. The monthly per capita income in the United States from dividends during the period 1959:1–1992:12 was less than 3 percent of the monthly personal income from all sources, whereas income from salaries and wages was about 63 percent during the same period. While these income flows ignore capital gains, these proportions remained relatively steady during this period.[12] This suggests that common stocks of all corporations constitute about a thirtieth of national income and probably national wealth as well. Another way to see this is as follows: As Diaz-Gimenez *et al.* (1992) point out, almost two-thirds of nongovernment tangible assets are owned by the household sector, and only one-third is owned by the corporate sector (p. 536, op. cit.). Approximately a third of the corporate assets are financed by equity (see Table 2, op. cit.). Hence, it appears that the return on stocks alone is unlikely to measure the return on aggregate wealth sufficiently accurately.

Apparently, the observation that stocks form only a small part of the total wealth is what motivated Stambaugh (1981 and 1982) to examine the sensitivity of the CAPM to different proxies for the market portfolio. In his seminal comparative study of the various market proxies, he finds that "even when stocks represent only 10 percent of the portfolio value, inferences about the CAPM are virtually identical to those obtained with a stock-only portfolio." However, he does not consider the return on human capital in his otherwise extensive study.

The commonly held view appears to be that human capital is not tradable and hence should be treated differently from other capital (see Mayers (1972)). This view is not entirely justified. First, note that mortgage loans, which are in most cases borrowing against future income, constitute about a third of all outstanding loans. At the end of 1986 the total market value of equities held by the households category was 0.80 GNP, whereas the outstanding stock of mortgages (0.60 GNP), consumer credit (0.16 GNP), and bank loans to the household sector (0.04 GNP) also amounted to 0.80 GNP (Table 4, Diaz-Gimenez *et al.* (1992)). Second, active insurance markets exist for hedging the risk in human capital. Examples include life insurance, unemployment insurance, and medical insurance. Hence, it does not appear inappropriate, as a first approximation, to take the view that human capital is just like any other form of physical capital, cash flows from which are traded through issuance of financial assets.

There is, however, an important difference between human capital and other physical assets owned by corporations. Typically, the entire cash flow that arises from the use of the physical assets employed by firms is promised away by issuing financial securities. This is not the case with human capital, where

---

[12] See Table 2.2 in *National Income and Product Account of the U.S.* published by the Bureau of Economic Analysis, the U.S. Department of Commerce.

only a portion of the labor income is secured by issuing mortgages. Also, in contrast to stocks, which are the residual claimants in the firm, the cash flow from labor income promised to mortgages comes from the top. Hence, factors that affect the return on human capital cannot be identified precisely enough by examining returns on financial assets like mortgages. We therefore follow a different strategy in measuring the return on human capital.

We assume that the return on human capital is an exact linear function of the growth rate in per capita labor income. While the use of the growth rate in per capita labor income is rather ad hoc, we can provide some rationale for using it. For example, suppose that, to a first order of approximation, the expected rate of return on human capital is a constant r, and that date-t per capita labor income L_t follows an autoregressive process of the form

$$L_t = (1 + g)L_{t-1} + \varepsilon_t.$$

In such a case, the realized capital-gain part of the rate of return on human capital (not corrected for additional investment in human capital made during the period) will be the realized growth rate in per capita labor income. To see this, note that under these assumptions, wealth due to human capital is

$$W_t = \frac{L_t}{r - g}.$$

The rate of change in wealth is then given by

$$R_t^{\text{labor}} = \frac{L_t - L_{t-1}}{L_{t-1}}.$$

Fama and Schwert (1977) arrive at a similar measure based on different lines of reasoning. Following the inter-temporal asset-pricing model, Campbell derives a measure for the return on human capital, which is the above current growth rate of labor income, plus a term that depends on expected future growth rates of labor income and expected future asset returns (see equation (3.3) in Campbell (1993b)). If both the forecastable part of the growth rates of labor income and the forecastable part of the returns on assets are not important, the term added to the above current growth rate of labor income will be very small. In this case, Campbell's measure and Fama-Schwert's measure for the return on human capital are approximately the same (see Campbell (1993b) for details). Motivated by these observations, we make the simple ad hoc assumption that the return on human capital is a linear function of the growth rate in per capita labor income.

It is possible that even when stocks constitute only a small fraction of total wealth, the stock-index portfolio return could well be an excellent proxy for the

The Conditional CAPM and the Cross-Section of Expected Returns   15

return on the portfolio of the aggregate wealth.[13] However, to allow for the possibility that this may not be the case, in our empirical work we consider the following proxy that incorporates a measure of the return on human capital. Let R_t^{labor} denote the growth rate in per capita labor income, which proxies for the return on human capital. We assume that the market return is a linear function of R_t^{vw} and R_t^{labor}, i.e.,

ASSUMPTION 2. *There are some constants ϕ_0, ϕ_{vw}, and ϕ_{labor} such that*

$$R_{mt} = \phi_0 + \phi_{vw}R_t^{vw} + \phi_{labor}R_t^{labor}. \tag{20}$$

Let us define the *labor-beta* as

$$\beta_i^{labor} = Cov(R_{it}, R_t^{labor})/Var(R_t^{labor}). \tag{21}$$

Then, by substituting (20) into (11), it follows from (18) and (21) that

$$\beta_i = b_{vw}\beta_i^{vw} + b_{labor}\beta_i^{labor}. \tag{22}$$

Under Assumptions 1 and 2, the unconditional expected return on any asset is a linear function of its vw-beta, prem-beta, and labor-beta. This can be seen by substituting equation (22) into the equation in Corollary 1 to get

COROLLARY 2. *Suppose that β_i^{γ} is not a linear function of β_i and that Assumptions 1 and 2 hold, then there are some constants c_0, c_{vw}, c_{prem}, and c_{labor} such that the equation*

$$E[R_{it}] = c_0 + c_{vw}\beta_i^{vw} + c_{prem}\beta_i^{prem} + c_{labor}\beta_i^{labor} \tag{23}$$

holds for every asset i.

We consider this to be the Premium-Labor model, and it forms the basis for the empirical study that follows. In the rest of this paper, it will be referred to as the "PL-model."

B. Econometric Tests

There are several ways to examine whether data are consistent with the PL-model. According to this model, the unconditional expected return on any asset is a linear function of its three betas only. A natural specification test is to examine whether any other variable has the ability to explain the cross-section of average returns not explained by the three-beta model. In particular, we investigate whether there are residual size effects in the PL-model. The rationale for testing a model against size effects has been discussed by Berk (1995). The *size* of a stock is defined as the logarithm of the market value of the stock. Let $\log(ME_i)$ denote the time-series average of size for asset i. We

---

[13] See Shanken (1987) and Kandel and Stambaugh (1987 and 1990), who show how the correlation between the market index proxy return and the unobserved wealth return is related to the mean-variance efficiency of the market-index proxy portfolio.

16   *The Journal of Finance*

examine whether any residual size effects exist by including $\log(\text{ME}_i)$ into the PL-model to get

$$E[R_{it}] = c_0 + c_{\text{size}} \log(\text{ME}_i) + c_{\text{vw}}\beta_i^{\text{vw}} + c_{\text{prem}}\beta_i^{\text{prem}} + c_{\text{labor}}\beta_i^{\text{labor}}. \quad (24)$$

If the PL-model holds, then the coefficient c_{size} should be zero, i.e., there should be no residual size effects.

The unconditional models in equations (23) and (24) can be consistently estimated by the cross-sectional regression (CSR) method proposed by Black, Jensen, and Scholes (1972) and Fama and MacBeth (1973). Notice that the PL-model nests the static CAPM as a special case. It facilitates direct comparison of the two models. For comparing the relative performance of the different empirical specifications, we use the R^2 in the cross-sectional regression as an informal and intuitive measure, which shows the fraction of the cross-sectional variation of average returns that can be explained by the model. We are also interested in examining whether c_{vw}, c_{prem}, c_{labor}, and c_{size} are different from zero after allowing for estimation errors. For this purpose, we need to estimate the sampling errors associated with the estimators for these parameters. In Appendix B, we show that the standard errors computed in the Fama-MacBeth procedure are biased, since it does not take into account the sampling errors in the estimated betas. Following the approach suggested by Shanken (1992), we derive a formula for correcting the bias (see Appendix B for details). In deriving the formula for the bias-correction, we made rather strong assumptions (see Assumptions 4 and 5 in Appendix B). Since these assumptions may not be satisfied in practice, we also evaluate the various CAPM specifications using the Generalized Method of Moments, which requires much weaker statistical assumptions.

For this purpose, consider the testable implications that arise from the following moment restriction imposed by the PL-model. Following Dybvig and Ingersoll (1982) we substitute the definition of β_i^{vw}, β_i^{labor}, and β_i^{prem} into the PL-model and rearrange the terms to get

$$E[R_{it}(\delta_0 + \delta_{\text{vw}}R_t^{\text{vw}} + \delta_{\text{prem}}R_{t-1}^{\text{prem}} + \delta_{\text{labor}}R_t^{\text{labor}})] = 1, \quad (25)$$

where δ_0, δ_{vw}, δ_{prem}, and δ_{labor} are the constants defined as follows:

$$\delta_0 = \frac{1}{c_0} + \frac{1}{c_0}\left[\frac{c_{\text{vw}}E[R_t^{\text{vw}}]}{\text{Var}(R_t^{\text{vw}})} + \frac{c_{\text{prem}}E[R_t^{\text{prem}}]}{\text{Var}(R_{t-1}^{\text{prem}})} + \frac{c_{\text{labor}}E[R_t^{\text{labor}}]}{\text{Var}(R_t^{\text{labor}})}\right]$$

$$\delta_{\text{vw}} = -\frac{c_{\text{vw}}}{c_0\text{Var}(R_t^{\text{vw}})} \qquad \delta_{\text{prem}} = -\frac{c_{\text{prem}}}{c_0\text{Var}(R_{t-1}^{\text{prem}})} \qquad \delta_{\text{labor}} = -\frac{c_{\text{labor}}}{c_0\text{Var}(R_t^{\text{labor}})}.$$

It is well known to financial economists (see Ross (1976)) that, so long as the financial market satisfies the law of one price, there will be at least some random variable d_t such that

$$E[R_{it}d_t] = 1, \quad (26)$$

The Conditional CAPM and the Cross-Section of Expected Returns   17

where d_t is generally referred to as a *stochastic discount factor*. Hansen and Richard (1987) point out that an asset-pricing model (like the CAPM) specifies the nature of this stochastic discount factor in terms of potentially observable variables. In our case the stochastic discount factor is given by

$$d_t(\delta) = \delta_0 + \delta_{vw}R_t^{vw} + \delta_{prem}R_{t-1}^{prem} + \delta_{labor}R_t^{labor}, \tag{27}$$

which depends on the parameters $\delta \equiv (\delta_0, \delta_{vw}, \delta_{prem}, \delta_{labor})'$.[14]

Suppose that there are N assets used in our econometric tests. Let 1_N be the N-dimensional vector of 1s, and

$$R_t \equiv (R_{1t}, \ldots , R_{Nt})'$$

$$Y_t \equiv (1, R_t^{vw}, R_t^{prem}, R_t^{labor})'.$$

Then $d_t(\delta) = Y_t'\delta$. If we let $w_t(\delta) = R_t d_t(\delta) - 1_N$, then $E[w_t(\delta)]$ is the vector of pricing errors of the model. Equation (25) implies that, when the PL-model is correctly specified, the N-dimensional pricing errors, $E[w_t(\delta)]$, should be zero. We can evaluate the relative performance of several competing model specifications by comparing the size of pricing errors. For this purpose, we therefore study the quadratic form $E[w_t(\delta)]'AE[w_t(\delta)]$, where A is a positive definite matrix (called weighting matrix). We should choose δ to minimize the pricing error by minimizing the value of the quadratic form, which leads to estimation of the parameters δ by the Generalized Method of Moments.

---

[14] Notice that we can rewrite the conditional CAPM given in equation (2) to get the following conditional stochastic discount factor representation: $E[R_{it}d_t|I_{t-1}] = 1$, where

$$d_t = \kappa_{0t-1} + \kappa_{1t-1}R_{mt}, \qquad \kappa_{0t-1} = \frac{1}{\gamma_{0t-1}} + \left[\frac{\gamma_{1t-1}}{\gamma_{0t-1}Var(R_{mt}|I_{t-1})}\right]E[R_{mt}|I_{t-1}],$$

and

$$\kappa_{1t-1} = -\frac{\gamma_{1t-1}}{\gamma_{0t-1}Var(R_{mt}|I_{t-1})}.$$

Cochrane (1992) suggests examining $E[R_{it}d_t|I_{t-1}] = 1$ empirically by assuming that κ_{0t-1} and κ_{1t-1} are linear functions of variables in the date $t-1$ information set I_{t-1}. If one assumes, as in Carhart *et al.* (1995), that (i) $\kappa_{1t-1} = \kappa_1$ (a constant) and (ii) $\kappa_{0t-1} = \kappa_{01} + \kappa_{02}R_{t-1}^{prem}$, the stochastic discount factor then becomes $d_t = \kappa_{01} + \kappa_{02}R_{t-1}^{prem} + \kappa_1 R_t^{vw}$, which resembles the one given in equation (25) with $\delta_{labor} = 0$. However, these assumptions are rather unreasonable. First, since κ_{1t-1} is a function of the conditional market risk premium, conditional zero-beta rate, and conditional variance of the market portfolio, it should be time-varying in nature. It is not reasonable to assume that κ_{1t-1} is a constant when the purpose is to evaluate the conditional CAPM with time-varying expected returns, variances, and covariances. Second, with assumption (i), it follows that $\kappa_{0t-1} = (1/\gamma_{0t-1}) - \kappa_1 E[R_{mt}|I_{t-1}]$. Thus, assumption (ii) implies that the conditionally expected market return is a linear function of R_{t-1}^{prem} and the *inverse* of the zero-beta rate. This is very hard to justify because the conditionally expected market return should, according to the conditional CAPM, be the sum of the market risk premium and the zero-beta rate (see equation (A1) in Appendix A). In contrast, to derive model (25), we only assume that the conditionally expected market risk premium is a linear function of the variables in the information set. This assumption can be justified under joint normality.

18 *The Journal of Finance*

Now the issue is how to choose the weighting matrix A. The most famous choice is the "optimal" weighting matrix suggested by Hansen and Singleton (1982). For expositional simplicity, let us now assume that w_t is i.i.d. over time. In this case, the weighting matrix suggested by Hansen and Singleton (1982) is $A = [Var(w_t(\delta))]^{-1}$. With this choice for the weighting matrix, they show that the minimized value of the sample analog of the quadratic form asymptotically has a χ^2 distribution with $N - K$ degrees of freedom, where K is the number of unknown parameters in the model. This asymptotic distribution can be used to test whether the pricing errors are zero. However, this weighting matrix will be different for different model specifications, and thus, we cannot use the value of the quadratic form to compare the relative size of the pricing errors associated with different models. Especially, if a model contains "more noise," i.e., the variance of $w_t(\delta)$ is larger, then the value of the quadratic form will be smaller. In this case, it would be misleading to conclude that the "more noisy" the model, the better it performs.

We therefore choose the weighting matrix suggested by Hansen and Jagannathan (1994), which is $A = (E[R_t R_t'])^{-1}$. Since this weighting matrix remains the same across various competing model specifications, it allows us to compare the performance of those models by the value of the quadratic form. Hansen and Jagannathan (1994) show that the value of the quadratic form is the squared distance from the candidate stochastic discount factor of a given model to the set of all the discount factors that price the N assets correctly. Thus, we refer to the square root of the quadratic form with this weighting matrix as the *Hansen-Jagannathan distance*, or simply, *HJ-distance*. Hansen and Jagannathan (1994) also show that the HJ-distance is the pricing error for the portfolio that is most mispriced by the model (see Appendix C for details). Since the weighting matrix suggested by Hansen and Jagannathan (1994) is generally not "optimal" in the sense of Hansen (1982), the minimized value of the sample analog of the quadratic form does not have a χ^2 distribution, and we thus cannot directly use Hansen's (1982) J-test for the overidentifying restrictions. In Appendix C, we therefore extend Hansen's (1982) results and show how to calculate the asymptotic distributions of the minimized quadratic form in the Generalized Method of Moments when the weighting matrix is chosen arbitrarily.

III. Empirical Results

A. Description of the Data

Though Fama and French (1992) use returns to common stocks of nonfinancial corporations listed in NYSE, AMEX (1962–90), and Nasdaq (1973–90) that are covered by CRSP as well as COMPUSTAT in their study, we study the returns to stocks of nonfinancial firms listed in NYSE and AMEX (1962–90) covered by CRSP alone. Nasdaq stocks are not included because we do not have monthly data for Nasdaq stocks available to us. This should not be an issue since Fama and French (1992) report that their results do not depend on the inclusion of Nasdaq stocks.

The Conditional CAPM and the Cross-Section of Expected Returns   19

It is well known that firms in the COMPUSTAT database may have some survivorship bias,[15] since stocks move in and out of the COMPUSTAT list depending on their performance. Kothari, Shanken, and Sloan (1995) provide indirect evidence for the existence of such bias—they point out that the annual returns are about 10 percentage points more for small firms in COMPUSTAT when compared to small firms that are only in CRSP. Breen and Korajczyk (1994) provide some direct evidence that supports the view that selection bias may be an important issue for tests that use standard sources of accounting data like COMPUSTAT. Fama and French (1993) attempt to address this problem by omitting the first two years of data, in response to COMPUSTAT's claim that no more than two years of data are included at the time a firm is added to the COMPUSTAT list. However, it is not clear whether this completely eliminates the bias in the COMPUSTAT tapes. With this in mind, we do not examine the relation between book-to-market equity and the cross-section of returns.[16] Hence, we are not constrained to limit our attention to stocks that are in CRSP as well as COMPUSTAT.[17]

We create 100 portfolios of NYSE and AMEX stocks as in Fama and French (1992). For every calendar year, starting in 1963, we first sort firms into size deciles based on their market value at the end of June. For each size decile, we estimate the beta of each firm, using 24 to 60 months of past-return data and the CRSP value-weighted index as the market index proxy. Following Fama and French (1992), we denote this beta as the "pre-ranking" beta estimate, or "pre-beta" for short. We then sort firms within each size decile into beta deciles based on their pre-betas. This gives us 100 portfolios, and we compute the return on each of these portfolios for the next 12 calendar months by equally weighting the returns on stocks in the portfolio. We repeat this procedure for each calendar year. This gives a time series of monthly returns (July 1963–December 1990, i.e., 330 observations) for each of the 100 portfolios.

The Fama and French (1992) sorting procedure produces an impressive dispersion in the characteristics of interest. Time-series averages of portfolio returns are given in Panel A of Table I. The rates of return range from a low of 0.51 percent to a high of 1.71 percent per month. The β_i^{vw}s of the portfolios are presented in Panel B of Table I. They range from a low of 0.57 to a high of 1.70. We calculate the size of a portfolio as the equally-weighted average of the

---

[15] See Chari, Jagannathan, and Ofer (1986).

[16] Chan, Jegadeesh, and Lakonishok (1995) report that the sample selection bias, if any, does not explain the superior performance of value stocks for the top quintile of the NYSE-AMEX stocks.

[17] Davis (1994), using a database that is free of survivorship bias, finds that book-to-market equity has significant explanatory power with respect to the cross-section of realized stock returns during the period of July 1940 through June 1963. It is worthwhile pointing out that we do not claim that the "book-to-market" variable does not help predict future returns on a stock. We are only pointing out that the COMPUSTAT data set has some selection bias and hence is unsuitable for econometric evaluation of asset-pricing models until we have a clearer understanding of the bias.

Table I

Basic Characteristics of the 100 Portfolios

Using stocks of nonfinancial firms listed in the NYSE and AMEX covered by CRSP, the 100 portfolios are formed in the same way as in Fama and French (1992). For every calendar year, starting from 1963, we first sort firms into size deciles based on their market value at the end of June. For each size category, we estimate the pre-beta of each firm by the slope coefficient in the regression of the 24 to 60 months of past-return data on a constant and the CRSP value-weighted index of the corresponding months. We then sort firms within each size decile into beta deciles based on their pre-betas. This gives 100 portfolios, and we compute the return on each of these portfolios for the next 12 calendar months by equally weighting the returns on stocks in the portfolio. We repeat this procedure for each calendar year. This gives a time series of monthly returns (July 1963–December 1990, i.e., 330 observations) for each of the 100 size-beta portfolios. β_i^{vw} is the slope in the regression of portfolio i's return on the CRSP value-weighted stock index return and a constant for the entire 330-month period. A portfolio size is calculated as the equally-weighted average of the logarithm of the market value (in million dollars) of the stocks in the portfolio. β_i^{prem} and β_i^{labor} are calculated in a similar way. The numbers given in Panel D are the part of β_i^{prem} orthogonal to a constant and β_i^{vw}, and the numbers in Panel E are the part of β_i^{labor} orthogonal to a constant, β_i^{vw} and β_i^{prem}.

	β-L	β-2	β-3	β-4	β-5	β-6	β-7	β-8	β-9	β-H
	Panel A: Time-Series Averages of Returns									
Size-S	1.44	1.53	1.56	1.71	1.36	1.44	1.37	1.33	1.46	1.34
Size-2	1.13	1.22	1.09	1.19	1.38	1.37	1.37	1.30	1.15	0.95
Size-3	1.26	1.27	1.22	1.26	1.16	1.29	1.34	1.19	1.12	0.89
Size-4	1.37	1.47	1.40	1.28	1.01	1.39	1.11	1.33	1.07	0.95
Size-5	0.97	1.53	1.10	1.28	1.18	1.04	1.35	1.07	1.23	0.82
Size-6	1.07	1.36	1.34	1.12	1.25	1.27	0.84	0.94	0.92	0.77
Size-7	0.99	1.18	1.13	1.19	0.96	0.99	1.11	0.91	0.90	0.83
Size-8	0.95	1.19	1.02	1.39	1.18	1.24	0.94	1.02	0.88	1.08
Size-9	0.94	0.92	1.05	1.17	1.15	1.03	1.02	0.84	0.80	0.51
Size-B	1.06	0.97	1.02	0.94	0.83	0.93	0.82	0.83	0.61	0.72
	Panel B: The Estimated β_i^{vw}s									
Size-S	0.90	0.99	1.01	1.13	1.17	1.21	1.20	1.31	1.44	1.54
Size-2	0.83	1.00	1.09	1.12	1.18	1.29	1.33	1.39	1.48	1.63
Size-3	0.78	0.93	1.09	1.11	1.18	1.27	1.29	1.40	1.42	1.70
Size-4	0.75	0.91	1.05	1.13	1.19	1.32	1.25	1.32	1.56	1.61
Size-5	0.57	0.78	1.10	1.10	1.12	1.20	1.25	1.43	1.45	1.54
Size-6	0.62	0.77	0.88	1.01	1.08	1.25	1.22	1.34	1.32	1.59
Size-7	0.64	0.84	1.01	1.07	1.16	1.21	1.26	1.26	1.31	1.54
Size-8	0.64	0.73	0.91	1.04	1.07	1.17	1.22	1.19	1.23	1.50
Size-9	0.62	0.78	0.88	0.96	1.04	1.05	1.13	1.17	1.22	1.34
Size-B	0.68	0.76	0.80	1.00	0.97	1.00	1.04	1.09	1.10	1.28
	Panel C: The Time-Series Averages of Size (log $million)									
Size-S	2.48	2.50	2.49	2.48	2.48	2.50	2.46	2.46	2.46	2.34
Size-2	3.71	3.72	3.73	3.73	3.71	3.71	3.72	3.72	3.72	3.72
Size-3	4.21	4.21	4.21	4.21	4.21	4.23	4.21	4.22	4.21	4.20
Size-4	4.67	4.65	4.64	4.65	4.65	4.65	4.65	4.64	4.64	4.64
Size-5	5.07	5.09	5.07	5.08	5.08	5.07	5.07	5.07	5.07	5.05
Size-6	5.47	5.48	5.47	5.48	5.48	5.48	5.48	5.48	5.47	5.48
Size-7	5.91	5.92	5.93	5.92	5.92	5.89	5.91	5.90	5.92	5.90
Size-8	6.44	6.42	6.43	6.39	6.43	6.41	6.43	6.42	6.40	6.40
Size-9	6.98	6.98	7.00	6.98	6.96	6.97	6.95	6.96	6.95	6.97
Size-B	8.11	8.26	8.22	8.19	8.16	8.18	8.06	8.03	7.92	7.81

The Conditional CAPM and the Cross-Section of Expected Returns   21

Table I—Continued

	β-L	β-2	β-3	β-4	β-5	β-6	β-7	β-8	β-9	β-H
			Panel D: The Estimated β_i^{prem} that is Orthogonal to β_i^{yw}							
Size-S	−0.03	0.30	0.20	0.08	0.43	0.25	0.16	0.25	0.46	0.24
Size-2	−0.47	0.41	0.47	−0.23	0.02	0.32	0.40	0.66	0.34	−0.03
Size-3	−0.04	0.10	0.41	0.27	−0.01	0.06	−0.50	−0.04	0.18	−0.38
Size-4	−0.04	0.37	−0.07	−0.28	0.24	0.13	0.71	−0.28	−0.26	−0.18
Size-5	−0.06	−0.13	0.18	0.08	0.06	0.17	0.11	0.14	−0.19	−0.79
Size-6	0.21	0.38	0.38	−0.01	0.12	0.62	−0.30	0.02	−0.45	−0.49
Size-7	−0.06	0.44	0.44	0.26	0.19	0.15	−0.07	0.06	0.31	0.05
Size-8	−0.44	−0.33	−0.02	0.16	0.41	0.11	0.05	−0.34	−0.69	−0.37
Size-9	−0.26	−0.34	0.14	0.09	−0.14	−0.13	0.15	−0.53	−0.03	−0.40
Size-B	−0.45	−0.07	−0.02	−0.26	−0.09	−0.64	−0.53	−0.34	−0.89	−0.25
			Panel E: The Estimated β_i^{labor} that is Orthogonal to β_i^{prem} and β_i^{yw}							
Size-S	1.23	1.15	0.71	0.48	0.65	0.19	1.38	0.73	1.06	0.73
Size-2	0.60	0.55	0.20	−0.10	0.51	0.53	−0.30	−0.84	0.35	−0.30
Size-3	0.32	0.19	−0.44	0.79	−0.29	0.07	0.94	0.13	0.13	0.52
Size-4	−0.04	0.48	0.46	−0.17	−0.05	−0.18	−1.40	0.15	0.30	0.42
Size-5	0.19	0.27	−0.15	0.30	0.16	−0.58	0.02	0.12	1.10	0.16
Size-6	−0.09	−0.05	−0.05	−0.08	0.02	−0.66	0.01	−0.52	−0.01	−1.04
Size-7	−0.66	−0.22	−0.38	−0.26	0.07	−0.07	−0.58	−0.21	−0.16	−0.45
Size-8	−0.25	0.16	−0.40	0.20	−0.53	−0.35	−0.76	−0.50	0.73	−0.78
Size-9	−0.38	−0.16	−0.27	−0.64	−0.07	−0.21	−0.25	−0.29	−0.39	−0.67
Size-B	0.32	−0.04	−0.04	−0.37	−0.24	0.01	−0.23	−0.43	0.02	−1.24

logarithm of market value of stocks (in million dollars). The time-series averages of portfolio size are presented in Panel C of Table I. They range from a low of 2.34 to a high of 8.26. Properties of these three characteristics of the portfolios are very similar to those of the portfolios formed by Fama and French (1992). The numbers given in Panel D are the part of β_i^{prem} orthogonal to a constant and β_i^{yw}, and the numbers in Panel E are the part of β_i^{labor} orthogonal to a constant, β_i^{yw} and β_i^{prem}.

The BAA- and AAA-bond yields are taken from Table 1.35 in the *Federal Reserve Bulletin* published by the Board of Governors of the Federal Reserve System. The data on personal income and population are taken from Table 2.2 in the *National Income and Product Account of the U.S.A.* published by the Bureau of Economic Analysis, U.S. Department of Commerce. The labor income used in this study is the difference between the total personal income and the dividend income. We construct the growth rate in per capita monthly labor income series using the formula,

$$R_t^{labor} = [L_{t-1} + L_{t-2}]/[L_{t-2} + L_{t-3}],$$

where R_t^{labor} denotes the growth rate in labor income that becomes known at the end of month t and L_{t-1} denotes the per capita labor income for month $t-1$, which becomes known at the end of month t. This dating convention is

22

The Journal of Finance

Table II

Evaluation of Various CAPM Specifications

This table gives the estimates for the cross-sectional regression model

$$E[R_{it}] = c_0 + c_{size} \log(ME_i) + c_{vw}\beta_i^{vw} + c_{prem}\beta_i^{prem} + c_{labor}\beta_i^{labor}$$

and the model for the moments

$$E[R_{it}(\delta_0 + \delta_{vw}R_t^{vw} + \delta_{prem}R_t^{prem} + \delta_{labor}R_t^{labor})] = 1,$$

with either a subset or all of the variables. Here, R_{it} is the return on portfolio i ($i = 1, 2, \ldots, 100$) in month t (July 1963–December 1990), R_t^{vw} is the return on the value-weighted index of stocks, R_{t-1}^{prem} is the yield spread between low- and high-grade corporate bonds, and R_t^{labor} is the growth rate in per capita labor income. The β_i^{vw} is the slope coefficient in the OLS regression of R_{it} on a constant and R_t^{vw}. The other betas are estimated in a similar way. The portfolio size, $\log(ME_i)$, is calculated as the equally-weighted average of the logarithm of the market value (in million dollars) of the stocks in portfolio i. The regression models are estimated by using the Fama-MacBeth procedure. The "corrected t- and p-values" take sampling errors in the estimated betas into account. The models for the moments are estimated by using the Generalized Method of Moments with the Hansen-Jagannathan weighting matrix. The minimized value of the GMM criterion function is the first item under the "HJ-dist," with the associated p-value immediately below it. All the R-squares and p-values are reported as percentages.

Panel A: The Static CAPM without Human Capital

Coefficient:	c_0	c_{vw}	c_{prem}	c_{labor}	c_{size}	R-square
Estimate:	1.24	−0.10				1.35
t-value:	5.17	−0.28				
p-value:	0.00	78.00				
Corrected-t:	5.16	−0.28				
Corrected-p:	0.00	78.01				
Estimate:	2.08	−0.32			−0.11	57.56
t-value:	5.79	−0.94			−2.30	
p-value:	0.00	34.54			2.14	
Corrected-t:	5.77	−0.94			−2.30	
Corrected-p:	0.00	34.60			2.17	

Coefficient:	δ_0	δ_{vw}	δ_{prem}	δ_{labor}	HJ-dist
Estimate:	0.97	1.55			0.6548
t-value:	89.01	1.09			
p-value:	0.00	27.59			0.22

Panel B: The Conditional CAPM without Human Capital

Coefficient:	c_0	c_{vw}	c_{prem}	c_{labor}	c_{size}	R-square
Estimate:	0.81	−0.31	0.36			29.32
t-value:	2.72	−0.87	3.28			
p-value:	0.66	38.45	0.10			
Corrected-t:	2.19	−0.70	2.67			
Corrected-p:	2.87	48.43	0.75			
Estimate:	1.77	−0.38	0.16		−0.10	61.66
t-value:	4.75	−1.10	2.50		−1.93	
p-value:	0.00	27.17	1.26		5.35	
Corrected-t:	4.53	−1.05	2.40		−1.84	
Corrected-p:	0.00	29.53	1.66		6.59	

The Conditional CAPM and the Cross-Section of Expected Returns   23

Table II—Continued

Panel B:—Continued

Coefficient:	δ_0	δ_{vw}	δ_{prem}	δ_{labor}	HJ-dist
Estimate:	1.48	2.05	-45.94		0.6425
t-value:	6.71	1.47	-2.36		
p-value:	0.00	14.14	1.83		0.98

Panel C: The Conditional CAPM with Human Capital

Coefficient:	c_0	c_{vw}	c_{prem}	c_{labor}	c_{size}	R-square
Estimate:	1.24	-0.40	0.34	0.22		55.21
t-value:	5.51	-1.18	3.31	2.31		
p-value:	0.00	23.76	0.09	2.07		
Corrected-t:	4.10	-0.88	2.48	1.73		
Corrected-p:	0.00	37.99	1.31	8.44		
Estimate:	1.70	-0.40	0.20	0.10	-0.07	64.73
t-value:	4.61	-1.18	3.00	2.09	-1.45	
p-value:	0.00	23.98	0.27	3.62	14.74	
Corrected-t:	4.14	-1.06	2.72	1.89	-1.30	
Corrected-p:	0.00	29.07	0.66	5.87	19.29	

Coefficient:	δ_0	δ_{vw}	δ_{prem}	δ_{labor}	HJ-dist
Estimate:	2.26	1.81	-65.72	-97.72	0.6184
t-value:	6.39	1.26	-3.10	-2.94	
p-value:	0.00	20.65	0.20	0.33	19.38

Panel D: The Static CAPM with Human Capital

Coefficient:	c_0	c_{vw}	c_{prem}	c_{labor}	c_{size}	R-square
Estimate:	1.67	-0.22		0.23		30.46
t-value:	6.91	-0.63		2.37		
p-value:	0.00	53.19		1.77		
Corrected-t:	5.71	-0.52		1.97		
Corrected-p:	0.00	60.49		4.87		
Estimate:	2.09	-0.32		0.05	-0.10	58.55
t-value:	5.80	-0.96		1.22	-2.15	
p-value:	0.00	33.78		22.29	3.19	
Corrected-t:	5.70	-0.95		1.20	-2.11	
Corrected-p:	0.00	34.46		22.93	3.48	

Coefficient:	δ_0	δ_{vw}	δ_{prem}	δ_{labor}	HJ-dist
Estimate:	1.37	1.22		-68.68	0.6422
t-value:	7.73	0.85		-2.32	
p-value:	0.00	39.65		2.01	1.94

consistent with the fact that the monthly labor income data are typically published with a one-month delay. We use a two-month moving average in per capita labor income to minimize the influence of measurement errors.

B. The Main Results

Using return data on the 100 portfolios described earlier, we first examine the traditional empirical CAPM specification,

$$E[R_{it}] = c_0 + c_{vw}\beta_i^{vw}. \tag{28}$$

The results are presented in Panel A of Table II. The t-value for c_{vw} is -0.28, and the corresponding p-value is 78 percent. The R^2 of the regression is only 1.35 percent, i.e., only 1.35 percent of the cross-sectional variation in average returns can be explained by this specification. The correction to the standard errors for estimation errors in the betas does not appear to be important. After the correction, the t-value remains as -0.28. Hence, we can conclude that c_{vw} is not significantly different from zero after allowing for sampling errors. When size is added to the model, the t-value for size is -2.30 and the corresponding p-value is only 2.14 percent. The R^2 goes up to 57.56 percent. The corrected t-value is not very different. The strong size effect suggests that the conventional specification of the CAPM is inconsistent with the data. In the GMM test that uses the Hansen-Jagannathan weighting matrix, the estimated HJ-distance is 0.6548 and the corresponding p-value is 0.22 percent, indicating that the pricing error is significantly different from zero. The p-value for the coefficient δ_{vw} in the moment restriction of the model is 27.59 percent, suggesting that R_t^{vw} does not play a significant role in constructing a stochastic discount factor that helps to explain the cross-sectional dispersion in expected returns on the 100 portfolios in our study. These results are consistent with what has been reported in the literature.

We next allow betas to vary over time, i.e., assume that the conditional CAPM holds, but still use the stock index as a proxy for the market return. This gives the following specification:

$$E[R_{it}] = c_0 + c_{vw}\beta_i^{vw} + c_{prem}\beta_i^{prem}. \tag{29}$$

The results are presented in Panel B of Table II. The estimated value of c_{prem}, using the Fama-MacBeth regression, is significantly different from zero. The t-value for c_{prem} is 3.28 with a p-value of 0.10 percent. The R^2 is 29.32 percent, which is a substantial improvement compared with 1.35 percent for the model in (28). The t-value for c_{prem} is 2.67 when the standard errors are corrected and the associated p-value is 0.75 percent. When size is added to equation (29), the t-value for c_{size} is -1.93 (p-value = 5.35 percent). When the standard errors are corrected, the t-value drops to -1.84 (p-value = 6.59 percent). Although there are still some size effects in model (29), they are much weaker than those in model (28). The GMM test with the HJ weighting matrix gives an estimated value of 0.6425 for HJ-distance with p-value of 0.98 percent. Hence, this specification reduces the pricing errors, but they are still significantly different from zero. The p-value for δ_{prem} in the moment restriction is 1.83 percent, which indicates that R_t^{prem} is a significant and important component of the stochastic discount factor.

The Conditional CAPM and the Cross-Section of Expected Returns 25

We now consider the main model developed in this paper:

$$E[R_{it}] = c_0 + c_{vw}\beta_i^{vw} + c_{prem}\beta_i^{prem} + c_{labor}\beta_i^{labor}, \qquad (30)$$

where the return on the market portfolio of all assets is assumed to be a linear function of the stock index and the growth rate of per capita labor income. Equation (30) is the same PL-model in equation (23). The estimation results are presented in Panel C of Table II. The estimated value of c_{labor}, using the Fama-MacBeth regression, is significantly different from zero (t-value = 2.31, p-value = 2.07 percent). The R^2 increases to 55.21 percent. However, when the standard errors are corrected, the t-value for c_{labor} drops to 1.73 (p-value = 8.44 percent). The coefficient c_{prem} remains significant. When size is added to the model, the t-value for the size coefficient is -1.45 and the associated p-value is 14.74 percent, which shows that size does not explain what is left unexplained in this model after controlling for sampling errors. When the standard errors are corrected, the p-value for size becomes even larger, reinforcing our conclusions. In the GMM test with the HJ weighting matrix, the estimated HJ-distance drops sharply to 0.6184 and the p-value jumps to 19.38 percent. Hence, the pricing errors of the PL-model are much smaller and not significantly different from zero. Notice that both R_t^{prem} and R_t^{labor} are significant in the GMM test, which is consistent with the results obtained from the Fama-MacBeth regression. While the point estimate of the slope coefficient c_{vw} is negative, it is not significantly different from zero, after allowing for sampling errors. Also, the estimated value of the average zero-beta rate is rather high when compared to the average T-bill rate and the average risk premium of stocks. Hence there is cause for concern even though our CAPM specification does substantially better than the static CAPM in explaining the cross-section of average returns on stocks. It appears that we are still missing some important aspect of reality in our modeling exercise.

In order to visually compare the performance of the different specifications, we plot the fitted expected return, computed by using the estimated parameter values in a model specification, against the realized average return. If the fitted expected returns and the realized average returns are the same, then all the points should lie on the 45-degree line through the origin. When β_i^{vw} alone is used, the fitted expected returns are all about the same, whereas the realized average returns vary substantially across the 100 portfolios (Figure 1). The performance substantially improves when β_i^{prem} and β_i^{labor} are also used (Figure 3). The fit is about as good as the model with size and β_i^{vw} (Figure 2). The distribution of the points around the 45-degree line in Figure 3 suggests that the improved performance of the CAPM using the specifications we suggest in this paper is not due to a few outliers. The distribution of the points around the 45-degree line does not significantly change when we add log(ME) as an additional explanatory variable (Figure 4).

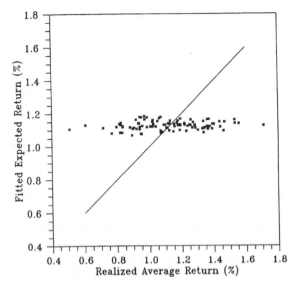

Figure 1. Fitted expected returns versus realized average returns. Each scatter point in the graph represents a portfolio, with the *realized average return* as the horizontal axis and the *fitted expected return* as the vertical axis. For each portfolio i, the realized average return is the time-series average of the portfolio return, and the fitted expected return is the fitted value for the expected return, $E[R_i]$, in the following regression model:

$$E[R_i] = c_0 + c_{vw}\beta_i^{vw},$$

where β_i^{vw} is the slope coefficient in the OLS regression of the portfolio return on a constant and the return on the value-weighted index portfolio of stocks. The straight line in the graph is the 45° line from the origin.

We may suspect that R_t^{labor} is the driving force behind the results for our main model. To determine if this is the case, we examine the following model:

$$E[R_{it}] = c_0 + c_{vw}\beta_i^{vw} + c_{labor}\beta_i^{labor}, \tag{31}$$

which can be obtained from the static CAPM by including the growth rate of labor income into the proxy for the market return. The estimated results for this specification are presented in Panel D of Table II. The coefficient corresponding to the growth rate of labor income is significant, both in the Fama-MacBeth regression and the GMM test using the HJ weighting matrix.[18] However, there is a strong residual size effect in the Fama-MacBeth regression. The HJ-distance is just slightly lower than that of model (28), and the

---

[18] Our empirical specification with labor income is similar to that used by Fama and Schwert (1977) when betas do not vary over time. The difference is that we use lagged labor income since labor income is published with a one-month lag. For a more detailed discussion of this issue, see Jagannathan and Wang (1993).

The Conditional CAPM and the Cross-Section of Expected Returns   27

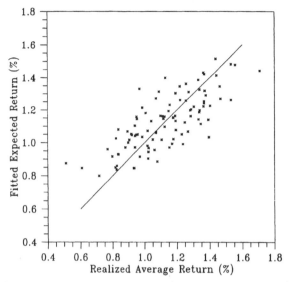

Figure 2. Fitted expected returns versus realized average returns. Each scatter point in the graph represents a portfolio, with the *realized average return* as the horizontal axis and the *fitted expected return* as the vertical axis. For each portfolio i, the realized average return is the time-series average of the portfolio return, and the fitted expected return is the fitted value for the expected return, $E[R_i]$, in the following regression model:

$$E[R_i] = c_0 + c_{\text{size}} \log(ME_i) + c_{vw}\beta_i^{vw},$$

where β_i^{vw} is the slope coefficient in the OLS regression of the portfolio return on a constant and the return on the value-weighted index portfolio of stocks, and the portfolio size, $\log(ME_i)$, is calculated as the equally-weighted average of the logarithm of the market value (in million dollars) of the stocks in portfolio i. The straight line in the graph is the 45° line from the origin.

p-value is only 1.94 percent. Thus, the pricing error of this model is still substantial. This suggests that it is necessary to allow for time variations in betas as well in order to explain the cross-section of expected returns on stocks.

C. Additional Investigations

The unconditional model we develop in this paper to some extent resembles the multi-factor model specified by Chen, Roll, and Ross (1986). A natural question that arises is whether the "lagged-prem factor" and the "labor-income-growth-rate factor" that we use in our specifications are just proxies for the macroeconomic factors that are identified by Chen, Roll, and Ross in their earlier work. Following them, we consider, besides the value-weighted stock index, four additional factors: (a) UTS_t is the monthly return spread between the long-term government bond and Treasury bill, (b) UPR_t is the return

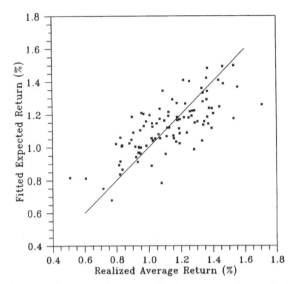

Figure 3. Fitted expected returns versus realized average returns. Each scatter point in the graph represents a portfolio, with the *realized average return* as the horizontal axis and the *fitted expected return* as the vertical axis. For each portfolio i, the realized average return is the time-series average of the portfolio return, and the fitted expected return is the fitted value for the expected return, $E[R_i]$, in the following regression model:

$$E[R_i] = c_0 + c_{vw}\beta_i^{vw} + c_{prem}\beta_i^{prem} + c_{labor}\beta_i^{labor},$$

where β_i^{vw} is the slope coefficient in the OLS regression of the portfolio return on a constant and the return on the value-weighted index portfolio of stocks, β_i^{prem} is the slope coefficient in the OLS regression of the portfolio return on a constant and the yield spread between low- and high-grade corporate bonds, and β_i^{labor} is the slope coefficient in the OLS regression of the portfolio return on a constant and the growth rate in per capita labor income. The straight line in the graph is the 45° line from the origin.

differential between a long-term corporate bond and long-term government bond, (c) MP_t is the growth rate in monthly industrial production in the United States, and (d) UI_t is the change of inflation rate. The betas are estimated using contemporaneous values of these variables. The UTS_t and MP_t are the same variable used by Chen, Roll, and Ross. While the UPR_t and UI_t used in our test should be similar to those corresponding factors used by Chen, Roll, and Ross, they may not be exactly the same since we do not have access to their data. The data series on inflation, corporate-bond return, and long-term government bond return are from Ibbotson Associates.[19] Monthly industrial production data are obtained from Table 2.10 in the *Federal Reserve Bulletin* published by the Board of Governors of the Federal Reserve System. We

---

[19] See *Stocks, Bonds, Bills and Inflation*, 1991 Year Book by Ibbotson Associates Inc.

The Conditional CAPM and the Cross-Section of Expected Returns   29

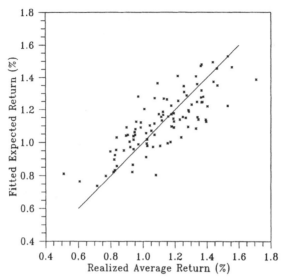

Figure 4. Fitted expected returns versus realized average returns. Each scatter point in
the graph represents a portfolio, with the *realized average return* as the horizontal axis and the
fitted expected return as the vertical axis. For each portfolio i, the realized average return is the
time-series average of the portfolio return, and the fitted expected return is the fitted value for the
expected return, $E[R_i]$, in the following regression model:

$$E[R_i] = c_0 + c_{size} \log(ME_i) + c_{vw}\beta_i^{vw} + c_{prem}\beta_i^{prem} + c_{labor}\beta_i^{labor},$$

where β_i^{vw} is the slope coefficient in the OLS regression of the portfolio return on a constant and
the return on the value-weighted index portfolio of stocks, β_i^{prem} is the slope coefficient in the OLS
regression of the portfolio return on a constant and the yield spread between low- and high-grade
corporate bonds, β_i^{labor} is the slope coefficient in the OLS regression of the portfolio return on a
constant and the growth rate in per capita labor income, and the portfolio size, $\log(ME_i)$, is
calculated as the equally-weighted average of the logarithm of the market value (in million dollars)
of the stocks in portfolio i. The straight line in the graph is the 45° line from the origin.

consider the following models:

$$E[R_{it}] = c_0 + c_{vw}\beta_i^{vw} + c_{UTS}\beta_i^{UTS} + c_{UPR}\beta_i^{UPR} + c_{MP}\beta_i^{MP} + c_{UI}\beta_i^{UI} \qquad (32)$$

$$E[R_{it}] = c_0 + c_{vw}\beta_i^{vw} + c_{prem}\beta_i^{prem} + c_{labor}\beta_i^{labor} + c_{UTS}\beta_i^{UTS} \qquad (33)$$
$$+ c_{UPR}\beta_i^{UPR} + c_{MP}\beta_i^{MP} + c_{UI}\beta_i^{UI},$$

where all the betas are calculated in the same way as β_i^{vw}.

The results are given in Table III. The top half of the table gives the
estimates for model (32). The R^2 for the model is 38.96 percent, which is
substantially less than the R^2 for the PL-model (55.21 percent). The HJ-
distance for equation (32) is 0.6529, which is larger than the HJ-distance for
the PL-model (0.6184). So, the R^2 and the HJ-distance consistently indicate
that the PL-model performs better than model (32). The p-value shows that the

30   *The Journal of Finance*

Table III

Comparison with the Factors Used by Chen, Roll, and Ross (1986)

This table gives the estimates for the cross-sectional regression model

$$E[R_{it}] = c_0 + c_{vw}\beta_i^{vw} + c_{prem}\beta_i^{prem} + c_{labor}\beta_i^{labor} + c_{UTS}\beta_i^{UTS} + c_{UPR}\beta_i^{UPR} + c_{MP}\beta_i^{MP} + c_{UI}\beta_i^{UI}$$

and the model for the moments

$$E[R_{it}(\delta_0 + \delta_{vw}R_t^{vw} + \delta_{prem}R_t^{prem} + \delta_{labor}R_t^{labor} + \delta_{UTS}UTS_t + \delta_{UPR}UPR_t + \delta_{MP}MP_t + \delta_{UI}UI_t)] = 1,$$

with either a subset or all of the variables. Here, R_{it} is the return on portfolio i ($i = 1, 2, \ldots, 100$) in month t (July 1963–December 1990), R_t^{vw} is the return on the value-weighted index of stocks, R_{t-1}^{prem} is the yield spread between low- and high-grade corporate bonds, R_t^{labor} is the growth rate in per capita labor income, UTS_t is the return spread between long-term government bonds and Treasury bills, UPR_t is the return differential between long-term corporate and long-term government bonds, MP_t is the growth rate in monthly industrial production in the United States, and UI_t is the change of inflation rate. The β_i^{vw} is the slope coefficient in the OLS regression of R_{it} on a constant and R_t^{vw}. The other betas are estimated in a similar way. The regression models are estimated by using the Fama-MacBeth procedure. The "corrected t- and p-values" take sampling errors in the estimated betas into account. The models for the moments are estimated by using the Generalized Method of Moments with the Hansen-Jagannathan weighting matrix. The minimized value of the GMM criterion function is the first item under the "HJ-dist," with the associated p-value immediately below it. All the R-squares and p-values are reported as percentages.

Coefficient:	c_0	c_{vw}	c_{prem}	c_{labor}	c_{UTS}	c_{UPR}	c_{MP}	c_{UI}	R-square
Estimate:	1.80	−0.44			−1.07	0.39	−0.02	−0.07	38.96
t-value:	7.18	−1.28			−2.44	1.63	−0.17	−1.95	
p-value:	0.00	20.14			1.46	10.33	86.27	5.13	
Corrected-t:	6.17	−1.10			−2.12	1.41	−0.15	−1.68	
Corrected-p:	0.00	26.99			3.38	15.93	88.19	9.34	

Coefficient:	δ_0	δ_{vw}	δ_{prem}	δ_{labor}	δ_{UTS}	δ_{UPR}	δ_{MP}	δ_{UI}	HJ-dist
Estimate:	0.97	1.15			2.81	3.40	2.30	8.08	0.6529
t-value:	28.47	0.76			0.88	0.45	0.19	0.23	
p-value:	0.00	44.77			37.96	65.19	85.12	81.70	0.16

Coefficient:	c_0	c_{vw}	c_{prem}	c_{labor}	c_{UTS}	c_{UPR}	c_{MP}	c_{UI}	R-square
Estimate:	1.37	−0.51	0.29	0.18	−0.17	0.19	0.07	−0.03	57.87
t-value:	6.33	−1.46	3.54	2.44	−0.46	0.92	0.61	−0.99	
p-value:	0.00	14.50	0.04	1.47	64.75	35.72	54.26	32.11	
Corrected-t:	4.97	−1.15	2.81	1.93	−0.36	0.72	0.48	−0.78	
Corrected-p:	0.00	25.17	0.50	5.39	71.91	46.89	63.24	43.53	

Coefficient:	δ_0	δ_{vw}	δ_{prem}	δ_{labor}	δ_{UTS}	δ_{UPR}	δ_{MP}	δ_{UI}	HJ-dist
Estimate:	2.38	1.73	−72.05	−104.33	−0.27	7.31	−5.91	−9.81	0.6152
t-value:	6.14	1.13	−3.19	−2.84	−0.08	0.86	−0.43	−0.27	
p-value:	0.00	25.86	0.14	0.46	94.01	38.95	66.68	78.80	22.06

HJ-distance for model (32) is significantly different from zero. The lower half of the table gives the results for model (33). Both the R^2 and the HJ-distance indicate that inclusion of the four additional factors in Chen, Roll, and Ross (1986) does not substantially improve the performance of the PL-model. More importantly, none of the coefficients corresponding to the factors in Chen, Roll,

The Conditional CAPM and the Cross-Section of Expected Returns   31

and Ross (1986) is significantly different from zero after taking sampling errors into account.

Earlier, we examined the possibility of model misspecification by checking whether firm size can explain the cross-sectional variation of expected returns that cannot be explained by our conditional CAPM specification. An alternative is to examine whether the betas with respect to the size and book-to-market factors, SMB_t and HML_t, introduced in Fama and French (1993), can explain the cross-sectional variation of expected returns not explained by our model. Although Berk (1995) shows that the log of size and the log of book-to-market equity should be correlated with expected returns in the cross-section, his observation does not imply that this correlation can be captured by the two factors. Hence, we are interested in examining whether the two factors that Fama and French (1993) identify from the data are proxying for the risk associated with the return on human capital and beta instability that we model.[20] For this purpose, we consider the following models:

$$E[R_{it}] = c_0 + c_{vw}\beta_i^{vw} + c_{SMB}\beta_i^{SMB} + c_{HML}\beta_i^{HML} \tag{34}$$

$$E[R_{it}] = c_0 + c_{vw}\beta_i^{vw} + c_{prem}\beta_i^{prem} + c_{labor}\beta_i^{labor}$$
$$+ c_{SMB}\beta_i^{SMB} + c_{HML}\beta_i^{HML}, \tag{35}$$

where all the betas are calculated in the same way as β_i^{vw}.

The empirical results are given in Table IV. The top half of the table gives the estimates for model (34). The R^2 is 55.12 percent, which is not much different from 55.21 percent, the R^2 for the PL-model. This means that the PL-model fits the data at least as well as model (34) does. Also, the estimated value of the zero-beta rate is not very different from the one obtained using the PL-model. However, the HJ-distance for model (34) is 0.6432, which is clearly larger than that for the PL-model (0.6184). In other words, although the two models do equally well on average, the pricing error for the portfolio that is most mispriced by model (34) is larger than the pricing error for the portfolio that is most mispriced by the PL-model. The p-value also shows that the HJ-distance for model (34) is significantly different from zero. The lower half of the table gives the estimates for model (35). The R^2 goes up from 55.21 to 64.04 percent when the two factors in Fama and French (1993) are included. This is about the same increase that is obtained when size is included. None of

---

[20] Daniel and Titman (1995) find that only part of the return premia on small capitalization and high book-to-market stocks can be explained by the betas with respect to the two factors introduced by Fama and French (1993). Hansen and Jagannathan (1994) point out that any given misspecified model can be "fixed" by adding a particular "modifying portfolio payoff" to the stochastic discount factor associated with the model. Equivalently, any given misspecified linear beta-pricing model can be "fixed" by adding one more beta, where the additional beta is computed with respect to the return on the "modifying portfolio." The results in Fama and French (1993) suggest that the modifying portfolio associated with the static CAPM is a portfolio of only two factors—the size and book-to-market factors. However, there is no theoretical explanation for this empirical regularity.

Table IV

Comparison with the Factors Used by Fama and French (1993)

This table gives the estimates for the cross-sectional regression model

$$E[R_{it}] = c_0 + c_{vw}\beta_i^{vw} + c_{prem}\beta_i^{prem} + c_{labor}\beta_i^{labor} + c_{SMB}\beta_i^{SMB} + c_{HML}\beta_i^{HML}$$

and the model for the moments

$$E[R_{it}(\delta_0 + \delta_{vw}R_t^{vw} + \delta_{prem}R_t^{prem} + \delta_{labor}R_t^{labor} + \delta_{SMB}SMB_t + \delta_{HML}HML_t)] = 1,$$

with either a subset or all of the variables. Here, R_{it} is the return on portfolio i ($i = 1, 2, \ldots, 100$) in month t (July 1963–December 1990), R_t^{vw} is the return on the value-weighted index of stocks, R_{t-1}^{prem} is the yield spread between low- and high-grade corporate bonds, R_t^{labor} is the growth rate in per capita labor income, and SMB_t and HML_t denote the respective Fama and French (1993) factors that are designed to capture the risks related to firm size and book-to-market equity. The β_i^{vw} is the slope coefficient in the OLS regression of R_{it} on a constant and R_t^{vw}. The other betas are estimated in a similar way. The regression models are estimated by using the Fama-MacBeth procedure. The "corrected t- and p-values" take sampling errors in the estimated betas into account. The models for the moments are estimated by using the Generalized Method of Moments with the Hansen-Jagannathan weighting matrix. The minimized value of the GMM criterion function is the first item under the "HJ-dist," with the associated p-value immediately below it. All the R-squares and p-values are reported as percentages.

Coefficient:	c_0	c_{vw}	c_{prem}	c_{labor}	c_{SMB}	c_{HML}	R-square
Estimate:	1.39	−0.45			0.33	0.25	55.12
t-value:	6.07	−0.95			1.53	0.96	
p-value:	0.00	34.34			12.60	33.59	
Corrected-t:	5.99	−0.94			1.51	0.95	
Corrected-p:	0.00	34.97			13.12	34.19	

Coefficient:	δ_0	δ_{vw}	δ_{prem}	δ_{labor}	δ_{SMB}	δ_{HML}	HJ-dist
Estimate:	0.98	2.62			−4.56	−0.94	0.6432
t-value:	35.00	1.35			−2.10	−0.28	
p-value:	0.00	17.78			3.60	77.91	0.65

Coefficient:	c_0	c_{vw}	c_{prem}	c_{labor}	c_{SMB}	c_{HML}	R-square
Estimate:	1.20	−0.38	0.22	0.11	0.16	0.22	64.04
t-value:	5.24	−0.80	3.32	2.25	0.78	0.84	
p-value:	0.00	42.41	0.09	2.44	43.79	40.24	
Corrected-t:	4.60	−0.70	2.95	1.99	0.68	0.74	
Corrected-p:	0.00	48.22	0.32	4.69	49.49	46.11	

Coefficient:	δ_0	δ_{vw}	δ_{prem}	δ_{labor}	δ_{SMB}	δ_{HML}	HJ-dist
Estimate:	2.17	2.62	−62.00	−89.33	−3.30	−0.59	0.6123
t-value:	6.09	1.26	−2.94	−2.67	−1.42	−0.18	
p-value:	0.00	20.90	0.32	0.77	15.52	85.98	18.58

the coefficients corresponding to the two factors in Fama and French (1993) is statistically significantly different from zero after taking sampling errors into account. These results suggest that the two Fama and French (1993) factors may proxy for the risk associated with the return on human capital and beta instability.

The Conditional CAPM and the Cross-Section of Expected Returns 33

In our study, we focus on the Black version of the conditional CAPM, which assumes that the borrowing and the lending rates are different. The zero-beta rate in such an environment should lie between the riskless borrowing and riskless lending rates. To examine whether this is true, we proceed as follows. We first assume that the riskless lending and borrowing rates are the same as the interest rate on one-month Treasury bills (T-bills). In that case the model should assign the right average return to T-bills as well. Let $R_{\text{TBill}t}$ denote the monthly return on the T-bills. Applying the PL-model to the T-bill, we have

$$E[R_{\text{TBill}t}] = c_0 + c_{\text{vw}}\beta_{\text{TBill}}^{\text{vw}} + c_{\text{prem}}\beta_{\text{TBill}}^{\text{prem}} + c_{\text{labor}}\beta_{\text{TBill}}^{\text{labor}}. \qquad (36)$$

Subtracting the above equation from the PL-model gives the relation between expected excess returns and betas for the 100 portfolios:

$$E[\tilde{R}_{it}] = c_{\text{vw}}\tilde{\beta}_i^{\text{vw}} + c_{\text{prem}}\tilde{\beta}_i^{\text{prem}} + c_{\text{labor}}\tilde{\beta}_i^{\text{labor}} \qquad i = 1, \ldots, 100, \qquad (37)$$

where $\tilde{R}_{it} = R_{it} - R_{\text{TBill}t}$ and $\tilde{\beta}_i^{\text{vw}} = \text{Cov}(\tilde{R}_{it}, R_t^{\text{vw}})/\text{Var}(R_t^{\text{vw}})$ for $i = 1, \ldots, 100$, and other $\tilde{\beta}$s are defined in a similar way. If the borrowing and lending rates are different, the relation given in (37) should be modified to include a positive intercept term, which should equal the difference between the average zero-beta rate and the average T-bill rate. One way to examine model misspecification is to estimate the above relation with an intercept term and test if it is positive and reasonable given our priors regarding what the difference between the zero-beta rate and T-bill rate should be. The moment restrictions implied by this model are

$$E[\tilde{R}_{it}(1 + \tilde{\delta}_{\text{vw}}R_t^{\text{vw}} + \tilde{\delta}_{\text{prem}}R_{t-1}^{\text{prem}} + \tilde{\delta}_{\text{labor}}R_t^{\text{labor}})] = 0,$$

where $\tilde{\delta}_{\text{vw}}$, $\tilde{\delta}_{\text{prem}}$, and $\tilde{\delta}_{\text{labor}}$ are the constants defined as follows:

$$\tilde{\delta}_{\text{vw}} = -\frac{c_{\text{vw}}}{\tilde{\delta}_0\text{Var}(R_t^{\text{vw}})} \qquad \tilde{\delta}_{\text{prem}} = -\frac{c_{\text{prem}}}{\tilde{\delta}_0\text{Var}(R_{t-1}^{\text{prem}})} \qquad \tilde{\delta}_{\text{labor}} = -\frac{c_{\text{labor}}}{\tilde{\delta}_0\text{Var}(R_t^{\text{labor}})}.$$

$$\tilde{\delta}_0 = 1 + \frac{c_{\text{vw}}E[R_t^{\text{vw}}]}{\text{Var}(R_t^{\text{vw}})} + \frac{c_{\text{prem}}E[R_t^{\text{prem}}]}{\text{Var}(R_{t-1}^{\text{prem}})} + \frac{c_{\text{labor}}E[R_t^{\text{labor}}]}{\text{Var}(R_t^{\text{labor}})}.$$

These moment restrictions can be tested using the Generalized Method of Moments as described in Section II-B. Notice that one should not subtract the T-bill return from any of the factors when calculating betas or constructing the stochastic discount factor since the zero-beta return may be different from the T-bill return. In contrast, the three-factor model for the excess returns specified in Fama and French (1993) is

$$E[\tilde{R}_{it}] = c_{\text{vw}}\ddot{\beta}_i^{\text{vw}} + c_{\text{SMB}}\tilde{\beta}_i^{\text{SMB}} + c_{\text{HML}}\tilde{\beta}_i^{\text{HML}}, \qquad (38)$$

where $\ddot{\beta}_i^{vw} = \mathrm{Cov}(\bar{R}_{it}, R_t^{vw} - R_{\mathrm{TBill}t})/\mathrm{Var}(R_t^{vw} - R_{\mathrm{TBill}t})$, which is the slope of regressing the excess asset return on the *excess* return of the CRSP value-weighted portfolio.

The results for excess returns are presented in Table V. The intercepts in the regressions for both the models are significantly different from zero, which suggests that the zero-beta rate is different from the T-bill rate. Neither our conditional CAPM specification nor the Fama-French three-factor specification assigns the right value to T-bills. The fact that the intercept term exceeds one percent per month suggests that both specifications are missing some important aspect of reality.

Ferson and Foerster (1994) point out that the GMM has rather poor finite sample properties. It is for this reason that we chose not to test the conditional CAPM directly, but rather to test its unconditional implications. This reduces the dimensionality of the problem and hence is likely to result in better finite sample statistical properties. This is also the reason we chose to use the weighting matrix suggested by Hansen and Jagannathan (1994) instead of the optimal GMM weighting matrix. Since the HJ weighting matrix does not depend on the unknown parameters that are being estimated, it is likely to improve the statistical properties of the GMM tests in finite samples.[21] Zhou (1994) provides some evidence that supports this view. In addition, we also formed portfolios of stocks by first sorting them into size quintiles and then pre-beta quintiles. We then repeated all the tests, using the time series of monthly returns on these 25 portfolios. The results for the 25 portfolios are qualitatively similar to those for the 100 portfolios reported in this paper.

IV. Conclusion

There are two major difficulties in examining the empirical support for the static CAPM. First, the real world is inherently dynamic and not static. Second, the return on the portfolio of aggregate wealth is not observable. These issues are typically ignored in empirical studies of the CAPM. It is commonly assumed that betas of assets remain constant over time, and the return on stocks measures the return on the aggregate wealth portfolio. Under these assumptions, Fama and French (1992) find that the relation between average return and beta is flat and that there is a strong size effect.

We argue that those two assumptions are not reasonable. Relaxing the first assumption naturally leads us to examine the conditional CAPM. We demonstrate that the empirical support for our conditional CAPM specification is rather strong. When betas and expected returns are allowed to vary over time by assuming that the CAPM holds period by period, the size effects and the statistical rejections of the model specifications become much weaker. When a proxy for the return on human capital is also included in measuring the return

---

[21] However, this issue is not explored in this paper. In a separate paper, we will compare the sampling properties of the optimal and HJ weighting matrices.

The Conditional CAPM and the Cross-Section of Expected Returns   35

Table V

Tests Using the Time Series of Monthly Excess Returns on the 100 Size-Beta Sorted Portfolios

This table gives the estimates for the following two regression models:

$$E[\tilde{R}_{it}] = c_{vw}\tilde{\beta}_i^{vw} + c_{prem}\tilde{\beta}_i^{prem} + c_{labor}\tilde{\beta}_i^{labor} \qquad E[\tilde{R}_{it}] = c_{vw}\ddot{\beta}_i^{vw} + c_{SMB}\tilde{\beta}_i^{SMB} + c_{HML}\tilde{\beta}_i^{HML}$$

and the two models for the moments

$$E[\tilde{R}_{it}(1 + \tilde{\delta}_{vw}R_t^{vw} + \tilde{\delta}_{prem}R_{t-1}^{prem} + \tilde{\delta}_{labor}R_t^{labor})] = 0$$

$$E[\tilde{R}_{it}(1 + \tilde{\delta}_{vw}\tilde{R}_t^{vw} + \tilde{\delta}_{SMB}R_t^{SMB} + \tilde{\delta}_{HML}R_t^{HML})] = 0.$$

Here, $\tilde{R}_{it} = R_{it} - R_t^{TBill}$, where R_{it} is the return on portfolio i ($i = 1, 2, \ldots, 100$) in month t (July 1963–December 1990) and R_t^{TBill} is the return on the T-bill. R_t^{vw} is the return on the value-weighted index of stocks and $\tilde{R}_t^{vw} = R_t^{vw} - R_t^{TBill}$. R_{t-1}^{prem} is the yield spread between low- and high-grade corporate bonds, R_t^{labor} is the growth rate in per capita labor income, and SMB_t and HML_t denote the respective Fama and French (1993) factors that are designed to capture the risks related to firm size and book-to-market equity. The $\tilde{\beta}_i^{vw}$ is the slope coefficient in the OLS regression of $\tilde{R}_{it}$ on a constant and R_t^{vw}. The other βs are estimated in a similar way. The $\ddot{\beta}_i^{vw}$ is the slope coefficient in the OLS regression of $\tilde{R}_{it}$ on a constant and $\tilde{R}_t^{vw}$. The regression models are estimated by using the Fama-MacBeth procedure. The "corrected t- and p-values" take sampling errors in the estimated betas into account. The models for the moments are estimated by using the Generalized Method of Moments with the Hansen-Jagannathan weighting matrix. The minimized value of the GMM criterion function is the first item under the "HJ-dist," with the associated p-value immediately below it. All the R-squares and p-values are reported as percentages.

Coefficient:	c_0	c_{vw}	c_{prem}	c_{labor}	c_{SMB}	c_{HML}	R-square
Estimate:	0.79	−0.40	0.34	0.22			55.21
t-value:	3.58	−1.18	3.31	2.31			
p-value:	0.03	23.76	0.09	2.07			
Corrected-t:	2.66	−0.88	2.48	1.73			
Corrected-p:	0.78	37.99	1.31	8.44			

Coefficient:	$\tilde{\delta}_{vw}$	$\tilde{\delta}_{prem}$	$\tilde{\delta}_{labor}$	$\tilde{\delta}_{SMB}$	$\tilde{\delta}_{HML}$	HJ-dist
Estimate:	−0.10	−48.21	−59.92			0.1443
t-value:	−0.25	−13.13	−9.25			
p-value:	80.10	0.00	0.00			96.49

Coefficient:	c_0	c_{vw}	c_{prem}	c_{labor}	c_{SMB}	c_{HML}	R-square
Estimate:	0.86	−0.47			0.33	0.24	55.20
t-value:	3.76	−0.99			1.56	0.92	
p-value:	0.02	32.20			11.91	35.97	
Corrected-t:	3.71	−0.98			1.54	0.90	
Corrected-p:	0.02	32.84			12.42	36.57	

Coefficient:	$\tilde{\delta}_{vw}$	$\tilde{\delta}_{prem}$	$\tilde{\delta}_{labor}$	$\tilde{\delta}_{SMB}$	$\tilde{\delta}_{HML}$	HJ-dist
Estimate:	−4.58			−0.45	−9.94	0.5348
t-value:	−3.34			−0.23	−3.80	
p-value:	0.08			81.79	0.01	26.48

on aggregate wealth, the pricing errors of the model are not significant at conventional levels. More importantly, firm size does not have any additional explanatory power.

Although the conditional model performs substantially better than the static model, we still advocate caution in interpreting these results as strong support for the conditional CAPM for the following reasons:

First, our modeling of the time variations in betas is rather simple. If one were to take seriously the criticism that the real world is inherently dynamic, then it may be necessary to model explicitly what is missing in a static model. In particular, in a dynamic world, investors may care about hedging against a variety of risks that do not arise in a static economy. One possibility is to extend Merton's inter-temporal CAPM for empirical analysis, along the lines suggested by Campbell (1993a and 1993b). However, the dynamic conditional CAPM has an undesirable feature. The econometrician has to take a stand on the nature of the information available to the investors. For example, while deriving the unconditional multi-factor model implied by the conditional CAPM, we assumed that the conditional market risk premium is a linear function of the yield spread between low- and high-grade bonds. An alternative is to follow Bansal, Hsieh, and Viswanathan (1993) and Bansal and Viswanathan (1993) and consider unconditional nonlinear factor models which may be relatively more robust to information-set misspecification.

Second, a number of events occur at deterministic monthly and yearly frequencies. It may be reasonable to expect that such events may influence the behavior of asset prices at these frequencies. Since such events are outside the scope of asset-pricing models like the CAPM, one strategy would be to study the performance of models by using annual data over a sufficiently long period of time, as in Amihud, Christensen, and Mendelson (1992), Jagannathan and Wang (1992), and Kothari, Shanken, and Sloan (1995). Such an approach has its own shortcomings, the most important of which is that the economy may not really be stationary. There is some need for developing statistical sampling theories for making inferences that are robust to the presence of such features, possibly along the lines of Bossaerts (1994).

Finally, we have to keep in mind that the CAPM, like any other model, is only an approximation of reality. Hence, it would be rather surprising if it turns out to be "100 percent accurate." The interesting question is not whether a particular asset-pricing model can be rejected by the data. The question is: "How inaccurate is the model?" Fama and French (1992) show that the static version of the CAPM is very inaccurate. We find that the conditional version of the CAPM explains the cross-section of stock returns rather well. In doing so, we implicitly assume that the portfolio of stocks used in our study is economically important. As we point out in Appendix B, it is possible to mask or highlight the model specification error through appropriate choice of the portfolios. We will not be surprised if subsequent studies form a set of portfolios for which the model we examine in this study performs rather differently. In order to reconcile these differing views, we need to devise methods for evaluating the economic importance of the data sets used in empirical studies of asset-pricing models. We intend to focus on this issue in our future research.

The conditional CAPM we study in this article is very different from what is commonly understood as the CAPM, and resembles the multi-factor model of Ross (1976). The model we evaluate has three betas, whereas the standard CAPM has only one beta. We chose this model because (i) the use of a better proxy for the return on the market portfolio results in a two-beta model in place of the classical one-beta model, and (ii) when the CAPM holds in a conditional sense, unconditional expected returns will be linear in the unconditional beta as well as a measure of beta-instability over time. When the CAPM holds conditionally, we need more than the unconditional beta calculated by using the value-weighted stock index to explain the cross-section of unconditional expected returns.

Appendix A: Modeling the Unconditional Expected Returns

We first show that when betas vary over time, $(\beta_i, \beta_i^\gamma)$ is a linear function of $(\bar{\beta}_i, \vartheta_i)$. We then show that if ϑ_i is a linear function of $\bar{\beta}_i$, the static CAPM will obtain even in the unconditional sense—i.e., unconditional expected returns will be linear in the market beta β_i. In this case, β_i^γ is also a linear function of β_i. Finally, we show that when β_i^γ is not a linear function of β_i, which should be the usual case, $(\beta_i, \beta_i^\gamma)$ will contain all the necessary information contained in $(\bar{\beta}_i, \vartheta_i)$. Hence, expected returns will be linear in $(\bar{\beta}_i, \vartheta_i)$ as well as $(\beta_i, \beta_i^\gamma)$.

To show that $(\beta_i, \beta_i^\gamma)$ is a linear function of $(\bar{\beta}_i, \vartheta_i)$, note that the market return R_{mt} also satisfies the conditional CAPM. This gives the following equations:

$$E[R_{mt}|I_{t-1}] = \gamma_{0t-1} + \gamma_{1t-1} \tag{A1}$$

$$\gamma_{1t-1} = E[R_{mt} - \gamma_{0t-1}|I_{t-1}]. \tag{A2}$$

We then define ε_{it} as

$$\varepsilon_{it} = R_{it} - \gamma_{0t-1} - (R_{mt} - \gamma_{0t-1})\beta_{it-1}. \tag{A3}$$

It follows from equations (2), (3), and (A3) that

$$E[\varepsilon_{it}|I_{t-1}] = 0 \tag{A4}$$

$$E[\varepsilon_{it}R_{mt}|I_{t-1}] = 0. \tag{A5}$$

These two equations together imply the following orthogonality conditions:

$$E[\varepsilon_{it}] = 0 \tag{A6}$$

$$E[\varepsilon_{it}R_{mt}] = 0 \tag{A7}$$

$$E[\varepsilon_{it}\gamma_{1t-1}] = 0. \tag{A8}$$

We can substitute equation (7) into (A3) to obtain

$$R_{it} = \gamma_{0t-1} + (R_{mt} - \gamma_{0t-1})\bar{\beta}_i + (R_{mt} - \gamma_{0t-1})(\gamma_{1t-1} - \gamma_1)\vartheta_i \qquad \text{(A9)}$$
$$+ (R_{mt} - \gamma_{0t-1})\eta_{it-1} + \varepsilon_{it}.$$

From the definition of covariance, the expression given above for R_{it} in (A9), and the orthogonality conditions in (A6), (A7), and (A8), we obtain

$$\text{Cov}(R_{it}, R_{mt}) = \text{Var}(R_{mt})\beta_i$$
$$= \text{Cov}(\gamma_{0t-1}, R_{mt}) + \text{Cov}(R_{mt} - \gamma_{0t-1}, R_{mt})\bar{\beta}_i \qquad \text{(A10)}$$
$$+ \text{Cov}((R_{mt} - \gamma_{0t-1})(\gamma_{1t-1} - \gamma_1), R_{mt})\vartheta_i$$
$$+ \text{Cov}((R_{mt} - \gamma_{0t-1})\eta_{it-1}, R_{mt}),$$

$$\text{Cov}(R_{it}, \gamma_{1t-1}) = \text{Var}(\gamma_{1t-1})\beta_i^{\gamma}$$
$$= \text{Cov}(\gamma_{0t-1}, \gamma_{1t-1}) + \text{Cov}(R_{mt} - \gamma_{0t-1}, \gamma_{1t-1})\bar{\beta}_i \qquad \text{(A11)}$$
$$+ \text{Cov}((R_{mt} - \gamma_{0t-1})(\gamma_{1t-1} - \gamma_1), \gamma_{1t-1})\vartheta_i$$
$$+ \text{Cov}((R_{mt} - \gamma_{0t-1})\eta_{it-1}, \gamma_{1t-1}).$$

Let us denote the conditional variance of the market return by $v_{t-1} = E[R_{mt}|I_{t-1}]$. Using equations (8), (9), (A1), and (A2), one can show that the last term in equation (A10) is

$$\text{Cov}((R_{mt} - \gamma_{0t-1})\eta_{it-1}, R_{mt}) = E[(v_{t-1} + \gamma_{1t-1}^2 + \gamma_{1t-1}\gamma_{0t-1})\eta_{it-1}], \qquad \text{(A12)}$$

and the last term in equation (A11) is

$$\text{Cov}((R_{mt} - \gamma_{0t-1})\eta_{it-1}, \gamma_{1t-1}) = E[\gamma_{1t-1}^2\eta_{it-1}]. \qquad \text{(A13)}$$

Then, equations (A10) and (A11) imply that there will be a linear relation between $(\beta_i, \beta_i^{\gamma})$ and $(\bar{\beta}_i, \vartheta_i)$, if the expressions in (A12) and (A13) are zero. Hence, we make the following additional assumption throughout the paper unless mentioned otherwise:

ASSUMPTION 3. *For each asset i, the residual beta* η_{it-1} *satisfies*

$$E[\eta_{it-1}v_{t-1}] = 0 \qquad \text{(A14)}$$

$$E[\eta_{it-1}\gamma_{1t-1}^2] = 0 \qquad \text{(A15)}$$

$$E[\eta_{it-1}\gamma_{1t-1}\gamma_{0t-1}] = 0. \qquad \text{(A16)}$$

According to the first equation in Assumption 3, the residual betas are uncorrelated with the conditional volatility of the market return. If the market return is conditionally homoskedastic, which is an assumption sometimes

The Conditional CAPM and the Cross-Section of Expected Returns   39

made by researchers, then the first equation in Assumption 3 is a consequence of equation (8). Since the residual betas do not affect the unconditional expected return, as was shown in Section I.C, we can ignore η_{it-1} by assuming that they are random noises that are uncorrelated with the market conditions, then all the equations in Assumption 3 will hold. Under Assumption 3, the following linear function for the betas follows from equations (A10) and (A11):

LEMMA 1. *There are constants* $\{b_{kl} : k = 1, 2; l = 0, 1, 2\}$ *such that*

$$\begin{pmatrix} \beta_i \\ \beta_i^\gamma \end{pmatrix} = \begin{pmatrix} b_{10} \\ b_{20} \end{pmatrix} + \begin{pmatrix} b_{11} & b_{12} \\ b_{21} & b_{22} \end{pmatrix} \begin{pmatrix} \bar{\beta}_i \\ \vartheta_i \end{pmatrix}. \tag{A17}$$

If the beta-prem sensitivity is a linear function of the expected beta, then the unconditional expected return will be linear in the market beta, i.e., the CAPM will hold unconditionally as well. This observation leads to the next lemma:

LEMMA 2. *If* ϑ_i *is a linear function of* $\bar{\beta}_i$, *then there are some constants* a_0 *and* a_1 *such that the equation*

$$E[R_{it}] = a_0 + a_1\beta_i \tag{A18}$$

holds for every asset i, i.e., the static CAPM will hold for unconditional expected returns.

Proof. Let $\vartheta_i = d_0 + d_1\bar{\beta}_i$ and substitute it into equation (10) to get

$$E[R_{it}] = [\gamma_0 + d_0\text{Var}(\gamma_{1t-1})] + [\gamma_1 + d_1\text{Var}(\gamma_{1t-1})]\bar{\beta}_i. \tag{A19}$$

Substitute $\vartheta_i = d_0 + d_1\bar{\beta}_i$ into the first equation in (A17) to obtain

$$\beta_i = (b_{10} + d_0 b_{12}) + (b_{11} + d_1 b_{12})\bar{\beta}_i, \tag{A20}$$

which implies that β_i is a linear function of $\bar{\beta}_i$. Since β_i is not a constant across assets, $b_{11} + d_1 b_{12}$ must be nonzero. So, we can substitute (A20) into equation (A19) to obtain equation (A18), which completes the proof.

One important special case arises when the conditional betas are uncorrelated with the market risk premium. In this case, we have $\vartheta_i = 0$, and thus, the single beta model (A18) in Theorem 2 holds. Chan and Chen (1988) derived equation (A18) by assuming

$$\beta_{it-1} = \bar{\beta}_i + \lambda_{t-1}(\bar{\beta}_i - \bar{\beta}^*) + \eta^*_{it-1}, \tag{A21}$$

where $\bar{\beta}^*$ is the cross-sectional average of $\bar{\beta}_i$, λ_{t-1} has zero mean, and η^*_{it-1} is the random noise. With this specification for the conditional betas, we have

$$\vartheta_i = \frac{\text{Cov}(\lambda_{t-1}, \gamma_{1t-1})}{\text{Var}(\gamma_{1t-1})}(\bar{\beta}_i - \bar{\beta}^*). \tag{A22}$$

Therefore, the assumption made by Chan and Chen (1988) implies that the beta-prem sensitivity ϑ_i is a linear function of $\bar{\beta}_i$, and hence, equation (A18) holds under their assumption.

The restriction that the beta-prem sensitivity is a linear function of the expected beta implies the following restriction on the premium betas:

LEMMA 3. *If ϑ_i is a linear function of $\bar{\beta}_i$, then β_i^{γ} is a linear function of β_i.*

Proof. We substitute $\vartheta_i = d_0 + d_1\bar{\beta}_i$ into equation (A17) to obtain

$$\beta_i = [b_{10} + d_0 b_{12}] + [b_{11} + d_1 b_{12}]\bar{\beta}_i \tag{A23}$$

$$\beta_i^{\gamma} = [b_{20} + d_0 b_{22}] + [b_{21} + d_1 b_{22}]\bar{\beta}_i. \tag{A24}$$

Since β_i is not constant across assets, we must have $b_{11} + d_1 b_{12} \neq 0$. We can then substitute equation (A23) into equation (A24) to express β_i^{γ} as a linear function of β_i, which completes the proof.

If the premium beta is not a linear function of the market beta, then, by Lemma 3, beta-prem sensitivity cannot be a linear function of the expected beta. In this case, the single-beta model in Lemma 2 will not hold, i.e., the CAPM will not hold unconditionally, even though it holds in a conditional sense. Instead, the unconditional expected return will be a linear function of *two* variables—the market beta and the premium beta. This fact is stated as Theorem 1 in Section I.C.

Now, let us prove Theorem 1. We first prove that the 2 by 2 matrix in equation (A17) is invertible. Suppose it is singular; then there is a nonzero vector (x, y) such that

$$(x, y)\begin{pmatrix} b_{11} & b_{12} \\ b_{21} & b_{22} \end{pmatrix} = 0, \tag{A25}$$

which implies that $x\beta_i + y\beta_i^{\gamma}$ is a constant across assets. Since β_i is not a constant across assets, we must have $y \neq 0$. But this means that β_i^{γ} is a linear function of β_i, which contradicts the assumption in Theorem 1. Now we can invert equation (A17) such that $(\bar{\beta}_i, \vartheta_i)$ are linear functions of $(\beta_i, \beta_i^{\gamma})$ and then substitute them into equation (10) to obtain equation (13).

Appendix B: The Cross-Sectional Regressions

For the purpose of developing the sampling theory, it is more convenient to write all the unconditional models that we have discussed into the following form:

$$E[R_{it}] = \sum_{k=1}^{K_1} c_{1k} z_{ik} + \sum_{k=1}^{K_2} c_{2k}\beta_{ik}, \tag{B1}$$

The Conditional CAPM and the Cross-Section of Expected Returns 41

where $\{z_{ik}\}_{k=1,\ldots,K_1}$ are K_1 observable characteristics of asset i, $\beta_{ik} = \mathrm{Cov}(R_{it}, y_{kt})/\mathrm{Var}(y_{kt})$, with $\{y_{kt}\}_{k=1,\ldots,K_2}$ being K_2 economic variables, and $\{c_{jk}\}$ are some coefficients. As an example, for equation (24), we can let $K_1 = 2$, $z_{i1} \equiv 1$, $z_{i2} = \log(\mathrm{ME}_i)$, $K_2 = 3$, $y_{1t} = R_t^{\mathrm{vw}}$, $y_{2t} = R_{t-1}^{\mathrm{prem}}$, $y_{3t} = R_t^{\mathrm{labor}}$, $\beta_{i1} = \beta_i^{\mathrm{vw}}$, $\beta_{i2} = \beta_i^{\mathrm{prem}}$, and $\beta_{i3} = \beta_i^{\mathrm{labor}}$.

Equation (B1) can be written in a more concise form as

$$E[R_i] = Zc_1 + Bc_2 = Xc, \qquad (B2)$$

where $R_t = (R_{1t}, \ldots, R_{Nt})'$, $c_1 = (c_{11}, \ldots, c_{1K1})'$, $c_2 = (c_{21}, \ldots, c_{2K2})'$, $c = (c_1' : c_2')'$, and $X = (Z : B)$, where

$$Z = \begin{pmatrix} z_{11} & \cdots & z_{1K_1} \\ \vdots & \ddots & \vdots \\ z_{N1} & \cdots & z_{NK_1} \end{pmatrix} \qquad B = \begin{pmatrix} \beta_{11} & \cdots & \beta_{1K_2} \\ \vdots & \ddots & \vdots \\ \beta_{N1} & \cdots & \beta_{NK_2} \end{pmatrix}.$$

In the cross-sectional regression method, we first estimate β_{ik} by the slope coefficient in the univariate regression of R_{it} on y_{kt} and a constant over time. Let $\hat{\beta}_{ik}$ be the estimated slope coefficient in this regression. Replacing all the betas in B by their estimates, we obtain an estimate of B which we denote by $\hat{B}$. Let $\hat{X} = (Z : \hat{B})$ and $\bar{R}$ be the time-series average of R_t, i.e., $\bar{R} = (1/T) \sum_{t=1}^{T} R_t$. The estimator of the parameters, denoted by $\hat{c}$, in the cross-sectional regression method is obtained by regressing $\bar{R}$ on $\hat{X}$, that is, $\hat{c} = (\hat{X}'\hat{X})^{-1} \hat{X}'\bar{R}$. Here, we assume that both X and $\hat{X}$ have the rank $K_1 + K_2$. If $\mathrm{plim}_{T\to\infty} \hat{B} = B$ and $\mathrm{plim}_{T\to\infty} \bar{R} = E[R_t]$, then $\mathrm{plim}_{T\to\infty} \hat{c} = c$, i.e., $\hat{c}$ is a consistent estimator of c.

Although the cross-sectional regression method does not provide a test for the linearity imposed by the model, it is still a very natural and intuitive tool for checking the ability of an unconditional model to explain the cross-sectional variation of average returns. The R^2 of the cross-sectional regression associated with a particular empirical specification provides a natural measure of how well that particular model does in explaining the cross-section of average returns. However, it is necessary to use caution in interpreting a low R^2 as indicating that a particular specification is bad in any absolute sense.

To see why, consider a hypothetical economy where the econometrician has observations on four assets. The betas with respect to a proxy market portfolio for the four assets are 0.5, 0.5, 2, and 2. The corresponding expected rates of returns are 12, 8, 24, and 20 percent. There are no measurement errors involved here. It can be verified that, in this case, the estimated regression equation will be

$$R_i = 6 + 8\beta_i + \hat{\varepsilon}_i \qquad i = 1, 2, 3, 4$$

and that the R^2 of the regression is 95 percent. Now consider forming four other portfolios (by an invertible linear transformation) from the four given assets as follows. Let $z = R_3 - R_4$ denote the payoff on the zero investment portfolio constructed by going long one dollar on the third asset and going short one dollar on the fourth asset. The beta of the payoff, z, is 0 by construction. Define the return on the four new portfolios by $R_1^* = R_1 + 3z$; $R_2^* = R_2 + 3z$; $R_3^* = R_3$; and $R_4^* = R_4$. Notice that the original four assets can be constructed as portfolios of these four new portfolios. The betas of the four portfolios defined this way are 0.5, 0.5, 2, and 2, respectively. The expected returns on these portfolios are 24, 20, 24, and 20 percent, respectively. Clearly, when these four portfolios are used, the relation between expected return and beta is flat (i.e., the R^2 is 0 percent). This shortcoming is not an issue for the way we use R^2 to compare the performance of different competing specifications of the CAPM, since we use the same set of portfolios across all model specifications.[22]

To assess the sampling errors associated with the estimated parameters, Fama and MacBeth (1973) suggest regressing R_t, instead of $\bar{R}$, on $\hat{X}$ for each period t to obtain

$$\hat{c}_t = (\hat{X}'\hat{X})^{-1}\hat{X}'R_t \tag{B3}$$

and then estimate the covariance matrix of $\sqrt{T}(\hat{c} - c)$ by

$$\hat{V} = \frac{1}{T} \sum_{t=1}^{T} (\hat{c}_t - \bar{c})(\hat{c}_t - \bar{c})', \tag{B4}$$

where $\bar{c} = (1/T) \sum_{t=1}^{T} \hat{c}_t$. It is easy to see that $\bar{c} = \hat{c}$. Substituting $\hat{c}_t = (\hat{X}'\hat{X})^{-1}\hat{X}'R_t$ into equation (B4), we have

$$\hat{V} = (\hat{X}'\hat{X})^{-1}\hat{X}' \left[\frac{1}{T} \sum_{t=1}^{T} (R_t - \bar{R})(R_t - \bar{R})' \right] \hat{X}(\hat{X}'\hat{X})^{-1}. \tag{B5}$$

In order to understand the properties of the estimated covariance matrix $\hat{V}$ provided by the Fama-MacBeth procedure, it is convenient to define $\mu = E[R_t]$ and use equation (B2) to write the average return as

$$\bar{R} = \hat{X}c + (\bar{R} - \mu) - (\hat{X} - X)c. \tag{B6}$$

Substituting it into the definition for $\hat{c}$, we can obtain

$$\hat{c} - c = (\hat{X}'\hat{X})^{-1}\hat{X}'(\bar{R} - \mu) - (\hat{X}'\hat{X})^{-1}\hat{X}'(\hat{B} - B)c_2. \tag{B7}$$

---

[22] Kandel and Stambaugh (1995) suggest using an alternative measure of goodness of fit that is invariant to portfolio formation for examining the performance of a given model. However, for comparing the relative performance of different models using the same set of assets, the OLS R^2 measure is quite appropriate.

The Conditional CAPM and the Cross-Section of Expected Returns   43

Suppose that $\sqrt{T}(\bar{R} - \mu)$ converges to a random variable $\tilde{u}$ in distribution and $\sqrt{T}(\hat{B} - B)$ converges to a random variable $\tilde{H}$ in distribution. If $\text{plim}_{T \to \infty} \hat{B} = B$, then

$$\sqrt{T}(\hat{c} - c) \xrightarrow{d} (X'X)^{-1}X'(\tilde{u} - \tilde{H}c_2). \tag{B8}$$

Here, $(X'X)^{-1}X'\tilde{u}$ is the sampling error of $\hat{c}$ from replacing expected returns by average returns, and $(X'X)^{-1}X'\tilde{H}c_2$ is the sampling error from replacing true beta by their estimates. The conventional consistent estimate for the variance of $\tilde{u}$ is

$$\frac{1}{T} \sum_{t=1}^{T} (R_t - \bar{R})(R_t - \bar{R})'.$$

Hence, a consistent estimate for the variance of $(X'X)^{-1}X'\tilde{u}$ is given by

$$(\hat{X}'\hat{X})^{-1}\hat{X}'\left[\frac{1}{T} \sum_{T=1}^{T} (R_t - \bar{R})(R_t - \bar{R})'\right]\hat{X}(\hat{X}'\hat{X})^{-1},$$

which is exactly $\hat{V}$ in view of equation (B5). If we can ignore the sampling error $\tilde{H}$ that is due to the errors associated with the estimated betas, then the consistent estimate for the variance of $\hat{c}$ is given by $\hat{V}$ obtained from the standard Fama-MacBeth procedure. If $\tilde{H}$ is not negligible, the standard error of $\hat{c}$ provided by the Fama-MacBeth procedure will generally be biased.

In general, it is difficult to assess the magnitude of the bias of the Fama-MacBeth procedure. However, under some additional assumptions, Shanken (1992) derives an expression for the bias when the betas are estimated using multiple regression. Since we use betas estimated from univariate OLS regressions, Shanken's formula is not directly applicable in our case.

In what follows, using methods similar to those used by Shanken (1992), we derive an expression for the sampling errors associated with parameters estimated using the cross-sectional regression method. We need to introduce two additional assumptions. For $i = 1, \ldots, N$, $k = 1, \ldots, K_2$, and $t = 1, \ldots, T$, define

$$\alpha_{ik} = E[R_{it}] - \beta_{ik}E[y_{kt}] \tag{B9}$$

$$e_{ikt} = R_{it} - \alpha_{ik} - \beta_{ik}y_{kt}. \tag{B10}$$

We then have

$$R_{it} = \alpha_{ik} + \beta_{ik}y_{kt} + e_{ikt} \tag{B11}$$

$$E[e_{ikt}] = 0 \tag{B12}$$

$$E[e_{ikt}y_{kt}] = 0. \tag{B13}$$

The two additional assumptions are as follows:

ASSUMPTION 4. *We assume that, for $i, j = 1, \ldots, N$ and $k, l = 1, \ldots, K_2$,*
$E[e_{ikt}|\{y_{ns}\}_{n=1,\ldots,K_2; s=1,\ldots,T}] = 0$ *and* $E[e_{ikt}e_{jlt}|\{y_{ns}\}_{n=1,\ldots,K_2; s=1,\ldots,T}]$
$= \sigma_{ijkl}$. *We then define*

$$\Sigma_{kl} \begin{pmatrix} \sigma_{11kl} & \cdots & \sigma_{1Nkl} \\ \vdots & \ddots & \vdots \\ \sigma_{N1kl} & \cdots & \sigma_{NNkl} \end{pmatrix}. \tag{B14}$$

ASSUMPTION 5. *Let* $\bar{y}_k = (1/T) \sum_{t=1}^{T} y_{kt}$. *We assume that the probability limit*

$$\operatorname*{plim}_{T \to \infty} \frac{1}{T} \sum_{t=1}^{T} (y_{kt} - \bar{y}_k)(y_{lt} - \bar{y}_l) = \omega_{kl}$$

exists for $k, l = 1, \ldots, K_2$, *and* $\omega_{kk} > 0$ *for* $k = 1, \ldots, K_2$.

Under Assumptions 4 and 5, the limiting distribution of the estimated parameter vector is given by the following:

THEOREM 2. *Suppose that when* $T \to \infty$, $\sqrt{T}(\hat{R}' - \mu', c_2'(\hat{B} - B)')'$ *converges to a joint normal distribution* $(\tilde{u}', c_2'\tilde{H}')'$, *with zero mean. Suppose that*

$$\operatorname*{plim}_{T \to \infty} \frac{1}{T} \sum_{t=1}^{T} (R_t - \bar{R})(R_t - \bar{R})' = \text{Var}(\tilde{u}) \tag{B15}$$

$$\operatorname*{plim}_{T \to \infty} \hat{B} = B. \tag{B16}$$

Then, under Assumptions 4 and 5, $\sqrt{T}(\hat{c} - c)$ *converges to a normal distribution with zero mean and variance* V + W, *where*

$$V = \operatorname*{plim}_{T \to \infty} \hat{V} \tag{B17}$$

$$W = \sum_{k,l=1}^{K_2} c_{2k} c_{2l} (\omega_{kk}^{-1} \omega_{kl} \omega_{ll}^{-1})(X'X)^{-1}X'\Sigma_{kl}X(X'X)^{-1}. \tag{B18}$$

Hence, under Assumptions 4 and 5, the bias of the Fama-MacBeth procedure is W. To obtain a consistent estimate of the sampling errors, we first use the Fama-MacBeth procedure to obtain $\hat{V}$, and then apply Theorem 2 to obtain a consistent estimate of W as

$$\hat{W} = \sum_{k,l=1}^{K_2} \hat{c}_{2k} \hat{c}_{2l} (\hat{\omega}_{kk}^{-1} \hat{\omega}_{kl} \hat{\omega}_{ll}^{-1})(\hat{X}'\hat{X})^{-1}\hat{X}'\hat{\Sigma}_{kl}\hat{X}(\hat{X}'\hat{X})^{-1}, \tag{B19}$$

where $\hat{\omega}_{kl}$ and $\hat{\Sigma}_{kl}$ are the sample analogs of ω_{kl} and Σ_{kl}.

The Conditional CAPM and the Cross-Section of Expected Returns   45

Theorem 2 can be proved as follows. First, we introduce some additional notations. By I_N (I_T) we denote the $N(T)$-dimensional identity matrix. By 1_T we denote a T-dimensional vector, with each of its elements equal to 1. Let $\bar{y}_k$ be the time-series sample average of y_{kt} and define

$$y_k \equiv (y_{k1} - \bar{y}_k, \ldots, y_{kT} - \bar{y}_k)'$$

$$b_k \equiv (\beta_{1k}, \ldots, \beta_{Nk})'$$

$$\hat{b}_k \equiv (\hat{\beta}_{1k}, \ldots, \hat{\beta}_{Nk})'$$

$$e_k \equiv (e_{1k1}, \ldots, e_{1kT}, \ldots, e_{Nk1}, \ldots, e_{NkT})'$$

$$Y \equiv (\{y_{kt}\}_{k=1, \ldots, K_2, t=1, \ldots, T}).$$

It follows from (B11) that

$$\bar{R} - \mu = \frac{1}{T} (1_N \otimes 1'_T) e_l, \qquad l = 1, \ldots, K_2, \tag{B20}$$

where $\otimes$ denotes the Kroneker product. By the definition of $\bar{\beta}_{ik}$, we have

$$\hat{b}_k - b_k = [I_N \otimes ((y'_k y_k)^{-1} y'_k)] e_k. \tag{B21}$$

In view of Assumption 4, equations (B20) and (B21) together imply

$$E[(\hat{b}_k - b_k)(\bar{R} - \mu)' | Y] \tag{B22}$$

$$= \frac{1}{T} [I_N \otimes ((y'_k y_k)^{-1} y'_k)] E[e_k e'_l | Y](I_N \otimes 1_T) \tag{B23}$$

$$= \frac{1}{T} [I_N \otimes ((y'_k y_k)^{-1} y'_k)](\Sigma_{kl} \otimes I_T)(I_N \otimes 1_T) \tag{B24}$$

$$= \frac{1}{T} \Sigma_{kl} \otimes [(y'_k y_k)^{-1} y'_k 1_T] \tag{B25}$$

$$= 0. \tag{B26}$$

This follows from the fact that $y'_k 1_T = 0$. Hence, $\hat{b}_k - b_k$ is uncorrelated with $\bar{R} - \mu$. Assumption 4 and equation (B20) also imply that Y is uncorrelated with $\bar{R} - \mu$. Therefore, $\tilde{u}$ and $\check{H}c_2$ should be uncorrelated with each other, and the asymptotic variance of $\sqrt{T}(\hat{c} - c)$ is given by

$$(X'X)^{-1}X'[\text{Var}(\tilde{u}) + \text{Var}(\check{H}c_2)]X(X'X)^{-1}. \tag{B27}$$

By Assumptions 4 and 5, we have

$$TE[(\hat{b}_k - b_k)(\hat{b}_l - b_l)'|y]$$

$$= T[I_N \otimes ((y_k'y_k)^{-1}y_k')](\Sigma_{kl} \otimes I_T)[I_N \otimes ((y_l'y_l)^{-1}y_l')]$$

$$= \Sigma_{kl} \otimes \left(\left(\frac{1}{T}y_k'y_k \right)^{-1} \left(\frac{1}{T}y_k'y_l \right) \left(\frac{1}{T}y_l'y_l \right)^{-1} \right)$$

$$\rightarrow \omega_{kk}^{-1}\omega_{kl}\omega_{ll}^{-1}\Sigma_{kl} \qquad (\text{as } T \rightarrow +\infty).$$

Thus,

$$\text{Var}(\tilde{H}c_2) = \sum_{k,l=1}^{K_2} c_{2k}c_{2l}\omega_{kk}^{-1}\omega_{kl}w_{ll}^{-1}\Sigma_{kl},$$

and

$$W = (X'X)^{-1}X'\text{Var}(\tilde{H}c_2)X(X'X)^{-1}$$

$$= \sum_{k,l=1}^{K_2} c_{2k}c_{2l}\omega_{kk}^{-1}\omega_{kl}\omega_{ll}^{-1}(X'X)^{-1}X'\Sigma_{kl}X(X'X)^{-1}.$$

From equations (B5) and (B15) and expression (B27), it follows that

$$V = (X'X)^{-1}X'\text{Var}(\tilde{u})X(X'X)^{-1} = \text{plim }\hat{V}.$$

This completes the proof.

Appendix C: The Hansen–Jagannathan Distance

If there is only one asset, then it is relatively straightforward to compare the performance of the different versions of the unconditional model implied by the conditional CAPM. All we have to do is to compare the pricing error— i.e., the difference between the market price of an asset and the hypothetical price assigned to it by the stochastic discount factor implied by a particular empirical specification. When there are many assets (100 in our study), it is rather difficult to compare the pricing errors across the different candidate stochastic discount factors for the model.

In view of this, we follow Hansen and Jagannathan (1994), who suggest examining the pricing error on the portfolio that is most mispriced by a given model. There is a practical problem in implementing this simple idea. Suppose there are at least two assets which do not have the same pricing error for a given candidate stochastic discount factor. Let R_{1t} and R_{2t} denote the corresponding gross returns. The date $t - 1$ prices of these payoffs are both 1, i.e., by investing one dollar at date $t - 1$ in asset i, the investor gets the payoff R_{it} at date t. A given asset-pricing model may not assign a price of 1 at date $t - 1$ to the payoff R_{it}. Suppose the pricing error is ψ_i, i.e., the model assigns a price of $1 + \psi_i$. Consider forming a zero-investment portfolio by going long one dollar

The Conditional CAPM and the Cross-Section of Expected Returns   47

in security 1 and short one dollar in security 2. The pricing error on this zero-investment portfolio is $\psi_1 - \psi_2$. So long as this is not zero, the pricing error on any portfolio of the two assets with a price of one dollar can be made arbitrarily large by adding a scale multiple of this zero-investment portfolio. The same problem arises if instead of examining the pricing error we examine the difference between the expected return on a portfolio and the expected return assigned by a particular asset-pricing model to that portfolio. To overcome this problem, it is necessary to examine the pricing error on portfolios that have the same "size." Hansen and Jagannathan (1994) suggest using the second moment of the payoff as a measure of "size," i.e., examine the portfolio which has the maximum pricing error among all portfolio payoffs that have the unit second moment.

Consider a portfolio of the N primitive assets defined by the vector of portfolio weights x. The date t payoff on this portfolio is given by $x'R_t$. It has a price of $x'1_N$ at the beginning of each date. The pricing error on this portfolio is $x'E[w_t(\delta)]$. The second moment of this portfolio payoff is $E[x'R_t]^2$, i.e., the norm of this portfolio is $\sqrt{E[x'R_t]^2}$. For a given vector of parameters δ, Hansen and Jagannathan (1994) show that the maximum pricing error per unit norm on any portfolio of these N assets is given by

$$\text{Dist}(\delta) \equiv \sqrt{E[w_t(\delta)]'G^{-1}E[w_t(\delta)]}, \qquad (C1)$$

where $G = E[R_t R_t']$ and is assumed to be nonsingular. We refer to Dist as the *HJ-distance*. It is also the least-square distance between the given candidate stochastic discount factor and the nearest point to it in the set of all discount factors that price assets correctly. (See Hansen and Jagannathan (1994) for details.)

Since the vector, δ, of parameters describing a particular asset-pricing model is unknown, a natural way to estimate them is to choose those values for δ that minimize Dist given in (C1). We can then assess the specification error of a given stochastic discount factor by examining the maximum pricing error Dist associated with it, as suggested by Hansen and Jagannathan (1994).

Let

$$D_T = \frac{1}{T} \sum_{t=1}^{T} R_t Y_t' \qquad (C2)$$

$$w_T(\delta) = \frac{1}{T} \sum_{t=1}^{T} w_t(\delta) = D_T \delta - 1_N \qquad (C3)$$

$$G_T = \frac{1}{T} \sum_{t=1}^{T} R_t R_t'. \qquad (C4)$$

The sample analog of the HJ-distance defined in (C1) is thus

$$\text{Dist}_T(\delta) = \sqrt{\min_\delta \; w_T'(\delta) G_T^{-1} w_T(\delta)}.$$ (C5)

We will therefore estimate δ_T by minimizing the sample analog of (C1), i.e., choose δ_T as the solution to

$$\min_\delta \; w_T(\delta)' G_T^{-1} w_T(\delta).$$ (C6)

The first order condition of the minimization problem is

$$D_T' G_T^{-1} w_T(\delta_T) = 0,$$ (C7)

which gives

$$\delta_T = (D_T' G_T^{-1} D_T)^{-1} D_T' G_T^{-1} 1_N.$$ (C8)

The estimator δ_T is equivalent to a GMM estimator defined by Hansen (1982) with the moment restriction $E[w(\delta)] = 0$ and the weighting matrix G^{-1}. It is also an extremum estimator described in Amemiya (1985). Therefore, under some regularity conditions, δ_T is consistent and has an asymptotic normal distribution. For details, we refer readers to Hansen (1982) or Chapter 4 of Amemiya (1985). We refer to G^{-1} as the HJ weighting matrix.

If the weighting matrix is optimal in the sense of Hansen (1982), then $T[\text{Dist}_T(\delta_T)]^2$ is asymptotically a random variable of χ^2 distribution with $N - K$ degrees of freedom, where K is the dimension of the vector δ of unknown parameters. However, G^{-1} is generally not optimal, and thus the distribution of $T[\text{Dist}_T(\delta_T)]^2$ is not $\chi^2(N - K)$. The following theorem shows that the asymptotic distribution of $T[\text{Dist}_T(\delta_T)]^2$ is a weighted sum of χ^2 distributed random variables, each of which has 1 degree of freedom.

THEOREM 3. *Suppose that for some δ_0 we have $\sqrt{T} w_T(\delta_0) \xrightarrow{d} N(0_N, S)$, where S is a positive definite matrix. Assume $D_T \xrightarrow{P} D$, where D is an $N \times K$ matrix of rank K, and assume $G_T \xrightarrow{P} G$, where G is nonsingular. Let*

$$A = S^{1/2} G^{-1/2} (I_N - (G^{-1/2})' D[D' G^{-1} D]^{-1} D' G^{-1/2})(G^{-1/2})'(S^{1/2})',$$ (C9)

where $S^{1/2}$ and $G^{1/2}$ are the upper-triangle matrices from the Cholesky decomposition of S and G, and I_N is the N-dimensional identity matrix. Then A has exactly $N - K$ nonzero eigenvalues, which are positive and denoted by $\lambda_1, \ldots, \lambda_{N-K}$, and the asymptotic sampling distribution of the HJ-distance is

$$T[\text{Dist}_T(\delta_T)]^2 \xrightarrow{d} \sum_{j=1}^{N-K} \lambda_j v_j \quad as \quad T \to \infty,$$ (C10)

where $v_1, \ldots, v_{N-K}$ are independent $\chi^2(1)$ random variables.

The Conditional CAPM and the Cross-Section of Expected Returns   49

Notice that, when all the eigenvalues are unity, $T[\text{Dist}_T(\delta_T)]^2$ has an asymptotic chi-square distribution with $N - K$ degrees of freedom. In this case, G^{-1} is optimal.

As long as we have a consistent estimate S_T of the matrix S, we can estimate the matrix A defined in Theorem 3 by

$$A_T = S_T^{1/2} G_T^{-1/2} (I_N - (G_T^{-1/2})' D_T [D_T' G_T^{-1} D_T]^{-1} D_T' G_T^{-1/2}) (G_T^{-1/2})' (S_T^{1/2})'. \quad (C11)$$

Then we can estimate the λ_js by the positive eigenvalues of A_T.

Let u be the asymptotic distribution of $T[\text{Dist}_T(\delta_T)]^2$, i.e.,

$$u \equiv \sum_{j=1}^{N-K} \lambda_j v_j,$$

and let $\psi(u)$ be the probability distribution function of u. Although $\psi(u)$ is not a known distribution function, we can still conveniently compute the p-value to test the null hypothesis that the discount factors are specified correctly. Let

$$\{v_{ij}\}_{i=1,\ldots,T^*;\, j=1,\ldots,N-K}$$

denote $T^*(N - K)$ independent random draws from a $\chi^2(1)$ distribution. These random draws can be easily obtained on computer. Then, we can obtain a set of independent samples, $\{u_i\}_{i=1}^{T^*}$, by letting

$$u_i = \sum_{j=1}^{N-K} \lambda_j v_{ij}.$$

By the Law of Large Numbers, for each nonnegative number a, we have, as $T^* \to \infty$,

$$\frac{1}{T^*} \sum_{i=1}^{T^*} I(u_i \leq a) \xrightarrow{p} \int_0^a d\psi(u) = \text{Prob}\{u \leq a\},$$

where $I(u \leq a)$ is an index function defined as

$$I(u \leq a) = \begin{cases} 1 & \text{if } u \leq a \\ 0 & \text{if } u > a. \end{cases} \quad (C12)$$

Here is the proof of Theorem 3. It follows from equation (C3) that

$$w_T(\delta_T) = w_T(\delta_0) + D_T(\delta_T - \delta_0). \quad (C13)$$

Multiplying both sides of equation (C13) by $D_T' G_T^{-1}$ and applying the first order condition (C7), we obtain

$$\delta_T - \delta_0 = -(D_T' G_T^{-1} D_T)^{-1} D_T' G_T^{-1} w_T(\delta_0). \quad (C14)$$

Substituting (C14) into (C13) gives

$$w_T(\delta_T) = (I_N - D_T(D'_T G_T^{-1} D_T)^{-1} D'_T G_T^{-1}) w_T(\delta_0). \qquad (C15)$$

After substituting (C15) into (C5) and some algebraic simplifications, we obtain

$$[\text{Dist}_T(\delta_T)]^2 = w_T(\delta_0)'(G_T^{-1} - G_T^{-1} D_T(D'_T G_T^{-1} D_T)^{-1} D'_T G_T^{-1}) w_T(\delta_0), \qquad (C16)$$

which gives

$$T[\text{Dist}_T(\delta_T)]^2 \xrightarrow{d} Z'(G^{-1} - G^{-1}D(D'G^{-1}D)^{-1}DG^{-1})Z, \qquad (C17)$$

where Z is the N-dimensional random vector of normal distribution with zero mean and covariance matrix S.

Let z be the N-dimensional random vector of normal distribution with zero mean and covariance matrix I_N. Then $Z = (S^{1/2})'z$. Substituting this into equation (C17), we have

$$T[\text{Dist}_T(\delta_T)]^2 \xrightarrow{d} z'Az, \qquad (C18)$$

where A is defined in (C9) and is obviously symmetric and positive semi-definite.

It is easy to check that

$$I_N - (G^{-1/2})'D(D'G^{-1}D)^{-1}D'G^{-1/2}$$

is symmetric and idempotent, and that its trace is $N - K$. Thus, we know that its rank is $N - K$, which implies that the rank of A is also $N - K$. It follows that A has exactly $N - K$ positive eigenvalues, denoted by $\lambda_1, \ldots, \lambda_{N-K}$. Then there is an orthogonal matrix H and a diagonal matrix Λ such that

$$\Lambda = \text{diag}\{\lambda_1, \ldots, \lambda_{N-K}, 0'_K\} \qquad (C19)$$

and $A = H'\Lambda H$. Let $x = Hz$, then $x \sim N(0_N, I_N)$. Then we have

$$T[\text{Dist}_T(\delta_T)]^2 \xrightarrow{d} x\Lambda x = \sum_{j=1}^{N-K} \lambda_j x_j^2. \qquad (C20)$$

Letting $v_j = x_j^2$ completes the proof.

REFERENCES

Amemiya, Takeshi, 1985, *Advanced Econometrics* (Harvard University Press, Cambridge, Mass.).
Amihud, Yakov, Bent Jesper Christensen, and Haim Mendelson, 1992, Further evidence in the risk-return relationship, Working paper No. S-93-11, New York University.
Bansal, Ravi, David A. Hsieh, and S. Viswanathan, 1993, A new approach to international arbitrage pricing, *Journal of Finance* 48, 1719–1747.

The Conditional CAPM and the Cross-Section of Expected Returns   51

Bansal, Ravi, and S. Viswanathan, 1993, No arbitrage and arbitrage pricing: A new approach, *Journal of Finance* 48, 1231–1262.

Banz, Rolf W., 1981, The relationship between return and market value of common stocks, *Journal of Financial Economics* 9, 3–18.

Basu, Sanjoy, 1983, The relationship between earnings yield, market value, and return for NYSE common stocks: Further evidence, *Journal of Financial Economics* 12, 51–74.

Berk, Jonathan B., 1995, A critique of size-related anomalies, *Review of Financial Studies* 8, 275–286.

Bernanke, Ben S., 1990, On the predictive power of interest rates and interest rate spreads, *New England Economic Review* (Federal Reserve Bank of Boston, Nov./Dec.), 51–68.

Bhandari, Laxmi Chand, 1988, Debt/equity ratio and expected common stock returns: Empirical evidence, *Journal of Finance* 43, 507–528.

Black, Fischer, 1972, Capital market equilibrium with restricted borrowing, *Journal of Business* 45, 444–455.

Black, Fischer, 1993, Beta and return, *Journal of Portfolio Management* 20, 8–18.

Black, Fischer, Michael C. Jensen, and Myron Scholes, 1972, The capital asset pricing model: Some empirical tests, in Michael Jensen, Ed.: *Studies in the Theory of Capital Markets* (Praeger, New York), pp. 79–121

Bodurtha, James N., Jr., and Nelson C. Mark, 1991, Testing the CAPM with time-varying risks and returns, *Journal of Finance* 46, 1485–1505.

Bollerslev, Tim, Robert F. Engle, and Jeffrey M. Wooldridge, 1988, A capital asset pricing model with time varying covariances, *Journal of Political Economy* 96, 116–131.

Bossaerts, Peter, 1994, Time series analysis of inefficient financial markets, Manuscript, California Institute of Technology.

Breen, William J., Larry R. Glosten, and Ravi Jagannathan, 1989, Economic significance of predictable variations in stock index returns, *Journal of Finance* 44, 1177–1190.

Breen, William J., and Robert A. Korajczyk, 1994, On selection biases in book-to-market based tests of asset pricing models, Working paper No. 167, Northwestern University.

Campbell, John Y., 1993a, Intertemporal asset pricing without consumption data, *American Economic Review* 83, 487–512.

Campbell, John Y., 1993b, Understanding risk and returns, Working paper No. 4554, NBER.

Carhart, Mark M., Robert J. Krail, Ross L. Stevens, and Kelly D. Welch, 1995, Testing the conditional CAPM, Manuscript, University of Chicago.

Chan, K. C., and Nai-fu Chen, 1988, An unconditional asset-pricing test and the role of firm size as an instrumental variable for risk, *Journal of Finance* 43, 309–325.

Chan, K. C., Nai-fu Chen, and David A. Hsieh, 1985, An exploratory investigation of the firm size effect, *Journal of Financial Economics* 14, 451–471.

Chan, Louis K. C., Narasimhan Jegadeesh, and Josef Lakonishok, 1995, Evaluating the performance of value versus glamour stocks: The impact of selection bias, *Journal of Financial Economics* 38, 269–296.

Chan, Louis K. C., and Josef Lakonishok, 1993, Are the reports of beta's death premature? *Journal of Portfolio Management* 19, 51–62.

Chari, V. V., Ravi Jagannathan, and Aharon R. Ofer, 1986, Seasonalities in security returns: The case of earnings announcements, *Journal Financial Economics* 21, 101–122.

Chen, Nai-Fu, 1991, Financial investment opportunities and the macroeconomy, *Journal of Finance* 46, 529–554.

Chen, Nai-Fu, Richard Roll, and Stephen A. Ross, 1986, Economic forces and the stock market, *Journal of Business* 59, 383–404.

Cochrane, John H., 1992, A cross-sectional test of a production based asset pricing model, Working paper No. 4025, NBER.

Connor, Gregory, and Robert A. Korajczyk, 1988a, Risk and return in an equilibrium APT: Application of a new test methodology, *Journal Financial Economics* 21, 255–289.

Connor, Gregory, and Robert A. Korajczyk, 1988b, The arbitrage pricing theory and multi-factor models of asset returns, Working paper, Kellogg Graduate School of Management, Northwestern University.

52   *The Journal of Finance*

Daniel, Kent, and Sheridan Titman, 1995, Evidence on the characteristics of cross sectional
    variation in stock returns, Manuscript, University of Chicago.
Davis, James L., 1994, The cross-section of realized stock returns: The pre-COMPUSTAT evi-
    dence, *Journal of Finance* 49, 1579–1593.
Diaz-Gimenez, Javier, Edward C. Prescott, Terry Fitzgerald, and Fernando Alvarez, 1992, Bank-
    ing in computable general equilibrium economics, *Journal of Economic Dynamics and Control*
    16, 533–559.
Dybvig, P. H., and J. E. Ingersoll, Jr., 1982, Mean-variance theory in capital markets, *Journal of
    Business* 55, 233–251.
Dybvig, P. H., and Stephen A. Ross, 1985, Differential information and performance measurement
    using a security market line, *Journal of Finance* 40, 383–400.
Fama, Eugene F., and Kenneth R. French, 1989, Business conditions and the expected returns on
    bonds and stocks, *Journal of Financial Economics* 25, 23–50.
Fama, Eugene F., and Kenneth R. French, 1992, The cross-section of expected stock returns,
    Journal of Finance 47, 427–466.
Fama, Eugene F., and Kenneth R. French, 1993, Common risk factors in the returns on bonds and
    stocks, *Journal of Financial Economics* 33, 3–56.
Fama, Eugene F., and James D. MacBeth, 1973, Risk, return and equilibrium: Empirical tests,
    Journal of Political Economy 81, 607–636.
Fama, Eugene F., and G. William Schwert, 1977, Human capital and capital market equilibrium,
    Journal of Financial Economics 4, 115–146.
Ferson, Wayne E., and Campbell R. Harvey, 1991, The variation of economic risk premiums,
    Journal of Political Economy 99, 385–415.
Ferson, Wayne E., and Campbell R. Harvey, 1993, The risk and predictability of international
    equity returns, *Review of Financial Studies* 6(3), 527–566.
Ferson, Wayne E., and S. R. Foerster, 1994, Finite sample properties of the generalized method of
    moments in tests of conditional asset pricing models, *Journal of Financial Economics* 36,
    29–35.
Ferson, Wayne E., and Robert A. Korajczyk, 1993, Do arbitrage pricing models explain the
    predictability of stock returns? Working paper, Kellogg Graduate School of Management,
    Northwestern University.
Gibbons, Michael R., 1982, Multivariate tests of financial models: A new approach, *Journal of
    Financial Economics* 10, 3–27.
Hansen, Lars Peter, 1982, Large sample properties of generalized method of moments estimators,
    Econometrica 50, 1029–1054.
Hansen, Lars Peter, and Ravi Jagannathan, 1991, Implications of security market data for models
    of dynamic economics, *Journal of Political Economy* 99, 225–262.
Hansen, Lars Peter, and Ravi Jagannathan, 1994, Assessing specification errors in stochastic
    discount factor models, Technical working paper No. 153, NBER.
Hansen, Lars Peter, and Scott F. Richard, 1987, The role of conditioning information in deducing
    testable restrictions implied by dynamic asset pricing models, *Econometrica* 55, 587–613.
Hansen, Lars Peter, and Kenneth Singleton, 1982, Generalized instrumental variables estimation
    in nonlinear rational expectations models, *Econometrica* 50, 1269–1286.
Harvey, Campbell R., 1989, Time-varying conditional covariances in tests of asset pricing models,
    Journal of Financial Economics 24, 289–318.
Jagannathan, Ravi, and Zhenyu Wang, 1992, The cross-section of expected stock returns: Do size
    and book to market equity measure systematic risk better than beta? Notes for The Berkeley
    Program in Finance on *"Are Betas Irrelevant? Evidence and Implications for Asset Manage-
    ment,"* September 13–15, 1992, Santa Barbara, California.
Jagannathan, Ravi, and Zhenyu Wang, 1993, The CAPM is alive and well, Staff report 165,
    Federal Reserve Bank of Minneapolis.
Jegadeesh, Narasimhan, 1992, Does market risk really explain the size effects? *Journal of
    Financial and Quantitative Analysis* 27, 337–351.
Kandel, Shmuel, and Robert F. Stambaugh, 1987, On correlations and inferences about mean-
    variance efficiency, *Journal of Financial Economics* 18, 61–90.

The Conditional CAPM and the Cross-Section of Expected Returns   53

Kandel, Shmuel, and Robert F. Stambaugh, 1990, A mean-variance framework for tests of asset pricing models, *Review of Financial Studies* 2, 125–156.

Kandel, Shmuel, and Robert F. Stambaugh, 1995, Portfolio inefficiency and the cross-section of expected returns, *Journal of Finance* 50, 157–184.

Keim, Donald B., and Robert F. Stambaugh, 1986, Predicting returns in the stock and bond markets, *Journal of Financial Economics* 17, 357–390.

Kothari, S. P., Jay Shanken, and Richard G. Sloan, 1995, Another look at the cross-section of expected stock returns, *Journal of Finance* 50, 185–224.

Lehmann, Bruce N., and David M. Modest, 1988, The empirical foundations of the arbitrage pricing theory, *Journal of Financial Economics* 21, 213–254.

Lintner, John, 1965, The valuation of risk assets and the selection of risky investments in stock portfolio and capital budgets, *Review of Economics and Statistics* 47, 13–37.

Long, J. B., 1974, Stock prices, inflation, and the term structure of interest rates, *Journal of Financial Economics* 1, 131–170.

Mandelker, G., 1974, Risk and return: The case of merging firms, *Journal of Financial Economics* 4, 303–335.

Mayers, David, 1972, Nonmarketable assets and capital market equilibrium under uncertainty, in Michael C. Jensen, Ed.: *Studies in the Theory of Capital Markets* (Praeger, New York), pp. 223–248

Merton, Robert C., 1973, An intertemporal capital asset pricing model, *Econometrica* 41, 867–887.

Merton, Robert C., 1980, On estimating the expected return on the market: An exploratory investigation, *Journal of Financial Economics* 8, 323–361.

Reinganum, Mark R., 1981, Misspecification of capital asset pricing: Empirical anomalies based on earnings yields and market values, *Journal of Financial Economics* 9, 19–46.

Roll, Richard, 1977, A critique of the asset pricing theory's tests; part I: On past and potential testability of the theory, *Journal of Financial Economics* 4, 129–176.

Ross, Stephen A., 1976, The arbitrage theory of capital asset pricing, *Journal of Economic Theory* 13, 341–360.

Shanken, Jay, 1985, Multivariate tests of the zero-beta CAPM, *Journal of Financial Economics* 14, 327–348.

Shanken, Jay, 1987, Multivariate proxies and asset pricing relations: Living with the roll critique, *Journal of Financial Economics* 18, 91–110.

Shanken, Jay, 1992, On the estimation of beta-pricing models, *Review of Financial Studies* 5, 1–33.

Sharpe, William F., 1964, Capital asset prices: A theory of market equilibrium under conditions of risk, *Journal of Finance* 19, 425–442.

Stambaugh, Robert F., 1981, Missing assets, measuring the market, and testing the capital asset pricing model, Doctoral dissertation, University of Chicago.

Stambaugh, Robert F., 1982, On the exclusion of assets from tests of the two-parameter model: A sensitivity analysis, *Journal of Financial Economics* 10, 237–268.

Stock, James, and Mark Watson, 1989, New indexes of coincident and leading economic indicators, in Olivier J. Blanchard and Stanley Fischer, Eds.: *NBER Macroeconomics Annual 1989*.

Zhou, Guofu, 1994, Analytical GMM tests: Asset pricing with time-varying risk premiums, *Review of Financial Studies* 7, 687–709.

[10]

THE JOURNAL OF FINANCE • VOL. LIV, NO. 4 • AUGUST 1999

Conditioning Variables and the Cross Section of Stock Returns

WAYNE E. FERSON and CAMPBELL R. HARVEY*

ABSTRACT

Previous studies identify predetermined variables that predict stock and bond returns through time. This paper shows that loadings on the same variables provide significant cross-sectional explanatory power for stock portfolio returns. The loadings are significant given the three factors advocated by Fama and French (1993) and the four factors of Elton, Gruber, and Blake (1995). The explanatory power of the loadings on lagged variables is robust to various portfolio grouping procedures and other considerations. The results carry implications for risk analysis, performance measurement, cost-of-capital calculations, and other applications.

EMPIRICAL ASSET PRICING is in a state of turmoil. The Capital Asset Pricing Model (CAPM; see Sharpe (1964) and Black (1972)) has long served as the backbone of academic finance and numerous important applications. However, studies have identified empirical deficiencies in the CAPM, challenging its preeminence. The most powerful challenges include market capitalization and related financial ratios that can predict the cross section of returns. For example, the firm "size-effect" drew attention as a challenge to the CAPM. Ratios of stock market price to earnings or the book value of equity are studied by Basu (1977), Banz (1981), Chan, Hamao, and Lakonishok (1991), and Fama and French (1992), among others.

With the CAPM under such strenuous attack the field is hungry for a replacement model.[1] There are some natural heirs waiting in the wings, including the intertemporal equilibrium models of Merton (1973) and Breeden

---

*Ferson is the Pigott-PACCAR Professor of Finance at the University of Washington and a Research Associate of the National Bureau of Economic Research (NBER). Harvey is the J. Paul Sticht Professor of International Business at Duke University, and a Research Associate of the NBER. We are grateful to Jonathan Berk, Chris Blake, Mark Carhart, Raymond Kan, Robert Korajczyk, Jay Shanken, Chu Zhang, and an anonymous referee for helpful comments and data. A. Roper provided research assistance. Ferson acknowledges financial support from the Pigott-PACCAR professorship at the University of Washington. Part of this work was completed while Ferson was a Visiting Scholar at the University of Miami. The paper has also benefited from workshops at the University of Miami, the University of Washington, the 1998 Conference on Financial Economics and Accounting, and the 1999 American Finance Association Meetings. (c) 1996, 1997, 1998, 1999 by Wayne E. Ferson and Campbell R. Harvey.

[1] The CAPM does have its erstwhile saviors. For example, studies find that dynamic versions of the CAPM with time-varying parameters and/or broader specifications for the market portfolio perform better than traditional formulations of the model. Examples include Harvey (1989), Ferson and Harvey (1991), Pannikkath (1993), Ferson and Korajczyk (1995), Jagannathan and Wang (1996), and Carhart et al. (1996). See Ghysels (1998) for a recent critique of conditional CAPMs.

(1979) and the Arbitrage Pricing Theory of Ross (1976). However, empirical implementations of these models have failed to produce much confidence in their explanatory power (e.g., Chan, Chen, and Hsieh (1985), Chen, Roll, and Ross (1986), Shanken and Weinstein (1990), Hansen and Singleton (1982), Connor and Korajczyk (1988), Lehmann and Modest (1988), and Roll (1995)).

One response to this hunger for a CAPM replacement has been to use the returns of attribute-sorted portfolios of common stocks to represent the factors in a multibeta model. For example, Fama and French (FF) (1993, 1995, 1996) advocate a three-factor "model," in which a market portfolio return is joined by a portfolio long in high book-to-market stocks and short in low book-to-market stocks (HML) and a portfolio that is long in small (i.e, low market capitalization) firms and short in large firms (SMB). Fama and French (1997) use this model for calculating the costs of equity capital for industry portfolios (see also Ibbotson Associates (1998)). Several recent studies use the FF three-factor model as an empirical asset pricing model. However, the model is controversial.

There is controversy over why the firm-specific attributes that are used to form the FF factors should predict returns. Some argue that such variables may be used to find securities that are systematically mispriced by the market (e.g., Graham and Dodd (1934), Lakonishok, Shleifer, and Vishny (1994), Haugen and Baker (1996), and Daniel and Titman (1997)). Others argue that the measures are proxies for exposure to underlying economic risk factors that are rationally priced in the market (e.g., Fama and French (1993, 1995, 1996)). A third view is that the observed predictive relations are largely the result of data snooping and various biases in the data (e.g., Black (1993), MacKinlay (1995), Breen and Korajczyk (1994), Kothari, Shanken, and Sloan (1995); see also Chan, Jegadeesh, and Lakonishok (1995)).

Berk (1995) emphasizes that, because returns are related mechanically to price by a present value relation, ratios that have price in the denominator are related to returns by construction. If the numerator of such a ratio can capture cross-sectional variation in the expected cash flows, the ratio is likely to provide a proxy for the cross section of expected returns. Ratios like the book-to-market are therefore likely to be related to the cross section of stock returns whether they are related to rationally priced economic risks or to mispricing effects. Ferson, Sarkissian, and Simin (1999) illustrate that spread portfolios like SMB or HML can appear to explain the cross section of stock returns even when the attributes used in the sort bear no relationship to risk. Since the FF factors are not derived from a theoretical model, such concerns about their interpretation are natural.

Given the prominence of the Fama–French three-factor model, we believe that it is interesting to test its empirical performance as an asset pricing model. The model was developed to explain unconditional mean (average) returns, and several studies explore its ability to explain average returns.[2]

---

[2] Fama and French (1993, 1996) find some nonzero alphas relative to the model, but interpret them as economically insignificant. Daniel and Titman (1997) find nonzero alphas using the FF model against a "characteristics-based" alternative for average returns. Berk (1997)

Conditioning Variables and the Cross Section of Stock Returns   1327

In this paper we test the FF model on conditional expected returns. Thus, we do not focus on alternative "factors" that may provide a better model of average returns. We concentrate instead on the ability of the model to capture common dynamic patterns in returns, modeled using a set of lagged, economy-wide predictor variables. Previous studies, including Fama and French (1996), explore the ability of the FF model to capture dynamic patterns in returns, such as the momentum effect of Jegadeesh and Titman (1993). We focus on common dynamic patterns, captured by a standard set of economy-wide instruments. These lagged instruments are used in numerous previous studies, including some by Fama and French (1988, 1989).

We find that simple proxies for time variation in expected returns, based on common lagged instruments, are also significant cross-sectional predictors of returns. The ability of these variables to explain the cross section of returns provides a powerful rejection of the FF model as a conditional asset pricing model. In some cases loadings on the lagged variables drive out the individual FF variables in cross-sectional regressions. The results are robust to variations in the empirical methods and to a variety of portfolio grouping procedures. We also reject the four-factor model advocated by Elton, Gruber, and Blake (1995). Our results raise a caution flag for researchers who would use the FF and Elton et al. models to control for systematic patterns in risk and expected return. Our results carry implications for risk analysis, performance measurement, cost-of-capital calculations, and other applications.

Our paper is related most closely to studies that use the loadings of stock portfolios on lagged economy-wide variables to explain the cross section of expected returns. Jagannathan and Wang (1996) and Jagannathan, Kubota, and Takehara (1998) show that asset covariances with labor income can be a powerful cross-sectional predictor in the United States and Japan. We use loadings on a larger set of lagged variables from the literature modeling time-series predictability.[3] The results show that size- and book-to-market-related factors leave out important cross-sectional information about expected returns, even in portfolios formed to maximize the potential explanatory power of these variables. The FF factors perform even worse in alternative designs.

The paper is organized as follows. Section I details the empirical methods. Here we propose a simple refinement of the standard Fama–MacBeth (1973) approach to cross-sectional regressions designed to improve its efficiency.

---

criticizes their sorting procedures and Davis, Fama, and French (1998) question the out-of-sample validity of their findings. Brennan, Chordia, and Subrahmanyam (1998) document cross-sectional attributes such as trading volume and exchange membership which also appear to reject the FF three-factor model.

[3] Conditional asset pricing studies use lagged instruments to model the time series of returns, and then test cross-sectional restrictions on the conditional expected returns. An early example of this approach is the so-called "latent variable" test, pioneered by Hansen and Hodrick (1983) and Gibbons and Ferson (1985); see Ferson, Foerster, and Keim (1993) for a review of this literature. Conversely, a few studies have observed that ratios such as book-to-market, originally identified as a cross-sectional predictor, have some time-series predictive power for aggregate returns (e.g., Pontiff and Schall (1998) and Kothari and Shanken (1997)).

Section II describes the data. Our empirical results are presented in Section III. Section IV explores some of the implications of the results. Section V discusses the robustness of the results to alternative portfolio grouping procedures, errors-in-variables, and other considerations. Some concluding remarks are offered in the final section.

I. The Empirical Framework

A. Time-Series Tests

We start with the null hypothesis that the FF three-factor model identifies the relevant risk in a linear return-generating process:

$$r_{i,t+1} = E_t(r_{i,t+1}) + \beta'_{it}\{r_{p,t+1} - E_t(r_{p,t+1})\} + \epsilon_{i,t+1}, \tag{1}$$

$$E_t(\epsilon_{i,t+1}) = 0,$$

$$E_t(\epsilon_{i,t+1} r_{p,t+1}) = 0,$$

where $r_{i,t+1}$ is the return for any stock or portfolio i, net of the return to a one-month Treasury bill, and $r_{p,t+1}$ is a vector of excess returns on the risk factor-mimicking portfolios. In the FF three-factor model, r_p is a 3×1 vector containing the market index excess return, HML, and SMB. The notation $E_t(\cdot)$ indicates the conditional expectation, given a common public information set at time t. The factor model expresses the unanticipated return, $r_{i,t+1} - E_t(r_{i,t+1})$, as a linear regression on the unanticipated parts of the factors. The third line says that the coefficient vectors β_{it} are the conditional betas of the return r_i on the factors. The error terms $\epsilon_{i,t+1}$ may be correlated across assets.[4]

Equation (1) captures the idea that $r_{p,t+1}$ are risk factors, but it says nothing about the determination of expected returns. We assume the following general model for the conditional expected returns and the betas:

$$E_t(r_{i,t+1}) = \alpha_{it} + \beta'_{it} E_t(r_{p,t+1}),$$

$$\beta_{it} = b_{0i} + b'_{1i} Z_t,$$

$$\alpha_{it} = \alpha_{0i} + \alpha'_{1i} Z_t, \tag{2}$$

where Z_t is an $L \times 1$ vector of mean zero information variables known at time t and the parameters of the model are b_{0i}, b_{1i}, α_{0i}, and α_{1i}. In the FF three-factor model, b_{0i} is 3×1, b_{1i} is $3 \times L$, α_{1i} is $1 \times L$, and α_{0i} is a scalar.

---

[4] The covariance matrix of these errors would be restricted to have bounded eigenvalues as the number of assets grows in the Arbitrage Pricing Theory, as shown by Chamberlain and Rothschild (1983).

Conditioning Variables and the Cross Section of Stock Returns   1329

Since we find that the lagged instruments have explanatory power beyond the FF three-factor model, we want to be sure that they do not simply proxy for time-variation in the FF factor betas. Given the evidence of time-varying conditional betas for stock portfolio returns (e.g., Ferson and Harvey (1991), Ferson and Korajczyk (1995), Braun, Nelson, and Sunier (1995)), it makes sense to allow for time-variation in the conditional betas. Thus, we allow the betas in equation (2) to depend on Z_t. The betas are modeled as linear functions of the predetermined instruments, following Shanken (1990), Ferson and Schadt (1996), and other studies. In equation (2), the relation over time between the lagged instruments and the betas for a given portfolio is assumed to be a fixed linear function, as b_{1i} is a fixed coefficient. However, we examine models estimated on rolling sample windows, an approach that allows b_{1i} to vary over time, thus relaxing the assumption of a fixed linear relation.

The hypothesis that the FF model explains expected returns says that the "alpha" term, α_{it}, in equation (2) is zero (i.e., the parameters α_{0i}, α_{1i} are zero). Assuming that alpha is zero is equivalent to assuming that the error term $\epsilon_{i,t+1}$ in equation (1) is not priced. Testing for $\alpha_{1i} = 0$ in system (2) asks whether the variables in Z_t can predict returns over and above their role as linear instruments for the betas.

Equation (2) follows empirical studies in which the alternative hypothesis specifies an alpha that is linear in instrumental variables. Examples include Fama and MacBeth (1973), who use the square of beta and a residual risk; Rosenberg and Marathe (1979), who use firm-specific accounting measures; and Daniel and Titman (1997), who use portfolio valuation ratios. Our example provides a natural test of the FF model, where mispricing related to the lagged, economy-wide instruments Z_t is the alternative hypothesis.

The models for both the betas and the alphas, as given by equation (2), are likely to be imperfect. The second and third equations of (2) may have independent error terms, reflecting possible misspecification of the alphas and the betas.

Combining equations (1) and (2), we derive the following econometric model:

$$r_{it+1} = (\alpha_{0i} + \alpha'_{1i} Z_t) + (b_{0i} + b'_{1i} Z_t) r_{p,t+1} + \epsilon_{i,t+1}. \tag{3}$$

An advantage of regression (3) is that it does not impose a functional form for the expected premiums, $E_t(r_{pt+1})$. This allows us to address the question of whether the lagged market indicators enter as proxies for time-variation in the conditional betas for specific factors, without concern about getting the right model for the expected returns on the factors.

B. Cross-Sectional Test Methodology

The cross-sectional regression approach of Fama and MacBeth (1973) is widely used to study asset pricing models and the cross-sectional structure of asset returns. In this approach returns are regressed each month, cross-sectionally, on a set of predetermined attributes of the firms or portfolios.

The attributes may include estimates of "betas" from a prior time period, as in Fama and MacBeth's study of the CAPM, or they may include other variables such as the book-to-market ratio of the portfolio, as in Fama and French (1992).

A cross-sectional regression using stock returns as the dependent variable is likely to have heteroskedastic and correlated errors, the latter due to the substantial correlation across stock returns in a given month. The usual regression standard errors are therefore not reliable. To test the hypothesis that the expected coefficient is zero, Fama and MacBeth suggest forming a *t*-ratio as the time series average of the monthly cross-sectional coefficients divided by the standard error of the mean, where the latter is computed from the time-series of the coefficient estimates. Shanken (1992) provides an analysis of the properties of this widely used approach. Jagannathan and Wang (1998) provide a recent asymptotic analysis, and Ahn and Gadarowski (1998) extend the analysis under autocorrelation and heteroskedasticity, where a single cross-sectional regression is used.

In Appendix A of this paper we show that the approach of Fama and MacBeth, which weights the monthly cross-sectional regression coefficients equally over time, can be easily improved. Under standard assumptions, the efficient generalized least squares (GLS) estimator of the pooled time-series and cross-sectional regression can be written as a weighted average of the time series of the Fama–MacBeth coefficients. The monthly estimates are weighted in inverse proportion to their variances. A measure of the total explanatory power of the system is also derived. We present results using the efficient-weighted estimators, as well as using the more traditional approach.

II. The Data

We obtain monthly returns on U.S. common stock portfolios for the period from July 1963 to December 1994. The portfolios are formed similarly to those of Fama and French (1993). Individual common stocks are placed into five groups according to their prior equity market capitalization, and independently on the basis of their ratios of book value to market value per share. This 5 × 5 classification scheme results in a sample of 25 equity portfolio returns. The appendix provides a more detailed description and Table I presents summary statistics for the returns. The means and standard deviations are annualized.

Our lagged instrumental variables, Z_t, follow from previous studies. These are: (1) the difference between the one-month lagged returns of a three-month and a one-month Treasury bill ("hb3"; see Campbell (1987), Harvey (1989), Ferson and Harvey (1991)); (2) the dividend yield of the Standard and Poors 500 (S&P 500) index ("div"; see Fama and French (1988)); (3) the spread between Moody's Baa and Aaa corporate bond yields ("junk"; see Keim and Stambaugh (1986) or Fama (1990)); (4) the spread between a ten-year and a one-year Treasury bond yield ("term"; see Fama and French (1989));

Conditioning Variables and the Cross Section of Stock Returns   1331

Table I
Summary Statistics

Returns on 25 value-weighted portfolios formed on size (as of June of the preceding year) and the ratio of book value to market value (as of the previous December) are summarized. Returns are measured in excess of a one-month Treasury bill return. S1 refers to the lowest 20 percent of market capitalization, S5 is the largest 20 percent, B1 refers to the lowest 20 percent of the book/market ratios, and B5 is the largest 20 percent. Market is the return on the value-weighted portfolio of all COMPUSTAT stocks used in forming the portfolios. HML is a high book/market less a low book/market return and SMB is a small firm return less a large firm return, as described in the text. The sample period is July 1963 through December 1994, which provides 378 observations. The sample means are annualized by multiplying by 12 and the sample standard deviations are multiplied by $12^{1/2}$. ρ_j is the sample autocorrelation at lag j.

Portfolio	Mean	Std. Dev.	ρ_1	ρ_2	ρ_3	ρ_4	ρ_{12}	ρ_{24}
S1/B1	8.89	26.18	0.21	0.02	−0.01	0.01	0.09	−0.01
S1/B2	14.18	23.01	0.20	0.00	−0.01	−0.00	0.10	−0.02
S1/B3	15.41	20.93	0.23	−0.01	−0.01	−0.02	0.14	−0.00
S1/B4	17.20	19.90	0.21	−0.01	−0.01	−0.02	0.16	−0.01
S1/B5	18.68	20.92	0.23	−0.02	−0.03	−0.04	0.22	0.06
S2/B1	11.60	24.35	0.16	−0.02	−0.02	−0.03	0.02	−0.06
S2/B2	14.36	21.34	0.17	−0.03	−0.02	−0.02	0.08	0.02
S2/B3	16.53	19.47	0.16	−0.04	−0.04	−0.02	0.09	−0.04
S2/B4	16.81	17.86	0.15	−0.04	−0.03	−0.01	0.12	0.01
S2/B5	18.55	20.34	0.16	−0.07	−0.07	−0.04	0.15	0.03
S3/B1	11.12	22.27	0.15	−0.02	−0.03	−0.05	0.02	−0.04
S3/B2	13.80	18.86	0.16	−0.03	−0.00	−0.04	0.05	−0.01
S3/B3	14.61	17.44	0.14	−0.02	−0.04	−0.03	0.03	−0.01
S3/B4	16.11	16.35	0.13	−0.04	−0.02	−0.04	0.09	0.06
S3/B5	18.48	18.78	0.11	−0.10	−0.06	−0.03	0.10	0.00
S4/B1	11.89	20.03	0.11	−0.02	−0.02	−0.02	0.01	−0.03
S4/B2	10.59	18.00	0.10	−0.04	−0.02	−0.02	0.01	−0.00
S4/B3	13.36	17.01	0.07	−0.05	−0.02	−0.06	0.02	0.00
S4/B4	15.21	16.44	0.07	−0.03	−0.03	−0.05	0.08	0.01
S4/B5	18.01	19.36	0.06	−0.04	−0.02	−0.02	0.06	−0.00
S5/B1	10.45	16.52	0.05	−0.01	−0.02	−0.01	0.05	−0.01
S5/B2	10.49	15.78	0.03	−0.06	0.00	−0.00	−0.00	−0.02
S5/B3	10.39	14.65	−0.05	−0.07	0.01	0.01	0.00	0.02
S5/B4	12.40	14.35	−0.07	0.01	0.05	−0.08	0.04	0.01
S5/B5	14.40	16.78	−0.02	−0.00	−0.03	−0.03	0.06	0.01
Market	11.26	15.12	0.04	−0.04	−0.01	−0.01	0.03	−0.01
SMB	3.23	9.91	0.18	0.06	−0.02	0.04	0.22	0.05
HML	5.40	8.88	0.20	0.06	−0.01	−0.06	0.10	0.10

and (5), the lagged value of a one-month Treasury bill yield ("Tbill"; see Fama and Schwert (1977), Ferson (1989), or Breen, Glosten, and Jagannathan (1989)).[5]

Table II summarizes time-series regressions of the 25 portfolios on the lagged instruments. The data are monthly for the July 1963 to December 1994 period. The regressions produce significant t-statistics for many of the variables. The adjusted R-squares vary from about six to 14 percent across

---

[5] Because of concerns about possible nonstationarity of the bill, we also examine results where the one-month yield is stochastically detrended by subtracting the lagged, twelve-month moving average.

Table II

In-Sample Predictability of Size and Book/Market Portfolios

Monthly excess returns are regressed on a set of lagged instrumental variables. The instrumental variables include "hb3," the lagged difference between three-month and one-month T-bill returns; "div," the lagged S&P 500 dividend yield; "junk," the lagged spread between Moody's Baa and Aaa yields; "term," the lagged spread between the 10-year and three-month Treasury yields. "Tbill" is the yield on the Treasury bill closest to 30 days to maturity from CRSP. The sample is July 1963 to December 1994 and the number of observations is 378. Returns on 25 value-weighted portfolios formed on size and the ratio of book value to market value are measured in excess of the return on a 30-day Treasury bill. S1 refers to the lowest 20 percent of market capitalization, S5 is the largest 20 percent, B1 refers to the lowest 20 percent of the book/market ratios and B5 is the highest 20 percent. Market is the return on the value-weighted portfolio of all COMPUSTAT stocks used in excess of the Ibbotson 30-day bill rate. HML is a high book/market less a low book/market return and SMB is a small firm return less a large firm return, as described in the text. Heteroskedasticity consistent t-ratios are on the second line below the coefficients. "R^2" is the coefficient of determination of the regression, with the adjusted R-square shown on the second line. "Autocorr" is the first-order autocorrelation of the regression residual, with its t-statistic on the second line.

				Variables				
	constant	hb3	div	junk	term	Tbill	R^2	Autocorr
S1/B1	-3.75	3.81	3.57	3.53	-1.24	-23.23	0.15	0.13
	-2.07	0.95	5.01	2.92	-3.40	-6.17	0.14	2.36
S1/B2	-3.21	2.93	2.83	3.33	-0.81	-18.27	0.14	0.12
	-2.00	0.89	4.26	3.11	-2.40	-5.06	0.13	2.20
S1/B3	-2.39	3.85	2.54	3.35	-0.83	-17.56	0.15	0.15
	-1.71	1.30	4.34	3.36	-2.81	-5.49	0.14	2.57
S1/B4	-1.50	4.63	2.24	3.13	-0.80	-16.51	0.15	0.13
	-1.13	1.73	3.99	3.31	-2.77	-5.30	0.14	2.26
S1/B5	-1.57	4.80	2.41	3.20	-0.83	-17.47	0.15	0.15
	-1.14	1.73	3.94	3.11	-2.73	-5.25	0.14	2.52
S2/B1	-3.05	4.11	2.98	2.86	-0.85	-19.19	0.13	0.09
	-1.74	1.06	4.22	2.47	-2.48	-5.36	0.12	1.73
S2/B2	-3.22	4.49	2.71	2.99	-0.76	-16.87	0.15	0.08
	-2.19	1.54	4.35	3.07	-2.51	-5.17	0.14	1.62
S2/B3	-1.70	5.68	1.95	2.70	-0.58	-13.69	0.13	0.08
	-1.26	2.09	3.36	2.94	-2.05	-4.39	0.12	1.46
S2/B4	-2.42	5.77	2.04	2.39	-0.51	-12.47	0.15	0.05
	-2.08	2.29	4.03	2.74	-1.91	-4.33	0.14	0.86
S2/B5	-1.67	6.56	2.15	2.46	-0.68	-14.35	0.13	0.09
	-1.24	2.35	3.57	2.50	-2.32	-4.41	0.12	1.56
S3/B1	-2.88	4.62	2.51	2.84	-0.70	-16.40	0.13	0.08
	-1.82	1.33	3.89	2.71	-2.17	-4.86	0.12	1.44
S3/B2	-2.50	5.89	2.15	2.79	-0.60	-14.23	0.16	0.07
	-1.94	2.20	3.86	3.14	-2.15	-4.79	0.15	1.30
S3/B3	-2.21	4.75	1.91	2.37	-0.45	-12.22	0.14	0.03
	-1.85	1.89	3.82	2.85	-1.79	-4.51	0.13	0.62
S3/B4	-0.63	5.64	1.61	2.10	-0.58	-12.10	0.13	0.03
	-0.57	2.48	3.48	2.69	-2.38	-4.64	0.12	0.56
S3/B5	-1.57	6.39	1.94	1.76	-0.55	-11.75	0.11	0.05
	-1.21	2.34	3.44	2.00	-2.01	-3.86	0.10	0.92

continued overleaf...

Conditioning Variables and the Cross Section of Stock Returns   1333

Table II—*Continued*

			Variables					
	constant	hb3	div	junk	term	Tbill	R^2	Autocorr
S4/B1	−1.99	6.60	2.00	2.27	−0.61	−13.41	0.12	0.04
	−1.40	1.97	3.48	2.31	−2.05	−4.56	0.11	0.84
S4/B2	−2.67	5.33	1.97	2.29	−0.46	−12.30	0.14	0.01
	−2.07	1.91	3.66	2.62	−1.70	−4.33	0.13	0.13
S4/B3	−1.67	4.97	1.69	2.56	−0.55	−12.04	0.14	0.04
	−1.47	2.18	3.39	3.20	−2.17	−4.38	0.12	0.67
S4/B4	−0.66	5.08	1.38	2.07	−0.48	−10.54	0.11	0.02
	−0.58	2.06	2.97	2.52	−1.97	−4.04	0.10	0.46
S4/B5	−0.90	6.39	1.59	2.55	−0.59	−12.11	0.11	0.03
	−0.67	2.36	2.83	2.74	−2.17	−4.02	0.10	0.48
S5/B1	−0.67	4.90	1.00	1.85	−0.30	−8.33	0.08	0.00
	−0.58	1.54	1.93	2.14	−1.24	−3.32	0.07	0.03
S5/B2	−1.87	4.51	1.31	1.85	−0.26	−8.32	0.10	0.04
	−1.70	1.65	2.76	2.29	−1.08	−3.37	0.09	0.63
S5/B3	−1.74	4.46	1.24	1.06	−0.12	−6.66	0.09	−0.11
	−1.72	1.66	2.81	1.37	−0.53	−2.91	0.07	−1.71
S5/B4	−0.86	3.19	1.02	1.89	−0.34	−7.57	0.08	−0.16
	−0.87	1.34	2.58	2.61	−1.58	−3.32	0.07	−2.89
S5/B5	0.14	5.34	0.78	2.32	−0.41	−8.46	0.08	−0.09
	0.12	2.13	1.64	2.94	−1.61	−3.19	0.07	−1.66
Market	−1.49	5.27	1.36	1.82	−0.33	−9.16	0.12	−0.04
	−1.43	1.95	2.93	2.40	−1.47	−3.91	0.11	−0.71
SMB	−1.20	−0.02	1.22	0.93	−0.40	−7.36	0.10	0.11
	−1.81	−0.01	4.68	1.97	−2.97	−5.36	0.08	1.92
HML	1.07	0.45	−0.46	−0.25	0.08	2.50	0.02	0.20
	1.77	0.28	−1.84	−0.48	0.52	1.70	0.00	3.10

the 25 portfolios. The residual autocorrelations are generally not large—approximately 0.1 on average—but there are some statistically significant autocorrelations for the small-firm portfolios. These no doubt reflect the nonsynchronous trading of these small stocks.[6]

The coefficients on the lagged variables show a great deal of spread across the portfolios. This is important, as cross-sectional dispersion in the coefficients is necessary to provide explanatory power for the cross section of stock returns.

Table II also reports regressions for the FF factor portfolios on the lagged instruments. Two of the FF factors, MARKET and SMB, produce similar R-squares to the 25 portfolios, but the HML portfolio is remarkable because its adjusted R-square is zero. This foreshadows the result that the HML portfolio does not help to explain time-varying conditional expected returns.

[6] The autocorrelations are estimated by regressing the fitted residual on its lagged value by OLS. A White (1980) t-ratio is reported for the slope coefficient of this regression in Table II.

The Journal of Finance

III. Empirical Evidence

A. Are the Betas Time-Varying?

As we show later, the lagged instruments track variation in expected returns that is not captured by the FF three-factor model. However, the lagged instruments may have explanatory power because they pick up time variation in the betas on the FF factors. This would imply that the FF model should be implemented in a conditional form—that is, with time-varying betas—but it would not indicate a fundamental shortcoming of the FF model.[7]

To examine the issue of time-varying betas, we report regressions in which we allow the lagged instruments to enter the models through the conditional betas. Table III presents the results of estimating the time-series regression (3) for each of the 25 portfolio returns. Both one-factor models, where the CRSP index is the market factor, and the FF three-factor model are examined; to save space we focus on the three-factor model in Table III.[8] The table reports the adjusted R-squares of the regressions and the right-tailed p-values of F-tests for the hypothesis that the interaction terms between the factor-mimicking portfolios and the lagged variables may be excluded from the regressions. In the three-factor model, the F-tests for 11 of the 25 portfolios produce p-values below 0.05 when the alphas are allowed to be time varying, and 12 cases reject constant betas on the assumption that the alphas are constant over time. A joint Bonferroni test strongly rejects the hypothesis that the betas are constant over time, in either specification. The evidence of Table III suggests that even if the FF factors are useful to control for "risk," it may be important to allow for the time-varying betas picked up by the lagged instruments.

B. Time-Series Evidence on the Three-Factor Model

Table IV presents further results from the time-series model given in equation (3). For the first two columns we regress the 25 size and book/market portfolio excess returns on a constant and the three FF factors. A t-test is conducted for the hypothesis that the intercept is equal to zero, similar to the results of Fama and French (1993, 1996), who found that the intercepts were close to zero. The null hypothesis is equivalent to the statement that a constant combination of the three FF factors is an unconditional (fixed-weight) minimum variance portfolio. This says that the three factors explain the unconditional expected returns of the 25 portfolios and, therefore, all fixed-weight portfolios formed from them. Like Fama and French (1993, 1996), we find little evidence against this hypothesis. Only four of 25 p-values

---

[7] Subsequent to an earlier version of this paper, Fama and French (1997) presented evidence of time-varying betas in their model when applied to industry portfolios. Eckbo, Norli, and Masulis (1998) provide evidence of time-varying betas for firms issuing new equity and their matching firms.

[8] More details are available at http://www.duke.edu/~charvey/Research/index.htm.

Conditioning Variables and the Cross Section of Stock Returns   1335

Table III

Tests for Time-Varying Betas in a Three-Factor Model

Returns on 25 value-weighted portfolios are measured in excess of the return on a 30-day Treasury bill and regressed on lagged instrumental variables, the excess returns of three-factor portfolios, the three-factor returns each multiplied by the instrumental variables, and a constant. The adjusted R-square of this regression is shown in the second column. A restricted regression is estimated where the portfolio returns are regressed only on the three-factor portfolios, the lagged instruments, and a constant. The p-value of an F-test comparing the two R-squares is presented in the third column, as a test for time-varying betas. In the three right-most columns a similar experiment is conducted (constant alphas), in which the lagged instruments do not appear except as interaction terms. The three factor-portfolios are the market return, a small minus large firm portfolio, and a high minus low book-to-market portfolio. The lagged instrumental variables are described in Table II. The sample period is July 1963 through December of 1994 and the number of observations is 378. S1 refers to the lowest 20 percent of market capitalization, S5 is the largest 20 percent, B1 refers to the lowest 20 percent of the book/market ratios, and B5 is the highest 20 percent. Bonferroni is the upper bound on the p-value of a joint test across the portfolios. #<0.05 is the number of p-values less than 0.05.

	Time-Varying Alphas			Constant Alphas		
Portfolio	R^2 Constant Betas	R^2 Time-Varying Betas	F-test (p-value)	R^2 Constant Betas	R^2 Time-Varying Betas	F-test (p-value)
S1/B1	0.673	0.685	0.002	0.651	0.659	0.014
S1/B2	0.693	0.703	0.004	0.681	0.689	0.020
S1/B3	0.688	0.701	0.001	0.673	0.682	0.012
S1/B4	0.647	0.663	0.001	0.633	0.645	0.007
S1/B5	0.608	0.624	0.002	0.592	0.604	0.008
S2/B1	0.783	0.787	0.037	0.774	0.777	0.125
S2/B2	0.786	0.795	0.002	0.775	0.779	0.047
S2/B3	0.758	0.769	0.001	0.756	0.763	0.009
S2/B4	0.765	0.775	0.001	0.758	0.764	0.019
S2/B5	0.706	0.721	0.000	0.702	0.711	0.007
S3/B1	0.835	0.838	0.040	0.832	0.834	0.107
S3/B2	0.845	0.850	0.006	0.838	0.839	0.210
S3/B3	0.803	0.807	0.026	0.800	0.801	0.147
S3/B4	0.795	0.800	0.018	0.791	0.794	0.057
S3/B5	0.730	0.737	0.013	0.729	0.733	0.069
S4/B1	0.879	0.878	0.730	0.878	0.877	0.736
S4/B2	0.900	0.904	0.001	0.898	0.901	0.004
S4/B3	0.861	0.862	0.126	0.859	0.859	0.272
S4/B4	0.785	0.787	0.199	0.786	0.788	0.152
S4/B5	0.751	0.761	0.002	0.751	0.761	0.003
S5/B1	0.878	0.881	0.024	0.877	0.878	0.179
S5/B2	0.911	0.913	0.010	0.911	0.914	0.008
S5/B3	0.832	0.837	0.009	0.831	0.836	0.012
S5/B4	0.772	0.773	0.356	0.774	0.775	0.231
S5/B5	0.643	0.648	0.067	0.644	0.649	0.062
Bonferroni			0.001			0.001
# < 0.05			11			12

The Journal of Finance

Table IV
Time-Varying Alphas in a Three-Factor Model

The first column shows the average annualized intercept (monthly figure × 12, in percent) in a regression of the portfolio excess return on a constant and three-factor portfolios. The second column presents the right-tailed p-value of a heteroskedasticity consistent test of whether this intercept is equal to zero. The third column reports the p-value of an F-test of whether the intercept is constant in a model with constant betas. The fourth column reports p-values of an F-test of the hypothesis that the intercept is constant in the model with time-varying betas. The alternative for the constant alpha tests is to model the alphas as linear functions of the lagged instrumental variables. The three-factor portfolios are the market return, a small minus large firm portfolio, and a high minus low book/market portfolio. The lagged instrumental variables are described in Table II. The sample is July 1963 to December 1994 and the number of observations is 378. Returns on 25 value-weighted portfolios formed on size and the ratio of book value to market value are measured in excess of the return on a 30-day Treasury bill. S1 refers to the lowest 20 percent of market capitalization, S5 is the largest 20 percent, B1 refers to the lowest 20 percent of the book/market ratios, and B5 is the highest 20 percent. Bonferroni is the upper bound on the p-value of a joint test across the portfolios. #<0.05 is the number of p-values less than 0.05.

Portfolio	Annual Intercept (Constant alpha, constant betas)	Test Zero Unconditional Alpha	Test Constant Alpha (Constant betas)	Test Constant Alpha (Time-varying betas)
S1/B1	−6.036	0.000	0.000	0.000
S1/B2	−1.924	0.036	0.002	0.002
S1/B3	−0.880	0.237	0.000	0.000
S1/B4	0.585	0.425	0.000	0.000
S1/B5	0.170	0.815	0.000	0.000
S2/B1	−0.917	0.320	0.002	0.002
S2/B2	−0.465	0.551	0.000	0.001
S2/B3	0.893	0.274	0.001	0.001
S2/B4	0.723	0.303	0.042	0.050
S2/B5	0.034	0.966	0.000	0.000
S3/B1	−1.100	0.239	0.000	0.000
S3/B2	0.100	0.908	0.002	0.003
S3/B3	−0.347	0.683	0.002	0.003
S3/B4	0.672	0.408	0.003	0.004
S3/B5	0.960	0.294	0.001	0.001
S4/B1	1.324	0.154	0.004	0.005
S4/B2	−2.322	0.011	0.000	0.000
S4/B3	−0.963	0.310	0.000	0.000
S4/B4	−0.040	0.969	0.000	0.000
S4/B5	0.476	0.693	0.015	0.019
S5/B1	2.295	0.002	0.000	0.000
S5/B2	−0.683	0.413	0.000	0.000
S5/B3	−1.240	0.222	0.000	0.000
S5/B4	−1.457	0.102	0.002	0.003
S5/B5	−1.678	0.196	0.079	0.092
Bonferroni	—	0.000	0.000	0.000
# < 0.05	—	4	24	24

(second column) are less than 0.05. The largest unconditional alpha is for the small-firm/value portfolio and is just over six percent per year; the second largest alpha is about 2.3 percent per year.

In the third column of Table IV we subject the FF model to a more stringent test, with a specific alternative hypothesis. We regress the portfolio excess returns over time on the three FF factors and the vector of lagged instruments. The F-test for the hypothesis that the lagged variables may be excluded from the regression is reported. This is implied by the hypothesis that the FF three-factor model with constant betas can explain the dynamic behavior of the *conditional* expected returns of the 25 portfolios, given the lagged instruments. Now we find strong evidence against the model. All of the p-values are less than 0.10, and all except one of the 25 are less than 0.05.[9]

Since we find evidence that conditional betas for the 25 portfolios on the FF variables are time-varying, the instruments could enter the model through the betas. In other words, by holding the betas fixed, the tests may be biased against the FF model. In the fourth column of Table IV we allow the betas to be time-varying. Each portfolio excess return is regressed on a constant intercept, the lagged instruments, the FF factors, and the products of the FF factors with the lagged instruments. This allows the FF factor betas to vary as a linear function of the lagged instruments. The null hypothesis that the alphas are constant (the lagged instruments may be excluded from the model of alpha) is tested with an F-test. Most of the p-values from this test are again small. We thus obtain a strong rejection of the FF three-factor model, even allowing for time-varying betas that depend on the instruments.

In summary, Fama and French (1993) found that the regression intercepts are close to zero for their three-factor model. However, conditional on the lagged instruments the alphas are time-varying and thus not zero. This implies that the FF three-factor model does not explain the conditional expected returns of these portfolios. Even a conditional version of the FF model, with time-varying betas, can be rejected.

C. Economic Significance of the Conditional Alphas

Though the time-series tests reject the FF model, the lagged instruments deliver only small increments to the already large time-series R-squares provided by the contemporaneous factors. We therefore conduct experiments to assess the economic significance of the conditional alphas.

In a first experiment we use the conditional alphas in a step-ahead "trading strategy" to assess the economic significance of the departures from the FF model. Each month we form portfolios using the conditional alphas of equation (3) estimated with trailing data. Each of the 25 size-sorted and book-to-market-sorted portfolios is assigned an alpha rank, and an equally

---

[9] Conditional pricing implies that the intercepts and the slopes on the lagged instruments are zero; we test the weaker implication that only the slopes are zero. Including the intercept would provide an even more powerful rejection of the FF model.

weighted combination of the top seven and bottom seven alpha portfolios is formed and held for one month. The procedure is repeated each month, producing a time-series of trading strategy returns for high-alpha and low-alpha portfolios. The models are estimated using either an expanding sample or a rolling, 60-month sample. We find that the subsequent returns of the high conditional alpha portfolios exceed those of the low conditional alpha portfolios by economically significant amounts. With the expanding sample, the difference in return is more than nine percent per year. With the rolling sample, it is more than eight percent per year. The standard deviations of the returns are slightly smaller in the high-alpha portfolios, which reinforces the economic significance of the conditional alphas.

In a second experiment we use the fitted values of the alphas, $\alpha_{0i} + \alpha'_{1i} Z_t$, from equation (3) in monthly cross-sectional regressions for $r_{i,t+1}$, where equation (3) is estimated using trailing data only. The three-factor betas for time t are also included in the regression. This means that the cross-sectional regression coefficient on the fitted alphas is the return for the month to a zero-net investment portfolio with three-factor betas equal to zero and a fitted alpha, based on past data, of one percent per month. If the FF model is correctly specified, the expected return of such a portfolio, and therefore the expected time-series average of the coefficient, should be zero.

The results of the cross-sectional regressions using a number of specifications for the fitted alphas and the FF factor betas may be found on the Internet. The results show that the fitted alphas are significant regressors in models with the three FF betas, producing t-ratios between 4.3 and 7.8, depending on the experiment. Including the fitted alphas in the regressions does not have much effect on the coefficients on the FF betas because the fitted alphas are constructed to be orthogonal to the FF betas in the cross section.[10] Thus, the regressions further illustrate the economic significance of the conditional alphas.

D. The Cross Section of Expected Stock Returns Revisited

Fama and French (1992) use cross-sectional regressions of stock portfolio returns on size and book-to-market to attack the CAPM. In this section we use a similar approach to examine the FF three-factor model in more detail. Consider the cross-sectional regression

$$r_{it+1} = \gamma_{0,t+1} + \gamma'_{t+1}\beta_{it} + \gamma_{4,t+1}\delta'_{it}Z_t + e_{it+1}; \qquad i = 1,\ldots,N, \qquad (5)$$

---

[10] This occurs because the factors are simple combinations of the test assets, which implies that a weighted average of the alphas must be zero. Consider the special case of a stacked regression model: $r = \alpha + r_p\beta + u$, where $r_p = rW$ is a combination of the test assets with weight given by the $n \times k$ matrix, W. Using the definition $\beta = (W'VW)^{-1}W'V$, where V is the covariance matrix of r, it is easy to show that $\alpha'V^{-1}\beta' = 0$.

Conditioning Variables and the Cross Section of Stock Returns   1339

where $\gamma_{o,t+1}$ is the intercept and $\gamma_{t+1} = (\gamma_{1,t+1}, \gamma_{2,t+1}, \gamma_{3,t+1})'$ and $\gamma_{4,t+1}$ are the slope coefficients. The β_{it} are the betas on the three FF variables, formed using information up to time t. The term $\delta'_{it} Z_t$ denotes the fitted conditional expected return, formed by regressing the return i on the lagged variables Z, using data up to date t, where δ_{it} is the time-series regression coefficient.[11] We use fit_{it} as a shorthand for this variable. The dating convention thus indicates when a coefficient or variable would be public information. The hypothesis that the FF factor betas explain the cross section of expected returns implies that the coefficient $\gamma_{4,t+1}$ is zero. The alternative hypothesis is that the FF variables do not explain the conditional expected returns, as captured by the lagged instruments.

Jagannathan and Wang (1998) study the asymptotic properties of cross-sectional regression models, allowing for heteroskedasticity in returns. They show that if an asset pricing model is misspecified, the coefficients are biased and, in some cases, the t-ratios do not conform to a limiting t distribution. Thus, the coefficients cannot be used to select significant factors. They emphasize, however, that including additional cross-sectional predictors in the model, the t-ratios for those variables provide a valid test of the null model. Their analysis justifies our use of the t-ratio on γ_4 as a test of the FF three-factor model.

Table V summarizes several versions of the cross-sectional regressions. The time-series averages of the cross-sectional regression coefficients are shown along with their Fama–MacBeth t-ratios. We examine one-factor models, where the CRSP value-weighted index is the factor, and three-factor models using the FF variables. Table V concentrates on the FF three-factor model.[12] We estimate the betas using either an expanding sample or a rolling, 60-month prior estimation period. When conditional betas are used (Panels C, D, G, and H) they are assumed to be linear functions of the lagged instruments. We estimate each cross-sectional regression model with and without the fitted expected returns in the regression, and we compare the results.

The FF model implies that the intercepts of the cross-sectional regressions should be zero. Table V shows that when the three-factor betas are the only regressors the intercept has a t-ratio of 0.80 using the expanding sample, and as large as 1.9 in other cases. The larger values may be interpreted as weak evidence against the FF three-factor model, similarly to Fama and French (1993, 1996).

When the fitted expected returns using the lagged market instruments (the "*fit*") are included in the cross-sectional regressions the results are dramatically different. The t-ratios of the *fit* are in excess of 5.7 in all of the

---

[11] The time-series regression is $r_{i\tau} = \delta'_{it} Z_{\tau-1} + v_{i\tau}$, $\tau = 1,\ldots,t$, so δ_{it} is estimated using data up to time t for returns and up to time $t - 1$ for the lagged instruments.

[12] Results for the one-factor models are available on the Internet. Consistent with Fama and French (1992), there is no significant relation between the returns on these portfolios and the market index betas. However, the fitted expected returns using the lagged market instruments are highly significant, with t-ratios in excess of seven.

Table V

Evidence on the Cross Section of Stock Returns

The average coefficients from monthly cross-sectional regressions are expressed as percentage per month. The dependent variables are value-weighted portfolio returns at time t, formed on size and the ratio of book-to-market, measured in excess of the return on a 30-day Treasury bill. The regressors are a constant, the betas on the three FF factors, and a fitted conditional expected return estimated with data up to time $t - 1$. The betas are from a time-series regression of the portfolio excess returns on the excess factor returns. The three FF factors are the market return (mkt), a small minus large market capitalization portfolio (smb), and a high minus a low book-to-market portfolio (hml). The fitted expected return is from a time-series regression of the portfolio return on lagged instrumental variables, using data to time $t - 1$. The instrumental variables used to form the fitted expected return (fit) are described in Table II. The sample is July 1963 to December 1994 and the number of time-series observations is 378. The number of cross-sectional regressions is 377. For the first 60 months we use the in-sample betas. After observation 60, the sample for estimating the beta grows by one observation in Panel A. In Panel B, the regressions use a 60-month rolling window to estimate the betas (the time-series predicted returns use an expanding sample). t-statistics are reported under the average coefficients. γ_0 is the average intercept.

γ_0	γ_1(mkt)	γ_2(smb)	γ_3(hml)	γ_4(fit)
	Panel A. With Expanding Sample Betas			
0.230	0.190	0.198	0.495	—
0.804	0.586	1.354	3.648	—
0.502	—	—	—	0.510
2.036	—	—	—	6.030
0.041	0.322	0.073	0.232	0.466
0.137	0.953	0.496	1.588	7.797
	Panel B. With 60-Period Rolling Sample Betas			
0.483	−0.049	0.208	0.473	—
1.865	−0.167	1.426	3.563	—
0.502	—	—	—	0.510
2.036	—	—	—	6.030
0.227	0.153	0.092	0.237	0.445
0.803	0.491	0.631	1.715	7.537
	Panel C. With Expanding Sample Conditional Betas			
0.217	0.235	0.195	0.416	—
0.872	0.974	1.426	3.473	—
0.502	—	—	—	0.510
2.036	—	—	—	6.030
0.201	0.341	0.173	0.176	0.387
0.785	1.392	1.284	1.411	6.659
	Panel D. With 60-Period Rolling Sample Conditional Betas			
0.190	0.276	0.195	0.360	—
0.868	1.548	1.508	3.392	—
0.502	—	—	—	0.510
2.036	—	—	—	6.030
0.254	0.211	0.160	0.205	0.355
1.138	1.243	1.293	2.041	6.250

continued overleaf...

Conditioning Variables and the Cross Section of Stock Returns 1341

Table V—*Continued*

γ_0	γ_1(mkt)	γ_2(smb)	γ_3(hml)	γ_4(fit)
	Panel E. WLS with Expanding Sample Betas			
0.236	0.186	0.229	0.466	—
0.826	0.555	1.561	3.482	—
0.467	—	—	—	0.523
1.859	—	—	—	6.107
0.066	0.301	0.106	0.246	0.435
0.219	0.880	0.718	1.714	7.438
	Panel F. WLS with 60-Period Rolling Sample Betas			
0.508	−0.070	0.242	0.440	—
1.929	−0.232	1.660	3.297	—
0.497	—	—	—	0.505
1.986	—	—	—	5.834
0.350	0.036	0.123	0.250	0.391
1.251	0.117	0.852	1.815	6.943
	Panel G. WLS with Expanding Sample Conditional Betas			
0.227	0.216	0.236	0.403	—
0.923	0.870	1.721	3.413	—
0.463	—	—	—	0.527
1.844	—	—	—	6.164
0.212	0.319	0.202	0.204	0.349
0.830	1.278	1.497	1.673	6.307
	Panel H. WLS with 60-Period Rolling Sample Conditional Betas			
0.208	0.246	0.247	0.345	—
0.960	1.360	1.893	3.220	—
0.502	—	—	—	0.511
1.992	—	—	—	5.866
0.314	0.158	0.196	0.211	0.324
1.430	0.924	1.587	2.105	5.730

panels. The FF three-factor model thus fails miserably when confronted with this alternative hypothesis. Although the magnitudes of the coefficients are difficult to interpret if the model is misspecified (Jagannathan and Wang (1998)), some of the patterns are interesting. With the *fit* in the regressions the coefficients on HML are consistently smaller, and the *t*-ratios become individually insignificant in many of the cases. The average coefficient on the market beta, γ_1(*mkt*), is usually larger in the presence of the fit. The intercepts are typically smaller and insignificant when the fit is included.

The coefficients and *t*-ratios in Table V show that the FF three-factor model is rejected. The *fit* thus provides a powerful alternative that allows us to detect patterns in the cross section of the conditional expected returns that the FF model does not capture. The rejection can also be turned around. If the fit delivered a perfect proxy for $E_t(r_{i,t+1})$, then in the cross section, the coefficients on β_{it} should have a mean of zero and the coefficient on the *fit* should be 1.0. The tests therefore reject the hypothesis that the *fit* completely captures expected returns. Of course, since the lagged instruments represent only a subset of publicly available information, and the regressions that determine the *fit* have estimation error, we do not expect the *fit* to provide a perfect proxy for expected returns. We discuss errors-in-variables in Section 5.A below.

The *t*-ratios in Table V allow a convenient economic interpretation of the rejections as they are proportional to a portfolio's Sharpe ratio (average excess return divided by standard deviation). For example, with a sample of 378 months and a *t*-ratio for the HML premium of 3.65 in Panel A, the Sharpe ratio of the HML premium is $3.65/\sqrt{378} = 0.188$. MacKinlay (1995) argues that such a high Sharpe ratio for monthly stock returns is implausible. With the *fit* in the regression, the Sharpe ratio for the HML premium is $1.58/\sqrt{378} = 0.081$, and that for the premium, $\gamma_4(fit)$, is $7.8/\sqrt{378} = 0.401$. Applying MacKinlay's interpretation here suggests that if we accept the FF three-factor as a model for both expected returns and risk control, then the portfolio strategy implied by the *fit* is an attractive, near-arbitrage opportunity. Alternatively, we interpret the evidence as a striking rejection of the FF three-factor model.

E. Are These "Useless" Factors?

Although the results of the cross-sectional regressions are striking, they should be interpreted with some caution. Kan and Zhang (1999) provide an analysis of bias in cross-sectional regressions when there is a "useless" factor that has a true beta in time series equal to zero. They show that such a useless factor beta may appear with a large *t*-ratio in a cross-sectional regression, as the design matrix of the regression is ill-conditioned. Jagannathan and Wang (1998) provide an asymptotic analysis that includes a useless factor as a special case, and Ahn and Gadarowski (1998) extend their results with more general assumptions about heteroskedasticity and autocorrelation. Given that the lagged instruments have relatively small R-squares in the time-series, it is possible that our results reflect a bias as described by these studies.

Kan and Zhang (1999) suggest using the stability of cross-sectional coefficients in subperiods as a diagnostic tool to indicate the useless factor bias, as the cross-sectional coefficients should be unstable in the presence of a useless factor. Our rolling estimators provide an opportunity to look for instability. We examine time-series plots of our cross-sectional coefficients. Figure 1 shows an example. The cross-sectional regression coefficients on the *fit* are graphed over time. Superimposed on the graph are the monthly coefficients for the betas on the market index, a factor that is as far from useless in the time-series regressions as we can imagine. Since the units of the regressors—market beta versus *fit*—are different, we multiply the coefficient on the *fit* by the ratio of the time series means of the coefficient

Conditioning Variables and the Cross Section of Stock Returns 1343

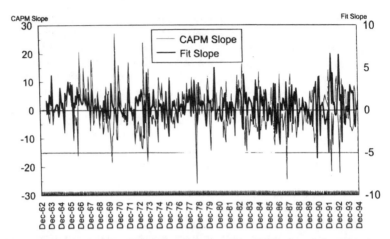

Figure 1. Comparison of cross-sectional slopes. The CAPM slope (left scale) shows the time series of monthly cross-sectional regression coefficients of size and book/market portfolio returns on their stock market betas. The fit slope (right scale) shows the time series of monthly cross-sectional regression coefficients of the portfolio returns on their *fit* values, scaled to have the same sample mean as the CAPM slopes. The figure illustrates that the fit slopes appear to be more stable over time than the CAPM slopes.

values. Scaled to the same means, the volatilities of the two time series are very different. The coefficients on the *fit* appear much more stable than those for the market beta. Indeed, to see the variation in both series on the same graph we use different scales: The *fit* coefficient is shown at a smaller scale than the market beta coefficient. Given this striking evidence, we do not believe that a useless factor story explains our results.

F. Results Using Efficient-Weighted Fama–MacBeth Regressions

Table VI summarizes cross-sectional regression results using the efficient-weighted version of the Fama–MacBeth coefficients, as derived in Appendix A. These essentially weight the coefficient each month in inverse proportion to the variance of the estimator from that month. A *t*-ratio for each coefficient is constructed similarly to Fama and MacBeth (1973), but the months are weighted to reflect the weighted estimator.

The results in Table VI confirm the finding that the *fit* allows us to reject the FF model in cross-sectional regressions. In three of the four cases, the *fit* *t*-ratio is significant given the FF factor loadings. Although the magnitudes should be interpreted with caution, as explained before, many of the patterns in the regression results are similar to those of Table V. Only in one of four cases does the coefficient on the HML loading produce a significant *t*-ratio when the fit is in the regression, and in no case is SMB significant. However, unlike the previous tables, the weighted average slope coefficient for HML is larger when the fit is in the regression.

Table VI

Efficient-Weighted Fama–MacBeth Regression Results

The efficient weighted average of the coefficients from monthly cross-sectional regressions are expressed as percentage per month, as derived in Appendix A. The dependent variables at time t are 25 value-weighted portfolio returns formed on size and the ratio of book-to-market, and measured in excess of the return on a 30-day Treasury bill. The regressors are a constant, the betas on the three FF factors, and a fitted conditional expected return estimated with data up to time $t - 1$. The three FF factors are the market return (mkt), a small minus large market capitalization portfolio (smb), and a high minus a low book-to-market portfolio (hml). The betas are from a time-series regression of the portfolio excess returns on the excess factor returns using data to time $t - 1$. The fitted expected returns (*fit*) are from time-series regressions of the returns on lagged instrumental variables, using data to time $t - 1$. The lagged instrumental variables are described in Table II. The sample is July 1963 to December 1994 and the number of time-series observations is 378. The number of cross-sectional regressions is 377. For the first 60 months we use the in-sample betas. After observation 60, the sample for estimating the beta grows by one observation in Panel A. In Panel B, the regressions use a 60-month rolling window to estimate the betas (the time-series predicted returns use an expanding sample). t-statistics are reported under the average coefficients. γ_0 is the weighted-average intercept. The overall R^2 is derived in Appendix A.

γ_0	γ_1(mkt)	γ_2(smb)	γ_3(hml)	γ_4(*fit*)	Overall R^2
\multicolumn{6}{c}{Panel A. With Expanding Sample Betas}
−0.073	0.453	0.796	0.275	—	0.0020
−0.123	0.601	1.990	1.442	—	—
0.410	—	—	—	1.912	0.0938
1.706	—	—	—	3.015	—
0.282	0.546	0.247	0.320	0.609	0.0946
0.480	0.734	0.627	1.616	0.275	—
\multicolumn{6}{c}{Panel B. With 60-Period Rolling Sample Betas}
0.051	−0.527	0.999	0.047	—	0.0025
0.052	−0.478	1.789	0.180	—	—
0.208	—	—	—	1.333	0.0938
0.822	—	—	—	2.022	—
−0.154	−0.897	0.504	0.171	6.032	0.0941
−0.171	−0.889	0.988	0.627	1.405	—
\multicolumn{6}{c}{Panel C. With Expanding Sample Conditional Betas}
−0.054	0.231	−0.341	−0.466	—	0.0042
−0.121	0.541	−1.032	−1.700	—	—
0.350	—	—	—	1.806	0.0938
1.472	—	—	—	2.960	—
−0.092	0.048	−0.409	−0.650	3.841	0.0950
−0.215	0.113	−1.231	−2.187	2.683	—
\multicolumn{6}{c}{Panel D. With 60-Period Rolling Sample Conditional Betas}
0.328	0.308	0.690	−0.019	—	0.0018
0.762	0.831	0.949	−0.069	—	—
0.207	—	—	—	1.400	0.0938
0.815	—	—	—	2.095	—
0.147	0.064	0.393	−0.079	2.321	0.0944
0.426	0.178	0.760	−0.304	1.975	—

Conditioning Variables and the Cross Section of Stock Returns 1345

We observed earlier that the increments to time-series regression R-squares, for the portfolio returns regressed on the contemporaneous factors, are small when the lagged instruments are included in the regressions. Table VI includes estimates of overall R-squares, as derived in Appendix A. The overall R-squares combine the time-series and cross-sectional dimensions of model explanatory power, where each return-month is weighted inversely to its variance. For the FF model, the R-squares vary from 0.2 to 0.42 percent across the experiments. These figures are much lower than the cross-sectional regression R-squares reported in previous studies, reflecting the relatively poor fit of the FF three-factor betas to the time-series of the expected returns. (Recall that the explanatory variables are predetermined betas, not the contemporaneous factor values.) When the predetermined value of the fit is in the regressions, the R-squares range from 9.3 percent to 9.5 percent. These figures are similar to those obtained from time-series regressions of returns on the lagged instruments themselves. The comparison shows that the fit provides a dramatic improvement in the overall explanatory power, illustrating that the FF three-factor model is strongly rejected.

G. Digging deeper

Given that the time-series instruments deliver such a powerful cross-sectional predictor of stock returns, it is interesting to know which of the lagged variables are relatively important in the cross-sectional regressions. We repeat the cross-sectional analysis of the preceding section, replacing the fitted expected returns with the estimated regression coefficient, δ, on a single lagged instrument, and we study the instruments one at a time in the presence of the FF three-factor betas. The results are on the Internet.

The cross-sectional coefficients on the individual δ's show a number of interesting patterns. No individual coefficient drives the cross-sectional explanatory power. However, the coefficients for the lagged excess return of the three-month bill, δ_{HB3}, and for the lagged one-month yield δ_{Tbill}, are consistently strongly significant cross-sectional predictors. For example, the t-ratios for the slope coefficient for δ_{HB3} are between 2.6 and 3.8 in all of the 48 different specifications we examine. For δ_{Tbill} the t-ratios are all between 2.1 and 4.1. This suggests that the FF three-factor model leaves out important patterns in expected stock returns that are related to cross-sectional differences in the portfolios' sensitivity to lagged interest rates.

H. Tests on a Four-Factor Model

The idea that the FF factor model may leave out important interest rate exposures is reflected in the work of Elton, Gruber, and Blake (EGB, 1995), who advocate a four-factor model. The first three factors are similar to those of the FF model, and the fourth factor is a low-grade bond portfolio excess return. We repeat the battery of tests described above using the EGB four-factor model as the null hypothesis, with data over the February 1979 to

December 1993 period, a total of 180 monthly observations.[13] The main results are summarized here, and are available by request or on the internet.

When we test for time-varying betas of the size- and book/market-sorted portfolios, as in Table III, we find evidence of time-varying betas in the four-factor model. The F-tests produce 10 out of 25 p-values less than 0.05, and the Bonferroni inequality implies that the p-value of a joint test across the 25 portfolios is less than 0.001. There is also evidence of time-varying alphas in this model, similar to Table IV. As a prelude to the cross-sectional regressions we examine the average cross-sectional correlations of the four-factor beta estimates and we find no strong correlations. This suggests that the $(x'x)$ matrix in the cross-sectional regressions should not be ill-conditioned due to colinearity of the regressors.

The cross-sectional regression analysis, similarly to Table V, reveals some interesting results for the four-factor model. In the presence of the bond-return factor, the betas on the EGB market, size, and value-growth factors are seldom individually significant in the cross-sectional regressions. By itself, the fitted expected return produces t-ratios between 3.8 and 5.8 in experiments corresponding to the eight panels of Table V. When the four-factor betas and the *fit* are in the regression, the t-ratios for the *fit* are between 3.3 and 5.6. No four-factor beta is individually significant in the presence of the *fit*.

In summary, the results for the EGB four-factor model are similar to the results for the FF three-factor model. Conditional on the lagged instruments the alphas in either model are time-varying and thus not zero. This implies that the models do not explain the conditional expected returns of these portfolios. Even conditional versions of the models, with time-varying betas, do not capture the dynamic patterns of the expected returns. The lagged instruments do not explain much the time-series variance of the returns. However, in cross-sectional regressions the *fit* is a relatively powerful regressor. Its Fama–MacBeth t-ratios are large even with the factor betas in the regression.

IV. Interpreting the Evidence

The preceding evidence shows that variables used to proxy for expected returns over time in the conditional asset pricing literature also provide a potent challenge for the Fama–French and Elton–Gruber–Blake variables in explaining the cross-section of conditional expected returns. These results carry implications for risk analysis in market efficiency studies, performance measurement, cost-of-capital calculations, and other applications.

Factor models are frequently used to control for risk in studies of market efficiency. This is typically done by regressing returns on the factors and taking the residuals, perhaps added to the intercept, as a measure of risk-adjusted returns. Alternatively, returns may be measured in excess of the return on a matching portfolio, constructed to have similar market capital-

---

[13] We are grateful to Chris Blake for providing data on the EGB factors.

Conditioning Variables and the Cross Section of Stock Returns   1347

ization and book/market ratio as the firm to be studied. Such an approach is required in a situation such as a study of initial public offerings (IPOs), as no prior returns data are available to estimate a regression model. If size and book/market are good proxies for risk, then the matching portfolio provides a risk adjustment. Our evidence casts serious doubt on the empirical validity of such a procedure. Matching the market, small-firm, and book/market exposure is expected to leave predictable dynamic behavior in the "risk-adjusted" returns. When studying the performance of portfolios based on a phenomenon that is correlated with aggregate economic activity, such as IPOs, the risk of falsely detecting "market inefficiencies" is likely to be especially acute. This is because the lagged instruments are likely to be correlated with the event in question.

Another recent application of the FF and EGB factor models is in measuring the performance of mutual funds. Here, a regression of the fund on the factor excess returns produces an intercept that is interpreted as a multi-beta version of Jensen's (1968) alpha. However, our evidence shows that even the hypothetical, mechanically constructed portfolios in our study have nonzero alphas in these models. The alphas are time-varying and can be modeled as simple functions of publicly available, lagged instruments. Since these portfolios can in principle be traded and the instruments are known, it should be a simple matter for a fund to "game" a performance measure constructed using these models. From this perspective, the performance of funds in relation to such strategies remains an open puzzle.[14]

Factor models for expected returns, and the CAPM in particular, have long been used in corporate cost-of-capital calculations. Here, the idea is to find an expected return commensurate with the risk of a project, and to discount prospective cash flows at the risk-adjusted return to determine its present value. Studies such as Fama and French (1997) have put the FF factor model to this application, and some have used it in practice. Of course, the lack of theoretical grounding for the FF model is a serious limitation in this context. For example, taken literally the model suggests that a firm could change its capital costs by altering its book value, other things equal. Our empirical evidence provides additional reasons to be suspicious of the FF model as a source of risk-adjusted discount rates.

Our empirical results may also be interpreted from a technical perspective, in view of portfolio efficiency. A portfolio is minimum-variance efficient if and only if expected returns in the cross section are a linear function of asset's covariances with the portfolio return (e.g., Roll (1977)). If betas on the FF factors provide a reasonable description of the cross section of the unconditional expected returns of these portfolios, then a combination of the factors is a fixed-weight, unconditionally efficient portfolio. If the lagged

---

[14] Becker et al. (1999) find that, although hypothetical portfolios of value stocks return more than growth stocks, portfolios of value-investing mutual funds grouped on similar criteria in their equity holdings do not offer higher returns than growth mutual funds. The difference is not explained by higher expense ratios for growth funds.

variables deliver a good proxy for the conditional expected returns at each date, given the lagged instruments Z_t, the *fit* is proportional in the cross section to betas on a *conditional* minimum-variance portfolio given Z_t. The Fama–MacBeth regressions use the actual future returns each month as the dependent variable. These may be viewed as equal to the unconditional expected returns plus noise, or as equal to the conditional expected returns plus a smaller-variance noise. The covariances with a conditionally efficient portfolio should therefore provide a more powerful regressor in the Fama–MacBeth approach, with smaller errors than would the covariances with an unconditionally efficient, fixed-weight portfolio.[15]

Although the portfolio efficiency interpretation of our results does not require a risk-based asset pricing model, if a risk-based model determines expected returns then the results carry implications about the model. These may provide direction for future research attempting to identify better-specified asset pricing models. In a risk-based asset pricing model, expected excess returns are proportional to securities covariances with a marginal utility of wealth. In essence, we should be looking for models in which the cross section of the conditional covariances with the marginal utility captures the cross section of the *fit*.

V. Robustness of the Results

We conduct a number of additional experiments to assess the sensitivity of our results to the portfolio grouping procedures and the empirical methods. The results of these experiments are described in this section. Tables of these results are available by request, or on the Internet.

A. Errors-in-Variables

The cross-sectional regressions are likely to be affected by errors-in-variables when the first-pass time-series regression coefficients appear on the right-hand side. If the factors are measured with error, we may falsely reject a model by introducing an explanatory variable that is correlated with the true factor betas. Kim (1997) explores the possibility that the CAPM is rejected by a book-to-market factor for this reason, and we cannot rule out a similar explanation for our rejections of the FF model. Since it is not clear what risks the FF factors may represent, it is hard to consider measuring those factors without error.

Errors in variables arise even when the first-pass regressions are unbiased, as a result of the sampling error in the first-pass estimator. This is the classic generated regressor problem, known to bias the second-pass, cross-

---

[15] We emphasize that the unconditional efficiency is defined here within the set of fixed-weight portfolios of the test assets. This is to distinguish from the notion of unconditional efficiency in Hansen and Richard (1987), which is defined over the set of all dynamic trading strategies that may depend on the conditioning information. See Bansal and Harvey (1997) and Ferson and Siegel (1997) for treatments of efficiency with dynamic trading strategies.

Conditioning Variables and the Cross Section of Stock Returns 1349

sectional regression slopes in finite samples and their standard errors even in infinite samples (see Pagan (1984), Shanken (1992), Kim (1995, 1997), and Kan and Zhang (1999) for recent analyses). The first-pass regression coefficients may also be biased in finite samples even without measurement errors in the factors (e.g., Stambaugh (1998), Kothari and Shanken (1997)).

Though measurement error problems are potentially complex, they are likely to be more severe in the time-series coefficients of the *fit* than in the estimates of the FF factor betas, because the explanatory power of a time-series regression on the contemporaneous FF factors is much higher than on the lagged instruments. Errors-in-variables therefore probably works against our ability to find that the lagged instruments are significant, suggesting that our results are conservative in view of measurement error. However, when there is correlated measurement error in a multiple regression the direction of the effect may be difficult to predict. We wish to be conservative about our evidence that the *fit* rejects the FF model. Therefore, we conduct experiments to assess the likely robustness of our results to measurement errors.

We repeat our analysis using the actual values of size and book/market in place of time-series betas on the FF factor-portfolios. As these attributes are likely to be measured more precisely than the time-series regression coefficients, this skews the measurement error further in favor of the FF model. We use data on 25 portfolios, sorted on the basis of book/market and size, together with the actual values of the log of the market capitalization (ln-Size) and the log of the book/market ratio (lnB/M) measured similarly to Fama and French (1992).[16] The data cover the July 1964 to December 1992 period, a total of 342 observations.

We repeat our previous tests for time-varying betas and alphas using this slightly different sample of returns, and the results are similar to those reported above. We find strong evidence of time-varying betas and alphas. Table VII focuses on the cross-sectional regressions, similar to those in Table V but using the actual lagged values of the attributes instead of the FF betas for SMB and HML. When the market betas, lnSize and lnB/M are used alone in the regressions, the results are as expected from Fama and French (1992). When the *fit* is included in the cross-sectional regressions, its *t*-ratios are 4.3 or larger in every case we consider. This is striking evidence against the FF three-factor model, especially in view of the measurement error issue.

As an additional check, we run cross-sectional regressions using betas on the FF factors and on the time-series of the fitted cross-sectional coefficients obtained from Table V, treating the latter as competing excess returns or "factors." This approach should place the *fit* at a further measurement error disadvantage, relative to the FF factors. We find that the *fit* loadings produce a Fama–MacBeth *t*-ratio larger than 1.95 in three of the four panels corresponding to Table V.

---

[16] These data are courtesy of Raymond Kan and Chu Zhang, to whom we are grateful. The sorting criteria are somewhat different than in our first sample; see Appendix B for details.

Table VII

Attributes and the Cross Section of Stock Returns

The average coefficients from monthly cross-sectional regressions are expressed as percentage per month. The dependent variables at time t are 25 value-weighted portfolios formed on size and the book/market ratio, and measured in excess of the return on a 30-day Treasury bill. The regressors are a constant, the portfolios' betas on a stock market factor, the portfolio size (natural log of market capitalization, lnSize), the log of the book/market ratio (ln(B/M)), and a fitted conditional expected return estimated with data up to time $t - 1$ (fit). The market betas are from time-series regressions of the returns on the excess market factor return using data to time $t - 1$. The fitted expected return is from a time-series regression of the portfolio returns on lagged instrumentals using data to time $t - 1$. The lagged instrumental variables are described in Table II. t-statistics are reported under the average coefficients. The sample is August 1964 to December 1992, the number of time-series observations is 342, and the number of cross-sectional regressions is 341. For the first 60 months we use the in-sample betas. After observation 60, the sample for estimating the beta grows by one observation in Panel A. In Panel B, the regressions use a 60-month rolling window to estimate the market betas (the time-series predicted returns use an expanding sample).

γ_0	$\gamma(\beta_{mkt})$	$\gamma(\text{lnSize})$	$\gamma(\ln(B/M))$	$\gamma(fit)$
	Panel A. With Expanding Sample Betas			
1.491	−0.017	−0.134	0.226	—
2.906	−0.043	−2.619	2.282	—
0.337	—	—	—	0.506
1.177	—	—	—	4.967
0.598	0.226	−0.063	0.188	0.308
1.242	0.547	−1.289	1.924	4.300
	Panel B. With 60-Period Rolling Sample Betas			
1.588	−0.217	−0.119	0.240	—
3.331	−0.677	−2.393	2.476	—
0.337	—	—	—	0.506
1.177	—	—	—	4.967
0.695	0.010	−0.050	0.199	0.328
1.536	0.032	−1.060	2.072	4.684
	Panel C. With Expanding Sample Conditional Betas			
1.479	0.012	−0.138	0.222	—
3.110	0.044	−2.759	2.287	—
0.337	—	—	—	0.506
1.177	—	—	—	4.967
0.770	−0.025	−0.056	0.199	0.324
1.686	−0.091	−1.187	2.065	4.663
	Panel D. With 60-Period Rolling Sample Conditional Betas			
1.480	0.046	−0.141	0.224	—
3.308	0.326	−2.766	2.299	—
0.337	—	—	—	0.506
1.177	—	—	—	4.967
0.834	0.042	−0.069	0.186	0.336
1.889	0.296	−1.480	1.910	4.529

Conditioning Variables and the Cross Section of Stock Returns   **1351**

Although these additional experiments increase our confidence that our results are robust to measurement errors, it seems impossible to completely resolve the measurement error issue without knowledge of the underlying "true" model of expected returns.

B. Results for Industry Portfolios

We replicate the tests of the previous sections using a sample of industry portfolio returns. The data are from Harvey and Kirby (1996) and are described in Appendix B. Industry portfolios are interesting in view of the evidence in Fama and French (1997), who use the FF three-factor model to estimate industry costs of capital. Since the FF factors are designed to explain the returns on size and book/market portfolios, we expect them to perform less well on portfolios grouped by alternative criteria.

We find strong evidence that the lagged market indicators enter as instruments for time-varying betas on the industry portfolios. The F-tests for 22 of the 25 portfolios produce p-values below 0.05, and a joint Bonferroni test strongly rejects the hypothesis that the three-factor betas are constant. Compared with our tests in Table III, this is consistent with the observation of Fama and French (1997) that the betas of industries vary over time more dramatically than portfolios sorted on size and book/market.

The portfolio excess returns are regressed on a constant and the three FF factors, and a t-test is conducted for the hypothesis that the intercept is equal to zero. Like the size and book/market portfolios, this test produces little evidence against the hypothesis that the FF variables can unconditionally price the 25 industry portfolios and fixed-weight combinations of their returns; only five of 25 p-values are less than 0.05.

We regress the portfolio excess returns on the three FF factors and the vector of lagged instruments. The F-test for the hypothesis that the vector of instruments may be excluded from the regression produces 25 p-values; all are less than 0.01. When we allow for both time-varying betas and time-varying alphas and test the hypothesis that the alphas are constant, we find 24 of the 25 p-values are below 0.01. In summary, the industry portfolio evidence against the FF three-factor model is even more striking than is the evidence based on the book/market portfolios.

We repeat our tests of the EGB four-factor model using the industry portfolios in place of the size- and book/market-sorted portfolios. We find slightly weaker evidence of time-varying betas and alphas here than in the other portfolio design. Still, the tests reject the hypotheses of constant betas or alphas. The cross-sectional regression analysis produces results generally similar to those described earlier.

C. Size, Book-to-Market, and Momentum Portfolios

Fama and French (1996) found that their three-factor model was most seriously challenged by the "momentum" anomaly described by Jegadeesh and Titman (1993). This is the observation that portfolios of stocks with relatively high returns over the past year tend to have high future returns. To see if our results are sensitive to portfolios grouped on momentum, we obtain data from Carhart, et al. (1996).[17] In each month t, Carhart et al. (1996) group the common stocks on the CRSP tape into thirds according to three independent criteria, producing 27 individual portfolio return series. The grouping criteria are (1) market equity capitalization, (2) the ratio of book equity to market equity, and (3) the past return for months $t - 2$ to $t - 12$. The data are available for the same sample period as our previous analysis, so we can conduct a controlled experiment by using the same lagged instrument data.

Conducting the tests for time-varying betas as in Table III, we find strong evidence that the betas on the FF factors vary with the lagged instruments. The largest of the 27 p-values from the F-tests is 0.029. Examining the alphas as in Table IV, we find that the unconditional alphas are larger than in the original 25 portfolios, consistent with the findings of Fama and French (1996). They are as large as -11 percent per year. Testing for zero unconditional alphas using F tests, 16 of the 27 p-values are less than 0.05 and the Bonferroni p-value is less than 0.001. Testing for constant alphas in conditional models with time-varying betas, the largest of the 27 p-values is less than 0.001.

We examine cross-sectional regressions and find, similarly to Table V, that the results are consistent with those using the other portfolio designs. When the fitted conditional expected return is used alone in the cross-sectional regressions, its t-ratio varies between 7.9 and 8.3. When all four variables are used, the t-ratio for fitted expected return remains strong, between 7.5 and 8.4.

D. Data Mining

The issue of data mining has been raised in previous studies, both in connection with the size and book/market effects in the cross section of stock returns and in connection with the lagged instruments in the time series of returns (e.g., Lo and MacKinlay (1990), Black (1993), Breen and Korajczyk (1994), Foster, Smith, and Whaley (1997)). With data mining, a chance correlation in the data may be "discovered" to be an interesting economic phenomenon. An empirical regularity that is dredged from the data by chance is not expected to hold up outside of the sample that generated it. Since many researchers use the same data in asset pricing studies, a collective form of data mining is a severe risk. Of particular concern here is the extent to which our results may be an artifact of data mining.

Although we can not rule out a potential data mining bias in our results, we have reasons to suspect this is not a serious problem. There have been out-of-sample studies that help to mitigate concerns about data mining in

---

[17] These data are courtesy of Mark Carhart, to whom we are grateful.

Conditioning Variables and the Cross Section of Stock Returns 1353

the cross-sectional analysis of book/market. For example, Chan, Hamao, and Lakonishok (1991) and Fama and French (1998) find book/market effects in the cross section of average returns in Japan and other countries. Davis, Fama, and French (1998) extend the results in U.S. data back to 1929. Barber and Lyon (1997) find the effects in a sample of U.S. firms that were not used by Fama and French in their original (1992) study.

There is also out-of-sample evidence that helps to mitigate concerns about data mining in the time-series predictive ability of the lagged instruments. The lagged Treasury bill rate, for example, was noted by Fama and Schwert (1977). If its explanatory power was a statistical fluke, it should not have remained a potent predictor, as it has, in more recent samples. Pesaran and Timmerman (1995) present an analysis of the ability of a set of lagged instruments, similar to ours, to predict returns in periods after they were discovered and promoted in academic studies.

We have an additional reason to believe that our results are not an artifact of data mining. Even if the lagged instruments are dredged from the data in previous studies, they are selected primarily for their ability to predict stock returns over time. We can think of no reason that a spurious time-series correlation with returns should produce a spurious ability to explain the cross-section of portfolio returns.

VI. Concluding Remarks

Previous studies identify predetermined variables with some power to explain the time series of stock and bond returns. This paper shows that loadings on the same variables also provide significant cross-sectional explanatory power for stock portfolio returns. We use time-series loadings on the lagged variables to conduct powerful tests of empirical models for the cross section of stock returns. We reject the three-factor model advocated by Fama and French (1993) even in a sample of equity portfolios similar to the one used to derive their factors. We also reject the four-factor model advocated by Elton, Gruber, and Blake (1995). The results are robust to variations in the empirical methods, and to a variety of portfolio grouping procedures.

Our focus is not to search for alternatives to the factors advocated by Fama and French and Elton, Gruber, and Blake. Our evidence does suggest that applications of these factor models should control for time-varying betas, and that doing so provides some improvement. However, even conditional versions of the models, with time-varying betas, appear to leave significant predictable patterns in their pricing errors.

Loadings on lagged instruments reveal information that is not captured by these popular factors for the cross section of expected returns. This should raise a caution flag for researchers who would use the FF or EGB factors in an attempt to control for systematic patterns in risk and expected return. The results carry implications for risk analysis, performance measurement, cost-of-capital calculations, and other applications.

Appendix A

A. Efficient Weighting of Fama–MacBeth Regressions

Consider a pooled time-series and cross-section regression model written similarly to Litzenberger and Ramaswamy (1979), as:

$$Y = X\gamma + U, \qquad E(UU') = \Omega, \tag{A1}$$

where Y is a $TN \times 1$ vector. The first N rows are the returns of N stock portfolios for the first month of the sample, followed by the second month, and so on. There are T months in the sample. The $TN \times K$ matrix X has a column of ones, and the remaining columns are the predetermined portfolio attributes, such as the betas, book-to-market ratios, or the fitted expected returns, stacked up like the dependent variable. The $K \times 1$ vector of parameters, γ, are the average risk premiums that we wish to estimate. The $TN \times TN$ covariance matrix is Ω.

Under standard assumptions the generalized least squares estimator is best linear unbiased and is given as:

$$\gamma_{GLS} = (X'\Omega^{-1}X)^{-1}X'^{-1}Y. \tag{A2}$$

We make the assumption that the error terms are uncorrelated over time but correlated across stock portfolios with a general $N \times N$ covariance matrix at date t, Ω_t. This implies that Ω has a block diagonal structure with the Ω_t's on the diagonal. Using this structure in equation (A2), the GLS estimator may be written as:

$$\gamma_{GLS} = (\Sigma_t X_t' \Omega_t^{-1} X_t)^{-1} (\Sigma_t X_t' \Omega_t^{-1} Y_t), \tag{A3}$$

where Σ_t indicates summation over time. Now, the GLS version of the Fama–MacBeth coefficient for month t may be written as

$$\gamma_{FM,t} = (X_t' \Omega_t^{-1} X_t)^{-1} (X_t' \Omega_t^{-1} Y_t). \tag{A4}$$

From equations (A3) and (A4) we can express the full GLS estimator as:

$$\gamma_{GLS} = \Sigma_t \{ (\Sigma_t X_t' \Omega_t^{-1} X_t)^{-1} (X_t' \Omega_t^{-1} X_t) \} \gamma_{FM,t}, \tag{A5}$$

which shows that the efficient GLS estimator is a weighted average of the Fama–MacBeth estimates with the weights for each date t proportional to $X_t' \Omega_t^{-1} X_t$.

From equation (A4) we calculate the variance of a typical Fama–MacBeth estimator for month t as $E\{(\gamma_{FM,t} - \gamma)(\gamma_{FM,t} - \gamma)'\} = (X_t'\Omega_t^{-1}X_t)^{-1}$. Thus, we can see that the efficient weighting of the FM estimators in equation (A5) places more weight on the months with lower variance estimators, and less weight on a month with an imprecise estimate.

The standard errors of the GLS estimates may be obtained from the usual expression: $Var(\gamma_{GLS}) = (\Sigma_t X_t'\Omega_t^{-1}X_t)^{-1}$. However, when N is large relative to T (e.g., a standard design with a rolling regression estimator of beta, $N=25$, and $T=60$), full covariance GLS is not practical. In such cases weighted least squares (WLS) may be used, which assumes that Ω_t is diagonal. But with a diagonal covariance matrix the standard error estimator does not capture the strong cross-sectional dependence in stock returns, which motivates the original Fama–MacBeth approach.

Fama and MacBeth (1973) suggest calculating a standard error for the overall coefficient from the time-series of the monthly estimates. The variance of the sample mean of the monthly estimates is $(1/T)(T^{-1}\Sigma_t\gamma_{FM,t}^2 - (T^{-1}\Sigma_t\gamma_{FM,t})^2)$, which assumes that the model errors are uncorrelated over time but cross-sectionally dependent.

We provide a simple modification of the approach of Fama and MacBeth for the efficient-weighted FM estimator. We first express $\gamma_{GLS} = \Sigma_t w_t \gamma_{FM,t}$, where the weight for each month, $w_t = ((\Sigma_t X_t'\Omega_t^{-1}X_t)^{-1}(X_t'\Omega_t^{-1}X_t))$. The variance may be obtained as

$$s^2(\gamma_{GLS}) = (1/T)(T^{-1}\Sigma_t w_t^2 \gamma_{FM,t}^2 - (T^{-1}\Sigma_t w_t \gamma_{FM,t})^2). \qquad (A6)$$

The standard errors for the efficient-weighted FM estimator are thus obtained by replacing $\gamma_{FM,t}$ by $w_t\gamma_{FM,t}$ in the usual calculation.

B. A Measure of Explanatory Power

The simplest measure of explanatory power in a regression model is the coefficient of determination, or R-squared. However, the usual R-squared is difficult to interpret in a cross-sectional regression for stock returns because of the strong cross-sectional dependence. Consider a standard, GLS-transformed version of equation (A1):

$$\tilde{Y} = \tilde{X}\gamma + \tilde{U}, \qquad E(\tilde{U}\tilde{U}') = I_{TN}, \qquad (A7)$$

where $\tilde{Y} = \Omega^{-1/2}Y$, $\tilde{X} = \Omega^{-1/2}X$, and $\tilde{U} = \Omega^{-1/2}U$. In the transformed model there is no time-series or cross-sectional correlation of the errors, and the errors are homoskedastic. We use the R-squared of the transformed model as a measure of the overall explanatory power. The GLS R-squared is advocated by Kan and Zhang (1999) for cross-sectional regressions. The overall measure here gives equal weight to the time-series and cross-sectional dimensions of explanatory power in the transformed model. Within a given cross section, observations with larger standard deviations are given smaller weight. In the time-series dimension, months with larger standard deviations of the error term are given smaller weights.

Define demeaned variables, $y_{it} = Y_{it} - N^{-1}T^{-1}\Sigma_t\Sigma_i Y_{it}$, demeaned using the grand mean, taken over both the time series and cross section. Stack the y_{it}'s into a $TN \times 1$ vector, y, using the same convention as before. The demeaned predictors x and the residuals, u, are defined analogously. A simple expression for the overall R-square measure uses the $TN \times 1$ vectors y, x, and u. The R-square for the transformed model (A7) is $1 - (u'\Omega^{-1}u)/(y'\Omega^{-1}y)$. Substituting the expression for γ_{GLS} with the assumed diagonal structure of Ω, we can express the R-square in terms of the demeaned N-vectors of the original data:

$$R^2 = (\Sigma_t y_t' \Omega_t^{-1} x_t)(\Sigma_t x_t' \Omega_t^{-1} x_t)^{-1}(\Sigma_t x_t' \Omega_t^{-1} y_t)/(\Sigma_t y_t' \Omega_t^{-1} y_t). \qquad (A8)$$

In a typical application such as ours, full covariance GLS is not practical. We therefore use a weighted least squares version of equation (A8). We replace Ω_t with a diagonal matrix using an estimate of the variance of the residuals for each test asset in a given month on the diagonals.

Appendix B

A. Book-to-Market and Size-Sorted Portfolios

Returns on 25 value-weighted portfolios of the common stock of firms listed on the New York Stock Exchange (NYSE) and covered by COMPUSTAT are formed. Following Dimension Fund Advisors' exclusion criteria, foreign firms, ADRs, and REITs are excluded. Portfolios are formed by ranking firms on their market capitalization (size) in June of each year and the ratio of book value to market value of equity (BE/ME) as of December of the preceding year. The size and BE/ME sorts are independent. Firms are ranked and sorted annually into five groups. Monthly portfolio returns are then computed from July of year $t+1$ to June of $t+2$ for each group. BE is Stockholder's Equity (A216) less Preferred Stock Redemption Value (A56) (or Liquidating Value (A10), or Par Value (A130), depending on availability), plus balance sheet deferred taxes (A35), if available. If Stockholders Equity is not available, it is calculated as Total Common Equity (A60) plus the par value of preferred stock (A130).

B. Industry Portfolios

Monthly returns on 25 portfolios of common stocks are from Harvey and Kirby (1996). The portfolios are value-weighted within each industry group. The industries and their SIC codes are listed in Table BI.

Conditioning Variables and the Cross Section of Stock Returns   1357

Table BI
Standard Industrial Classifications for Industry Portfolios

Number	Industry	SIC Codes
1	Aerospace	372, 376
2	Transportation	40, 45
3	Banking	60
4	Building Materials	24, 32
5	Chemicals/Plastics	281, 282, 286–289, 308
6	Construction	15–17
7	Entertainment	365, 483, 484, 78
8	Food/Beverages	20
9	Healthcare	283, 284, 385, 80
10	Industrial Machinery	351–356
11	Insurance/Real Estate	63–65
12	Investments	62, 67
13	Metals	33
14	Mining	10, 12, 14
15	Motor Vehicles	371, 551, 552
16	Paper	26
17	Petroleum	13, 29
18	Printing/Publishing	27
19	Professional Services	73, 87
20	Retailing	53, 56, 57, 59
21	Semiconductors	357, 367
22	Telecommunications	366, 381, 481, 482, 489
23	Textiles/Apparel	22, 23
24	Utilities	49
25	Wholesaling	50, 51

REFERENCES

Ahn, Seugn C., and C. Gadarowski, 1998, Two-pass cross-sectional regression of factor pricing models: Minimum distance approach, Working paper, Arizona State University.

Bansal, Ravi, and Campbell R. Harvey, 1997, Dynamic trading strategies, Working paper, Duke University.

Banz, Rolf W., 1981, The relationship between return and market value of common stocks, *Journal of Financial Economics* 9, 3–18.

Barber, B. M., and J. D. Lyon, 1997, Firm size, book-to-market ratio and security returns: A holdout sample of financial firms, *Journal of Finance* 52, 875–901.

Basu, Sanjoy, 1977, The investment performance of common stocks in relation to their price-earnings ratios: A test of the efficient markets hypothesis, *Journal of Finance* 32, 663–682.

Becker, C., W. Ferson, D. Myers and M. Schill, 1999, Conditional market timing with benchmark investors, *Journal of Financial Economics* 52, 119–148.

Berk, Jonathan B., 1995, A critique of size-related anomalies, *Review of Financial Studies* 8, 275–286.

Berk, Jonathan B., 1997, Sorting out sorts, Working paper, University of California at Berkeley.

Black, Fischer, 1972, Capital market equilibrium with restricted borrowing, *Journal of Business* 45, 444–455.

Black, Fischer, 1993, Beta and return, *Journal of Portfolio Management* 20, 8–18.

Braun, Phillip, Daniel Nelson, and Alain Sunier, 1995, Good news, bad news, volatility and betas, *Journal of Finance* 50, 1575–1604.

Breeden, Douglas T., 1979, An intertemporal asset pricing model with stochastic consumption and investment opportunities, *Journal of Financial Economics* 7, 265–296.

Breen, William, Lawrence R. Glosten, and Ravi Jagannathan, 1989, Economic significance of predictable variations in stock index returns, *Journal of Finance* 44, 1177–1190.

Breen, William J., and Robert A. Korajczyk, 1994, On selection biases in book-to-market based tests of asset pricing models, Working paper, Northwestern University.

Brennan, M., T. Chordia, and A. Subrahmanyam, 1998, Alternative factor specifications, security characteristics, and the cross-section of expected stock returns, *Journal of Financial Economics* 49, 345–73.

Campbell, John Y., 1987, Stock returns and the term structure, *Journal of Financial Economics* 18, 373–400.

Carhart, Mark M., Robert J. Krail, Ross L. Stevens, and Kelly D. Welch, 1996, Testing the conditional CAPM, Working paper, University of Chicago.

Chamberlain, Gary, and M. Rothschild, 1983, Arbitrage, factor structure and mean variance analysis on large asset markets, *Econometrica* 51, 1281–1304.

Chan, K. C., Nai-fu Chen, and David Hsieh, 1985, An exploratory investigation of the firm size effect, *Journal of Financial Economics* 14, 451–472.

Chan, Louis K.C., Yasushi Hamao, and Josef Lakonishok, 1991, Fundamentals and stock returns in Japan, *Journal of Finance* 46, 1739–1764.

Chan, Louis K. C., Narasimhan Jegadeesh, and Josef Lakonishok, 1995, Evaluating the performance of value versus glamor stocks: The impact of selection bias, *Journal of Financial Economics* 38, 269–296.

Chen, Nai-fu, Richard Roll, and Stephen A. Ross, 1986, Economic forces and the stock market, *Journal of Business* 59, 383–403.

Connor, Gregory, and Robert A. Korajczyk, 1988, Risk and return in an equilibrium APT: Applications of a new test methodology, *Journal of Financial Economics* 21, 255–289.

Daniel, Kent, and Sheridan Titman, 1997, Evidence on the characteristics of cross-sectional variation in stock returns, *Journal of Finance* 52, 1–33.

Davis, James, E. Fama, and Kenneth French, 1998, Characteristics, covariances and average returns: 1929–1997, Working paper, University of Chicago.

Eckbo, Espen, O. Norli, and Ronald Masulis, 1998, Conditional long-run performance following security offering: Is there a new issues puzzle? Working paper, Dartmouth College.

Elton, Edwin J., Martin J. Gruber, and Christopher R. Blake, 1995, Fundamental economic variables, expected returns, and bond fund performance, *Journal of Finance* 50, 1229–1256.

Fama, Eugene F., 1990, Stock returns, expected returns, and real activity, *Journal of Finance* 45, 1089–1108.

Fama, Eugene F., and Kenneth R. French, 1988, Dividend yields and expected stock returns, *Journal of Financial Economics* 22, 3–25.

Fama, Eugene F., and Kenneth R. French, 1989, Business conditions and expected stock returns, *Journal of Financial Economics* 25, 23–50.

Fama, Eugene F., and Kenneth R. French, 1992, The cross-section of expected returns, *Journal of Finance* 47, 427–465.

Fama, Eugene F., and Kenneth R. French, 1993, Common risk factors in the returns on stocks and bonds, *Journal of Financial Economics* 33, 3–56.

Fama, Eugene F., and Kenneth R. French, 1995, Size and book-to-market factors in earnings and returns, *Journal of Finance* 50, 131–155.

Fama, Eugene F., and Kenneth R. French, 1996, Multifactor explanations of asset pricing anomalies, *Journal of Finance* 51, 55–87.

Fama, Eugene F., and Kenneth R. French, 1997, Industry cost of equity, *Journal of Financial Economics* 43, 153–194.

Fama, Eugene F., and Kenneth R. French, 1998, Value versus growth: The international evidence, *Journal of Finance* 53, 1975–1999.

Conditioning Variables and the Cross Section of Stock Returns   1359

Fama, Eugene F., and James D. MacBeth, 1973, Risk, return and equilibrium: Empirical tests, *Journal of Political Economy* 81, 607–636.

Fama, Eugene F., and G. William Schwert, 1977, Asset returns and inflation, *Journal of Financial Economics* 5, 115–146.

Ferson, Wayne E., 1989, Changes in expected security returns, risk and the level of interest rates, *Journal of Finance* 44, 1191–1218.

Ferson, Wayne E., Stephen Foerster, and Donald B. Keim, 1993, Tests of general latent variable models and mean variance spanning, *Journal of Finance* 48, 131–156.

Ferson, Wayne E., and Campbell R. Harvey, 1991, The variation of economic risk premiums, *Journal of Political Economy* 99, 385–415.

Ferson, Wayne, and Robert Korajczyk, 1995, Do arbitrage pricing models explain the predictability of stock returns? *Journal of Business* 68, 309–349.

Ferson, Wayne, Sergei Sarkissian, and Timothy Simin, 1999, The alpha factor asset pricing model: A parable, *Journal of Financial Markets* 2, 49–68.

Ferson, Wayne, and Rudi Schadt, 1996, Measuring fund strategy and performance in changing economic conditions, *Journal of Finance* 51, 425–462.

Ferson Wayne, and Andrew F. Siegel, 1997, The efficient use of conditioning information in portfolios, Working paper, University of Washington.

Foster, F. Douglas, Tom Smith, and Robert E. Whaley, 1997, Assessing goodness-of-fit of asset pricing models: The distribution of the maximal R^2, *Journal of Finance* 52, 591–608.

Ghysels, Eric, 1998, On stable factor structures in the pricing of risk: Do time-varying betas help or hurt?, *Journal of Finance* 53, 549–574.

Gibbons, Michael R., and Wayne E. Ferson, 1985, Tests of asset pricing models with changing expectations and an unobservable market portfolio, *Journal of Financial Economics* 14, 217–236.

Graham, Benjamin, and D. Dodd, 1934, *Security Analysis* (McGraw-Hill, New York).

Hansen, Lars P., and Robert J. Hodrick, 1983, Risk averse speculation in forward foreign exchange markets: An econometric analysis of linear models; in Jacob A. Frenkel, ed.: *Exchange Rates and International Macroeconomics* (University of Chicago Press, Chicago, IL).

Hansen, Lars P., and Scott Richard, 1987, The role of conditioning information in deducing testable restrictions implied by asset pricing models, *Econometrica* 50, 1269–1286.

Hansen, Lars P., and Kenneth Singleton, 1982, Generalized instrumental variables estimation of nonlinear rational expectations models, *Econometrica* 55, 587–613.

Harvey, Campbell R., 1989, Time-varying conditional covariances in tests of asset pricing models, *Journal of Financial Economics* 24, 289–318.

Harvey, Campbell R., and Chris Kirby, 1996, Analytic tests of factor pricing models, Working paper, Duke University.

Haugen, Robert A., and Nardin L. Baker, 1996, Commonality in the determinants of expected stock returns, *Journal of Financial Economics* 41, 401–440.

Ibbotson Associates, 1998, *Cost of Capital Quarterly 1998 Yearbook* (Ibbotson Associates, Chicago, IL).

Jagannathan, Ravi, Keiichi Kubota, and Y. Takehara, 1998, The relation between labor-income risk and average returns: Empirical evidence for the Japanese stock market, *Journal of Business* 71, 319–347.

Jagannathan, Ravi, and Zhenwu Wang, 1996, The conditional CAPM and the cross-section of expected returns, *Journal of Finance* 51, 3–54.

Jagannathan, Ravi, and Zhenwu Wang, 1998, Asymptotic theory for estimating beta pricing models using cross-sectional regressions, *Journal of Finance* 53, 1285–1309.

Jegadeesh, Narasimhan, and Sheridan Titman, 1993, Returns of buying winners and selling losers, *Journal of Finance* 48, 65–91.

Jensen, Michael C., 1968, The performance of mutual funds in the period 1945–1964, *Journal of Finance* 23, 389–446.

Kan, Raymond, and Chu Zhang, 1999, Two-pass tests of asset pricing models with useless factors, *Journal of Finance* 54, 203–235.

Keim, Donald B., and Robert F. Stambaugh, 1986, Predicting returns in the bond and stock markets, *Journal of Financial Economics* 17, 357–390.

Kim, Dongcheol, 1995, The errors in the variables problem in the cross-section of expected stock returns, *Journal of Finance* 50, 1605–1634.

Kim, Dongcheol, 1997, A reexamination of firm size, book-to-market, and earnings price in the cross-section of expected stock returns, *Journal of Financial and Quantitative Analysis* 32, 463–489.

Kothari, S. P., and Jay Shanken, 1997, Book-to-market time series analysis, *Journal of Financial Economics* 44, 169–203.

Kothari, S. P., Jay Shanken, and Richard G. Sloan, 1995, Another look at the cross-section of expected stock returns, *Journal of Finance* 50, 185–224.

Lakonishok, Josef, Andrei Shliefer, and Robert W. Vishny, 1994, Contrarian investment, extrapolation and risk, *Journal of Finance* 49, 1541–1578.

Lehmann, Bruce N., and David M. Modest, 1988, The empirical foundations of the arbitrage pricing theory, *Journal of Financial Economics* 21, 213–254.

Litzenberger, Robert H., and Krishna Ramaswamy, 1979, The effect of personal taxes and dividends on capital asset prices: Theory and empirical evidence, *Journal of Financial Economics* 7, 163–195.

Lo, Andrew, and A. Craig MacKinlay, 1990, Data snooping biases in test of financial models, *Review of Financial Studies* 3, 175–208.

MacKinlay, A. Craig, 1995, Multifactor models do not explain deviations from the CAPM, *Journal of Financial Economics* 38, 3–28.

Merton, Robert C., 1973, An intertemporal capital asset pricing model, *Econometrica* 41, 867–887.

Pagan, Adrian, 1984, Econometric issues in the analysis of regressions with generated regressors, *International Economic Reveiew* 25, 221–247.

Pannikkath, Sunil K., 1993, Dynamic asset pricing and the cross-section of expected stock returns, Working paper, Washington University in St. Louis.

Pesaran, M., and Alan Timmermann, 1995, Predictability of stock returns: Robustness and economic significance, *Journal of Finance* 50, 1201–1228.

Pontiff, Jeffrey, and Lawrence Schall, 1998, Book-to-market as a predictor of market returns, *Journal of Financial Economics* 49, 141–160.

Roll, Richard, 1977, A critique of the asset pricing theory's tests—part I: On past and potential testability of the theory, *Journal of Financial Economics* 4, 349–357.

Roll, Richard, 1995, Value and growth; in T. Daniel Coggin and Frank J. Fabozzi, eds.: *Handbook of Equity Style Management* (Association for Investment Management and Research, Charlottesville, VA).

Rosenberg, Barr, and Vinay Marathe, 1979, Tests of capital asset pricing hypotheses, *Research in Finance* 1, 115–223.

Ross, Stephen A., 1976, The arbitrage theory of capital asset pricing, *Journal of Economic Theory* 13, 341–360.

Shanken, Jay, 1990, Intertemporal asset pricing: An empirical investigation, *Journal of Econometrics* 45, 99–120.

Shanken, Jay, 1992, On the estimation of beta pricing models, *Review of Financial Studies* 5, 1–34.

Shanken, Jay, and Mark I. Weinstein, 1990, Macroeconomic variables and asset pricing: estimation and tests, Working paper, University of Rochester.

Sharpe, William. F., 1964, Capital asset prices: A theory of market equilibrium under conditions of risk, *Journal of Finance* 19, 425–442.

Stambaugh, Robert F., 1998, Predictive regressions, Working paper, Wharton School.

White, Halbert, 1980, A heteroskedasticity-consistent covariance matrix estimator and a direct test for heteroskedasticity, *Econometrica*, 48, 817–838.

Part V
Tests of the Linear Risk Tolerance CAPMs

[11]

Journal of Financial Economics 6 (1978) 11–32. © North-Holland Publishing Company

GENERALIZED TWO PARAMETER ASSET PRICING MODELS

Some Empirical Evidence

Robert R. GRAUER*

Simon Fraser University, Burnaby, British Columbia V5A 1S6, Canada

Received September 1976, revised version received November 1977

A series of empirically refutable generalized two parameter asset pricing models that linearly relate risk and return are identified for the power (and quadratic) utility members of the linear risk tolerance capital asset pricing models. Five possible power utility models and the mean variance model are tested to determine whether one model might provide a more accurate description of security pricing. The major empirical result is that the data do not allow us to distinguish between the models.

1. Introduction

Empirical testing of positive theories of asset pricing has overwhelmingly rested on the mean variance capital asset pricing model (MV CAPM). However, the model itself has received less than full-fledged support in recent empirical tests [Friend and Blume (1970), Black, Jensen, and Scholes (1972), Blume and Friend (1973), Fama and MacBeth (1973)]. Moreover, from a theoretical view it suffers from a number of deficiencies. These two factors have led several authors [Roll (1973), Hakansson (1974a), Rubinstein (1975), Kraus and Litzenberger (1972, 1975), Grauer (1976a)] either implicitly or explicitly to suggest that one of the power linear risk tolerance (LRT) utility functions may form the basis of a better positive theory of capital asset pricing.

While most of the empirical work on CAPMs has been conducted from an MV perspective, it has not been exclusively concerned with tests of that model. Some, in fact, has compared an equilibrium formulation of the 'growth optimal' model [which is consistent with logarithmic utility (only) and which, in turn, can be viewed as a special case of the power LRT models]. Employing weekly stock market data from the 1960s Roll (1973) found the two models to be empirically indistinguishable. Essentially the same conclusion was reached by

*The research was supported by grants from the Canada Council, Simon Fraser University's President's Research Fund and the University of Toronto Commerce and Finance Research Fund. I thank M. Brennan, P. Halpern, J. Herzog, R. Koopman, A. Kraus, J. MacBeth, J. Watts, and the referee, E. Fama, for helpful comments, and D. McKinnon and R. Whaley for computational assistance. Naturally I fall heir to any errors or omissions.

Fama and MacBeth (1974) and Kraus and Litzenberger (1975) employing monthly data.

In a somewhat different context Friend and Blume (1975) working with a continuous-time form of the MV CAPM and employing cross-sectional data on household asset holdings reported that the data are consistent with an aggregate utility function on the order of $-w^{-1}$. Grauer (1976b), however, conducted tests of the various power LRT models based on their ability to predict the relative market values of portfolios of common stocks and bonds and found that none of the models fared very well.

In this paper conventional econometric techniques are employed to determine whether one of the power LRT CAPMs or generalized two parameter models may provide a better positive theory of security pricing than does the MV CAPM. Alternatively the research can be viewed as an attempt to measure an 'aggregate' or 'composite' individual's utility function based on the observed market behavior of investors. Section 2 reviews the LRT CAPMs; shows how the power LRT CAPMs can be formulated as empirically refutable generalized two parameter models, where risk (appropriately measured) and expected return are linearly related; and presents a hypothetical example to develop more fully the theory and to illustrate how the empirical tests will be conducted. Section 3 presents the testable implications of the generalized two parameter models. Section 4 contains an explanation of the empirical methodology. Section 5 reports and discusses the results of the empirical tests. Section 6 contains a summary and conclusions.

2. Theoretical background

2.1. Empirically testable generalized two parameter models derived from the LRT utility functions

By invoking the standard assumptions that borrowing and lending can take place at the riskfree rate, all investments are infinitely divisible and can be sold short, taxes are non-existent, and all investors share homogeneous beliefs and identical decision horizons, we can derive the LRT CAPMs from the LRT utility functions for which the separation property holds, namely:

$$u_i(w) = 1/\gamma(w+a_i)^\gamma, \qquad \gamma < 1, \tag{1}$$

$$u_i(w) = -(a_i-w)^\gamma, \qquad \gamma > 1 \text{ and } a_i \text{ large}, \tag{2}$$

$$u_i(w) = -\exp(a_i w_i), \qquad a_i < 0, \tag{3}$$

where the a_i are allowed to vary among investors to reflect differing degrees of risk aversion, but a common γ value must be shared by all investors.[1]

[1]Quadratic utility is a special case of (2) where $\gamma = 2$ and (1) reduces to $\log(w+a_i)$ when $\gamma = 0$.

A CAPM based on any of the polynomial families of utility functions in (2) (where a family corresponds to a given γ value) will imply that risky assets are inferior goods, while a model based on any of the power families in (1) will imply that risky assets are normal goods. It is this feature of the power families which makes them desirable candidates for study.[2]

Let: z_j be the dollar amount invested in asset j (asset 1 being riskless); w_0 and $w_1 = \Sigma_{j=2}^{J} z_j(r_j - r) + w_0(1+r)$ be initial and end-of-period wealth; r_j, r, and r_M be the rate of return on asset j, the riskless asset and the market portfolio respectively; $u(\cdot)$ be the utility function of a 'composite' individual defined on end-of-period wealth; $u'(\cdot)$ be the first derivative of the utility function; $E(\cdot)$ be the expectation operator; $\text{cov}(\cdot)$ be covariance; and S_{j0} be the aggregate present value of asset j.

In LRT economies, where the aggregation property holds,[3] Rubinstein (1974) has derived a generalized valuation equation equivalent to

$$E(r_j) = r + [E(r_M) - r] \frac{\text{cov}(r_j, u'(w_1))}{\text{cov}(r_M, u'(w_1))}. \tag{4}$$

Eq. (4) provides a general statement of how securities are priced in an LRT economy but it lacks empirical content as it contains unobservable utility information. However, it can be shown to yield empirically refutable results.

Note that, because the 'composite' of all investors holds the unlevered market portfolio, $w_1 = w_0(1 + r_M)$. Assume that tastes are quadratic, then it is well known that (4) reduces to the familiar and empirically testable MV CAPM valuation equation

$$E(r_j) = r + [E(r_M) - r]\beta_j. \tag{5}$$

Now if we restrict attention to any one of the power utility functions in (1), the first derivative of the utility function is given by

$$u'(w_1) = [w_0^c(1 + d + r_M)^c],$$

where $c \equiv \gamma - 1$ and $d \equiv a/w_0$. Substituting this result into (4) yields

---

[2]The power families allow the theorist to bypass the internal logical inconsistencies of a MV model based on normality. Specifically, normality conflicts with the empirical reality of limited liability, or more generally with the idea of finite returns in a finite time period, and with the opportunity for riskless borrowing and lending. On the other hand, to be able to make use of the expected utility theorem with power utility functions it is assumed that the von Neumann–Morgenstern postulates have been modified in such a way as to permit unbounded utility functions.

[3]Rubinstein's aggregation theorem provides alternative sets of sufficient conditions under which equilibrium security rates of return are determined as if there existed only identical individuals whose resources, beliefs, and tastes are composites of the (at least partially) heterogeneous resources, beliefs, and tastes of actual individuals in the economy.

$$E(r_j) = r + [E(r_M) - r] \, Risk_j, \tag{6}$$

where $Risk_j = \text{cov}(r_j, (1+d+r_M)^c)/\text{cov}(r_M, (1+d+r_M)^c)$.

Clearly, different values of c and d yield a whole series of simple empirically testable two parameter valuation equations that linearly relate 'reward' (expected return) to 'risk', but only for the special case of quadratic utility ($c = 1, d = -1$) will the 'risk' measure be the familiar beta coefficient.[4] While the MV CAPM describes how securities are priced in terms of two parameters, expected return and beta, the generalized two parameter models describe how, in given LRT economies including the MV or quadratic utility economy as a special case, securities are priced in terms of two parameters, expected return and Risk. A particularly interesting aspect of the models is that the specific Risk terms implicitly capture the effect of all the relevant moments (and comoments) that determine security pricing whether they are just the mean and variance in a quadratic utility model or all the moments in the power utility models.

2.2. An example involving three risky securities[5]

Before moving to the empirical tests we consider a hypothetical equilibrium example involving three risky securities as a means of demonstrating the efficacy of the research technique and of introducing some further theoretical and empirical considerations that will reduce the area of search for relevant c, d combinations.

Envision the following scenario. All the assumptions of the asset pricing models hold exactly. Investors perceive the ex ante return distribution to be as given in table 1 and can borrow and lend at the same riskless rate of interest. For purposes of illustration assume that everyone has a logarithmic utility function as in (1). In equilibrium each investor will hold the market portfolio of

---

[4]For quadratic utility saying that $d \equiv a/w_0 = -1$ is a notational convenience to emphasize the similarity between the models. As is shown below, for the power utility models, the constant d is a well defined economic quantity that guarantees borrowing and lending cancel in aggregate. In the case of quadratic utility d is not defined but as it is a constant it does not affect the covariance.

[5]The example was constructed: (i) to illustrate the efficacy of the empirical methodology, (ii) to show that beta is not the measure of Risk in a power LRT economy, and (iii) to show that the concept of a zero-beta portfolio is not meaningful if the market portfolio is not MV efficient. In addition, the present draft shows that if the market portfolio is not MV efficient not only does $E(r_z)$ not equal r but the expected returns on zero-beta portfolios are not equal. It has recently come to my attention that in the context of the MV model, Fama (1976), Roll (1977) and Ross (1977) have emphasized the importance of the market portfolio being MV efficient and the idea that $E(r_z)$ does not equal r if the market proxy is not the true market portfolio but is still MV efficient. While the present section was completely independently developed, I have no doubt that their work has influenced my interpretation of the empirical results in section 5. I thank a referee for pointing out Fama's work.

risky assets in conjunction with some combination of the riskless asset. In the example, the equilibrium weights in the market portfolio were calculated to be (0.2613, 0.5774, 0.1613).[6]

Table 1

The ex ante return distribution for individual securities.

Security	Return	State					
		1	2	3	4	5	6
1	$1+r$	1.05	1.05	1.05	1.05	1.05	1.05
2	$1+r_{2S}$	0.	0.	1.5	1.5	1.5	1.5
3	$1+r_{3S}$	1.0	1.0	1.0	1.0	2.5	2.5
4	$1+r_{4S}$	0.6	1.8	0.6	1.8	0.6	1.8
Probability Π_{2S}		0.05	0.05	0.4	0.4	0.05	0.05

Summary statistics

$E(r_2) = 0.35$ Skewness $(r_2) = -2.67$
$E(r_3) = 0.15$ Skewness $(r_3) = +2.67$
$E(r_4) = 0.20$ Skewness $(r_4) = 0.$

Variance–covariance matrix

	2	3	4
2	0.2025	0.0225	0.
3	0.0225	0.2025	0.
4	0.	0.	0.3600

Now suppose that a social scientist did not know that the true process of equilibrium price formation was based on logarithmic tastes but he was supplied with the true ex ante rates of return and asked to determine the pricing process. His first guess might be that the true pricing process is consistent with the MV CAPM. Thus he would run an empirical analogue of (5),

$$\bar{r}_j - r = a_0 + a_1 \, \beta_j (\bar{r}_M - r) + e_j, \tag{7}$$

[6]For the power utility functions the individual's expected utility problem was reformulated as:

$$\text{Max } E \, 1/\gamma \left[\sum_{j=2}^{J} v_j(r_j - r) + 1 + r \right]^{\gamma}, \qquad \gamma < 1,$$
$$\{v_j\}$$

where $v_j = z_j^i/(w_0^i + a_i/(1+r))$, and the i's indicate individuals. The expected utility problem was then solved by numerical analysis employing an alogrithm by Best (1975). The calculated solutions were (0.564, 1.247, 0.348). Because of the separation property exhibited by the LRT utility functions everyone holds the same mix of risky assets, which in equilibrium must be the market portfolio. Forming the set of ratios, $[v_k/\Sigma_{j=2}^{J} v_j]$, yielded the equilibrium market value weights.

where $\bar{r}_j$ denotes average return on asset j [but is actually identical to $E(r_j)$ in the example]. If the MV CAPM correctly describes the process a_0 will equal 0 and $a_1 = 1.$[7] Clearly something is amiss as the slope of the regression shown in the first panel of fig. 1 is negative. (Note this result occurs with ex ante data and involves none of the other econometric difficulties we face in the empirical section of the paper.)

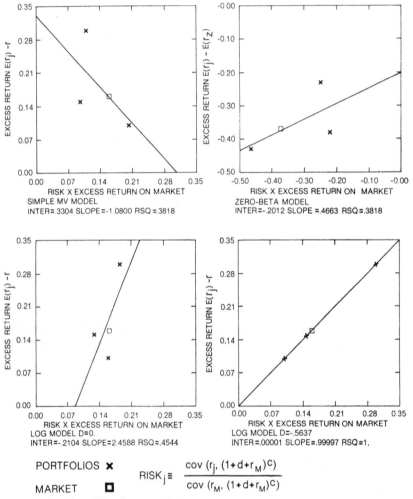

Fig. 1. Estimated risk return tradeoffs for the three risky security example.

[7]In the example the risk measure is multiplied by the excess return so that the true slope and intercept will lie on the 45° line in fig. 1. In the empiricial work that follows we revert to the more standard form of regressing the excess return on the risk measure so that the results may be more easily compared to previous work on the MV CAPM.

Given the result of his first test our social scientist may find the zero-beta model an appealing alternative to the simple MV model because of its apparent empirical success in explaining security pricing in terms of a two factor model,

$$r_j = a_j + b_j r_M + (1 - b_j) r_z + e_j$$

(as in Black, Jensen, and Scholes), and/or because he may feel that the equilibrium pricing process he has been asked to study really involves rigidities in borrowing and lending. Thus, defining the return on the minimum variance zero-beta portfolio, z, as r_z, he would run the cross sectional regression

$$\bar{r}_j - \bar{r}_z = a_0 + a_1 \beta_j (\bar{r}_M - \bar{r}_z) + e_j,$$

an empirical analogue of Black's (1972) zero-beta pricing equation,

$$E(r_j) = E(r_z) + (E(r_M) - E(r_z)) \beta_j.$$

In one sense this formulation might be considered to provide a better explanation of security pricing than does the simple MV model (because at least the model is consistent with a positive 'reward' to 'risk' tradeoff) until a closer inspection of the second panel of fig. 1 indicates that all the securities, including the market portfolio are plotting in the third quadrant!

This plot can be explained by recalling some of the properties of the zero-beta model. Black (1972), Merton (1972), and Sharpe (1970) have shown that the MV feasible frontier can be generated by two basic (but non-unique) MV frontier portfolios. In an equilibrium context we can choose the two portfolios to be the MV efficient market portfolio and the zero-beta portfolio, or alternatively stated the zero-beta MV feasible frontier portfolio (which incidentally is inefficient). Black noted two other properties of zero-beta portfolios: (i) $r \leq E(r_z) < E(r_M)$, and (ii) every portfolio with beta equal to zero must have the same expected return.

Because the zero-beta model has been derived in an MV framework it may be that all of the properties of the model do not hold in a non MV model. What perhaps is surprising is that in the example: (i) The market portfolio is not MV efficient. [Given the same opportunity set, including unrestricted borrowing and lending at the same riskless rate, and an economy populated by MV decision-makers the market value weights would have been (0.6582, 0.1519, 0.1899)]. (ii) For the minimum variance zero-beta portfolio that we calculated, $E(r_z) > E(r_M)$.[8] (iii) For the three zero-beta portfolios calculated in this example,

---

[8] The return on the zero-beta portfolio was calculated from the formula $r_{zs} = x_j r_{js} + x_k r_{ks}$, $j, k = 1, 2, 3$, where $x_j = -\beta_k/(\beta_j - \beta_k)$ and $x_k = (1 - x_j)$. The minimum variance zero beta portfolio was taken to be the one that minimized σ_z^2 when the σ_z^2's from the j, k pairs (1, 2), (1, 3), (2, 3) were compared. In an MV model this selection process may not have identified the MV zero-beta feasible frontier portfolio (discussed below) but it does not affect the observations made in the text.

the $E(r_z)$ values were $(0.582, -0.915, 0.245)$. [For the corresponding MV economy the three $E(r_z)$ values were equal to five percent as they should have been, given the equal riskless borrowing and lending opportunity.] (iv) The minimum variance zero-beta portfolio that we calculated did not exhibit limited liability in two of the six states of nature.

The moral to be derived from this example is straightforward: a test of whether $E(r_z) - r = 0$ is a joint test of the assumption that there in unrestricted riskless borrowing and lending at the known rate r and that the market portfolio is MV efficient. In the empirical work that follows we generalize the concept of the zero-beta portfolio to zero-risk portfolios, with returns r_0, and it is well to remember that tests of whether $E(r_0) - r = 0$ are joint tests of whether there is unrestricted borrowing and lending and that the composition of the market portfolio is consistent with the specific tastes under consideration.

Our social scientist, who is now batting 0 for 2, decides to fit the empirical analogue of (6) for various values of c and d, i.e.,

$$\bar{r}_j - r = a_0 + a_1 \, Risk_j \, (\bar{r}_M - r) + e_j. \tag{8}$$

Setting $c = -1$ and $d = 0$ is equivalent to testing a 'growth optimal' model or to assuming that 'composite' investors have utility functions of the form $\ln(w_1)$. Even though the example was constructed where everyone had logarithmic utility, the regression results are less than satisfactory, as is shown in the third panel of fig. 1. However, with $c = -1$ and $d = -0.5637$, the fourth panel indicates that the fit is essentially perfect. Immediately the question arises: Why is $d = -0.5637$? The answer is found in the market clearing condition for the riskless asset. In these models, with no exogenous government or foreign sector, borrowing must equal lending or the net supply of the riskless asset must be zero for (6) to hold; a condition satisfied if $d = -0.5637$.[9]

This example clearly illustrates that it is empirically possible to infer investor tastes from observed market return data. But it also indicates that one may have

---

[9]Formally consider the market clearing conditions in an economy where there are I identical individuals. For the $j-1$ risky assets, the conditions for demand to equal supply are

$$Iv_j w_0(1 + d/(1+r)) = S_{j0}, \qquad j = 2, \ldots, J,$$

while for the riskless asset, demand equals supply (equals zero):

$$Iw_0\left[1 - (1 + d/(1+r)) \sum_{j=2}^{J} v_j\right] = S_{10} = 0.$$

In the example

$$\sum_{j=2}^{J} v_j = 2.159.$$

Substituting into the above equation and simplifying, confirms that the market clears if $d = -0.5637$.

to be close to clairvoyant to find the correct c, d combination. As computational costs prevent testing an unlimited number of possibilities we apply an eclectic mix of theoretical argument and empirical evidence to narrow the area of search.

Although all the empirical work has tested the MV CAPM in a multiperiod setting or, more accurately, as if it held period by period in a multiperiod setting, it is really a single period equilibrium model.[10] While we cannot completely circumvent the single period equilibrium context, if we narrow the search to the power utility models where a_i (and hence d) ≤ 0, not only will risky assets be normal goods but the models will be consistent with individual multiperiod discrete-time decision making. The next step is to provide some idea as to the range of d values. The example showed that d may be quite large and negative. This could be interpreted as implying that the 'composite' individuals had a positive subsistence level of wealth. However, there is a lower bound on how negative d may be. If $u(w_1) = 1/\gamma(w_1 + a)^\gamma$, then $(w_0 + a/(1+r))$ must be positive and thus $d \equiv a/w_0 > -(1+r)$. On the other hand, Hakansson (1974b) has shown, in a multiperiod discrete-time wealth accumulation model, that if the utility function of terminal wealth is continuous monotone-increasing and bounded both above and below by an appropriately shifted power function, then the induced utility of wealth functions will converge to a power function of the form $1/\gamma w^\gamma$, which implies that d is close to zero.[11] A corroborating empirical finding by Friend and Blume (1975) was that the assumption of constant proportional risk aversion ($d = 0$) is as a first approximation a fairly accurate description of the market place.

Given these arguments, the strong theoretic appeal of a generalized logarithmic utility function, and the desirability of investigating a wide range of tastes, the following six c, d combinations were chosen for further study:

c	d	Utility function	Functional form
1	-1	quadratic	$u(w_1) = -(a - w_1)^2$
-0.5	0	square root	$u(w_1) = -2w_1^{1/2}$
-1	0	logarithmic	$u(w_1) = \ln w_1$
-1	-0.5	generalized logarithmic	$u(w_1) = \ln(w_0(0.5 + r_M))$
-2	0	negative one power	$u(w_1) = -w_1^{-1}$
-6	0	negative five power	$u(w_1) = -\frac{1}{5} w_1^{-5}$

[10]It is emphasized that we are working with a discrete-time model. Merton (1973) has derived a continuous-time MV CAPM independent of the specific form of investor tastes. In discrete-time the picture is not so clear. The reader is referred to Hakansson (1974a, 1977) for a discussion of the multiperiod nature of the MV CAPM in discrete time.

[11]In a multiperiod setting the assumption that d is a constant, while it may provide a good approximation, is an approximation nonetheless for two reasons. First, d may vary with a change in tastes. For example, with the war babies becoming of investment age we may find that aggregate investment behaviour exhibits a lower degree of risk aversion. Second, with no change in tastes, the value of a in the induced utility functions of wealth will change over time as investors move closer to their decision horizons. [See for example Hakansson (1974a).]

3. Testable implications

As stated earlier, the research is designed to determine whether one of the power LRT CAPMs may provide a better positive theory of security pricing than does the MV CAPM. Eq. (6) provides a framework for generating testable hypotheses about specific models and estimating the 'true' c, d parameters. The estimation and testing aspects are intimately entwined in the sense that, if we cannot reject hypotheses concerning a specific model, then that specific model provides a possible 'true' set of c, d values. We might then argue that from the set of non-rejected models the one that yields the closest parameter estimates is the 'true' model.

Specifically, we begin with eq. (6) and generalize it to encompass a zero-risk form. Define r_0 as the return on a zero-risk portfolio, then (6) becomes

$$E(r_j) = E(r_0) + (E(r_M) - E(r_0))\, Risk_j. \qquad (9)$$

Generalizing the results of Black, Jensen and Scholes and Fama and MacBeth (1973) we propose the following stochastic generalization of (9),

$$r_{jt} = a_{0t} + a_{1t} Risk_{jt} + a_{2t} Risk_{jt}^2 + e_{jt}, \qquad (10)$$

where a_{0t} and a_{1t} are permitted to vary from period to period and are meant to be the counterparts of $E(r_0)$ and $E(r_M) - E(r_0)$ respectively, while the $Risk_j^2$ term is added to test for linearity.

In the context of the MV CAPM, Fama and MacBeth (1974) have shown that the least squares estimates a_{0t} and a_{1t} from the cross-sectional regressions (10) (with $Risk_j^2$ suppressed and $Risk_j = Beta_j$) are proxies for r_{zt} and $r_{Mt} - r_{zt}$ respectively. It is easy to verify that this result generalizes and that in general the estimates a_{0t} and a_{1t} (with $Risk_j^2$ suppressed) correspond to the return on a zero-risk portfolio, r_{0t}, and the excess return $r_{Mt} - r_{0t}$ respectively.

In sum, with the stochastic generalization of (6) and (9) that is given by (10), the testable implications of the generalized two parameter models are: (i) linearity, (ii) a positive expected return–risk tradeoff, and (iii) the joint hypothesis that there are no restrictions on riskless borrowing or lending and the composition of the market portfolio is consistent with the specific tastes under consideration. Finally, the model which most closely supports linearity, $a_{2t} = 0$, a positive risk–return tradeoff, $a_{1t} > 0$, and the joint hypothesis that there are no restrictions on riskless borrowing or lending and the composition of the market portfolio is consistent with the specific tastes under consideration, $a_{0t} = r_t$ and $a_{1t} = r_{Mt} - r_t$, will be taken to be the 'true' model.

4. Methodology

4.1. The general approach

The difficulties in testing the simple MV two parameter model (5) have been well documented.[12] Clearly we face the same difficulty with the generalized risk measures employed in this paper. The first and most obvious problem is that the models are stated in ex ante terms while empirical work must be concerned with ex post data. Thus, it is assumed that investors correctly assess return distributions so that the data observed ex post are drawings from the ex ante distributions assessed by investors. The second problem is closely related to the first but more subtle. Basically it is an 'errors in variables' problem, caused from having to estimate the true risk measures, that may cause the slope of the estimated risk-reward tradeoff to be downward biased. Almost all the empirical studies have employed a grouping technique to circumvent this problem.

In this paper the actual method employed is similar to that employed by Fama and MacBeth (1973). Three periods are used to construct a time series of risk return data needed to test the LRT CAPMs: a formation period (to group securities into portfolios based on individual security risk measures), an estimation period (to re-estimate the individual security risk measures used in calculating the portfolio risk measures), and a test period (over which the portfolio returns and risk measures are calculated). The tests themselves are conducted by running a series of cross-sectional regressions on the time series of portfolio returns and risk measures to determine if one of the 'risk–return' tradeoffs in (6) holds.

4.2. The details

The monthly data used in the tests were taken from a merged University of Chicago Center for Research in Security Prices (CRSP) and Compustat data base. The monthly returns on the market portfolio were taken to be Fisher's Arithmetic Performance Index. The proxy for the riskfree rate was the one month rate on U.S. Treasury Bills subsequent to 1941 and the monthly rate on Bankers' Acceptances prior to 1941.

For each of the 6 models rates of return and risk measures were generated for that model's set of 20 (risk measure) ranked portfolios. The following steps were undertaken:

(1) In each year for which there were at least 36 observations from the previous 60 months (the formation period), at least 36 observations from the

---

[12]See Jensen (1972b) for a summary of the research. Blume (1970), Friend and Blume (1970), Miller and Scholes (1972), Black, Jensen and Scholes (1972), Blume and Friend (1973), Roll (1973) and Fama and MacBeth (1973) have originated and developed the econometric procedures we employ here.

subsequent 60 months (the estimation period), and at least 1 observation from the 12 months subsequent to the estimation period (the test period), the 6 risk measures for each stock were calculated over both the formation and estimation periods. (The first formation and estimation periods were only 48 months long and the first test period 24 months long so that two more years of risk return data could be generated.)

(2) The stocks were then ranked from largest to smallest for each of the 6 risk measures calculated in the formation period.

(3) Twenty portfolios were selected for each of the 6 risk measures by assigning the highest 5 percent of the ranked stocks to portfolio 1, the next 5 percent to portfolio 2, and so on. [More accurately, if n stocks were available for selection in year t, $n/20$ stocks were assigned to each of the 20 portfolios. The remainder from $j = $ mod $(n, 20)$ was distributed such that one extra stock was included in each of the first j portfolios.]

(4) Over the 12 month test period, for each of the 6 sets of 20 portfolios, monthly returns and the corresponding monthly portfolio risk measures were calculated as the averages of the returns (in the test period) and the risk measures (calculated over the estimation period) of the individual securities contained in the portfolios in each month. Thus in the event of the delisting of a stock in some month during the test period the portfolio return and risk measures were calculated as averages of the stocks remaining in the portfolio.

(5) Steps 1 to 4 were repeated for each year until January 1966 so that 6 sets of monthly returns on 20 portfolios were created for the 456 month period from January 1934 to December 1971.

For each of the 6 sets of 20 portfolios in each month of the period from January 1934 to December 1971, a cross-sectional regression of the form

$$r_{pt} = a_{0t} + a_{1t}Risk_{pt} + a_{2t}Risk_{pt}^2 + e_{pt}, \qquad p = 1, ..., 21, \qquad (11)$$

was run in two forms with $Risk_p^2$ included and excluded. (The market portfolio provided the twenty-first observation.) The 456 month time-series of data on the a_{it}'s provided input for the tests. The tests on the individual models were conducted using simple t tests while the Hotelling T^2 test was employed in order to determine whether the models differed.

5. Results

Table 2 shows a profile of the risk–return characteristics of selected portfolios. To save space only the statistics for the 1934–71 period are shown for all 6 models. For the MV model the statistics for two half periods and the 1935–6/68 period (studied by Fama and MacBeth) are presented for comparative purposes. The table shows that for any particular model the average returns do not differ appreciably over the range of risk measures.

Table 2

Expected return–risk profile for twenty-one portfolios.[a]

	1	2	3	4	5	6	7	8	9	10	11	12	13	14	15	16	17	18	19	20	21
Mean variance model 1/34 to 12/71																					
Mean risk	1.440	1.304	1.254	1.188	1.137	1.086	1.038	1.007	0.965	0.958	0.917	0.905	0.874	0.813	0.803	0.697	0.707	0.647	0.587	0.488	1.000
Mean rate of return	0.017	0.015	0.014	0.016	0.015	0.014	0.015	0.013	0.013	0.015	0.013	0.013	0.012	0.013	0.011	0.013	0.013	0.013	0.010	0.009	0.013
Mean variance model 1/34 to 12/52																					
Mean risk	1.445	1.292	1.258	1.170	1.089	1.058	1.005	0.976	0.904	0.897	0.854	0.845	0.794	0.718	0.716	0.613	0.624	0.595	0.527	0.416	1.000
Mean rate of return	0.019	0.017	0.016	0.020	0.017	0.015	0.017	0.015	0.013	0.017	0.015	0.015	0.014	0.013	0.011	0.014	0.015	0.013	0.010	0.009	0.016
Mean variance model 1/53 to 12/71																					
Mean risk	1.435	1.315	1.249	1.206	1.186	1.114	1.071	1.037	1.026	1.020	0.981	0.965	0.954	0.908	0.890	0.782	0.790	0.700	0.646	0.561	1.000
Mean rate of return	0.014	0.012	0.013	0.013	0.013	0.013	0.012	0.011	0.014	0.013	0.012	0.011	0.010	0.013	0.012	0.012	0.010	0.013	0.009	0.010	0.011
Mean variance model 1/35 to 6/68																					
Mean risk	1.441	1.302	1.256	1.190	1.142	1.088	1.033	1.000	0.957	0.947	0.911	0.895	0.864	0.809	0.791	0.692	0.690	0.623	0.568	0.457	1.000
Mean rate of return	0.018	0.016	0.016	0.018	0.017	0.015	0.016	0.014	0.014	0.016	0.014	0.013	0.013	0.013	0.012	0.013	0.012	0.014	0.010	0.010	0.014
Square root utility model 1/34 to 12/71																					
Mean risk	1.436	1.300	1.253	1.207	1.125	1.089	1.054	0.998	0.990	0.933	0.939	0.897	0.871	0.826	0.800	0.724	0.700	0.659	0.592	0.493	1.000
Mean rate of return	0.016	0.015	0.015	0.017	0.015	0.013	0.014	0.013	0.014	0.014	0.014	0.012	0.013	0.012	0.011	0.012	0.013	0.013	0.010	0.009	0.013
Logarithmic utility model 1/34 to 12/71																					
Mean risk	1.433	1.293	1.268	1.205	1.125	1.091	1.054	0.986	0.998	0.951	0.924	0.907	0.871	0.825	0.795	0.730	0.701	0.661	0.597	0.495	1.000
Mean rate of return	0.016	0.015	0.014	0.016	0.016	0.014	0.014	0.013	0.014	0.014	0.013	0.013	0.013	0.012	0.011	0.012	0.013	0.013	0.010	0.009	0.013
Generalized logarithmic utility model 1/31 to 12/71																					
Mean risk	1.432	1.298	1.251	1.200	1.141	1.099	1.049	0.997	0.985	0.948	0.934	0.908	0.886	0.841	0.799	0.743	0.711	0.670	0.597	0.514	1.000
Mean rate of return	0.016	0.014	0.016	0.015	0.015	0.015	0.014	0.013	0.014	0.013	0.014	0.013	0.014	0.012	0.011	0.012	0.012	0.013	0.011	0.009	0.013
Negative one utility model 1/34 to 12/71																					
Mean risk	1.434	1.291	1.265	1.196	1.140	1.094	1.053	0.991	0.990	0.950	0.930	0.909	0.883	0.819	0.812	0.726	0.709	0.659	0.598	0.504	1.000
Mean rate of return	0.016	0.014	0.015	0.016	0.016	0.014	0.014	0.013	0.014	0.013	0.013	0.013	0.013	0.012	0.011	0.012	0.013	0.013	0.010	0.009	0.013
Negative five utility model 1/34 to 12/71																					
Mean risk	1.424	1.280	1.265	1.188	1.138	1.101	1.063	1.008	0.987	0.948	0.920	0.917	0.901	0.855	0.794	0.774	0.730	0.680	0.615	0.529	1.000
Mean rate of return	0.016	0.014	0.016	0.015	0.015	0.014	0.015	0.013	0.013	0.013	0.013	0.013	0.015	0.013	0.012	0.012	0.012	0.013	0.010	0.010	0.013

[a]The first 20 portfolios were formed on the basis of risk groupings. The twenty-first portfolio is this study's proxy for the market portfolio – Fisher's Arithmetic Performance Index.

As expected, the six models differed somewhat in the assignment of securities to the 20 portfolios, but not dramatically so. Moreover, the average rates of return ranked by portfolio are similar, but slight differences exist there as well. Finally, the risk measures generated from the various models, while similar in magnitude, reveal that the more risk averse utility functions assign higher risk values to low (risk) ranked portfolios than do their less risk averse counterparts.

Table 3 contains the data for testing the major implications of the asset pricing models. The table contains statistics for 7 time periods, the 6 risk measures, and the 2 versions of test equation (11). Panel A suppresses the $Risk_p^2$ term while panel B reports the results for (11) itself. For each period and each model the table shows: $\bar{a}_j$, the average of the month-by-month regression coefficient estimates, a_{jt}; $s(a_j)$, the standard deviation of the monthly estimates; and $\bar{R}_t^2$ and $s(R_t^2)$, the mean and standard deviation of the month-by-month coefficients of determination, R_t^2, which are adjusted for degrees of freedom. Finally, t-statistics for testing the hypothesis that $\bar{a}_j = 0$ (or some other value) are presented. The t-statistics are of the form:

$$t(d_j) = (\bar{d}_j/s(d_j))\sqrt{(n)},$$

where d_{jt} is the deviation of a_{jt} from zero (or r or $r_M - r$ as the case may be) and n is the number of months in the period, which is also the number of estimates d_{jt} used to compute $\bar{d}_j$ and $s(d_j)$. As is always the case in the asset pricing literature, we caution the reader that, because the underlying variables are most likely not normally distributed, care should be taken not to interpret the results of the t-tests too literally.

5.1. Tests of the major hypotheses of the generalized two parameter models

We consider the three testable implications of the models: (i) linearity, (ii) positive expected return–risk tradeoffs, and (iii) the joint hypothesis that there are no restrictions on riskless borrowing or lending and that the composition of the market portfolio is consistent with the specific tastes under consideration, in order.

Linearity.   For each model the test of linearity is fundamental. It is equivalent to testing whether the composition of the market portfolio is consistent with investment decisions generated by the specific tastes under consideration. If the linearity hypothesis is rejected for the MV model we can conclude that the market portfolio (or more accurately market portfolio proxy) is not MV efficient. For the power models rejection of linearity implies that the market portfolio is not priced as if all investors were driven by the specific type of utility function being assumed and that the market for borrowing and lending does not clear.

The $t(a_2)$ values in table 3 panel B indicate that a_2 is not significantly different from zero in any but the 6/1943–52 subperiod for the MV, square root, and logarithmic utility models. Thus, we cannot reject the hypothesis of linearity for any of the models.

Positive risk–return tradeoff. To provide a viable positive theory of security pricing the models should, at a minimum, exhibit a positive risk–return tradeoff. But the reader is cautioned that this hypothesis is intimately related to linearity. Roll (1977, p. 136) points out that in the MV model if the market portfolio is known to be MV efficient then linearity and a positive risk–return tradeoff are both implied. Almost the same result holds for the power models. If we know that the market portfolio is consistent with (say) logarithmic utility decision-making and also know the d value that guarantees market clearing in the bond market then linearity and a positive risk–return tradeoff obtains. However, if we are studying a world where there is some exogenous supply of the riskless asset so that borrowing and lending among investors does not cancel any generalized logarithmic model will predict the correct relative market value weights but it will not necessarily lead to a positive linear risk–return tradeoff. (Note the numerical example illustrates exactly this phenomenon.) The results in panel A of table 3 show that there is a positive tradeoff for all the models except in the 1953–6/62 subperiod for the MV, square root, and logarithmic models. But the slope is too 'flat' in all cases.

Joint hypothesis: *No restrictions on borrowing or lending and composition of the market portfolio is consistent with the specific tastes under consideration.*[13] In the ex ante example it was shown that one could infer the true process of price determination by finding the exact risk–return tradeoff that matched (9). In a similar manner the empirical test of whether $E(a_{0t}) = r_t$ is the crucial test in attempting to determine which of the 6 models best fits the historic record. We may concentrate on testing whether the average intercept differs from the average risk-free rate because it can be shown that (from the nature of the construction of the market index and the properties of ordinary least squares regression) a test of the hypothesis that $E(a_{0t}) = r_t$ is simultaneously a test of the hypothesis that $E(a_{1t}) = E(r_{Mt}) - r_t$. [See Kraus and Litzenberger (1976, p. 1097).[14]] In particular, we employ the values of the intercept to help identify which of the 6 models may provide the more accurate description of security pricing.

---

[13]In the MV model Roll (1977) also recognizes the nature of the joint hypothesis. But he is critical of joint hypotheses in general.

[14]The equality of the tests holds strictly only if the market proxy return is constructed to be the average of the n stock returns in the sample. As this is not exactly the case in the current study we present the slope values and t-statistics in table 3 but concentrate on the intercept test in the text.

Table 3

Summary results for the regression.

$$r_{pt} = a_{0t} + a_{1t}Risk_{pt} + a_{2t}Risk^2 + e_{pt}$$

Panel A

	$\bar{a}_0$	$\bar{a}_1$	$\bar{a}_2$	$\bar{d}_0{}^a$	$\bar{d}_1{}^b$	$s(a_0)$	$s(a_1)$	$s(a_2)$	$s(d_0)$	$s(d_1)$	$t(a_0)$	$t(a_1)$	$t(a_2)$	$t(d_0)$	$t(d_1)$	$\bar{R}^2$	$s(R^2)$
MV model																	
1934 –71	0.00739	0.00646	—	0.00579	−0.00528	0.034	0.064	—	0.034	0.034	4.66	2.15	—	3.64	−3.30	0.26	0.25
1934 –6/43	0.00502	0.01209	—	0.00487	−0.00537	0.043	0.100	—	0.043	0.042	1.26	1.30	—	1.22	−1.35	0.29	0.28
7/1943–52	0.00960	0.00441	—	0.00887	−0.00848	0.028	0.052	—	0.027	0.029	3.73	0.90	—	3.45	−3.14	0.27	0.25
1953 –6/72	0.01189	−0.00008	—	0.01010	−0.00865	0.025	0.034	—	0.025	0.025	5.03	−0.02	—	4.26	−3.63	0.22	0.24
7/1962–71	0.00303	0.00941	—	−0.00068	0.00136	0.037	0.053	—	0.037	0.037	0.88	1.91	—	−0.20	0.39	0.24	0.24
1934 –52	0.00731	0.00825	—	0.00687	−0.00692	0.036	0.079	—	0.036	0.036	3.08	1.57	—	2.90	−2.88	0.28	0.27
1953 –71	0.00746	0.00467	—	0.00471	−0.00364	0.032	0.044	—	0.032	0.032	3.54	1.59	—	2.22	−1.72	0.23	0.24
1935 –6/68	0.00678	0.00801	—	0.00545	−0.00490	0.032	0.061	—	0.032	0.033	4.23	2.61	—	3.40	−2.98	0.26	0.26
Square root model																	
1934 –71	0.00725	0.00656	—	0.00565	−0.00518	0.034	0.065	—	0.034	0.034	4.57	2.15	—	3.55	−3.24	0.26	0.25
1934 –6/43	0.00399	0.01306	—	0.00384	−0.00439	0.043	0.102	—	0.043	0.043	0.99	1.37	—	0.95	−1.09	0.30	0.28
7/1943–52	0.00961	0.00433	—	0.00887	−0.00856	0.027	0.053	—	0.025	0.028	3.74	0.88	—	3.46	−3.21	0.27	0.25
1953 –6/72	0.01201	−0.00019	—	0.01021	−0.00876	0.025	0.034	—	0.025	0.025	5.13	−0.06	—	4.35	−3.71	0.21	0.24
7/1962–71	0.00339	0.00904	—	−0.00032	0.00098	0.37	0.052	—	0.037	0.037	0.99	1.84	—	−0.09	0.29	0.24	0.24
1934 –52	0.00680	0.00870	—	0.00636	−0.00647	0.036	0.081	—	0.036	0.036	2.84	1.62	—	2.66	−2.68	0.28	0.27
1953 –71	0.00770	0.00442	—	0.00494	−0.00389	0.032	0.044	—	0.032	0.032	3.69	1.51	—	2.36	−1.85	0.23	0.24
1935 –6/68	0.00667	0.00808	—	0.00534	−0.00482	0.032	0.062	—	0.032	0.033	4.19	2.61	—	3.35	−2.98	0.26	0.25
Logarithmic model																	
1934 –71	0.00716	0.00664	—	0.00557	−0.00510	0.034	0.065	—	0.034	0.035	4.49	2.19	—	3.48	−3.15	0.26	0.26
1934 –6/43	0.00436	0.01265	—	0.00421	−0.00481	0.044	0.100	—	0.044	0.044	1.06	1.35	—	1.03	−1.16	0.30	0.28
7/1943–52	0.00919	0.00479	—	0.00846	−0.00810	0.027	0.053	—	0.027	0.028	3.62	0.97	—	3.33	−3.05	0.27	0.26
1953 –6/72	0.01195	−0.00013	—	0.01015	−0.00870	0.025	0.034	—	0.025	0.025	5.08	−0.04	—	4.30	−3.66	0.21	0.25
7/1962–71	0.00316	0.00927	—	−0.00055	0.00121	0.037	0.053	—	0.037	0.037	0.92	1.88	—	−0.16	0.35	0.24	0.23
1934 –52	0.00677	0.00872	—	0.00633	−0.00645	0.036	0.080	—	0.036	0.037	2.81	1.65	—	2.63	−2.63	0.29	0.27
1953 –71	0.00755	0.00457	—	0.00480	−0.00375	0.032	0.044	—	0.032	0.032	3.60	1.55	—	2.27	−1.78	0.23	0.24
1935 –6/68	0.00652	0.00823	—	0.00519	−0.00468	0.032	0.062	—	0.032	0.033	4.05	2.68	—	3.22	−2.83	0.26	0.26

Generalized logarithmic model

1934 –71	0.00697	–0.00680	0.00537	–0.00494	0.034	0.065	0.034	0.035	4.34	2.23	3.33	–3.03	0.26	0.25
1934 –6/43	0.00502	–0.01182	0.00486	–0.00563	0.043	0.100	0.043	0.044	1.23	1.26	1.20	–1.38	0.31	0.28
7/1943–52	0.00811	–0.00587	0.00738	–0.00701	0.029	0.055	0.028	0.030	3.04	1.14	2.77	–2.51	0.27	0.26
1953 –6/72	0.01155	–0.00028	0.00975	–0.00829	0.026	0.034	0.026	0.026	4.83	0.09	4.06	–3.43	0.20	0.23
7/1962–71	0.00322	–0.00921	–0.00050	0.00115	0.037	0.053	0.037	0.037	0.93	1.86	–0.14	0.33	0.24	0.23
1934 –52	0.00657	–0.00885	0.00612	–0.00632	0.037	0.081	0.032	0.037	2.70	1.66	2.52	–2.56	0.29	0.27
1953 –71	0.00738	–0.00475	0.00463	–0.00357	0.032	0.045	0.032	0.032	3.49	1.61	2.18	–1.68	0.22	0.23
1935 –6/68	0.00621	–0.00850	0.00488	–0.00441	0.032	0.062	0.032	0.033	3.85	2.73	3.02	–2.67	0.26	0.25

Minus one power utility model

1934 –71	0.00701	–0.00679	0.00541	–0.00495	0.034	0.064	0.034	0.034	4.42	2.25	3.40	–3.08	0.25	0.26
1934 –6/43	0.00435	–0.01261	0.00420	–0.00484	0.043	0.099	0.043	0.043	1.08	1.36	1.04	–1.20	0.30	0.28
7/1943–52	0.00874	–0.00525	0.00800	–0.00763	0.028	0.054	0.028	0.029	3.35	1.05	3.08	–2.81	0.27	0.26
1953 –6/72	0.01175	–0.00008	0.00995	–0.00849	0.025	0.034	0.025	0.025	4.96	0.02	4.19	–3.56	0.20	0.24
7/1962–71	0.00321	–0.00922	–0.00051	0.00116	0.036	0.053	0.036	0.036	0.94	1.87	–0.15	0.34	0.24	0.23
1934 –52	0.00654	–0.00893	0.00610	–0.00624	0.036	0.080	0.036	0.037	2.73	1.69	2.55	–2.56	0.29	0.27
1953 –71	0.00748	–0.00465	0.00472	–0.00367	0.032	0.044	0.032	0.032	3.58	1.58	2.25	–1.75	0.22	0.23
1935 –6/68	0.00626	–0.00848	0.00493	–0.00442	0.032	0.062	0.032	0.033	3.88	2.73	3.05	–2.68	0.26	0.26

Minus five power utility model

1934 –71	0.00639	–0.00733	0.00479	–0.00441	0.036	0.067	0.036	0.035	3.84	2.33	2.88	–2.67	0.25	0.25
1934 –6/43	0.00333	–0.01342	0.00317	–0.00404	0.046	0.104	0.046	0.044	0.77	1.37	0.74	–0.98	0.29	0.28
7/1943–52	0.00745	–0.00644	0.00672	–0.00645	0.030	0.057	0.030	0.031	2.66	1.21	2.40	–2.20	0.27	0.26
1953 –6/72	0.01177	–0.00007	0.00997	–0.00850	0.025	0.034	0.026	0.026	4.94	0.02	4.17	–3.53	0.20	0.23
7/1962–71	0.00301	–0.00941	–0.00070	0.00136	0.037	0.054	0.037	0.037	0.87	1.88	–0.20	0.39	0.24	0.23
1934 –52	0.00539	–0.00993	0.00494	–0.00524	0.039	0.084	0.039	0.038	2.10	1.79	1.93	–2.08	0.28	0.27
1953 –71	0.00739	–0.00474	0.00464	–0.00357	0.032	0.045	0.032	0.032	3.48	1.60	2.18	–1.67	0.22	0.23
1935 –6/68	0.00553	–0.00911	0.00421	–0.00380	0.034	0.065	0.034	0.034	3.29	2.82	2.50	–2.24	0.25	0.25

continued overleaf...

Panel B

$$r_{pt} = a_{0t} + a_{1t}Risk_{pt} + a_{2t}Risk_{pt}^2 + e_{pt}$$

	$\bar{a}_0$	$\bar{a}_1$	$\bar{a}_2$	$\bar{d}_0{}^a$	$\bar{d}_1{}^b$	$s(a_0)$	$s(a_1)$	$s(a_2)$	$s(d_0)$	$s(d_1)$	$t(a_0)$	$t(a_1)$	$t(a_2)$	$t(d_0)$	$t(d_1)$	$\bar{R}^2$	$s(R^2)$
MV model																	
1934 –71	0.00331	0.01521	−0.00448	0.00171	0.00347	0.068	0.157	0.076	0.068	0.145	1.03	2.06	−1.25	0.53	0.51	0.29	0.25
1934 –6/43	0.00950	0.00130	0.00592	0.00935	−0.01615	0.067	0.174	0.084	0.067	0.151	1.51	0.08	0.75	1.49	−1.14	0.32	0.28
7/1943–52	−0.00481	0.03640	−0.01672	−0.00555	0.02352	0.062	0.162	0.080	0.063	0.145	−0.82	2.39	−2.24	−0.95	−1.73	0.31	0.26
1953 –6/62	−0.00914	0.00650	−0.00361	−0.00735	−0.00207	0.045	0.109	0.056	0.044	0.101	−2.19	0.64	−0.69	1.77	−0.22	0.26	0.23
7/1962–71	−0.00061	0.01665	−0.00351	−0.00432	0.00860	0.091	0.175	0.082	0.091	0.172	−0.07	1.02	−0.46	−0.51	0.53	0.27	0.24
1934 –52	0.00234	0.01885	−0.00540	0.00190	0.00368	0.065	0.169	0.083	0.065	0.149	0.54	1.69	−0.99	0.44	0.37	0.31	0.24
1953 –71	0.00427	0.01158	−0.00356	0.00151	0.00326	0.071	0.145	0.070	0.071	0.141	0.90	1.20	−0.77	0.32	0.35	0.26	0.27
1935 –6/68	0.00276	0.01669	−0.00447	0.00143	0.00379	0.063	0.151	0.071	0.063	0.135	0.88	2.22	−1.26	0.46	0.56	0.29	0.26
Square root model																	
1934 –71	0.00210	0.01786	−0.00586	0.00050	0.00612	0.067	0.158	0.075	0.067	0.142	0.67	2.41	−1.68	0.16	0.92	0.28	0.26
1934 –6/43	0.00499	0.01123	0.00088	0.00484	−0.00622	0.069	0.185	0.083	0.069	0.152	0.77	0.65	0.11	0.75	−0.44	0.32	0.28
7/1943–52	−0.00491	0.03652	−0.01684	−0.00564	0.02364	0.062	0.161	0.079	0.062	0.144	−0.85	2.42	−2.29	−0.98	1.76	0.30	0.25
1953 –6/62	0.00963	0.00547	−0.00310	0.00783	0.00310	0.044	0.104	0.054	0.044	0.098	2.34	0.56	−0.61	1.90	−0.34	0.25	0.24
7/1962–71	−0.00130	0.01822	−0.00437	0.00501	0.01017	0.087	0.170	0.079	0.087	0.166	−0.16	1.15	−0.59	−0.61	0.65	0.26	0.24
1934 –52	0.00004	0.02388	−0.00798	−0.00040	0.00871	0.065	0.174	0.081	0.065	0.148	0.01	2.07	−1.48	−0.09	0.89	0.31	0.24
1953 –71	0.00416	0.01185	−0.00374	0.00141	0.00353	0.069	0.141	0.068	0.069	0.136	0.91	1.27	−0.83	0.31	0.39	0.25	0.24
1935 –6/68	0.00211	0.01825	−0.00534	0.00079	0.00534	0.063	0.153	0.071	0.063	0.134	0.68	2.39	−1.51	0.25	0.80	0.28	0.25
Logarithmic model																	
1934 –71	0.00204	0.01796	−0.00593	0.00044	0.00622	0.067	0.159	0.074	0.067	0.141	0.65	2.41	−1.71	0.14	0.94	0.28	0.26
1934 –6/43	0.00453	0.01295	−0.00049	0.00437	−0.00450	0.071	0.194	0.085	0.071	0.155	0.68	0.71	−0.06	0.65	−0.31	0.32	0.28
7/1943–52	−0.00432	0.03468	−0.01564	−0.00506	0.02179	0.060	0.159	0.077	0.060	0.140	−0.77	2.33	−2.18	−0.90	1.66	0.31	0.26
1953 –6/62	0.00972	0.00514	−0.00288	0.00793	−0.00343	0.044	0.104	0.054	0.044	0.098	2.36	0.53	−0.57	1.93	−0.37	0.25	0.24
7/1962–71	−0.00178	0.01909	−0.00473	−0.00549	0.01103	0.086	0.167	0.078	0.086	0.163	−0.22	1.22	−0.65	−0.68	0.72	0.26	0.24
1934 –52	0.00010	0.02381	−0.00806	−0.00034	0.00864	0.066	0.177	0.081	0.066	0.148	0.02	2.03	−1.51	−0.08	0.88	0.31	0.27
1953 –71	0.00397	0.01211	−0.00381	0.00122	0.00380	0.068	0.139	0.067	0.068	0.134	0.88	1.31	−0.86	0.27	0.43	0.25	0.24
1935 –6/68	0.00200	0.01830	−0.00532	0.00067	0.00539	0.062	0.154	0.070	0.062	0.133	0.64	2.38	−1.52	0.22	0.81	0.29	0.26

Generalized logarithmic model

Period																
1934 –71	0.00288	0.01604	−0.00490	0.00128	0.00430	0.072	0.171	0.080	0.072	0.153	0.85	2.01	−1.32	0.38	0.60	0.28	0.25
1934 –6/43	0.00652	0.00971	0.00065	0.00636	−0.00775	0.087	0.222	0.097	0.087	0.187	0.80	0.47	0.07	0.78	−0.44	0.33	0.28
7/1943–52	−0.00378	0.03197	−0.01360	−0.00451	0.01908	0.065	0.170	0.083	0.065	0.151	−0.62	2.00	−1.75	−0.74	1.35	0.31	0.26
1953 –6/62	0.00814	0.00810	−0.00414	0.00635	−0.00047	0.046	0.106	0.056	0.046	0.102	1.89	0.81	−0.79	1.48	−0.05	0.24	0.22
7/1962–71	0.00065	0.01437	−0.00252	−0.00306	0.00632	0.082	0.165	0.078	0.082	0.160	0.08	0.93	−0.35	−0.40	0.42	0.26	0.23
1934 –52	0.00137	0.02084	−0.00647	0.00093	0.00567	0.077	0.198	0.090	0.077	0.170	0.27	1.59	−1.08	0.18	0.50	0.32	0.27
1953 –71	0.00440	0.01124	−0.00333	0.00164	0.00292	0.067	0.138	0.067	0.067	0.134	1.00	1.23	−0.75	0.37	0.33	0.25	0.23
1935 –6/68	0.00092	0.02043	−0.00634	−0.00040	0.00752	0.069	0.169	0.078	0.069	0.148	0.27	2.42	−1.63	−0.12	1.02	0.29	0.25

Minus one power utility model

Period																
1934 –71	0.00293	0.01573	−0.00470	0.00133	0.00399	0.069	0.164	0.077	0.069	0.146	0.91	2.05	−1.31	0.41	0.58	0.28	0.26
1934 –6/43	0.00660	0.00815	0.00190	0.00645	−0.00930	0.076	0.200	0.088	0.076	0.163	0.93	0.44	0.23	0.91	−0.61	0.33	0.28
7/1943–52	−0.00279	0.03062	−0.01322	−0.00353	0.01774	0.065	0.169	0.082	0.065	0.150	−0.46	1.94	−1.73	−0.58	1.26	0.31	0.27
1953 –6/62	0.00890	0.00656	−0.00342	0.00711	−0.00201	0.046	0.108	0.056	0.046	0.103	2.07	0.65	−0.65	1.65	−0.21	0.24	0.23
7/1962–71	−0.00098	0.01759	−0.00405	−0.00470	0.00954	0.084	0.165	0.078	0.084	0.161	−0.13	1.14	−0.56	−0.60	0.63	0.25	0.24
1934 –52	0.00191	0.01939	−0.00566	0.00146	0.00422	0.071	0.185	0.085	0.071	0.157	0.41	1.58	−1.01	0.31	0.41	0.32	0.27
1953 –71	0.00396	0.01208	−0.00374	0.00121	0.00377	0.068	0.139	0.068	0.068	0.135	0.88	1.31	−0.83	0.27	0.42	0.25	0.24
1935 –6/68	0.00264	0.01642	−0.00419	0.00131	0.00351	0.064	0.157	0.073	0.064	0.138	0.82	2.09	−1.15	0.41	0.51	0.28	0.26

Minus five power utility model

Period																
1934 –71	0.00400	0.01290	−0.00305	0.00241	0.00116	0.076	0.175	0.083	0.076	0.160	1.13	1.57	−0.78	0.68	0.15	0.27	0.25
1934 –6/43	0.00766	0.00476	0.00408	0.00751	−0.01269	0.093	0.223	0.101	0.093	0.197	0.88	0.23	0.43	0.86	−0.69	0.31	0.28
7/1943–52	−0.00140	0.02593	−0.01017	0.00213	−0.01304	0.069	0.182	0.092	0.069	0.164	0.22	1.52	−1.18	−0.33	0.85	0.30	0.26
1953 –6/62	0.00805	0.00882	−0.00472	0.00625	0.00025	0.046	0.106	0.055	0.046	0.101	1.88	0.89	−0.91	1.46	0.03	0.24	0.22
7/1962–71	0.00171	0.01211	−0.00139	−0.00200	0.00405	0.087	0.171	0.078	0.087	0.165	0.21	0.76	−0.19	0.25	0.26	0.25	0.22
1934 –52	0.00313	0.01534	−0.00304	0.00269	0.00018	0.082	0.204	0.097	0.082	0.181	0.58	1.14	−0.47	0.49	0.01	0.31	0.27
1953 –71	0.00488	0.01046	−0.00306	0.00213	0.00215	0.069	0.142	0.068	0.069	0.137	1.06	1.11	−0.68	0.46	0.24	0.24	0.22
1935 –6/68	0.00135	0.01858	−0.00507	0.00002	0.00568	0.072	0.172	0.081	0.072	0.153	0.38	2.16	−1.26	0.00	0.74	0.28	0.25

[a] $d_{0t} \equiv a_{0t} - r_t$.
[b] $d_{1t} \equiv a_{1t} - (r_{Mt} - r_t)$.

B

Turning to table 3, it is apparent from the t tests that the hypothesis $E(a_{0t}) = r_t$ must be rejected for all the models except in the first and fourth quarters of the sample period. Therefore, we reject the joint hypotheses that there is riskless borrowing and lending and that the market proxy is consistent with investment decisions determined by any of the LRT CAPMs considered here. But whether one wishes to make a blanket indictment of the LRT CAPMs, based on these results, depends on how close he believes the market proxy is to the true market portfolio. My judgment (strongly bolstered by reading Roll) is that we should be highly skeptical of the results, and further research employing either different data containing a better proxy for the true market portfolio or a different research design is called for before the issue can be settled.

5.2. Do the models differ?

A key part of the research was not only to determine which model might best describe security pricing but also whether the 6 models differed. With even a casual glance at table 3 one is struck by the similarity between the models across all the statistics. But somewhat tenuously we might argue that the more risk-averse models offer the better description of security pricing because the intercepts are smaller, the coefficients on the squared risk term are never significantly different from zero, and the slopes are never negative. (On the other hand, the adjusted coefficients of determination are slightly lower.) Of course the argument would carry more weight if we could establish a statistical difference between the models.

With a large sample it is sometimes possible to detect significant differences between apparently small quantities. The highly significant t-values on the intercept coefficients is a case in point. To determine whether the models differed, we tested for differences in the 6 time series of intercepts generated from eq. (11) (with $Risk^2$ excluded). The tests must allow for the interdependence between the models arising from time dependent measurements. The tests were conducted employing the Hotelling T^2 statistic because it allows for the interdependence between the models induced by time and does not make the strong assumptions regarding the homogeneity of variances and covariances between models as would say a two-way analysis of variance design. [See Morrison (1967, ch. 4).] The results (not shown) revealed no differences between the models. The close similarity of the models may be best described by the fact that the intercepts in panel A of table 3 were correlated on the order of 0.95 to 0.99.

Clearly the tests failed to differentiate between the models. Unfortunately, ambiguity again surrounds any conclusions we may wish to draw. Probably, the majority of researchers would argue that the models are empirically identical, citing either the approximate normality of return distributions or a 'compact return' distribution argument to back up their claim that in the stock market all risk averters are approximately MV decision-makers. On the other hand, one might believe that there is an underlying difference between the models and it is only the particular research design (accentuated by a poor market proxy) that has caused the failure to detect a significant difference between the models. Again, this appears to be an area calling for further research.

6. Summary and conclusions

A series of empirically refutable generalized two parameter asset pricing models that linearly relate risk and return were identified for the power (and quadratic) utility members of the LRT CAPMs. Five possible power utility models and the MV model were tested to determine whether one model might provide a more accurate description of security pricing. Three interrelated hypotheses were tested: linearity, a positive risk–return tradeoff, and a joint hypothesis of no restrictions on riskless borrowing and lending and that the composition of the market portfolio is consistent with decision-making governed by the specific LRT tastes under consideration. All the models passed the first two tests and failed the third. There was a slight indication that the more risk averse models better described security pricing but no statistically significant differences between the 6 models were detected. Finally it was noted (echoing Roll) that any conclusions drawn from the results of the tests should be greeted with a healthy dose of skepticism because the market proxy did not correspond to the true market portfolio.

References

Best, Michael J., 1975, A feasible conjugate direction method to solve linearly constrained optimization problems, Journal of Optimization Theory and Applications 16, July, 25–38.

Black, Fischer, 1972, Capital market equilibrium with restricted borrowing, Journal of Business 45, July, 444–455.

Black, Fischer, Michael C. Jensen and Myron Scholes, 1972, The capital asset pricing model: Some empirical tests, in: Michael C. Jensen, ed., Studies in the theory of capital markets.

Blume, Marshall E., 1970, Portfolio theory: A step towards its practical application, Journal of Business 43, April, 152–173.

Blume, Marshall E. and Irwin Friend, 1973, A new look at the capital asset pricing model, Journal of Finance 28, March, 19–34.

Fama, Eugene F., 1976, Foundations of finance (Basic Books, New York).

Fama, Eugene F. and James D. MacBeth, 1973, Risk, return, and equilibrium: empirical tests, Journal of Political Economy 81, May, 607–636. ·

Fama, Eugene F. and James D. MacBeth, 1974, Long-term growth in a short-term market, Journal of Finance 29, June, 857–885.

Friend, Irwin and Marshall Blume, 1970, Measurement of portfolio performance under uncertainty, American Economic Review 60, September, 561–575.

Friend, Irwin and Marshall Blume, 1975, The demand for risky assets, American Economic Review 65, December, 900–922.

Grauer, Robert R., 1976a, Beta as a measure of risk in linear risk tolerance economies, Finance Working Paper No. 49, Institute of Business and Economic Research, University of California, Berkeley.

Grauer, Robert R., 1976b, The inference of tastes and beliefs from bond and stock market data, Simon Fraser University Department of Economics and Commerce Discussion Paper. Forthcoming in the Journal of Financial and Quantitative Analysis.

Hakansson, Nils H., 1977, The capital asset pricing model: Some open and closed ends, Finance Working Paper No. 22, Institute of Business and Economic Research, University of California, Berkeley, June 1974a, and in: Irwin Friend and James Bicksler, eds., Risk and return in finance, vol. 1 (Ballinger, Cambridge, MA).

Hakansson, Nils H., 1974, Convergence to isoelastic utility and policy in multiperiod portfolio choice, Journal of Financial Economics 1, September, 201–224.

Jensen, Michael C., ed., 1972a, Studies in the theory of capital markets (Praeger, New York).

Jensen, Michael C., 1972b, Capital markets: Theory and evidence, Bell Journal of Economics and Management Science 3, Autumn, 357–398.

Kraus, Alan and Robert Litzenberger, 1975, Market equilibrium in a multiperiod state preference market with logarithmic utility, Journal of Finance 30, December, 1213–1227.

Kraus, Alan and Robert Litzenberger, 1976, Skewness preference and the valuation of risky assets, Research Paper No. 130, Graduate School of Business, Stanford University, December 1972, and Journal of Finance 31, September, 1085–1100.

Merton, Robert C., 1972, An analytic derivation of the efficient portfolio frontier, Journal of Financial and Quantitative Analysis 7, September, 1851–1871.

Merton, Robert C., 1973, An intertemporal capital asset pricing model, Econometrica 41, September, 867–887.

Miller, Merton H. and Myron Scholes, 1972, Rates of return in relation to risk: A reexamination of some recent findings, in: Michael C. Jensen, ed., Studies in the theory of capital markets.

Morrison, Donald F., 1967, Multivariate statistical methods (McGraw-Hill, New York).

Roll, Richard, 1973, Evidence on the growth optimum model, Journal of Finance 28, June, 551–566.

Roll, Richard, 1977, A critique of the asset pricing theory's tests: Part 1 – On past and potential testability of the theory, Journal of Financial Economics 4, March, 129–176.

Ross, Stephen A., 1977, The capital asset pricing model (CAPM): Short-sale restrictions and related issues, Journal of Finance 32, March, 177–183.

Rubinstein, Mark, 1974, An aggregation theorem for securities markets, Journal of Financial Economics 1, September, 225–244.

Rubinstein, Mark, 1976, The strong case for the generalized logarithmic utility model as the premier model of financial markets, Finance Working Paper No. 34, Institute of Business and Economic Research, University of California, Berkeley, February 1975, and Journal of Finance 31, May.

Sharpe, William F., 1970, Portfolio analysis and capital markets (McGraw-Hill, New York).

Part VI
Tests of the Consumption-Based CAPM

[12]

THE JOURNAL OF FINANCE • VOL. XLIV, NO. 2 • JUNE 1989

Empirical Tests of the Consumption-Oriented CAPM

DOUGLAS T. BREEDEN, MICHAEL R. GIBBONS, and
ROBERT H. LITZENBERGER*

ABSTRACT

The empirical implications of the consumption-oriented capital asset pricing model (CCAPM) are examined, and its performance is compared with a model based on the market portfolio. The CCAPM is estimated after adjusting for measurement problems associated with reported consumption data. The CCAPM is tested using betas based on both consumption and the portfolio having the maximum correlation with consumption. As predicted by the CCAPM, the market price of risk is significantly positive, and the estimate of the real interest rate is close to zero. The performances of the traditional CAPM and the CCAPM are about the same.

IN AN INTERTEMPORAL ECONOMY, Rubinstein (1976), Breeden and Litzenberger (1978), and Breeden (1979) demonstrate that equilibrium expected excess returns are proportional to their "consumption betas." This contrasts with the market-oriented capital asset pricing model (hereafter, CAPM) derived in a single-period economy by Sharpe (1964) and Lintner (1965). While tests of the CAPM by Black, Jensen, and Scholes (1972), Fama and MacBeth (1973), Gibbons (1982), and others find a positive association between average excess returns and betas using a proxy for the market portfolio, the relation is not proportional. This paper studies similar empirical issues for the consumption-oriented capital asset pricing model (hereafter, CCAPM).

Even though the relevant market portfolio includes all assets, most empirical research focuses on common stocks for which accurately measured data are available. In contrast, reported consumption data are estimates of the relevant consumption flows, and the data are subject to measurement problems not found with stock indexes. In this paper the tests of the CCAPM incorporate some adjustments for these measurement problems.

The outline of the paper is as follows. Section I provides an alternative derivation of the CCAPM. Section II examines four econometric problems associated with measured consumption: the durables problem, the problem of

*Duke University; Stanford University and visiting the University of Chicago (1988-1989); and University of Pennsylvania, respectively. We are grateful for the comments we have received from seminar participants at a number of universities. Special thanks go to Eugene Fama, Wayne Ferson, Bruce Lehmann, Bill Schwert, Jay Shanken, Kenneth Singleton, René Stulz, and an anonymous referee. Over the years this paper has benefited also from research assistance by Susan Cheng, Hal Heaton, Chi-Fu Huang, Charles Jacklin, and Ehud Ronn. Financial support was provided in part to all authors by the Stanford Program in Finance. Breeden (1981-1982) and Gibbons (1982-1983) acknowledge with thanks financial support provided for this research by Batterymarch Financial Management.

measured consumption as an integral of spot consumption rates, the problem that consumption data are reported infrequently, and the problem of pure sampling error in consumption measures. Time series properties of consumption measures are also discussed in Section II. Section III analyzes the empirical characteristics of estimated consumption betas for various stock and bond portfolios. The composition of the portfolio whose return has the highest correlation with the growth rate of real, per capita consumption is also discussed in Section III. This portfolio is used in some of the tests of the model. Section IV presents empirical tests of the consumption and market-oriented CAPMs based on their implications for unconditional moments. Section V concludes the paper with a review of the results obtained.

I. A Synthesis of the CCAPM Theory

The Rubinstein (1976) derivation of the CCAPM assumes that, over a discrete time interval, the joint distribution of all assets' returns with each individual's optimal consumption is normal. More generally, Breeden and Litzenberger (1978) derive the CCAPM in a discrete-time framework for the *subset of assets* whose returns are jointly lognormally distributed with aggregate consumption. Breeden's (1979) continuous-time derivation of the CCAPM applies instantaneously to all assets, based on the assumption that assets' returns and individuals' optimal consumption paths follow diffusion processes. In all these papers, utility functions are time additive.

Since the CCAPM is well known, a standard review is unnecessary. The following synthesis provides a theoretical basis that is more relevant for the subsequent empirical work. In particular, theoretical predictions are derived for easily estimated models which are based on unconditional moments of returns using discretely sampled data.

Let $\{\tilde{R}_{it}, i = 1, \cdots, M\}$ be the rates of return on risky assets from time $t - 1$ to time t. M may be less than the number of all risky assets in the economy. Let $\tilde{R}_{zt}$ be the rates of return on a portfolio whose return is uncorrelated with the growth rate in aggregate consumption. All individuals are assumed to have time-additive, monotonically increasing, and strictly concave von Neumann-Morgenstern utility functions for lifetime consumption. Identical beliefs, a fixed population with infinite lifetimes, a single consumption good, and capital markets that permit an unconstrained Pareto-optimal allocation of consumption are also assumed. From the first-order conditions for individual k's optimal consumption and portfolio plan, it follows that

$$\mathscr{E}[(\tilde{R}_{it} - \tilde{R}_{zt})[U^{k'}(\tilde{C}_t^k)/U^{k'}(C_{t-1}^k)] \mid \phi_{t-1}] = 0, \forall \ i, k, \qquad (1)$$

where ϕ_{t-1} describes the full information set at time $t - 1$. This relation holds for any sampling interval. This is well known (e.g., see Lucas (1978)).

An individual achieves an optimal portfolio by adjusting the portfolio weights and consumption plans until relation (1) holds for all assets. Breeden and Litzenberger (1978) show that, in a capital market that permits an unconstrained Pareto-optimal allocation of consumption, each individual's consumption at a given date is an increasing function of *aggregate* consumption. Furthermore, each

Empirical Tests of the CCAPM   233

individual's optimal marginal utility of consumption at a given date t is equal to a scalar, a_k, times a monotonically decreasing function of aggregate consumption, $g\,(C_t,t)$, which is identical for all individuals. The assumption that all individuals have the same subjective rate of time preference implies that the time dependence of the aggregate marginal utility function is the same for all dates, so $g\,(C_t,t) = f\,(C_t)$. Thus, in equilibrium in a Pareto-efficient capital market, the growth rate in the marginal utility of consumption would be identical for all individuals and equal to the growth rate in the "aggregate marginal utility" of consumption. That is,

$$\frac{U'(C_t)}{U'(C_{t-1})} = \frac{f(C_t)}{f(C_{t-1})} \cong 1 - [-C_{t-1}f'(C_{t-1})/f(C_{t-1})]c_t^*, \qquad (2)$$

where c_t^* is the growth rate in aggregate consumption per capita and where the approximation follows from a first-order Taylor series. The term in square brackets is aggregate relative risk aversion evaluated at C_{t-1}. If we take relative risk aversion as approximately constant and denote it as b, we can combine (1) with these approximations in (2) and find (ignoring the approximations)[1]

$$\mathscr{E}\{(\tilde{R}_{it} - \tilde{R}_{zt})(1 - b\tilde{c}_t^*)|\phi_{t-1}\} = 0. \qquad (3)$$

Since (3) is zero conditional on any information, it also holds in terms of unconditional expectations:

$$\mathscr{E}\{(\tilde{R}_{it} - \tilde{R}_{zt})(1 - b\tilde{c}_t^*)\} = 0. \qquad (4)$$

The return on an asset may be stated as a linear function of the growth rate in aggregate consumption per capita, c_t^*, plus a disturbance. This disturbance term is assumed to be uncorrelated with $\tilde{c}_t^*$ for a proper subset of assets ($i = 1, \cdots, M$). These conditions, combined with the assumption of constant unconditional consumption betas and alphas, imply

$$\tilde{R}_{it} = \alpha_{ci}^* + \beta_{ci}^*\tilde{c}_t^* + \tilde{u}_{it}^*, \quad \forall i = 1, \cdots, M,$$

$$\mathscr{E}\{\tilde{u}_{it}^*\} = 0 \quad \text{and} \quad \mathscr{E}\{\tilde{u}_{it}^*\tilde{c}_t^*\} = 0, \qquad (5)$$

where $\beta_{ci}^* \equiv \operatorname{cov}(\tilde{R}_{it}, \tilde{c}_t^*)/\operatorname{var}(\tilde{c}_t^*)$, $\alpha_{ci}^* \equiv \mu_i - \beta_{ci}^*\mathscr{E}\{\tilde{c}_t^*\}$, and $\mu_i \equiv \mathscr{E}\{\tilde{R}_{it}\}$. Asterisks indicate parameters in relation to true consumption growth. Later asterisks are removed to indicate parameters in relation to measured consumption growth.

For a zero consumption beta portfolio consisting of just the M assets,

$$\tilde{R}_{zt} = \gamma_0 + \tilde{\mu}_{zt}^*,$$

$$\mathscr{E}\{\tilde{u}_{zt}\} = 0,$$

$$\mathscr{E}\{\tilde{u}_{zt}\tilde{c}_t^*\} = 0. \qquad (6)$$

Substituting the right-hand side (hereafter, RHS) of (5) and (6) into relation (4) gives the CCAPM:

$$\mu_i - \gamma_0 = \gamma_1^*\beta_{ci}^*, \quad \forall i = 1, \cdots, M, \qquad (7)$$

[1] The approximation can be avoided by making an additional distributional assumption that $\operatorname{cov}(\tilde{u}_{it}^*, \tilde{X}_t) = 0$, where $X_t \equiv f(\tilde{c}_t)/f(\tilde{c}_{t-1})$ and $\tilde{u}_{it}^*$ is defined in (5) below. All the following results go through, and $\gamma_1^* \equiv \operatorname{cov}(\tilde{c}_{t1} - \tilde{X}_t)/E(\tilde{X}_t)$. The market price of consumption beta risk, γ_1^*, appears in equation (7) below.

where $\gamma_1^* \equiv b \; \mathrm{var}(\tilde{c}_t^*)/[1 - b\mathscr{E}\,(\tilde{c}_t^*)]$. The market price of consumption beta risk, γ_1^*, increases as the variability of consumption increases. If $[1 - b\mathscr{E}\,(\tilde{c}_t^*)] > 0$ and $\mathscr{E}\,(\tilde{c}_t^*) > 0$, then γ_1^* also increases as relative risk aversion increases.

This model only gives the CCAPM for a proper subset of assets—those assets that have a conditionally linear relation with c_t^* over the measurement interval. Assets which do not satisfy (5) still are priced according to their joint distributions of payoffs with consumption, but higher order co-moments with consumption are required for pricing over discrete intervals. Since in the continuous-time model all assets' returns and consumption are locally jointly normally distributed, the CCAPM applies to all assets as long as returns can be measured over instantaneous intervals. However, since the available data are measured discretely, the CCAPM in (7) is more useful for empirical tests.

In continuous time with time-additive utility, Breeden (1979) demonstrates that Merton's (1973) intertemporal multi-beta asset pricing model is equivalent to a single-beta CCAPM. However, Cornell (1981) emphasizes that the conditional consumption beta in such a representation need not be constant. The tests presented in this paper are tests of restrictions on the unconditional co-moments of assets returns and consumption growth. As Grossman and Shiller (1982) point out, such tests do not ignore Cornell's (1981) concerns about changes in the conditional moments. An advantage of tests based on unconditional moments is that a specification of the changes in conditional moments is not required. To the extent that changes in the conditional moments could be modeled, the resulting tests may be more powerful. For examples of such tests see Gibbons and Ferson (1985), Hansen and Singleton (1983), and Litzenberger and Ronn (1986). Since the CCAPM has predictions for conditional and unconditional expectations, failure to reject the "unconditional CCAPM" is a necessary, but not sufficient, condition for acceptance of the model.

II. Econometric Problems Associated with Measured Consumption

In this section, a distinction is made between the appropriate theoretical definition of aggregate consumption per capita and the consumption reported by the Department of Commerce. Four measurement problems are examined: 1) the reporting of expenditures, rather than consumption, 2) the reporting of an integral of consumption rates, rather than the consumption rate at a point in time, 3) infrequent reporting of consumption data relative to stock returns, and 4) reporting aggregate consumption with sampling error since only a subset of the total population of consumption transactions is measured.

The CCAPM prices assets with respect to changes in aggregate consumption between two points in time. In contrast, the available data on aggregate "consumption" provide total expenditures on goods and services over a period of time. These differences between consumption in theory and its measured counterpart suggest the first two problems. First, goods and services need not be consumed in the same period that they are purchased. Second, measured aggregate consumption is closer to an integral of consumption over a period of time than to "spot" consumption (at a point in time). This second problem creates a "summation bias."

Empirical Tests of the CCAPM 235

While returns on stocks are available on an intraday basis, corresponding consumption data are not available. Currently, only quarterly data are provided back to 1939, and monthly reporting begins in 1959. Infrequent reporting of aggregate expenditures on consumption is the measurement problem analyzed in the third subsection. The fourth subsection demonstrates that sampling error in aggregate consumption does not bias the statistical tests.

A. Description of the Consumption Data

Exploring the empirical implications of the CCAPM for a long sample period requires aggregate consumption data from different sources. The tables in Sections III and IV focus on a time series for consumption that requires "splicing" the data at two points. Each of these three data sources is discussed in turn.

As is discussed later, powerful tests of any asset pricing model require precise estimations for the relevant betas. Precision of the estimators improves if the variability of the consumption measure increases, holding everything else constant. Since consumption was quite variable in the 1930s, we want to include this time period in our empirical work.[2] Unfortunately, aggregate consumption data are not available, except for annual sampling intervals, from 1929 to 1939. However, nominal personal income less transfer payments is available on a monthly basis from the U.S. Department of Commerce,[3] and these income numbers are used to approximate quarterly consumption for this decade.

From 1929 to 1939 a regression of annual consumption data on personal income yields

$$z_{1t} = 0.00186 + 0.56z_{2t} + \hat{v}_t, \qquad R^2 = 0.94, \qquad (8)$$
$$\phantom{z_{1t} =} (0.39) \qquad (11.51)$$

where $z_{1t} \equiv$ annual growth of real nondurables and services consumption per capita, $z_{2t} \equiv$ annual growth of real personal income less transfer payments per capita, and t-statistics are in parentheses. The data for the above regression are deflated by the average level of the Consumer Price Index (CPI) from the U.S. Bureau of Labor Statistics. The population numbers, which are used to calculate per capita values, are from the *Statistical Abstract of the United States* and reflect the resident population of the U.S. The monthly numbers on personal income less transfer payments are used to infer the consumption numbers based on the above regression equation. From these monthly estimates of consumption, quarterly growth rates are constructed.

From 1939 through 1958 the spliced consumption data rely on quarterly expenditures on nondurable goods and services based on national income accounting. From 1939 through 1946, the data are deflated by the average level of the monthly CPI for the relevant quarter. From 1947 through 1958, real consumption data are available from the Commerce Department. Only seasonally

---

[2] There is no doubt that part of the unusual volatility of consumption during the 1930s is due to data construction, not variation in true consumption.

[3] For both the annual and monthly data, see *National Income and Product Statistics of the United States, 1929–46.* This appeared as a supplement to the *Survey of Current Business,* July 1947.

adjusted numbers for consumption are available.[4] Average total U.S. population during a quarter as reported by the Commerce Department is used to calculate the per capita numbers. Various issues of *Business Conditions Digest, Business Statistics*, and *The National Income and Product Accounts of the United States* report the relevant data.

The consumption data from 1959 to 1982 are constructed in essentially the same manner as that from 1947 to 1958.[5] However, since the government started publishing monthly numbers during this latter period, these monthly numbers are used to compute growth in real consumption per capita over a quarter. For example, growth in a first quarter is based on expenditures during March, relative to expenditures during the prior December.

In later sections, the term "spliced" consumption data refers to the data base constructed in the above manner, which combines the quarterly observations on monthly income data from 1929 to 1938, the quarterly consumption expenditures from 1939 to 1958, and the quarterly observations on the monthly consumption expenditures from 1959 to 1982.

For the whole time period (1929–1982), the consumption data are based on expenditures on nondurables plus services, following Hall (1978). This is an attempt to minimize the measurement problem associated with expenditures versus current consumption of goods and services. No attempt is made to extract the consumption flow from durable goods.[6] While monthly sampling of consumption data is available after 1958, most of the tables do not rely on this information. As the sampling interval decreases, "nondurables" become more durable. However, some of the calculations have been repeated using monthly sampling intervals, and these results are summarized in the text and footnotes.

B. Interval versus Spot Consumption (the Summation Bias)

Ignoring other measurement problems, the reported ("interval") consumption rate for a quarter is the integral of the instantaneous ("spot") consumption rates during the quarter. The CCAPM relates expected quarterly returns on assets (e.g., from January 1 to March 31) and the covariances of those returns with the change in the spot consumption rate from the beginning of the quarter to the end of the quarter. This subsection derives the relation between the desired population covariances (and betas) of assets' returns relative to spot consumption changes and the population covariances (and betas) of assets' returns relative to changes in interval consumption. The variance of interval consumption changes is shown to have only two thirds the variance of spot consumption changes, while the autocorrelation of interval consumption is 0.25 due to the integration of spot

---

[4] Since the seasonal adjustment smoothes expenditures, such an adjustment may be desirable if the transformed expenditures better resemble actual consumption. Of course, seasonal adjustment is inappropriate if it removes seasonals in true consumption.

[5] The only exception to this occurs for the population number for December 1978. This number is adjusted from the published tables because there is an obvious typographical error.

[6] Alternative treatments for this measurement problem exist in the literature. For example, Marsh (1981) postulates a latent variable model to estimate the parameters of the CCAPM. A more recent attempt is made by Dunn and Singleton (1986), using an econometric approach that relies on the specification of preferences for the representative economic agent.

Empirical Tests of the CCAPM   237

rates. These latter results are reported by Working (1960) and generalized by Tiao (1972). Similar results on time aggregation have been used in studies of stock prices and corporate earnings (Lambert (1978) and Beaver, Lambert, and Morse (1980)). In an independent and contemporaneous paper, Grossman, Melino, and Shiller (1987) derive maximum-likelihood estimates of CCAPM parameters, explicitly accounting for time aggregation of consumption data. Our bias corrections are much simpler but give similar results.

Without loss of generality, consider a two-quarter period with $t = 0$ being the beginning of the first quarter and $t = T$ being the end of the first quarter. All discussion will analyze annualized consumption rates, so $T = 0.25$ for a quarter. Initially, let the change in the spot consumption rate over a quarter be the cumulative of n discrete changes, $\{\tilde{\Delta}_1^C, \tilde{\Delta}_2^C, \cdots, \tilde{\Delta}_n^C\}$ for the first quarter, and $\{\tilde{\Delta}_{n+1}^C, \tilde{\Delta}_{n+2}^C, \cdots, \tilde{\Delta}_{2n}^C\}$ for the second quarter. That is, $\tilde{C}_T = C_0 + \sum_1^n \tilde{\Delta}_i^C$. Similarly, let the wealth at time T from buying one share of an asset at time 0 (and reinvesting any dividends) equal its initial price plus n random increments $\{\tilde{\Delta}_i^a\}: P_T = P_0 + \sum_i^n \tilde{\Delta}_i^a$.[7]

Changes in consumption, $\tilde{\Delta}_i^C$, are assumed to be homoscedastic and serially uncorrelated. Similar assumptions are made for the asset's return, $\tilde{\Delta}_i^a$, with variance σ_a^2. The contemporaneous covariation of an asset's return with consumption changes is σ_{ac}, and noncontemporaneous covariances are assumed to be zero. The variance of the change in the spot consumption from the beginning of a quarter to the end of the quarter is $\text{var}(\tilde{C}_T - \tilde{C}_0) = \text{var}(\sum_1^n \tilde{\Delta}_i^C) = \sigma_C^2 T$.

The first quarter's *reported* annualized consumption, C_{Q1}, is a summation of the consumption during the quarter, annualized by multiplying by 4 (or $1/T$):

$$C_{Q1} = (1/T) \sum_{j=1}^n C_j \Delta t = (1/T) \sum_{j=1}^n (C_0 + \sum_{i=1}^j \Delta_i^C) \Delta t. \qquad (9)$$

The annualized consumption rate for the second quarter, C_{Q2}, is the same as (9), but with the first summation for j being $n + 1$ to $2n$.

Continuous movements in consumption and asset prices can be approximated by letting the number of discrete movements per quarter, n, go to infinity ($\Delta t \to 0$). Doing this, the change in reported consumption becomes[8]

$$C_{Q2} - C_{Q1} = \int_0^T (t/T)\Delta_t^C \, dt + \int_T^{2T} ((2T - t)/T)\Delta_t^C \, dt. \qquad (10)$$

---

[7] The summation bias is developed for price changes and consumption changes, not rates of return and consumption growth rates. When the prior period's price and consumption are fixed, the results of this section apply. However, in tests involving unconditional moments, the prior period's price and consumption are random. Since it is difficult to derive a closed-form solution for the summation bias in terms of rates, the subsequent analysis ignores this distinction.

[8] To see this, represent C_{Q2} and C_{Q1} as in (9) and take the difference:

$$C_{Q2} - C_{Q1} = (1/T) \left\{ \sum_1^{n+1} \Delta_i^C + \sum_1^{n+2} \Delta_i^C + \cdots + \sum_1^{2n} \Delta_i^C \right\} \Delta t$$

$$-(1/T) \left\{ \sum_1^1 \Delta_i^C + \sum_1^2 \Delta_i^C + \cdots + \sum_i^n \Delta_i^C \right\} \Delta t$$

$$= n^{-1} \{ \Delta_2^C + 2\Delta_3^C + \cdots + (n-1)\Delta_n^C + n\Delta_{n+1}^C + (n-1)\Delta_{n+2}^C + \cdots + \Delta_{2n}^C \}.$$

Letting n become large gives equation (10).

Given the independence of spot consumption change over time, (10) implies that the variance of reported annualized consumption changes is

$$\text{var}(\tilde{C}_{Q2} - \tilde{C}_{Q1}) = \int_0^T ((t/T)^2 \sigma_C^2) \, dt$$

$$+ \int_T^{2T} ((2T - t)/T)^2 \sigma_C^2 \, dt = (2/3)\sigma_C^2 T. \tag{11}$$

Thus, the population variance of reported (interval) consumption changes for a quarter is two thirds of the population variance for changes in the spot consumption from the beginning of a quarter to the end of the quarter. The averaging caused by the integration leads to the lower variance for reported consumption.

Next, consider the covariance of an asset's quarterly return with quarterly changes in the consumption. The covariance of the change in spot consumption from the beginning of a quarter to the end of the quarter with an asset's return over the same period is $\sigma_{aC}T$, given the i.i.d. assumption. With reported, interval consumption data, the covariance can be computed from (10):

$$\text{cov}(\tilde{C}_{Q2} - \tilde{C}_{Q1}, \hat{P}_{2T} - \hat{P}_T) = T^{-1} \int_T^{2T} (2T - t)\sigma_{aC} \, dt = T\sigma_{aC}/2. \tag{12}$$

Thus, from (12) the population covariance of an asset's quarterly return with reported (interval) consumption is half the population covariance of the asset's return with spot consumption changes.

Given (11) and (12), betas measured relative to reported quarterly consumption changes are ¾ times the corresponding betas with spot consumption:

$$\beta_{ac}^{sum} = \frac{(1/2)\sigma_{aC}T}{(2/3)\sigma_C^2 T} = (3/4)\beta_{ac}^{spot}. \tag{13}$$

Since the CCAPM relates quarterly returns to "spot betas," the subsequent empirical tests multiply the mean-adjusted consumption growth rates by ¾ to obtain unbiased "spot betas." The ¾ relation of interval betas to spot betas in (17) is a special case of the multiperiod differencing relation: $\beta_{ac}^{sum} = \beta_{ac}^{spot} [K - (1/2)]/[K - (1/3)]$, where K is the differencing interval. Thus, monthly data sampled quarterly (i.e., $K = 3$) should give interval betas that are $(5/2)/(8/3) = 0.9375$ times the spot betas. When quarterly consumption growth rates are calculated from monthly data, the quarterly numbers are mean adjusted and multiplied by 0.9375.

Although changes in spot consumption are uncorrelated, changes in reported, interval consumption rates have positive autocorrelation. To see this, use (10) to compute the covariance of the reported consumption change from Q1 to Q2 with the reported change from Q2 to Q3, noting that all covariance arises from the time overlap from T to $2T$:

$$\text{cov}(\tilde{C}_{Q3} - \tilde{C}_{Q2}, \tilde{C}_{Q2} - \tilde{C}_{Q1}) = \int_T^{2T} ((t - T)(2T - t)/T^2)\sigma_C^2 \, dt = (1/6)\sigma_C^2 T. \tag{14}$$

The first-order autocorrelation in reported consumption is 0.25 since

$$\rho_1 = \text{cov}(\tilde{C}_{Q3} - \tilde{C}_{Q2}, \tilde{C}_{Q2} - \tilde{C}_{Q1})/\text{var}(\tilde{C}_{Q2} - \tilde{C}_{Q1}) = \frac{(1/6)\sigma_C^2 T}{(2/3)\sigma_C^2 T} = 0.25. \quad (15)$$

By similar calculations, higher order autocorrelation is zero. Table I presents the time series properties of reported *unspliced* quarterly consumption growth rates. First-order autocorrelation of quarterly real consumption growth for the entire 1939–1982 period is estimated to be 0.29, which is insignificantly different from the theoretical value of 0.25 at usual levels of significance. Higher order autocorrelations are not significantly different from zero. Thus, the model for reported consumption is not rejected by the sample autocorrelations.

Monthly growth rates of real consumption from 1959 to 1982 exhibit negative autocorrelation of −0.28, which is significantly different from zero and from the hypothesized 0.25. This may be caused by vagaries such as bad weather and strikes in major industries, which cut current consumption temporarily but are followed by catch-up purchases. Quarterly growth rates in consumption computed from the monthly series again have positive autocorrelation of 0.13, more closely in line with the value 0.0625 (or 1/16) predicted by the summation bias.[9] The longer the differencing interval, the less affected the data are by temporary fluctuations and measurement errors in consumption.

Chen, Roll, and Ross (1986) and Hansen and Singleton (1983) use monthly data on unadjusted consumption growth. Since those data's autocorrelation statistics suggest significant departures from the random-walk assumption, the statistics they present warrant re-examination. The use of larger differencing intervals should be fruitful.

C. Infrequent Reporting of Consumption: The Maximum Correlation Portfolio

Since the returns on many assets are available for a longer time and are reported more frequently than consumption, more precise evidence on the CCAPM can be provided if only returns were needed to test the theory. Fortunately, Breeden's (1979, footnote 8) derivation of the CCAPM justifies the use of betas measured relative to a portfolio that has maximum correlation with growth in aggregate consumption, in place of betas measured relative to aggregate consumption. This result is amplified below, as it is shown that securities' betas measured relative to this maximum correlation portfolio (hereafter, MCP) are equal to their consumption betas divided by the consumption beta of the MCP. If a riskless asset exists, then the consumption beta of the MCP can be changed by adjusting leverage. Our MCP excludes the riskless asset, resulting in a consumption beta of 2.9.

In the following, the first M assets have a linear relation with consumption as in equation (5). The CCAPM holds with respect to these M assets when betas are measured relative to the MCP obtained from these M assets. Second, for *any* *subset N* (where $N \leq M$) of these M assets, the CCAPM holds for that subset when betas are measured relative to the MCP obtained from these N assets.

---

[9] The derivation of this prediction is similar to the derivation of equation (15).

Table I

Time Series Properties of Percentage Changes in Real, Per Capita Consumption of Nondurable Goods and Services

Data are seasonally adjusted as reported by the Department of Commerce in the *Survey of Current Business*. T denotes the number of observations, while $\hat{c}$ and $\widehat{SD}(c)$ are the sample mean and standard deviation, respectively. Under the hypothesis that the observations are serially uncorrelated, the asymptotic standard errors for the sample autocorrelations are $1/\sqrt{T}$, as given by $SD^*(\hat{\rho}_k)$. Under the hypothesis that $\rho_1 = 0.25$ and $\rho_k = 0 \ \forall \ |k| > 1$, $SD(\rho_1)$ and $SD(\rho_k)$ report the asymptotic standard errors using the results of Bartlett (1946). The test statistic for the joint hypothesis that all autocorrelations are zero for lags 1 through 12 is given by Q_{12}, the modified Box-Pierce Q-statistic. Q_{12} is asymptotically distributed as chi-square with 12 degrees of freedom. The p-value is the probability of drawing a Q_{12} statistic larger than the current value under the null hypothesis.

Time Period	T	$\hat{c}$	$\widehat{SD}(c)$	$\hat{\rho}_1$	$\hat{\rho}_2$	$\hat{\rho}_3$	$\hat{\rho}_4$	$\hat{\rho}_8$	SD^* $(\hat{\rho}_k)$	$\widehat{SD}$ $(\hat{\rho}_1)$	$\widehat{SD}$ $(\hat{\rho}_4)$	Q_{12}	p-Value
					Panel A: Quarterly Consumption Data								
39Q2–82Q4	175	0.00543	0.00951	0.29	0.03	−0.00	0.07	0.02	0.08	0.07	0.08	23.93	0.02
39Q2–52Q4	55	0.00665	0.01517	0.30	0.03	−0.04	0.08	0.08	0.13	0.12	0.14	11.26	0.51
53Q1–67Q4	60	0.00463	0.00549	0.21	0.09	0.11	−0.01	−0.22	0.13	0.12	0.14	11.25	0.51
68Q1–82Q4	60	0.00511	0.00487	0.36	0.01	0.26	0.09	−0.31	0.13	0.12	0.14	25.95	0.01
					Panel B: Monthly Consumption Data								
1959–1982	287	0.00178	0.00447	−0.28	−0.02	−0.14	−0.12	−0.19	0.06	0.05	0.06	43.09	0.00
1959–1970	143	0.00199	0.00467	−0.31	−0.11	0.18	−0.08	−0.17	0.08	0.08	0.09	33.49	0.00
1971–1982	144	0.00156	0.00427	−0.24	0.07	0.09	−0.16	−0.16	0.08	0.08	0.09	20.56	0.06
				Panel C: Quarterly Sampling of Monthly Consumption Data									
59Q2–82Q4	95	0.00521	0.00568	0.13	−0.13	0.20	0.04	−0.17	0.10	0.09	0.11	13.42	0.34
59Q2–70Q4	47	0.00576	0.00506	0.13	−0.15	0.13	−0.03	−0.04	0.15	0.13	0.15	10.61	0.56
71Q1–82Q4	47	0.00468	0.00623	0.12	−0.07	0.22	−0.10	−0.26	0.14	0.13	0.15	11.40	0.50

Empirical Tests of the CCAPM 241

The following notation will be used throughout the paper. Let μ be the $N \times 1$ vector unconditional expected returns, let $\mathbf{1}$ be an $N \times 1$ vector of ones, and let β_c^* be the $N \times 1$ vector of unconditional consumption betas. Let $\tilde{R}_{mcp}$ be the return on the MCP that excludes the riskless asset, let $\beta_{c,nb}^*$ be the unconditional consumption beta of this "no borrowing" MCP, and let β_{mcp} be the $N \times 1$ vector of unconditional MCP betas. The $N \times N$ unconditional covariance matrix for returns is $\mathbf{V}$, which is assumed to be nonsingular.

Consider the following portfolio problem: find the minimum-variance portfolio that has a consumption beta of $\beta_{c,nb}^*$ (i.e., with no borrowing). The consumption beta of a portfolio is the product of its correlation coefficient with consumption and the portfolio's standard deviation, divided by the standard deviation of consumption. By constraining the consumption beta to be fixed and then minimizing variance, the resulting portfolio has the maximum correlation with consumption, i.e., the MCP. Mathematically, the MCP solves

$$\min_{|\mathbf{w}|}: \mathbf{w}'\mathbf{V}\mathbf{w} + 2\lambda(\beta_{c,nb}^* - \mathbf{w}'\beta_c^*), \tag{16}$$

where λ is a Lagrange multiplier. The weights (i.e., $\mathbf{w}$) in the MCP are not constrained to unity since the risky assets may be combined with a riskless asset without any effect on the correlation coefficient, the variance, or the consumption beta. Alternatively, if the weights obtained sum to the value S, those same weights multiplied by $1/S$ sum to unity and have the same correlation with consumption. Thus, the existence or nonexistence of a riskless asset does not affect the MCP analysis.

The first-order conditions imply

$$\mathbf{w}_{mcp} = \lambda \mathbf{V}^{-1}\beta_c^*. \tag{17}$$

Since $\beta_{c,nb}^* = \mathbf{w}_{mcp}'\beta_c^*$, $\lambda = \beta_{c,nb}^*/(\beta_c^{*'}\mathbf{V}^{-1}\beta_c^*)$. Pre-multiplying (17) by $\mathbf{w}_{mcp}'\mathbf{V}$ and simplifying implies $\mathbf{w}_{mcp}'\mathbf{V}\mathbf{w}_{mcp} = \lambda\beta_{c,nb}^*$. The MCP betas of risky assets are

$$\beta_{mcp} = \frac{\mathbf{V}\mathbf{w}_{mcp}}{\mathbf{w}_{mcp}'\mathbf{V}\mathbf{w}_{mcp}} = \frac{\lambda\beta_c^*}{\lambda\beta_{c,nb}^*} = \beta_c^*/\beta_{c,nb}^*, \tag{18}$$

using the facts just derived.

In words, (18) states that assets' betas measured relative to the MCP are proportional to their betas relative to true consumption. Substituting (18) into the zero-beta CCAPM and using the CCAPM to get the expected excess return on the MCP implies

$$\mu - \gamma_0\mathbf{1} = \beta_{mcp}(\mu_{mcp} - \gamma_0), \tag{19}$$

Where $\mu_{mcp} \equiv \mathscr{E}(\tilde{R}_{mcp,t})$. Thus, the CCAPM may be restated (and tested) in terms of the MCP, and the testable implication is that the MCP is ex ante mean-variance efficient. Obviously, any zero-consumption beta portfolio also has a zero beta relative to the MCP.

The above result also suggests an intuitive interpretation of the portfolio weights for the MCP. Equation (17) implies

$$\mathbf{w}_{mcp} = \lambda\mathbf{V}^{-1}\beta_c^* = \theta\mathbf{V}^{-1}\mathbf{V}_{ac}^*, \tag{20}$$

where $\theta \equiv \lambda/\mathrm{var}(\tilde{c}) = \dfrac{\beta^*_{c,nb}}{(\beta^{*'}_c \mathbf{V}^{-1}\beta^*_c)\mathrm{var}(\tilde{c}^*)}$ and $\mathbf{V}^*_{ac}$ is the $N \times 1$ vector of covariances of returns with consumption. From (20), the MCP's weights are proportional to the coefficients in a multiple regression of consumption on the various risky assets' returns, with θ being the factor of proportionality. Actually, θ equals $\beta^*_{c,nb}$ divided by the coefficient of determination (R^2) of the multiple regression just described. To see this, note that the weights in the multiple regression, $\mathbf{w}^*_c$, are $\mathbf{w}^*_c = \mathbf{V}^{-1}\mathbf{V}^*_{ac}$, and the R^2 in the regression is

$$R^2 = (\mathbf{w}^{*'}_c \mathbf{V}\mathbf{w}^*_c)/\mathrm{var}(\tilde{c}^*) = (\beta^{*'}_c \mathbf{V}^{-1}\beta^*_c)\mathrm{var}(\tilde{c}^*), \qquad (21)$$

which shows that $\theta = \beta^*_{c,nb}/R^2$. If there is a riskless asset, a unit beta MCP has weights that equal the regression's coefficients divided by the R-squared value of the regression (with any residual wealth in the riskless asset). Betas with respect to such a unit-beta MCP equal the assets' direct consumption betas (see equation (18)).

The optimization problem of (16) does not involve a constraint on means, so a MCP is not tautologically a mean-variance efficient portfolio. However, the CCAPM does imply mean-variance efficiency of that MCP in equilibrium. This implication is tested later in our paper.

D. Sampling Error In Reported Consumption

In this section the problem of pure sampling error in reported consumption is examined. These errors are assumed to be random and uncorrelated with economic variables. Continue with $\tilde{c}^*_t$ as the true growth rate of real consumption from $t - 1$ to t, and let $\tilde{c}_t$ be the reported growth rate. The measurement error, $\tilde{\epsilon}_t$, is such that

$$\tilde{c}_t = \tilde{c}^*_t + \tilde{\epsilon}_t \qquad (22)$$

$$\mathscr{E}(\tilde{\epsilon}_t) = 0, \qquad \mathrm{cov}(\tilde{\epsilon}_t, \tilde{c}^*_t) = 0,$$

$$\mathrm{cov}(\tilde{\epsilon}_t, \tilde{R}_{it}) = 0, \qquad \forall\, i = 1, \cdots, N. \qquad (23)$$

Substituting (22) into the CCAPM of (7) gives

$$\mu_i - \gamma_0 = \gamma^*_1 \beta^*_{ci} = \gamma^*_1 \mathrm{cov}(\tilde{R}_{it}, \tilde{c}_t - \tilde{\epsilon}_t)/\mathrm{var}(\tilde{c}^*_t) \qquad (24)$$

$$= \gamma^*_1 \frac{\mathrm{var}(\tilde{c}_t)\mathrm{cov}(\tilde{R}_{it}, \tilde{c}_t)}{\mathrm{var}(\tilde{c}^*_t)\mathrm{var}(\tilde{c}_t)} = \gamma_1\beta_{ci},$$

where β_{ci} is the beta asset of i with respect to reported consumption, and $\gamma_1 \equiv \gamma^*_1[\mathrm{var}(\tilde{c}_t)/\mathrm{var}(\tilde{c}^*_t)]$. As long as the variance of the measurement error is positive, the variance of measured consumption exceeds the variance of true consumption. From (24), the slope coefficient, γ_1, in the relation between excess returns and betas with reported consumption is biased upward as an estimate of the price of risk, γ^*_1.

Sampling error in reported consumption does not cause a bias in the coefficients of a multiple regression of consumption growth on risky asset returns. However, the coefficient of determination for such a regression is downward biased. While the portfolio weights of the MCP are calculated by taking ratios of the regression coefficients divided by this R^2, the downward bias in R^2 affects all the weights in a proportional fashion. Thus, this has no effect on the subsequent tests.

Some other important measurement errors in aggregate consumption data involve interpolation (i.e., expenditures for all items are sampled every month), to which the analysis of this subsection is not applicable. This problem is similar to one faced by Fama and Schwert (1977, 1979) in their analysis of components of the CPI. Unfortunately, the interpolation problems with consumption are exacerbated by the summation bias, and it is difficult to disentangle the two effects. For example, either problem leads to serial correlation in consumption, noncontemporaneous correlation between aggregate consumption and returns, and more serious effects as sampling interval becomes shorter.[10] If the summation bias were not present, presumably an approach similar to that in Scholes and Williams (1977) would be appropriate. Perhaps the combination of interplation and summation bias explains the pattern of serial correlations in monthly data on consumption growth (see Panel B of Table I). Interpolation is yet another reason for avoiding monthly sampling intervals.

III. Empirical Characteristics of Consumption Betas and the MCP

Since existing empirical research on the CCAPM is not extensive, we summarize how consumption betas vary across different assets. Several types of assets will be studied, including government and corporate bonds and equities.

Monthly returns on individual securities are gathered from the Center for Research in Security Prices (CRSP) at the University of Chicago. Twelve portfolios of these stocks are formed by grouping firms using the first two digits of their SIC numbers. The grouping closely followed a classification used by Sharpe (1982), with the major exception being that Sharpe's "consumer goods" category is subdivided. This subdivision should increase the dispersion of consumption betas in the sample. While other groupings of stocks have been suggested (e.g., see Stambaugh (1982)), Sharpe's scheme is selected because the industry portfolios are reasonable and capture some important correlation patterns among stocks. Table II provides more details on the classification scheme. To represent the return on a "buy and hold" strategy, relative market values are used to weight the returns in a given portfolio. Every return on the CRSP tape from 1926 through 1982 is included, which should minimize problems with survivorship bias.[11]

---

[10] Interpolation should result in serial correlation in the residuals in regressions of returns on consumption growth. (Equation (26) below is such a regression.) Yet, when we examine the residuals, the autocorrelations are not striking. On the other hand, when we run a multiple regression of returns on a leading value of consumption, current consumption, and lagged consumption, we do get an interesting pattern. Generally, the coefficient on the lead value is insignificant, the coefficient on current consumption is significant and positive, and the coefficient on lagged consumption is significant and negative. Usually, the absolute value of the coefficient on the lagged value is about half the value of the coefficient on current consumption. However, as we note in the text, the significance of the coefficient on lagged consumption is predictable if only a summation bias is present.

[11] However, all firms with a SIC number of 39 (i.e., miscellaneous manufacturing industries) are excluded to avoid any possible problems with a singular covariance matrix when the CRSP value-weighted index is added to the sample.

Table II

Estimated Betas Relative to 1) Growth in Real, Per Capita Consumption[a], 2) Maximum-Correlation Portfolio for Consumption, and 3) CRSP Value-Weighted Index

NA denotes not available. The maximum correlation portfolio (MCP) is constructed from the seventeen assets given in Table III. The weights of the MCP are determined by maximizing the sample correlation between the return on the portfolio and the growth rate of real consumption; see Table III for more details.

Asset (SIC Codes)	Number of Firms			Spliced Consumption, Quarterly 1929–1982 (T = 215)			Max.-Correlation Cons. Portfolio, Monthly 1926–1982 (T = 684)			CRSP Value-Weighted Index Monthly 1926–1982 (T = 684)		
	1/26	6/54	12/82	$\hat{\beta}_c$	$t(\hat{\beta})$	R^2	$\hat{\beta}_{MCP}$	$t(\hat{\beta})$	R^2	$\hat{\beta}_{RKSV}$	$t(\hat{\beta})$	R^2
U.S. Treasury bills	–	–	–	−0.11	−1.27	0.01	0.03	3.86	0.02	0.01	2.04	0.01
Long-term govt. bonds	NA	NA	NA	−0.01	−0.02	0.00	0.07	2.53	0.01	0.07	4.93	0.03
Long-term corp. bonds	NA	NA	NA	0.24	0.91	0.00	0.07	2.52	0.01	0.08	6.62	0.06
Junk bond premium	NA	NA	NA	2.45	6.85	0.18	0.63	18.52	0.33	0.33	20.45	0.38
Petroleum (13, 29)	46	51	69	4.31	6.37	0.16	1.41	20.61	0.38	0.92	38.63	0.69
Finance & real estate (60–69)	16	43	234	5.85	6.30	0.16	1.50	18.81	0.34	1.19	75.95	0.89
Consumer durables (25, 30, 36, 37, 50, 55, 57)	69	157	180	6.86	6.80	0.18	1.79	22.03	0.42	1.29	80.79	0.91

Basic industries (10, 12, 14, 24, 26, 28, 33)	94	207	194	5.45	6.95	0.18	1.48	21.98	0.41	1.09	100.80	0.94
Food & tobacco (1, 20, 21, 54)	64	103	81	3.25	5.69	0.13	0.99	18.62	0.34	0.76	58.15	0.83
Construction (15–17, 32, 52)	5	28	53	7.36	7.06	0.19	1.57	19.16	0.35	1.20	61.22	0.85
Capital goods (34, 35, 38)	39	120	191	5.31	6.74	0.18	1.45	21.10	0.39	1.08	85.90	0.92
Transportation (40–42, 44, 45, 47)	78	85	46	5.15	4.97	0.10	1.27	13.52	0.21	1.19	49.04	0.78
Utilities (46, 48, 49)	24	102	176	3.73	6.10	0.15	1.04	19.40	0.35	0.75	46.34	0.76
Textiles & trade (22, 23, 31, 51, 53, 56, 59)	46	101	119	5.63	7.84	0.22	1.66	30.49	0.58	0.95	48.73	0.78
Services (72, 73, 75, 80, 82, 89)	3	4	57	4.21	4.18	0.08	1.65	12.97	0.20	0.80	12.82	0.19
Leisure (27, 58, 70, 78, 79)	12	31	59	7.35	6.95	0.18	1.85	23.03	0.44	1.22	49.82	0.78
CRSP value-weighted	NA	NA	NA	4.92	7.06	0.19	1.37	23.73	0.45	1.00	—	—

[a] The spliced consumption data are scaled to adjust for the summation bias problem. Real growth in per capita consumption is multiplied by 0.75 for observations between 1939Q2 and 1959Q1, and by 0.9375 otherwise.

While methods which handle data on individual securities rather than aggregate portfolios could be dveloped, this route was not followed.[12] The dimensionality of the parameter space is enormous when analyzing a large cross-section of securities, and conventional methods for statistical inference may become unreliable. Also, a grouping procedure by industry decreases the number of statistics to be reported—probably without a disastrous loss of information.

Several types of assets should be represented, for Stambaugh (1982) finds the statistical results are not robust to the assets under study. Short-term Treasury bills, long-term government bonds, and high-grade long-term corporate bonds are included using the data in Ibbotson and Sinquefield (1982). In addition, the recent work by Chen, Roll, and Ross (1986) suggests that the difference in returns is between low-grade long-term corporate bonds (or "junk" bonds) and long-term government bonds is useful in explaining expected returns, so these returns are included as well.[13] To capture the spread between junk bonds and government bonds, a return is calculated on a portfolio which buys junk bonds by shorting long-term government bonds and then invests in short-term T-bills.[14] This portfolio's return is referred to as the "junk bond premium." Returns on junk bonds relative to government bonds primarily reflect changes in investors' perceptions concerning the probability of default. This is related to their perceptions of current and future economic conditions, which should be related to consumption growth. In fact, our statistical analysis shows a strong relation between junk bond returns and real consumption growth.

Returns are expressed in real terms and on a simple basis without continuously compounding. Returns are deflated by the Consumer Price Index, as reported by the U.S. Bureau of Labor Statistics on a monthly basis for the entire sample period. For purposes of testing the CAPM, the CRSP value-weighted index is used as the proxy for the market portfolio.[15]

Table II reports estimated betas for various assets. (The construction of the MCP is described below.) The table reveals that different measures of risk are highly correlated. In fact, the correlation between the market betas and the consumption betas (or the MCP betas) is 0.96 (or 0.94). Of course, while the risk measures are highly correlated, the rankings of the risk measures for the various assets are not exactly the same.

As discussed by Breeden (1980), industries' consumption betas should be related to price and income elasticities of demand and to supply elasticities. Goods with high income elasticities of demand should have high consumption

[12] Using different econometric methods, Mankiw and Shapiro (1985) have analyzed a version of the CCAPM using individual securities. However, they only rely on quarterly consumption data from 1959 to 1982.

[13] We are grateful to Roger Ibbotson, who made these data available to us. Since Ibbotson's data ended in 1978, the data are extended through 1982 using the monthly return on a mutual fund which is managed by Vanguard. This portfolio, the High Yield Bond Fund, is based on an investment strategy very similar to the one used by Ibbotson in constructing his return series.

[14] The investment in short-term T-bills is convenient but not necessary. The asset pricing models are specified assuming that the assets are held with some net capital invested.

[15] See Roll (1977) for a discussion of the potential consequences of selecting a proxy for the true market portfolio. The reader should keep in mind that one usual form of the consumption-based theory includes the market portfolio as part of the statement. Nevertheless, the theoretical results hold when any security replaces the market portfolio (Breeden (1979)).

betas, ceteris paribus. This appears to be borne out in the data, for consumer durables, construction, and recreation and leisure all have high consumption betas. While the services portfolio may have a high income elasticity, it does not have a high consumption beta. However, the number of firms in that portfolio is quite low (<5) for the first thirty years, and the R-squared is also low (0.08). Goods with lower income elasticities of demand, such as utilities, petroleum, food and agriculture, and transportation, have the lowest consumption betas of the stock portfolios.

Section II. C discusses the usefulness of a maximum correlation portfolio. Equation (20) suggests a way to calculate the weights in an MCP. Table III reports the results of running a regression of consumption growth on the returns from the twelve industry portfolios, four bond portfolios, and the CRSP value-weighted index for the period 1929–1982. Consumption growth is adjusted so that the summation bias in the estimated covariances between consumption and the returns on assets is removed. Table III gives the coefficients after they are rescaled so that they sum to one hundred percent, for the MCP in Section IV does not use the riskless asset.

The composition of the MCP in Table III helps to explain why Chen, Roll, and Ross (1986) found such an unimportant role for aggregate consumption. The MCP gives large absolute weights to long-term government bonds (−31%), the

Table III

Estimated Weights for the Maximum-Correlation Portfolio for Consumption Based on Spliced Quarterly Data from 1929–1982

All data are in real terms. (Consumption growth is scaled to adjust for the summation bias). The coefficient of determination for the above regression is 0.25, and the F-statistic for testing the joint significance of all the coefficients is 3.93 with a p-value of 0.0001. Before running real consumption growth on the returns, the data are mean adjusted. Then consumption growth is multiplied by two for observations between 1939Q2 and 1959Q1, and by 1.2 otherwise.

Asset	Weight	t-Statistic
U.S. Treasury bills	0.01	0.02
Long-term government bonds	0.54	1.05
Long-term corporate bonds	−0.31	−0.64
Junk bond premium	0.59	2.71
Petroleum	0.27	1.13
Banking, finance and real estate	−0.17	0.38
Consumer durables	0.10	0.44
Basic industries	0.33	0.90
Agriculture, food, and tobacco	−0.35	−1.45
Construction	−0.11	−0.80
Capital goods	0.03	0.11
Transportation	−0.29	−2.25
Utilities	0.18	0.72
Textiles, retail stores, and wholesalers	0.49	2.69
Services	0.08	1.39
Recreation and leisure	0.13	1.17
CRSP value-weighted index	−0.51	−0.38
	1.00	

junk bond premium (59%), and the CRSP index (-51%). Since these three variables were included as factors in Chen, Roll, and Ross (1986), aggregate consumption may be dominated as an additional factor given multicollinearity and measurement error.

The weights reported in Table III seem extreme, for the MCP involves large short positions in assets. Placing restrictions on the estimated weights would eliminate the extreme positions but could sacrifice some consistency with the underlying theory. The collinearity among the assets makes it difficult to estimate any single weight with precision, but the fitted value from the regression may be useful for our purposes. To see how the MCP tracks consumption growth, the following regression is run using spliced quarterly data from 1929 to 1982 (again, consumption has been scaled so that the reported beta is free of the summation bias):[16]

$$R_{MCP,t} = 0.00828 + 2.90c'_t + \hat{u}_{MCP,t}, \; R^2 = 0.33,$$
$$\phantom{R_{MCP,t} = } (2.62) \qquad (10.19) \tag{25}$$

where t-statistics are given in parentheses. Since the MCP places no funds in the minimum-variance zero-beta portfolio, it need not have a unit beta. Even though the correlation between the MCP and consumption growth is 0.57, the theory of Section II. C still predicts that the MCP should be mean-variance efficient relative to the assets that it contains. Furthermore, the estimated risk measures when using actual consumption growth versus the MCP give similar rankings, and the sample correlation between the two sets of betas in Table II is 0.98.

Unlike the CRSP value-weighted index, the MCP has fixed weights since the entire sample period is used in the estimation reported in Table III. Constant weights are appropriate for the empirical work focuses on unconditional moments.[17] Moreover, estimating the weights by subperiods is not practical since quarterly data limit the number of available observations.

To better understand the MCP, Table IV compares it with the CRSP value-weighted index, a portfolio that has been studied extensively. According to Table III, the CRSP index has a negative weight in the MCP (-51%), yet the two portfolios are positively correlated. For the overall period, the correlation is 0.67. Furthermore, the MCP has roughly half the mean and standard deviation as the proxy for the market. Risk aversion combined with the CAPM predicts that the

---

[16] For observations between 1939Q2 and 1959Q1, $c'_t = 0.75(c_t - \bar{c})$. Otherwise, $c'_t = 0.9375 \, (c_{it} - \bar{c})$, where $\bar{c}$ is the sample mean of c_t for the entire time period. By reducing the sizes of the consumption growth deviations, the slope coefficient is scaled up so as to be consistent (at least with regard to the summation bias).

[17] Even if second moments change conditional on predetermined information, working with a constant weight MCP is still appropriate for investigations involving unconditional moments. However, certain forms of heteroscedasticity may pose a problem for our statistical inference even in large samples. There is evidence of heteroscedasticity. We divided the overall period into four subperiods (1929Q2–1939Q1, 1939Q2–1947Q1, 1947Q2–1959Q1, and 1959Q2–1982Q4) and examined the constancy of the covariance matrix across all four periods. The covariance matrix is 18×18 involving the returns on seventeen assets in Table III and consumption growth. Using a likelihood-ratio test and an asymptotic approximation involving the F-distribution (Box (1949)), the F-statistic is 3.378 with degrees of freedom of 513 and 43165.7. The p-value is less than 0.001.

Table IV

Descriptive Statistics on Real Returns from Treasury Bills, the CRSP Value-Weighted Index, and the Maximum-Correlation Portfolio (MCP) for Consumption Based on Monthly Data, 1926–1982

The sample means are annualized by multiplying by 12. The sample standard deviations are annualized by multiplying by $\sqrt{12}$. (Since returns on T-bills are serially correlated, the annualized standard deviation is not the approximate standard deviation for annual holding periods.) Correlations between the CRSP return and the MCP return for the four periods are 0.67, 0.75, 0.59, and 0.41, respectively. The maximum-correlation portfolio (MCP) is constructed from the seventeen assets given in Table III. The weights of the MCP are determined by maximizing the sample correlation between the return on the portfolio and the growth rate of real consumption; see Table III for more details.

Date	Number of Observations	Mean of T-bills	t-Statistic for Mean of T-bills	Standard Deviation
1926–1982	684	0.0013	0.48	0.0204
1926–1945	240	0.0100	1.77	0.0253
1946–1965	240	−0.0082	−1.74	0.0211
1966–1982	204	0.0023	0.89	0.0106

Date	Number of Observations	Mean of CRSP Return	t-Statistic for Mean of CRSP Return	Standard Deviation
1926–1982	684	0.0767	2.88	0.2013
1926–1945	240	0.1002	1.61	0.2782
1946–1965	240	0.1039	3.70	0.1257
1966–1982	204	0.0172	0.44	0.1615

Date	Number of Observations	Mean of MCP Return	t-Statistic for Mean of MCP Return	Standard Deviation
1926–1982	684	0.0370	2.83	0.0987
1926–1945	240	0.0598	1.98	0.1351
1946–1965	240	0.0382	2.62	0.0651
1966–1982	204	0.0086	0.46	0.0786

mean of the market is positive, and the CCAPM makes the same prediction about the mean of the MCP. The point estimates for both portfolios are consistent with these predictions. However, when the standard deviation of the return is large in 1926–1945, the mean of the MCP is marginally significant while the market proxy is not.

IV. Testing the CCAPM and the CAPM

The usefulness of the risk measures in predicting expected returns is examined in this section. Two issues are studied. First, does expected return increase as the risk increases? Second, is the relation between risk and return linear? These two issues are synonymous with the question of mean-variance efficiency for a given portfolio. In addition, estimates of the expected real return on the zero-beta portfolio will be compared with the real return on a nominally riskless bill.

The empirical implications of the CCAPM in terms of aggregate consumption are examined first. Then the empirical results are extended by testing the mean-variance efficiency of the maximum-correlation portfolio. Finally, the CAPM is studied by testing the ex ante efficiency of the CRSP index.

Since the relevant econometric methodology is detailed by Gibbons (1982), only a brief development is provided here. In the case of the CCAPM, a regression similar to the market model is assumed to be a well-specified statistical model. That is, the joint distribution between the return on an asset and real growth in per capita consumption, $\tilde{c}_t$, is such that the disturbance term in the following regression has mean zero and is uncorrelated with $\tilde{c}_t$. Such an assumption justifies the following regression model:

$$\tilde{R}_{it} = \alpha_{ci} + \beta_{ci}\tilde{c}'_t + \tilde{u}_{it}, \qquad \forall\, i = 1, \cdots, N, \quad t = 1, \cdots, T. \qquad (26)$$

Further, it is assumed that

$$\mathscr{E}(\tilde{u}_{is}\tilde{u}_{jt}) = \begin{cases} \sigma_{ij} & \forall\, s = t, \\ 0 & \text{otherwise.} \end{cases} \qquad (27)$$

Since $\tilde{c}'_t$ has already been mean-adjusted, μ_i is equal to α_{ci}.[18] Also, $\tilde{c}'_t$ has been scaled so that the summation bias is avoided.

Using the CCAPM as modified in Section II. D to account for sampling error in consumption provides

$$\mu_i = \gamma_0 + \gamma_1\beta_{ci}. \qquad (28)$$

The theoretical relation in (28) imposes a parameter restriction on (26) of the form:

$$\alpha_{ci} = \gamma_0 + \gamma_1\beta_{ci}. \qquad (29)$$

Pooling the time-series regressions in (26) across all N assets and then imposing the parameter restriction given in (29) provides a framework in which to estimate the expected return on the zero-beta portfolio, γ_0, and the market price of beta risk, γ_1. In addition, the parameter restriction may be tested.

There are various econometric methods for estimating the above model. Many of these are asymptotically (as T approaches infinity) equivalent to a full maximum-likelihood procedure. In the past, these alternatives have been selected because of computational considerations. However, results by Kandel (1984) and extended by Shanken (1985) make full maximum likelihood easy to implement.[19]

---

[18] Consumption growth is adjusted by its sample mean, not the unknown population mean. Our statistical inference that follows is conditional on the sample mean equal to its population counterpart. We overstate the significance of our tests as a result.

[19] Shanken (1982) shows that the full maximum-likelihood estimator may have desirable properties as the number of assets, N, used in estimating the model becomes large.

Shanken establishes that the full maximum-likelihood estimators for γ_0 and γ_1 can be found by minimizing the following function:

$$L(\gamma_0, \gamma_1) = (1/(1 + (\gamma_1^2/s_c^2)))\mathbf{e}'(\gamma)\hat{\mathbf{\Sigma}}^{-1}\mathbf{e}(\gamma), \qquad (30)$$

where

$\mathbf{e}(\gamma) \equiv \bar{\mathbf{R}} - \gamma_0\mathbf{1}_N - \gamma_1\hat{\beta}_c,$
$\hat{\mathbf{\Sigma}} \equiv T^{-1}\sum_{t=1}^{T}\hat{\mathbf{u}}_t\hat{\mathbf{u}}_t',$
$s_c^2 \equiv T^{-1}\sum_{t=1}^{T}c_t'^2;$
$\hat{\beta}_c \equiv N \times 1$ vector with typical element $\hat{\beta}_{ci}$, where $\hat{\beta}_{ci}$ is the usual unrestricted ordinary least-squares estimator of β_{ci} in (26),
$\hat{\mathbf{u}}_t \equiv N \times 1$ vector with typical element $\hat{u}_{it}$, where $\hat{u}_{it}$ is the residual in (26) when ordinary least squares is performed, and
$\bar{\mathbf{R}} \equiv N \times 1$ vector with typical element $\bar{R}_i$, the sample mean of the return on asset i.

The concentrated-likelihood function is proportional to equation (30),[20] in which γ_0 and γ_1 are the only unknowns.

The first-order conditions for minimizing (30) involve a quadratic equation. The concentrated-likelihood function for the overall time period is graphed in Figure 1, a and b. Figure 1b suggests that, in the neighborhood of the maximum-likelihood estimates, γ_0 is estimated more precisely than γ_1 and there is negative correlation between the two estimates. Figure 1a has a coarser grid than Figure 1b. Figure 1a suggests that higher values for $\hat{\gamma}_1$ will not dramatically affect the maximized value of the likelihood function, but lower values for $\hat{\gamma}_1$ will have an impact.

Table V provides the point estimates of γ_0 and γ_1 along with the asymptotic standard errors. The subperiods in Table V correspond to the points where the data are spliced (see Section II. *A*). Unlike many studies on asset pricing models, the estimates of the expected return on the zero-beta asset are quite small. With the exception of the first subperiod, the point estimates are less than or equal to fifteen basis points (annualized), and in many cases the rate is negative (but only significant and negative in the second subperiod). This suggests that one implication of a riskless asset version of the CCAPM is consistent with the data. Table IV provides some information about the ex post real return on short-term Treasury bills during this time period, and in all cases the estimate of γ_0 is smaller than the sample mean in Table IV. Another implication of the CCAPM is that the market price of risk should be positive, for the expected return increases as the risk increases. This implication is verified for all periods, and

---

[20] Shanken derives this result by first maximizing the likelihood function with respect to β_{ci} and σ_y. These estimators depend on γ_0 and γ_1. Shanken then substitutes the estimators for β_{ci} and σ_y back into the original likelihood function, which then depends on only γ_0 and γ_1. This new function is the concentrated-likelihood function. After some algebra he discovers that maximizing the concentrated-likelihood function is equivalent to minimizing (30) above. Note that full maximum likelihood refers to maximizing the likelihood function with respect to σ_y as well as γ_0, γ_1, and β_{ci}.

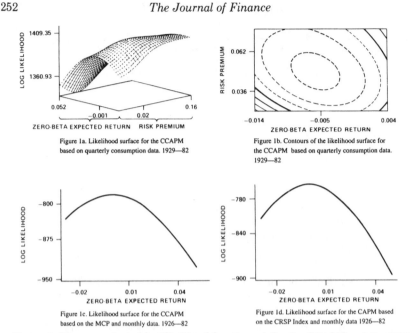

Figure 1a. Likelihood surface for the CCAPM
based on quarterly consumption data. 1929—82

Figure 1b. Contours of the likelihood surface for
the CCAPM based on quarterly consumption data.
1929—82

Figure 1c. Likelihood surface for the CCAPM
based on the MCP and monthly data. 1926—82

Figure 1d. Likelihood surface for the CAPM based
on the CRSP Index and monthly data 1926—82

Figure 1. The concentrated log likelihood functions, *l*, for the CCAPM and the CAPM.
The relevant parameters of these functions are the expected annualized return on the "zero-beta"
portfolio, γ_0, and the expected annualized premium for consumption-beta risk, γ_1.

the point estimate is statistically significant in most rows of Table V.[21] While
the magnitude of the estimate of γ_1 seems large, Section II. *D* shows that γ_1 is
biased upwards relative to γ_1^* by the variance of the sampling error in reported
consumption. Reflecting the large standard errors in some subperiods, the variation in $\hat{\gamma}_1$ across subperiods is striking. Since γ_1 does reflect the variance in
measurement error for consumption, the high value of $\hat{\gamma}_1$ in the earlier subperiods
(except 1929–1939) may be the result.

The CCAPM also implies that the relation between expected returns and betas
is linear, or the null hypothesis is the equality given in (29). This null hypothesis
is tested against a vague alternative that the equality does not hold.

Gibbons (1982) suggests a likelihood ratio for testing hypotheses like (29).
Such an approach relies on an asymptotic distribution as *T* becomes large.
However, the methodology may have undesirable small sample properties, espe-

---

[21] In addition to the full maximum-likelihood procedure, the two step GLS estimator suggested in
Gibbons (1982) was used. This estimator is not as desirable as the full maximum-likelihood approach
as the number of securities approaches infinity, and it should be downward biased due to a
phenomenon similar to errors-in-variables for simple regressions. Since consumption betas are
measured less precisely than market betas, the difference between the full maximum likelihood and
two-step GLS should be larger in this application than in past tests of the CAPM. In fact, the GLS
estimate of γ_1 is usually half the value reported in Table V. On the other hand, the simulations by
Amsler and Schmidt (1985) suggest that the finite sample behavior of the GLS estimator is better
than the maximum-likelihood alternative. Since the sign of the estimate from either approach is the
same across any row in Table V and since the significance from zero is the same across any row
(except for one subperiod), the GLS results are not reported, but they are available on request to the
authors.

Empirical Tests of the CCAPM 253

Table V

Estimating and Testing the CCAPM Using Aggregate Consumption Data

All data are annualized and in real terms $(\hat{R}_{it})$, and consumption growth $(\tilde{c}'_t)$ is adjusted to correct for the summation bias. The model is fit to seventeen assets (twelve industry portfolios, four boud portfolios, and the CRSP value-weighted index). The econometric model is

$$\hat{R}_{it} = \alpha_{ci} + \beta_{ci}\tilde{c}'_t + \hat{u}_{it},$$
$$\mathscr{E}(\hat{u}_t\hat{u}'_s) = \Sigma \text{ if } t = s, 0 \text{ otherwise.}$$
$$H_0: \alpha_{ci} = \gamma_0 + \gamma_1\beta_{ci}, \forall \ i = 1,\cdots, 17.$$

The data are annualized by multiplying the quarterly returns by 4 and monthly returns by 12. $F(\beta_{ci} = \beta_{cj})$ is the F-statistic for testing the hypothesis that $\beta_{ci} = \beta_{cj} \ \forall$ $i \neq j$, while $F(\beta_{ci} = 0)$ tests the hypothesis that $\beta_{ci} = 0, \ \forall \ i = 1,\cdots, 17$. Both $\hat{\gamma}_0$ and $\hat{\gamma}_1$ are estimates from a full maximum-likelihood procedure, and their respective standard errors (given in parentheses below the estimates) are based on the inverse of the relevant information matrix. The likelihood ratio (LR) provides a test of the null hypothesis that expected returns are linear in consumption betas as implied by the CCAPM. The likelihood ratio is adjusted by Bartlett's (1938) correction. In all cases, p-value is the probability of seeing a higher statistic than the one reported under the null hypothesis. If the test statistics are independent across subperiods, then the last four rows can be aggregated into one summary measure. In the case of the likelihood-ratio test, the overall results yield a χ^2_{60} random variable with a realization equal to 69.06. (This yields a p-value equal to 0.198.) For the F-statistic, the overall results yield a standardized normal random variable with a realization equal to 0.68, which implies 0.25 as a p-value.

Date	Number of Observations	F-test: Betas Equal (p-Value)	F-test: Betas = Zero (p-Value)	$\hat{\gamma}_0$ (SE($\hat{\gamma}_0$))	$\hat{\gamma}_1$ (SE($\hat{\gamma}_1$))	LR Test of H_0 (p-Value)
Panel A: Spliced Quarterly Consumption Data, Adjusted for Summation Bias, 1929–1982						
1929Q2– 1982Q4	215	3.874 (<0.001)	3.912 (<0.001)	−0.0061 (0.0044)	0.0478 (0.0133)	28.03 (0.021)
1929Q2– 1939Q1	40	4.319 (0.001)	4.241 (0.001)	0.0484 (0.0091)	0.0329 (0.0189)	26.45 (0.034)
1939Q2– 1947Q1	32	0.502 (0.908)	1.410 (0.261)	−0.2558 (0.0859)	0.5850 (0.2507)	6.84 (0.962)
1947Q2– 1959Q1	48	1.006 (0.476)	1.182 (0.334)	−0.0699 (0.0469)	0.2928 (0.1865)	14.82 (0.464)
1959Q2– 1982Q4	95	2.257 (0.009)	2.277 (0.008)	0.0015 (0.0028)	0.0187 (0.0062)	20.95 (0.138)
Panel B: Unspliced Quarterly Consumption Data, Adjusted for Summation Bias, 1947–1982						
1947Q2– 1982Q4	144	1.342 (0.182)	1.695 (0.052)	−0.0325 (0.0256)	0.2136 (0.1430)	19.87 (0.177)
1959Q2– 1982Q4	96	1.398 (0.165)	1.450 (0.137)	−0.0007 (0.0040)	0.0528 (0.0179)	16.29 (0.363)
Panel C: Unspliced Monthly Consumption Data, Adjusted for Summation Bias, 1959–1982						
1959 Feb– 1982 Dec	287	1.316 (0.186)	1.581 (0.069)	−0.0008 (0.0034)	0.0804 (0.0263)	10.47 (0.789)

cially when the number of assets is large (Stambaugh (1982)). The simulation by Amsler and Schmidt (1985) indicates that Barlett's (1938) correction, which was suggested by Jobson and Korkie (1982), improves the small sample performance of the likelihood ratio even when the number of assets is large. This correction is applied in all of the following tables.[22]

For the overall period using spliced data, the linear equality between reward and risk implied by the CCAPM is rejected at the traditional levels of significance. The last column of Table V reports the statistic in Panel A. This rejection is confirmed by Shanken's (1985, 1986) lower bound statistic, which suggests that the inference is robust to the asymptotic approximation of the likelihood ratio.[23] However, as noted at the bottom of Table V, aggregation of the results for each subperiod fails to reject the CCAPM at traditional levels of significance. The subperiod of 1929–1939 is the most damaging to the model. Given the nature of the consumption data used for this time period (see Section II. A), such behavior is troubling, for the rejection of the CCAPM may be due to measurement problems. On the other hand, the F-statistics given in the third and fourth columns of Table V suggest another interpretation. These F-statistics examine the joint significance of the risk measures across the assets as well as the significance of the dispersion of the risk measures across the assets. If all the risk measures were equal, then tests of (29) would lack power, and γ_0 and γ_1 would not be identified. In the first subperiod the risk measures are estimated with the most precision, and as a result tests against the null are more powerful.

Panel A of Table V is based on spliced quarterly consumption data. That is, monthly income predicts consumption for 1929–1939, and monthly consumption forms the basis of the quarterly numbers from 1959 to 1982. The above statistics are also calculated using the unspliced quarterly data from 1947 to 1982 with quarterly sampling intervals and on unspliced monthly data from 1959 to 1982 with monthly sampling intervals. The spliced data are considered first because the time series is longer and the measurement problems are less severe for quarterly observations than for monthly.

However, the results based on the spliced data are the least favorable to the CCAPM. Panels B and C in Table V suggest that the linearity hypothesis is *never* rejected with the unspliced monthly numbers and the unspliced quarterly numbers. Shanken's upper bound test confirms this result except for the subperiod 1947Q2-1982Q4. Also, the market price of consumption beta risk is also higher (with one exception) for the unspliced results.[24]

---

[22] The Lagrange multiplier test (suggested by Stambaugh (1982)) and the CSR test (suggested by Shanken (1986)) were also computed for all time periods without dramatically different results and not reported here. Both tests are monotonic transforms of the likelihood ratio (Shanken (1985)). The choice of which statistic to report is somewhat arbitrary. Since the geometric interpretation of the likelihood ratio follows, this statistic is reported in the tables.

[23] For all results we confirmed the inferences with Shanken's (1985, 1986) tests which have upper or lower bounds based on *finite sample* distributions. If the null hypothesis is not rejected with the upper bound, then it would not be rejected using an exact distribution. Similarly, if one rejects with the lower bound, such a result holds with a finite sample distribution.

[24] These results are consistent with those of Wheatley (1986), who re-examined Hansen and Singleton's (1983) tests of the CCAPM. Using 1959–1981 data, Wheatley showed by simulation that measurement error in consumption biased their test statistics. After correcting for that bias, he was unable to reject the CCAPM.

Empirical Tests of the CCAPM   255

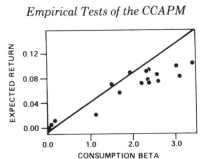

Figure 2a. 1929Q2 1982Q4

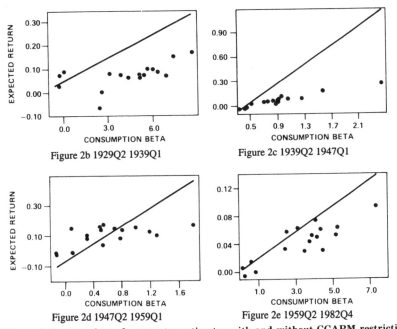

Figure 2b 1929Q2 1939Q1   Figure 2c 1939Q2 1947Q1

Figure 2d 1947Q2 1959Q1   Figure 2e 1959Q2 1982Q4

Figure 2. Scatter plots of parameter estimates with and without CCAPM restriction.
All data are annualized and in real terms, and consumption growth is adjusted to correct for
summation bias. Seventeen assets (twelve industry portfolios, four bond portfolios, and the CRSP
value-weighted index) are used. The intercept and slope of the solid straight line in each plot are
determined by the maximum-likelihood estimates for the expected return on the "zero-beta" asset
and premium for consumption-beta risk, respectively (*not* the ordinary least squares fit of the points).
All points should fall on this line if the CCAPM is true. The seventeen points on each plot represent
unrestricted estimates of expected return, $E(\tilde{R}_{it})$, and consumption beta, β_{ci}. (Note that the scale
varies across the scatter plots.)

Except for the subperiod 1929–1939 (and its effect on the results for the overall
time period), Table V provides positive support for the CCAPM. To provide a
more intuitive interpretation of the empirical results, Figure 2 informally examines the deviations for the null hypothesis. Figure 2 plots the unrestricted mean
returns against the unrestricted estimates of betas. The straight line represents

the relation estimated by maximum likelihood. Despite the rejection of the theory by formal tests, the relation between expected returns and betas is reasonably linear[25]—perhaps more than could have been anticipated given the poor quality of the consumption data. In some of the plots (e.g., Figure 2d), a straight line fit to the points would be flat. Given the measurement error in the consumption betas, this flatness is expected. To better understand the "empirical validity" of the CCAPM, the efficiency of the maximum-correlation portfolio will now be considered.

Section II. C demonstrates that the MCP is ex ante mean-variance efficient under the CCAPM. This result is derived when the covariance matrix among returns on securities and consumption growth is known, which is not the case here. Thus, all the statistical inference concerning the ex ante efficiency of the MCP is conditional on the portfolio being the desired theoretical construct. Estimation error in the portfolio weights is ignored.

Following Gibbons (1982), consider testing the efficiency of any portfolio p when the riskless asset is not observed. Assume that the following regression is well specified in the sense that the error term has a zero mean and is uncorrelated with $\tilde{R}_{pt}$:

$$\tilde{R}_{it} = \alpha_{pi} + \beta_{pi}\tilde{R}_{pt} + \tilde{u}_{it}. \tag{31}$$

If portfolio p is efficient, then the following parameter restriction holds:

$$\alpha_{pi} = \gamma(1 - \beta_{pi}), \tag{32}$$

where γ is the expected return on the portfolio which is uncorrelated with p. Similar to the econometric model of (26) and (29) above, (31) and (32) are combined and then estimated by a full maximum-likelihood procedure. Furthermore, when (32) is treated as a null hypothesis, both a likelihood ratio and an asymptotic F are calculated. In the tests that follow, the maximum-correlation portfolio or the CRSP index is used as portfolio p.[26]

Figure 1, c and d, graphs the concentrated-likelihood function relative to possible estimates of the expected return on the zero-beta portfolio in the case of the MCP and CRSP index, respectively. Table VI summarizes the statistical results for both portfolios as well. Like Table V, the third column of Table VI indicates a small expected return on the zero-beta asset. Further, the point estimate when using the MCP never exceeds that when using the CRSP index. Also, the overall period rejects the efficiency of either the maximum-correlation portfolio or the CRSP index, as indicated by the last column of the table. (This rejection would occur even without relying on asymptotic theory to approximate the sampling distribution, for the lower bound test also rejects.) Unlike Table V, the rejection of the model does not stem from just the first subperiod. These

---

[25] Like beauty, perceived linearity is in the eyes of the beholder. One reviewer of this paper thought the graphs in Figure 2 revealed remarkable nonlinearities.

[26] Panels A and B of Table VI are based on sixteen assets, not seventeen as in Table V. The regressions using the CRSP index as the dependent variable have been excluded because otherwise the covariance matrix of the residuals would be singular.

Empirical Tests of the CCAPM 257

Table VI

Estimating and Testing the Mean-Variance Efficiency of the Maximum-Correlation Portfolio (MCP) and the CRSP Value-Weighted Index, 1926–1982

All returns ($\hat{R}_{it}$) are annualized and in real terms. The model is fit to sixteen assets (twelve industry and four bond portfolios). The econometric model is

$$\hat{R}_{it} = \alpha_{pi} + \beta_{pi}\hat{R}_{pt} + \tilde{u}_{it},$$
$$\mathscr{E}(\tilde{u}_t \tilde{u}'_s) = \Sigma \text{ if } t = s, 0 \text{ otherwise.}$$
$$H_0: \alpha_{pi} = \gamma(1 - \beta_{pi}), \forall\ i = 1, \cdots, 16.$$

$\hat{R}_{pt}$ is either the return on MCP or a CRSP index. The maximum correlation portfolio (MCP) is constructed from the seventeen assets given in Table III. The weights of the MCP are determined by maximizing the sample correlation between the return on the portfolio and the growth rate of real consumption; see Table III for more details. The data are annualized by multiplying the monthly returns by 12. $\tilde{\gamma}$ is an estimate from a full maximum-likelihood procedure, and the standard errors (given in parentheses below the estimates) are based on the inverse of the relevant information matrix. The likelihood ratio (LR) provides a test of the null hypothesis that a given portfolio is efficient. The ratio is adjusted by Bartlett's (1938) correction. The p-value is the probability of seeing a higher statistic than the one reported under the null hypothesis. If the tests are independent across subperiods, then the last three rows in each panel can be aggregated into one summary measure based on either the likelihood ratio or the F-test. These aggregate test statistics always have p-values less than 0.0001.

Date	Number of Observations	$\hat{\gamma}$ (SE($\hat{\gamma}$))	LR Test (p-Value)
Panel A: Mean-Variance Efficiency Tests on the MCP			
1926–1982	684	−0.0009 (0.0027)	26.86 (0.029)
1926–1945	240	0.0064 (0.0054)	49.21 (<0.001)
1946–1965	240	−0.0151 (0.0049)	40.96 (<0.001)
1966–1982	204	0.0016 (0.0024)	19.25 (0.203)
Panel B: Mean-Variance Efficiency Tests on CRSP Index			
1926–1982	684	0.0000 (0.0027)	26.77 (0.031)
1926–1945	240	0.0076 (0.0053)	49.98 (<0.001)
1946–1965	240	−0.0125 (0.0047)	36.62 (0.001)
1966–1982	204	0.0016 (0.0024)	19.23 (0.204)

stronger rejections are probably due to the increased number of observations, which provides more precision. The joint significance of the betas across assets, as well as the significance of the dispersion of the betas across assets, is unrelated in Table VI, but it is much higher than the comparable F-statistics reported in Table V. Unfortunately, the test of efficiency of the MCP assumes that the portfolio weights are estimated without error, which is obviously not the case. If this measurement error were taken into account, the p-value would increase (see Kandel and Stambaugh (1988)).

The likelihood ratio test in Table VI can be given a geometrical interpretation based on the position of either the MCP or the CRSP index relative to the ex post efficiency frontier (Kandel 1984)). The mean-variance frontier is a parabola. A line joining the points corresponding to any given frontier portfolio and the minimum-variance portfolio intersects the mean axis at a point corresponding to the expected return of all portfolios having a zero beta relative to the frontier portfolio. When graphed with the variance on the horizontal axis, the slope of this line is equal to half the slope of the tangent at the point corresponding to the frontier portfolio (Gonzales-Gaviria (1973), pp. 58–61).

Building on this geometric relation, Figure 3 presents a graphical interpretation of the test statistic based on the ex post frontier. The maximum-likelihood estimates of the expected return on a portfolio having a zero beta relative to a test portfolio p (either MCP or CRSP in Figure 3) is denoted as γ. A line joining the mean axis at $\hat{\gamma}$ and the ex post minimum variance portfolio intersects the ex post frontier at a point (A or B in Figure 3) corresponding to the frontier portfolio having ex post zero-beta portfolios whose mean returns are equal to $\hat{\gamma}$. Let x equal the slope of this line. This portfolio would be the test portfolio, p, if and only if the test portfolio were ex post mean-variance efficient. Now consider a line joining the point corresponding to the test portfolio, p, and $\hat{\gamma}$. Denote the slope of this line by y. The LRT is equal to $T\ln(x/y)$ and is directly testing whether the slope of the second line is significantly less than the slope of the first line. A significantly lower slope for the second line implies rejection of the null hypothesis that the test portfolio is ex ante mean-variance efficient. The results of Table IV suggest that the two lines in either Figure 3a or 3b do have statistically different slopes.

Figure 3 also provides a comparison of the inefficiency of the MCP versus the CRSP index. For example, Figure 3a provides the unconstrained ex post frontier as well as a parabola which represents the maximum-likelihood estimate of the frontier assuming that the MCP is efficient. Figure 3b provides similar information in the case of the CRSP index. The scales of Figure 3a and 3b are equal, and there is little difference between the frontier constrained so that MCP is efficient versus a case where the CRSP index is efficient. Figure 3c, which has a very fine grid, is provided to see the difference between the two constrained frontiers.

Based on Table VI and Figure 3, the relative merits of the CCAPM versus the CAPM are difficult to discern. The inefficiency of either the MCP or the CRSP index is about the same. The two models are hard to compare because they are inherently non-nested hypotheses, which makes formal inference difficult. How-

Empirical Tests of the CCAPM   259

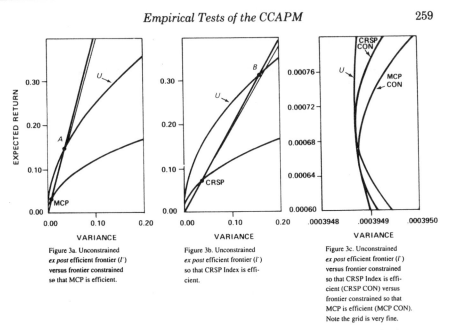

Figure 3a. Unconstrained *ex post* efficient frontier (*Γ*) versus frontier constrained so that MCP is efficient.

Figure 3b. Unconstrained *ex post* efficient frontier (*Γ*) so that CRSP Index is efficient.

Figure 3c. Unconstrained *ex post* efficient frontier (*Γ*) versus frontier constrained so that CRSP Index is efficient (CRSP CON) versus frontier constrained so that MCP is efficient (MCP CON). Note the grid is very fine.

Figure 3. A geometrical interpretation of the likelihood-ratio test, LRT, of ex ante efficiency for the MCP and CRSP value-weighted index based on monthly real returns, 1926–1982. The sample means and variances are annualized by multiplying by twelve. The LRT equals $T \ln(x/y)$. x is the slope of the straight line that passes through the maximum-likelihood estimate of the expected return on the zero-beta portfolio, $\hat{\gamma}$, and the global minimum variance point of the ex post frontier. y is the slope of the straight line that passes through $\hat{\gamma}$ and the test portfolio (either the MCP or CRSP index). The ex post frontier is based on sixteen assets (twelve industry portfolios and four bond portfolios) and either the MCP or CRSP index.

ever, the apparent inefficiency of the MCP is overstated since the portfolio weights are estimated with error.

V. Conclusion

This paper tests the consumption-oriented CAPM and compares the model with the market-oriented CAPM. Two econometric problems peculiar to consumption data are analyzed. First, real consumption reported for a quarter is an integral of instantaneous consumption rates during the quarter, rather than the consumption rate on the last day of the quarter. This "summation bias" lowers the variance of measured consumption growth and creates positive autocorrelation, even when the true consumption rate has no autocorrelation. This summation bias also underestimates the covariance between measured consumption and asset returns by half the true values, with the result that measured consumption betas are ¾ of their true values. The empirical work accounts of these problems.

A second major econometric problem is the paucity of data points for consumption growth rates. Some tests use the consumption data (adjusted for the summation bias). However, alternative tests are based on the returns of the portfolio of assets (the "MCP") that is most highly correlated with the growth rate of real consumption. The CCAPM implies that expected returns should be linearly related to betas calculated with respect to the MCP. Interestingly, the MCP has a correlation of 0.67 with the CRSP value-weighted index. Apart from stocks, a major component of the MCP is the return on a "junk bond" portfolio. Thus, the correlation between average returns and the sensitivity of returns on various assets to junk bond returns, which has been discussed by Chen, Roll, and Ross (1983), may be attributed to the correlation between junk bond returns and real growth in consumption.

A number of tests of the consumption-oriented CAPM are examined. Unlike past studies on asset pricing, the estimated return on the zero-beta asset is quite small. Except for one subperiod, all the estimates are less than or equal to fifteen basis points (annualized). This suggests that some of the implications of a riskless real asset version of the CCAPM are consistent with the data. Another implication of the CCAPM is that the market price of risk should be positive; in other words, the expected return increases as the risk increases. This implication is verified for all periods, and the point estimate is statistically significant in most of the subperiods.

Based on the quarterly consumption data for the overall period, the linear equality between reward and risk implied by the CCAPM is rejected at the 0.05 level. However, a plot suggests that the relation is reasonably linear given the poor quality of the consumption data. Analysis by subperiods reveals that the time period from 1929 through 1939 seems to be the most damaging to the model. In fact, when the model is estimated by subperiods and then the results are aggregated across subperiods, no rejection occurs at the usual levels of significance. The first subperiod may be rejecting the model because the risk measures are estimated more precisely due to the large fluctuations in consumption and asset returns in the 1930s. The added precision should increase the power of tests. On the other hand, the quality of the data for this time period is particularly suspicious. While the CCAPM is by no means a perfect description of the data, we found the fit better than we anticipated.

For the overall period (1926–1982), the mean-variance efficiency is rejected for both the CRSP value-weighted index and the portfolio with maximum correlation with consumption (the MCP). This rejection occurs in a number of time periods, not just the 1929–1939 subperiod. Given that the estimated risk measures for both models are highly correlated, this similarity in the performances by the CAPM and the CCAPM is predictable. Since these tests permit the use of monthly, not quarterly, data, the rejection could be attributed to the increased power of the tests due to additional observations. On the other hand, the statistical significance of the rejection of the efficiency of the MCP is overstated since the portfolio weights are unknown and had to be estimated.

REFERENCES

Amsler, C. and P. Schmidt, 1985, A Monte Carlo investigation of the accuracy of multivariate CAPM tests, *Journal of Financial Economics* 14, 359–376.

Bartlett, M., 1938, Further aspects of the theory of multiple regression, *Proceedings of the Cambridge Philosophical Society* 34, 33–47.

——, 1946, On the theoretical specification and sampling properties of autocorrelated time series, *Supplement to the Journal of the Royal Statistical Society* 8, 27–41.

Beaver, W., R. Lambert, and D. Morse, 1980, The information content of security prices, *Journal of Accounting and Economics* 2, 3–28.

Black, F., 1972, Capital market equilibrium with restricted borrowing, *Journal of Business* 45, 444–454.

——, M. Jensen, and M. Scholes, 1972, The capital asset pricing model: Some empirical findings, in M. Jensen, ed.: *Studies in the Theory of Capital Markets* (Praeger, New York).

Box, G., 1949, A general distribution theory for a class of likelihood criteria, *Biometrika* 36, 317–346.

Breeden, D., 1979. An intertemporal asset pricing model with stochastic consumption and investment opportunities, *Journal of Financial Economics* 7, 265–296.

——, 1980, Consumption risk in futures markets, *Journal of Finance* 35, 503–520.

—— and R. Litzenberger, 1978, Prices of state-contingent claims implicit in option prices, *Journal of Business* 51, 621–651.

Chen, N., R. Roll, and S. Ross, 1986, Economic forces and the stock market, *Journal of Business* 59, 383–404.

Cornell, B., 1981. The consumption based asset pricing model: A note on potential tests and applications, *Journal of Financial Economics* 9, 103–108.

Dunn, K. and K. Singleton, 1986, Modeling the term structure of interest rates under nonseparable utility and durability of goods, *Journal of Financial Economics* 17, 27–56.

Fama, E., 1976, *Foundations of Finance* (Basic Books, New York).

—— and J. MacBeth, 1973, Risk, return and equilibrium: Empirical tests, *Journal of Political Economy* 81, 607–636.

—— and G. Schwert, 1977, Asset returns and inflation, *Journal of Financial Economics* 5, 115–146.

—— and G. Schwert, 1979, Inflation, interest, and relative prices, *Journal of Business* 52, 183–209.

Ferson, W., 1983, Expected real interest rates and consumption in efficient financial markets: Empirical tests, *Journal of Financial and Quantitative Analysis* 18, 477–498.

Gibbons, M., 1982. Multivariate tests of financial models: A new approach, *Journal of Financial Economics* 10, 3–27.

—— and W. Ferson, 1985, Testing asset pricing models with changing expectations and an unobservable market portfolio, *Journal of Financial Economics* 14, 217–236.

Gonzales-Gaviria, N., 1973, Inflation and capital asset market prices: Theory and tests, Ph.D. dissertation, Graduate School of Business, Stanford University.

Grossman, S. and R. Shiller, 1982, Consumption correlatedness and risk measurement in economies with non-traded assets and heterogeneous information, *Journal of Financial Economics* 10, 195–210.

——, A. Melino, and R. Shiller, 1987, Estimating the continuous-time consumption-based asset-pricing model, *Journal of Business and Economic Statistics* 5, 315–328.

Hall, R., 1978, Stochastic implications of the life cycle-permanent income hypothesis: Theory and evidence, *Journal of Political Economy* 86, 971–987.

Hansen, L. and K. Singleton, 1982, Generalized instrumental variables estimation of nonlinear rational expectations models, *Econometrica* 50, 1269–1286.

—— and K. Singleton, 1983, Stochastic consumption, risk aversion, and the temporary behavior of asset returns, *Journal of Political Economy* 91, 249–265.

Ibbotson, R. and R. Sinquefield, 1982, *Stocks, Bonds, Bills and Inflation: Updates* (1926–1982) (R. G. Ibbotson Associates Inc., Chicago, IL).

Jobson, J. and R. Korkie, 1982, Potential performance and tests of portfolio efficiency, *Journal of Financial Economics* 10, 433–466.

Kandel, S., 1984, The likelihood ratio test statistic of mean-variance efficiency without a riskless asset, *Journal of Financial Economics* 13, 575–592.

—— and R. Stambaugh, 1988, A mean-variance framework for tests of asset pricing models, Unpublished manuscript, Graduate School of Business, University of Chicago.

Lambert, R., 1978, The time aggregation of earnings series, Unpublished manuscript, Graduate School of Business, Stanford University.

Lintner, J., 1965, The valuation of risk assets and the selection of risky investments in stock portfolios and capital budgets, *Review of Economics and Statistics* 47, 13–37.

262   *The Journal of Finance*

Litzenberger, R. and E. Ronn, 1986, A utility-based model of common stock returns, *Journal of Finance* 41, 67–92.

Lucas, R., 1978, Asset prices in an exchange economy, *Econometrica* 46, 1429–1445.

Mankiw, N. and M. Shapiro, 1985, Risk and return: Consumption beta versus market beta, Unpublished manuscript, Cowles Foundation, Yale University.

Marsh, T., 1981, Intertemporal capital asset pricing model and the term structure of interest rates, Ph.D. dissertation, University of Chicago.

Merton, R., 1973, An intertemporal capital asset pricing model, *Econometrica* 41, 867–887.

Roll, R., 1977, A critique of the asset pricing theory's test—Part 1: On past and potential testability of the theory, *Journal of Financial Economics* 4, 129–176.

Rubinstein, M., 1976, The valuation of uncertain income streams and the pricing of options, *Bell Journal of Economics and Management Science* 7, 407–425.

Scholes, M. and J. Williams, 1977, Estimating betas from nonsynchronous data, *Journal of Financial Economics* 5, 309–327.

Shanken, J., 1982, An asymptotic analysis of the traditional risk-return model, Unpublished manuscript, School of Business Administration, University of California, Berkeiey.

———, 1985, Multivariate tests of the zero-beta CAPM, *Journal of Financial Economics* 14, 327–348.

———, 1986, Testing portfolio efficiency when the zero-beta rate is unknown: A note, *Journal of Finance* 41, 269–276.

Sharpe, W., 1964, Capital asset prices: A theory of market equilibrium under conditions of risk, *Journal of Finance* 19, 425–442.

———, 1982, Factors in New York Stock Exchange security returns, 1931–1979, *Journal of Portfolio Management* 8, 5–19.

Stambaugh, R., 1982, On the exclusion of assets from tests of the two-parameter model: A sensitivity analysis, *Journal of Financial Economics* 10, 237–268.

Stulz, R., 1981, A model of international asset pricing, *Journal of Financial Economics* 9, 383–406.

Tiao, G., 1972, Asymptotic behavior of temporal aggregates of time series, *Biometrika* 59, 525–531.

Wheatley, S. 1986, Some tests of the consumption based asset pricing model, Unpublished manuscript, School of Business Administration, University of Washington, Seattle.

Working, H., 1960, A note of the correlation of first differences of averages in a random chain, *Econometrica* 28, 916–918.

[13]

THE JOURNAL OF FINANCE • VOL. LV, NO. 4 • AUGUST 2000

Asset Pricing at the Millennium

JOHN Y. CAMPBELL*

ABSTRACT

This paper surveys the field of asset pricing. The emphasis is on the interplay between theory and empirical work and on the trade-off between risk and return. Modern research seeks to understand the behavior of the stochastic discount factor (SDF) that prices all assets in the economy. The behavior of the term structure of real interest rates restricts the conditional mean of the SDF, whereas patterns of risk premia restrict its conditional volatility and factor structure. Stylized facts about interest rates, aggregate stock prices, and cross-sectional patterns in stock returns have stimulated new research on optimal portfolio choice, intertemporal equilibrium models, and behavioral finance.

This paper surveys the field of asset pricing. The emphasis is on the interplay between theory and empirical work. Theorists develop models with testable predictions; empirical researchers document "puzzles"—stylized facts that fail to fit established theories—and this stimulates the development of new theories.

Such a process is part of the normal development of any science. Asset pricing, like the rest of economics, faces the special challenge that data are generated naturally rather than experimentally, and so researchers cannot control the quantity of data or the random shocks that affect the data. A particularly interesting characteristic of the asset pricing field is that these random shocks are also the subject matter of the theory. As Campbell, Lo, and MacKinlay (1997, Chap. 1, p. 3) put it:

> What distinguishes financial economics is the central role that uncertainty plays in both financial theory and its empirical implementation. The starting point for every financial model is the uncertainty facing investors, and the substance of every financial model involves the impact of uncertainty on the behavior of investors and, ultimately, on mar-

* Department of Economics, Harvard University, Cambridge, Massachusetts, and NBER (john_campbell@harvard.edu). This paper is a survey of asset pricing presented at the 2000 annual meeting of the American Finance Association, Boston, Massachusetts. I am grateful for the insights and stimulation provided by my coauthors, students, and colleagues in the NBER Asset Pricing Program, without whom I could not even attempt such a survey. Franklin Allen, Nick Barberis, Geert Bekaert, Lewis Chan, John Cochrane, David Feldman, Will Goetzmann, Martin Lettau, Sydney Ludvigson, Greg Mankiw, Robert Shiller, Andrei Shleifer, Pietro Veronesi, Luis Viceira, and Tuomo Vuolteenaho gave helpful comments on the first draft. I acknowledge the financial support of the National Science Foundation.

ket prices. . . . The random fluctuations that require the use of statistical theory to estimate and test financial models are intimately related to the uncertainty on which those models are based.

For roughly the last 20 years, theoretical and empirical developments in asset pricing have taken place within a well-established paradigm. This paradigm emphasizes the structure placed on financial asset returns by the assumption that asset markets do not permit the presence of arbitrage opportunities—loosely, opportunities to make riskless profits on an arbitrarily large scale. In the absence of arbitrage opportunities, there exists a "stochastic discount factor" that relates payoffs to market prices for all assets in the economy. This can be understood as an application of the Arrow–Debreu model of general equilibrium to financial markets. A state price exists for each state of nature at each date, and the market price of any financial asset is just the sum of its possible future payoffs, weighted by the appropriate state prices. Further assumptions about the structure of the economy produce further results. For example, if markets are complete then the stochastic discount factor is unique. If the stochastic discount factor is linearly related to a set of common shocks, then asset returns can be described by a linear factor model. If the economy has a representative agent with a well-defined utility function, then the SDF is related to the marginal utility of aggregate consumption. Even recent developments in behavioral finance, which emphasize nonstandard preferences or irrational expectations, can be understood within this paradigm.

From a theoretical perspective, the stability of the paradigm may seem to indicate stagnation of the field. Indeed Duffie (1992, Pref., pp. xiii–xiv) disparages recent progress by contrasting it with earlier theoretical achievements:

> To someone who came out of graduate school in the mid-eighties, the decade spanning roughly 1969–79 seems like a golden age of dynamic asset pricing theory. . . . The decade or so since 1979 has, with relatively few exceptions, been a mopping-up operation.

Without denying the extraordinary accomplishments of the earlier period, I hope to show in this paper that the period 1979 to 1999 has also been a highly productive one. Precisely because the conditions for the existence of a stochastic discount factor are so general, they place almost no restrictions on financial data. The challenge now is to understand the economic forces that determine the stochastic discount factor or, put another way, the rewards that investors demand for bearing particular risks. We know a great deal more about this subject today than we did 20 years ago. Yet our understanding is far from perfect, and many exciting research opportunities remain.

Any attempt to survey such a large and active field must necessarily be limited in many respects. This paper concentrates on the trade-off between risk and return. Most of the literature on this subject makes the simplifying assumption that investors have homogeneous information. I therefore neglect the theory of asymmetric information and its applications to corporate finance, market microstructure, and financial intermediation. I concentrate on the U.S. financial markets and do not discuss international finance. I mention issues in financial econometrics only in the context of applications to risk-return models, and I do not review the econometric literature on changing volatility and nonnormality of asset returns. I do not draw implications of the asset pricing literature for asset management, performance evaluation, or capital budgeting. I leave most continuous-time research, and its applications to derivative securities and corporate bonds, to the complementary survey of Sundaresan (2000). I draw heavily on earlier exposition in Campbell et al. (1997) and Campbell (1999). The latter paper reports comparative empirical results on aggregate stock and bond returns in other developed financial markets.

I. Asset Returns and the Stochastic Discount Factor

The basic equation of asset pricing can be written as follows:

$$P_{it} = \mathrm{E}_t[M_{t+1}X_{i,t+1}], \tag{1}$$

where P_{it} is the price of an asset i at time t ("today"), E_t is the conditional expectations operator conditioning on today's information, $X_{i,t+1}$ is the random payoff on asset i at time $t + 1$ ("tomorrow"), and M_{t+1} is the stochastic discount factor, or SDF. The SDF is a random variable whose realizations are always positive. It generalizes the familiar notion of a discount factor to a world of uncertainty; if there is no uncertainty, or if investors are risk-neutral, the SDF is just a constant that converts expected payoffs tomorrow into value today.

Equation (1) can be understood in two ways. First, in a discrete-state setting, the asset price can be written as a state-price-weighted average of the payoffs in each state of nature. Equivalently, it can be written as a probability-weighted average of the payoffs, multiplied by the ratio of state price to probability for each state. The conditional expectation in equation (1) is just that probability-weighted average. The absence of arbitrage opportunities ensures that a set of positive state prices exists and hence that a positive SDF exists. If markets are complete, then state prices and the SDF are unique.

Second, consider the optimization problem of an agent k with time-separable utility function $U(C_{kt}) + \delta U(C_{k,t+1})$. If the agent is able to freely trade asset i, then the first-order condition is

$$U'(C_{kt})P_{it} = \delta\mathrm{E}_t[U'(C_{k,t+1})X_{i,t+1}], \tag{2}$$

which equates the marginal cost of an extra unit of asset i, purchased today, to the expected marginal benefit of the extra payoff received tomorrow. Equation (2) is consistent with equation (1) for $M_{t+1} = \delta U'(C_{k,t+1})/U'(C_{kt})$, the discounted ratio of marginal utility tomorrow to marginal utility today. This marginal utility ratio, for investors who are able to trade freely in a set of assets, can always be used as the SDF for that set of assets.

Equation (1) allows for the existence of assets—or investment strategies—with zero cost today. If P_{it} is nonzero, however, one can divide through by P_{it} (which is known at time t and thus can be passed through the conditional expectations operator) to obtain

$$1 = E_t[M_{t+1}(1 + R_{i,t+1})], \tag{3}$$

where $(1 + R_{i,t+1}) \equiv X_{i,t+1}/P_{it}$. This form is more commonly used in empirical work.

The origins of this representation for asset prices lie in the Arrow–Debreu model of general equilibrium and in the application of that model to option pricing by Cox and Ross (1976) and Ross (1978), along with the Arbitrage Pricing Theory of Ross (1976). A definitive theoretical treatment in continuous time is provided by Harrison and Kreps (1979), and the discrete-time representation was first presented and applied empirically by Grossman and Shiller (1981). Hansen and Richard (1987) develop the discrete-time approach further, emphasizing the distinction between conditional and unconditional expectations. Textbook treatments are given by Ingersoll (1987) and Duffie (1992). Cochrane (1999) restates the whole of asset pricing theory within this framework.

How are these equations used in empirical work? A first possibility is to impose minimal theoretical structure, using data on asset returns alone and drawing implications for the SDF. Work in this style, including research that simply documents stylized facts about means, variances, and predictability of asset returns, is reviewed later in this section. A second possibility is to build a time-series model of the SDF that fits data on both asset payoffs and prices; work along these lines, including research on the term structure of interest rates, is reviewed in Section II. A third approach is microeconomic. One can use equation (2), along with assumed preferences for an investor, the investor's intertemporal budget constraint, and a process for asset returns or equivalently for the SDF, to find the investor's optimal consumption and portfolio rules. This very active area of recent research is reviewed in Section III. Fourth, one can assume that equation (2) applies to a representative investor who consumes aggregate consumption; in this case C_{kt} is replaced by aggregate consumption C_t, and equation (2) restricts asset prices in relation to consumption data. Work along these lines is discussed in Section IV. Finally, one can try to explain equilibrium asset prices as arising from the interactions of heterogeneous agents. Section V discusses models with rational agents who are heterogeneous in their information, income, preferences, or constraints. Section VI discusses recent research on behavioral finance, in which some agents are assumed to have nonstandard preferences or irrational expectations, whereas other agents have standard preferences and rational expectations. Section VII concludes.

A. Mean and Variance of the SDF

A.1. The Real Interest Rate

Asset return data restrict the moments of the SDF. The one-period real interest rate is closely related to the conditional mean of the SDF, conditioning on information available at the start of the period. If there is a short-term riskless real asset f with a payoff of one tomorrow, then equation (1) implies that

$$\mathrm{E}_t M_{t+1} = P_{ft} = \frac{1}{1 + R_{f,t+1}}. \tag{4}$$

The expected SDF is just the real price of the short-term riskless real asset or, equivalently, the reciprocal of its gross yield.

Of course, there is no truly riskless one-period real asset in the economy. Short-term Treasury bills are riskless in nominal terms rather than real terms, and even inflation-indexed bonds have an indexation lag that deprives them of protection against short-term inflation shocks. In practice, however, short-term inflation risk is sufficiently modest in the United States and other developed economies that nominal Treasury bill returns are a good proxy for a riskless one-period real asset. This means that the conditional expectation of the SDF is pinned down by the expected real return on Treasury bills. This return is fairly low on average (Campbell (1999) reports a mean log return of 0.8 percent per year in quarterly U.S. data over the period 1947.2 to 1996.4). It is also fairly stable (the standard deviation is 1.76 percent in the same data set, and perhaps half of this is due to ex post inflation shocks). In fact, Fama (1975) argued that in the 1950s and 1960s the real interest rate was actually constant. Since the early 1970s, however, there have been some lower-frequency variations in the real interest rate; it was very low or even negative during the late 1970s, much higher in the early 1980s, and drifted lower during the late 1980s. A reasonable model of the SDF must therefore have a conditional expectation that is slightly less than one, does not move dramatically in the short run, but has some longer-term variation. Such behavior can be captured using persistent linear time-series models (standard in the literature on the term structure of interest rates, discussed in Section II.B.2) or regime-switching models (Gray (1996), Garcia and Perron (1996)).

There is also a great deal of research on the time-series properties of the nominal interest rate. One can define a "nominal stochastic discount factor" as the real SDF times the price level today, divided by the price level tomorrow. The expectation of the nominal SDF is the price of a short-term risk-free nominal asset. This work is less relevant for the equilibrium issues discussed in this paper, however, as the nominal SDF cannot be related to optimal consumption in the same way as the real SDF. Much of this literature is surveyed by Campbell et al. (1997, Chap. 11) and Sundaresan (2000).

A.2. Risk Premia

Risk premia restrict the volatility of the SDF. Comparing equation (3) for a risky asset and for the riskless asset, we have $0 = E_t[M_{t+1}(R_{i,t+1} - R_{f,t+1})] = E_t M_{t+1} E_t (R_{i,t+1} - R_{f,t+1}) + \text{Cov}_t(M_{t+1}, R_{i,t+1} - R_{f,t+1})$. Rearranging, the expected excess return on any asset satisfies

$$E_t(R_{i,t+1} - R_{f,t+1}) = \frac{-\text{Cov}_t(M_{t+1}, R_{i,t+1} - R_{f,t+1})}{E_t M_{t+1}}. \tag{5}$$

The expected excess return is determined by risk, as measured by the negative of covariance with the SDF, divided by the expected SDF or equivalently the price of a riskless asset. An asset whose covariance with the SDF is large and negative tends to have low returns when the SDF is high, that is, when marginal utility is high. In equilibrium such an asset must have a high excess return to compensate for its tendency to do poorly in states of the world where wealth is particularly valuable to investors.

Because the correlation between the SDF and the excess return must be greater than minus one, the negative covariance in equation (5) must be less than the product of the standard deviations of the excess return and the SDF. Rearranging, we have

$$\frac{\sigma_t(M_{t+1})}{E_t M_{t+1}} \geq \frac{E_t(R_{i,t+1} - R_{f,t+1})}{\sigma_t(R_{i,t+1} - R_{f,t+1})}. \tag{6}$$

In words, the Sharpe ratio for asset i—the asset's risk premium divided by its standard deviation—puts a lower bound on the volatility of the SDF. The tightest lower bound is achieved by finding the risky asset, or portfolio of assets, with the highest Sharpe ratio. This bound was first stated by Shiller (1982). Hansen and Jagannathan (1991) have extended it to a setting with many risky assets but no riskless asset, showing how to construct a frontier relating the lower bound on the volatility of the SDF to the mean of the SDF. This frontier contains the same information as the familiar mean-variance efficient frontier relating the lower bound on the variance of a portfolio return to the mean portfolio return. The lower bound is achieved by an SDF that is a linear combination of a hypothetical riskless asset and the risky assets under consideration. Hansen and Jagannathan also derive a tighter bound by using the restriction that the SDF must always be positive. Cochrane and Hansen (1992) present further empirical results, and Hansen and Jagannathan (1997) extend the methodology to consider the pricing errors that can be made by a false economic model for the SDF. They show that the largest possible pricing errors are bounded by the standard deviation of the difference between the false SDF and the true SDF, in a manner analogous to equation (6).

As written, all the quantities in equation (6) are conditional on information at time t, that is, they have time subscripts. Fortunately it is simple to derive an unconditional version by returning to equation (3) and taking unconditional expectations; the form of equation (6) is unchanged. The only subtlety is that the unconditional mean SDF is the unconditional mean price of a riskless asset, which is not the same as the reciprocal of the unconditional mean riskless real interest rate.

A.3. The Equity Premium Puzzle

It is not hard to find assets that imply surprisingly large numbers for the volatility of the SDF. The aggregate U.S. stock market is the best-known example. In postwar quarterly U.S. data summarized by Campbell (1999) the annualized Sharpe ratio for a value-weighted stock index is about one-half, implying a minimum annualized standard deviation of 50 percent for the SDF. This is a large value for a random variable whose mean must be close to one and whose lower bound is zero. As we shall see later in the paper, it is also very large relative to the predictions of simple equilibrium models. The annualized standard deviation of aggregate consumption growth in postwar U.S. data is about one percent. A representative-agent model with power utility must therefore have a very large coefficient of relative risk aversion, on the order of 50, to match the standard deviation of the SDF. Mehra and Prescott (1985) first drew the attention of the profession to this phenomenon and named it the "equity premium puzzle."

Of course, there is considerable uncertainty about the moments that enter equation (6). Cecchetti, Lam, and Mark (1994) and Hansen, Heaton, and Luttmer (1995) develop statistical methods, based on Hansen's (1982) Generalized Method of Moments (GMM), to estimate a confidence interval for the volatility of the SDF. Mean asset returns are particularly hard to estimate because, as Merton (1980) pointed out, the precision of the estimate depends on the total length of calendar time rather than the number of observations per se. Fortunately U.S. stock market data are available for a period of almost two centuries (Schwert (1990) presents data starting in 1802); this long span of data means that even a lower confidence bound on the volatility of the SDF is quite large.

Some authors have argued that these results are misleading. If academic studies focus on long-term U.S. data precisely because the economy and the stock market have performed so well, then there is an upward selection bias in measured average U.S. returns (Brown, Goetzmann, and Ross (1995)). Most other developed stock markets have offered comparable returns to the United States in the postwar period (Campbell (1999)), but Jorion and Goetzmann (1999) show that price returns in many of these other markets were low in the early twentieth century; this may indicate the importance of selection bias, although it is possible that lower returns were compensated by higher dividend yields in that period.

Rietz (1988) argues that the U.S. data are misleading for a different reason. Investors may have rationally anticipated the possibility of a catastrophic event that has not yet occurred. This "peso problem" implies that sample volatility understates the true risk of equity investment. One difficulty with this argument is that it requires not only a potential catastrophe but one that affects stock market investors more seriously than investors in short-term debt instruments. Many countries that have experienced political upheaval or defeat in war have seen very low returns on short-term government debt and on equities. A peso problem that affects both asset returns equally will not necessarily affect the estimated volatility of the SDF. The major example of a disaster for stockholders that spared bondholders is the Great Depression of the 1930s, but of course this event is already included in long-term U.S. data.

A.4. Predictability of Aggregate Stock Returns

Further interesting results are available if one uses conditioning information. There is an enormous literature documenting the predictability of aggregate stock returns from past information, including lagged returns (Fama and French (1988a), Poterba and Summers (1988)), the dividend-to-price ratio (Campbell and Shiller (1988a), Fama and French (1988b), Hodrick (1992)), the earnings-to-price ratio (Campbell and Shiller (1988b)), the book-to-market ratio (Lewellen (1999)), the dividend payout ratio (Lamont (1998)), the share of equity in new finance (Nelson (1999), Baker and Wurgler (2000)), yield spreads between long-term and short-term interest rates and between low- and high-quality bond yields (Campbell (1987), Fama and French (1989), Keim and Stambaugh (1986)), recent changes in short-term interest rates (Campbell (1987), Hodrick (1992)), and the level of consumption relative to income and wealth (Lettau and Ludvigson (1999a)). Many of these variables are related to the stage of the business cycle and predict countercyclical variation in stock returns (Fama and French (1989), Lettau and Ludvigson (1999a)).

A number of econometric pitfalls are relevant for evaluating these effects. First, return predictability appears more striking at long horizons than at short horizons; the explanatory power of a regression of stock returns on the log dividend-to-price ratio, for example, increases from around two percent at a monthly frequency to 18 percent at an annual frequency and 34 percent at a two-year frequency in postwar quarterly U.S. data (Campbell (1999)). The difficulty is that the number of nonoverlapping observations decreases with the forecast horizon, and it is essential to adjust statistical inference for this. Standard adjustments work poorly when the size of the overlap is large relative to the sample size; Richardson and Stock (1989) suggest an alternative approach to handle this case. Second, many of the variables that appear to predict returns are highly persistent, and their innovations are correlated with return innovations. Even when returns are measured at short horizons, this can lead to small-sample biases in standard test statistics. Nelson and Kim (1993) and others use Monte Carlo methods to adjust for this problem.

Despite these difficulties, the evidence for predictability survives at reasonable if not overwhelming levels of statistical significance. Most financial economists appear to have accepted that aggregate returns do contain an important predictable component. Even the recent increase in U.S. stock prices, which has weakened the purely statistical evidence for mean-reversion and countercyclical predictability, has not broken this consensus because it is difficult to rationalize the runup in prices with reasonable dividend or earnings forecasts and constant discount rates (Heaton and Lucas (1999)).

Conditioning information can be used to learn about the SDF in two different ways. First, one can create a "managed portfolio" that increases the portfolio weight on stocks when one or more predictive variables suggest that stock returns will be high. The managed portfolio can then be included in the basic Hansen–Jagannathan analysis. To the extent that the managed portfolio has a higher Sharpe ratio than the unmanaged stock index, the Hansen–Jagannathan volatility bound will be sharpened.

Second, one can explicitly track the time variation in expected returns and volatilities. Campbell (1987), Harvey (1989, 1991), and Glosten, Jagannathan, and Runkle (1993) use GMM techniques to do this. They find that some variables that predict returns also predict movements in volatility, but there is also substantial countercyclical variation in Sharpe ratios. These results could be used to construct a time-varying volatility bound for the SDF.

For future reference, I note that much empirical work uses logarithmic versions of the SDF equations reviewed in this section. If one assumes that the SDF and asset returns are conditionally jointly lognormal, then one can use the formula for the conditional expectation of a lognormal random variable Z, $\ln(E_t[Z]) = E_t(\ln(Z)) + 1/2\text{Var}_t(\ln(Z))$. Applied to equation (4), this delivers an expression for the riskless interest rate $r_{f,t+1} = -E_t m_{t+1} - \sigma_{mt}^2/2$, where $r_{f,t+1} \equiv \ln(1 + R_{f,t+1})$, $m_{t+1} \equiv \ln(M_{t+1})$, and $\sigma_{mt}^2 = \text{Var}_t(m_{t+1})$. Applied to equation (4), it delivers an expression for the log risk premium, adjusted for Jensen's Inequality by adding one-half the own variance, $E_t r_{i,t+1} - r_{f,t+1} + \sigma_i^2/2 = -\sigma_{imt}$, where $\sigma_{imt} \equiv \text{Cov}_t(r_{i,t+1}, m_{t+1})$. In lognormal intertemporal equilibrium models, such as the representative-agent model with power utility, these equations are more convenient than equations (4) and (5).

A.5. Government Bond Returns

A largely separate literature has studied the behavior of the term structure of government bond yields. Until 1997, all U.S. Treasury bonds were nominal. Thus the great bulk of the literature studies the pricing of nominal bonds of different maturities. There are several important stylized facts.

First, the U.S. Treasury yield curve is upward-sloping on average. McCulloch and Kwon (1993), for example, report monthly zero-coupon bond yields that have been estimated from prices of coupon-bearing Treasury bonds. Using this data set and the sample period 1952:1 to 1991:2, Campbell et al. (1997, Chap. 10) report an average spread of 10-year zero-coupon log yields over one-month Treasury bill yields of 1.37 percent (137 basis points). This number can be taken as an estimate of the expected excess return on 10-year bonds if there is no expected upward or downward drift in nominal interest rates.[1]

Second, the U.S. Treasury yield curve is highly convex on average. That is, its average slope declines rapidly with maturity. The average yield spread over the one-month bill yield is 33 basis points at three months, 77 basis points at one year, and 96 basis points at two years. There is very little further change in average yields from two to 10 years.

Hansen and Jagannathan (1991) point out that the steep slope of the short-term Treasury yield curve implies high volatility of the SDF. The risk premia on longer-term Treasury bills over one- or three-month Treasury bills are small; but the volatility of excess returns in the Treasury bill market is also small, so Sharpe ratios are quite high. High Sharpe ratios of this sort, resulting from small excess returns divided by small standard deviations, are of course highly sensitive to transactions costs or liquidity services provided by Treasury bills. He and Modest (1995) and Luttmer (1996) show how to modify the basic Hansen–Jagannathan methodology to handle transactions costs and portfolio constraints, whereas Bansal and Coleman (1996) and Heaton and Lucas (1996) emphasize that liquidity services may depress Treasury bill returns relative to the returns on other assets.

A third stylized fact is that variations in U.S. Treasury yield spreads over time forecast future excess bond returns. This is true both at the short end of the term structure and at the long end, and it is true whether one measures a simple yield spread or the difference between a forward rate and a current spot rate (Shiller, Campbell, and Schoenholtz (1983), Fama and Bliss (1987), Campbell and Shiller (1991)). The predictability of excess bond returns contradicts the expectations hypothesis of the term structure, according to which expected excess bond returns are constant over time.

Just as in the literature on predictability of excess stock returns, it is important to keep in mind that the standard tests for unpredictability of returns may be subject to small-sample biases and peso problems. Small-sample biases arise because yield spreads are persistent and their innovations are correlated with bond returns, whereas peso problems arise if investors anticipate the possibility of a regime switch in interest rates that is not

---

[1]An alternative measure of the expected excess return is the realized average excess return over the sample period. In 1952 to 1991, this number is actually negative because nominal interest rates drifted upward over this period. Because there cannot be an upward drift in interest rates in the very long run, the realized average excess return over 1952 to 1991 is probably a downward-biased estimate of the term premium.

observed in the data sample. Bekaert, Hodrick, and Marshall (1998) consider both issues but conclude that there is indeed some genuine predictability of U.S. Treasury bond returns.

This evidence has implications for the relation between yield spreads and future movements in interest rates. If term premia are constant over time, then yield spreads are optimal predictors of future movements in interest rates. More generally, yield spreads contain predictions of both interest rates and term premia. In postwar U.S. data, short-term rates tend to increase when yield spreads are high, consistent with the expectations hypothesis, but long rates tend to fall, counter to that hypothesis (Campbell and Shiller (1991)). Looking across data sets drawn from different countries and time periods, yield spreads predict interest rate movements more successfully when the interest rate has greater seasonal or cyclical variation and less successfully when the monetary authority has smoothed the interest rate so that it follows an approximate random walk (Mankiw and Miron (1986), Hardouvelis (1994)).

B. Factor Structure of the SDF

The SDF can also be used to understand the enormous literature on multifactor models. Historically, this literature began with the insight of Sharpe (1964) and Lintner (1965), sharpened by Roll (1977), that if all investors are single-period mean-variance optimizers, then the market portfolio is mean-variance efficient, which implies a beta pricing relation between all assets and the market portfolio. Ross (1976) points out that this conclusion can also be reached using an asymptotic no-arbitrage argument and the assumption that the market portfolio is the only source of common, undiversifiable risk. More generally, if there are several common factors that generate undiversifiable risk, then a multifactor model holds.

Within the SDF framework, these conclusions can be reached directly from the assumption that the SDF is a linear combination of K common factors $f_{k,t+1}$, $k = 1 \ldots K$. For expositional simplicity I assume that the factors have conditional mean zero and are orthogonal to one another. If

$$M_{t+1} = a_t - \sum_{k=1}^{K} b_{kt} f_{k,t+1},$$

(7)

then the negative of the covariance of any excess return with the SDF can be written as

$$-\text{Cov}_t(M_{t+1}, R_{i,t+1} - R_{f,t+1}) = \sum_{k=1}^{K} b_{kt} \sigma_{ikt} = \sum_{k=1}^{K} (b_{kt} \sigma_{kt}^2) \left(\frac{\sigma_{ikt}}{\sigma_{kt}^2} \right) = \sum_{k=1}^{K} \lambda_{kt} \beta_{ikt}.$$

(8)

Here σ_{ikt} is the conditional covariance of asset return i with the kth factor, σ_{kt}^2 is the conditional variance of the kth factor, $\lambda_{kt} \equiv b_{kt}\sigma_{kt}^2$ is the "price of risk" of the kth factor, and $\beta_{ikt} \equiv \sigma_{ikt}/\sigma_{kt}^2$ is the "beta" or regression coefficient of asset return i on that factor. This equation, together with equation (5), implies that the risk premium on any asset can be written as a sum of the asset's betas with common factors times the risk prices of those factors.

This way of deriving a multifactor model is consistent with the earlier insights. In a single-period model with quadratic utility, for example, consumption equals wealth and the marginal utility of consumption is linear. In this case the SDF must be linear in future wealth, or equivalently linear in the market portfolio return. In a single-period model with K common shocks and completely diversifiable idiosyncratic risk, the SDF can depend only on the common shocks.

It is important to note the conditioning information in equation (8). Both the betas and the prices of risk are conditional on information at time t. Unfortunately, this conditional multifactor model does not generally imply an unconditional multifactor model of the same form. The relevant covariance for an unconditional model is the unconditional covariance $-\text{Cov}(M_{t+1}, R_{i,t+1} - R_{f,t+1}) = -\text{Cov}(a_t - \sum_{k=1}^{K} b_{kt} f_{k,t+1}, R_{i,t+1} - R_{f,t+1})$, and this involves covariances of the coefficients a_t and b_t with returns in addition to covariances of the factors $f_{k,t+1}$ with returns. One way to handle this problem is to model the coefficients themselves as linear functions of observable instruments: $a_t = a'z_t$ and $b_t = b'z_t$, where z_t is a vector of instruments including a constant. In this case one obtains an unconditional multifactor model in which the factors include the original $f_{k,t+1}$, the instruments z_t, and all cross-products of $f_{k,t+1}$ and z_t. Cochrane (1996) and Lettau and Ludvigson (1999b) implement this approach empirically, and Cochrane (1999, Chap. 7) provides a particularly clear explanation. Jagannathan and Wang (1996) develop a related approach including instruments as factors but excluding cross-product terms.

B.1. The Cross-Sectional Structure of Stock Returns

Early work on the Sharpe–Lintner Capital Asset Pricing Model (CAPM) tended to be broadly supportive. The classic studies of Black, Jensen, and Scholes (1972) and Fama and MacBeth (1973), for example, found that high-beta stocks tended to have higher average returns than low-beta stocks and that the relation was roughly linear. Although the slope of the relation was too flat to be consistent with the Sharpe–Lintner version of the CAPM, this could be explained by borrowing constraints of the sort modeled by Black (1972).

During the 1980s and 1990s, researchers began to look at other characteristics of stocks besides their betas. Several deviations from the CAPM, or "anomalies," were discovered. First, Banz (1981) reported the *size effect* that small (low-market-value) stocks have higher average excess returns than can be explained by the CAPM. Small stocks do have higher betas and higher average returns than large stocks, but the relation between average return and beta for size-sorted portfolios is steeper than the CAPM security market line. Fama and French (1992) drew further attention to the size effect by sorting stocks by both size and beta and showing that high-beta stocks have no higher returns than low-beta stocks of the same size. Second, several authors found a *value effect* that returns are predicted by ratios of market value to accounting measures such as earnings or the book value of equity (Basu (1983), Rosenberg, Reid, and Lanstein (1985), Fama and French (1992)). This is related to the finding of DeBondt and Thaler (1985) that stocks with low returns over the past three to five years outperform in the future. Third, Jegadeesh and Titman (1993) documented a *momentum effect* that stocks with high returns over the past three to 12 months tend to outperform in the future.

Empirically, these anomalies can be described parsimoniously using multi-factor models in which the factors are chosen atheoretically to fit the empirical evidence. Fama and French (1993) introduced a three-factor model in which the factors include the return on a broad stock index, the excess return on a portfolio of small stocks over a portfolio of large stocks, and the excess return on a portfolio of high book-to-market stocks over a portfolio of low book-to-market stocks. Carhart (1997) augmented the model to include a portfolio of stocks with high returns over the past few months. These models broadly capture the performance of stock portfolios grouped on these characteristics, with the partial exception of the smallest value stocks.

There is considerable debate about the interpretation of these results. The first and most conservative interpretation is that they are entirely spurious, the result of "data snooping" that has found accidental patterns in historical data (Lo and MacKinlay (1990), White (2000)). Some support for this view, in the case of the size effect, is provided by the underperformance of small stocks in the 15 years since the effect was first widely publicized.

A second view is that the anomalies result from the inability of a broad stock index to proxy for the market portfolio return. Roll (1977) takes the extreme position that the CAPM is actually untestable, because any negative results might be due to errors in the proxy used for the market. In response to this, Stambaugh (1982) has shown that tests of the CAPM are insensitive to the addition of other traded assets to the market proxy, and Shanken (1987) has shown that empirical results can only be reconciled with the CAPM if the correlation of the proxy with the true market is quite low.

Recent research in this area has concentrated on human capital, the present value of claims to future labor income. Because labor income is about two-thirds of U.S. GDP and capital income is only one-third of GDP, it is clearly important to model human capital as a component of wealth. Jagannathan and Wang (1996) argue that labor income growth is a good proxy for the return to human capital and find that the inclusion of this variable as a factor reduces evidence against the CAPM. In a similar spirit, Liew and Vassalou (2000) show that excess returns to value stocks help to forecast GDP growth, and Vassalou (1999) introduces GDP forecast revisions as an additional risk factor in a cross-sectional model.

A third view is that the anomalies provide genuine evidence against the CAPM but not against a broader rational model in which there are multiple risk factors. Fama and French (1993, 1996) have interpreted their three-factor model as evidence for a "distress premium"; small stocks with high book-to-market ratios are firms that have performed poorly and are vulnerable to financial distress (Chan and Chen (1991)), and they command a risk premium for this reason.

Fama and French do not explain why distress risk is priced, that is, why the SDF contains a distress factor. Given the high price of distress risk relative to market risk, this question cannot be ignored; in fact MacKinlay (1995) expresses skepticism that any rational model with omitted risk factors can generate sufficiently high prices for those factors to explain the cross-sectional pattern of stock returns.

One possibility is that the distress factor reflects the distinction between a conditional and unconditional asset pricing model. The CAPM may hold conditionally but fail unconditionally. If the risk premium on the market portfolio moves over time, and if the market betas of distressed stocks are particularly high when the market risk premium is high, then distressed stocks will have anomalously high average returns relative to an unconditional CAPM even if they obey a conditional CAPM exactly. Jagannathan and Wang (1996) try to capture this by using a yield spread between low- and high-quality bonds as an additional risk factor proxying for the market risk premium. Cochrane (1996) and Lettau and Ludvigson (1999b) introduce additional risk factors by interacting the market return with the dividend-to-price ratio and long-short yield spread, and a consumption-wealth-income ratio. These approaches reduce deviations from the model, and Lettau and Ludvigson are particularly successful in capturing the value effect. Campbell and Cochrane (2000) take a more theoretical approach, showing that a model with habit formation in utility, of the sort described in Section IV below, implies deviations from an unconditional CAPM of the magnitude found in the data even though the CAPM holds conditionally.

Alternatively, the CAPM may fail even as a conditional model, but the data may be described by an intertemporal CAPM of the sort proposed by Merton (1973). In this case additional risk factors may be needed to capture time variation in investment opportunities that are of concern to long-term investors. This possibility is discussed further in Section IV.

A fourth view is that the anomalies do not reflect any type of risk but are "mistakes" that disappear once market participants become aware of them. Keim (1983) pointed out that the small-firm effect was entirely attributable to excess returns on small firms in the month of January. A seasonal excess return of this sort is very hard to relate to risk, and if it is not purely the result of data snooping it should be expected to disappear once it becomes well-known to investors. Indeed the January effect does seem to have diminished in recent years.

The most radical view is that the anomalies reflect enduring psychological biases that lead investors to make irrational forecasts. Lakonishok, Shleifer, and Vishny (1994) argue that investors irrationally extrapolate past earnings growth and thus overvalue companies that have performed well in the past. These companies have low book-to-market ratios and subsequently underperform once their earnings growth disappoints investors. Supporting evidence is provided by La Porta (1996), who shows that earnings forecasts of stock market analysts fit this pattern, and by La Porta et al. (1997), who show that the underperformance of stocks with low book-to-market ratios is concentrated on earnings announcement dates. This view has much in common with the previous one and differs only in predicting that anomalies will remain stable even when they have been widely publicized.

All these views have difficulties explaining the momentum effect. Almost any model in which discount rates vary can generate a value effect: stocks whose discount rates are high, whether for rational or irrational reasons, have low prices, high book-to-market ratios, and high subsequent returns. It is much harder to generate a momentum effect in this way, and Fama and French (1996) do not attempt to give a rational risk-based explanation for the momentum effect. Instead they argue that it may be the result of data snooping or survivorship bias (Kothari, Shanken, and Sloan (1995)). Psychological models also have difficulties in that momentum arises if investors underreact to news. Such underreaction is consistent with evidence for continued high returns after positive earnings announcements (Bernard (1992)), but it is hard to reconcile with the overreaction implied by the value effect. Several recent attempts to solve this puzzle are discussed in Section VI.

II. Prices, Returns, and Cash Flows

A. Solving the Present Value Relation

The empirical work described in Section I takes the stochastic properties of asset returns as given and merely asks how the first moments of returns are determined from their second moments. Although this approach can be informative, ultimately it is unsatisfactory because the second moments of asset returns are just as endogenous as the first moments. The field of asset pricing should be able to describe how the characteristics of payoffs determine asset prices, and thus the stochastic properties of returns.

When an asset lasts for only one period, its price can be determined straightforwardly from equation (1). The difficulty arises when an asset lasts for many periods and particularly when it makes payoffs at more than one date. There are several ways to tackle this problem.

A.1. Constant Discount Rates

First, if an asset has a constant expected return, then its price is a linear function of its expected future payoffs. From the definition of return, $1 + R_{t+1} = (P_{t+1} + D_{t+1})/P_t$, if the expected return is a constant R, then

$$P_t = \frac{E_t(P_{t+1} + D_{t+1})}{1 + R}. \tag{9}$$

This model is sometimes called the martingale model or random walk model of stock prices because, even though the stock price itself is not a martingale in equation (9), the discounted value of a portfolio with reinvested dividends is a martingale (Samuelson (1965)). The expectational difference equation (9) can be solved forward. If one assumes that the expected discounted future price has a limit of zero, $\lim_{K \to \infty} \mathrm{E}_t P_{t+K}/(1 + R)^K = 0$, then one obtains

$$P_t = \mathrm{E}_t \sum_{i=1}^{\infty} \frac{D_{t+i}}{(1 + R)^i}. \tag{10}$$

The right-hand side of equation (10) is sometimes called the "fundamental value" of an asset price, although it is important to keep in mind that this expression holds only under the very special condition of a constant discount rate.

Models of "rational bubbles" (Blanchard and Watson (1982), Froot and Obstfeld (1991)) challenge the assumption just made that the expected future discounted price has a limit of zero. Such models entertain the possibility that future prices are expected to grow forever at the rate of interest, in which case a bubble term B_t that satisfies $B_t = \mathrm{E}_t B_{t+1}/(1 + R)$ can be added to the right-hand side of equation (10). The theoretical conditions that allow bubbles to exist are extremely restrictive, however. Negative bubbles are ruled out by limited liability that puts a floor of zero on the price of an asset; this implies that a bubble can never start once an asset is trading, because $B_t = 0$ implies $B_{t+1} = 0$ with probability one (Diba and Grossman (1988)). General equilibrium considerations also severely limit the circumstances in which bubbles can arise (Santos and Woodford (1997)).

An important special case arises when the expected rate of dividend growth is a constant, $\mathrm{E}_t(D_{t+1}/D_t) = (1 + G)$. In this case equation (10) simplifies to the Gordon (1962) growth model, $P_t = \mathrm{E}_t D_{t+1}/(R - G)$. This formula relates prices to prospective dividends, the discount rate, and the expected dividend growth rate; it is widely used by both popular writers (Glassman and Hassett (1999)) and academic writers (Heaton and Lucas (1999)) to interpret variations in prices relative to dividends, such as the spectacular runup in aggregate stock prices at the end of the 1990s. A difficulty with such applications is that they assume changes in R and G that are ruled out by assumption in the Gordon model. Thus the Gordon formula can only provide a rough guide to the price variations that occur in a truly dynamic model.

At the end of the 1970s most finance economists believed that equation (10) was a good approximate description of stock price determination for at least the aggregate market. LeRoy and Porter (1981) and Shiller (1981) challenged this orthodoxy by pointing out that aggregate stock prices seem to be far more volatile than plausible measures of expected future dividends. Their work assumed that both stock prices and dividends are stationary around a stochastic trend; Kleidon (1986) and Marsh and Merton (1986) responded that stock prices follow unit-root processes, but Campbell and Shiller (1988a, 1988b) and West (1988) found evidence for excess volatility even allowing for unit roots.

A.2. A Log-Linear Approximate Framework

Campbell and Shiller (1988a) extended the linear present-value model to allow for log-linear dividend processes and time-varying discount rates. They did this by approximating the definition of log return, $r_{t+1} = \log(P_{t+1} + D_{t+1}) - \log(P_t)$, around the mean log dividend-to-price ratio, $(\overline{d_t - p_t})$, using a first-order Taylor expansion. The resulting approximation is $r_{t+1} \approx k + \rho p_{t+1} + (1 - \rho)d_{t+1} - p_t$, where ρ and k are parameters of linearization defined by $\rho \equiv 1/(1 + \exp(\overline{d_t - p_t}))$ and $k \equiv -\log(\rho) - (1 - \rho)\log(1/\rho - 1)$. When the dividend-to-price ratio is constant, then $\rho = P/(P + D)$, the ratio of the ex-dividend to the cum-dividend stock price. In the postwar quarterly U.S. data of Campbell (1999), the average price-to-dividend ratio has been 26.4 on an annual basis, implying that ρ should be about 0.964 in annual data.

Solving forward, imposing the "no-bubbles" terminal condition that $\lim_{j\to\infty} \rho^j(d_{t+j} - p_{t+j}) = 0$, taking expectations, and subtracting the current dividend, one gets

$$p_t - d_t = \frac{k}{1 - \rho} + \mathrm{E}_t \sum_{j=0}^{\infty} \rho^j[\Delta d_{t+1+j} - r_{t+1+j}]. \tag{11}$$

This equation says that the log price-to-dividend ratio is high when dividends are expected to grow rapidly or when stock returns are expected to be low. The equation should be thought of as an accounting identity rather than a behavioral model; it has been obtained merely by approximating an identity, solving forward subject to a terminal condition, and taking expectations. Intuitively, if the stock price is high today, then from the definition of the return and the terminal condition that the dividend-to-price ratio is non-explosive, there must either be high dividends or low stock returns in the future. Investors must then expect some combination of high dividends and low stock returns if their expectations are to be consistent with the observed price.

Campbell (1991) extends this approach to obtain a decomposition of returns. Substituting equation (11) into the approximate return equation gives

$$r_{t+1} - \mathrm{E}_t r_{t+1} = (\mathrm{E}_{t+1} - \mathrm{E}_t) \sum_{j=0}^{\infty} \rho^j \Delta d_{t+1+j} - (\mathrm{E}_{t+1} - \mathrm{E}_t) \sum_{j=1}^{\infty} \rho^j r_{t+1+j}. \tag{12}$$

This equation says that unexpected stock returns must be associated with changes in expectations of future dividends or real returns. An increase in expected future dividends is associated with a capital gain today, whereas an increase in expected future returns is associated with a capital loss today. The reason is that with a given dividend stream, higher future returns can only be generated by future price appreciation from a lower current price.

Equation (12) can be used to understand the relation between the predictability of excess returns, described in Section I.A.4, and the excess volatility of prices and returns discussed in Section II.A.2. The equation implies that the variance of unexpected returns is the variance of "dividend news" (the first term on the right-hand side), plus the variance of "expected return news" (the second term on the right-hand side), plus twice the covariance between the two types of news. Revisions in expected future returns move prices today and generate volatility in unexpected returns. The discounted sums on the right-hand side of equation (12) imply that this effect is greater, the more persistent the revisions in expected future returns; thus considerable extra volatility is created by predictability of returns from slow-moving variables such as dividend-to-price or market-to-book ratios.[2]

A.3. Alternatives to the Use of Dividends

Both the linear present value model with constant discount rates and the log-linear approximate model relate asset prices to expected future dividends. The use of dividends is not arbitrary but results from the accounting identity that links returns, prices, and dividends. Nonetheless the presence of dividends creates several difficulties for empirical work.

First, many companies pay cash to shareholders partly by repurchasing shares on the open market. This strategy is tax-advantaged and has become increasingly popular in recent years. Share repurchases do not invalidate any of the formulas given above, but they do make it essential to apply these formulas correctly. One can work on a per-share basis, measuring price per share and traditional dividends per share; in this case repurchases are not counted as dividends, but they do affect future dividends per share by reducing the number of shares. Alternatively, one can work on a total-value basis, measuring the market value of the company and the sum of its cash payments to shareholders, including both traditional dividends and repurchases. Liang and Sharpe (1999) emphasize that the exercise of executive stock options leads to share issues that must be set against repurchases. They estimate that the dividend yield on the S&P 500 index in the late 1990s rises by about one percent when net repurchases are added to traditional dividends.[3]

Second, many companies seem to be postponing the payment of dividends until much later in their life cycle. This means that current dividends are observed for fewer companies. Fama and French (1999) report that in 1993 to 1997, non-dividend-payers accounted for almost one-quarter of the value of the aggregate stock market, a tenfold increase in their value share since the mid-1960s. These firms must eventually pay cash to shareholders in some way, but it is clearly not fruitful to model their dividends as following a stable stochastic process.

In response to these difficulties, there is increasing interest in present-value models in which earnings, rather than dividends, are the driving variable. Ohlson (1990, 1995) assumes a constant discount rate and shows that

[2] One can understand a rational bubble as the limiting case where the price movement is so persistent (in fact, explosive) that it has no effect on the expected return at all.

[3] Cash paid by acquiring firms to shareholders of acquired firms is another form of indirect payout. The quantitative importance of this is hard to judge.

under clean-surplus accounting, the market value of a firm can be written as the book value of its equity, plus the discounted present value of future surplus earnings (earnings in excess of the discount rate times book value). Vuolteenaho (1999) combines this approach with the log-linear approximate framework, allowing for time-varying discount rates. He shows that cash flow news accounts for a greater fraction of return volatility for a typical stock than for the market as a whole, because cash flow news is largely idiosyncratic. Ang and Liu (1998) combine the Ohlson model with an explicit model of the SDF.

A.4. Exact Solution Methods

Although the log-linear framework of Section II.A.2 delivers useful insights, it does rely on an approximation of return. Two other approaches are available to get more accurate results. First, one can work with a discrete-state model in which dividend growth and returns, or the expectations of these variables, follow a Markov chain. Under this assumption one can solve for prices in each discrete state by solving a system of linear equations. This approach has been used by Mehra and Prescott (1985), Kandel and Stambaugh (1991), and others. The discrete-state model can be specified a priori or can be chosen using Gaussian quadrature methods to approximate an estimated continuous-state model.

A second exact approach treats an asset paying dividend at many future dates as the sum of many assets, each of which pays a dividend at a single future date. These single-payment or "zero-coupon" assets are often easier to model. This approach is most natural, and has been developed furthest, in the literature on fixed-income securities that I now describe.

B. Affine-Yield Models

B.1. Theoretical Structure

Consider a real zero-coupon bond that makes a single payment of one unit of consumption at time $t + n$. The bond price at time t, P_{nt}, must satisfy the general SDF relation equation (1), which in this special case becomes

$$P_{nt} = E_t[M_{t+1}P_{n-1,t+1}].$$ (13)

This equation can be solved forward to obtain

$$P_{nt} = E_t[M_{t+1}M_{t+2}\ldots M_{t+n}].$$ (14)

Just as the price of a single-period real bond is the expectation of the single-period SDF in equation (4), so the price of an n-period real bond is the expectation of the n-period SDF (the product of n successive single-period SDF's). This is natural because an n-period real bond is the riskless real asset for an investor with a horizon of n periods (Modigliani and Sutch (1966)). Equation (14) makes it clear that a model of bond prices is equivalent to a time-series model of the SDF.

The yield on an n-period bond, Y_{nt}, is defined to be the discount rate that equates the bond's price to the present value of its future payment: $P_{nt} = 1/(1 + Y_{nt})^n$. Taking logs, $y_{nt} = -(1/n)p_{nt}$, so the log bond yield is just a linear transformation of the log bond price. Affine-yield models have the property that all log bond yields are linear ("affine") in a set of state variables describing the movements of the SDF. This property holds only under restrictive conditions on the SDF. Classic papers by Vasicek (1977) and Cox, Ingersoll, and Ross (1985) present simple examples; recent work has sought to characterize more generally the conditions on the SDF required for an affine-yield structure. Most of this work is set in continuous time and is surveyed by Sundaresan (2000). In the discrete-time framework used here, if we define a vector z_t containing the log SDF m_t and all state variables relevant for predicting its future values m_{t+i}, then an affine-yield model requires that both the conditional mean and the conditional variance-covariance matrix of z_{t+1} should be linear in z_t. The model also requires some restrictions on the conditional distribution of z_{t+1}; a normal distribution is sufficient but not necessary (Backus, Foresi, and Telmer (1998)). The simplest example is a univariate homoskedastic normal AR(1) process for m_{t+1}, which gives a discrete-time version of the Vasicek (1977) model of the term structure. A normal AR(1) process for m_{t+1} with a variance proportional to the level of m_{t+1} gives a discrete-time version of the Cox et al. (1985) model. In continuous time the affine-yield restrictions are similar. It is possible to allow for jumps in the state vector provided that the jump intensity is itself linear in the state variables.

Dai and Singleton (2000) present a careful analysis of the substantive restrictions imposed by the affine-yield structure. There are two basic issues. First, the affine-yield model limits the way in which volatility (driven either by a diffusion term or by jump intensity in continuous time) can vary with state variables. Variances can be constant or, more generally, linear in state variables but cannot vary nonlinearly. Second, the implied variance-covariance matrix of the state vector must be positive definite. This places few restrictions on the correlations of state variables when volatility is constant but is much harder to ensure when volatility is time-varying.

The affine-yield structure makes it possible to solve recursively for the unknown coefficients relating log bond yields to state variables. Starting from the terminal condition that the bond price at maturity is one (so the log bond price is zero), one can work out the term structure of interest rates to price bonds of arbitrary maturity. Coupon bonds can then be priced, if desired, as packages of zero-coupon bonds, one for each date at which a coupon payment is made.

The affine-yield structure can also be extended to study assets with uncertain future payoffs. There are three ways to do this. First, one can assume that the expected asset returns are unaffected by payoff uncertainty, which will be the case if the payoff uncertainty is uncorrelated with the SDF.

Gibbons and Ramaswamy (1993), for example, assume that inflation uncertainty is uncorrelated with the SDF, so inflation risk is unpriced, and study the real returns on nominal bonds. Second, one can change the numeraire to units in which future payoffs are known. Nominal Treasury bonds, for example, have uncertain real payoffs but certain nominal payoffs. One can define a nominal SDF, the real SDF times the ratio of the price level today to the price level tomorrow, and then use an affine model of the nominal SDF. The advantage of this approach is its simplicity; the disadvantage is that it is hard to relate the nominal SDF to the real risks that affect investors. Third, one can explicitly model the time-series process for the payoffs in relation to the SDF. If the state vector includes those variables that determine the payoffs, and if the previous assumptions on the state vector continue to hold, then the log asset price continues to be linear in the log state vector and the advantages of the affine framework are preserved. Campbell and Viceira (2000) apply this approach to nominal bonds; Bakshi and Chen (1997), Ang and Liu (1998), Bekaert and Grenadier (1999), and Berk, Green, and Naik apply it to stocks.

B.2. *Empirical Applications to U.S. Treasury Bonds*

Section I.A.5 reported several stylized facts about U.S. Treasury bond yields. Both the shape of the average yield curve and the time variation of term premia are inconsistent with single-factor affine-yield models of the nominal term structure. In single-factor models, the convexity of the average yield curve is related to the rate at which shocks to the short-term interest rate die out; but time-series evidence implies that interest-rate shocks die out much more slowly than would be implied by the rapidly declining slope of the average yield curve (Gibbons and Ramaswamy (1993)). As for term premia, they are counterfactually constant in a single-factor Vasicek (1977) model with constant volatility. A single-factor Cox et al. (1985) model with volatility linear in the level of the short-term interest rate can generate time variation in term premia, but in this model the yield spread is inversely related to volatility. If term premia are positive on average, they move positively with volatility so they move inversely with the yield spread, contrary to the empirical evidence (Backus et al. (1998)).

These problems have led to an explosion of research on more complex models of the nominal term structure. These include multifactor affine models that include both persistent state variables to fit the slowly decaying autocorrelations of interest rates and transitory state variables to fit the rapidly declining slope of the average yield curve; nonaffine models that allow for a nonlinear effect of the level of the interest rate on its volatility and drift; and regime-switching models that allow for occasional discrete changes in interest-rate behavior. Practitioners have gone in a somewhat different direction, introducing time-dependent parameters into simple affine models, but this does not build the understanding of the underlying economic structure that is the ultimate goal of academic research. Most of this work is set in continuous time and is reviewed by Sundaresan (2000).

Several issues remain unresolved by this research. First, real-interest-rate risk and inflation risk are conceptually distinct and may have very different risk prices. This distinction is blurred when term-structure models are fit directly to nominal interest rates. It can be addressed either by looking at inflation data jointly with nominal interest rates (Gibbons and Ramaswamy (1993), Campbell and Viceira (2000)) or by studying inflation-indexed bonds, which have been actively traded in the U.K. for 15 years (Brown and Schaefer (1994)) and have been issued in the United States since 1997. There is some evidence that both inflation risk and real-interest-rate risk are priced, so that the real term structure is upward sloping but flatter than the nominal term structure; however more work is needed on this subject.

Second, it is important to reconcile the characterization of the SDF provided by bond market data with the evidence from stock market data. Term-structure models of the SDF are ultimately unsatisfactory unless they can be related to the deeper general-equilibrium structure of the economy. Researchers often calibrate equilibrium models to fit stock market data alone, but this is a mistake because bonds carry equally useful information about the SDF. The short-term real interest rate is closely related to the conditional expected SDF and thus to the expected growth rate of marginal utility; in a representative-agent model with power utility of consumption, this links the real interest rate to expected consumption growth as discussed in Section IV.A. The risk premium on long-term bonds is also informative; it is small relative to the equity premium, and this remains true even if one divides by the standard deviation of return to calculate a Sharpe ratio. This fact is consistent with risk-based models of the equity premium in which the SDF is more highly correlated with stocks than with bonds, but it runs counter to models that explain the equity premium as the result of liquidity services from short-term Treasury debt that drive down the equilibrium short-term interest rate (Bansal and Coleman (1996)). Unless long-term Treasury bonds also provide liquidity services, the liquidity-based model should imply a large yield spread of long-term over short-term Treasury debt.

Third, the short-term nominal interest rate is an important driving variable in any nominal term-structure model. One cannot ignore the fact that the short rate is directly controlled by the monetary authority, which responds to macroeconomic conditions by changing the rate in discrete jumps. Balduzzi, Bertola, and Foresi (1997) and Piazzesi (1999) address this issue.

III. Consumption and Portfolio Choice for Long-Term Investors

The general theory outlined in Section I can also be used to understand the microeconomic theory of portfolio choice. In a one-period model, the connection is particularly clear. If an investor k lives off financial wealth and consumes all wealth tomorrow, then the investor's consumption tomorrow, $C_{k,t+1}$, is just the payoff $X^*_{k,t+1}$ on the optimal portfolio: $C_{k,t+1} = X^*_{k,t+1}$. Using the relation between the SDF and the growth rate of the marginal utility of consumption, we have $M_{t+1} = \theta_t U_k'(X_{k,t+1}^*)$, where θ_t known at time t captures time discounting and marginal utility of consumption at time t. Inverting this relation,

$$X_{k,t+1}^* = U_k'^{-1}(M_{t+1}/\theta_t). \tag{15}$$

Given an exogenous SDF that summarizes the available asset returns, this equation determines the payoffs on the optimal portfolio for an investor with utility function U_k. In the classic case where U_k is quadratic, U_k' is linear and the optimal portfolio can be found using the mean-variance analysis of Markowitz (1952). In a CAPM equilibrium where M_{t+1} is linear in the return on the market portfolio, an investor with linear U_k' holds a mix of a riskless asset and the market. If M_{t+1} is highly volatile, then the optimal portfolio payoff and consumption are also highly volatile unless the investor is highly risk averse (U_k' is rapidly declining).

The difficult task faced by modern portfolio theory is to extend these insights to a multiperiod setting in which investors seek to finance a stream of consumption over a long lifetime. Financial economists have understood for at least 30 years that the solution to a multiperiod portfolio choice problem can be very different from the solution to a static portfolio choice problem. Samuelson (1969) derived restrictive conditions under which these two solutions are the same (portfolio choice is "myopic"). For an investor with no labor income who maximizes the expected value of a time-separable von Neumann–Morgenstern utility function, sufficient conditions for myopic portfolio choice are either log utility (with constant relative risk aversion equal to one), or both power utility (constant relative risk aversion) and returns that are independently and identically distributed (IID) over time.

Merton (1969, 1971, 1973) shows that if investment opportunities are varying over time, then long-term investors generally care about shocks to investment opportunities—the productivity of wealth—and not just about wealth itself. They may seek to hedge their exposures to wealth productivity shocks, and this gives rise to intertemporal hedging demands for financial assets. Brennan, Schwartz, and Lagnado (1997) have coined the phrase "strategic asset allocation" to describe this farsighted response to time-varying investment opportunities.

Unfortunately the intertemporal consumption and portfolio choice problem is hard to solve in closed form. Cox and Huang (1989) made conceptual progress by showing that a version of equation (15) must hold for each future date in a multiperiod model, but this does not generally lead to a closed-form solution. Few solutions have been available outside those trivial cases where the Merton model reduces to the static model, severely limiting the empirical applicability of the Merton model and its influence on asset management practices. Very recently this situation has begun to change as a result of several related developments. First, computing power and numerical methods have advanced to the point at which realistic multiperiod portfolio choice problems can be solved numerically using discrete-state approximations. Second, financial theorists have discovered some new closed-form solutions to the Merton model. Third, approximate analytical solutions have been developed. These solutions are based on perturbations of known exact solutions. They offer analytical insights into investor behavior in models that fall outside the still limited class that can be solved exactly.

A. Specification of Utility

A first important issue is the specification of utility. Ross (1998) points out that the investment horizon can affect portfolio choice, even with IID returns, once we relax the assumption of power utility. However only a few utility specifications are consistent with the observation that interest rates and risk premia have remained stationary over more than a century of U.S. economic growth. Most models of utility imply that trends in per capita consumption and wealth would generate counterfactual trends in financial variables. For this reason most research works either with power utility or with generalizations that retain the scale-independence of power utility.[4]

One appealing generalization of power utility has been proposed by Epstein and Zin (1989, 1991) and Weil (1989), building on the work of Kreps and Porteus (1978). This model moves outside the von Neumann–Morgenstern framework of expected utility to separate the coefficient of relative risk aversion from the elasticity of intertemporal substitution in consumption. The Epstein–Zin objective function can be written as

$$U(C_t, E_t(U_{t+1})) = \left[(1-\delta)C_t^{1-\gamma/\theta} + \delta\left(E_t(U_{t+1}^{1-\gamma})\right)^{1/\theta}\right]^{\theta/1-\gamma}, \qquad (16)$$

where C_t is consumption at time t, $\gamma > 0$ is the relative risk aversion coefficient, $\psi > 0$ is the elasticity of intertemporal substitution, $0 < \delta < 1$ is the time discount factor, $\theta \equiv (1-\gamma)/(1-1/\psi)$, and $E_t(\cdot)$ is the conditional expectation operator. For time-separable power utility, $\gamma = 1/\psi$ and hence $\theta = 1$. In this case the nonlinear recursive equation (16) becomes a linear equation that can be solved forward to deliver the familiar time-separable power utility function.

Epstein–Zin utility is harder to work with than time-separable power utility, but Epstein and Zin have used the assumption that the investor has no labor income and lives entirely off financial wealth to show that the intertemporal marginal rate of substitution takes the form $\delta(C_{t+1}/C_t)^{-\theta/\psi}$ $(1 + R_{p,t+1})^{\theta-1}$, where $R_{p,t+1}$ is the investor's portfolio return. If consump-

---

[4] Models of income risk or noise trading, however, sometimes assume constant absolute risk aversion for tractability. To prevent trending risk premia, such models can assume a trend in the number of risk-averse investors (equivalently a trend in the risk-bearing capacity of the economy) to counteract the trend in the scale of the economy. Campbell and Kyle (1993) is an example.

tion and returns are jointly lognormal, this implies that expected consumption growth is linear in the expected portfolio return with slope coefficient ψ, and that each asset's risk premium must equal a weighted average of the asset's covariance with the optimal portfolio return (as in the static CAPM) and optimal consumption growth (as in the consumption CAPM).

Giovannini and Weil (1989) have shown that in this model, portfolio choice is myopic when $\gamma = 1$ for any value of ψ. Thus Samuelson's conditions for myopic portfolio choice can be relaxed slightly in this framework. When $\psi = 1$, the consumption-to-wealth ratio is constant for any value of γ, but portfolio choice is affected by intertemporal hedging demand unless $\gamma = 1$. Campbell (1993, 1996) and Campbell and Viceira (1999, 2000) have used the Epstein–Zin model with $\psi = 1$ as a benchmark case and have derived approximate solutions that are accurate if ψ is sufficiently close to one. Numerical work suggests that accuracy is acceptable for ψ less than about three.

An alternative rationale for this form of preferences is provided by Maenhout (1999). He builds on the work of Anderson, Hansen, and Sargent (1999) to show that Epstein–Zin preferences may result from power utility, together with a preference for "robustness" (choices that deliver desirable outcomes in the face of model uncertainty, evaluated using the worst plausible model). Equivalent "stochastic differential utility" preferences have been formulated in continuous time by Duffie and Epstein (1992) and have been used to study long-term portfolio choice by Schroder and Skiadas (1999).

It is possible to construct other models of utility that preserve the desirable scale-independence of power utility. One strategy is to write utility as a power function of some variable other than consumption: for example, consumption relative to a habit or subsistence level that captures the past history of consumption. This approach is discussed in Section IV.B. Another strategy is to model a reference point that grows with consumption or wealth and to define utility relative to this reference point in a scale-independent way. This approach is discussed in Section VI.B.1. For the rest of this section, however, I will follow the bulk of the microeconomic portfolio choice literature and consider investors who have power or Epstein–Zin utility.

B. Time-Varying Investment Opportunities

B.1. Variation in Real Interest Rates

One of the most obvious ways in which investment opportunities vary is that real interest rates change over time. Real affine-yield models surveyed in Section II.B capture this variation and derive implications for long-term bond yields. If there were no variation in real interest rates, inflation-indexed bonds would have constant prices and would be perfect substitutes for cash; thus any coherent model of the demand for long-term real bonds must be an intertemporal rather than a static model. Nominal interest rates are also influenced by inflation shocks, but here too an intertemporal model is appropriate to capture the effects of changing real interest rates.

Investment advisers often argue that long-term bonds are appropriate for conservative long-term investors. In fact, the recommended investment allocations of several financial columnists and mutual-fund companies summarized by Canner, Mankiw, and Weil (1997) systematically increase the ratio of bonds to stocks for more conservative investors. Bond returns are risky in the short term, however, so this advice contradicts the mutual-fund theorem of Tobin (1958), according to which all investors should hold the same portfolio of risky assets, the tangency portfolio of mean-variance analysis. Conservative investors should hold less of this portfolio and more of a short-term safe asset, but the relative proportions of different risky assets—including stocks and bonds—should be the same for conservative investors as for aggressive investors. Canner et al. call this contradiction the *asset allocation puzzle*.

The Tobin mutual-fund theorem takes a short-term perspective, defining a short-term safe asset as riskless and long-term bonds as risky. Such a perspective is inappropriate for a long-term investor who cares about the distribution of wealth at a fixed date in the distant future. Short-term assets are not safe for such an investor, because they must be rolled over at uncertain future interest rates. Instead, a long-term zero-coupon bond that matures on the terminal date is the safe asset for this investor (Modigliani and Sutch (1966)).

This insight has recently been extended to the more realistic case in which the investor cares about the stream of consumption that can be financed by wealth, rather than the distribution of wealth at any particular date. Brennan and Xia (1998) consider a power-utility investor with a finite horizon, able to buy inflation-indexed bonds at interest rates determined by the Vasicek (1977) model. They show that as risk aversion increases, the investor's portfolio converges to an inflation-indexed coupon bond maturing at the horizon. Wachter (1998) proves a more general version of this result.

Campbell and Viceira (2000) fit a two-factor homoskedastic model of the SDF to data on U.S. nominal interest rates, stock returns, and inflation. They consider an infinitely lived investor with Epstein–Zin utility, derive a portfolio solution that is exact when $\psi = 1$ and approximate otherwise, and show that the share of nominal bonds relative to stocks increases with risk aversion when bonds are inflation-indexed or when inflation risk is moderate as it has been in the United States in the last 15 years. In this way they resolve the asset allocation puzzle.

B.2. Variation in Risk Premia

It is often argued that stocks are relatively safer for long-term investors (Siegel 1999). If asset returns are IID, this cannot be true because the means and variances of all asset returns increase in proportion with the investment horizon. Thus any claim of this sort must be based on predictability of stock returns. In fact, the empirical evidence summarized in Section I.A.4 does imply that the variance of stock returns increases more slowly than proportionally with the investment horizon. Poterba and Summers (1988) present direct evidence for this effect based on the predominantly negative univariate autocorrelations of stock returns, and Campbell (1991) reports indirect evidence based on the predictability of stock returns from the dividend-to-price ratio and the negative correlation between innovations to the stock return and the dividend-to-price ratio. Predictability of this sort, that reduces long-term risk relative to short-term risk, is often called mean reversion.

If stock returns are mean-reverting, this again implies that investment opportunities are time-varying. Once again an intertemporal model is needed to calculate optimal investment allocations. Kim and Omberg (1996) solve the portfolio choice problem of a long-lived investor, with power utility defined over wealth at a distant future date, who faces a constant riskless interest rate and a time-varying equity premium that follows a homoskedastic AR(1) process. They show that when the stock return is negatively correlated with innovations to the equity premium, then the investor increases the average allocation to stocks if risk aversion is greater than one. Wachter (1999) derives a similar result for an investor who has power utility defined over consumption, in the special case where the innovations to the stock return and the equity premium are perfectly correlated. Campbell and Viceira (1999) consider an infinitely lived investor with Epstein–Zin utility defined over consumption. Their solution is exact when $\psi = 1$ and approximate otherwise. They estimate the parameters of the model from postwar U.S. data and find that the estimated mean reversion dramatically increases the average optimal equity allocation of a conservative long-term investor.

In all these models the investor optimally times the market, altering the allocation to stocks as the equity premium changes. Thus the models do not support the buy-and-hold policy recommended by Siegel (1999) for long-term investors.[5] This also raises the issue of consistency with general equilibrium; with a constant supply of stocks not all investors can buy or sell stocks at the same time, so these models cannot be used to describe the behavior of a representative agent in general equilibrium. Models with time-varying risk aversion, of the sort described in Section IV.B, solve the complementary problem of finding preferences that make a representative agent content to buy and hold the market in the face of a time-varying equity premium.

Brennan, Schwartz, and Lagnado (1996), Campbell, Chan, and Viceira (1999), and Lynch (1999) combine time-varying real interest rates with time-varying risk premia. They estimate more complex empirical models in which both bonds and stocks can be used to hedge against changes in investment opportunities. The estimated predictability of stock returns tends to imply that hedging demand is largest for stocks. Brandt (1999) uses a nonparametric approach, avoiding the specification of a parametric model, and obtains generally similar results. Balduzzi and Lynch (1999) show how transactions costs can affect optimal long-term portfolios.

---

[5] A buy-and-hold policy may be a constrained optimum if investors are unable to leverage their equity holdings. In this case, however, the constrained problem must be solved from first principles because the constraint affects the optimal consumption policy in addition to the optimal portfolio.

All these models assume that investors know the parameters of the model for asset returns. This is clearly unrealistic given the substantial uncertainty among financial economists about these parameters. Bawa, Brown, and Klein (1979) provided an early treatment of parameter uncertainty in a short-horizon model with IID asset returns, and Kandel and Stambaugh (1996) have considered the effects on a short-horizon investor of uncertainty about return predictability. Williams (1977), Dothan and Feldman (1986), and Gennotte (1986) point out that in a long-horizon setting, optimal portfolios are affected by the fact that investors can learn about parameters over time. Brennan (1998) and Barberis (2000) explore this issue empirically. If an investor learns about the mean stock return by observing realized returns, then a positive stock return will lead the investor to revise upward his estimate of the mean stock return. This makes stock returns positively correlated with expected future stock returns, the opposite of the mean-reversion effect. Hedging demand is correspondingly reversed, and the stock demand of conservative long-term investors is reduced. Xia (1999) considers the possibility of learning about the degree of mean-reversion itself. Future research will undoubtedly push further in the direction of integrating the estimation and portfolio choice problems; Brandt (1999) shows one way to do this by directly estimating an optimal portfolio rule rather than a process for asset returns.

C. Labor Income and Portfolio Choice

Labor income can also have important effects on portfolio choice for long-term investors. An important paper on this topic is Bodie, Merton, and Samuelson (hereafter BMS) (1991). These authors show that exogenous, riskless labor income is equivalent to an implicit holding of riskless assets. Previous results apply to total asset holdings, so riskless labor income tilts explicit asset holdings toward risky assets. Exogenous labor income that is perfectly correlated with risky assets, on the other hand, is equivalent to an implicit holding of risky assets and tilts the financial portfolio toward safe assets. BMS also consider the possibility that investors can vary their labor supply endogenously. They find that this increases the willingness to take risks because investors can absorb financial losses both by cutting consumption and by adjusting labor supply.

BMS do not consider idiosyncratic risk in labor income that cannot be hedged using financial assets. Recent theoretical work shows that such background risk can have important effects on consumption and portfolio decisions; Gollier (2000) provides a textbook treatment. Here too it is extremely challenging to extend two-period results to a more realistic multiperiod setting. Viceira (1999) shows that lognormally distributed labor income risk, uncorrelated with financial asset risk, reduces the tilt toward risky assets but does not reverse it. This type of risk also has a large effect in stimulating wealth accumulation through precautionary saving as emphasized by Carroll (1997).

Bertaut and Haliassos (1997), Heaton and Lucas (1997), Cocco, Gomes, and Maenhout (1998), and Storesletten, Telmer, and Yaron (1998) have explored the effects of realistically calibrated labor income risk on portfolio choice over the life cycle. Because the ratio of labor income to wealth rises early in adult life and then gradually declines, the willingness to take equity risk follows a similar pattern. Dammon, Spatt, and Zhang (1999) have explored the life-cycle portfolio effects of the tax code and particularly the adjustment of the capital gains tax basis at death. They find that the tax code deters elderly investors from selling stocks, and thus increases their average allocation to equities.

IV. Equilibrium Models with a Representative Agent

The theory of intertemporal optimization relates the SDF to the marginal utility process for an unconstrained investor. This in turn restricts the consumption of such an investor. The research summarized in Section III uses this fact to solve for the optimal consumption and portfolio choice of investors with exogenously specified utility functions who face exogenous asset return processes (equivalently, an exogenous SDF).

Lucas (1978) pointed out that this logic can be reversed to derive the equilibrium SDF implied by an exogenous consumption process and utility specification. He assumed that the economy can be described by a representative investor, with a standard utility function, who consumes aggregate consumption. The first-order conditions of this investor determine the SDF. Asset prices can be determined explicitly by modeling payoffs jointly with the SDF, using methods described in Section II. Lucas modeled the aggregate stock market as paying a dividend equal to aggregate consumption; this is equivalent to the traditional assumption in finance that the stock market is the "market portfolio" of all wealth.

A. *Three Puzzles*

With the standard assumption of power utility, this approach leads to three puzzles. First, the average return on the stock market is too high to be readily explained by the model. The SDF implied by power utility is $\delta(C_{t+1}/C_t)^{-\gamma}$, the time discount factor times aggregate consumption growth raised to the power $-\gamma$. If we assume joint lognormality of consumption growth and asset returns for expositional convenience, the negative covariance of the log return on asset i with the log SDF becomes $\gamma\sigma_{ic}$, the coefficient of risk aversion times the covariance of asset i with log consumption growth. This should equal the risk premium on asset i. But empirically, U.S. consumption growth is very smooth (Campbell (1999) reports a standard deviation of about one percent in quarterly postwar U.S. data). Thus the covariance of risky assets with consumption growth cannot be large, no matter how highly correlated with consumption growth these assets may be. To explain the equity premium, the coefficient of risk aversion must be a much higher number than has traditionally been considered plausible. This is the *equity premium puzzle* of Mehra and Prescott (1985).

Second, the volatility of stock returns is too high to be readily explained by the model. Stock returns are driven by innovations to consumption growth, which affect both expected future dividends and discount rates. Expected log dividend growth equals expected log consumption growth $E_t \Delta c_{t+1}$, and in a homoskedastic lognormal model with constant risk premia, the expected log stock return is a constant plus $\gamma E_t \Delta c_{t+1}$, risk aversion times expected consumption growth. Using the approximate log-linear formula for stock returns, equation (12), the implied return on the aggregate stock market, $r_{e,t+1}$, is

$$r_{e,t+1} - E_t r_{e,t+1} = (\Delta c_{t+1} - E_t \Delta c_{t+1}) + (1 - \gamma)(E_{t+1} - E_t) \sum_{j=1}^{\infty} \rho^j \Delta c_{t+1+j}.$$

$$(17)$$

If consumption growth is IID (this appears to be approximately true in postwar U.S. data), then expected future consumption growth is constant and the unexpected stock return should equal current unexpected consumption growth. More generally, variations in expected future consumption growth cause offsetting variations in expected future dividend growth and expected future stock returns—the offset is exact if risk aversion $\gamma = 1$—and this makes it hard to generate large variations in current stock returns. Campbell (1999) calls this the *stock market volatility puzzle*.

One response to the equity premium puzzle is to accept the possibility that risk aversion might be higher than was traditionally considered reasonable. Our intuition about risk aversion has been built through thought experiments, but Kandel and Stambaugh (1991) point out that the results of such experiments are very sensitive to details of their specification, including particularly the size of the gamble one considers.

Within the power utility framework, increasing risk aversion has the unfortunate side effect of lowering the elasticity of intertemporal substitution (EIS). Although there is direct evidence that the EIS is fairly small (Hall (1988), Campbell and Mankiw (1989)—but see Attanasio and Weber (1993) and Beaudry and van Wincoop (1996) for somewhat larger estimates), extremely small values for the EIS imply that investors have an overpowering preference for a flat consumption path. Given the historical upward drift in consumption, this implies an extremely strong desire to borrow from the future. Unless this is offset by a low or even negative rate of time preference, the result is a counterfactually high real interest rate. Weil (1989) calls this the *risk-free rate puzzle*.

Epstein–Zin utility can be helpful in resolving the risk-free rate puzzle. It, like the model of habit formation discussed in Section IV.B, allows the EIS to differ from the reciprocal of risk aversion. Thus one can postulate high risk aversion to resolve the equity premium puzzle without driving the EIS to an unreasonably low value.

There is no such straightforward escape from the stock market volatility puzzle. The lognormal model with power utility explains variation in stock prices relative to dividends as resulting from predictable variation in future consumption growth that moves expected future dividends and real interest rates. Unfortunately, real interest rates are too stable to explain large swings in stock prices (Campbell (1991)), and there is very little evidence that stock price-to-dividend ratios predict future consumption growth, dividend growth, or real interest rates (Campbell (1999)). This suggests that the volatility of stock returns must be explained by changes in the equity premium itself.

One way to generate time variation in the equity premium is from time variation in volatility. Schwert (1989) presents evidence that the conditional volatility of stock returns moves countercyclically along with forecasts of stock returns, and Bollerslev, Engle, and Wooldridge (1988) derive implications of exogenous movements in return volatility for the equity premium. Of course, it is desirable to derive movements in return volatility from underlying fundamentals; accordingly Abel (1988), Kandel and Stambaugh (1991), Veronesi (1999), and Whitelaw (2000) model heteroskedasticity or time-varying uncertainty about the consumption (dividend) process. A difficulty with these efforts is that the evidence for heteroskedasticity in aggregate consumption is fairly weak. This suggests that it is worthwhile to build a model in which risk aversion changes over time so that the price of risk, rather than the quantity of risk, is time-varying.

B. Habit Formation and Time-Varying Risk Aversion

Sundaresan (1989) and Constantinides (1990) have argued for the importance of habit formation, a positive effect of today's consumption on tomorrow's marginal utility of consumption.

Several modeling issues arise at the outset. Writing the period utility function as $U(C_t, X_t)$, where X_t is the time-varying habit or subsistence level, the first issue is the functional form for $U(\cdot)$. Abel (1990) has proposed that $U(\cdot)$ should be a power function of the ratio C_t/X_t, whereas most other researchers have used a power function of the difference $C_t - X_t$. The second issue is the effect of an agent's own decisions on future levels of habit. In standard "internal habit" models such as those in Constantinides (1990) and Sundaresan (1989), habit depends on an agent's own consumption and the agent takes account of this when choosing how much to consume. In "external habit" models such as those in Abel (1990) and Campbell and Cochrane (1999), habit depends on aggregate consumption that is unaffected by any one agent's decisions. Abel calls this "catching up with the Joneses." The third issue is the speed with which habit reacts to individual or aggregate consumption. Abel (1990) and Ferson and Constantinides (1991) make habit depend on one lag of consumption, whereas Sundaresan (1989), Constantinides (1990), Heaton (1995), and Campbell and Cochrane (1999) assume that habit reacts only gradually to changes in consumption.

The choice between ratio models and difference models of habit is important because ratio models have constant risk aversion whereas difference models have time-varying risk aversion. In Abel's (1990) ratio model, external habit adds a term to the equation describing the riskless interest rate but does not change the equation that describes the excess return of risky assets over the riskless interest rate. The effect on the riskless interest rate has to do with intertemporal substitution. Holding consumption today and

1546   *The Journal of Finance*

expected consumption tomorrow constant, an increase in consumption yes-
terday increases the marginal utility of consumption today. This makes the
representative agent want to borrow from the future, driving up the real
interest rate.

This instability of the riskless real interest rate is a fundamental problem
for habit-formation models. Time-nonseparable preferences make marginal utility volatile even when consumption is smooth, because consumers derive utility from consumption relative to its recent history rather than from the absolute
level of consumption. But unless the consumption and habit processes take particular forms, time-nonseparability also creates large swings in expected marginal utility at successive dates, and this implies large movements in the real
interest rate. I now present an alternative specification in which it is possible
to solve this problem and in which risk aversion varies over time.

Campbell and Cochrane (1999) build a model with external habit formation in which a representative agent derives utility from the difference between consumption and a time-varying subsistence or habit level. They assume
that log consumption follows a random walk with mean g and innovation
$\epsilon_{c,t+1}$. This is a fairly good approximation for U.S. data. The utility function
of the representative agent is a time-separable power utility function, with
curvature γ, of the difference between consumption C_t and habit X_t. Utility
is only defined when consumption exceeds habit.

It is convenient to capture the relation between consumption and habit by
the surplus consumption ratio S_t, defined by $S_t \equiv (C_t - X_t)/C_t$. The surplus
consumption ratio is the fraction of consumption that exceeds habit and is
therefore available to generate utility. If habit X_t is held fixed as consumption C_t varies, the local coefficient of relative risk aversion is $-Cu_{CC}/u_C =
\gamma/S_t$, where u_C and u_{CC} are the first and second derivatives of utility with
respect to consumption. Risk aversion rises as the surplus consumption ratio
S_t declines, that is, as consumption approaches the habit level. Note that γ,
the curvature parameter in utility, is no longer the coefficient of relative risk
aversion in this model.

To complete the description of preferences, one must specify how the habit
X_t evolves over time in response to aggregate consumption. Campbell and Cochrane suggest an AR(1) model for the log surplus consumption ratio, $s_t \equiv \log(S_t)$:

$$s_{t+1} = (1 - \varphi)\bar{s} + \varphi s_t + \lambda(s_t)\epsilon_{c,t+1}. \qquad (18)$$

The parameter φ governs the persistence of the log surplus consumption
ratio, whereas the "sensitivity function" $\lambda(s_t)$ controls the sensitivity of s_{t+1}
and thus of log habit x_{t+1} to innovations in consumption growth $\epsilon_{c,t+1}$. This
modeling strategy ensures that the habit process implied by a process for
s_{t+1} always lies below consumption.

To derive the asset pricing implications of this model, one first calculates
the SDF as

$$M_{t+1} = \delta \left(\frac{S_{t+1}}{S_t}\right)^{-\gamma} \left(\frac{C_{t+1}}{C_t}\right)^{-\gamma}. \qquad (19)$$

The SDF is driven by proportional innovations in the surplus consumption ratio and also by proportional innovations in consumption. If the surplus consumption ratio is only a small fraction of consumption, then small shocks to consumption can be large shocks to the surplus consumption ratio; thus the SDF can be highly volatile even when consumption is smooth. This volatility is itself time-varying because it depends on the level of the surplus consumption ratio.

The logic of Hansen and Jagannathan (1991) implies that the largest possible Sharpe ratio is given by the conditional standard deviation of the log SDF. This is $\gamma\sigma(1 + \lambda(s_t))$, so a sensitivity function that varies inversely with s_t delivers a time-varying, countercyclical Sharpe ratio.

The same mechanism helps to stabilize the riskless real interest rate. When the surplus consumption ratio falls, investors have an intertemporal-substitution motive to borrow from the future, but this is offset by an increased precautionary savings motive created by the volatility of the SDF. Campbell and Cochrane parameterize the model so that these two effects exactly cancel. This makes the riskless real interest rate constant, a knife-edge case that helps to reveal the pure effects of time-varying risk aversion on asset prices. With a constant riskless rate, real bonds of all maturities are also riskless, and there are no real term premia. Thus the equity premium is also a premium of stocks over long-term bonds.

When this model is calibrated to fit the first two moments of consumption growth, the average riskless interest rate, and the Sharpe ratio on the stock market, it also roughly fits the volatility, predictability, and cyclicality of stock returns. The model does not resolve the equity premium puzzle, because it relies on high average risk aversion, but it does resolve the stock market volatility puzzle.

It is important to understand the mechanism by which this resolution takes place. Any scale-independent model implies that wealth and consumption are cointegrated, so over sufficiently long horizons their growth rates must have the same volatility. Because the volatility of wealth seems to be far higher than the volatility of consumption in the short run, the question is how these volatilities are reconciled in the long run. The two possibilities are that consumption growth is positively autocorrelated, so the variance of consumption growth increases more than proportionally with the horizon, or that stock returns are negatively autocorrelated, so the variance of wealth increases less than proportionally with the horizon. The Campbell–Cochrane model assumes random walk consumption and implies negative autocorrelation of stock returns. The Constantinides (1990) model of habit formation, by contrast, assumes IID asset returns and implies positive autocorrelation of consumption growth.

Campbell and Cochrane (2000) develop cross-sectional implications of the habit-formation model. Because the model is driven by a single shock, the stock market return is almost perfectly correlated with the innovation to consumption. This implies that either a conditional consumption CAPM or a conditional version of the traditional CAPM provides a good conditional description of returns. Unconditionally, however, the consumption CAPM works poorly because the SDF is a time-varying function of consumption growth. The market return partly captures this time variation so the unconditional CAPM works better. A scaled version of the CAPM works better still. These results apply to artificial data generated by the habit-formation model, not to real data, but they do suggest the importance of using conditional models to evaluate cross-sectional anomalies as in the recent work of Cochrane (1996), Jagannathan and Wang (1996), and Lettau and Ludvigson (1999b).

V. Equilibrium Models with Heterogeneous Agents

The previous section assumed that assets can be priced as if there is a representative agent who consumes aggregate consumption. An alternative view is that aggregate consumption is not an adequate proxy for the consumption of investors.

A. Heterogeneous Constraints

One simple explanation for a discrepancy between these two measures of consumption is that there are two types of agents in the economy: constrained agents who are prevented from trading in asset markets and simply consume their labor income each period, and unconstrained agents. The consumption of the constrained agents is irrelevant to the determination of equilibrium asset prices, but it may be a large fraction of aggregate consumption. Campbell and Mankiw (1989) argue that predictable variation in consumption growth, correlated with predictable variation in income growth, suggests an important role for constrained agents, whereas Mankiw and Zeldes (1991) and Brav, Constantinides, and Geczy (1999) use U.S. panel data to show that the consumption of stockholders is more volatile and more highly correlated with the stock market than the consumption of nonstockholders. Heaton and Lucas (1999) and Vissing-Jørgensen (1997) build general equilibrium models in which a limited fraction of the population participates in the stock market. They argue that an increased participation rate, along with reduced costs of diversification, may help to explain recent increases in stock prices. Such effects are likely to be even more important in countries with low stock market capitalization and concentrated equity ownership.

 This view suggests an approach to asset pricing in which one assumes that there is a representative investor who holds the market portfolio but does not necessarily consume aggregate consumption. Consumption becomes unobservable and must be substituted out of an intertemporal model. Merton's (1973) intertemporal CAPM is the classic example of this approach. More recently Campbell (1993, 1996) has developed an empirical discrete-time version of this model in which priced factors are innovations to variables that forecast future returns on the market portfolio. For reasons discussed in Section III.B.2, the estimated mean reversion of aggregate stock market returns increases the demand for stocks by the representative investor if the coefficient of relative risk aversion is greater than one. This increase in equity demand means that the risk aversion needed to fit the equity premium is large, in line with the consumption-based literature of Section IV, rather than small, as suggested by Friend and Blume (1975) using a static model that ignores mean reversion. This work deepens the equity premium puzzle by showing that the puzzle arises even if one ignores aggregate consumption data.

One might hope that an intertemporal CAPM of this sort, with additional priced risks beyond shocks to the market, could explain the cross-sectional anomalies in stock returns. This line of research is promising but is hampered by the Roll (1977) critique that aggregate wealth itself is very hard to measure.

B. *Heterogeneous Income*

It is also possible that utility-maximizing stock market investors are heterogeneous in important ways. If investors are subject to large idiosyncratic risks in their labor income and can share these risks only indirectly by trading a few assets such as stocks and Treasury bills, their individual consumption paths may be much more volatile than aggregate consumption. Even if individual investors have the same power utility function, so that any individual's consumption growth rate raised to the power $-\gamma$ would be a valid SDF, the aggregate consumption growth rate raised to the power $-\gamma$ may not be a valid SDF.

This problem is an example of Jensen's Inequality. Because marginal utility is nonlinear, the average of investors' marginal utilities of consumption is not generally the same as the marginal utility of average consumption. The problem disappears when investors' individual consumption streams are perfectly correlated with one another as they will be in a complete markets setting. Grossman and Shiller (1982) point out that it also disappears in a continuous-time model when the processes for individual consumption streams and asset prices are diffusions.

Recently Constantinides and Duffie (1996) have provided a simple framework within which the effects of heterogeneity can be understood. Constantinides and Duffie postulate an economy in which individual investors k have different consumption levels C_{kt}. The cross-sectional distribution of individual consumption is lognormal, and the change from time t to time $t + 1$ in individual log consumption is cross-sectionally uncorrelated with the level of individual log consumption at time t. All investors have the same power utility function with time discount factor δ and coefficient of relative risk aversion γ.

In this economy each investor's own intertemporal marginal rate of substitution is a valid SDF. Hence the cross-sectional average of investors' intertemporal marginal rates of substitution, M^*_{t+1}, is a valid SDF. However the marginal utility of the cross-sectional average of investors' consumption, M^{RA}_{t+1}, is *not* a valid SDF when marginal utility is nonlinear. This false SDF would be used incorrectly by an economist who ignores the aggregation problem in the economy.

1550   *The Journal of Finance*

The difference between the logs of these two variables is

$$m^*_{t+1} - m^{RA}_{t+1} = \frac{\gamma(\gamma + 1)}{2} \operatorname{Var}^*_{t+1} \Delta c_{k, t+1}, \tag{20}$$

where $\operatorname{Var}^*_{t+1}$ denotes a cross-sectional variance measured at time $t + 1$. The time series of this difference can have a nonzero mean, helping to explain the risk-free rate puzzle, and a nonzero variance, helping to explain the equity premium puzzle. If the cross-sectional variance of log consumption growth is negatively correlated with the level of aggregate consumption, so that idiosyncratic risk increases in economic downturns, then the true SDF m^*_{t+1} will be more strongly countercyclical than the representative-agent SDF constructed using the same preference parameters; this has the potential to explain the high price of risk without assuming that individual investors have high risk aversion. Mankiw (1986) makes a similar point in a two-period model.

An important unresolved question is whether the heterogeneity we can measure has the characteristics that are needed to help resolve the asset pricing puzzles. In the Constantinides–Duffie model the heterogeneity must be large to have important effects on the SDF; a cross-sectional standard deviation of log consumption growth of 20 percent, for example, is a cross-sectional variance of only 0.04, and it is variation in this number over time that is needed to explain the equity premium puzzle. Interestingly, the effect of heterogeneity is strongly increasing in risk aversion because $\operatorname{Var}^*_{t+1} \Delta c_{k, t+1}$ is multiplied by $\gamma(\gamma + 1)/2$ in equation (20). This suggests that heterogeneity may supplement high risk aversion but cannot altogether replace it as an explanation for the equity premium puzzle.

Cogley (1998) looks at consumption data and finds that measured heterogeneity has only small effects on the SDF. Lettau (1997) reaches a similar conclusion by assuming that individuals consume their income and calculating the risk-aversion coefficients needed to put model-based SDFs inside the Hansen–Jagannathan volatility bounds. This procedure is conservative in that individuals trading in financial markets are normally able to achieve some smoothing of consumption relative to income. Nevertheless Lettau finds that high individual risk aversion is still needed to satisfy the Hansen–Jagannathan bounds.

These conclusions may not be surprising given the Grossman–Shiller (1982) result that the aggregation problem disappears in a continuous-time diffusion model. In such a model, the cross-sectional variance of consumption is locally deterministic, and hence the false SDF M^{RA}_{t+1} correctly prices risky assets. In a discrete-time model the cross-sectional variance of consumption can change randomly from one period to the next, but in practice these changes are likely to be small. This limits the effects of consumption heterogeneity on asset pricing.

It is also important to note that idiosyncratic shocks are assumed to be permanent in the Constantinides–Duffie model. Heaton and Lucas (1996) calibrate individual income processes to microdata from the Panel Study of

Income Dynamics (PSID). Because the PSID data show that idiosyncratic income variation is largely transitory, Heaton and Lucas find that investors can minimize its effects on their consumption by borrowing and lending. This prevents heterogeneity from having any large effects on aggregate asset prices.

To get around this problem, several recent papers have combined heterogeneity with constraints on borrowing. Heaton and Lucas (1996) and Krusell and Smith (1997) find that borrowing constraints or large costs of trading equities are needed to explain the equity premium. Constantinides, Donaldson, and Mehra (1998) focus on heterogeneity across generations. In a stylized three-period overlapping generations model young agents have the strongest desire to hold equities because they have the largest ratio of labor income to financial wealth. If these agents are prevented from borrowing to buy equities, the equilibrium equity premium is large.

C. Heterogeneous Preferences

Heterogeneity in preferences may also be important. Several authors have recently argued that trading between investors with different degrees of risk aversion or time preference, possibly in the presence of market frictions or portfolio insurance constraints, can lead to time variation in the market price of risk (Dumas (1989), Grossman and Zhou (1996), Wang (1996), Sandroni (1997), Chan and Kogan (1999)). Intuitively, risk-tolerant agents hold more risky assets so they control a greater share of wealth in good states than in bad states; aggregate risk aversion therefore falls in good states, producing effects similar to those of habit formation.

VI. Behavioral Finance

Behavioral finance has been one of the most active areas in asset pricing during the 1990s. Shiller (1984) and Summers (1986) are two key early references; the field has now matured to the point where textbook treatments are possible (Shiller (1999), Shleifer (2000)).

Behavioral finance models contain two key ingredients. First, they postulate nonstandard behavior, driven by irrationality or nonstandard preferences, on the part of at least some investors. Ideally the postulated behavior is supported by experimental or empirical evidence. Second, they assume that rational investors with standard preferences are limited in their desire or ability to offset the asset demands of the first group of investors. This means that irrational expectations or nonstandard preferences affect the prices of financial assets.

These models cannot be tested using data on aggregate consumption or the market portfolio, because rational utility-maximizing investors neither consume aggregate consumption (some is accounted for by nonstandard investors) nor hold the market portfolio (instead they shift in and out of the stock market). This makes it hard to test behavioral models without having detailed information on the investment strategies of different market participants.

1552   *The Journal of Finance*

A. Limits to Arbitrage

In the first phase of this research, the description of nonstandard investors was rudimentary. These investors were called "noise traders." Their demands for risky assets were assumed to follow simple exogenous processes. Papers of this sort include Shiller (1984), De Long et al. (1990), Cutler, Poterba, and Summers (1991), and Campbell and Kyle (1993). The main emphasis of this work is on the factors that limit the ability of utility-maximizing investors to absorb the demands of noise traders at constant prices. (This absorption of demand is often called "arbitrage" but should not be confused with the technical use of the term to mean a riskless profit opportunity.)

The basic factor is risk, and this can be enough by itself. In Campbell and Kyle (1993), for example, markets are perfect and investors are infinitely lived, but utility maximizers charge a price for bearing fundamental risk when they are asked to buy more risky assets from noise traders. The effects of risk aversion are reinforced if investors have short horizons. De Long et al. (1990) assume an overlapping generations structure in which utility-maximizing investors are forced to sell their asset holdings after one period. In this case utility maximizers are exposed to price fluctuations caused by noise trading and also to fundamental risk, and their willingness to offset noise is correspondingly reduced. The wealth or capital of utility maximizers is also relevant. A shock to noise demand that moves prices away from fundamental value reduces the wealth of utility maximizers and may reduce their trading capacity. This factor is likely to be particularly important if utility-maximizing investors are financed by uninformed outside lenders, who react to losses by cutting lending (Shleifer and Vishny (1997), Xiong (1999)). This point appears highly relevant for understanding the events of fall 1998, particularly the collapse of the hedge fund Long Term Capital Management.

Because risk is the key factor limiting the ability of utility maximizers to offset noise-trader demands, noise traders cannot create diversifiable random variation in asset prices. The effects of noise trading must either be systematic—that is, correlated with pervasive common factors in the economy—or must be limited to isolated instances. Lee, Shleifer, and Thaler (1991), for example, argue that noise traders determine the premia and discounts on closed-end funds and that these premia tend to move with the returns on small stocks. Small-stock returns are a systematic risk factor in the Fama–French (1993) model, whether for fundamental reasons or because they reflect systematic shifts in noise trader demands. Shleifer (1986) and Wurgler and Zhuravskaya (1999) argue that noise traders bid up the prices of stocks when they are included in the S&P 500 index. Because only one or a few stocks are included in the index at any one time, this effect cannot be readily diversified away. Noise traders may similarly affect the prices of initial public offerings if only one or a few IPOs are available at any one time.

B. Modeling Nonstandard Behavior

Recent behavioral research has placed greater emphasis on the modeling of nonstandard investor behavior and has sought to explain the aggregate predictability and cross-sectional patterns in stock returns summarized in Section I. Some models alter standard assumptions about preferences, whereas others assume particular forms of irrational expectations.

B.1. Prospect Theory

Preference-based behavioral models often work with the prospect theory of Kahneman and Tversky (1979). According to this theory, people do not judge outcomes on an absolute scale but compare outcomes with an initial reference point. Their objective function has a kink at the reference point, so risk aversion is locally infinite at that point. The objective function is concave for "gains" (outcomes above the reference point) but is convex for "losses" (outcomes below the reference point). All these properties are based on experimental evidence, but such evidence can be hard to interpret because experimental rewards and penalties are necessarily small and may not reveal people's attitudes toward larger risks. For this reason many applications modify the model to drop certain features, particularly the convexity of the objective function in the realm of losses. A related model of "first-order risk aversion," with kinked utility at a reference point but without convexity in the realm of losses, is developed by Epstein and Zin (1990) (see also Gul (1991)).

Several important issues arise in using prospect theory, and experimental evidence gives little guidance. A first issue is the time horizon: at what intervals do investors evaluate outcomes using the Kahneman–Tversky objective function? A second issue is the determination and updating of the reference point. A third issue is the argument of the objective function. In a standard intertemporal model, investors care about consumption rather than wealth. Many papers in the behavioral literature argue instead that wealth is the argument of the objective function. Some go further and claim that investors have a separate "mental account" for each asset, evaluating outcomes on an asset-by-asset basis.

Benartzi and Thaler (1995) argue that wealth-based prospect theory can explain the equity premium puzzle if investors evaluate their wealth frequently and update their reference points to current wealth levels. In this case the kink at the reference point is always relevant and makes investors, in effect, highly risk-averse. Epstein and Zin (1990) find a similar effect in their model of first-order risk aversion.

Barberis, Huang, and Santos (hereafter BHS) (2000) combine a standard power utility function in consumption with wealth-based prospect theory. They show that the Benartzi–Thaler model, with high but constant risk aversion, fails to explain the stock market volatility puzzle. Appealing to experimental evidence of Thaler and Johnson (1990), they argue that aversion to losses varies with past outcomes; past success reduces effective risk aversion as investors feel they are "gambling with house money." This creates a time-varying price of risk that explains aggregate stock market volatility in a similar manner to Campbell and Cochrane (1999). The BHS model has a lower aversion to consumption risk than the Campbell–

Cochrane model, because it generates risk-averse behavior not only from standard aversion to consumption fluctuations but also from direct aversion to wealth fluctuations.

Gomes (1999) explores the effects of wealth-based prospect theory on the demand for risky assets in partial equilibrium. Gomes shows that a decline in asset prices with fixed expected payoffs can actually reduce asset demands as increased risk aversion, caused by reduced wealth, outweighs higher expected returns. At a certain point, however, there is a discontinuous jump in asset demand as investors become risk-loving in the domain of losses. Gomes also shows that the kink in the Kahneman–Tversky objective function makes it optimal for investors to hold no stock when the equity premium is small; this is quite different from the standard result that a risk-averse investor should always take some amount of a favorable gamble, and it might help to explain the existence of investors who do not participate in the stock market.

Shefrin and Statman (1985) reported empirical evidence that many investors are reluctant to realize losses. This is a particular puzzle because the tax code favors realizing losses and delaying the realization of gains. Odean (1998) argues that prospect theory can explain this phenomenon. However such an argument requires a separate mental account for each stock and also requires that investors treat unrealized losses differently from realized ones (i.e., realization triggers evaluation of the objective function). These radical assumptions are not implied by prospect theory itself.

B.2. Irrational Expectations

A number of papers have explored the consequences of relaxing the assumption that investors have rational expectations and understand the behavior of dividend and consumption growth. In the absence of arbitrage, there exist positive state prices that can rationalize the prices of traded financial assets. These state prices equal subjective state probabilities multiplied by ratios of marginal utilities in different states. Thus given any model of utility, there exist subjective probabilities that produce the necessary state prices and in this sense explain the observed prices of traded financial assets. The interesting question is whether these subjective probabilities are sufficiently close to objective probabilities, and sufficiently related to known psychological biases in behavior, to be plausible.

Many of the papers in this area work in partial equilibrium and assume that stocks are priced by discounting expected future dividends at a constant rate. This assumption makes it easy to derive any desired behavior of stock prices directly from assumptions on dividend expectations. Barsky and De Long (1993), for example, assume that investors believe dividends to be generated by a doubly integrated process, so that the dividend growth rate has a unit root. These expectations imply that rapid dividend growth increases stock prices more than proportionally, so that the price-to-dividend ratio rises when dividends are growing strongly. If dividend growth is in fact stationary, then the high price-to-dividend ratio is typically followed by dividend disappointments, low stock returns, and reversion to the long-run mean price-to-dividend ratio. Under this assumption of stationary dividend growth, Barsky and DeLong's model produces overreaction of stock prices to dividend news. At the cross-sectional level, it explains the value effect. At the aggregate level, the model can account for the volatility puzzle and the predictability of stock returns.

It is harder to build a model of irrational expectations that explains the cross-sectional momentum effect together with the value effect. Three recent attempts to do this include Barberis, Shleifer, and Vishny (hereafter BSV) (1998), Daniel, Hirshleifer, and Subrahmanyam (hereafter DHS) (1998), and Hong and Stein (1999). BSV assume that investors entertain two different models of dividends. In the first model, dividend growth is negatively autocorrelated so dividends are mean-reverting, whereas in the second model, dividend growth is positively autocorrelated so dividends display trends. Investors never change either model but use Bayesian methods to update their priors about the probability that each model is true. BSV assume that dividends in fact follow a random walk, so both models are false; the mean-reverting model makes investors underreact to news, whereas the trending model makes them overreact. In this setting a string of good or bad news can induce investors to switch from the mean-reverting model to the trending model, so the model can produce both underreaction and overreaction depending on recent events.

The BSV model assumes a representative irrational investor. DHS (1998) and Hong and Stein (1999), by contrast, assume that there are multiple investors who receive both private signals and public information. In the DHS model, all investors are symmetrical and overconfident; they place too great a weight on their own private signal and too little on public information. Furthermore, investors react to public information that is consistent with their private signal by increasing their overconfidence but react to inconsistent public information by a smaller reduction in overconfidence; DHS call this "biased self-attribution." These assumptions imply that private information triggers short-run overreaction, which initially increases as investors react in a biased manner to subsequent public information. Only when the weight of public information becomes overwhelming do investors abandon their overconfident misvaluation. Thus the model produces both short-run momentum and long-run reversal.

Hong and Stein (1999) assume that there are two types of irrational investors. "Newswatchers" receive private signals about fundamental value, which diffuse gradually through the newswatching population. These investors form price expectations based on their signals but are imperfectly rational in that they do not learn from market prices. "Momentum investors" have no private information and trade on the basis of the most recent change in price. These investors are imperfectly rational in that they do not trade optimally based on the entire history of price changes. The interaction between these two groups produces both a momentum effect, as private information gradually affects prices and is reinforced by momentum trading, and a value effect, as momentum investors drive prices beyond fundamental value.

Another potentially important form of irrationality is a failure to understand the difference between real and nominal magnitudes. Modigliani and Cohn (1979) argued that investors suffer from inflation illusion, in effect discounting real cash flows at nominal interest rates. Ritter and Warr (1999) and Sharpe (1999) argue that inflation illusion may have led investors to bid up stock prices as inflation has declined since the early 1980s. An interesting issue raised by this literature is whether misvaluation is caused by a high *level* of inflation (in which case it is unlikely to be important today) or whether it is caused by *changes* in inflation from historical benchmark levels (in which case it may contribute to high current levels of stock prices).

A limitation of all these models is that they do not consider general equilibrium issues. If the models are supposed to apply to individual assets, then the misvaluations they produce are diversifiable and so can easily be arbitraged away by rational investors. If, on the other hand, the models apply to the market as a whole, then it is important to consider the implications for consumption. Using for simplicity the fiction that dividends equal consumption, investors' irrational expectations about dividend growth should be linked to their irrational expectations about consumption growth. Interest rates are not exogenous but, like stock prices, are determined by investors' expectations. Thus it is significantly harder to build a general equilibrium model with irrational expectations.

To see how irrationality can affect asset prices in general equilibrium, consider first a static model in which log consumption follows a random walk with drift. Investors understand that consumption is a random walk, but they underestimate its drift. Such irrational pessimism lowers the average risk-free rate, increases the equity premium, and has an ambiguous effect on the price-to-dividend ratio. Thus pessimism has the same effects on asset prices as a low rate of time preference and a high coefficient of risk aversion, and it can help to explain both the risk-free rate puzzle and the equity premium puzzle (Hansen, Sargent, and Tallarini (1997)).

To explain the volatility puzzle, a more complicated model of irrationality is needed. Suppose now that log consumption growth follows an AR(1) process but that investors overestimate the persistence of this process. In this model the equity premium falls when consumption growth has been rapid and rises when consumption growth has been weak. This model, which can be seen as a general equilibrium version of Barsky and De Long (1993), fits the apparent cyclical variation in the market price of risk. One difficulty with this story is that it has strong implications for bond market behavior. Consumption growth drives up the riskless interest rate and the real bond premium even while it drives down the equity premium. Cecchetti, Lam, and Mark (1997) handle this problem by allowing the degree of investors' irrationality itself to be stochastic and time-varying.

VII. Conclusion

This review of the past 20 years of asset pricing research suggests three main developments. First, we now have a rich set of stylized facts about interest rates, aggregate stock prices, and cross-sectional patterns in stock returns. Although some of these facts may turn out to be the result of data snooping, most of them are likely to survive as the subject of legitimate interest. Second, we have developed a variety of models in response to these facts. Even though these models fall within the general outlines established by an earlier generation of theorists, the details are new and important. Third, asset pricing is concerned with the sources of risk and the economic forces that determine the rewards for bearing risk. Summers (1985) infamously compared financial economists with "ketchup economists" obsessed with the relative prices of different-sized bottles of ketchup. He alleged that "financial economists, like ketchupal economists . . . are concerned with the interrelationships between the prices of different financial assets. They ignore what seems to many to be the more important question of what determines the overall level of asset prices" (p. 634). This accusation may never have been fair, but it certainly does not describe the field today.

A number of important issues remain as challenges for the new millennium. Some of these grow out of the literature I have described, and others I have not touched on at all.

First, we have only a poor understanding of how transactions costs can affect asset prices. Amihud and Mendelson (1986) have argued that transactions costs significantly reduce the prices of small stocks and may help to explain the small-firm effect. He and Modest (1995) and Luttmer (1996) have extended the Hansen–Jagannathan volatility bounds to allow for transactions costs. The bigger challenge is to explain how transactions costs—both in adjusting portfolios and in adjusting consumption, particularly of durable goods and housing—affect the prices of assets in general equilibrium. Recent work by Constantinides (1986), Grossman and Laroque (1990), Heaton and Lucas (1996), Vayanos (1998), and others makes a start on this task, but we still need simple, tractable models that incorporate these frictions.

Second, there is tantalizing evidence that extra risk factors suggested by dynamic asset pricing models can help to explain cross-sectional patterns in stock returns. Some of these extra factors proxy for omitted components of wealth, notably human capital; others capture time variation in the underlying model for the SDF. More work is needed to refine our understanding of these factor models. Here it will be helpful to use information from government and corporate bond markets as well as from stock markets. Ultimate success will require a much deeper understanding of the relation between the SDF and the equilibrium of the real economy.

Despite the promise of such research, in my opinion it is unrealistic to hope for a fully rational, risk-based explanation of all the empirical patterns that have been discovered in stock returns. A more reasonable view is that rational models of risk and return describe a long-run equilibrium toward which financial markets gradually evolve. Some deviations from such models can be quickly arbitraged away by rational investors; others are much harder to arbitrage and may disappear only after a slow process of learning and institutional innovation. The value effect, for example, may result in part from investors' irrational extrapolation of poor earnings growth—put another way, their reluctance to hold badly managed companies in declining industries. This effect may disappear only as mutual funds become available that disguise the identities of companies in a value portfolio.

If this view is correct, a third challenge for empirical research is to devise ways to track the changing strength of asset pricing patterns over time. Some effects, such as the January effect in small-stock returns or the earnings announcement effect, may disappear quite quickly after they become widely known. Others may be much more stable. Relatively little academic work has explored such issues systematically.

Fourth, an important function of asset markets is to enable investors to share risks. Despite the extraordinary financial innovation that has occurred in the last 30 years, many risk-sharing arrangements are still quite primitive. It is particularly hard for investors to share risks that affect large subgroups of the population, falling between the purely idiosyncratic risks covered by insurance contracts and the aggregate risks that can be hedged using bonds and stock indexes. An important role for academic research is to evaluate potential financial innovations, including financial instruments that are indexed to inflation, house prices, or components of national or world income. Shiller (1994) describes an agenda for exploring many of these issues.

Fifth, there are some fascinating public policy questions that relate to the field of asset pricing. Two important examples are the debate over proposals to invest Social Security funds in risky assets and the question of how the Treasury should optimally structure the public debt. As risk management issues confront both households and governments, asset pricing will remain an active and relevant field of economics.

REFERENCES

Abel, Andrew B., 1988, Stock prices under time-varying dividend risk: An exact solution in an infinite-horizon general equilibrium model, *Journal of Monetary Economics* 22, 375–393.

Abel, Andrew B., 1990, Asset prices under habit formation and catching up with the Joneses, *American Economic Review Papers and Proceedings* 80, 38–42.

Amihud, Yakov, and Haim Mendelson, 1986, Asset pricing and the bid-ask spread, *Journal of Financial Economics* 17, 223–249.

Anderson, E., Lars P. Hansen, and Thomas J. Sargent, 1999, Risk and robustness in equilibrium, Working paper, University of Chicago.

Ang, Andrew, and Jun Liu, 1998, A generalized earnings model of stock valuation, Working paper, Stanford University.

Attanasio, Orazio, and Gulielmo Weber, 1993, Consumption growth, the interest rate, and aggregation, *Review of Economic Studies* 60, 631–649.

Backus, David, Silverio Foresi, Abon Mozumdar, and Liuren Wu, 1998, Predictable changes in yields and forward rates, NBER Working paper 6379.

Backus, David, Silverio Foresi, and Chris Telmer, 1998, Discrete-time models of bond pricing, NBER Working paper 6736.

Baker, Malcolm, and Jeffrey Wurgler, 2000, The equity share in new issues and aggregate stock returns, *Journal of Finance*, forthcoming.

Bakshi, Gurdip, and Zhiwu Chen, 1997, Stock valuation in dynamic economies, Working paper, University of Maryland.

Balduzzi, Pierluigi, Giuseppe Bertola, and Silverio Foresi, 1997, A model of target changes and the term structure of interest rates, *Journal of Monetary Economics* 39, 223–249.

Balduzzi, Pierluigi, and Anthony Lynch, 1999, Transaction costs and predictability: Some utility cost calculations, *Journal of Financial Economics* 52, 47–78.

Bansal, Ravi, and Wilbur J. Coleman II, 1996, A monetary explanation of the equity premium, term premium, and riskfree rate puzzles, *Journal of Political Economy* 104, 1135–1171.

Banz, Rolf W., 1981, The relation between return and market value of common stocks, *Journal of Financial Economics* 9, 3–18.

Barberis, Nicholas C., 2000, Investing for the long run when returns are predictable, *Journal of Finance* 55, 225–264.

Barberis, Nicholas C., Ming Huang, and Tano Santos, 2000, Prospect theory and asset prices, *Quarterly Journal of Economics*, forthcoming.

Barberis, Nicholas C., Andrei Shleifer, and Robert W. Vishny, 1998, A model of investor sentiment, *Journal of Financial Economics* 49, 307–343.

Barsky, Robert, and J. Brad De Long, 1993, Why does the stock market fluctuate?, *Quarterly Journal of Economics* 107, 291–311.

Basu, Sanjoy, 1983, The relationship between earnings yield, market value, and return for NYSE common stocks: Further evidence, *Journal of Financial Economics* 12, 129–156.

Bawa, Vijay, Stephen Brown, and Roger Klein, 1979, *Estimation Risk and Optimal Portfolio Choice* (North-Holland, Amsterdam).

Beaudry, Paul, and Eric van Wincoop, 1996, The intertemporal elasticity of substitution: An exploration using a U.S. panel of state data, *Economica* 63, 495–512.

Bekaert, Geert, and Steven R. Grenadier, 1999, Stock and bond pricing in an affine economy, Working paper, Stanford University.

Bekaert, Geert, Robert J. Hodrick, and David A. Marshall, 1998, Peso problem explanations for term structure anomalies, NBER Working Paper 7346.

Benartzi, Shlomo, and Richard H. Thaler, 1995, Myopic loss aversion and the equity premium puzzle, *Quarterly Journal of Economics* 110, 73–92.

Berk, Jonathan B., Richard C. Green, and Vasant Naik, 1999, Optimal investment, growth options, and security returns, *Journal of Finance* 54, 1553–1607.

Bernard, Victor, 1992, Stock price reactions to earnings announcements, in Richard Thaler, ed.: *Advances in Behavioral Finance* (Russell Sage Foundation, New York).

Bertaut, Carol C., and Michael Haliassos, 1997, Precautionary portfolio behavior from a life-cycle perspective, *Journal of Economic Dynamics and Control* 21, 1511–1542.

Black, Fischer, 1972, Capital market equilibrium with restricted borrowing, *Journal of Business* 45, 444–454.

Black, Fischer, Michael Jensen, and Myron Scholes, 1972, The capital asset pricing model: Some empirical tests, in Michael Jensen, ed.: *Studies in the Theory of Capital Markets* (Praeger, New York).

Blanchard, Olivier J., and Mark Watson, 1982, Bubbles, rational expectations, and financial markets, in Paul Wachtel, ed.: *Crises in the Economic and Financial Structure: Bubbles, Bursts, and Shocks* (Lexington, Lexington, Mass.).

Bodie, Zvi, Robert C. Merton, and William F. Samuelson, 1991, Labor supply flexibility and portfolio choice in a life cycle model, *Journal of Economic Dynamics and Control* 16, 427–449.

Bollerslev, Timothy, Robert F. Engle, and Jeffrey Wooldridge, 1988, A capital asset pricing model with time varying covariances, *Journal of Political Economy* 96, 116–131.

Brandt, Michael, 1999, Estimating portfolio and consumption choice: A conditional Euler equations approach, *Journal of Finance* 54, 1609–1645.

Brav, Alon, George Constantinides, and Christopher C. Geczy, 1999, Asset pricing with hetero-geneous consumers and limited participation: Empirical evidence, Working paper, Duke University.

Brennan, Michael J., 1998, The role of learning in dynamic portfolio decisions, *European Finance Review* 1, 295–306.

Brennan, Michael J., Eduardo S. Schwartz, and Ronald Lagnado, 1996, The use of Treasury bill futures in strategic asset allocation programs, Working paper, Anderson Graduate School of Management, UCLA.

Brennan, Michael J., Eduardo S. Schwartz, and Ronald Lagnado, 1997, Strategic asset allocation, *Journal of Economic Dynamics and Control* 21, 1377–1403.

Brennan, Michael J., and Yihong Xia, 1998, Resolution of a financial puzzle, Working paper, Anderson Graduate School of Management, UCLA.

Brown, Roger H., and Stephen M. Schaefer, 1994, The term structure of real interest rates and the Cox, Ingersoll, and Ross model, *Journal of Financial Economics* 35, 3–42.

Brown, Stephen, William Goetzmann, and Stephen A. Ross, 1995, Survival, *Journal of Finance* 50, 853–873.

Campbell, John Y., 1987, Stock returns and the term structure, *Journal of Financial Economics* 18, 373–399.

Campbell, John Y., 1991, A variance decomposition for stock returns, *Economic Journal* 101, 157–179.

Campbell, John Y., 1993, Intertemporal asset pricing without consumption data, *American Economic Review* 83, 487–512.

Campbell, John Y., 1996, Understanding risk and return, *Journal of Political Economy* 104, 298–345.

Campbell, John Y., 1999, Asset prices, consumption, and the business cycle, in John Taylor and Michael Woodford, eds.: *Handbook of Macroeconomics*, Vol. 1 (North-Holland, Amsterdam).

Campbell, John Y., Yeung Lewis Chan, and Luis M. Viceira, 1999, A multivariate model of strategic asset allocation, Working paper, Harvard University.

Campbell, John Y., and John H. Cochrane, 1999, By force of habit: A consumption-based explanation of aggregate stock market behavior, *Journal of Political Economy* 107, 205–251.

Campbell, John Y., and John H. Cochrane, 2000, Explaining the poor performance of consumption-based asset pricing models, *Journal of Finance*, forthcoming.

Campbell, John Y., and Albert S. Kyle, 1993, Smart money, noise trading, and stock price behavior, *Review of Economic Studies* 60, 1–34.

Campbell, John Y., Andrew W. Lo, and A. Craig MacKinlay, 1997, *The Econometrics of Financial Markets* (Princeton University Press, Princeton, N.J.).

Campbell, John Y., and N. Gregory Mankiw, 1989, Consumption, income, and interest rates: Reinterpreting the time-series evidence, in O. J. Blanchard and S. Fischer, eds.: *National Bureau of Economic Research Macroeconomics Annual* 4 (MIT Press, Cambridge, Mass.).

Campbell, John Y., and Robert J. Shiller, 1988a, The dividend-price ratio and expectations of future dividends and discount factors, *Review of Financial Studies* 1, 195–228.

Campbell, John Y., and Robert J. Shiller, 1988b, Stock prices, earnings, and expected dividends, *Journal of Finance* 43, 661–676.

Campbell, John Y., and Robert J. Shiller, 1991, Yield spreads and interest rates: A bird's eye view, *Review of Economic Studies* 58, 495–514.

Campbell, John Y. and Luis M. Viceira, 1999, Consumption and portfolio decisions when expected returns are time varying, *Quarterly Journal of Economics* 114, 433–495.

Campbell, John Y., and Luis M. Viceira, 2000, Who should buy long-term bonds? *American Economic Review*, forthcoming.

Canner, Niko, N. Gregory Mankiw, and David N. Weil, 1997, An asset allocation puzzle, *American Economic Review* 87, 181–191.

Carhart, Mark M., 1997, On persistence in mutual fund performance, *Journal of Finance* 52, 57–82.

Carroll, Christopher D., 1997, Buffer-stock saving and the life cycle/permanent income hypothesis, *Quarterly Journal of Economics* 112, 1–55.

Cecchetti, Stephen G., Pok-Sang Lam, and Nelson C. Mark, 1994, Testing volatility restrictions on intertemporal marginal rates of substitution implied by Euler equations and asset returns, *Journal of Finance* 49, 123–152.

Cecchetti, Stephen G., Pok-Sang Lam, and Nelson C. Mark, 1997, Asset pricing with distorted beliefs: Are equity returns too good to be true?, Working paper, Ohio State University.

Chan, K. C., and Nai-fu Chen, 1991, Structural and return characteristics of small and large firms, *Journal of Finance* 46, 1467–1484.

Chan, Yeung Lewis, and Leonid Kogan, 1999, Heterogeneous preferences and the dynamics of asset prices, Working paper, Harvard University.

Cocco, Joao, Francisco Gomes, and Pascal Maenhout, 1998, Consumption and portfolio choice over the life cycle, Working paper, Harvard University.

Cochrane, John H., 1996, A cross-sectional test of an investment-based asset pricing model, *Journal of Political Economy* 104, 572–621.

Cochrane, John H., 1999, *Asset Pricing*, Unpublished manuscript, University of Chicago.

Cochrane, John H., and Lars Peter Hansen, 1992, Asset pricing lessons for macroeconomics, in O. J. Blanchard and S. Fischer, eds.: *NBER Macroeconomics Annual 1992* (MIT Press, Cambridge, Mass.).

Cogley, Timothy, 1998, Idiosyncratic risk and the equity premium: Evidence from the Consumer Expenditure Survey, Working paper, Federal Reserve Bank of San Francisco.

Constantinides, George, 1986, Capital market equilibrium with transactions costs, *Journal of Political Economy* 94, 842–862.

Constantinides, George, 1990, Habit formation: A resolution of the equity premium puzzle, *Journal of Political Economy* 98, 519–543.

Constantinides, George, John Donaldson, and Rajnish Mehra, 1998, Junior can't borrow: A new perspective on the equity premium puzzle, NBER Working paper 6617.

Constantinides, George, and Darrell Duffie, 1996, Asset pricing with heterogeneous consumers, *Journal of Political Economy* 104, 219–240.

Cox, John C., and Chi-fu Huang, 1989, Optimal consumption and portfolio policies when asset prices follow a diffusion process, *Journal of Economic Theory* 39, 33–83.

Cox, John C., Jonathan E. Ingersoll, Jr., and Stephen A. Ross, 1985, A theory of the term structure of interest rates, *Econometrica* 53, 385–407.

Cox, John C., and Stephen A. Ross, 1976, The valuation of options for alternative stochastic processes, *Journal of Financial Economics* 3, 145–166.

Cutler, David, James Poterba, and Lawrence Summers, 1991, Speculative dynamics, *Review of Economic Studies* 58, 529–546.

Dai, Qiang, and Kenneth J. Singleton, 2000, Specification analysis of affine term structure models, *Journal of Finance*, forthcoming.

Dammon, Robert M., Chester S. Spatt, and Harold H. Zhang, 1999, Optimal consumption and investment with capital gains taxes, Working paper, Carnegie Mellon University.

Daniel, Kent, David Hirshleifer, and Avanidhar Subrahmanyam, 1998, Investor psychology and security market under- and overreactions, *Journal of Finance* 53, 1839–1885.

DeBondt, Werner F. M., and Richard H. Thaler, 1985, Does the stock market overreact?, *Journal of Finance* 40, 793–805.

De Long, J. Bradford, Andrei Shleifer, Lawrence Summers, and Michael Waldmann, 1990, Noise trader risk in financial markets, *Journal of Political Economy* 98, 703–738.

Diba, Behzad, and Herschel I. Grossman, 1988, The theory of rational bubbles in stock prices, *Economic Journal* 98, 746–757.

Dothan, M., and David Feldman, 1986, Equilibrium interest rates and multiperiod bonds in a partially observable economy, *Journal of Finance* 41, 369–382.

Duffie, Darrell, 1992, *Dynamic Asset Pricing Theory* (Princeton University Press, Princeton, N.J.).

Duffie, Darrell, and Lawrence Epstein, 1992, Stochastic differential utility and asset pricing, *Econometrica* 60, 353–394.

Dumas, Bernard, 1989, Two-person dynamic equilibrium in the capital market, *Review of Financial Studies* 2, 157–188.

Epstein, Lawrence, and Stanley Zin, 1989, Substitution, risk aversion, and the temporal behavior of consumption and asset returns: A theoretical framework, *Econometrica* 57, 937–969.

Epstein, Lawrence, and Stanley Zin, 1990, First-order risk aversion and the equity premium puzzle, *Journal of Monetary Economics* 26, 387–407.

Epstein, Lawrence, and Stanley Zin, 1991, Substitution, risk aversion, and the temporal behavior of consumption and asset returns: An empirical investigation, *Journal of Political Economy* 99, 263–286.

Fama, Eugene F., 1975, Short-term interest rates as predictors of inflation, *American Economic Review* 65, 269–282.

Fama, Eugene F., and Robert Bliss, 1987, The information in long-maturity forward rates, *American Economic Review* 77, 680–692.

Fama, Eugene F., and Kenneth R. French, 1988a, Permanent and temporary components of stock prices, *Journal of Political Economy* 96, 246–273.

Fama, Eugene F., and Kenneth R. French, 1988b, Dividend yields and expected stock returns, *Journal of Financial Economics* 22, 3–27.

Fama, Eugene F., and Kenneth R. French, 1989, Business conditions and expected returns on stocks and bonds, *Journal of Financial Economics* 25, 23–49.

Fama, Eugene F., and Kenneth R. French, 1992, The cross-section of expected stock returns, *Journal of Finance* 47, 427–465.

Fama, Eugene F., and Kenneth R. French, 1993, Common risk factors in the returns on stocks and bonds, *Journal of Financial Economics* 33, 3–56.

Fama, Eugene F., and Kenneth R. French, 1996, Multifactor explanations of asset pricing anomalies, *Journal of Finance* 51, 55–84.

Fama, Eugene F., and Kenneth R. French, 1999, Disappearing dividends: Changing firm characteristics or increased reluctance to pay?, Working paper, University of Chicago and MIT.

Fama, Eugene F., and J. MacBeth, 1973, Risk, return, and equilibrium: Empirical tests, *Journal of Political Economy* 71, 607–636.

Ferson, Wayne E., and George Constantinides, 1991, Habit persistence and durability in aggregate consumption: Empirical tests, *Journal of Financial Economics* 29, 199–240.

Friend, Irwin, and Marshall E. Blume, 1975, The demand for risky assets, *American Economic Review* 65, 900–922.

Froot, Kenneth, and Maurice Obstfeld, 1991, Intrinsic bubbles: The case of stock prices, *American Economic Review* 81, 1189–1217.

Garcia, René, and Pierre Perron, 1996, An analysis of the real interest rate under regime shifts, *Review of Economics and Statistics* 78, 111–125.

Gennotte, Gerard, 1986, Optimal portfolio choice under incomplete information, *Journal of Finance* 41, 733–746.

Gibbons, Michael R., and Krishna Ramaswamy, 1993, A test of the Cox, Ingersoll, and Ross model of the term structure, *Review of Financial Studies* 6, 619–658.

Giovannini, Alberto, and Philippe Weil, 1989, Risk aversion and intertemporal substitution in the capital asset pricing model, NBER Working paper 2824.

Glassman, James K., and Kevin A. Hassett, 1999, *Dow 36,000: The New Strategy for Profiting from the Coming Rise in the Stock Market* (Times Books).

Glosten, Lawrence, Ravi Jagannathan, and David Runkle, 1993, On the relation between the expected value and the volatility of the nominal excess return on stocks, *Journal of Finance* 48, 1779–1801.

Gollier, Christian, 2000, *The Economics of Risk and Time* (MIT Press, Cambridge, Mass.), forthcoming.

Gomes, Francisco, 1999, Loss aversion and the demand for risky assets, Working paper, Harvard University.

Gordon, Myron, 1962, *The Investment, Financing, and Valuation of the Corporation* (Irwin, Homewood, Ill.).

Gray, Stephen F., 1996, Modelling the conditional distribution of interest rates as a regime-switching process, *Journal of Financial Economics* 42, 27–62.

Grossman, Sanford J., and Guy Laroque, 1990, Asset pricing and optimal portfolio choice in the presence of illiquid durable consumption goods, *Econometrica* 58, 25–51.

Grossman, Sanford J., and Robert J. Shiller, 1981, The determinants of the variability of stock market prices, *American Economic Review* 71, 222–227.

Grossman, Sanford J., and Robert J. Shiller, 1982, Consumption correlatedness and risk measurement in economies with nontraded assets and heterogeneous information, *Journal of Financial Economics* 10, 195–210.

Grossman, Sanford J., and Z. Zhou, 1996, Equilibrium analysis of portfolio insurance, *Journal of Finance* 51, 1379–1403.

Gul, Faruk, 1991, A theory of disappointment aversion, *Econometrica* 59, 667–686.

Hall, Robert E., 1988, Intertemporal substitution in consumption, *Journal of Political Economy* 96, 221–273.

Hansen, Lars P., 1982, Large sample properties of generalized method of moments estimators, *Econometrica* 50, 1029–1054.

Hansen, Lars P., John Heaton, and Erzo Luttmer, 1995, Econometric evaluation of asset pricing models, *Review of Financial Studies* 8, 237–274.

Hansen, Lars P., and Ravi Jagannathan, 1991, Restrictions on intertemporal marginal rates of substitution implied by asset returns, *Journal of Political Economy* 99, 225–262.

Hansen, Lars P., and Ravi Jagannathan, 1997, Assessing specification errors in stochastic discount factor models, *Journal of Finance* 52, 557–590.

Hansen, Lars P., and Scott Richard, 1987, The role of conditioning information in deducing testable restrictions implied by dynamic asset pricing models, *Econometrica* 55, 587–613.

Hansen, Lars P., Thomas J. Sargent, and Thomas Tallarini, 1997, Robust permanent income and pricing, Working paper, University of Chicago.

Hardouvelis, Gikas A., 1994, The term structure spread and future changes in long and short rates in the G7 countries: Is there a puzzle? *Journal of Monetary Economics* 33, 255–283.

Harrison, John M., and David Kreps, 1979, Martingales and arbitrage in multiperiod securities markets, *Journal of Economic Theory* 20, 381–408.

Harvey, Campbell R., 1989, Time-varying conditional covariances in tests of asset pricing models, *Journal of Financial Economics* 24, 289–317.

Harvey, Campbell R., 1991, The world price of covariance risk, *Journal of Finance* 46, 111–157.

He, Hua, and David Modest, 1995, Market frictions and consumption-based asset pricing, *Journal of Political Economy* 103, 94–117.

Heaton, John, 1995, An empirical investigation of asset pricing with temporally dependent preference specifications, *Econometrica* 63, 681–717.

Heaton, John, and Deborah Lucas, 1996, Evaluating the effects of incomplete markets on risk sharing and asset pricing, *Journal of Political Economy* 104, 668–712.

Heaton, John, and Deborah Lucas, 1997, Market frictions, saving behavior and portfolio choice, *Macroeconomic Dynamics* 1, 76–101.

Heaton, John, and Deborah Lucas, 1999, Stock prices and fundamentals, *NBER Macroeconomics Annual* (MIT Press, Cambridge, Mass) 213–242.

Hodrick, Robert J., 1992, Dividend yields and expected stock returns: Alternative procedures for inference and measurement, *Review of Financial Studies* 5, 357–386.

Hong, Harrison, and Jeremy C. Stein, 1999, A unified theory of underreaction, momentum trading, and overreaction in asset markets, *Journal of Finance* 54, 2143–2184.

Ingersoll, Jonathan E., Jr., 1987, *Theory of Financial Decision Making* (Rowman and Littlefield, Totowa, N.J.).

Jagannathan, Ravi, and Z. Wang, 1996, The conditional CAPM and the cross-section of expected returns, *Journal of Finance* 51, 3–53.

Jegadeesh, Narasimhan, and Sheridan Titman, 1993, Returns to buying winners and selling losers: Implications for stock market efficiency, *Journal of Finance* 48, 65–91.

Jorion, Philippe, and William N. Goetzmann, 1999, Global stock markets in the twentieth century, *Journal of Finance* 54, 953–980.

Kahneman, Daniel, and Amos Tversky, 1979, Prospect theory: An analysis of decision under risk, *Econometrica* 47, 263–291.

Kandel, Shmuel, and Robert F. Stambaugh, 1991, Asset returns and intertemporal preferences, *Journal of Monetary Economics* 27, 37–91.

Kandel, Shmuel, and Robert F. Stambaugh, 1996, On the predictability of stock returns: An asset allocation perspective, *Journal of Finance* 51, 385–424.

Keim, Donald, 1983, Size-related anomalies and stock return seasonality: Further empirical evidence, *Journal of Financial Economics* 12, 13–32.

Keim, Donald, and Robert Stambaugh, 1986, Predicting returns in stock and bond markets, *Journal of Financial Economics* 17, 357–390.

Kim, Tong Suk, and Edward Omberg, 1996, Dynamic nonmyopic portfolio behavior, *Review of Financial Studies* 9, 141–161.

Kleidon, Allan, 1986, Variance bounds tests and stock price valuation models, *Journal of Political Economy* 94, 953–1001.

Kothari, S. P., Jay Shanken, and Richard G. Sloan, 1995, Another look at the cross-section of expected stock returns, *Journal of Finance* 50, 185–224.

Kreps, David M., and E. L. Porteus, 1978, Temporal resolution of uncertainty and dynamic choice theory, *Econometrica* 46, 185–200.

Krusell, Per, and A. A. Smith, Jr., 1997, Income and wealth heterogeneity, portfolio choice, and equilibrium asset returns, Working paper, University of Rochester and Carnegie Mellon University.

Lakonishok, Josef, Andrei Shleifer, and Robert W. Vishny, 1994, Contrarian investment, extrapolation, and risk, *Journal of Finance* 49, 1541–1578.

Lamont, Owen, 1998, Earnings and expected returns, *Journal of Finance* 53, 1563–1587.

La Porta, Rafael, 1996, Expectations and the cross-section of returns, *Journal of Finance* 51, 1715–1742.

La Porta, Rafael, Josef Lakonishok, Andrei Shleifer, and Robert W. Vishny, 1997, Good news for value stocks: Further evidence on market efficiency, *Journal of Finance* 52, 859–874.

Lee, Charles M. C., Andrei Shleifer, and Richard Thaler, 1991, Investor sentiment and the closed-end fund puzzle, *Journal of Finance* 46, 75–110.

LeRoy, Stephen, and Richard Porter, 1981, The present value relation: Tests based on variance bounds, *Econometrica* 49, 555–577.

Lettau, Martin, 1997, Idiosyncratic risk and volatility bounds, Working paper, CentER, Tilburg University.

Lettau, Martin, and Sydney Ludvigson, 1999a, Consumption, aggregate wealth, and expected stock returns, Working paper, Federal Reserve Bank of New York.

Lettau, Martin, and Sydney Ludvigson, 1999b, Resurrecting the (C)CAPM: A cross-sectional test when risk premia are time-varying, Working paper, Federal Reserve Bank of New York.

Lewellen, Jonathan, 1999, The time-series relations among expected return, risk, and book-to-market, *Journal of Financial Economics* 54, 5–43.

Liang, J. Nellie, and Steven A. Sharpe, 1999, Share repurchases and employee stock options and their implications for S&P 500 share retirements and expected returns, Working paper, Federal Reserve Board.

Liew, Jimmy, and Maria Vassalou, 2000, Can book-to-market, size, and momentum be risk factors that predict economic growth?, *Journal of Financial Economics*, forthcoming.

Lintner, John, 1965, The valuation of risky assets and the selection of risky investments in stock portfolios and capital budgets, *Review of Economics and Statistics* 47, 13–37.

Lo, Andrew W., and A. Craig MacKinlay, 1990, Data-snooping biases in tests of financial asset pricing models, *Review of Financial Studies* 3, 431–468.

Lucas, Robert E., Jr., 1978, Asset prices in an exchange economy, *Econometrica* 46, 1429–1446.

Luttmer, Erzo, 1996, Asset prices in economies with frictions, *Econometrica* 64, 1439–1467.

Lynch, Anthony W., 1999, Portfolio choice and equity characteristics: Characterizing the hedging demands induced by return predictability, Working paper, New York University.

MacKinlay, A. Craig, 1995, Multifactor models do not explain deviations from the CAPM, *Journal of Financial Economics* 38, 3–28.

Maenhout, Pascal, 1999, Robust portfolio rules and asset pricing, Working paper, Harvard University.

Mankiw, N. Gregory, 1986, The equity premium and the concentration of aggregate shocks, *Journal of Financial Economics* 17, 211–219.

Mankiw, N. Gregory, and Jeffrey A. Miron, 1986, The changing behavior of the term structure of interest rates, *Quarterly Journal of Economics* 101, 211–221.

Mankiw, N. Gregory, and Stephen P. Zeldes, 1991, The consumption of stockholders and non-stockholders, *Journal of Financial Economics* 29, 97–112.

Markowitz, Harry, 1952, Portfolio selection, *Journal of Finance* 7, 77–91.

Marsh, Terry, and Robert C. Merton, 1986, Dividend variability and variance bounds tests for the rationality of stock market prices, *American Economic Review* 76, 483–498.

McCulloch, J. Huston, and H. Kwon, 1993, U.S. term structure data, 1947–1991, Working Paper 93–6, Ohio State University.

Mehra, Rajnish, and Edward Prescott, 1985, The equity premium: A puzzle, *Journal of Monetary Economics* 15, 145–161.

Merton, Robert C., 1969, Lifetime portfolio selection under uncertainty: The continuous time case, *Review of Economics and Statistics* 51, 247–257.

Merton, Robert C., 1971, Optimum consumption and portfolio rules in a continuous-time model, *Journal of Economic Theory* 3, 373–413.

Merton, Robert C., 1973, An intertemporal capital asset pricing model, *Econometrica* 41, 867–887.

Merton, Robert C., 1980, On estimating the expected return on the market: An exploratory investigation, *Journal of Financial Economics* 8, 323–361.

Modigliani, Franco, and Richard A. Cohn, 1979, Inflation and the stock market, *Financial Analysts Journal* 35, 24–44.

Modigliani, Franco, and Richard Sutch, 1966, Innovations in interest rate policy, *American Economic Review* 56, 178–197.

Nelson, Charles, and M. Kim, 1993, Predictable stock returns: The role of small sample bias, *Journal of Finance* 48, 641–661.

Nelson, William R., 1999, Three essays on the ability of the change in shares outstanding to predict stock returns, Ph.D. dissertation, Yale University.

Odean, Terrance, 1998, Are investors reluctant to realize their losses?, *Journal of Finance* 53, 1775–1798.

Ohlson, J. A., 1990, A synthesis of security valuation theory and the role of dividends, cash flows, and earnings, *Journal of Contemporary Accounting Research* 6, 648–676.

Ohlson, J. A., 1995, Earnings, book values, and dividends in equity valuation, *Journal of Contemporary Accounting Research* 11, 661–687.

Piazzesi, Monika, 1999, An econometric model of the yield curve with macroeconomic jump effects, Working paper, Stanford University.

Poterba, James, and Lawrence H. Summers, 1988, Mean reversion in stock returns: Evidence and implications, *Journal of Financial Economics* 22, 27–60.

Richardson, Matthew, and James H. Stock, 1989, Drawing inferences from statistics based on multiyear asset returns, *Journal of Financial Economics* 25, 323–348.

Rietz, Tom, 1988, The equity risk premium: A solution?, *Journal of Monetary Economics* 21, 117–132.

Ritter, Jay R., and Richard S. Warr, 1999, The decline of inflation and the bull market of 1982 to 1997, Working paper, University of Florida.

Roll, Richard, 1977, A critique of the asset pricing theory's tests: Part I, *Journal of Financial Economics* 4, 129–176.

Rosenberg, Barr, Kenneth Reid, and Ronald Lanstein, 1985, Persuasive evidence of market inefficiency, *Journal of Portfolio Management* 11, 9–17.

Ross, Stephen A., 1976, The arbitrage theory of capital asset pricing, *Journal of Economic Theory* 13, 341–360.

Ross, Stephen A., 1978, A simple approach to the valuation of risky streams, *Journal of Business* 51, 453–475.

Ross, Stephen A., 1998, Samuelson's fallacy of large numbers revisited, Working paper, MIT.

Samuelson, Paul A., 1965, Proof that properly anticipated prices fluctuate randomly, *Industrial Management Review* 6, 41–49.

Samuelson, Paul A., 1969, Lifetime portfolio selection by dynamic stochastic programming, *Review of Economics and Statistics* 51, 239–246.

Sandroni, A., 1997, Asset prices, wealth distribution, and intertemporal preference shocks, Working paper, University of Pennsylvania.

Santos, M. S., and Michael Woodford, 1997, Rational asset pricing bubbles, *Econometrica* 65, 19–57.

Schroder, Mark, and Costis Skiadas, 1999, Optimal consumption and portfolio selection with stochastic differential utility, *Journal of Economic Theory* 89, 68–126.

Schwert, G. William, 1989, Why does stock market volatility change over time?, *Journal of Finance* 44, 1115–1153.

Schwert, G. William, 1990, Indexes of U.S. stock prices from 1802 to 1987, *Journal of Business* 63, 399–426.

Shanken, Jay, 1987, Multivariate proxies and asset pricing relations: Living with the Roll critique, *Journal of Financial Economics* 18, 91–110.

Sharpe, Steven A., 1999, Stock prices, expected returns, and inflation, Working paper, Board of Governors of the Federal Reserve System.

Sharpe, William, 1964, Capital asset prices: A theory of market equilibrium under conditions of risk, *Journal of Finance* 19, 425–442.

Shefrin, Hersh, and Meir Statman, 1985, The disposition to sell winners too early and ride losers too long: Theory and evidence, *Journal of Finance* 40, 777–790.

Shiller, Robert J., 1981, Do stock prices move too much to be justified by subsequent changes in dividends?, *American Economic Review* 71, 421–436.

Shiller, Robert J., 1982, Consumption, asset markets, and macroeconomic fluctuations, *Carnegie Mellon Conference Series on Public Policy* 17, 203–238.

Shiller, Robert J., 1984, Stock prices and social dynamics, *Brookings Papers on Economic Activity* 2, 457–498.

Shiller, Robert J., 1994, *Macro Markets: Creating Institutions for Managing Society's Largest Economic Risks* (Oxford University Press, Oxford).

Shiller, Robert J., 1999, Human behavior and the efficiency of the financial system, in John Taylor and Michael Woodford, eds.: *Handbook of Macroeconomics Vol. 1* (North-Holland, Amsterdam).

Shiller, Robert J., John Y. Campbell, and Kermit L. Schoenholtz, 1983, Forward rates and future policy: Interpreting the term structure of interest rates, *Brookings Papers on Economic Activity* 1, 173–217.

Shleifer, Andrei, 1986, Do demand curves for stocks slope down?, *Journal of Finance* 41, 579–590.

Shleifer, Andrei, 2000, *Inefficient Markets: An Introduction to Behavioral Finance* (Oxford University Press, Oxford).

Shleifer, Andrei, and Robert W. Vishny, 1997, The limits of arbitrage, *Journal of Finance* 52, 35–55.

Siegel, Jeremy, 1999, *Stocks for the Long Run*, 2nd ed. (Irwin).

Stambaugh, Robert F., 1982, On the exclusion of assets from tests of the two parameter model, *Journal of Financial Economics* 10, 235–268.

Storesletten, Kjetil, Chris I. Telmer, and Amir Yaron, 1998, Asset pricing with idiosyncratic risk and overlapping generations, Working paper, Carnegie Mellon University.

Summers, Lawrence H., 1985, On economics and finance, *Journal of Finance* 40, 633–635.

Summers, Lawrence H., 1986, Do we really know that financial markets are efficient? in J. Edwards et al., eds.: *Recent Developments in Corporate Finance* (Cambridge University Press, New York).

Sundaresan, Suresh M., 1989, Intertemporally dependent preferences and the volatility of consumption and wealth, *Review of Financial Studies* 2, 73–88.

Sundaresan, Suresh M., 2000, Continuous-time methods in finance: A review and an assessment, *Journal of Finance*, forthcoming.

Thaler, Richard H., and Eric J. Johnson, 1990, Gambling with the house money and trying to break even: The effects of prior outcomes on risky choice, *Management Science* 36, 643–660.

Tobin, James, 1958, Liquidity preference as behavior towards risk, *Review of Economic Studies* 25, 68–85.

Vasicek, Oldrich, 1977, An equilibrium characterization of the term structure, *Journal of Financial Economics* 5, 177–188.

Asset Pricing at the Millennium 1567

Vassalou, Maria, 1999, The Fama-French factors as proxies for fundamental economic risks, Working paper, Columbia University.

Vayanos, Dimitri, 1998, Transactions costs and asset prices: A dynamic equilibrium model, *Review of Financial Studies* 11, 1–58.

Veronesi, Pietro, 1999, Stock market overreaction to bad news in good times: A rational expectations equilibrium model, *Review of Financial Studies* 12, 975–1007.

Viceira, Luis M., 1999, Optimal portfolio choice for long-horizon investors with nontradable labor income, NBER Working paper 7409.

Vissing-Jørgensen, Annette, 1997, Limited stock market participation, Working paper, MIT.

Vuolteenaho, Tuomo, 1999, What drives firm-level stock returns? Working paper, University of Chicago.

Wachter, Jessica, 1998, Risk aversion and allocation to long-term bonds, Working paper, Harvard University.

Wachter, Jessica, 1999, Portfolio and consumption decisions under mean-reverting returns: An exact solution for complete markets, Working paper, Harvard University.

Wang, Jiang, 1996, The term structure of interest rates in a pure exchange economy with heterogeneous investors, *Journal of Financial Economics* 41, 75–110.

Weil, Philippe, 1989, The equity premium puzzle and the riskfree rate puzzle, *Journal of Monetary Economics* 24, 401–421.

West, Kenneth D., 1988, Dividend innovations and stock price volatility, *Econometrica* 56, 37–61.

White, Halbert, 2000, A reality check for data snooping, *Econometrica*, forthcoming.

Whitelaw, Robert F., 2000, Stock market risk and return: An equilibrium approach, *Review of Financial Studies*, forthcoming.

Williams, Joseph, 1977, Capital asset prices with heterogeneous beliefs, *Journal of Financial Economics* 5, 219–239.

Wurgler, Jeffrey, and Ekaterina Zhuravskaya, 1999, Does arbitrage flatten demand curves for stocks? Working paper, Harvard University.

Xia, Yihong, 1999, Learning about predictability: The effect of parameter uncertainty on dynamic asset allocation, Working paper, UCLA.

Xiong, Wei, 1999, Imperfect arbitrage with wealth effects, Working paper, Duke University.

Part VII
Tests of the Arbitrage Pricing Theory

[14]

THE JOURNAL OF FINANCE • VOL. XXXV, NO. 5 • DECEMBER 1980

The Journal of FINANCE

VOL. XXXV	DECEMBER 1980	No. 5

An Empirical Investigation of the Arbitrage Pricing Theory

RICHARD ROLL and STEPHEN A. ROSS

ABSTRACT

Empirical tests are reported for Ross' [48] arbitrage theory of asset pricing. Using data for individual equities during the 1962–72 period, at least three and probably four "priced" factors are found in the generating process of returns. The theory is supported in that estimated expected returns depend on estimated factor loadings, and variables such as the "own" standard deviation, though highly correlated (simply) with estimated expected returns, do not add any further explanatory power to that of the factor loadings.

THE ARBITRAGE PRICING THEORY (APT) formulated by Ross [48] offers a testable alternative to the well-known capital asset pricing model (CAPM) introduced by Sharpe [51], Lintner [30] and Mossin [38]. Although the CAPM has been predominant in empirical work over the past fifteen years and is the basis of modern portfolio theory, accumulating research has increasingly cast doubt on its ability to explain the empirical constellation of asset returns.

More than a modest level of disenchantment with the CAPM is evidenced by the number of related but different theories, e.g., Hakansson [18], Mayers [34], Merton [35], Kraus and Litzenberger [23]; by anomalous empirical evidence, e.g., Ball [2], Basu [4], Reinganum [40]; and by questioning of the CAPM's viability as a scientific theory, e.g., Roll [41]. Nonetheless, the CAPM retains a central place in the thoughts of academic scholars and of finance practitioners such as portfolio managers, investment advisors, and security analysts.

There is good reason for its durability: it is compatible with the single most widely-acknowledged empirical regularity in asset returns, their common variability. Apparently, intuition readily ascribes such common variation to a single factor which, with a random disturbance, generates returns for each individual asset via some (linear) functional relationship. Oddly, though, this intuition is wholly divorced from the formal CAPM theory. To the contrary, elegant deriva-

Graduate School of Management, University of California, Los Angeles, and School of Organization and Management, Yale University, respectively.

tions of the CAPM equation have been concocted beginning from the first principles of utility theory; but the model's popularity is not due to such analyses, for they make all too obvious the assumptions required for the CAPM's validity and make no use of the common variability of returns. A review of recent finance texts (e.g., Van Horne, [54, pp. 57–63]) reveals that rationalizations of the CAPM are based instead on the dichotomy between diversifiable and non-diversifiable risk, a distinction which refers to a linear generating process, not to the CAPM derived from utility theory.

The APT is a particularly appropriate alternative because it agrees perfectly with what appears to be the intuition behind the CAPM. Indeed, the APT is based on a linear return generating process *as a first principle*, and requires no utility assumptions beyond monotonicity and concavity. Nor is it restricted to a single period; it will hold in both the multiperiod and single period cases. Though consistent with every conceivable prescription for portfolio diversification, no particular portfolio plays a role in the APT. Unlike the CAPM, there is no requirement that the market portfolio be mean variance efficient.

There are two major differences between the APT and the original Sharpe [50] "diagonal" model, a single factor generating model which we believe is the intuitive grey eminence behind the CAPM. First, and most simply, the APT allows more than just one generating factor. Second, the APT demonstrates that since any market equilibrium must be consistent with no arbitrage profits, every equilibrium will be characterized by a linear relationship between each asset's expected return and its return's response amplitudes, or loadings, on the common factors. With minor caveats, given the factor generating model, the absence of riskless arbitrage profits—an easy enough condition to accept a priori—leads immediately to the APT. Its modest assumptions and its pleasing implications surely render the APT worthy of being the object of empirical testing.

To our knowledge, though, there has so far been just one published empirical study of the APT, by Gehr [17]. He began with a procedure similar to the one reported here. We can claim to have extended Gehr's analysis with a more comprehensive set of data (he used 24 industry indices and 41 individual stocks) and to have carried the analysis farther—to a stage actually required if the tests are to be definitive. Nonetheless, Gehr's paper is well worth reading and it must be given precedence as the first empirical work directly on this subject.

Another empirical study related to the APT is an early paper by Brennan [6], which is unfortunately still unpublished. Brennan's approach was to decompose the residuals from a market model regression. He found two factors present in the residuals and concluded that "the true return generating process must be represented by at least a two factor model rather than by the single factor diagonal model" (p. 30). Writing before the APT, Brennan saw clearly that "it is not possible to devise cross-sectional tests of the Capital Asset Pricing Model, since only in the case of a single factor model is it possible to relate *ex ante* and *ex post* returns" (p. 34). Of course, the APT's empirical usefulness rests precisely in its ability to permit such cross-sectional tests whether there is one factor or many.

The possibility of multiple generating factors was recognized long ago. Farrar

[15] and King [22], for example, employed factor analytic methods. Their work focused on industry influences and was pure (and very worthwhile) empiricism. Since the APT was not available to predict the cross-sectional effects of industry factors on expected returns, no tests were conducted for the presence of such effects.

More recently, Rosenberg and Marathe [44] have analyzed what they term "extra-market" components of return. They find unequivocal empirical support for the presence of such components. Rosenberg and Marathe's work employs extraneous "descriptor variables" to predict intertemporal changes in the CAPM's parameters. They state that "the appropriateness of the multiple-factor model of security returns, with loadings equal to predetermined descriptors, as opposed to a single-factor or market model, is conclusively demonstrated" (p. 100). But, they do not ascertain the *separate* influences of these multiple factors on individual expected returns, and focus instead on a combined influence working through the market portfolio. In other words, they assume the CAPM and decompose the single market beta into its constitutent parts.

Regarding the market portfolio as a construct which captures the influences of many factors follows the theoretical ideas in Rosenberg [45] and Sharpe [52]. Thus, Rosenberg and Marathe's work does not provide a definitive test of the APT.

There are a number of other recent papers which are more or less related to this one. In particular, Langetieg [25], Lee and Vinso [28], and Meyers [36] contain evidence of more than just a single market factor influencing returns. In contrast, Kryzanowski and To [24] give a formal test for the presence of additional factors but find "that only the first factor is non-trivial" (p. 23).

Nevertheless, there seems to be enough evidence in past empirical work to conclude that there may exist multiple factors in the returns generating processes of assets. The APT provides a solid theoretical framework for ascertaining whether those factors, if they exist, are "priced," i.e., are associated with risk premia. The purpose of our paper is to use the APT framework to investigate both the existence and the pricing questions.

In the following section, (I), a more complete discussion of the unique testable features of the APT is provided. Then section II gives our basic tests. It concludes that three factors are definitely present in the "prices" (actually in the expected returns) of equities traded on the New York and American Exchanges. A fourth factor may be present also but the evidence there is less conclusive.

Sections III and IV present two additional tests of the APT. The most important and powerful is in section III, where the APT is compared against a specific alternative hypothesis that "own" variance influences expected returns. If the APT is true, the "own" variance should not be important, even though its sample value is known to be highly correlated cross-sectionally with sample mean returns. We find that the "own" variance's sample influence arises spuriously from skewness in the returns distribution.

In section IV, we present a test of the consistency of the APT across groups of assets. Although the power of this test is probably weak, it gives no indication whatsoever of differences among groups.

Our conclusion is that the APT performs well under empirical scrutiny and that it should be considered a reasonable model for explaining the cross-sectional variation in average asset returns.

I. The APT and its Testability

A. The APT

This section outlines the APT in a fashion that makes it suitable for empirical work. A detailed development of theory is presented in Ross [47, 48] and the intent here is to highlight those conclusions of the theory which are tested in subsequent sections.

The theory begins with the traditional neoclassical assumptions of perfectly competitive and frictionless asset markets. Just as the CAPM is derived from the assumption that random asset returns follow a multivariate normal distribution, the APT also begins with an assumption on the return generating process. Individuals are assumed to believe (homogeneously) that the random returns on the set of assets being considered are governed by a k-factor generating model of the form:

$$\tilde{r}_i = E_i + b_{i1}\tilde{\delta}_1 + \cdots + b_{ik}\tilde{\delta}_k + \tilde{\epsilon}_i,$$

$$i = 1, \cdots, n. \tag{1}$$

The first term in (1), E_i, is the expected return on the ith asset. The next k terms are of the form $b_{ij}\tilde{\delta}_j$ where $\tilde{\delta}_j$ denotes the mean zero j^{th} factor common to the returns of all assets under consideration. The coefficient b_{ij} quantifies the sensitivity of asset i's returns to the movements in the common factor $\tilde{\delta}_j$. The common factors capture the systematic components of risk in the model. The final term, $\tilde{\epsilon}_i$, is a noise term, i.e., an unsystematic risk component, idiosyncratic to the ith asset. It is assumed to reflect the random influence of information that is unrelated to other assets. In keeping with this assumption, we also have that

$$E\{\tilde{\epsilon}_i \mid \tilde{\delta}_j\} = 0,$$

and that $\tilde{\epsilon}_i$ is (quite) independent of $\tilde{\epsilon}_j$ for all i and j. Too strong a dependence in the $\tilde{\epsilon}_i$'s would be like saying that there are more than simply the k hypothesized common factors. Finally, we assume for the set of n assets under consideration, that n is much greater than the number of factors, k.

Before developing the theory, it is worth pausing to examine (1) in a bit more detail. The assumption of a k-factor generating model is very similar in spirit to a restriction on the Arrow-Debreu tableau that displays the returns on the assets in different states of nature. If the $\tilde{\epsilon}_i$ terms were omitted, then (1) would say that each asset i has returns r_i that are an exact linear combination of the returns on a riskless asset (with identical return in each state) and the returns on k other factors or assets or column vectors, $\delta_1, \cdots, \delta_k$. In such a setting, the riskless return and each of the k factors can be expressed as a linear combination of $k + 1$ other returns, say r_1 through r_{k+1}. Any other asset's return, since it is a linear combination of the factors, must also be a linear combination of the first $k + 1$

assets' returns. And thus, portfolios of the first $k + 1$ assets are perfect substitutes for all other assets in the market. Since perfect substitutes must be priced equally, there must be restrictions on the individual returns generated by the model. This is the core of the APT: there are only a few systematic components of risk existing in nature. As a consequence, many portfolios are close substitutes and as such, they must have the same value.

What are the common or systematic factors? This question is equivalent to asking what causes the particular values of covariance terms in the CAPM. If there are only a few systematic components of risk, one would expect these to be related to fundamental economic aggregates, such as GNP, or to interest rates or weather (although no causality is implied by such relations). The factor model formalism suggests that a whole theoretical and empirical structure must be explored to better understand what economic forces actually affect returns systematically. But in testing the APT, it is no more appropriate for us to examine this issue than it would be for tests of the CAPM to examine what, if anything, causes returns to be multivariate normal. In both instances, the return generating process is taken as one of the primitive assumptions of the theory. We do consider the basic underlying causes of the generating process of returns to be a potentially important area of research, but we think it is an area that can be investigated separately from testing asset pricing theories.

Now let us develop the APT itself from the return generating process (1). Consider an individual who is currently holding a portfolio and is contemplating an alteration of his portfolio. Any new portfolio will differ from the old portfolio by investment proportions x_i ($i = 1, \cdots, m$), which is the dollar amount purchased or sold of asset i as a fraction of total invested wealth. The sum of the x_i proportions,

$$\sum_i x_i = 0,$$

since the new portfolio and the old portfolio put the same wealth into the n assets. In other words, additional purchases of assets must be financed by sales of others. Portfolios that use no wealth such as $\underline{x} \equiv (x_1, \cdots x_n)'$ are called arbitrage portfolios.

In deciding whether or not to alter his current holdings, an individual will examine all the available arbitrage portfolios. The additional return obtainable from altering the current portfolio by n is given by

$$\underline{x}\tilde{r} \equiv \sum_i x_i \tilde{r}_i$$

$$= (\sum_i x_i E_i) + (\sum_i x_i b_{i1})\tilde{\delta}_1 + \cdots + (\sum_i x_i b_{ik})\tilde{\delta}_k + \sum_i x_i \tilde{\epsilon}_i$$

$$\equiv \underline{x}E + (\underline{x}b_1)\tilde{\delta}_1 + \cdots + (\underline{x}b_k)\tilde{\delta}_k + \underline{x}\tilde{\epsilon}.$$

Consider the arbitrage portfolio chosen in the following fashion. First, we will keep each element, x_i, of order $1/n$ in size; i.e., we will choose the arbitrage portfolio $\underline{x}$ to be well diversified. Second, we will choose $\underline{x}$ in such a way that it

---

[1] An underscored symbol indicates a vector or matrix.

has no systematic risk; i.e., for each j

$$\underline{x}\underline{b}_j \equiv \sum_i x_i b_{ij} = 0.$$

Any such arbitrage portfolio, $\underline{x}$, will have returns of

$$
\begin{aligned}
\underline{x}\tilde{r} &= (\underline{x}E) + (\underline{x}\underline{b}_1)\delta_1 + \cdots + (\underline{x}\underline{b}_k)\delta_k + (\underline{x}\tilde{\epsilon}) \\
&\approx \underline{x}E + (\underline{x}\underline{b}_1)\delta_1 + \cdots + (\underline{x}\underline{b}_k)\delta_k \\
&= \underline{x}E.
\end{aligned}
$$

The term $(\underline{x}\tilde{\epsilon})$ is (approximately) eliminated by applying the law of large numbers. For example, if σ^2 denotes the average variance of the $\tilde{\epsilon}_i$ terms, and if, for simplicity, each x_i exactly equals $\pm 1/n$, then

$$
\begin{aligned}
\text{Var}(\underline{x}\tilde{\epsilon}) &= \text{Var}(1/n \sum_i \tilde{\epsilon}_i) \\
&= [\text{Var}(\tilde{\epsilon}_i)]/n^2 \\
&= \sigma^2/n,
\end{aligned}
$$

where we have assumed that the ϵ_i are mutually independent. It follows that for large numbers of assets, the variance of $\underline{x}\tilde{\epsilon}$ will be negligible, and we can diversify away the unsystematic risk.

Recapitulating, we have shown that it is possible to choose arbitrage portfolios with neither systematic *nor* unsystematic risk terms! If the individual is in equilibrium and is content with his current portfolio, we must also have $\underline{X}E = 0$. No portfolio is an equilibrium (held) portfolio if it can be improved upon without incurring additional risk or committing additional resources.

To put the matter somewhat differently, in equilibrium all portfolios of these n assets which satisfy the conditions of using no wealth and having no risk must also earn no return on average.

The above conditions are really statements in linear algebra. Any vector, x, which is orthogonal to the constant vector and to each of the coefficient vectors, $\underline{b}_j (j = 1, \cdots, k)$, must also be orthogonal to the vector of expected returns. An algebraic consequence of this statement is that the expected return vector, $\overline{E}$, must be a linear combination of the constant vector and the $\underline{b}_j$ vectors. In algebraic terms, there exist $k + 1$ weights, $\lambda_0, \lambda_1, \cdots, \lambda_k$ such that

$$E_i = \lambda_0 + \lambda_1 b_{i1} + \cdots + \lambda_k b_{ik}, \quad \text{for all} \quad i. \tag{2}$$

If there is a riskless asset with return, E_0, then $b_{0j} = 0$ and

$$E_0 = \lambda_0,$$

hence we will write

$$E_i - E_0 = \lambda_1 b_{i1} + \cdots + \lambda_k b_{ik},$$

with the understanding that E_0 is the riskless rate of return if such an asset exists.

and is the common return on all "zero-beta" assets, i.e., assets with $b_{ij} = 0$, for all j, whether or not a riskless asset exists.

If there is a single factor, then the APT pricing relationship is a line in expected return, E_i, systematic risk, b_i, space:

$$E_i - E_0 = \lambda b_i.$$

Figure 1 can be used to illustrate our argument geometrically. Suppose, for example, that assets 1, 2, and 3 are presently held in positive amounts in some portfolio and that asset 2 is above the line connecting assets 1 and 3. Then a portfolio of 1 and 3 could be constructed with the same systematic risk as asset 2, but with a lower expected return. By selling assets 1 and 3 in the proportions they represent of the initial portfolio and buying more of asset 2 with the proceeds, a new position would be created with the same overall risk and a greater return. Such arbitrage opportunities will be unavailable *only* when assets lie along a line. Notice that the intercept on the expected return axis would be E_0 when no arbitrage opportunities are present.

The pricing relationship (2) is the central conclusion of the APT and it will be the cornerstone of our empirical testing, but it is natural to ask what interpretation can be given to the λ_j factor risk premia. By forming portfolios with unit systematic risk on each factor and no risk on other factors, each λ_j can be interpreted as

$$\lambda_j = E^j - E_0,$$

the excess return or market risk premium on portfolios with only systematic factor j risk. Then (2) can be rewritten as,

$$E_i - E_0 = (E^1 - E_0)b_{i1} + \cdots + (E^k - E_0)b_{ik}. \qquad (3)$$

Is the "market portfolio" one such systematic risk factor? As a well diversified portfolio, indeed a convex combination of diversified portfolios, the market

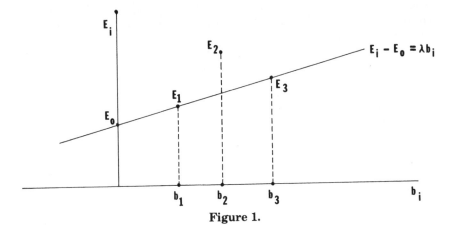

Figure 1.

portfolio probably should not possess much idiosyncratic risk. Thus, it might serve as a substitute for one of the factors. Furthermore, individual asset b's calculated against the market portfolio would enter the pricing relationship and the excess return on the market would be the weight on these b's. But, it is important to understand that *any* well-diversified portfolio could serve the same function and that, in general, k well-diversified portfolios could be found that approximate the k factors *better* than any single market index. In general, the market portfolio plays no special role whatsoever in the APT, unlike its pivotal role in the CAPM, (Cf. Roll [41, 42] and Ross [49]).

The lack of a special role in the APT for the market portfolios is particularly important. As we have seen, the APT pricing relationship was derived by considering any set of n assets which followed the generating process (1). In the CAPM, it is crucial to both the theory and the testing that all of the universe of available assets be included in the measured market portfolio. By contrast, the APT yields a statement of relative pricing on subsets of the universe of assets. As a consequence, the APT can, in principle, be tested by examining only subsets of the set of all returns. We think that in many discussions of the CAPM, scholars were actually thinking intuitively of the APT and of process (1) with just a single factor. Problems of identifying that factor and testing for others were not considered important.

To obtain a more precise understanding of the factor risk premia, $E^j - E_0$, in (3), it is useful to specialize the APT theory to an explicit stochastic environment within which individual equilibrium is achieved. Since the APT is valid in intertemporal as well as static settings and in discrete as well as in continuous time, the choice of stochastic models is one of convenience alone. The only critical assumption is the returns be generated by (1) over the shortest trading period.

A particularly convenient specialization is to a rational anticipations intertemporal diffusion model. (See Cox, Ingersoll and Ross [8] for a more elaborate version of such a model and for the relevant literature references.) Suppose there are k exogenous, independent (without loss of generality) factors, s^j, which follow a multivariate diffusion process and whose current values are sufficient statistics to determine the current state of the economy. As a consequence, the current price, p_i, of each asset i will be a function only of $s = (s^1, \cdots, s^k)$ and the particular fixed contractual conditions which define that asset in the next differential time unit. Similarly the random return, dr_i, on asset i will depend on the random movements of the factors. By the diffusion assumption we can write

$$d\tilde{r}_i = E_i \, dt + b_{i1} \, d\tilde{s}^1 + \cdots + b_{ik} \, d\tilde{s}^k. \qquad (4)$$

It follows immediately that the conditions of the APT are satisfied exactly—with $d\tilde{\varepsilon}_i = 0$ and the APT pricing relationship (3) must hold exactly to prevent arbitrage. In this setting, however, we can go further and examine the premia, $E^j - E_0$, themselves.

If individuals in this economy are solving consumption withdrawal problems, then the current utility of future consumption, e.g., the discounted expected value of the utility of future consumption, V, will be a function only of the individual's current wealth, w, and the current state of nature, s. The individual will optimize

Arbitrage Pricing   1081

by choosing a consumption withdrawal plan, c, and an optimal portfolio choice, x, so as to maximize the expected increment in V; i.e.,

$$\max_{\underline{x}, c} E\{dV\}.$$

At an optimum, consumption will be withdrawn to the point where its marginal utility equals the marginal utility of wealth,

$$u'(c) = V_w.$$

The individual portfolio choice will result from the optimization of a locally quadratic form exactly as in the static CAPM theory with the additional feature that covariances of the change in wealth, $d\bar{w}$, with the changes in state variables, $\bar{d}s^i$, will now be influenced by portfolio choice and will, in general, alter the optimal portfolio. By solving this optimization problem and using the marginal utility condition, $u'(c) = V_w$, the individual equilibrium sets factor risk premia equal to

$$E^j - E_0 = (R/c)(\partial c/\partial s^j)\sigma_j^2;$$

where $R = -(wV_{ww})/V_w$, the individual coefficient of relative risk aversion and σ_j^2 is the local variance of (independent) factor s_j. (The interested reader is referred to Cox, Ingersoll and Ross [8] for details.) Notice that the premia $E^j - E_0$ can be negative if consumption moves counter to the state variable. In this case portfolios which bear positive factor s^j risk hedge against adverse movements in consumption, but too much can be made of this, since by simply redefining s^j to be $-s^j$ the sign can be reversed. The sign, therefore, is somewhat arbitrary and we will assume it is normalized to be positive. Aggregating over individuals yields (3).

One special case of particular interest occurs when state dependencies can be ignored. In the log case, $R = 1$, for example, or any case with a relative wealth criteria (see Ross [48]) the risk premia take the special form

$$E^j - E_0 = R(\textstyle\sum_i x_i b_{ij})\sigma_j^2$$

where x is the individual optimal portfolio. This form emphasizes the general relationship between b_j and σ_j^2. Normalizing $\sum_i x_i b_{ij}$ to unity by scaling s^j, we have

$$E^j - E_0 = R\sigma_j^2.$$

The risk premium of factor j is proportional to its variance and the constant of proportionality is a measure of relative risk aversion.

For other utility functions, individual consumption vectors can be expressed in terms of portfolios of returns and similar expressions can be obtained. In effect, since the weighted state consumption elasticities for all individuals satisfy the APT pricing relationships, they must all be proportional.[2]

---

[2] Breeden [5] has developed the observation that homogenous beliefs about E's and b's imply perfect correlation between individual random consumption changes. His results depend on the assumption, made also by APT, that $k < N$.

The risk premium can be written in general as

$$E^j - E_0 = \left[\sum_l w_l R_l \left(\frac{1}{c_l} \right) \frac{\partial c_l}{\partial s_j} \right] \sigma_j^2$$

where l indexes individual agents, w_l is the proportion of total wealth held by agent l, R_l is his coefficient of relative risk aversion, $\frac{1}{c_l} \frac{\partial c_l}{\partial s_j}$ is the partial elasticity of his consumption with respect to changes in the jth factor, and σ_j^2 is the variance of the jth factor. Not very much is known about the term in parentheses and, all other things being equal, about all we can conclude is that risk premia should be larger, the larger the own variance of the factor. We would not expect this result to be specialized to the diffusion model and, in general, we would expect, with beta weights appropriately normalized, that factors with larger own variances would have larger associated risk premia.[3]

Let us return now to the general APT model and aggregate it to a testable market relationship. The key point in aggregation is to make strong enough assumptions on the homogeneity of individual anticipations to produce a testable theory. To do so with the APT we need to assume that individuals agree on both the factor coefficients, b_{ij}, and the expected returns, E_i. It now follows that the pricing relationship (2) which holds for each individual holds at the market level as well. Notice that individual and aggregate risk premia must coincide when there are homogenous beliefs on the expected returns and the factor coefficients.

As with the CAPM, the purpose of assuming homogenous anticipations is not to facilitate the algebra of aggregation. Rather, it is to take the final step to a testable theory. We can now make the rational anticipations assumption that (1) not only describes the *ex ante* individual perceptions of the returns process but also that *ex post* returns are described by the same equation. This fundamental intertemporal rationality assumption permits the *ex ante* theory to be tested by examining *ex post* data. In the next section we will discuss the possibilities for empirical testing which derive from this assumption.

B. Testing the APT

Our empirical tests of the APT will follow a two step procedure. In the first step, the expected returns and the factor coefficients are estimated from time series data on individual asset returns. The second step uses these estimates to test the basic cross-sectional pricing conclusion, (2), of the APT. This procedure is analogous to familiar CAPM empirical work in which time series analysis is used to obtain market betas, and cross-sectional regressions are then run of expected returns, estimated for various time periods, on the estimated betas. While flawed in some respects, the two step procedure is free of some major conceptual difficulties in CAPM tests. In particular, the APT applies to subsets

---

[3] We have not, of course, developed a complete rational anticipations model in diffusion setting, but it should be clear from this outline that the APT is compatible with the more specific results of Merton [35], Lucas [31], Cox, Ingersoll, and Ross [8], and Ross [48].

of the universe of assets; this eliminates the need to justify a particular choice of a surrogate for the market portfolio.

If we assume that returns are generated by (1), then the basic hypothesis we wish to test is the pricing relationship,

H_0: There exist non-zero constants, $(E_0, \lambda_1, \cdots, \lambda_k)$

such that

$$E_i - E_0 = \lambda_1 b_{i1} + \cdots + \lambda_k b_{ik}, \quad \text{for all } i.$$

The theory should be tested by its conclusions, not by its assumptions. One should not reject the APT hypothesis that assets were priced as if (2) held by merely observing that returns do not exactly fit a k-factor linear process. The theory says nothing about how close the assumptions must fit. Rejection is justified only if the conclusions are inconsistent with the observed data.[4]

To estimate the b coefficients, we appeal to the statistical technique of factor analysis. In factor analysis, these coefficients are called factor loadings and they are inferred from the sample covariance matrix, $\hat{V}$. From (1), the population variance, $\underline{V}$, is decomposed into

$$\underline{V} = \underline{B \Lambda B'} + \underline{D}, \tag{5}$$

where $\underline{B} = [b_{ij}]$ is the matrix of factor loadings, $\underline{\Lambda}$ is the matrix of factor covariances, and $\underline{D}$ is the diagonal matrix of own asset variances, $\sigma_i^2 = E\{\epsilon_i^2\}$.

From (5), $\underline{V}$ will be unaltered by any transformation which leaves $\underline{B \Lambda B'}$ unaltered. In particular, if $\underline{G}$ is an orthogonal transformation matrix, $\underline{GG'} = I$, then

$$\underline{V} = \underline{B \Lambda B'} + \underline{D}$$

$$= \underline{BGG'\Lambda GG'B'} + \underline{D}$$

$$= (\underline{BG})(\underline{G'\Lambda G})(\underline{BG})' + \underline{D}$$

If $\underline{B}$ is to be estimated from $\hat{V}$, then all transforms $\underline{BG}$ will be equivalent. For example, it clearly makes no difference in (1) if the first two factors switch places. More importantly, we could obviously scale up factor j's loadings and scale down factor j by the same constant g and since $bz_{ij}\delta_j = gb_{ij}\left(\dfrac{1}{g}\delta_j\right)$ the distributions of returns would be unaltered. To some extent we can eliminate ambiguity by restricting the factors to be orthonormal so they are independent and have unit variance. Alternatively, we could maintain the independence of the factors and construct the loadings for each factor to have a particular norm value, e.g., to

---

[4] This is a strongly positive view. Testing the APT involves testing H_0 and *not* testing the k-factor model. The latter tests may be of interest in their own right just as any examination of the distribution of returns is of interest, but it is irrelevant for the APT. As Friedman [16, pp. 19–20] points out: one would not be inclined to reject the hypothesis that the leaves on a tree arranged themselves so as to maximize the amount of sunlight they received by observing that trees did not have free will. Similarly, one should not reject the conclusions derived from firm profit maximization on the basis of sample surveys in which managers claim that they trade off profit for social good.

sum to 1 (or −1) and let the factor variances vary. From a theoretical viewpoint these are all equivalent constraints. While they alter the form of the APT null hypotheses, H_0, the statistical rejection region is unaffected.

To see this note that if

$$E_i - E_0 = \underline{b}_i \cdot \lambda,$$

or, in matrix form,

$$\underline{E} - E_0 = \underline{B}\lambda,$$

then

$$\underline{E} - E_0 = (\underline{B}G)(\underline{G'\lambda})$$

and the linear hypothesis remains true with the exact weights altered by the orthogonal transform.[5] This is a very sensible result. The APT concludes that excess expected returns lie in the space spanned by the factor loadings. Orthogonal transforms leave that space unchanged, altering only the directions of the defining basis vectors, the column vectors of the loadings. As a consequence, we will adopt a statistically convenient restriction to estimate B, keeping the arbitrariness of the procedure in mind. Notice that this is quite different from the ordinary uses of factor analysis. We are not "rotating" the factors in an arbitrary fashion to try to "interpret" them. Rather, our results are independent of the rotation chosen.

Once the expected returns, E_i, and the loadings, B, have been estimated, we can then move to the test of H_0. The general procedure is to examine cross-sectional regressions of the form

$$E_i = E_0 + \lambda_1 \hat{b}_{i1} + \cdots + \lambda_k \hat{b}_{ik},$$

where E_0 and $\lambda_1, \cdots, \lambda_k$ are to be estimated. The theory will not be rejected if the joint hypothesis that $\lambda_1 = \cdots = \lambda_k = 0$, is rejected. This is the usual state of statistical testing; we cannot "prove" that a theory is true against an unspecified alternative. We can only fail to reject it.

In Section III a specific alternative will be proposed, namely that the "own" variances, $\sigma_{\epsilon_i}^2$, affect excess returns, and the APT will be tested against this alternative. (This is probably the standard structure which most tests of the APT will take. A specific alternative will be proposed in which some idiosyncratic feature of the assets not reflected in their loadings is hypothesized to explain returns.)

We deal with the specifics of the above tests below, but for the present point out some of the major deficiencies of the procedure. The estimates of b_{ij} found in

---

[5] Notice, that if we knew the λ_i weights, we could obviously use them to aggregate the factors into a single factor which "explains" excess returns. In this trivial sense the number of factors does not matter. Without further assumptions, though, this begs the question since the λ_i weights must first be estimated to find the proper combination of the factors. For example, if we chose G such that its first column is proportional to λ, then $G'\lambda$ will be a vector with only the first entry non-zero. Under this rotation only a single factor is used to explain excess returns, but as noted above, the result has no empirical content.

the first step are, of course, just estimates and, as such, are subject to sampling error. Let $\bar{e}_i$ and $\tilde{\beta}_{ij}$ denote the respective sample errors,

$$\hat{E}_i = E_i + \bar{e}_i$$

and

$$\hat{b}_{ij} = b_{ij} + \tilde{\beta}_{ij}.$$

Under the null hypothesis, then, the cross-sectional regression for any period will be of the form

$$\hat{E}_i = E_i + \bar{e}_i$$

$$= E_0 + \lambda_1 b_{i1} + \cdots + \lambda_k b_{ik} + \bar{e}_i$$

$$= E_0 + \lambda_1 \hat{b}_{i1} + \cdots + \lambda_k \hat{b}_{ik} + \xi_i,$$

where the regression error

$$\xi_i \equiv \bar{e}_i - \lambda_1 \tilde{\beta}_{i1} - \cdots - \lambda_k \tilde{\beta}_{ik}.$$

Since the factor analytic estimation procedure to be employed is a maximum likelihood procedure, in a multivariate normal world the estimates will be asymptotically consistent; but very little is known about their small sample properties. In general, we expect ξ_i to be correlated with $\hat{b}_i$ and the cross-sectional regression to suffer from the usual errors-in-variables problems. Clearly, there is a considerable amount of statistical analysis to be carried out before one can feel comfortable with this approach. As a consequence, we stress the tentative and "first try" nature of the empirical work which follows.

II. Empirical Results

A. Data

The data are described in Table I. In selecting them, several more or less arbitrary choices were necessary. For instance, although daily data were available through 1977, the calculations reported in this paper used data only through 1972. The motivation was to secure a calibration or "holdout" sample without sacrificing the advantages of a large estimation sample, large enough for some statistical reliability even after aggregating the basic daily returns into monthly returns. The calibration sample is thereby reserved for later replication and for investigation of problems such as non-stationarity. The cutoff data of 31 December 1972 was selected also to correspond with other published studies of asset pricing, most of which used a pre-1973 period. This should facilitate a comparison of the results.

In our empirical analysis, estimated covariance matrices of returns were computed for groups of individual assets. Calculation of covariances necessitates simultaneous observations—so the beginning and ending dates were specified in order to exclude exceedingly short-lived securities. Although this assured a reasonably large time series sample for every group, there remained some variation across groups in number of observations. This was due evidently to suspen-

Table I

Data Description

Source:	Center for Research in Security Prices
	Graduate School of Business
	University of Chicago
	Daily Returns File
Selection Criterion:	By alphabetical order into groups of 30 individual securities from those listed on the New York or American Exchanges on *both* 3 July 1962 and 31 December 1972. The (alphabetically) last 24 such securities were not used since complete groups of 30 were required.
Basic Data Unit:	Return adjusted for all capital changes and including dividends, if any, between adjacent trading days; i.e., $[(p_{j,t} + d_{j,t})/p_{j,t-1}] - 1$, where p = price, d = dividend, j = security index, t = trading day index.
Maximum Sample Size per Security:	2619 daily returns
Number of Selected Securities	1260, (42 groups of 30 each)

sion of trading, temporary delisting, or simply to missing data for individual securities. None of the 42 groups contained data for all 2619 trading days. The minimum sample size was still 1445 days, however, and only three groups had less than 2000 days. Thirty-six groups (86%) had at least 2400 observations.

The group size of 30 individual securities was a compromise. For some purposes, such as estimating the number of return generating factors present in the economy, the best group size would have included *all* individual assets; but this would have dictated a covariance matrix larger than the processing capacity of the computer. For other purposes, such as comparing covariance structures across groups, statistical power increases with the number of groups, *cet. par.* Unfortunately, the *ceteris* are not *paribus*; for the number of securities *per* group also improves power and the reliability of estimates. We guessed that 30 securities per group would confer reasonable precision for all of the tests envisaged initially and we stuck with 30 as the work proceeded.

B. Estimating the Factor Model

The analysis proceeds in the following stages:
1) For a group of individual assets, (in this case, a group of 30 selected alphabetically), a sample product-moment covariance matrix is computed from a time series of returns, (of New York and American Exchange listed stocks from July 1962 through December 1972).
2) A maximum-likelihood factor analysis is performed on the covariance matrix. This estimates the number of factors and the matrix of loadings.
3) The individual-asset factor loading estimates from the previous step are used to explain the cross-sectional variation of individual estimated expected returns. The procedure here is similar to a cross-sectional generalized least squares regression.
4) Estimates from the cross-sectional model are used to measure the size and statistical significance of risk premia associated with the estimated factors.

This procedure is similar to estimating the size and significance of factor "scores."

5) Steps (1) through (4) are repeated for all groups and the results are tabulated.

The first stage is straightforward and should require no further explanation. There was only one curiosity: every element in the covariance matrix was divided by one-half the largest of the 30 individual variances. This was done to prevent rounding error in the factor analysis and it has no effect whatever on the results since factor analysis is scale free.

In the second stage, an optimization technique suggested by Jöreskog [20] was employed in the form of a program described by Jöreskog and Sörbom [21]. There are several available choices of types of factor analysis. In addition to the maximum likelihood method, there are generalized least squares, unweighted least squares, and approximate methods, among others. The maximum-likelihood method is usually preferable since more is known about its statistical properties, (Cf. Lawley and Maxwell [26]). As we shall see later, however, there may be some problems attendant to the M.L.E. method because the likelihood function involved is that of a multivariate gaussian distribution. To the extent that the data have been generated by a non-gaussian probability law, unknown biases and inconsistencies may be introduced.

Assuming away these problems for the moment, the M.L.E. method provides the capability of estimating the number of factors. This can be accomplished by specifying an arbitrary number of factors, say k, then solving for the maximum likelihood conditional on a covariance matrix generated by exactly k factors. Of course k is set less than the number of securities in the group of 30. A second value of the likelihood function is also found; this one being conditional on the observed sample covariance matrix without any restriction as to number of factors. Then a likelihood ratio, (first likelihood value divided by second), is computed. Under the null hypothesis of exactly k factors, twice the natural logarithm of the likelihood ratio is distributed asymptotically as chi-square with $\frac{1}{2}[(n - k)^2 - (n + k)]$ degrees of freedom. Thus, if the computed chi-square statistic is large (small), then more (fewer) than k factors are required to explain the structure of the generating process. So $k + 1$ ($k - 1$) factors are specified and another chi-square statistic is computed. The process terminates when the chi-square statistic indicates a pre-selected level, (usually 50%), that an additional factor is required.

We used the alphabetically first group of 30 securities to estimate the number of factors in the way just described, but with the added intention of retaining more factors than a 50% probability level would dictate. We could afford these extra, perhaps superfluous, factors since the third stage of our procedure provides a direct check on the true number of factors in the underlying generating process. An estimated factor introduced spuriously at the factor analysis stage would not be "priced" in the cross-sectional regression; its estimated coefficient should not differ significantly from zero. We wanted to allow the possibility of spurious factors because the same number of true (priced) factors should be present in every group *and* the first group might have been unrepresentative. Fewer than the true number of common factors could have been estimated for group one because of sampling variation. The third stage protects against too many factors estimated at stage two but it does not protect against too few.

For five factors using daily returns over the entire sample period, the chi-square statistic computed from the first group was 246.1. The number of degrees of freedom was 295 and the probability level (.980) implied only two chances in 100 that at least six factors were present in the data. Thus, we specified five factors, retaining this same number in the factor analysis computation for all 42 groups. Table II presents frequencies of the chi-square statistic for the 42 groups of daily returns. The monthly returns used later display a similar pattern.

As the table shows, in 38.1% of the groups, (16 of 42), the likelihood ratio test implied more than a 90% chance that five factors were sufficient. Over three-quarters of the groups had at least an even chance that five were enough. Some sampling variation in the estimated number of factors is inevitable; but the results indicate clearly that five is conservative in the sense of including, with high probability, at least as many estimated factors as there are true factors. Note, however, that a formal goodness-of-fit test using the results in Table II would not quite be legitimate. Since the original covariance matrices were computed over the same time period for all groups, there is probably some statistical dependence across the groups. Thus, the cross-group sample of any statistic is not likely to be a random sample. Since there is positive cross-sectional dependence among the returns, there is also likely to be positive cross group dependence in any statistic calculated from their returns.

With five factors, the model envisaged for each security can be written

$$\tilde{r}_{jt} \equiv \tilde{R}_{jt} - E_j = b_{1j}\tilde{\delta}_{1t} + \cdots + b_{5j}\tilde{\delta}_{5t} + \tilde{\epsilon}_{jt} \tag{6}$$

where R_{jt} is the daily return for day t and security j, E_j is the expected return for j, the b_j's are factor coefficients, the $\tilde{\delta}$'s are the true common factors, and $\tilde{\epsilon}_{jt}$ is a random disturbance completely unrelated to anything else including its own values in other periods. In matrix notation, a group of n individual securities whose returns conform to (6) can be expressed as

$$\tilde{r}_t = \underline{B}\tilde{\delta}_t + \tilde{\epsilon}_t$$

where $\tilde{r}_t$ and $\tilde{\epsilon}_t$ are $(n \times 1)$ column vectors, $\underline{B}$ is an $(n \times 5)$ matrix and $\tilde{\delta}_t$ is a (5×1) vector. Without loss of generality, the factors can be assumed orthogonal and scaled to have unit variance. Then the null hypothesis represented by equation (6) implies that the covariance matrix of returns takes the form

$$\underline{V} = \underline{BB'} + \underline{D}$$

Table II

Probability that no more than five factors are needed to explain returns	.9	.8	.7	.6	.5	.4	.3	.2	.1	0
Frequency (%)	38.1	16.7	7.14	2.38	11.9	2.38	4.76	4.76	9.52	2.38

Cross-sectional distribution of the Chi-square statistic from a likelihood ratio test that no more than five factors are necessary to explain daily returns, 42 covariance matrices of 30 securities each, NYSE and AMEX listed securities, 1962–72.

where $\underline{D}$ is a (diagonal) matrix whose j^{th} diagonal element is the variance of $\tilde{\epsilon}_{jt}$.

As noted in Section I, although maximum likelihood factor analysis provides a unique estimate of $\underline{V}$, this estimate is compatible with an infinity of estimates for $\underline{B}$, "all equally good from a statistical point of view. In this situation, all the statistician can do is to select a particular solution, one which is convenient to find, and leave the experimenter to apply whatever rotation he thinks desirable" (Lawley and Maxwell [26, p. 11]).

Our program chooses an estimate $\hat{\underline{B}}$ of $\underline{B}$ such that the matrix $\hat{\underline{B}}'\hat{\underline{D}}^{-1}\hat{\underline{B}}$ is diagonal and arranged with its diagonal elements in descending order of magnitude. This constitutes a restriction that guarantees uniqueness, except that $-\hat{\underline{B}}$ is statistically equivalent and, in fact, any column of $\hat{\underline{B}}$ can be reversed in sign. The problem of sign reversal is solved quite easily for the restricted estimates, (see below), but the general non-uniqueness of factor loadings is very troublesome. Essentially, one cannot ascertain with certainty that the first factor in one group of securities is the same as the first factor in another group. For instance, factor number one in group A could conceivably correspond to factor number three in group $K (K \neq A)$. Thus, when the cross-sectional distributions of the loading coefficients are tabulated, there could be a mixing of estimates which apply to different "true" factors.

C. A First Test of the APT

The factor model can be written as

$$\tilde{\underline{R}}_t = \underline{E} + B\tilde{\underline{\delta}}_t + \tilde{\underline{\epsilon}}_t$$

and the arbitrage pricing theory requires

$$\underline{E} = \lambda_0 + \underline{B}\lambda.$$

Combining the two gives the basic factor process under the null hypothesis that the APT is true,

$$\tilde{\underline{r}}_t = \tilde{\underline{R}}_t - \lambda_0 = \underline{B}\lambda + (\underline{B}\tilde{\underline{\delta}}_t + \tilde{\underline{\epsilon}}_t), \tag{7}$$

or, more compactly,

$$\tilde{\underline{r}}_t = \underline{B}\lambda + \underline{\xi}_t, \tag{8}$$

where $\underline{\xi}_t$ is the mean zero disturbance at date t caused by intertemporal variation in the factors $\tilde{\underline{\delta}}_t$ and in the diversifiable component $\tilde{\underline{\epsilon}}_t$.

It might seem natural to test the APT via (8) by first estimating the factor loadings, $\underline{B}$, and the mean return vector $\bar{\underline{r}} = \Sigma \underline{r}_t/T$ *from time series, and then running a simple OLS cross-sectional regression analogous to* (8),

$$\bar{\underline{r}} = \hat{\underline{B}}\hat{\lambda} + \hat{\underline{\xi}} \tag{9}$$

where $\hat{\lambda}$ the OLS regression coefficients, would be the estimated risk premia. A closer examination of (7), however, reveals that this procedure would be biased toward finding risk premia for "priced" factors, even when their true prices are actually zero. To see why, notice that the mean value of $\tilde{\underline{\delta}}_t$, say $\bar{\underline{\delta}} = \Sigma \tilde{\underline{\delta}}_t/T$, must, with probability one, not be exactly zero in any sample. Thus, the cross-sectional regression (9) actually should be written

$$\bar{r} = \hat{B}(\lambda + \bar{\delta}) + \bar{\epsilon}$$

so that $E(\hat{\lambda}) = \lambda + \bar{\delta}$ will be biased by the time series *sample* mean of the factors, $\bar{\delta}$. Of course, the bias should decrease with larger time series sample sizes, but since $\bar{\delta}$ will not be exactly zero, however large the time series, $E(\hat{\lambda}) \neq 0$ even when $\lambda = 0$.

To correct this problem, we have employed a method analagous to that of Fama and MacBeth [14] but adapted to the factor analytic framework. The Fama-MacBeth procedure calculates a cross-sectional regression like (9) *for every time period t,*

$$r_t = \hat{B}\hat{\lambda}_t + \xi_t$$

and then uses the time series of $\hat{\lambda}_t$ to estimate the standard error of the average value of $\hat{\lambda}$. This yields an inference about whether the true λ is non-zero.

A more efficient procedure exploits the factor analysis already conducted with the time series during the estimation of $\underline{B}$. The factor loadings $\hat{B}$ are chosen such that $\hat{V} \equiv \hat{B}\,\hat{B}' + \underline{D}$ is the estimated covariance matrix of $B\,\hat{\delta}_t + \bar{\epsilon}_t$, the disturbance term in (7). Thus, a natural generalized least squares cross-sectional regression for each day t is

$$\hat{\lambda}_t = (\hat{B}'\hat{V}^{-1}\hat{B})^{-1}\hat{B}'\hat{V}^{-1}r_t \equiv \Gamma r_t \tag{10}$$

which yields GLS estimates of the risk premia. Furthermore, it can be proven (Lawley and Maxwell [26, pp. 88–89]) that the covariance matrix of the estimates $\hat{\lambda}_t$ from (10) is given by

$$\underline{B}'\underline{V}^{-1}\underline{B}. \tag{11}$$

This matrix is particularly convenient since it is constrained to be diagonal by the factor analysis. As a consequence, the estimated risk premia are mutually independent and admit simple t-tests of significance.

For instance, we will report below significance tests for

$$\bar{\lambda} = \Gamma\bar{r} \tag{12}$$

whose covariance matrix is

$$\frac{1}{T}\underline{B}'\underline{V}^{-1}\underline{B}, \tag{13}$$

provided the returns are independent over time. Notice that the time series behavior of the estimated factor "scores," the $\bar{\delta}$'s, is accounted for by the matrix $\underline{V}$, thereby eliminating the problem created by non-zero $\bar{\delta}$ in the simple OLS cross-section (9).

There remain, however, some tricky econometric problems in this procedure. First, equation (11) ignores any estimation errors present in $\hat{B}$. This means essentially that the significance tests for $\hat{\lambda}$ are only asymptotically correct. There could be an understatement or an overstatement of significance for small samples. We have no way to ascertain the extent of this problem, but we doubt that it introduces a serious error because our sample sizes are "large" by usual statistical standards.

A second difficulty concerns the signs of $\hat{\lambda}$. Since the factor loadings ($\underline{B}$) are not unique with respect to sign, neither are their coefficients $\underline{\lambda}$ in (7). Any rotated set of factors would have produced just as adequate a set of loadings. This implies that no importance can be ascribed to the numerical values of $\hat{\underline{\lambda}}$; only their statistical significance is relevant.

Finally, in the cross-sectional models (10) and (12), a value for the zero-beta or risk-free coefficient, λ_0 in (7), must be assumed. It might be thought that $\hat{\lambda}_0$ could be obtained easily by adding a column of 1's to $\hat{B}$ and computing regression (10) with an augmented matrix of loadings, $[\underline{1}:\underline{B}]$ an augmented Γ and the total return R_t, in place of the excess return $\underline{r}_t$, as

$$\hat{\underline{\lambda}}_t = \Gamma \underline{R}_t,$$

where $\hat{\underline{\lambda}}_t$ now contains an estimate for λ_0 as its first element. Unfortunately, although we report the result of this regression below, it is less satisfactory because the augmented covariance matrix of the estimated risk premia is

$$[\underline{1}:\underline{B}]'\underline{V}^{-1}[\underline{1}:\underline{B}]$$

which is not diagonal except in the fortuitous case when the constant vector is orthogonal to the loadings.

The trade-off, then, is between using a rather arbitrary value of λ_0 in the cross-sectional excess return regression (10) or allowing the data to determine λ_0 but bearing the consequence that the estimates $\hat{\underline{\lambda}}$ are no longer statistically independent. In many applications, mutual independence is merely a nicety since F-tests can be used when dependence among the coefficients is present. In our case, however, constraining the sample design to the independent case is especially important because the $\hat{\lambda}$'s at best are some unknown linear combinations of the true $\underline{\lambda}$'s and testing for the number of priced factors or non-zero λ_j's, is thereby reduced to a simple t-test.

Perhaps this will be clarified by considering the results in Table III. The top panel assumes a λ_0 of 6% per annum during the sample period, July 1962 through December 1972. The first results in Table III give the percentage of the groups in which more than a specified number of factors were associated with statistically significant risk premia, $\hat{\underline{\lambda}}$ estimated by (12) and (13). With daily data, 88.1% of the groups had at least one significant factor risk premium, 57.1% had two or more significant factors and in one-third of the groups at least three risk premia were significant. These percentages are far in excess of what would be expected by chance alone under the null hypothesis of no effect. The next row of Table III gives the relevant percentages which would be expected under this null hypothesis. If $\underline{\lambda} = 0$, the chance of observing at least a given number of $\hat{\lambda}_j$'s significant at the 95% level is the upper tail of the binomial distribution with probability of success $p = .05$. For example, the probability of observing at least two significant

Table III

Cross-sectional generalized least squares regressions of arithmetic
mean sample returns on factor loadings, (42 groups of 30
individual securities per group, 1962–72 daily returns, standard
errors of risk premia (λ) computed from time series)

1 FACTOR	2 FACTORS	3 FACTORS	4 FACTORS	5 FACTORS
I.	$\bar{R}_j - 6\% = \hat{\lambda}_1\, \hat{b}_{j1} + \cdots + \hat{\lambda}_5\, \hat{b}_{j5}$ (λ_0 assumed at 6%)			

Percentage of groups with at least this many factor risk premia significant at the
95% level

88.1	57.1	33.3	16.7	4.8

Expected Percentage of groups with at least this many risk premia significant at
the 95% level given no true risk premia ($\underline{\lambda} = 0$)

22.6	2.26	.115	.003	.00003

Percentage of groups with factor's risk premium significant at the 95% level in
natural order from factor analysis

76.2	50.0	28.6	23.8	21.4

II.	$\bar{R}_j = \hat{\lambda}_0 + \hat{\lambda}_1\, \hat{b}_{j1} + \cdots + \hat{\lambda}_5\, \hat{b}_{j5}$ (λ_0 estimated)			

Percentage of groups with at least this many factor risk premia significant at the
95% level

69.0	47.6	7.1	4.8	0

Percentage of groups with this factor's risk premium significant at the 95% level in
natural order from factor analysis

35.7	31.0	23.8	21.4	16.7

λ's, given $\underline{\lambda} = 0$, is $1 - (.95)^5 - 5(.05)(.95)^4 = .0226$. Notice that this calculation
requires zero correlation among the λ_j's .

If, in fact, four factors are truly significant, then the 4.8 observed significance
percentage for five factors (see line 1 of Table III), is almost precisely what one
would expect at the 95% level. Similarly, if three are truly significant, the 16.7%
of the groups in which at least four are found to be significant exceeds the 9.75%
which would occur by chance alone. The disparity is much greater if less than
three factors are significant. We can conclude then, that at least three factors are
important for pricing, but that it is unlikely that more than four are present.

The second set of results, still with λ_0 assumed equal to 6%, report the
percentage of groups in which the first, second, and remaining factors produced
by the factor analysis have significant associated risk premia. As noted above,
the first factor is selected as the one with the largest diagonal element in
$\hat{B}'D^{-1}\hat{B}$, the second has the second largest diagonal element, and so forth, but
there is no assurance that corresponding factors agree across different groups.
Nevertheless, it is of some interest to examine the significance of the ordered
factors and this is reported in the third line of Table III. As can be seen, all
factors are significantly greater than the chance level (5%) with particularly heavy
weight on the first two. The remaining three are significant, but this may be more
a consequence of mixing the order of factors across the groups than of anything
important.

The second part of Table III reports similar statistics but with the constant λ_0 estimated instead of assumed. Now the t statistics are no longer independent across the factors and we cannot apply the simple analysis above. But, the statistical results seem to conform well with the previous findings. Perhaps most striking is that at least two factors are significant in 47.6% of the groups while in only 7.1% are three or more significant. This suggests that the three significant factors obtained with λ_0 set equal to 6% may be an over-estimate due to the incorrect choice of the zero-beta return λ_0. When the intercept is estimated, two factors emerge as significant for pricing. However, because the $\hat{\lambda}_j$'s are not mutually independent, there is no standard of comparison for these percentages. As is to be expected, the results for the ordered factors are less significant than those for the λ_0 equal to 6% case, at least for the first and second factors produced by the factor analysis.

The next section (III) tests the APT against a specific alternative. Section IV presents a test for the equivalence of factor structure across the 42 groups.

III. Tests of the APT Against a Specific Alternative

In the previous section, we presented evidence that equity returns seem to depend on several common factors, perhaps as many as four. This many seem to be "priced", i.e., associated with non-zero risk premia which compensate for undiversifiable variation present in the generating process. Although these results are reassuring for the APT, there remains a possibility that other variables also are "priced" even though they are not related to undiversifiable risk. According to the theory, such variables should not explain expected returns; so if some were found to be empirically important, the APT would be rejected.

In this section, we report an investigation of one particular variable, the total variance of individual returns, or the "own" variance. The total variance would not affect expected returns if the APT is valid because its diversifiable component would be eliminated by portfolio formation and its non-diversifiable part would depend only upon the factor loadings and factor variances. It is a particularly good choice to use in an attempt to reject the APT because of its long-documented high positive correlation with sample mean returns.[6] If this sample correlation arises either from statistical estimation errors or else from its relation to factor loadings, the APT would enjoy an additional element of empirical support. If the correlation cannot be ascribed to these causes, however, then this would constitute evidence against the theory.

The procedure of this section is relatively straightforward: cross-sectionally (across individual assets), we regress estimates of expected returns on the five factor loading estimates described in the previous section *and* on

$$s_j = [\textstyle\sum_{t=1}^{T} (R_{jt} - R_j)/T]^{1/2}, \quad j = 1, \cdots, N$$

the standard deviation of individual returns. This test is less efficient for detecting

---

[6] See, e.g., Douglas [10] and Lintner [30]. The "own" variance received very careful scrutiny in Miller and Scholes [37], and has been the object of recent theoretical inquiry in Levy [29].

The Journal of Finance

"priced" factors than the factor analysis based test reported previously. Now, however, there is no alternative to using an ordinary regression approach since the extra variable s_j is not a factor loading and is not produced by the factor analysis.

Some evidence on the apparent explanatory power of the own standard deviation, s_j, is presented in Table IV. On average over the 42 groups of securities, the t-statistic (coefficient/standard error of coefficient) was 2.17 for s_j. 45.2% of the groups displayed statistically significant effects of s_j on mean sample returns at the 95% level of significance. In contrast, the F-test that at least some (one or more) factor loading had an effect on the mean return was significant at the 95% level for only 28.6% of the 42 groups.

A caution mentioned earlier in connection with all of our results should be reiterated: there was probably some positive dependence across groups, so the percentage of groups whose statistics exceed a critical value may overstate the actual significance of the relation between explanatory variables and expected returns. Nevertheless, the magnitude of the numbers would certainly appear to support a conclusion that the relation is statistically significant. The "explained"

Table IV

Cross-sectional regression[a] of estimated expected returns on factor loadings and individual total standard deviations of return (summary for 42 groups of 30 individual securities per group, 1962–72 daily returns)

Arithmetic Mean	Standard Error of Mean	Percentage of Groups Whose Statistic Exceeds 95% Critical Level[b]
Across 42 Groups		
t-statistic, test for most significant factor loading having no effect on expected return.		
2.19	.162	47.6
t-statistic: test for individual total standard deviation having no effect on expected return.		
2.17	.303	45.2
F-statistic: test for no effect by any factor loading on expected return (in addition to the effect of standard deviation).		
2.21	.295	28.6

[a] The regression equation for group g is

$$\bar{R}_j = \lambda_{0g} + \lambda_{1g} b_{1j} + \cdots + \lambda_{5g} b_{5j} + \lambda_{6g} s_j + \xi \quad j = 1, \cdots, 30$$

where $\bar{R}_j$ is the sample arithmetic mean return for security j, b_{kj} is security j's loading on factor k, the λ's are regression coefficients, s_j is individual asset j's total standard deviation of daily returns during the sample period and ξ_j is a residual.

[b] With 30 observations per group and six explanatory variables, the 95% critical value is 2.06 for the t-statistic and 2.64 for the F-statistic.

variation is quite high: the coefficient of multiple determination (adjusted R^2) is .743 on average over the 42 groups. Even the group with lowest explained variation has an R^2 of .561 (and recall that these are individual assets!). Without s included, the average adjusted R^2 is .563 and the minimum R^2 over the 42 groups is .166.

The apparently significant explanatory power of the "own" standard deviation (s) suggests that the arbitrage pricing theory may be false. Since arbitrageurs should be able to diversify away the non-common part of s, it should not be priced. There is reason, however, for a closer examination before rejecting the APT entirely.

A possible source of a spurious effect of the own variance on expected return is skewness in the distribution of individual returns. Positive skewness can create positive dependence between the *sample* mean and *sample* standard deviation (and vice versa for negative skewness). Miller and Scholes [37] argued convincingly that skewness could explain the sample mean's dependence on "own" variance. Our results below tend to support the Miller-Scholes argument within the APT context.

The distribution of individual daily returns are indeed highly skewed. Table V gives some sample results. As indicated there, 1213 out of 1260 individual assets, (96.3%), had positive estimated measures of skewness. There was considerable variation across assets, too. Although the sampling distribution of the skewness measure SK is not known and is difficult to tabulate even under the assumption of lognormality, there appears to be too much cross-sectional variation in SK to be ascribed to chance alone. Thus, individual assets probably differ in their population skewness. Note that intertemporal aggregation to monthly returns reduces the skewness only slightly.

Skewness is cross-sectionally correlated positively with the mean return and even more strongly with the standard deviation. Some part of this correlation may itself arise from sampling variation and some part too could be present in the population parameters. There is really no way to sort this out definitively. The strong cross-sectional regressions in the last panels of Table V suggest that attempts to expunge the spurious sampling dependence between sample mean return and standard deviation by exploiting the measured sample skewness, either as an additional variable in the cross-sectional regression or as a basis for skewness-sorted groups which might have less remaining spurious dependence, are probably doomed to weak and ambiguous results.[7] Also, such methods would be biased against finding a true effect of standard deviation, if one exists.

A procedure[8] which is charming in its simplicity and seems to resolve many of the statistical problems occasioned by skewness can be used if the observations are not too serially dependent: simply estimate each parameter from a different set of observations. In the present application, for example, we are concerned with sampling dependencies among estimates of all three parameters, expected return, factor loadings, and "own" standard deviation. If the time-series obser-

---

[7] As Martin [33] shows, using sample skewness and standard deviation both as additional explanatory variables causes severe econometric problems.

[8] We are grateful to Richard McEnally for suggesting this procedure.

Table V

Information About Skewness for Daily and Monthly Returns 1260 New York and American Listed Assets, 1962–72

Data Interval	Percent Positive	Mean	Standard Deviation	Smallest	Largest	with $\bar{R}$	with $\text{Log}_e(s_j)$
						Correlation	

					Product—Moment Skewness Measure, SK		
Daily	96.3	.681	.551	−2.06	4.56	.211	.452
Monthly	90.0	.654	.688	−1.04	5.94	.212	.520

Cross-Asset Regressions

Data Interval	b_1	$t_{\hat{b}_1}$	b_2	$t_{\hat{b}_2}$	Adjusted R^2

$$(\bar{R}_j - \bar{R}_{.5,j})/\log_e(s_j) = b_0 + b_1 SK_j \quad j = 1, \cdots, 1260$$

Data Interval	b_1	$t_{\hat{b}_1}$	b_2	$t_{\hat{b}_2}$	Adjusted R^2
Daily	1.82	20.6	—	—	.251
Monthly	1.14	36.6	—	—	.515

$$\bar{R}_j - \bar{R}_{.5,j} = b_0 + b_1 SK_j + b_2 \log_e(s_j) \quad j = 1, \cdots, 1260$$

Data Interval	b_1	$t_{\hat{b}_1}$	b_2	$t_{\hat{b}_2}$	Adjusted R^2
Daily	5.17	7.87	29.2	68.0	.838
Monthly	7.33	24.6	8.17	32.1	.728

Definitions:

R_{jt} = Return for asset j in interval t

T = Total number of intervals in sample

$\bar{R}_j = \sum_t R_{jt}/T$

$\bar{R}_{.5,j}$ = Sample mean after excluding the 25% smallest and 25% largest values of R_{jt}

$s_j = [\sum_t (R_{jt} - \bar{R}_j)^2/T]^{1/2}$

$SK_j = [\sum_t (R_{jt} - \bar{R}_j)^3/T]/s_j^3$

vations are temporarily uncorrelated such dependencies could be removed by using observations 1, 4, 7, 10, ... to estimate the expected return, observations 2, 5, 8, 11, ... to estimate the factor loadings, and 3, 6, 9, 12, ... to estimate the standard deviation of returns. With complete intertemporal independence, there would be no sampling covariation among the estimates and only the cross-asset population relationships would remain.

The daily returns for each asset are indeed close to independent over time. There may be some slight negative dependence but it has a low order of magnitude. Unfortunately, this is not true for the squared returns. There is positive intertemporal dependence in absolute price changes or in squared changes. This implies that the standard deviation of returns and the factor loadings estimated from non-overlapping adjacent days would still retain some sampling dependence. But since there are so many available time series observations (2619), we have the luxury of skipping days and estimating the parameters from non-overlapping observations "insulated" be at least one day. Table VI summarizes the results obtained with daily observations, using days 1, 7, 13, . . . for the estimated expected returns, observations 3, 9, 15, . . . for the factor loadings, and 5, 11, 17, . . . for the standard deviations. This has had the effect of reducing the number of time series observations used in the estimation of each parameter from 2619 to 436. Note that the factor loadings were estimated in the usual way but for covariance matrices computed only with observations 3, 9, 15, ...

These results are to be compared with those reported in Table IV where all estimates were computed from the same sample observations. Only nine of the 42 groups now display a significant t-statistic for s. Given the possibility of cross-group interdependence, this is only the weakest conceivable evidence for an effect by s on expected returns. The remaining effect drops even further when more "insulating" days are inserted between observations used to estimate the parameters. When three days are skipped rather than just one day, only seven groups out of 42 (16.7%) display significant effects for s at the 95% level. This supports

Table VI

Cross-sectional regressions of estimated expected returns on factor loadings and individual total standard deviations of return (summary for 42 groups of 30 individual securities per groups, 1962–72 daily observations with estimators taken from non-overlapping subsamples) [a]

Arithmetic Mean	Standard Error of Mean	Percentage of Groups Whose Statistic Exceeds 95% Critical Level[b]
Across 42 Groups		
t-statistic: test for most significant factor loading having no effect on expected return.		
2.27	.111	57.1
t-statistic, test for individual total standard deviation of return having no effect on expected return.		
.941	.204	21.4
F-statistic, test for no effect by any factor loading on expected return (in addition to the effect of standard deviation).		
2.24	.183	31.0

[a] The estimated returns are obtained from daily observations 1, 7, 13, $\cdots$2617; the factor loadings from observations 3, 9, $\cdots$2619; the standard deviations from observations 5, 11, $\cdots$2615.

[b] The regression equation and 95% critical values are given in nn. a and b of Table IV.

the argument that serial dependence in *squared* returns may be responsible for the small remaining effect of *s* shown in Table VI.

In contrast to the reduced impact of standard deviation, the estimated influence of the factor loadings have increased, (though admittedly only by a small amount). For example, the most significant factor loading now has a *t*-statistic of at least 2.06 in 57.1% of the groups.

Again, the groups are not independent; so caution should be exercised when interpreting the results. The results are not definitive but they *are* consistent with most of the frequently-observed sampling dependence between standard deviation and mean return being attributable to effects working through factor loadings and to spurious effects due to skewness.

As a final test, we conducted an experiment similar to that developed by Fama and MacBeth [14]. Here is an outline of the procedure:

a) Using daily observations 3, 9, 15, ... the five factor loadings $b_{1j}, \ldots b_{5j}$ are estimated for each asset in each of the 42 groups of 30 assets.

b) Using daily observations 5, 11, 17, ... the "own" standard deviation of return s_j is computed for each asset.

c) Using observations 1, 7, 13, ... the following cross-sectional regression is computed for each group, g. $R_{jt} = \hat{\lambda}_{0gt} + \hat{\lambda}_{1gt}b_{1j} + \ldots + \hat{\lambda}_{5gt}b_{5j} + \hat{\lambda}_{6gt}s_j + \xi_{jt}$, $j = 1, \ldots 30$ within each group and for all groups $g = 1, \ldots 42$. This yields 42 time series of vectors, $\hat{\lambda}_{gt} = \hat{\lambda}_{0gt}, \ldots \hat{\lambda}_{6gt}$, of estimated factors $\hat{\lambda}_{1gt}$ through $\hat{\lambda}_{5gt}$, of the riskless interest rate and of the effect of "own" standard deviation $\hat{\lambda}_{6gt}$.

d) The time series of $\hat{\lambda}_{6gt}$ is used to compute a standard error for the mean value, i.e., for $\bar{\lambda}_{6g} = \Sigma_t \hat{\lambda}_{6gt}/T$, in order to test for the significant presence of an "own" variance effect.

The results indicate that just three of the 42 groups (7.1%) display a significant effect of *s* on expected return at the 95% level. Since just one less group, two out of 42, would be fewer than the number to be expected by pure chance, there seems to be little remaining reason to reject the hypothesis that individual expected returns are unaffected by the "own" variance of returns.

This procedure also could be used to estimate the significance of different factors. However, due to the factor identification problem, the time series of factor values from one group will probably not be the same as the factor values for a different group. Furthermore, the resulting tests are less powerful than the factor-analysis based tests reported in Section II. They do indicate, however, that 17 groups (40.5%) have at least one significant factor and ten groups (23.8%) have at least two significant. This is an indication of fewer significant factors than in the factor-analysis tests but such a result is to be anticipated with a less powerful method.[9]

[9] Following Fama-MacBeth [14], a test of market efficiency can be conducted by regarding that the $\hat{\lambda}$ as excess returns on portfolios. (They can be interpreted as portfolios that load exclusively on a given factor). The returns should be serially uncorrelated in an efficient market. We found the first ten lagged autocorrelations, each subsuming six trading days, to be insignificantly different from zero. For example, the ten lagged serial correlation coefficients of $\hat{\lambda}_{11}$, (the first factor of the first group), are .00726, .0432, −.0197, −.0123, −.0201, −.112, −.0412, −.000979, −.0624, .0739. The sample size is 430 ± 5, (depending on the lag).

IV. A Test for the Equivalence of Factor Structure Across Groups

One of the most troubling econometric problems in the two preceding sections was due to the technological necessity of splitting assets into groups. Since the calculations were made for each group separately, but over the same time interval, the results are potentially susceptible to spurious sampling dependence among the groups. Also, due to the factor identification problem, there is no good way to ascertain whether the *same* three (or four) factors generate the returns in every group. It's conceivable, (but we think unlikely) that each of the 42 groups displays three *different* factors. This would imply that the actual number of common factors is 3×42, or at least some number considerably larger than three.

Even if the APT is true, the same underlying common factors can be "rotated" differently in each group. However, there is one parameter, the intercept term (λ_0 in eq.(2)) which should be identical across groups, whatever the sample rotation of the generating factors. Recall that λ_0 should be the expected return on either the riskless rate of interest or on an asset with no sensitivity to the common factors. This suggests that a simple test of the APT and of the cross-group consistency of factor structure can involve ascertaining whether the λ_0's estimated for the 42 groups are significantly different.

Since the test must also correct for inter-group dependence, a reasonable approach would use the time series estimated intercepts from the Fama-MacBeth type cross-sectional regressions computed in the last part of Section III; (Cf. pp. 46–48). For each group g, $\hat{\lambda}_{0gt}$ is the cross-sectional intercept for day t, from a cross-sectional regression on the factor landings ($\hat{b}$'s) and the "own" standard deviation (s_j) estimated from different but interleaved observations. Since each group has a time series $\hat{\lambda}_{0g}$ whose members are possibly correlated across groups, the appropriate test is Hotelling's T^2 for differences in adjacent groups.[10] That is, let

$$Z_{g/2,t} = \hat{\lambda}_{0,g-1,t} - \hat{\lambda}_{0,g,t} \quad g = 2, 4, 6, \dots .$$

be computed for each naturally-ordered pair of groups with a "sufficient" number of observations. We assumed that 400 was a sufficient number. There were 38 groups with at least 400 observations from the calendar observations used in the regressions (i.e., from observation 1, 7, 13, ...). Thus, there were 19 time-series for $Z_{g/2}$, $(g = 2, \dots 38)$.

The composite null hypothesis to be tested is

$$H_0: E(Z_{g/2}) = 0, g = 2, 4, \dots 38$$

and Hotelling's T^2 conducts this test by using the quadratic form

$$T^2 = N \bar{Z} \, \underline{\Sigma}^{-1} \, \bar{Z}$$

where $\bar{Z}$ is the vector of sample means of the $\bar{Z}_{g/2,t}$'s and $\underline{\Sigma}$ is their sample covariance matrix. The sample size is N. Since simultaneous observations are required to compute the covariance matrix, if any stock in any of the 38 groups

---

[10] See Press [39, ch. 6] for a general explanation of Hotelling's T².

had a missing observation, that observation could not be used. This resulted in a further reduction to 188 simultaneous observations.

Hotelling's T^2 value for these observations was 16.9 and the corresponding F statistic with 19 and 169 degrees of freedom was located at the .298 fractile of the null distribution. Thus, there is absolutely no evidence that the intercept terms were different across groups.

However, we do admit that this test is probably quite weak. There is a very low degree of explanatory power in the daily cross-sectional regressions and thus the sampling variation of each λ_{0gt} is quite large. Furthermore, Hotelling's test in small samples requires multi-variate normality. It is known, however, to be asymptotically robust and in the bivariate case is robust even for quite modest sample sizes much smaller than ours; (Cf. Chase and Bulgren [7]).

V. Conclusion

The empirical data support the APT against both an unspecified alternative—a very weak test—and the specific alternative that own variance has an independent explanatory effect on excess returns. But, as we have emphasized, these tests are only the beginning and should be viewed in that light.

A number of the empirical anomalies in the recent literature could be re-examined in the context of these results. For example, the APT would predict that insofar as price-earnings ratios have explanatory power for excess returns, they must be surrogates for the factor loadings. This provides the basis for an alternative test of the APT. On the longer term agenda, the statistical underpinnings of our analysis must be shored. Work on the small sample properties of factor analysis is scarce, and for nonnormal distributions, results appear to be nonexistent.

Lastly, of course, an effort should be directed at identifying a more meaningful set of sufficient statistics for the underlying factors. While this is not a necessary component of tests of the APT, it is an interesting and worthwhile pursuit of its own.

The issue in all of this, of course, is not whether the APT is true or false. Like all the theories that are not empty, it is false that some degree of precision in the testing: if we test long enough, all interesting theories are rejected. Rather, the question is what we will learn from these tests on how well the theory performs in competition with specific alternatives. At stake is the basic intuition of the APT that systematic variability alone affects expected returns, and this is the central theme of modern asset pricing theory.

Acknowledgement

The comments and suggestions of listeners to our preliminary results on this subject have been invaluable in improving many half-baked procedures. To the extent that our soufflé is finally ready to come out of the oven, we owe a particular debt to participants in seminars at Berkeley/Stanford, Laval, Karlsruhe, and Southern California, and to the participants in the conference on "new issues in

Arbitrage Pricing 1101

the asset pricing model" held at Coeur d'Alene, Idaho, and sponsored by Washington State University. This work originated while the authors were Leslie Wong summer fellows at the University of British Columbia in 1977. Comments by Michael Brennan, Thomas Copeland and Richard McEnally have been especially helpful. Of course, no one but us can be held responsible for remaining errors.

REFERENCES

1. J. Aitcheson and J.A.G. Brown. *The Lognormal Distribution.* Cambridge: Cambridge University Press, 1957.
2. Ray Ball. "Anomalies in Relationships Between Securities' Yields and Yield—Surrogates." *Journal of Financial Economics* (June/September 1978), 103-26.
3. Fischer Black. "Capital Market Equilibrium with Restricted Borrowing." *Journal of Business* 45 (July 1972), 444-54.
4. S. Basu. "Investment Performance of Common Stock in Relation to Their Price-Earnings Ratios: A Test of the Efficient Market Hypothesis." *Journal of Finance* 23 (June 1977), p. 663-82.
5. Douglas T. Breeden. "An Inter-Temporal Asset Pricing Model with Stochastic Consumption and Investment Opportunities." Unpublished manuscript, University of Chicago, Graduate School of Business, August 1978.
6. M. J. Brennan. "Capital Asset Pricing and the Structure of Security Returns." Unpublished manuscript, University of British Columbia, May 1971.
7. G. R. Chase and William G. Bulgren. "A Monte Carlo Investigation of the Robustness of T^2." *Journal of the American Statistical Association* 66 (September 1971), 499-502.
8. John C. Cox, Jonathan E. Ingersoll, Jr. and Stephen A. Ross. "A Theory of the Term Structure." *Econometrica.* (forthcoming).
9. Peter K. Clark. "A Subordinated Stochastic Process Model with Finite Variance for Speculative Prices." *Econometrica* 41 (January 1973), 135-55.
10. George W. Douglas. "Risk in the Equity Market: An Empirical Appraisal of Market Efficiency." *Yale Economic Essays* 9 (Spring 1969), 3-45.
11. Eugene F. Fama. "Efficient Capital Markets: A Review of Theory and Empirical Work." *Journal of Finance* 25 (May 1970), 383-417.
12. Eugene F. Fama. *Foundations of Finance.* New York: Basic Books, 1976.
13. Eugene F. Fama. "The Behavior of Stock Market Prices." *Journal of Business* 38 (January 1965), 34-105.
14. Eugene F. Fama and James D. MacBeth. "Risk, Return, and Equilibrium: Empirical Tests." *Journal of Political Economy* 38 (May 1973) 607-36.
15. D. E. Farrar. *The Investment Decision Under Uncertainty.* Englewood Cliffs, N.J.: Prentice-Hall dissertation series, 1962.
16. Milton Friedman. "The Methodology of Positive Economics," in *Essays in Positive Economics.* Chicago: University of Chicago Press, 1953.
17. Adam Gehr, Jr. "Some Tests of the Arbitrage Pricing Theory." *Journal of the Midwest Finance Association* (1975), 91-105.
18. Nils H. Hakansson. "Capital Growth and the Mean-Variance Approach to Portfolio Selection." *Journal of Financial and Quantitative Analysis* 6 (January 1971), 517-557.
19. Der-Ann Hsu, Robert B. Miller, and Dean W. Wichern. "On the Stable Paretian Behavior of Stock Market Prices." *Journal of the American Statistical Association* 69 (March 1974), 108-13.
20. Karl G. Jöreskog. "Some Contributions to Maximum Likelihood Factor Analysis." *Psychometrika* 32 (December 1967), 443-82.
21. Karl G. Jöreskog and Dag Sörbom. *EFAP, Exploratory Factor Analysis Program.* National Educational Resources, Inc., 1976.
22. Benjamin F. King. "Market and Industry Factors in Stock Price Behavior." *Journal of Business* 39 (January 1966, supp.), 139-90.

23. Alan Kraus and Robert Litzenberger. "Skewness Preference and the Valuation of Risk Assets." *Journal of Finance* 31 (September 1976), 1085–1100.

24. Lawrence Kryzanowski and To Minh Chan. "General Factor Models and the Structure of Security Returns." Working paper, Concordia University, Faculty of Commerce and Administration, (September 1979).

25. Terence C. Langetieg. "An Application of a Three-Factor Performance Index to Measure Stockholder Gains from Merger." *Journal of Financial Economics* 6 (December 1978), 365–83.

26. D. N. Lawley and A. E. Maxwell. *Factor Analysis as a Statistical Method.* London: Butterworths, 1963.

27. Cheng F. Lee. "Functional Form, Skewness Effect, and the Risk-Return Relationship." Abstracted in *Journal of Financial and Quantitative Analysis.* (March 1977), 55–72.

28. Cheng F. Lee and Joseph D. Vinso. "Single vs. Simultaneous Equation Models in Capital Asset Pricing: The Role of Firm-Related Variables." *Journal of Business Research* (1980), 65–80.

29. Haim Levy. "Equilibrium in an Imperfect Market: A Constraint on the Number of Securities in the Portfolio." *American Economic Review* (September 1978).

30. John Lintner. "The Valuation of Risk Assets and the Selection of Risky Investments in Stock Portfolios and Capital Budgets." *Review of Economics and Statistics* 47 (February 1965), 13–37.

31. Robert E. Lucas, Jr. "Asset Prices in an Exchange Economy." *Econometrica* 46 (November 1978), 1429–45.

32. Benoit Mandelbrot. "The Variation of Certain Speculative Prices." *Journal of Business* 36 (October 1963), 394–419.

33. Charles G. Martin. "Ridge Regression Estimates of the *Ex Post* Risk-Return Tradeoff on Common Stock." *Review of Business and Economic Research* 13 (Spring 1978), 1–15.

34. David Mayers. "Non-Marketable Assets and Capital Market Equilibrium Under Uncertainty." 223–248 in Michael C. Jensen, ed., *Studies in the Theory of Capital Markets.* New York: Praeger, 1972.

35. Robert C. Merton. "An Inter-Temporal Capital Asset Pricing Model." *Econometrica* 41 (September 1973), 867–87.

36. Stephen L. Meyers. "A Re-examination of Market and Industry Factors in Stock Price Behaviors." *Journal of Finance* 28 (June 1973), 695–706.

37. Merton H. Miller and Myron Scholes. "Rates of Return in Relation to Risk: A Re-examination of Some Recent Findings." 47–48 in Michael C. Jensen, ed., *Studies in the Theory of Capital Markets.* New York: Praeger, 1972.

38. Jan Mossin. "Equilibrium in a Capital Asset Market." *Econometrica* 34 (October 1966), 768–83.

39. S. James Press. *Applied Multivariate Analysis.* New York: Holt, Rinehart, and Winston, Inc., 1972.

40. Marc R. Reinganum. "Misspecification of Capital Asset Pricing: Empirical Anomalies Based on Earnings Yields and Forecasts." Unpublished manuscript, Graduate School of Business, University of Chicago, 1978.

41. Richard Roll. "A Critique of the Asset Pricing Theory's Tests." *Journal of Financial Economics* 4 (May 1977), 129–76.

42. Richard Roll. "Ambiguity When Performance is Measured by the Securities Market Line." *Journal of Finance* 33 (September 1978), 1051–69.

43. Richard Roll. "Testing a Portfolio for Ex Ante Mean/Variance Efficiency." In E. Elton and M. Gruber, eds., *TIMS Studies in the Management Sciences.* Amsterdam: North-Holland, 1979.

44. Barr Rosenberg and Vinay Marathe. "Tests of Capital Asset Pricing Hypotheses." Unpublished manuscript, University of California, Berkeley, 1977.

45. Barr Rosenberg. "Extra-Market Components of Covariance in Security Returns." *Journal of Financial and Quantitative Analysis* 9 (March 1974), 263–74.

46. Barr Rosenberg and Michael Houglet. "Error Rates in CRSP and Compustat Data Bases and Their Implications." *Journal of Finance* 29 (September 1974), 1303–10.

47. Stephen A. Ross. "Return Risk, and Arbitrage." In Irwin Friend, and James L. Bicksler, eds., *Risk and Return in Finance*, I, 189–218. Cambridge, Mass.: Ballinger, 1977.

Arbitrage Pricing   1103

48. Stephen A. Ross. "The Arbitrage Theory of Capital Asset Pricing." *Journal of Economic Theory* 13 (December 1976), 341–60.

49. Stephen A. Ross. "The Current Status of the Capital Asset Pricing Model (CAPM)." *Journal of Finance* 33 (June 1978), 885–90.

50. William F. Sharpe. "A Simplified Model for Portfolio Analysis." *Management Science* 9 (January 1963), 277–93.

51. William F. Sharpe. "Capital Asset Prices: A Theory of Market Equilibrium Under Conditions of Risk." *Journal of Finance* 19 (September 1964), 425–42.

52. William F. Sharpe. "The Capital Asset Pricing Model: A 'Multi-Beta' Interpretation." In H. Levy and M. Sarnat, eds., *Financial Decision Making Under Uncertainty*. New York: Academic Press, 1977.

53. Ledyard R. Tucker and Charles Lewis. "A Reliability Coefficient for Maximum Likelihood Factor Analysis." *Psychometrika* 38 (March 1973), 1–10.

54. James C. Van Horne. *Financial Management and Policy*, 4th ed. Englewood Cliffs, N.J. Prentice-Hall, 1977.

[15]

Nai-Fu Chen
University of Chicago

Richard Roll
University of California, Los Angeles

Stephen A. Ross
Yale University

Economic Forces and the Stock Market*

I. Introduction

Asset prices are commonly believed to react sensitively to economic news. Daily experience seems to support the view that individual asset prices are influenced by a wide variety of unanticipated events and that some events have a more pervasive effect on asset prices than do others. Consistent with the ability of investors to diversify, modern financial theory has focused on pervasive, or "systematic," influences as the likely source of investment risk.[1] The general conclusion of theory is that an additional component of long-run return is required and obtained whenever a particular asset is influenced by systematic economic news and that no extra reward can be earned by (needlessly) bearing diversifiable risk.

This paper tests whether innovations in macroeconomic variables are risks that are rewarded in the stock market. Financial theory suggests that the following macroeconomic variables should systematically affect stock market returns: the spread between long and short interest rates, expected and unexpected inflation, industrial production, and the spread between high- and low-grade bonds. We find that these sources of risk are significantly priced. Furthermore, neither the market portfolio nor aggregate consumption are priced separately. We also find that oil price risk is not separately rewarded in the stock market.

* The authors are grateful to their respective universities, to the Center for Research in Security Prices, to the National Science Foundation for research support, and to Ceajer Chan for computational assistance. The comments of Bradford Cornell, Eugene Fama, Pierre Hillion, Richard Sweeney, and Arthur Warga were most helpful, as were the comments of participants in workshops at Claremont Graduate School, Stanford University, the University of Toronto, the University of California, Irvine, the University of Alberta, the University of Chicago, and unknown referees. The University of British Columbia provided a stimulating research environment where part of the first revision was written during August 1984.

1. For example, the APT (Ross 1976) and the models of Merton (1973) and Cox, Ingersoll, and Ross (1985) are consistent with this view.

(*Journal of Business*, 1986, vol. 59, no. 3)

The theory has been silent, however, about which events are likely to influence all assets. A rather embarrassing gap exists between the theoretically exclusive importance of systematic "state variables" and our complete ignorance of their identity. The comovements of asset prices suggest the presence of underlying exogenous influences, but we have not yet determined which economic variables, if any, are responsible.

Our paper is an exploration of this identification terrain. In Section II, we employ a simple theoretical guide to help choose likely candidates for pervasive state variables. In Section III we introduce the data and explain the techniques used to measure unanticipated movements in the proposed state variables. Section IV investigates whether exposure to systematic state variables explains expected returns. As specific alternatives to the pricing influence of the state variables identified by our simple theoretical model, Section IV considers the value- and the equally weighted market indices, an index of real consumption, and an index of oil prices. Each of these is found to be unimportant for pricing when compared with the identified economic state variables. Section V briefly summarizes our findings and suggests some directions for future research.

II. Theory

No satisfactory theory would argue that the relation between financial markets and the macroeconomy is entirely in one direction. However, stock prices are usually considered as responding to external forces (even though they may have a feedback on the other variables). It is apparent that all economic variables are endogenous in some ultimate sense. Only natural forces, such as supernovas, earthquakes, and the like, are truly exogenous to the world economy, but to base an asset-pricing model on these systematic physical factors is well beyond our current abilities. Our present goal is merely to model equity returns as functions of macro variables and nonequity asset returns. Hence this paper will take the stock market as endogenous, relative to other markets.

By the diversification argument that is implicit in capital market theory, only general economic state variables will influence the pricing of large stock market aggregates. Any systematic variables that affect the economy's pricing operator or that influence dividends would also influence stock market returns. Additionally, any variables that are necessary to complete the description of the state of nature will also be part of the description of the systematic risk factors. An example of such a variable would be one that has no direct influence on current cash flows but that does describe the changing investment opportunity set.

Stock prices can be written as expected discounted dividends:

$$p = \frac{E(c)}{k},$$ (1)

where c is the dividend stream and k is the discount rate. This implies that actual returns in any period are given by

$$\frac{dp}{p} + \frac{c}{p} = \frac{d[E(c)]}{E(c)} - \frac{dk}{k} + \frac{c}{p}.$$ (2)

It follows (trivially) that the systematic forces that influence returns are those that change discount factors, k, and expected cash flows, $E(c)$.[2]

The discount rate is an average of rates over time, and it changes with both the level of rates and the term-structure spreads across different maturities. Unanticipated changes in the riskless interest rate will therefore influence pricing, and, through their influence on the time value of future cash flows, they will influence returns. The discount rate also depends on the risk premium; hence, unanticipated changes in the premium will influence returns. On the demand side, changes in the indirect marginal utility of real wealth, perhaps as measured by real consumption changes, will influence pricing, and such effects should also show up as unanticipated changes in risk premia.

Expected cash flows change because of both real and nominal forces. Changes in the expected rate of inflation would influence nominal expected cash flows as well as the nominal rate of interest. To the extent that pricing is done in real terms, unanticipated price-level changes will have a systematic effect, and to the extent that relative prices change along with general inflation, there can also be a change in asset valuation associated with changes in the average inflation rate. Finally, changes in the expected level of real production would affect the current real value of cash flows. Insofar as the risk-premium measure does not capture industrial production uncertainty, innovations in the rate of productive activity should have an influence on stock returns through their impact on cash flows.

III. Constructing the Economic Factors

Having proposed a set of relevant variables, we must now specify their measurement and obtain time series of unanticipated movements. We could proceed by identifying and estimating a vector autoregressive model in an attempt to use its residuals as the unanticipated innova-

---

2. Since we are only concerned with intuition, we are ignoring the second-order terms from the stochastic calculus in deriving eq. (2). Also notice that the expectation is taken with respect to the martingale pricing measure (see Cox et al. 1985) and not with respect to the ordinary probability distribution.

tions in the economic factors. It is, however, more interesting and (perhaps) robust out of sample to employ theory to find single equations that can be estimated directly. In particular, since monthly rates of return are nearly serially uncorrelated, they can be employed as innovations without alteration. The general impact of a failure adequately to filter out the expected movement in an independent variable is to introduce an errors-in-variables problem. This has to be traded off against the error introduced by misspecification of the estimated equation for determining the expected movement.

A somewhat subtler version of the same problem arises with procedures such as vector autoregression. Any such statistically based time-series approach will find lagged stock market returns having a significant predictive content for macroeconomic variables. In the analysis of pricing, then, we will indirectly be using lagged stock market variables to explain the expected returns on portfolios of stocks. Whatever econometric advantages such an approach might offer, it is antithetical to the spirit of this investigation, which is to explore the pricing influence of exogenous macroeconomic variables. For this reason, as much as for any other, we have chosen to follow the simpler route in constructing the time series we use.[3]

Throughout this paper we adopt the convention that time subscripts apply to the end of the time period. The standard period is 1 month. Thus, $E(\quad|t - 1)$ denotes the expectation operator at the end of month $t - 1$ conditional on the information set available at the end of month $t - 1$, and $X(t)$ denotes the value of variable X in month t, or the growth that prevailed from the end of $t - 1$ to the end of t.

A. Industrial Production

The basic series is the growth rate in U.S. industrial production. It was obtained from the *Survey of Current Business*. If $IP(t)$ denotes the rate of industrial production in month t, then the monthly growth rate is

$$MP(t) = \log_e IP(t) - \log_e IP(t - 1), \qquad (3)$$

and the yearly growth rate is

$$YP(t) = \log_e IP(t) - \log_e IP(t - 12) \qquad (4)$$

(see table 1 for a summary of variables).

Because $IP(t)$ actually is the flow of industrial production during month t, $MP(t)$ measures the change in industrial production lagged by at least a partial month. To make this variable contemporaneous with other series, subsequent statistical work will lead it by 1 month. Except for an annual seasonal, it is noisy enough to be treated as an innovation.

---

3. In addition, the pricing tests reported below used portfolios that have induced autocorrelations in their returns arising from the nontrading effect.

TABLE 1   **Glossary and Definitions of Variables**

Symbol	Variable	Definition or Source
	Basic Series	
I	Inflation	Log relative of U.S. Consumer Price Index
TB	Treasury-bill rate	End-of-period return on 1-month bills
LGB	Long-term government bonds	Return on long-term government bonds (1958–78: Ibbotson and Sinquefield [1982]; 1979–83: CRSP)
IP	Industrial production	Industrial production during month (*Survey of Current Business*)
Baa	Low-grade bonds	Return on bonds rated Baa and under (1953–77: Ibbotson [1979], constructed for 1978–83)
EWNY	Equally weighted equities	Return on equally weighted portfolio of NYSE-listed stocks (CRSP)
VWNY	Value-weighted equities	Return on a value-weighted portfolio of NYSE-listed stocks (CRSP)
CG	Consumption	Growth rate in real per capita consumption (Hansen and Singleton [1982]; *Survey of Current Business*)
OG	Oil prices	Log relative of Producer Price Index/Crude Petroleum series (Bureau of Labor Statistics)
	Derived Series	
$MP(t)$	Monthly growth, industrial production	$\log_e[IP(t)/IP(t-1)]$
$YP(t)$	Annual growth, industrial production	$\log_e[IP(t)/IP(t-12)]$
$E[I(t)]$	Expected inflation	Fama and Gibbons (1984)
$UI(t)$	Unexpected inflation	$I(t) - E[I(t)\|t-1]$
$RHO(t)$	Real interest (ex post)	$TB(t-1) - I(t)$
$DEI(t)$	Change in expected inflation	$E[I(t+1)\|t] - E[I(t)\|t-1]$
$URP(t)$	Risk premium	$Baa(t) - LGB(t)$
$UTS(t)$	Term structure	$LGB(t) - TB(t-1)$

The monthly series of yearly growth rates, $YP(t)$, was examined because the equity market is related to changes in industrial activity in the long run. Since stock market prices involve the valuation of cash flows over long periods in the future, monthly stock returns may not be highly related to contemporaneous monthly changes in rates of industrial production, although such changes might capture the information pertinent for pricing. This month's change in stock prices probably reflects changes in industrial production anticipated many months into the future. Therefore, subsequent statistical work will lead this variable by 1 year, similar to the variable used in Fama (1981).

Because of the overlap in the series, YP(t) is highly autocorrelated. A procedure was developed for forecasting expected YP(t) and a series of unanticipated changes in YP(t), and changes in the expectation itself were examined for their influence on pricing. The resulting series offered no discernible advantage over the raw production series, and, as a consequence, they have been dropped from the analysis.[4]

B. Inflation

Unanticipated inflation is defined as

$$\text{UI}(t) = \text{I}(t) - \text{E}[\text{I}(t)|t - 1], \qquad (5)$$

where I(t) is the realized monthly first difference in the logarithm of the Consumer Price Index for period t. The series of expected inflation, $\text{E}[\text{I}(t)|t - 1]$ for the period 1953–78, is obtained from Fama and Gibbons (1984). If RHO(t) denotes the ex post real rate of interest applicable in period t and TB($t - 1$) denotes the Treasury-bill rate known at the end of period $t - 1$ and applying to period t, then Fisher's equation asserts that

$$\text{TB}(t - 1) = \text{E}[\text{RHO}(t)|t - 1] + \text{E}[\text{I}(t)|t - 1]. \qquad (6)$$

Hence, TB($t - 1$) $-$ I(t) measures the ex post real return on Treasury bills in the period. From a time-series analysis of this variable, Fama and Gibbons (1984) constructed a time series for $\text{E}[\text{RHO}(t)|t - 1]$. Our expected inflation variable is defined by subtracting their time series for the expected real rate from the TB($t - 1$) series.

Another inflation variable that is unanticipated and that might have an influence separable from UI is

$$\text{DEI}(t) = \text{E}[\text{I}(t + 1)|t] - \text{E}[\text{I}(t)|t - 1], \qquad (7)$$

the change in expected inflation. We subscript this variable with t since it is (in principle) unknown at the end of month $t - 1$. While, strictly speaking, DEI(t) need not have mean zero, under the additional assumption that expected inflation follows a martingale this variable may be treated as an innovation, and it may contain information not present in the UI variable. This would occur whenever inflation forecasts are influenced by economic factors other than past forecasting errors. (Notice that the UI series and the DEI series will contain the information in a series of innovations in the nominal interest rate, TB.)[5]

4. Results that include these series are available in an earlier draft of the paper, which is available from the authors on request.

5. As an aside, the resulting unanticipated inflation variable, UI(t), is perfectly negatively correlated with the unanticipated change in the real rate. This follows from the observation that the Fisher equation (6) holds for realized rates as well as for expectations. The UI(t) series also has a simple correlation of .98 with the unanticipated inflation series in Fama (1981).

C. Risk Premia

To capture the effect on returns of unanticipated changes in risk premia, we will employ another variable drawn from the money markets. The variable, UPR, is defined as

$$\text{UPR}(t) = \text{``Baa and under'' bond portfolio return } (t) - \text{LGB}(t), \quad (8)$$

where $\text{LGB}(t)$ is the return on a portfolio of long-term government bonds obtained from Ibbotson and Sinquefield (1982) for the period 1953–78. From 1979 through 1983, $\text{LGB}(t)$ was obtained from the Center for Research in Securities Prices (CRSP) data file. Again, UPR is not formally an innovation, but, as the differences in two return series, it is sufficiently uncorrelated that we can treat it as unanticipated, and we will use it as a member of the set of economic factors.

The low-grade bond return series is for nonconvertible corporate bonds, and it was obtained from R. G. Ibbotson and Company for the period prior to 1977. A detailed description of the sample is contained in Ibbotson (1979). The low-grade series was extended through 1983 by choosing 10 bonds whose ratings on January 1966 were below Baa. By 1978 these bonds still were rated below Baa, but their maturity was shorter than that of the long-term government bond series. These 10 bonds were then combined with three that were left over from the Ibbotson series at the end of 1978 to create a low-grade bond portfolio of 13 bonds in all. The returns on this portfolio were then used to extend the UPR series beyond 1977 and through 1983. Two further difficulties with the series are that the ratings have experienced considerable inflation since the mid-1950s and that the low-grade series contains bonds that are unrated.

The UPR variable would have mean zero in a risk-neutral world, and it is natural to think of it as a direct measure of the degree of risk aversion implicit in pricing (at least insofar as the rating agencies maintain constant standards for their classifications). We hoped that UPR would reflect much of the unanticipated movement in the degree of risk aversion and in the level of risk implicit in the market's pricing of stocks.[6]

D. The Term Structure

To capture the influence of the shape of the term structure, we employ another interest rate variable,

$$\text{UTS}(t) = \text{LGB}(t) - \text{TB}(t - 1). \quad (9)$$

---

6. It could be argued that UPR captures a leverage effect, with highly levered firms being associated with lower ratings. Furthermore, UPR is also similar to a measure of equity returns since a substantial portion of the value of low-grade bonds comes from the same sort of call option (behind secured debt) as for ordinary stock.

Again, under the appropriate form of risk neutrality,

$$E[UTS(t)|t - 1] = 0, \tag{10}$$

and this variable can be thought of as measuring the unanticipated return on long bonds. The assumption of risk neutrality is used only to isolate the pure term-structure effects; the variable UPR is used to capture the effect of changes in risk aversion.

E. Market Indices

The major thrust of our effort is to examine the relation between non-equity economic variables and stock returns. However, because of the smoothing and averaging characteristics of most macroeconomic time series, in short holding periods, such as a single month, these series cannot be expected to capture all the information available to the market in the same period. Stock prices, on the other hand, respond very quickly to public information. The effect of this is to guarantee that market returns will be, at best, weakly related and very noisy relative to innovations in macroeconomic factors.

This should bias our results in favor of finding a stronger linkage between the time-series returns on market indices and other portfolios of stock returns than between these portfolio returns and innovations in the macro variables. To examine the relative pricing influence of the traditional market indices we used the following variables:

$$EWNY(t) = \text{return on the equally weighted NYSE index;}$$
$$\tag{11}$$
$$VWNY(t) = \text{return on the value-weighted NYSE index.}$$

These variables should reflect both the real information in the industrial production series and the nominal influence of the inflation variables.

F. Consumption

In addition to the macro variables discussed above, we also examined a time series of percentage changes in real consumption, CG. The series is in real per capita terms and includes service flows. It was constructed by dividing the CITIBASE series of seasonally adjusted real consumption (excluding durables) by the Bureau of Census's monthly population estimates. The CG series extends from January 1959 to December 1983, and it is an extension of a series obtained from Lars Hansen for the period through 1979. A detailed description of its construction can be found in Hansen and Singleton (1983).

G. Oil Prices

It is often argued that oil prices must be included in any list of the systematic factors that influence stock market returns and pricing. To test this proposition and to examine another alternative to the macro variables discussed above, we formed the OG series of realized

monthly first differences in the logarithm of the Producer Price Index/
Crude Petroleum series (obtained from the Bureau of Labor Statistics,
U.S. Department of Labor, DRI series no. 3884). The glossary in table
1 summarizes the variables.

H.   Statistical Characteristics of the Macro Variables

Table 2 displays the correlation matrix for the state variables. The
correlation matrices of table 2 are computed for several different pe-

TABLE 2   **Correlation Matrices for Economic Variables**

Symbol	EWNY	VWNY	MP	DEI	UI	UPR	UTS
			A. January 1953–November 1983				
VWNY	.916						
MP	.103	.020					
DEI	−.163	−.119	.063				
UI	−.163	−.112	−.067	.378			
UPR	.105	.042	.216	.266	.018		
UTS	.227	.248	−.159	−.394	−.103	−.752	
YP	.270	.270	.139	−.003	−.005	.113	.099
			B. January 1953–December 1972				
VWNY	.930						
MP	.147	.081					
DEI	−.130	−.122	.020				
UI	−.081	−.021	−.203	.388			
UPR	.265	.214	.213	.068	−.072		
UTS	.110	.108	−.059	−.210	−.041	−.688	
YP	.260	.238	.128	−.013	−.032	.128	.063
			C. January 1973–December 1977				
VWNY	.883						
MP	.022	−.118					
DEI	−.314	−.263	.004				
UI	−.377	−.352	−.004	.505			
UPR	.341	.231	.227	.032	−.289		
UTS	.217	.313	−.350	−.280	.026	−.554	
YP	.335	.361	.107	−.124	−.334	.221	.174
			D. January 1978–November 1983				
VWNY	.937						
MP	.092	−.010					
DEI	−.143	−.073	.169				
UI	−.055	−.024	.168	.375			
UPR	−.275	−.319	.248	.458	.259		
UTS	.424	.431	−.277	−.512	−.239	−.890	
YP	.269	.261	.193	.053	.247	.018	.115

NOTE.—VWNY = return on the value-weighted NYSE index; EWNY = return on the equally
weighted NYSE index; MP = monthly growth rate in industrial production; DEI = change in
expected inflation; UI = unanticipated inflation; UPR = unanticipated change in the risk premium
(Baa and under return − long-term government bond return); UTS = unanticipated change in the
term structure (long-term government bond return − Treasury-bill rate); and YP = yearly growth
rate in industrial production.

TABLE 3   Autocorrelations of the Economic Variables, January 1953–November 1983

Symbol	ρ_1	ρ_2	ρ_3	ρ_4	ρ_5	ρ_6	ρ_7	ρ_8	ρ_9	ρ_{10}	ρ_{11}	ρ_{12}	Adjusted Box/Pierce (24)
YP	.9615	.8896	.7937	.6838	.5658	.4477	.3290	.2088	.0919	−.0196	−.1233	−.2109	1,639
MP	−.0990	−.1711	−.1204	.0413	.0778	.0241	.0765	.0240	−.1558	−.2122	−.1914	.8030	632.9
DEI	−.0432	−.0864	−.0094	−.0719	.0284	.0130	−.0874	.1662	.1101	−.0290	.0297	.0007	43.33
UI	.1804	.1314	.0567	.0483	.0490	−.0454	−.0398	.0535	.1391	.1536	.1361	.1875	85.50
UPR	−.1053	.0491	−.1340	.0882	−.0196	.0422	−.1297	.0117	−.0494	−.0733	.0834	.0264	52.81
UTS	.0267	−.0052	−.1637	.0383	.0739	.0750	−.0929	−.0278	.0023	−.0105	.1693	−.0029	57.15
CG	−.2458	−.0269	.1190	.0192	−.0460	.0082	.0497	−.0496	.0121	.0470	.1364	−.1324	53.06
OG	.4088	.2194	.1523	.1613	.0954	.1447	.1594	.0674	.0969	.0976	.0609	−.0038	159.0
EWNY	.1447	−.0133	.0141	.0554	.0518	−.0213	−.0959	−.0861	.0072	−.0140	.0043	.0997	40.43
VWNY	.0677	−.0223	.0456	.0936	.0909	−.0755	−.0779	−.0258	.0147	−.0515	−.0320	.0655	37.24

NOTE.—YP = yearly growth rate in industrial production; MP = monthly growth rate in industrial production; DEI = change in expected inflation; UI = unanticipated inflation; UPR = unanticipated change in the risk premium (Baa and under return − long-term government bond return); UTS = unanticipated change in the term structure (long-term government bond return − Treasury-bill rate); CG = growth rate in real per capita consumption; OG = growth rate in oil prices; EWNY = return on the equally weighted NYSE index; and VWNY = return on the value-weighted NYSE index.

riods; part A covers the entire 371-month sample period from January 1953 through November 1983, and the remaining parts cover three subperiods, with breaks at December 1977 and January 1973. We have broken the sample at this time because it is often argued that the oil price jump in 1973 presaged a structural shift in the macro variables. (The work of Litterman and Weiss [1983] supports this view, but, although we have performed no formal tests, the correlation matrix does not appear to differ markedly across the subperiods.)

With the exception of the market indices, the strongest correlation is between UPR and UTS. This is to be expected since they both use the long-term bond series, $LGB(t)$. The resulting collinearity tends to weaken the individual impact of these variables. Substituting an Aaa corporate bond series for treasuries in the definition of UPR did, in fact, improve the significance of both UPR and UTS, but the improvement was not sufficiently important to make a qualitative difference in our findings.

The production series, YP and MP, are correlated with each other and with each of the other variables except DEI and UI, which are also strongly correlated. These latter two series are correlated because they both contain the $EI(t)$ series, and the negative correlation between DEI and UTS occurs for a similar reason. A number of other correlations are not negligible, but the variables are far from perfectly correlated, and no one variable can be substituted for any other.

Table 3 displays the autocorrelations for the state variables computed over the entire sample period, January 1953–November 1983. There are no surprises here; as expected, YP is highly autocorrelated. The variables generally display mild autocorrelations, and many of them have seasonals at the 12-month lag. The MP series, in particular, has a peak in its lag at 12 months (repeated at 24 months), warning that this variable is highly seasonal. As noted above, the autocorrelation in the state variables implies the existence of an errors-in-variables problem that will bias estimates of the loadings of the stock returns on these variables and will bias downward estimates of statistical significance.

IV. The Economic State Variables and Asset Pricing

A. Basic Results

Using the state variables[7] defined above implies that individual stock returns follow a factor model of the form

---

7. We did the following experiment to find out if asset prices do, in fact, react to news associated with our proposed economic state variables. We first extracted the most important stock factors (common covariations) during the period 1953–72, using the Chen (1983) algorithm. Five factors were chosen on the basis of previous empirical studies (see Roll and Ross 1980; Brown and Weinstein 1983). The factors can be thought of as portfolios constructed to capture the common movements in stock market returns.

$$R = a + b_{MP}MP + b_{DEI}DEI + b_{UI}UI$$
$$+ b_{UPR}UPR + b_{UTS}UTS + e, \tag{12}$$

where the betas are the loadings on the state variables, a is the constant term, and e is an idiosyncratic error term. To ascertain whether the identified economic state variables are related to the underlying factors that explain pricing in the stock market, a version of the Fama-MacBeth (1973) technique was employed. The procedure was as follows. (a) A sample of assets was chosen. (b) The assets' exposure to the economic state variables was estimated by regressing their returns on the unanticipated changes in the economic variables over some estimation period (we used the previous 5 years). (c) The resulting estimates of exposure (betas) were used as the independent variables in 12 cross-sectional regressions, one regression for each of the next 12 months, with asset returns for the month being the dependent variable. Each coefficient from a cross-sectional regression provides an estimate of the sum of the risk premium, if any, associated with the state variable and the unanticipated movement in the state variable for that month. (d) Steps b and c were then repeated for each year in the sample, yielding for each macro variable a time series of estimates of its associated risk premium. The time-series means of these estimates were then tested by a t-test for significant difference from zero.

To control the errors-in-variables problem that arises from the use at step c of the beta estimates obtained in step b and to reduce the noise in individual asset returns, the securities were grouped into portfolios. An effort was made to construct the portfolios so as to spread their expected returns over a wide range in an effort to improve the discriminatory power of the cross-sectional regression tests. To accomplish this spreading we formed portfolios on the basis of firm size. Firm size is known to be strongly related to average return (see Banz 1981), and we hoped that it would provide the desired dispersion without biasing the tests of the economic variables. (It has been facetiously noted that size may be the best theory we now have of expected returns. Unfortunately, this is less of a theory than an empirical observation.)[8]

The time series of those five factors were then each regressed on the state variables. An economic variable is significantly related to stock movements if and only if it is significantly related to at least one of the five common stock factors. The null hypothesis for each variable is the restriction across the equations that the five regression coefficients for that variable (one to each of the factor regressions) are jointly zero. The null hypothesis was rejected for the production growth, the term structure, and the risk premium variables. The support for the inflation variables, however, was weak. When a market index was included in the list of state variables, the significance of the other variables remained unchanged, except for the production variable, which became insignificantly related to the time series of the factors.

8. A number of alternative experiments were run in which securities were grouped into portfolios according to (a) their betas on a market index, (b) the standard deviation of their returns in a market-model regression (i.e., their residual variability), and (c) the

Table 4 reports the results of these tests on 20 equally weighted portfolios, grouped according to the total market values of their constituent securities at the beginning of each test period. Each part of table 4 is broken into four subperiods beginning with January 1958, the first month preceded by the requisite 60 months of data used to estimate exposures. Part A of table 4 examines the state variables, YP, MP, DEI, UI, UPR, and UTS. Over the entire sample period MP, UI, and UPR are significant, while UTS is marginally so. The inflation-related variables, DEI and UI, were highly significant in the 1968–77 period and insignificant both earlier and later. The yearly production series, YP, was not significant in any subperiod, and, as can be seen from part B, deleting it had no substantive effect on the remaining state variables. Although the coefficients have the same signs as in the overall period, they are generally smaller in absolute magnitude and less significant in the last subperiod, 1978–84.[9]

While we have not developed a theoretical foundation for the signs of the state variables, it is worth noting that their signs are, at least, plausible. The positive sign on MP reflects the value of insuring against real systematic production risks. Similarly, UPR has a positive risk premium since individuals would want to hedge against unanticipated increases in the aggregate risk premium occasioned by an increase in uncertainty. Since changes in inflation have the general effect of shifting wealth among investors, there is no strong a priori presumption that would sign the risk premia for UI or DEI, but the negative signs on the premia for these variables probably mean that stock market assets are generally perceived to be hedges against the adverse influence on other assets that are, presumably, relatively more fixed in nominal terms.

As for UTS, the negative risk premium indicates that stocks whose returns are inversely related to increases in long rates over short rates are, ceteris paribus, more valuable. One interpretation of this result is that UTS measures a change in the long-term real rate of interest (remember that inflation effects are included in the other variables). After long-term real rates decrease, there is subsequently a lower real return on any form of capital. Investors who want protection against this possibility will place a relatively higher value on assets whose price increases when long-term real rates decline, and such assets will carry a negative risk premium. Thus, stocks whose returns are cor-

---

level of the stock price. These efforts were not successful. The first two of these grouping techniques failed completely to spread portfolio returns out of sample and had to be discarded. Grouping by the level of the stock price did spread returns, although not as well as did size, but the state variables were then individually only marginally significant, and the market indices were of no significance. The sensitivity of the results to different grouping techniques is an important area for research.

9. This subperiod had only about two-thirds as many observations as did the first two subperiods.

TABLE 4   **Economic Variables and Pricing (Percent per Month × 10), Multivariate Approach**

A

Years	YP	MP	DEI	UI	UPR	UTS	Constant
1958–84	4.341	13.984	−.111	−.672	7.941	−5.87	4.112
	(.538)	(3.727)	(−1.499)	(−2.052)	(2.807)	(−1.844)	(1.334)
1958–67	.417	15.760	.014	−.133	5.584	.535	4.868
	(.032)	(2.270)	(.191)	(−.259)	(1.923)	(.240)	(1.156)
1968–77	1.819	15.645	−.264	−1.420	14.352	−14.329	−2.544
	(.145)	(2.504)	(−3.397)	(−3.470)	(3.161)	(−2.672)	(−.464)
1978–84	13.549	8.937	−.070	−.373	2.150	−2.941	12.541
	(.774)	(1.602)	(−.289)	(−.442)	(.279)	(−.327)	(1.911)

B

	MP	DEI	UI	UPR	UTS	Constant
1958–84	13.589	−.125	−.629	7.205	−5.211	4.124
	(3.561)	(−1.640)	(−1.979)	(2.590)	(−1.690)	(1.361)
1958–67	13.155	.006	−.191	5.560	−.008	4.989
	(1.897)	(.092)	(−.382)	(1.935)	(−.004)	(1.271)
1968–77	16.966	−.245	−1.353	12.717	−13.142	−1.889
	(2.638)	(−3.215)	(−3.320)	(2.852)	(−2.554)	(−.334)
1978–84	9.383	−.140	−.221	1.679	−1.312	11.477
	(1.588)	(−.552)	(−.274)	(.221)	(−.149)	(1.747)

C

	EWNY	MP	DEI	UI	UPR	UTS	Constant
1958–84	5.021	14.009	−.128	−.848	8.130	−5.017	6.409
	(1.218)	(3.774)	(−1.666)	(−2.541)	(2.855)	(−1.576)	(1.848)
1958–67	6.575	14.936	−.005	−.279	5.747	−.146	7.349
	(1.199)	(2.336)	(−.060)	(−.558)	(2.070)	(−.067)	(1.591)
1968–77	2.334	17.593	−.248	−1.501	12.512	−9.904	3.542
	(.283)	(2.715)	(−3.039)	(−3.366)	(2.758)	(−2.015)	(.558)
1978–84	6.638	7.563	−.132	−.729	5.273	−4.993	9.164
	(.906)	(1.253)	(−.529)	(−.847)	(.663)	(−.520)	(1.245)

D

	VWNY	MP	DEI	UI	UPR	UTS	Constant
1958–84	−2.403	11.756	−.123	−.795	8.274	−5.905	10.713
	(−.633)	(3.054)	(−1.600)	(−2.376)	(2.972)	(−1.879)	(2.755)
1958–67	1.359	12.394	.005	−.209	5.204	−.086	9.527
	(.277)	(1.789)	(.064)	(−.415)	(1.815)	(−.040)	(1.984)
1968–77	−5.269	13.466	−.255	−1.421	12.897	−11.708	8.582
	(−.717)	(2.038)	(−3.237)	(−3.106)	(2.955)	(−2.299)	(1.167)
1978–84	−3.683	8.402	−.116	−.739	6.056	−5.928	15.452
	(−.491)	(1.432)	(−.458)	(−.869)	(.782)	(−.644)	(1.867)

NOTE.—VWNY = return on the value-weighted NYSE index; EWNY = return on the equally weighted NYSE index; MP = monthly growth rate in industrial production; DEI = change in expected inflation; UI = unanticipated inflation; UPR = unanticipated change in the risk premium (Baa and under return − long-term government bond return); UTS = unanticipated change in the term structure (long-term government bond return − Treasury-bill rate); and YP = yearly growth rate in industrial production. *t*-statistics are in parentheses.

related with long-term bond returns, abstracting from unanticipated changes in inflation or in expected inflation and holding all other characteristics equal, will be more valuable than stocks that are uncorrelated or negatively correlated with long-term bond returns.

To test the pricing influence on the market indices, EWNY and VWNY were added to the set of state variables (actually, they were substituted for YP). It would not be inconsistent with asset-pricing theory to discover, for example, that the betas on the market portfolio were sufficient to capture the pricing impact of the macroeconomic state variables, and it would certainly rationalize past efforts that have focused on examining the efficiency of a market index. In some sense, then, an important test of the independent explanatory influence of the macroeconomic variables on pricing is to see how they fare in direct competition with a market index.

Parts C and D of table 4 report the results of such tests. Using the EWNY as a substitute for YP and including MP, DEI, UI, UPR, and UTS, we find in part C that the market index fails to have a statistically significant effect on pricing in any subperiod. On the other hand, the original macroeconomic variables have about the same significance as they did in part B. Nor are these results affected by the choice of market index; part D of table 4 reports similar results when using the VWNY.

By contrast with the tests reported in table 4, table 5 reports on tests that purposely have been designed to enhance the impact of the market indices. The tests discussed above were "fair" in the sense that the time-series regressions that measured the betas and the subsequent cross-sectional regressions that estimated their pricing influence gave each variable an a priori equal opportunity to be significant; that is, the design treated the variables in a symmetric fashion. The tests reported in table 5 are asymmetric in that they are weighted a priori to favor the market indices.

The tests in table 4 can be interpreted from the perspective of the arbitrage pricing theory. They are tests of whether the set of economic variables can be usefully augmented by the inclusion of a market index. In this sense they are tests of whether the market contains missing priced factors or, alternatively, whether the factors fail to have pricing significance as against the market. The tests in table 5 are best interpreted as tests whose null hypothesis is the CAPM, or, rather more simply, the efficiency of the index. If the index is efficient, then the factors should not improve on its pricing ability. Of course, all these interpretations are subject to the caveat that the factors may only help to improve the estimate of the "true" market portfolio either by accounting for missing assets or through their correlations with measurement errors in the market beta estimates.

TABLE 5   **Economic Variables and Pricing**

Years	VWNY	MP	DEI	UI	UPR	UTS	Constant
				A			
1958–84	14.527	...	...	...	...	...	−5.831
	(2.356)						(−.961)
1958–67	5.005	...	...	...	...	...	6.853
	(.673)						(.928)
1968–77	17.987	...	...	...	...	...	−15.034
	(1.460)						(−1.254)
1978–84	23.187	...	...	...	...	...	−10.802
	(1.935)						(−.907)
				B			
1958–84	−9.989	12.185	−.145	−.912	9.812	−5.448	10.714
	(−2.014)	(3.153)	(−1.817)	(−2.590)	(3.355)	(−1.609)	(2.755)
1958–67	−5.714	13.024	.004	−.193	6.104	−.593	9.527
	(−1.008)	(1.852)	(.057)	(−.369)	(1.994)	(−.260)	(1.983)
1968–77	−17.396	14.467	−.291	−1.614	14.367	−9.227	8.584
	(−1.824)	(2.214)	(−3.388)	(−3.297)	(3.128)	(−1.775)	(1.167)
1978–84	−5.515	7.725	−.150	−.935	8.602	−6.986	15.454
	(−.513)	(1.303)	(−.574)	(−1.051)	(1.064)	(−.681)	(1.867)
				C			
1958–84	11.507	10.487	−.190	−.738	8.126	−7.073	−3.781
	(1.189)	(2.761)	(−2.459)	(−2.215)	(2.869)	(−2.194)	(−.402)
1958–67	22.311	9.597	.001	−.163	3.186	.697	−11.734
	(1.950)	(1.494)	(.012)	(−.341)	(1.474)	(.337)	(−1.015)
1968–77	11.689	13.381	−.293	−1.422	13.007	−12.981	−9.488
	(.622)	(1.947)	(−3.590)	(−2.814)	(2.697)	(−2.214)	(−.526)
1978–84	−4.188	7.624	−.316	−.584	8.211	−9.735	15.732
	(−.207)	(1.286)	(−1.246)	(−.716)	(1.039)	(−1.123)	(.803)

NOTE.—VWNY = return on the value-weighted NYSE index; EWNY = return on the equally weighted NYSE index; MP = monthly growth rate in industrial production; DEI = change in expected inflation; UI = unanticipated inflation; UPR = unanticipated change in the risk premium (Baa and under return − long-term government bond return); and UTS = unanticipated change in the term structure (long-term government bond return − Treasury-bill rate). *t*-statistics are in parentheses.

Part A of table 5 reports the results of a simple test of the pricing influence of the ordinary CAPM betas computed from the VWNY index in the absence of the state variables. The VWNY-index betas are significant and positively related to average returns over the entire period, although they are significant only in the last subperiod. Part B of table 5 reports a more demanding test of the pricing influence of the index. These results differ from part D of table 4 because the cross sections were run with the simple betas for the VWNY index (instead of betas from a multivariate time-series regression). The betas for the state variables came from multivariate time-series regressions with only those variables included (they are the same as those used in part B of table 4). The VWNY betas are significant over the entire period but appear with a negative sign, and a comparison with part B of table 4 reveals that neither the coefficients nor the significance of the factor betas is altered substantially by the inclusion of the market index. (The results for the EWNY were essentially the same.)

Part C of table 5 reports on a final test in which, instead of estimating the index betas for the VWNY in the same fashion as for the other variables, the estimates were obtained from a single multiple regression that was run over the testing period from 1958 to 1983. The resulting market-index beta estimates were then used in each of the cross-sectional tests along with the betas for the other variables. The betas for the other variables were estimated as before, from time-series multiple regressions. (The betas for variables other than the market index came from part D of table 4.) It was thought that using the index-beta estimates from the testing period would lessen the ability of the other variables to show up as significant in pricing merely through their correlation with measurement errors in the index betas. Once again, the market index was insignificant overall, and the other variables were unaltered by its inclusion. The results for the EWNY were similar and are not reported.

The insignificance for pricing of the stock market indices contrasts sharply with their significance in time series. In the time-series regressions, EWNY and VWNY were by far the most statistically significant variables. For example, the average t-statistics for EWNY ranged between 11.7 and 29.9 over the 20 portfolios. The largest t-statistic for any other variable was only 3.4 when the indices were not included (for UPR and the smallest portfolio), and this fell to 2.5 when the VWNY was included, and most were considerably smaller. Although stock market indices "explain" much of the intertemporal movements in other stock portfolios, their estimated exposures (their betas) do not explain cross-sectional differences in average returns after the betas of the economic state variables have been included. This suggests that the "explanatory power" of the market indices may have less to do with economics and more to do with the statistical observation that large, positively weighted portfolios of random variables are correlated.

B. Consumption and Asset Pricing

Because of the current interest in consumption-based asset pricing models, we also examined the influence of the real consumption series. In a one-good intertemporal asset-pricing model, assets will be priced according to their covariances with aggregate (marginal utility of) consumption (see Lucas 1978; Breeden 1980; or Cox et al. 1985). There is nothing in this analysis that requires that consumption represents any particular state variable, and, in fact, the model is consistent with multistate descriptions of the economy. As a consequence, consumption-based theories predict that, when factors that represent state variables are included along with consumption, they will be rejected as having an influence on pricing.

Put formally, the consumption beta theories argue that

$$E - r = b_c^* k,$$ (13)

where $E - r$ is the vector of excess returns, k is a risk-premium measure, and b_c is the vector of consumption betas. The intuition of the theory is that individuals will adjust their intertemporal consumption streams so as to hedge against changes in the opportunity set. In equilibrium, assets that move with consumption, that is, assets for which $b_c > 0$, will be less valuable than will those that can insure against adverse movements in consumption, that is, those for which $b_c < 0$. It follows from risk aversion that the risk-premium measure, k, should be positive.

The alternative hypothesis that we will examine states that

$$E - r = b_c^* k + b_q^*,$$ (14)

where b is a vector of betas on the economic state variables used above, and q is the vector of associated risk premia. The null hypothesis of the consumption beta models would be that k is positive and that q is zero. Of course, it can always be argued that the other variables pick up changes in the relative pricing of different consumption goods or correct errors in the measurement of real consumption. Alternatively, although our updating procedure is an attempt to deal with intertemporal changes in the beta coefficients, it could also be argued that the factors could be correlated with such changes (see Cornell [1981] for a discussion of this possibility).

Table 6 reports the results of these tests using the CG series of real per capita consumption growth described in Section III. Because of data collection timing, the CG series, like the monthly production series, MP, may actually measure consumption changes with a lag. To deal with this problem, we led the CG series forward by 1 month. The results with the contemporaneous CG series are uniformly less favorable for its pricing influence and are not reported.

TABLE 6   Pricing with Consumption

Years	CG	MP	DEI	UI	UPR	UTS	Constant
1964–84	.68	14.964	−.166	−.846	8.813	−6.921	2.289
	(.108)	(3.800)	(−1.741)	(−2.250)	(2.584)	(−1.790)	(.628)
1964–77	−.485	18.150	.166	−.946	11.442	−9.191	−1.910
	(−.659)	(3.535)	(−2.419)	(−2.494)	(3.288)	(−2.412)	(−.442)
1978–84	1.173	8.592	−.166	−.645	3.556	−2.382	10.687
	(.998)	(1.476)	(−.659)	(−.770)	(.474)	(−.272)	(1.609)

NOTE.—t-statistics are in parentheses.

TABLE 7   Pricing with Oil Price Changes

Years	OG	MP	DEI	UI	UPR	UTS	Constant
1958–84	2.930	12.728	− .095	− .391	11.844	− 8.726	4.300
	(.996)	(1.406)	(− 1.193)	(− 1.123)	(4.294)	(− 2.770)	(1.340)
1958–67	4.955	14.409	.078	.119	8.002	− 1.022	2.663
	(1.978)	(.921)	(1.102)	(.204)	(2.604)	(− .421)	(.556)
1968–77	1.038	4.056	− .223	− 1.269	16.170	− 16.055	− 1.344
	(.251)	(.296)	(− 2.737)	(− 2.975)	(3.839)	(− 3.154)	(− .243)
1978–84	2.738	22.718	− .159	.134	11.152	− 9.264	14.702
	(.303)	(1.228)	(− .598)	(.156)	(1.465)	(− 1.024)	(2.240)

NOTE.—CG = growth rate in real per capita consumption; OG = growth rate in oil prices; VWNY = return on the value-weighted NYSE index; EWNY = return on the equally weighted NYSE index; MP = monthly growth rate in industrial production; DEI = change in expected inflation; UI = unanticipated inflation; UPR = unanticipated change in the risk premium (Baa and under return − long-term government bond return); and UTS = unanticipated change in the term structure (long-term government bond return − Treasury-bill rate). t-statistics are in parentheses.

Since the CG series begins in 1959, the tests were conducted only for the period beginning in 1964, 5 years later. In these tests the consumption betas and the factor betas are estimated simultaneously and then the risk premia are measured from the cross-sectional tests. Over the entire period and in no subperiod are the consumption betas significant for pricing. Furthermore, their signs are negative, and a comparison with the results of part B of table 4 shows that the coefficients and the significance of the state variables are unaltered by the presence of the CG betas.

To summarize the results of this subsection, the rate of change in consumption does not seem to be significantly related to asset pricing. The estimated risk premium is insignificant and has the wrong sign.

C. Oil and Asset Pricing

Oil prices are often mentioned as being an important economic factor even though there is no a priori reason to believe that innovations in oil prices should have the same degree of influence as, for example, interest rate variables or industrial production. To examine the independent influence of oil prices on asset pricing, we used the methods described above to test the impact of the OG series of petroleum price changes.

Table 7 reports on these tests. As with the consumption tests, the OG series was led by 1 month to enhance its influence. The oil betas were insignificant for pricing in the overall period and in two of the subperiods. As a comparison with part B of table 4 shows, inclusion of oil growth did reduce the significance of industrial production, but it increased the significance of the risk-premium variable (UPR) and the term-structure variable (UTS). The risk associated with oil price changes was not priced in the stock market during the critical 1968–77 subperiod, when the OPEC cartel became important (or in the later subperiods).

V. Conclusion

This paper has explored a set of economic state variables as systematic influences on stock market returns and has examined their influence on asset pricing. From the perspective of efficient-market theory and rational expectations intertemporal asset-pricing theory (see Cox et al. 1985), asset prices should depend on their exposures to the state variables that describe the economy. (This conclusion is consistent with the asset-pricing theories of Merton [1973], Cox et al. [1985], or the APT [Ross 1976].)

In Part II of this paper we used simple arguments to choose a set of economic state variables that, a priori, were candidates as sources of systematic asset risk. Several of these economic variables were found to be significant in explaining expected stock returns, most notably, industrial production, changes in the risk premium, twists in the yield curve, and, somewhat more weakly, measures of unanticipated inflation and changes in expected inflation during periods when these variables were highly volatile. We do not claim, of course, that we have exhaustively characterized the set of influential macro variables, but the set that was chosen performed well against several other potential pricing variables. Perhaps the most striking result is that even though a stock market index, such as the value-weighted New York Stock Exchange index, explains a significant portion of the time-series variability of stock returns, it has an insignificant influence on pricing (i.e., on expected returns) when compared against the economic state variables. We also examined the influence on pricing of exposure to innovations in real per capita consumption. These results are quite disappointing to consumption-based asset-pricing theories; the consumption variable was never significant. Finally, we examined the impact of an index of oil price changes on asset pricing and found no overall effect.

Our conclusion is that stock returns are exposed to systematic economic news, that they are priced in accordance with their exposures, and that the news can be measured as innovations in state variables whose identification can be accomplished through simple and intuitive financial theory.

References

Banz, Rolf W. 1981. The relationship between returns and market values of common stocks. *Journal of Financial Economics* 9:3–18.

Breeden, Douglas. 1979. An intertemporal asset pricing model with stochastic consumption and investment opportunities. *Journal of Financial Economics* 7:256–96.

Brown, S., and Weinstein, M. 1983. A new approach to testing asset pricing models: The bilinear paradigm. *Journal of Finance* 38:711–43.

Chen, Nai-Fu. 1983. Some empirical tests of the theory of arbitrage pricing. *Journal of Finance* 38:1393–1414.

Cornell, Bradford. 1981. The consumption based asset pricing model: A note on potential tests and applications. *Journal of Financial Economics* 9:103–8.

Cox, John; Ingersoll, Jonathan; and Ross, Stephen A. 1985. An intertemporal general equilibrium model of asset prices. *Econometrica* 53:363–84.

Fama, Eugene. 1981. Stock returns, real activity, inflation and money. *American Economic Review* 71:545–65.

Fama, Eugene, and Gibbons, Michael. 1984. A comparison of inflation forecasts. *Journal of Monetary Economics* 13:327–48.

Fama, Eugene, and MacBeth, James D. 1973. Risk, return, and equilibrium: Empirical tests. *Journal of Political Economy* 38:607–36.

Hansen, Lars, and Singleton, Kenneth. 1983. Stochastic consumption, risk aversion, and the temporal behavior of asset returns. *Journal of Political Economy* 91:249–65.

Ibbotson, Roger. 1979. The corporate bond market: Structure and returns. Unpublished manuscript. Chicago: University of Chicago.

Ibbotson, Roger, and Sinquefield, Rex. 1982. *Stocks, Bonds, Bills and Inflation: The Past and the Future*. Charlottesville, Va.: Financial Analysts Research Foundation.

Litterman, Robert, and Weiss, Laurence. 1983. Money, real interest rates, and output: A reinterpretation of postwar U.S. data. NBER Working Paper no. 1077. Chicago: University of Chicago.

Lucas, Robert E., Jr. 1978. Asset prices in an exchange economy. *Econometrica* 46:1429–45.

Merton, Robert C. 1973. An intertemporal capital asset pricing model. *Econometrica* 41:867–87.

Roll, R., and Ross, S. 1980. An empirical investigation of the arbitrage pricing theory. *Journal of Finance* 35:1073–1103.

Ross, Stephen A. 1976. The arbitrage theory of capital asset pricing. *Journal of Economic Theory* 13:341–60.

[16]

THE JOURNAL OF FINANCE • VOL. XXXVII, NO. 5 • DECEMBER 1982

The Journal of FINANCE

| VOL. XXXVII | DECEMBER 1982 | NO. 5 |

The Arbitrage Pricing Theory: Is it Testable?

JAY SHANKEN*

ABSTRACT

This paper challenges the view that the Arbitrage Pricing Theory (APT) is inherently more susceptible to empirical verification than the Capital Asset Pricing Model (CAPM). The usual formulation of the testable implications of the APT is shown to be inadequate, as it precludes the very expected return differentials which the theory attempts to explain. A recent competitive-equilibrium extension of the APT may be testable in principle. In order to implement such a test, however, observation of the return on the true market portfolio appears to be necessary.

THE CAPITAL ASSET PRICING Model (CAPM) has, for many years, been the major framework for analyzing the cross-sectional variation in expected asset returns. The main implication of the theory is that expected return should be linearly related to an asset's covariance with the return on the market portfolio:

$$E_i = \gamma_0 + \gamma_1 \beta_i$$

where

$$\beta_i = \sigma_{im}/\sigma_m^2 \qquad (1)$$

is the "beta coefficient" of asset i, E_i its expected return, and γ_0 and γ_1 are constants that do not depend on i.

This simple relation has been the focus of intensive empirical scrutiny for more than a decade. Roll [16], in an influential article, suggests that the CAPM is testable in principle, but he argues that "(a) No correct and unambiguous test has appeared in the literature, and (b) There is practically no possibility that such a test can be accomplished in the future." These conclusions are a consequence of our inability to observe the exact composition of the true market portfolio.

The Arbitrage Pricing Theory (APT) of Ross [18, 19] has been proposed as a testable alternative, and perhaps the natural successor to the CAPM (Ross [21], p. 894). An important intuition in modern portfolio theory is that it is the

* University of California at Berkeley. Thanks to David Babbel, Michael Brennan, Greg Connor, Ken Dunn, Mark Rubinstein, Jeff Skelton, Sheridan Titman, participants in seminars at Berkeley and Stanford and especially Jim Ohlson and Rex Thompson for their helpful comments.

covariability of an asset's return with the return on other assets, rather than its total variability, that is important from the perspective of a risk averse investor who holds a well-diversified portfolio of many assets. Ross's seminal contribution was his insight that this intuition can be transformed into a theory of asset pricing with implications similar to (1).

Whereas derivation of the CAPM requires very specific technical assumptions (quadratic utility or multivariate normality of returns, for example), Ross's theory exploits the concept of a "large" (many assets) security market, consistent with the intuition described above. The market portfolio plays no special role in this theory. Rather, it is the covariability of an asset's return with those random factors which systematically influence the returns on most assets, that is reflected in the expected return relation. This ability of the APT to accommodate several sources of "systematic risk" has been considered by many an advantage in comparison with the CAPM.

Brennan [1] has described the APT as "a minimalist model of security market equilibrium" that is "logically prior to our other utility based models, and should be tested before the predictions of stronger utility specifications are considered." The body of empirical literature concerned with testing the APT is growing at a rapid rate. In addition to the early work of Gehr [8] are studies by Chen [5], Roll and Ross [17], Oldfield and Rogalski [14], P. Brennan [2], Gibbons [9], Reinganum [15], and Brown and Weinstein [3]. The goal of this paper is to provide a critical perspective on this important area of empirical research. Our concern is not with the particular experimental designs and statistical methods used. We address the more fundamental question of what it means to test the APT. The arguments presented below challenge the view that the APT is inherently more susceptible to empirical verification than the CAPM.

The paper is organized as follows. Section I provides an overview of the Ross APT. Section II discusses the inadequacy of the usual formulation of the testable implications of the theory. Section III considers the interpretation of empirical investigations of the APT. Section IV summarizes the main conclusions. Technical arguments have been placed in appendices.

I. An Overview of the Ross APT

The APT assumes returns conform to a K-factor linear model $(K < N)$:

$$R_i = E_i + \beta_{i1}\delta_1 + \cdots + \beta_{iK}\delta_K + \epsilon_i \qquad i = 1, N$$

R_i is the random return on asset i, and E_i its expected return. The δ_k are mean zero common factors and the ϵ_i are mean zero asset specific disturbances assumed to be uncorrelated with the δ_k and with each other. In the language of factor analysis, the β_{ik} are the factor loadings. N is the number of assets under consideration. In matrix notation,

$$R = E + B\delta + \epsilon \tag{2}$$

where R, E, and ϵ are $N \times 1$, B is $N \times K$, and δ is $K \times 1$. Let D be the diagonal covariance matrix of ϵ.

A decomposition as in (2) will hold whenever returns are regressed on an arbitrary set of random variables measured as deviations from the mean. In general, however, the ϵ_i will be correlated, thereby violating the factor model definition. An example is the usual "market model" in which δ is the return on a market proxy (see Fama [7], Chapter 3). There is considerable empirical evidence documenting correlation between market model disturbances (see King [12]). Sometimes it is convenient to treat the disturbances as if they were uncorrelated, however. This is often referred to as the Sharpe single index model. Only in this case does the market model constitute a factor model ($K = 1$) in the strict sense used here.

A special case that conveys the basic idea behind the APT, but is too restrictive to be of practical interest, occurs when $\epsilon \equiv 0$, i.e., there are no asset-specific disturbances. In this case, absence of riskless arbitrage implies the existence of a constant γ_0 and a K-vector γ_1 such that

$$E = \gamma_0 1_N + B\gamma_1 \tag{3}$$

Ross's argument is as follows. Consider an arbitrage portfolio with no systematic risk; i.e., an N-vector X such that

$$X'1_N = 0 \quad \text{and} \quad X'B = 0$$

Assuming $\epsilon \equiv 0$ in (2),

$$X'R = X'E$$

Since the portfolio requires no net investment and is riskless we must have, in the absence of arbitrage,

$$X'E = 0$$

In the language of linear algebra, *any* vector orthogonal to 1_N and the columns of B is orthogonal to E. It follows that E must be a linear combination of 1_N and the columns of B, as stated in (3).

When asset specific disturbances are introduced, the situation is complicated considerably. In this case, zero investment and zero systematic risk imply

$$X'R = X'E + X'\epsilon$$

If N is "large" and the arbitrage portfolio is well diversified, then laws of large numbers suggest that the asset specific risk will be *approximately* diversified away so that

$$X'R \approx X'E \quad \text{and hence} \quad X'E \approx 0$$

Even if we overlook the approximation, there is a technical problem. We have considered a well diversified X, while the linear algebra leading to (3) requires that $X'E = 0$ for *any* X orthogonal to 1_N and B.

Ross [18] still manages to prove a result in the spirit of (3) for the general model with asset specific disturbances. The result is considerably weaker than (3), however. Specifically, as the number of assets under consideration approaches infinity, the sum of squared deviations from (3) converges; i.e., there exist γ_0 and γ_1 such that

$$\sum_{i=1}^{\infty} [E_i - \gamma_0 - \beta_i\gamma_1]^2 < \infty \tag{4}$$

where β_i is the ith row of B. In order that (4) hold, "most" of the deviations from linearity must be "small," although any particular deviation may be "large."[1]

A test of the APT must, of course, be implemented with a finite set of data. Since any finite sum of squared deviations is clearly finite, (4) is not an empirically testable condition. We should like to know, therefore, whether any empirically testable bound on the deviations is implied by the theory. The arguments in Appendix A suggest that this is not the case. What, then, have empirical investigations of the APT actually tested? This is considered in the next section.

II. The Usual Empirical Formulation

Empirical investigations of the APT have attempted to test the following proposition:

> *If* a set of asset returns conforms to a K-factor model, *then* the expected return vector is equal to a linear combination of a unit vector and the factor loading vectors   (5)

i.e., If (2) then (3).

We shall refer to (5) as the empirical formulation of the APT. Given the discussion of Section I, we know that *(5) is not literally an implication of the APT.* Nonetheless, it might be viewed as a reasonable representation of the *intuitive* content of the theory. Its rejection could not be equated with rejection of the theory. Its acceptance in an empirical test would be consistent with the theory, however, and might (power considerations aside) be interpreted as evidence in favor of the theory. A theory that cannot be rejected is not necessarily preferable to the CAPM, though.

Proponents of the APT have emphasized that, in contrast to the CAPM, the APT may be tested by merely observing subsets of the set of all returns (Roll and Ross [17], p. 1080).[2] Provided that observable returns conform to a factor model, the matrix of factor loadings can be estimated by the statistical technique of factor analysis (see Morrison [13], Chapter 9). The number of factors must be known in advance, though they need not be observable. There is an issue of uniqueness, however. If A is any $K \times K$ nonsingular matrix, then B and δ in (2) may be replaced by BA and $A^{-1}\delta$. The factor model definition is still satisfied, but with factors $A^{-1}\delta$ and loading matrix BA. As Roll and Ross ([17], p. 1084) note, this is of no concern from the perspective of the APT. The empirical formulation of the APT in (5) is a statement about the relation between the expected return vector E and the space spanned by the loading vectors and a unit vector.[3] Since that space is unaltered when B is replaced by BA, there is really no

---

[1] Formally: for every $\varepsilon > 0$, there exists an integer M such that for all $i > M$, $|E_i - \gamma_0 - \beta_i \gamma_1| < \varepsilon$.

[2] As Roll and Ross note, "the APT yields a statement of relative pricing on subsets of the universe of assets." This contrasts with the CAPM which is a preference based equilibrium model, not an arbitrage model. See Huberman [10] for a clarification of the no-arbitrage condition underlying the APT.

[3] The space spanned by a given set of vectors is the set of all vectors which are linear combinations of those given vectors.

problem. The particular factor analytic estimation technique used simply chooses some basis for that space.

In light of the difficulties in measuring the true market portfolio, a theory which permits estimation of the appropriate risk measures without observation of the corresponding "factors" is certainly appealing. Some might argue that this apparent immunity from measurement problems more than compensates for the ambiguity surrounding the approximate nature of the risk-return relation. Another source of ambiguity should be considered, however.

Let us say that two sets of securities are *equivalent* if the corresponding sets of obtainable portfolio returns are identical. In this case, the two sets of securities are merely different packagings of the same underlying returns. Given perfect markets with no transaction costs, investors would be indifferent between equivalent sets. This simple idea plays an important role in many applications of arbitrage theory (for example, the Modigliani-Miller theory of corporate capital structure, and the theory of option pricing). The return on the equity of a firm may be viewed as the return on a portfolio whose components correspond to the underlying assets (long positions) and liabilities (short positions) of the firm. Alternative packagings of the underlying returns may, of course, be obtained by forming portfolios of stocks. The empirical formulation of the APT in (5) does not discriminate between different packagings. It would seem natural, therefore, to inquire as to the relation between the factors in the respective factor models for two equivalent sets of securities.

If, intuitively, we identify factors with the pervasive forces in the economy, then we might expect the same set of factors to be obtained from equivalent sets of securities. This is not the case, however. The basic idea may be illustrated with a simple example. Consider two securities which conform to the following 1-factor model:

$$R_1 = E_1 + \delta + \epsilon_1$$
$$R_2 = E_2 - \delta + \epsilon_2 \qquad (6)$$

where

$$\text{var}(\delta) = 1 \quad \text{and} \quad \text{var}(\epsilon_1) = \text{var}(\epsilon_2) = \sigma^2 > 0$$

Let $R_1^* = R_1$ and $R_2^* = \alpha R_1 + (1 - \alpha) R_2$. Thus R_2^* is the return on a portfolio of the initial securities. R_2^* may be written as

$$R_2^* = [\alpha E_1 + (1 - \alpha) E_2] + (2\alpha - 1)\delta + [\alpha\epsilon_1 + (1 - \alpha)\epsilon_2]$$

Now $\text{cov}[\epsilon_1, \alpha\epsilon_1 + (1 - \alpha)\epsilon_2] = \alpha\sigma^2$. Unless $\alpha = 0$, R_1^* and R_2^* will not conform to a 1-factor model with factor δ. The disturbance term for R_2^*, relative to δ, is a mixture of ϵ_1 and ϵ_2, and is not uncorrelated with ϵ_1.

Consider the covariance between R_1^* and R_2^*:

$$\text{cov}(R_1^*, R_2^*) = \alpha\text{var}(R_1) + (1 - \alpha)\text{cov}(R_1, R_2)$$
$$= \alpha(1 + \sigma^2) + (1 - \alpha)(- 1)$$

Let $\alpha = 1/(2 + \sigma^2)$, so that $\text{cov}(R_1^*, R_2^*) = 0$. Since $\alpha \neq 0$, R_1^* and R_2^* violate the

1-factor model. But any set of uncorrelated returns conforms to the simplest possible factor model: a 0-factor model. To see this, write R_1^* and R_2^* as

$$R_1^* = E_1^* + \epsilon_1^*$$

$$R_2^* = E_2^* + \epsilon_2^* \tag{7}$$

where $E_i^* = E(R_i^*)$ and $\epsilon_i^* = R_i^* - E_i^*$, $i = 1, 2$. By the choice of α, $\text{cov}(\epsilon_1^*, \epsilon_2^*) = 0$. Therefore (7) is a legitimate factor model with $K = 0$. It is easily verified that $\{R_1, R_2\}$ and $\{R_1^*, R_2^*\}$ are equivalent sets.[4]

It has been shown that equivalent sets of securities need not conform to the same factor model. In particular, the number of factors in the respective models need not be the same. Therefore, this is not an instance of the phenomenon described earlier, which involved an arbitrary invertible transformation of one set of factors into another basis for the same factor space.[5] Whereas that phenomenon poses no problem, the present consideration does. The empirical formulation of the APT in (5), together with (6), implies the existence of γ_0 and γ_1 such that[6]

$$\begin{bmatrix} E_1 \\ E_2 \end{bmatrix} = \gamma_0 \begin{bmatrix} 1 \\ 1 \end{bmatrix} + \gamma_1 \begin{bmatrix} 1 \\ -1 \end{bmatrix} \tag{8}$$

On the other hand, (5) and (7) imply the existence of γ_0^* such that

$$\begin{bmatrix} E_1^* \\ E_2^* \end{bmatrix} = \gamma_0^* \begin{bmatrix} 1 \\ 1 \end{bmatrix} \tag{9}$$

But equivalence means that R_1 and R_2 are equal to portfolios of R_1^* and R_2^*, so that $E_1 = E_2 = \gamma_0^*$ as well. (8) and (9) will not be consistent unless $\gamma_1 = 0$ and $\gamma_0 = \gamma_0^*$.

Let us summarize the observations above. First, equivalent sets of securities may conform to very different factor structures. Second, the usual empirical formulation of the APT, when applied to these structures, may yield different and inconsistent implications concerning expected returns for a given set of securities. The implications will be consistent if and only if all of the securities have the same expected return. While the example above considered only two securities, the conclusions apply, aside from a few mild technical restrictions, to any *finite* set of securities (see Appendix B).[7]

In light of these observations, (5) cannot be considered an adequate formulation of the empirical content of a testable theory of asset pricing. It rules out the very expected return differentials which the theory seeks to explain.[8] We have already noted that the exact risk-return relation of (5) is not literally an implication of the Ross APT. The positing of such a relation might, therefore, be considered the main source of difficulty. But our observations concerning the factor models of

---

[4] R_2 may be recovered by shorting $\alpha/(1 - \alpha)$ units of R_1^* and buying $1/(1 - \alpha)$ units of R_2^*.

[5] The factor space is the set of random variables which are linear combinations of the given factors.

[6] The case $N = 2$ is clearly without content and is considered for the purpose of illustration only. The same conclusions hold for any finite N. See Appendix B.

[7] Note that the CAPM suggests no particular relation between the expected returns of uncorrelated securities, since their covariances with the market may vary.

[8] Ingersoll [11] has made a similar assertion independently.

equivalent sets of securities are disturbing (and revealing) quite apart from this issue.

The phenomenon is actually more general than the previous discussion might suggest. The following proposition is proved in Appendix B: given a vector of returns R and (almost) any other vector of random variables δ, there exists an equivalent set of securities with return vector R^*, which conforms to a factor model with factors δ. Given this undesirable degree of flexibility, how are we to identify the "true" factors? Indeed, does such a phrase have a well-defined meaning? The securities we observe in the market constitute a particular packaging of the underlying returns in the economy. Are we to assume that the "relevant" factor model is the one which corresponds to this particular packaging? These issues are addressed in the following section.

III. Interpreting Empirical Studies of the APT

Given a vector of security returns, suppose that, using the best available statistical methods, we are unable to reject the expected return relation (3). Should this be interpreted as evidence in support of the APT? The following discussion suggests that such an interpretation may be inappropriate. Let δ be the return on a mean-variance efficient portfolio of securities, and let R be a vector of returns on a proper subset of the securities which enter δ.[9] The proposition of Appendix B implies the existence of an equivalent vector of returns R^*, which conforms to a one-factor model with δ as the factor.

Suppose the vector of returns used in an empirical test happens to be R^*. Note that the factor loadings on δ are just the usual beta coefficients with respect to δ. Since δ is mean-variance efficient, the expected return relation (3) must hold exactly (see Fama [7], Roll [16], or Ross [20]). An empirical test of the APT based on R^* necessarily will appear to support the theory (given a large enough sample of data). It would generally be wrong to attribute any *economic* significance to such a result, however, since the validity of (3), in this case, is simply a *mathematical* consequence of the mean-variance efficiency of δ.

The scenario described above might seem a bit improbable. It is intended more to illustrate what is possible than what is likely. What does seem plausible is that some of the factors in a given factor model representation of returns might be highly correlated with the return on a mean-variance efficient portfolio. In that case, it would not be surprising to find some of those factors "priced" in an APT empirical investigation. Such an empirical result would be of questionable economic significance, however.

These remarks are very close in spirit to the "Roll Critique" of tests of the CAPM. Roll argues that empirical investigations of the CAPM which use proxies for the true market portfolio are really tests of the mean-variance efficiency of those proxies, not tests of the CAPM. The CAPM implies that a particular portfolio, the market portfolio, is efficient. The theory is not testable unless *that* portfolio is observable and used in the tests.

Similarly, it is argued here that factor-analytic empirical investigations of the

---

[9] If δ consisted solely of securities in R, then Σ (see Appendix B) would be singular.

APT are not necessarily tests of that theory. In the case of the APT, we are confronted with the task of identifying the relevant factor structure, rather than the true market portfolio.[10] Whereas we have a reasonably clear notion of what is meant by "the true market portfolio," it is not clear in what sense, if any, a uniquely "relevant factor structure" exists. We noted in Section II that there are, in general, many factor structures corresponding to equivalent sets of securities. The APT does not appear to provide a criterion for singling out one structure as the "relevant" one.

The recent work of Connor [6] on "Asset Pricing in Factor Economies" is pertinent in this regard. Building on the earlier work of Ross, Connor obtains an exact pricing relation by introducing assumptions about the aggregate structure of the economy. As he notes, his theory relies on principles of competitive equilibrium rather than on an arbitrage technique. Significant, from our present perspective, is the central role played by the market portfolio. A crucial condition in the Connor "equilibrium APT" is that *idiosyncratic risk, defined relative to a given factor structure, is completely diversified away in the market portfolio.* It is important to appreciate the relative nature of this condition. The same economy might satisfy the condition with respect to one factor representation of returns and fail to satisfy it with respect to an alternative representation.

This diversification condition provides us with a basis for evaluating and interpreting factor-analytic investigations of the APT. We argued earlier against attaching much economic significance to factor-analytic results. Suppose, however, it can be shown that the factors (implicitly) identified in a factor analysis explain all of the variation in the return on the market portfolio.[11] In this case, it might be appropriate to interpret the results of the investigation as reflecting on the validity of the "equilibrium APT."[12] Without observing the return on the true market portfolio, however, it is unlikely that the diversification condition can ever be conclusively verified in practice. Thus the "equilibrium APT" appears to be subject to substantially the same difficulties encountered in testing the CAPM.

Additional insight into the relation between Connor's work and the inadequacy of the usual empirical formulation of the APT may be obtained by reconsidering the case of the 0-factor model, i.e., a set of mutually uncorrelated returns. If there are no "systematic factors," then all risk is, by definition, idiosyncratic. The condition that idiosyncratic risk be diversified away in the market portfolio requires, in this case, that the variance of the market return be zero. Given the substantial variation in all commonly observed market proxies, we can reject this condition with some confidence. Thus, from the perspective of the "equilibrium

[10] An alternative would be to abandon the notion of a "relevant" factor structure, and view the APT as having implications for approximate asset pricing relative to any set of "factors." The implied degree of approximation would presumably differ for different sets of factors. Appendix A notes some problems with the view, but is, by no means, conclusive.

[11] See Shanken and Tajirian [22] for some empirical evidence related to this condition.

[12] Connor employs a more general concept of "factor structure" than that used here and in the empirical APT literature. Since he does not require that the factor model disturbances be uncorrelated, the empirical implications of his work are not limited to factors obtained (implicitly) by factor analysis.

APT," the existence of a 0-factor representation of returns (appropriately) fails to take on any economic significance.

IV. Summary and Conclusions

It is generally accepted that the Capital Asset Pricing Model (CAPM) is not truly testable in a strict sense. Much of this acceptance can be attributed to the persuasive analysis of Roll, who argues that the CAPM is not testable unless the market portfolio of all assets is used in the empirical test. The Arbitrage Pricing Theory (APT) of Ross has been proposed as a testable alternative to the CAPM. Its proponents suggest that it suffices to merely consider subsets of the universe of existing assets to test the APT. The rapidly growing volume of empirical analysis purporting to test the theory indicates that this view has achieved a significant level of acceptance in the finance research community. Our previous observations suggest that this acceptance may not be warranted.

Ross's theory does not (even in the limit as the number of assets $\rightarrow \infty$) imply an exact linear risk-return relation. The testability of the theory could reasonably be questioned on this ground alone. Perhaps of greater concern is the inadequacy of the usual empirical formulation of the intuitive content of the theory. This formulation states that if a (large) set of asset returns conforms to a factor model, then the expected return vector should be equal to a linear combination of the loading vectors and a unit vector. This proposition is appealing in that it appears to capture the spirit of the theory, and is susceptible to statistical testing via factor analytic methods. But taken literally, it is actually equivalent to the proposition that all securities have the same expected return.

This surprising conclusion is a consequence of a previously unnoticed property of the factor model representation of returns. The factor model can be manipulated rather arbitrarily by repackaging a given set of securities. A new set of returns and a corresponding factor model can be produced, with virtually any prespecified random variables as the factors. By itself, therefore, factor analysis is not an adequate tool for identifying the random components of returns that should be relevant to asset pricing.

This conclusion is compatible with the recent work of Connor, who extends the earlier work of Ross. Connor's competitive equilibrium analysis highlights the role of certain aggregate features of the economy in asset pricing. Factor analysis is merely concerned with statistical correlations and is blind to aggregate economic considerations. The failure of the usual empirical formulation of the APT to discriminate between alternative factor representations on the basis of such considerations is its fundamental weakness. Unfortunately, since the market portfolio plays a prominent role in Connor's "equilibrium APT," it appears to be subject to substantially the same difficulties encountered in testing the CAPM.

Appendix A

In this appendix it is argued that Ross's APT does not imply an empirically testable bound on the sum of squared deviations in (4). It is necessary to first review some essential features of the proof in Ross [18]. Consider the problem of minimizing the variance of an arbitrage portfolio with no systematic risk and expected return $c > 0$; i.e.,

$$\text{minimize } X'DX$$

subject to

$$X'1_N = 0$$

$$X'\beta = 0$$

and $\quad X'E = c \qquad\qquad\qquad$ (A.1)

More specifically, consider an infinite sequence of such problems implicitly indexed by N, the number of assets in the subset under consideration. Let a be the minimum variance obtained in (A.1). Given some mild assumptions on preferences and boundedness of the elements of D, Ross shows that utility maximization implies the sequence of a values must be bounded away from zero. Intuitively, a sequence of a's approaching zero would constitute a sort of arbitrage opportunity in the limit.

Now let

$$e \equiv E - \gamma_0 1_N - \gamma_1 \beta$$

with γ_0 and γ_1 chosen so as to minimize the expression $e'D^{-1}e$. γ_0 and γ_1 so defined are identical to the coefficients from a generalized least squares regression of E on 1_N and β with nonsingular covariance matrix D. e is the corresponding vector of residuals. A key result in Ross's analysis (Ross [18], p. 349, 357) is that

$$e'D^{-1}e = c^2/a \qquad\qquad\qquad (A.2)$$

If the elements of D are bounded above, say by u, then

$$e'e \leqq uc^2/a \qquad\qquad\qquad (A.3)$$

It might appear that (A.3) provides an upper bound on the finite sum of squared deviations $e'e$, which could conceivably be tested. But (A.2) and (A.3) are purely algebraic facts, devoid of any economic content. The economics enters when we recall that utility maximization implies the sequence of a's is bounded away from zero. It follows from (A.3) that the sum of squared deviations remains bounded above as the number of assets approaches infinity. Therefore, the theory yields an economic restriction on the expected returns in an infinite sequence of economies. There does not appear to be a restriction on any particular economy in the sequence.

Appendix B

This appendix generalizes the results of the two asset example of Section II. Let R be an N-vector of security returns with positive-definite covariance matrix V. Let δ be a K-vector of mean zero random variables jointly distributed with R. As noted in Section I, we can regress each of the components of R on δ to obtain the following representation:

$$R = E + B\delta + \epsilon \tag{B.1}$$

where $E(\delta) = E(\epsilon) = 0$, so that $E = E(R)$. Let $\sum$ be the covariance matrix of ϵ. In general, $\sum$ will not be diagonal, so that (B.1) is not a factor model representation. We shall assume $\sum$ is positive definite. While this rules out some potential random vectors δ, it is a fairly general assumption which should encompass many cases. In particular, in the $K = 0$ case $\sum = V$ and hence is positive definite.

Let Q be an $N \times N$ nonsingular matrix such that

$$Q'Q = \sum^{-1}$$

Such a matrix always exists, given our assumptions (this fact is used to show that a generalized least squares regression is equivalent to an ordinary least squares regression on transformed variables (see Theil [23], p. 23). Assume that the row sums of Q are all nonzero (if we imagine that the parameters of $\sum$ have been generated by some random continuous process, then the row sums will be nonzero with probability one). Let D be the diagonal matrix with i^{th} entry equal to the reciprocal of row sum i of matrix Q, and let $P \equiv DQ$. Then $P1_N = 1_N$, i.e., the row sums of P are all equal to one.

Premultiplication of a return vector by P generates a vector of portfolio returns. Transforming the representation (B.1) we obtain

$$R^* = E^* + B^*\delta + \epsilon^*$$

where

$$R^* = PR, \quad E^* = PE, \quad B^* = PB \quad \text{and} \quad \epsilon^* = P\epsilon \tag{B.2}$$

P has been constructed so that

$$\text{Var}(\epsilon^*) = P \sum P' = DQ \sum Q'D' = D^2$$

is diagonal. Therefore, the representation (B.2) is a legitimate K-factor model. The usual empirical formulation of the APT (see (5) of Section II) implies that there exist γ_0 and γ_1 such that

$$E^* = \gamma_0 1_N + B^* \gamma_1 \tag{B.3}$$

Premultiplication of both sides of (B.3) by P^{-1} gives

$$P^{-1}E^* = \gamma_0 P^{-1} 1_N + P^{-1}B^* \gamma_1$$

Using (B.2) and noting that $P1_N = 1_N$ implies $P^{-1}1_N = 1_N$, we obtain

$$E = \gamma_0 1_N + B \gamma_1 \tag{B.4}$$

(B.4) is the usual APT expected return relation, with risk measured relative to the random vector δ. Since δ is essentially arbitrary, many such relations may be deduced for the same expected return vector E. The existence of many distinct representations for E is not, in itself, a problem (recall that in the mean-variance context, a different representation exists for each mean-variance efficient portfolio of the securities in R). To the contrary, it might appear that the APT may be tested using any random vector δ. Unfortunately, this view is untenable, since it leads to a logical contradiction.

This may be seen by letting $K = 0$ in the argument leading to (B.4); i.e., let δ be the empty set (vector). In this case, we have the existence of a single number γ_0, such that

$$E = \gamma_0 1_N \tag{B.5}$$

Thus the empirical formulation of the APT, from which (B.5) was deduced, rules out the very expected return differentials which the theory attempts to explain.

REFERENCES

1. M. Brennan. "Discussion." *Journal of Finance* 36 (May 1981), 352–3.
2. P. Brennan. "A Test of the Arbitrage Pricing Model." Unpublished manuscript, University of British Columbia, Vancouver, Canada, 1981.
3. S. Brown and M. Weinstein. "A New Approach to Testing Asset Pricing Models: The Bilinear Paradigm." Unpublished manuscript, Bell Laboratories, Holmdell, NJ: 1982.
4. G. Chamberlain and M. Rothschild. "Arbitrage and Mean-Variance Analysis on Large Asset Markets." Unpublished manuscript, University of Wisconsin, 1981.
5. N. Chen. "Some Empirical Tests of the Theory of Arbitrage Pricing." Working Paper No. 69, University of Chicago, 1982.
6. G. Connor. "Asset Pricing in Factor Economies." Doctoral dissertation, Yale University, 1982.
7. E. Fama. *Foundations of Finance.* New York: Basic Books, Inc., 1976.
8. A. Gehr. "Some Tests of the Arbitrage Pricing Theory." *Journal of the Midwest Finance Association,* 1975.
9. M. Gibbons. "Empirical Examination of the Return Generating Process of the Arbitrage Pricing Theory." Unpublished manuscript, Stanford University, 1981.
10. G. Huberman. "A Simple Approach to Arbitrage Pricing Theory." Working Paper No. 44, University of Chicago, 1980.
11. J. Ingersoll. "Some Results in the Theory of Arbitrage Pricing." Working Paper No. 67, University of Chicago, 1982.
12. B. King. "Market and Industry Factors in Stock Price Behavior." *Journal of Business* 39 (1966), 139–90.
13. D. Morrison. *Multivariate Statistical Methods.* 2nd edition. New York: McGraw-Hill, 1976.
14. G. Oldfield and R. Rogalski. "Treasury Bill Factors and Common Stock Returns." *Journal of Finance* 36 (May 1981), 337–50.
15. M. Reinganum. "The Arbitrage Pricing Theory: Some Empirical Results." *Journal of Finance* 36 (May 1981), 313–21.
16. R. Roll. "A Critique of the Asset Pricing Theory's Tests." *Journal of Financial Economics* (May 1977), 129–76.
17. —— and S. Ross. "An Empirical Investigation of the Arbitrage Pricing Theory." *Journal of Finance* 35 (December 1980), 1073–1103.
18. S. Ross. "The Arbitrage Theory of Capital Asset Pricing." *Journal of Economic Theory,* December 1976, 341–60.
19. ——. "Return, Risk, and Arbitrage." In I. Friend and J. Bicksler (eds.), *Risk and Return in Finance.* Cambridge: Ballinger, 1977.
20. ——. "The Capital Asset Pricing Model (CAPM), Short-Sale Restrictions and Related Issues." *Journal of Finance* 32 (March 1977), 177–83.
21. ——. "The Current Status of the Capital Asset Pricing Model (CAPM)." *Journal of Finance* 33 (June 1978), 885–901.
22. J. Shanken and A. Tajirian. "Equity Factors and the Market Portfolio." Unpublished manuscript, University of California, Berkeley, 1982.
23. H. Theil. *Principles of Econometrics.* New York: John Wiley & Sons, Inc., 1971.

Part VIII
Tests of an Investment-Based CAPM Using the Generalized Method of Moments

[17]

A Cross-Sectional Test of an Investment-Based Asset Pricing Model

John H. Cochrane

University of Chicago, Federal Reserve Bank of Chicago, and National Bureau of Economic Research

I examine a factor pricing model for stock returns. The factors are returns on physical investment, inferred from investment data via a production function. I examine the model's ability to explain variation in expected returns across assets and over time. The model is not rejected. It performs about as well as the CAPM and the Chen, Roll, and Ross factor model, and it performs substantially better than a simple consumption-based model. I also provide an easy technique for estimating and testing dynamic, conditional asset pricing models—one simply includes factors and returns scaled by instruments in an unconditional estimate—and for comparing such models.

I. Introduction

The *investment return* is the marginal rate at which a firm can transfer resources through time by increasing investment today and decreasing it at a future date, leaving its production plan unchanged at all other dates. I examine whether cross-sectional and time-series variation in expected stock returns can be explained by investment returns, inferred from investment data via an adjustment cost production function.

Why? The identity of the macroeconomic risks that drive asset

I have benefited greatly from conversations with Lars Hansen on the methods used in this paper. I am grateful to Mark Carhart, Gene Fama, Ken French, and especially Wayne Ferson and Masao Ogaki for many useful comments. This research was partially supported by the University of Chicago Graduate School of Business and the National Science Foundation.

[*Journal of Political Economy*, 1996, vol. 104, no. 3]

prices and expected returns is a central question of finance, and an important question for macroeconomics. There is a wealth of tantalizing empirical evidence for a link between macroeconomic events and asset returns: many of the variables that forecast stock and bond returns also forecast investment growth or growth in gross national product; stock and bond returns are correlated with contemporaneous and subsequent economic activity; and expected returns are related to the covariances of returns with macroeconomic variables. But there is as yet no accepted economic explanation for this evidence.

Ideally, the consumption-based asset pricing model should provide a framework for digesting this empirical evidence and for identifying the macroeconomic shocks that drive asset returns. But the empirical performance of the consumption-based model has been disappointing, despite a two-decade specification search. Mechanically, this poor performance results from the fact that nondurable consumption growth barely moves over the business cycle, and it is poorly correlated with stock returns. Economically, the poor performance may be due to measurement error in consumption data; a poor understanding of the representative agent's utility function; or taxes, transactions costs, borrowing constraints, and other frictions that can "delink" many consumers' intertemporal consumption choices from high-frequency asset market movements.[1]

Much of finance studies reduced-form models that explain an asset's expected return by its covariance with other assets' returns, rather than covariance with macroeconomic risks. Though these models may successfully *describe* variation in expected returns, they will never *explain* it. To say that an asset's expected return varies over the business cycle because (say) the market expected return varies leaves unanswered the question, What real risks cause the market expected return to vary? Furthermore, fishing for asset return factors with no explicit connection to real risks can result in models that price assets by construction in a given data set (ex post mean-variance efficient portfolios).

In this context, the basic idea of this paper is to infer the presence of real macroeconomic shocks by watching firms' investment decisions, just as the consumption-based model tries to infer the presence of systematic shocks by watching consumption decisions.

This paper extends the work in Cochrane (1991). That paper explained time-series variation in the market return with a single investment return, inferred from gross fixed investment data with an ad-

---

[1] Cochrane and Hansen (1992) give a literature review and a summary of "puzzles" that characterize the empirical failure of the consumption-based model. Cochrane (1989) and Luttmer (1992) calculate effects of small frictions.

justment cost production function. It showed that some adjustment cost is necessary to produce investment return variation anything like that observed in market returns. It showed that variation in the expected market return is largely matched by variation in the expected investment return and that market returns and investment returns have the same association with subsequent economic activity. This paper explains *cross-sectional* as well as time-series variation in expected stock returns by reference to investment returns.

However, the factor pricing model studied in this paper is not a pure production-based asset pricing model. A pure production-based model uses *no* assumptions on preferences or restrictions on the space of asset returns and reads any asset return off a producer's first-order conditions, just as the consumption-based model uses no technology assumptions (i.e., is valid for any production technology) and reads asset prices from a consumer's first-order conditions. The standard production functions I use here do not have general cross-sectional asset pricing implications, since there is nothing a producer can do to transform goods *across states*.

The techniques I use to estimate and test dynamic, conditional factor models are derived from the work of Hansen (1982), Hansen and Singleton (1982), Hansen and Richard (1987), and Hansen and Jagannathan (1991*b*). Knez (1991) and Snow (1991) use similar techniques to study factor pricing models; Braun (1991) uses them to investigate consistent pricing of asset and investment returns and tests whether the inverse of a single investment return can explain a cross section of assets; and De Santis (1992) uses them to study international capital market integration.

II. Investment Returns: Definition and Construction

To construct investment returns from production data, I use adjustment cost technologies of the form

$$y_t = f(k_t, l_t) - c(i_t, k_t), \tag{1}$$

$$k_{t+1} = (1 - \delta)(k_t + i_t), \tag{2}$$

where y_t is output, $f(k_t, l_t)$ is the production function, k_t is capital stock, l_t is labor input, i_t is investment, δ is the depreciation rate, and $c(i_t, k_t)$ is the adjustment cost function. The adjustment cost reflects the fact that it is hard to produce in periods of high investment. For example, it is hard to write papers while a new computer is being installed. This is the standard sort of production function used to justify the *q*-theory of investment.

The one-period investment return is the amount of extra output the firm can sell at $t + 1$ if it invests an additional unit at t, leaving all variables at $t + 2, t + 3, \ldots$ unchanged. The Appendix goes through the algebra to show that the one-period investment return for the technology specified in (1)–(2) is given by

$$r_{t+1}^i = (1 - \delta) \frac{1 + f_k(t + 1) + c_i(t + 1) - c_k(t + 1)}{1 + c_i(t)}, \tag{3}$$

where

$$c_i(t) \equiv \frac{\partial c(i_t, k_t)}{\partial i_t},$$

and so forth.

The denominator $1 + c_i(t)$ in equation (3) reflects the fact that some output is lost to adjustment costs when investment is increased at time t. This term is equal to marginal q: the marginal rate of transformation between installed and uninstalled capital. The extra time t investment gives rise to extra capital stock at $t + 1$: $f_k(t + 1)$ is the extra output that results from the extra capital stock, and $c_k(t + 1)$ captures the effect of extra capital at $t + 1$ on time $t + 1$ adjustment costs. At $t + 1$, the firm must *lower* investment to restore the capital stock at $t + 2$ to its original value. The lowered investment lowers $t + 1$ adjustment costs, and this means that more can be sold. The term $1 + c_i(t + 1)$ captures these effects.

The investment return is random: it depends on events at $t + 1$ as well as events at t. A positive productivity shock at time $t + 1$ implies an unexpectedly high return to investment from t to $t + 1$. Do not confuse the investment return with the expected investment return, the required return, or other ex ante concepts.

I use the following parametric specification of technology:

$$y_t = mpk \, k_t + mpl \, l_t - \frac{\eta}{2} \left(\frac{i_t}{k_t} \right) i_t. \tag{4}$$

In this case, the investment return (3) becomes

$$r_{t+1}^i = (1 - \delta) \frac{1 + mpk + \eta(i_{t+1}/k_{t+1}) + (\eta/2)(i_{t+1}/k_{t+1})^2}{1 + \eta(i_t/k_t)}. \tag{5}$$

Though this function is not pretty, the investment return it specifies is approximately proportional to growth in the investment/capital ratio or, since capital does not vary much, growth in investment.

For given values of the parameters $\{\eta, \delta, mpk\}$, I form investment/capital ratios by accumulating capital according to equation (2) starting from the steady-state investment/capital ratio

$$\frac{i_0}{k_0} = \left[E\left(\frac{i_t}{i_{t-1}}\right)\Big/(1 - \delta)\right] - 1.$$

Then, given η and mpk, I construct the investment returns from their definition (5).

One might object to the excessive simplicity of this technology. But the most obvious complications—such as taxes, declining marginal products, substitutability between capital and labor, and marginal productivity shocks—affect the dividend or one-period cash flow portion of the investment return. The adjustment cost influences the price change term $(1 + c_i$ or $1 + \eta[i/k]$, the marginal rate of transformation between installed and uninstalled capital), which dominates the investment return as it does stock returns.[2] Furthermore, most of these complications have low-frequency effects on the level of prices or q. By looking at investment and stock *returns*, we essentially first-difference out the effects of these complications. On the other hand, complications to the adjustment cost technology such as gestation lags may have first-order effects on the results.

III. Factor Pricing Model

What can one do with investment returns? If there are no arbitrage opportunities, then there is a stochastic discount factor m, such that any asset return r_j and investment return r_k^i obey (see, e.g., Ross 1978; Hansen and Richard 1987; Hansen and Jagannathan 1991*b*)

$$1 = E(mr_j); \quad 1 = E(mr_k^i). \tag{6}$$

The marginal utility growth of a nonsatiated owner of the firm is one such m; E can be interpreted as a conditional or unconditional expectation. I shall be specific about conditioning information below.

Braun (1991) tests two immediate implications of this fact. First, one can expand the space of returns on which one tests any asset pricing model (model for m) to include investment returns. In this way, one tests whether the asset pricing model can account for macroeconomic events as well as stock market events. Second, one can test for the absence of arbitrage or consistent pricing between the set of asset and investment returns by trying to construct nonnegative m's that satisfy equations (6).

---

[2] Braun (1991) found that tests of producer first-order conditions were insensitive to these issues in detailed experiments, for just the reasons given above. Sharathchandra (1991) models a concave technology with production function shocks but no adjustment costs and obtains an essentially constant investment return.

INVESTMENT-BASED ASSET PRICING   577

I concentrate on *asset* pricing. What can one learn about asset returns r from investment returns r^i? I study the hypothesis that a factor pricing model holds; namely, *the investment returns are factors for the asset returns.* More formally, an investment return factor pricing model says that there exists a discount factor that is a function of only the investment returns and yet prices both asset and investment returns:

$$m = \sum_k b_k r_k^i \tag{7}$$

satisfies equation (6) for all asset returns r_j and investment returns r_k^i.

The law of one price implies that there is always a discount factor m that is a linear combination of the investment and asset returns and that prices both. Mechanically, one can choose b's to construct

$$m = \sum_j b_j r_j + \sum_k b_k r_k^i$$

so as to satisfy equations (6) exactly, in sample or in population. The factor pricing model restriction is that the asset returns can be excluded from this construction. This restriction is equivalent to the statement that expected excess returns are proportional to the covariance or betas of any return with the investment returns. It is also equivalent to the statement that the investment returns span the mean-variance frontier of investment and asset returns.

Why should investment returns be factors for asset returns? Factor pricing models are derived by arbitrage assumptions or by preference assumptions. We can assume that the firms on the New York Stock Exchange (NYSE) are claims to different combinations of N production technologies, plus idiosyncratic components that have small prices. Alternatively, we can invoke preference assumptions under which the returns on the N active production processes, which are the only nondiversifiable payoffs in the economy and add up to aggregate wealth, drive marginal utility growth and hence price assets (see, e.g., Brock 1982; Cox, Ingersoll, and Ross 1985).[3]

The number and nature of the intertemporal technologies that drive asset returns or, equivalently, the appropriate level of aggregation of the capital stock are a modeling choice. "My car" and "your

---

[3] Time-separable preferences are the central assumption. If preferences are not time-separable, then past investment returns could affect current asset returns. One could, of course, account for potential nonseparabilities by including past investment returns as additional factors. With general preferences in discrete time, nonlinear functions of investment returns might also enter m; one can regard linearity either as an assumption on preferences or as a first-order approximation as in the log utility example below.

car" are both ways of getting consumption services from today to tomorrow, but one hopes that their behavior across states of nature that affect asset returns is sufficiently similar that we can aggregate them into "cars." However, there is no reason to believe a priori that all the intertemporal investment opportunities in the economy can be summarized by one or two aggregated production functions. I follow the "spirit of the arbitrage pricing theory" and hope that only a few investment return factors will suffice, but this is an additional modeling assumption, not a prediction of theory. Models with highly disaggregated investment opportunities may turn out to be more useful for some purposes.

Following the factor pricing tradition, I estimate the loadings of the investment return factors in the discount factor—the b's—as free parameters. In complete general equilibrium models—models in which we can solve for consumption and asset returns ex post, not just state $1 = E(mR)$—the b's can be derived from economic theory as well. For example, in the standard one-sector stochastic growth model with log utility, Cobb-Douglas production, and full depreciation, we have[4]

$$m_{t+1} = \beta \frac{c_t}{c_{t+1}} = \frac{1}{r_{t+1}^i} \approx 1 - (r_{t+1}^i - 1),$$

where β is the subjective discount factor. This model predicts $b_0 = 2$, $b_1 = -1$. I estimate the b's rather than construct a complete general equilibrium model, in order to focus on production technologies and firm behavior rather than preferences and sources of shocks. More theory is better only if it is the right theory.

IV. Empirical Methods

A. A GMM Test of Factor Pricing Models

The statement of the factor pricing model above maps naturally into the generalized method of moments (GMM) framework for estima-

[4] The model is

$$\max E \sum_{j=0}^{\infty} \beta^j \ln(c_j)$$

subject to $c_t + i_t = y_t = \lambda_t i_{t-1}^\alpha$, $\quad \ln \lambda_t = \rho \ln \lambda_{t-1} + \epsilon_t$.

The investment return is $r_{t+1}^i = \alpha \lambda_{t+1} i_t^{\alpha-1} = \alpha y_{t+1}/i_t$. The solution to the model gives $c_t = (1 - \alpha\beta)y_t$ and $i_t = \alpha\beta y_t$. Substituting this solution into the investment return, we obtain

$$r_{t+1}^i = \frac{1}{\beta}\frac{c_{t+1}}{c_t} = \frac{1}{m_{t+1}}.$$

tion and testing. Let r_{t+1} denote a vector of returns and p_t denote a vector of prices. (The "price" of a return is one, and that of an excess return or difference between two returns is zero.) I suppress time subscripts when they are clear. The natural set of moment conditions to exploit is $p = E(mr)$ or

$$E(mr - p) = 0. \tag{8}$$

Let f_{t+1} denote a vector of pricing factors (one factor may be a constant). A linear factor pricing model is $m = f'b$, where b is a vector of coefficients.

Following the standard GMM procedure (Hansen 1982; Hansen and Singleton 1982), I estimate the parameters b to minimize a weighted combination of the sample moments (8). Using Hansen's notation, let E_T denote the sample mean, $E_T \equiv (1/T) \Sigma_{t=1}^T$; let W denote a weighting matrix; and denote the sample moments g_T,

$$g_T \equiv E_T(mr - p) = E_T(rf')b - E_T(p). \tag{9}$$

The GMM objective is to choose b to minimize a weighted sum of squares of the pricing errors across assets,

$$J_T = g_T' W g_T. \tag{10}$$

Econometric issues aside, this objective is a natural and intuitive way to pick parameters in order to make the model fit as well as possible.

Since the parameters b enter linearly in the minimization, we can find their estimates analytically. Let D denote the matrix of cross–second moments between returns and factors:

$$D = \frac{\partial g_T}{\partial b} = E_T(rf').$$

Let $\hat{b}$ denote the estimate of b. Then the first-order conditions to the minimization of (10) are

$$\frac{\partial g_T'}{\partial b} W g_T = D'W(D\hat{b} - E_T p) = 0. \tag{11}$$

Solving, and assuming that at least one element of $E_t p$ is not equal to zero,[5] we get

$$\hat{b} = (D'WD)^{-1}D'WE_T(p). \tag{12}$$

---

[5] If all elements of p are zero, which occurs when only excess returns are used, then b is identified only up to a constant $(0 = E(mr) \Rightarrow 0 = E(2mr))$. In this case, one can impose one element of b arbitrarily (e.g., $b_0 = 1$) and solve for the others, one can add a normalization such as $1 = E(m)$ as an additional moment, or one can add a single return in levels to the system such as the real Treasury-bill return to obtain a $p \neq 0$. I follow the last strategy.

This estimate has a natural interpretation: $\hat{\mathbf{b}}$ is the coefficient in a generalized least squares (GLS) cross-sectional regression of the mean price vector $E_T(\mathbf{p})$ on the second moments $\mathbf{D}$. Since the asset pricing model (8) or (9) says that prices should be proportional to second moments, this estimate is a natural way of choosing parameters to make the model hold as well as possible.

The GMM distribution theory (Hansen 1982) gives an asymptotic joint normal distribution for the estimates $\hat{\mathbf{b}}$. Denote by $\mathbf{S}$ a consistent estimate of the covariance matrix of the sample pricing errors $\mathbf{g}_T$, which is also the spectral density at zero of $m\mathbf{r} - \mathbf{p}$, or

$$\mathbf{S} = \text{consistent estimate of} \sum_{j=-\infty}^{\infty} E[(m_t \mathbf{r}_t - \mathbf{p}_t)(m_{t-j} \mathbf{r}_{t-j} - \mathbf{p}'_{t-j})].$$

Then Hansen (1982) shows that $\hat{\mathbf{b}}$ is asymptotically normal with variance-covariance matrix

$$\text{var}(\hat{\mathbf{b}}) = \frac{1}{T} (\mathbf{D}'\mathbf{WD})^{-1} \mathbf{D}'\mathbf{WSWD}(\mathbf{D}'\mathbf{WD})^{-1} \qquad (13)$$

If $\mathbf{W}$ is chosen equal to $\mathbf{S}^{-1}$, the GMM estimator is "optimal" or "efficient" in the sense that this variance matrix is as small as possible. In this case, the variance formula specializes to the more familiar form

$$\text{var}(\hat{\mathbf{b}}) = \frac{1}{T} (\mathbf{D}'\mathbf{S}^{-1}\mathbf{D})^{-1}. \qquad (14)$$

It is interesting to know whether the pricing errors are in fact equal to zero, after one accounts for estimation and sampling error. Hansen (1982, lemma 4.1) also gives us a distribution theory for the pricing errors $\mathbf{g}_T$:

$$\text{var}(\mathbf{g}_T) = \frac{1}{T} [\mathbf{I} - \mathbf{D}(\mathbf{D}'\mathbf{WD})^{-1}\mathbf{D}'\mathbf{W}]\mathbf{S}[\mathbf{I} - \mathbf{D}(\mathbf{D}'\mathbf{WD})^{-1}\mathbf{D}'\mathbf{W}]'. \qquad (15)$$

(While $\mathbf{S}$ is the variance-covariance matrix of the sample pricing errors evaluated at the true parameters, $\text{var}[\mathbf{g}_T(\mathbf{b})]$, the terms in brackets account for the fact that linear combinations of pricing errors are set to zero in parameter estimation, giving us $\text{var}[\mathbf{g}_T(\hat{\mathbf{b}})]$.) We can use this formula to construct standard errors for the pricing errors on individual assets or groups of pricing errors. In particular, we can test whether all pricing errors are zero by forming

$$\mathbf{g}'_T [\text{var}(\mathbf{g}_T)]^+ \mathbf{g}_T \sim \chi^2(\#\text{moments} - \#\text{parameters}). \qquad (16)$$

INVESTMENT-BASED ASSET PRICING   581

The "+" denotes pseudo-inversion,[6] since the variance-covariance matrix is singular with rank #moments − #parameters. When one uses the efficient estimator, $\mathbf{W} = \mathbf{S}^{-1}$, this test reduces to the celebrated J_T test of overidentifying restrictions:

$$TJ_T = T\mathbf{g}_T'\mathbf{S}^{-1}\mathbf{g}_T \sim \chi^2(\#\text{moments} - \#\text{parameters}). \qquad (17)$$

This is the basic test whether we can statistically reject a given observable factor model against a nonspecific alternative.

It can be more interesting to test a model against *specific* alternatives, that is, to ask, Given factors $\mathbf{f}_1$, are factors $\mathbf{f}_2$ important for pricing assets? There are two ways to perform such tests, corresponding to Wald and likelihood ratio philosophies. Start with a general model that includes both sets of factors, $m = \mathbf{b}_1'\mathbf{f}_1 + \mathbf{b}_2'\mathbf{f}_2$. First, we can use the sampling theory (13) or (14) to form t or χ^2 tests for $\mathbf{b}_2 = \mathbf{0}$. Second, we can compare the minimized objective $J_T = \mathbf{g}_T'\mathbf{S}^{-1}\mathbf{g}_T$ of a restricted system that excludes a given set of factors to the objective of the unrestricted system that includes all factors. If the excluded factors are not important for asset pricing, the J_T should not rise much. Precisely, if we use the same weighting matrix to estimate both systems (I use the weighting matrix from the unrestricted system), then

$$TJ_T(\text{restricted}) - TJ_T(\text{unrestricted}) \sim \chi^2(\#\text{ of restrictions})$$

(Newey and West 1987a). It is important *not* to simply compare J_T statistics from two estimates, but rather to use the same weighting matrix. A model can achieve a low J_T by simply blowing up the $\mathbf{S}$ matrix rather than improving the moment conditions.

To perform the GMM estimation, I start with an identity weighting matrix, $\mathbf{W} = \mathbf{I}$, which forms "first-stage" estimates of the parameters $\mathbf{b}$. I use these first-stage estimates to form an estimate of the matrix $\mathbf{S}$ and then use $\mathbf{S}^{-1}$ as the weighting matrix for "second-stage" estimates. I iterate this procedure, finding third-stage estimates and so forth. This does not change the asymptotic distribution theory, but Ferson and Foerster (1994) find that this procedure gives better small-sample performance. I also found that it produces results that are more stable across small variations in the model setup. Hansen, Heaton, and Luttmer (1995) suggest that one instead minimize $\mathbf{g}_T'(\mathbf{b})\mathbf{S}(\mathbf{b})^{-1}\mathbf{g}_T(\mathbf{b})$ directly as a function of parameters $\mathbf{b}$, and they find that this procedure can work well in small samples. This procedure

---

[6] One way to pseudo-invert a variance-covariance matrix is to perform an eigenvalue decomposition, $\mathbf{V} = \mathbf{Q}\boldsymbol{\Lambda}\mathbf{Q}'$, with $\boldsymbol{\Lambda}$ a diagonal matrix of eigenvalues. Let $\boldsymbol{\Lambda}^+$ be a diagonal matrix with $1/\lambda_j$ for nonzero eigenvalues λ_j and zero for zero eigenvalues. Then $\mathbf{V}^+ = \mathbf{Q}\boldsymbol{\Lambda}^+\mathbf{Q}'$. In practice, it helps to multiply $\mathbf{V}$ by a large number initially to help distinguish small nonzero eigenvalues from rounding errors.

has the great advantage that it is invariant to normalization choices when **b** is not completely identified and to the choice of the initial weighting matrix. However, I have an analytic formula for $\hat{\mathbf{b}}$ only when the weighting matrix is held fixed, so the iterative strategy is much quicker.

When the factors are investment returns, I estimate production function parameters in addition to the factor weights **b**. Since these parameters enter nonlinearly, a search is required. The programming is harder, but the GMM methodology extends trivially.

B. Conditional Estimates and Conditional Factor Models

So far, I have considered *unconditional* factor models and estimates of unconditional moments. It is easy to include the effects of conditioning information by scaling the returns or the factors by instruments, as follows. (Scaling returns is Hansen and Singleton's [1982] use of instruments in a moment condition. Scaling factors is analogous to linear models of conditional betas, as in Ferson, Kandel, and Stambaugh [1987], Harvey [1989], and Shanken [1990].)

Scaling Returns

To test the conditional predictions of an asset pricing model,

$$\mathbf{p}_t = E(m_{t+1}\mathbf{r}_{t+1}|I_t), \tag{18}$$

we can expand the set of returns to include returns scaled by instruments and then proceed as before; that is, we use the moment conditions

$$E[\mathbf{p}_t \otimes \mathbf{z}_t] = E[m_{t+1}(\mathbf{r}_{t+1} \otimes \mathbf{z}_t)], \quad \mathbf{z}_t \in I_t, \tag{19}$$

where $\otimes$ denotes the Kronecker product (multiply every asset return by every instrument).

Equation (19) is an implication of equation (18): multiply both sides of (18) by z_t and take unconditional expectations. Conversely, if (19) holds for *all* variables z_t in an information set I_t, then (18) holds. Thus expanding the payoff space to include scaled returns as in (19) can test *all* the implications of (18), so that no generality is lost in principle. Of course, the usual instrument selection problem remains. If $z_t \in I_t$, then $z_t^2 \in I_t$; "every variable" in I_t means every variable and every measurable function of every variable, so in principle one has to include a lot of variables. In practice, one hopes to capture most of the predictability of $m\mathbf{r}$ with a few well-chosen and thoughtfully transformed instruments, as one hopes to capture the information in the thousands of available assets in a few well-chosen portfolios.

This scaling procedure also has an intuitive interpretation. The scaled returns $r_{t+1}z_t$ are the returns on managed portfolios in which the manager invests more or less according to the signal z_t. Thus we have shown that one can test all the *conditional* implications of an asset pricing model by performing *unconditional* tests on managed portfolio returns!

Scaling Factors

To test a model in which the factors are expected only to conditionally price assets, we can expand the set of factors to include factors scaled by instruments:

$$m_{t+1} = \mathbf{b}'(\mathbf{f}_{t+1} \otimes \mathbf{z}_t).$$

To motivate scaling factors, note that we have supposed so far that the discount factor m is a *fixed* linear combination of a given set of factors. However, the discount factor m might be a linear combination of factors with weights that vary as a vector of instruments z varies across different information sets:

$$m_{t+1} = \mathbf{b}(\mathbf{z}_t)' \mathbf{f}_{t+1}.$$

A conditional factor model does not imply an unconditional factor model: the model $0 = E_t[\mathbf{r}_{t+1}\mathbf{f}'_{t+1}\mathbf{b}(\mathbf{z}_t)]$ does not imply that there is a $\mathbf{b}$ such that $0 = E[\mathbf{r}_{t+1}\mathbf{f}'_{t+1}\mathbf{b}]$.

It is sufficient to consider $\mathbf{b}$'s that vary linearly with the instruments, since nonlinear functions can be expressed as linear functions of additional instruments. With one instrument z and one factor f then, the conditional factor model is

$$m_{t+1} = (b_0 + z_t b_1) f_{t+1}.$$

Scaling the factors f by the instruments z achieves the same result. The last equation is equivalent to

$$m_{t+1} = b_0 f_{t+1} + b_1 (f_{t+1} \times z_{t+1}).$$

Therefore, given the choice of instruments, performing the GMM estimation and testing with scaled factors is in principle a completely general test of a dynamic, conditional factor pricing model based on the instruments. Again, the only complaint one can make is that more or other instruments (or functions of instruments) should have been included.

Scaling

To keep scaling returns and scaling factors distinct, I refer to the former as "conditional estimates" and the latter as a "scaled factor pricing model." The two are distinct: If one had a model that predicted constant b's, then it would be appropriate to scale the returns (perform conditional estimates) but not the factors. One can also examine the unconditional implications of a scaled factor pricing model, scaling the factors but not the returns.

Consumers may observe finer information sets, that is, more instruments z, than we do. This fact potentially reduces the power of tests that include scaled returns but does not bias them. Omitting instruments is exactly the same as omitting potential assets (managed portfolios). However, a conditional factor pricing model with respect to a fine information set does not imply a conditional factor pricing model with respect to a coarser information set, as it does not imply an unconditional factor model. Equivalently, conditional mean-variance efficiency does not imply unconditional mean-variance efficiency, though the converse is true (Hansen and Richard 1987). Thus a rejection of any factor model that is derived as a conditional factor pricing model with respect to consumers' information may still be attributed to an insufficiently rich set of instruments. But scaling factors does provide a very easy method for estimating and testing generally specified conditional factor pricing models given an information set.

C. Relation to Traditional Statements and Tests of Factor Models

Factor Models

The statement that the discount factor m is a linear function of factors is equivalent to the conventional statements of factor pricing models in terms of betas and factor risk premia. (This fact has been known at least since Ross [1978] or Dybvig and Ingersoll [1982].) Precisely, the model

$$m = \mathbf{b'f}; \quad 1 = E(mr) \tag{20}$$

implies the traditional statement of a factor pricing model,

$$E(r) = r^0 + \boldsymbol{\beta'}\boldsymbol{\lambda}, \tag{21}$$

where $\boldsymbol{\beta}$ is a vector of multiple regression coefficients of returns on the variable factors and r^0 is a constant across assets. Conversely, (21) implies that there exists a discount factor of the form $m = \mathbf{b'f}$.

To prove this statement, define the riskless or zero beta rate

$$r^0 = \frac{1}{E(m)} = \frac{1}{E(\mathbf{f'})\mathbf{b}};$$

INVESTMENT-BASED ASSET PRICING   585

denote the variable factors $\tilde{\mathbf{f}}$, that is,

$$\mathbf{f} = \begin{bmatrix} 1 \\ \tilde{\mathbf{f}} \end{bmatrix};$$

define $\boldsymbol{\beta}$ as

$$\boldsymbol{\beta} \equiv \mathrm{cov}(\tilde{\mathbf{f}}, \tilde{\mathbf{f}}')^{-1} \mathrm{cov}(\tilde{\mathbf{f}}, r);$$

and define $\boldsymbol{\lambda}$ as the price of the demeaned variable factors, brought forward at the risk-free rate,

$$\boldsymbol{\lambda} = -r^0 E[m(\tilde{\mathbf{f}} - E\tilde{\mathbf{f}})].$$

With these definitions, one can simply manipulate either (20) or (21) to obtain the other. These definitions also allow one to obtain $\boldsymbol{\beta}$, $\boldsymbol{\lambda}$ estimates from a GMM estimate of $\mathbf{b}$ together with the factor variance-covariance matrix or to obtain estimates and tests of $\mathbf{b}$ from cross-section or time-series regression estimates of $\boldsymbol{\beta}$, $\boldsymbol{\lambda}$.[7]

One can rewrite an element λ_j of $\boldsymbol{\lambda}$ as

$$\lambda_j = -r^0[E(mf_j) - E(m)E(f_j)] = E(f_j) - r^0 E(mf_j).$$

If a factor f_j is an excess return, then $0 = E(mf_j)$, and we recover the familiar result that λ_j is the mean of the excess return factor $E(f_j)$. If a factor is a return, then $1 = E(mf_j)$, and we recover $\lambda_j = E(f_j) - r^0$.

The b's are *not* the same as the $\boldsymbol{\beta}$'s: $\mathbf{b}$ are the regression coefficients of m on $\mathbf{f}$, and $\boldsymbol{\beta}$ are the regression coefficients of r on $\mathbf{f}$. One tests whether "factor j is priced" by testing whether $\lambda_j = -r^0 E[m(\tilde{f}_j - E\tilde{f}_j)] = 0$. This hypothesis does *not* answer the question whether factor j is marginally useful in pricing other assets. To test whether factor j helps to price assets, one tests whether $b_j = 0$, that is, whether one can construct an m that prices the set of assets under examination without factor f_j. Since

$$\boldsymbol{\lambda} = -r^0 E[(\tilde{\mathbf{f}} - E\tilde{\mathbf{f}})\mathbf{f}'\mathbf{b}] = -r^0 \,\mathrm{cov}(\tilde{\mathbf{f}}, \mathbf{f}')\mathbf{b},$$

---

[7] Mechanically,

$$1 = E(mr) = E(r\mathbf{f}')\mathbf{b} = E(r)E(\mathbf{f}')\mathbf{b} + \mathrm{cov}(r, \mathbf{f}')\mathbf{b},$$

$$E(r) = \frac{1 - \mathrm{cov}(r, \mathbf{f}')\mathbf{b}}{E(\mathbf{f}')\mathbf{b}} = \frac{1 - \mathrm{cov}(r, \tilde{\mathbf{f}}')\tilde{\mathbf{b}}}{E(\mathbf{f}')\mathbf{b}}$$

$$= \frac{1 - \mathrm{cov}(r, \tilde{\mathbf{f}}')\mathrm{cov}(\tilde{\mathbf{f}}, \tilde{\mathbf{f}}')^{-1}\mathrm{cov}(\tilde{\mathbf{f}}, \tilde{\mathbf{f}}')\tilde{\mathbf{b}}}{E(\mathbf{f}')\mathbf{b}} = r^0 - r^0 \boldsymbol{\beta}' \,\mathrm{cov}(\tilde{\mathbf{f}}, \mathbf{f}')\mathbf{b}$$

$$= r^0 - r^0 \boldsymbol{\beta}' E[(\tilde{\mathbf{f}} - E\tilde{\mathbf{f}}')\mathbf{f}'\mathbf{b}] = r^0 + \boldsymbol{\beta}'\boldsymbol{\lambda}.$$

The same steps backward prove "only if." Given either model, there is a model of the other form. They are not *unique*. We can add to m any random variable orthogonal to returns, and we can add risk factors with zero $\boldsymbol{\beta}$ or $\boldsymbol{\lambda}$, leaving pricing implications unchanged.

the hypotheses $b_j = 0$ and $\lambda_j = 0$ are equivalent only if the factors are orthogonal: if $\text{cov}(\mathbf{f}, \mathbf{f}')$ is diagonal.

The inclusion of scaled factors and scaled returns in an $m = \mathbf{b}'\mathbf{f}$, $\mathbf{p} = E(m\mathbf{r})$ model captures variation in conditional betas and factor risk premia $\boldsymbol{\lambda}$ in a very simple structure. Most tests of factor pricing models include auxiliary assumptions, such as constant conditional betas, constant conditional factor risk premia, constant conditional covariances, or complex time-series models for these quantities. Furthermore, the factors $\mathbf{f}$ do *not* have to be conditionally mean zero (white noise), conditionally or unconditionally orthogonal, or conditionally or unconditionally homoskedastic, as is often assumed.

The model $m = \mathbf{b}'\mathbf{f}$ is a factor *pricing* model. A factor *structure* on the covariance matrix of returns is sometimes used to derive factor pricing, but factor pricing does not imply or require a factor structure. The use of the same word "factor" for a pricing factor, a covariance factor structure, and a discount factor is unfortunate, but it is too late for me to try to change it.

Empirical Procedures

The moment conditions or pricing errors are proportional to expected return errors or α's. By the same argument as given above for the equivalence of $m = \mathbf{b}'\mathbf{f}$ and β, λ models, we have

$$\mathbf{g} = E(m\mathbf{r}) - \mathbf{p} = \frac{1}{r^0}[E(\mathbf{r}) - \boldsymbol{\beta}'\boldsymbol{\lambda} - r^0\mathbf{p}] = \frac{\boldsymbol{\alpha}}{r^0},$$

and conversely, we can recover expected return error α estimates from GMM estimates via

$$\boldsymbol{\alpha} = \frac{\mathbf{g}}{E(m)}. \tag{22}$$

The GMM objective is to minimize a weighted sum of squared pricing errors, which we can write in terms of α's as

$$\mathbf{g}_T(\mathbf{b})'\mathbf{W}\mathbf{g}_T(\mathbf{b}) = \frac{\boldsymbol{\alpha}_T(\mathbf{b})'\mathbf{W}\boldsymbol{\alpha}_T(\mathbf{b})}{(r^0)^2}.$$

Except for scaling by r^0, we can think of GMM as minimizing α's. The resulting χ^2 test has the form $\mathbf{g}_T' \times (\text{covariance matrix})^{-1} \times \mathbf{g}_T$, which is obviously analogous to the Gibbons, Ross, and Shanken (1989) test statistic, $\boldsymbol{\alpha}_T' \times (\text{covariance matrix})^{-1} \times \boldsymbol{\alpha}_T$.

Generalized method of moments minimizes the pricing errors in a way that is similar to a Fama-MacBeth (1973) cross-sectional regression. To see this, consider the special case in which the factors are

mean zero and only excess returns are considered, and ignore for
the moment the distinction between sample and population moments.
Then the model can be written as

$$0 = E(m\mathbf{r}^e); \quad m = 1 + \tilde{\mathbf{f}}'\mathbf{b}, \quad E(\tilde{\mathbf{f}}) = 0$$

($E(m)$ is not identified by excess returns, so I normalize to $E(m) = 1$).
The first-order conditions for the GMM minimization are then

$$\text{cov}(\tilde{\mathbf{f}}, \mathbf{r}^{e\prime})\mathbf{W}[E(\mathbf{r}^e) - \text{cov}(\mathbf{r}^e, \tilde{\mathbf{f}}')\hat{\mathbf{b}}] = 0,$$

which we solve for

$$\hat{\mathbf{b}} = [\text{cov}(\tilde{\mathbf{f}}, \mathbf{r}^{e\prime})\mathbf{W}\,\text{cov}(\mathbf{r}^e, \tilde{\mathbf{f}}')]^{-1}\text{cov}(\mathbf{f}, \mathbf{r}^{e\prime})\mathbf{W}E(\mathbf{r}^e).$$

The first-stage GMM estimate ($\mathbf{W} = \mathbf{I}$) is thus a cross-sectional ordinary least squares (OLS) regression of expected returns on covari-
ances. The second-stage GMM estimate is a corresponding GLS estimate.

In the more general case, the GMM estimate (eq. [12]) runs a cross-
sectional regression of mean prices on second moments. This slight
refinement allows the distribution theory to reflect the sampling error
induced by estimating sample means of the factors.

V. Estimating and Testing the Investment Return Factor Model

A. Setup

I use two investment technologies, corresponding to gross private
domestic nonresidential and residential investment. (The Appendix
details the sources and transformations used for all data.) I assume
that each investment series corresponds to a technology of the form
(4), so that its investment returns are given by (5).

For asset returns, I use the 10 portfolios of NYSE stocks sorted by
market value (size) maintained by the Center for Research in Security
Prices (CRSP). There is a large spread in the mean returns of these
portfolios: the small-firm decile's mean excess return is almost twice
that of the large-firm decile. Any asset pricing model must explain
this spread in mean returns by a spread in assets' covariance with risk
factors. Since the investment returns are based on quarterly average
investment, I transformed the asset returns to quarterly average returns rather than use end-of-quarter to end-of-quarter returns. I include moment conditions for investment returns along with the moment conditions generated by asset returns, since both sets of returns
should be correctly priced by this or any model and since it is interesting and important to check whether the asset pricing model can ac-

count in this way for macroeconomic events. I created excess returns by subtracting the 3-month Treasury-bill return in each case, to focus on risk premia. I also include the level of the ex post real Treasury-bill rate as an asset, in order to identify the level of the discount factor m.[8]

I use two instruments: the term premium (yield on long-term government bonds less yield on 3-month Treasury bills) and the dividend/price ratio of the equally weighted NYSE portfolio. I also considered the default premium (yield on BAA corporate bonds minus yield on AAA corporate bonds); with the dividend/price ratio, it produces similar results. These instruments are popular forecasters of stock returns. In the first-stage estimation, the moments corresponding to scaled returns are treated equally with the nonscaled returns, so it is convenient that the scale of the two is roughly comparable. To this end, I used $1 + 100 \times [(d/p) - 0.04]$ in place of the raw dividend/price ratio.[9] To avoid overlap with the averaged return series, I lag the instruments twice: an instrument used for the return from the first to second quarter is known by the last day of December.

Scaling factors and assets by instruments can lead to an explosion of moment conditions and scaled factors. I prune this explosion in three ways, beyond the already limited set of assets and instruments. First, I do not scale the Treasury-bill return by the instruments. Such scaling asks whether the model can capture variation over time in the real Treasury-bill return. I want to focus on whether the model can capture the much larger variation over time in risk premia, represented by scaled excess stock returns. Second, I scale the variable factors by the instruments, but I do not include the instruments themselves (constant scaled by instruments) as factors. Such factors help the model to capture variation in risk-free rates (varying $E_t(m)$), but they do not help the model capture time-varying risk premia. Third, I use only deciles 1, 2, 5, and 10 in the conditional estimates (return times instrument). With all 10 deciles I would have 37 moment conditions in 186 data points. The iterated GMM estimates behaved badly with 37×37 covariance matrices. I hope that deciles 2, 5, and 10 capture most of the cross-sectional information in (span the frontier of) the original 10 deciles; I include decile 1 as well in order to examine the well-known size anomaly.

---

[8] Of course, the system $1 = E(mr^{tb})$; $0 = E[m(\mathbf{r} - r^{tb})]$ is equivalent to the system $1 = E(mr^{tb})$; $\mathbf{1} = E[m\mathbf{r}]$, since either set of moments is a linear combination of the other. In a one-step efficient GMM estimate, min $\mathbf{g}_T(b)'\mathbf{S}^{-1}(b)\mathbf{g}_T(b)$, the two setups would yield exactly the same result. However, iterated and first-stage GMM estimates are affected by the initial choice of moments.

[9] This transformation is supposed to be data-independent. If I were to use $[(d/p) - E(d/p)]/\sigma(d/p)$, I would have to adjust the distribution theory for estimation of the mean and variance of d/p, not a straightforward task. The estimates *are* sensitive to scaling choices of the instruments, so it is important to choose instruments with a reasonable scale.

INVESTMENT-BASED ASSET PRICING   589

If we allow all the production function parameters $\{\eta, \delta, mpk\}$ to vary, the system is overparameterized. Examining the definition of the investment return (5), one can see that the parameters δ and mpk basically affect the mean of the investment return, and η affects its mean and standard deviation. None of the parameters substantially affects the cross-correlations of investment returns with other variables; they are basically given by the cross-correlation of investment growth with the other variables. Furthermore, the mean and standard deviation of the factors are not separately identified, since the factors can be rescaled at will by choice of b. As a result, the minimization surface has a valley in it, and the minimization program soon crashes with a singular gradient matrix $\partial \mathbf{g}_T / \partial [\eta \; \delta \; mpk]$. Therefore, I present results in which η and δ are held fixed, minimizing only over mpk. I tried choosing each of the parameters and choosing the parameters sequentially (first η, then mpk, etc.); both procedures produce similar results.

The tables below present results imposing no autocorrelation in the construction of the **S** matrix, since the null hypothesis of the central conditional models predicts that lagged mr should not predict mr. I also tried using four Newey-West (1987*b*) lags to construct standard errors, and the results overall are not much changed, indicating little autocorrelation.

B.   Iterated GMM Estimates and Tests of the Investment Return Model

Table 1 presents estimates and tests of the investment return factor model. Start with the simple unconditional estimates of the nonscaled factor model, panel A. The marginal product of capital parameters mpk are plausible and highly significant. They have about the same value (0.05–0.06) and are highly significant in all the following estimates, so I do not present them in the following tables, though they are estimated any time an investment return is estimated. The b's measure which factors are important for pricing assets. The residential factor prices significantly ($t = -2.61$), but the nonresidential factor does not ($t = 1.37$). They are jointly significant (*p*-value for joint $b_m, b_r = 0$ is 3 percent). In interpreting the b's, keep in mind that the discount factor m is proportional to the minimum *second-moment* return, which is on the lower portion of the minimum variance frontier. Since the investment returns are typically on the upper portion of the minimum variance frontier, b's may be negative. Finally, the J_T test of overidentifying restrictions does not reject the model (*p*-value 24 percent).

In the conditional estimates (with scaled returns), panel B, both investment return factors are individually significant (t on $b = 1.94$

TABLE 1

Iterated GMM Estimates and Tests of Investment Return Factor Model

A. Nonscaled Model $m = b_0 + b_{nr}r^i_{nr} + b_r r^i_r$

	PARAMETER ESTIMATES				
	mpk_{nr}	mpk_r	b_0	b_{nr}	b_r
	Unconditional Estimates $(1 = E(mr^{tb})$, $\ 0 = E(mr^e)$ [13 moments])				
Coefficient	.058	.063	-19	71	-51
t-statistic	38	44	$-.40$	1.37	-2.61
	Conditional Estimates $(1 = E(mr^{tb})$, $\ 0 = E(mr^e \otimes z)$ [19 moments])				
Coefficient			-36	123	-86
t-statistic			$-.56$	1.94	-5.57

	TESTS			
	All b	b_{nr}, b_r	J_T	Stock J_T
	Unconditional Estimates			
χ^2	382	7.0	10.4	
Degrees of freedom	3	2	8	
p-value (%)	.00	3.1	24	
	Conditional Estimates			
χ^2	35	22	22	
Degrees of freedom	2	14	12	
p-value (%)	.00	7.4	4.0	

B. Scaled Factor Model $m = b_0 + \mathbf{b}'(\mathbf{r}^i \otimes \mathbf{z})$: Conditional Estimates $(1 = E(mr^{tb})$, $0 = E(mr^e \otimes z))$

	PARAMETER ESTIMATES						
	b_0	b_{nr}	b_r	$b_{nr \cdot tp}$	$b_{r \cdot tp}$	$b_{nr \cdot dp}$	$b_{r \cdot dp}$
Coefficient	-29	157	-126	48	-48	-57	56
t-statistic	$-.46$	1.48	-2.00	3.42	-3.42	-2.12	2.11

	TESTS					
	Joint $b = 0$					
	No b_0	Unscaled	Scaled	All nr	All r	J_T
Wald χ^2	32.8	4.1	18.4	12.2	13.6	
p-value (%)	.001	13	.1	.7	.4	
$\Delta J_T \chi^2$	54	4.2	26	11.1	10.9	10.6
p-value (%)	.00	12	.003	1.1	1.2	39
Degrees of freedom	6	2	4	3	3	10

Note.—In the unconditional estimates, $\mathbf{r}^e$ is the 10 CRSP size decile portfolio and two investment excess returns, and r^{tb} is the real Treasury-bill return. The conditional estimates use the deciles 1, 2, 5, 10, and investment excess returns, scaled by instruments, and the real Treasury-bill return. Investment returns are functions of nonresidential (nr) and residential (r) gross fixed investment, eq. (5) with parameters $\eta = 3.0$, $\delta = .05$ throughout. mpk_{nr} and mpk_r are always estimated, even when not shown. Instruments are the constant, term premium (tp), and equally weighted dividend/price ratio (dp). The p-value is the percentage probability of obtaining a χ^2 value as high or higher.

and -5.57) and jointly highly significant (p-value < 0.00 percent). Adding moments should sharpen the precision of estimates, and it does. However, the J_T statistic now provides some evidence against the model (p-value 7 percent). A J_T test formed using only the stock returns, explained in some detail below, produces slightly more evidence against the model, with a 4 percent p-value.

The natural response to the rejection of the conditional estimates is to include scaled factors, panel B. The scaled factors are individually and jointly significant. The table presents Wald tests, based on the joint distribution of the b in equation (14), as well as tests on the increase in J_T when groups of the factors are omitted from the model. It is comforting that the two procedures yield quite similar results. The unscaled factors are only marginally jointly significant (p-value 13 percent), but the scaled factors are highly jointly significant. Also, the residential and nonresidential factors are significant as subgroups. Finally, the J_T test does not reject the overall model (p-value 39 percent).

C. First-Stage Estimates and Tests

Every first-year econometrics student is advised that GLS is best but OLS is pretty good. The GLS estimates can be more efficient with a good estimate of the covariance matrix, but GLS estimates can be terrible if the covariance matrix is poorly modeled. The OLS estimates are consistent and robust to many misspecifications. Thus one is often advised to make sure that GLS estimates are not too different from OLS estimates, or even to estimate parameters by the inefficient but robust OLS, correcting standard errors for residual correlation or heteroskedasticity.

The same advice applies to GMM. Efficient GMM estimates use the estimated covariance matrix of the sample moments to find linear combinations of those moments that are the most precisely measured. Generalized method of moments weights those linear combinations more highly in estimation, in order to improve efficiency, and then evaluates the model by testing whether those most precisely estimated linear combinations of moments are in fact zero. The dangers of this procedure if the **S** matrix is poorly measured are the same as those of GLS. The estimate may pay too much attention to portfolios that spuriously seem nearly risk-free in a small sample and hence seem to have well-measured pricing errors. Statistical issues aside, efficient GMM may pay close attention to economically uninteresting but statistically well-measured moments.

To make this observation precise, diagonalize the **S** matrix, $\mathbf{S} = \mathbf{Q\Lambda Q}'$, where **Q** is an orthonormal matrix with eigenvectors in its columns and Λ is a diagonal matrix of eigenvalues. Since $\mathbf{S}^{-1} = (\mathbf{Q}'\Lambda\mathbf{Q})^{-1} = \mathbf{Q}'\Lambda^{-1}\mathbf{Q}$, we can define

$$\mathbf{r}^* = \mathbf{Q}'\mathbf{r}; \quad \mathbf{p}^* = \mathbf{Q}'\mathbf{p}$$

and write the efficient GMM objective as

$$\min\{[E(m\mathbf{r}^* - \mathbf{p}^*)]'\Lambda^{-1}[E(m\mathbf{r}^* - \mathbf{p}^*)]\}.$$

The efficient GMM estimate first forms portfolios of the original assets with weights given by the eigenvalues of $\mathbf{S}$; then it pays more attention to the portfolios corresponding to small eigenvalues of $\mathbf{S}$—the ones whose pricing errors are most precisely measured.

The smallest four eigenvalues of $\mathbf{S}$ in this case are 1/64,000, 1/22,600, 1/14,200, and 1/7,800, so the first eigenvector is by far the most important in the estimation and testing. Figure 1 presents the corresponding portfolio weights: the first column of $\mathbf{Q}$. (Figure 1 rescales the weights so that they sum to one.) By far, the most important assets in this portfolio are the two investment returns. The investment returns have a good deal less variance than the stock returns, and so their means are more precisely measured. The portfolio places practically no weight on the Treasury-bill return. The asset and investment return moments are formed from m times excess returns, or m times a number typically around 0.02 (investment) or 0.10 (asset). The Treasury-bill rate moment is formed from m times a

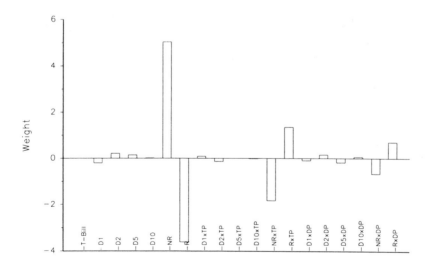

Fig. 1.—Portfolio (eigenvector) corresponding to largest eigenvalue of $\mathbf{S}^{-1}$

number typically around 1.01. Therefore, the quite high volatility of the discount factor m translates into a high variance of mr^{tb} and thus a high sampling variability for this moment.

The portfolio graphed in figure 1 also features large long and short positions in similar assets. This is a common feature of portfolios formed to minimize variance in a sample. The original portfolios are highly correlated, so their sample variance-covariance matrix and hence the **S** matrix are nearly singular. Small sampling errors in means and covariances make it look like there are nearly riskless portfolios.

So, GMM does exactly what we ask it to. We ask it to measure parameters "efficiently," which means to weight more heavily sources of information with less estimated sampling variation. Then GMM evaluates the model (via the J_T statistic) by asking whether the pricing errors on these low sampling error portfolios are in fact zero, after accounting for sampling information.

But is this what we want GMM to do? Perhaps not.

Evaluation: J_T Tests on a Restricted Set of Moments

Perhaps we do not want to accept or reject the model on the basis of how well it prices the portfolio graphed in figure 1. One alternative is to use only a subset of assets in the overidentifying restrictions test. Using the expression (15) for the variance-covariance matrix of the moment conditions, we can form an analogue to the J_T test in equations (16) and (17) using only an interesting subset of moments.

I conduct such tests for all moments excluding the Treasury-bill rate, and for the stock returns alone, to check that the model is not evaluated only on its ability to price investment returns. In all but one case, these tests produce numerically the same values as the J_T test in table 1. To see how this is possible, recall that the GMM estimate sets some linear combinations of moments to zero in sample in order to estimate parameters. Suppose that the first moment of a two-moment GMM estimate is set to zero in estimation, that is,

$$\left[\left(\frac{\partial \mathbf{g}_T}{\partial \mathbf{b}}\right)' \mathbf{W}\right] \mathbf{g}_T = \begin{bmatrix} 1 & 0 \end{bmatrix} \begin{bmatrix} g_{1T} \\ g_{2T} \end{bmatrix} = 0.$$

Now, the J_T test is based only on the second moment. If we test only the second moment, we obtain exactly the same test statistic and degrees of freedom as the J_T test. In the one case in table 1 in which the stock return J_T test was different from the J_T test, marked "Stock J_T," the stock return only test gives slightly more statistical evidence against the model, lowering the p-value from 7 percent to 4 percent.

Thus the iterated GMM estimates and tests survive an important robustness check: *evaluating* this model on only the asset moments does not make much difference, even though the *estimates* concentrate on the investment return moments.

Estimation: First-Stage GMM

If we are uncomfortable estimating and evaluating a model on the basis of portfolios such as figure 1, perhaps we should instead ask GMM to weight assets more evenly or, in an economically more interesting way, in estimation as well as in testing. I use an identity weighting matrix, so that all moments are weighted equally. This is the first-stage GMM estimate and test.[10] The only tricky part of first-stage or fixed weighting matrix estimates is that one must use the corresponding standard error, moment variance, and overidentifying restrictions test formulas, equations (13) and (16), rather than their more familiar special cases for an optimal weighting matrix, equations (14) and (17). In addition, the test based on the increase in GMM objective no longer has a χ^2 distribution, so I examine only Wald tests of joint b's for model comparisons.

Table 2 presents *first-stage* estimates and tests of the investment return factor model. The estimates and test statistics are quite similar to their iterated GMM counterparts in table 1, with the decrease in precision that one expects of a less efficient estimate: the significance levels of the b's and χ^2 tests are lower. The one qualitative difference is that the evidence against the nonscaled factor model is much weaker; I return to this point below. Overall, the iterated GMM esti-

---

[10] Hansen and Jagannathan (1991a) advocate an alternative prespecified weighting matrix, the second-moment matrix of returns,

$$\min\{E(m\mathbf{r} - \mathbf{p})' E(\mathbf{rr}')^{-1} E(m\mathbf{r} - \mathbf{p})\}.$$

This weighting matrix, like the one-step efficient GMM outlined in n. 8, has an important advantage over the identity matrix: it produces an estimate that is invariant to units and portfolio formation. In particular, it is invariant to the choice of units of the instruments; using $2z$ in place of z makes no difference, where it would double the attention the identity weighting matrix pays to returns scaled by z ratios. Because of this sensitivity, I had to carefully choose the units of the instruments. On the other hand, the return second-moment matrix is very nearly singular: $E(\mathbf{rr}') = E(\mathbf{r})E(\mathbf{r}') + \text{cov}(\mathbf{r}, \mathbf{r}')$, so one takes an already near-singular covariance matrix and adds a singular matrix, typically one with much larger elements. Therefore, its eigenvectors feature much stronger long and short positions, and no more economic justification, than the eigenvectors of the **S** matrix as graphed in fig. 1. Estimates with this weighting matrix can produce large pricing errors on the original assets. Also, I use the root mean square error (RMSE) expected return errors or α's and plots of α's as a diagnostic. Using the identity weighting matrix, GMM picks parameters to do best by this diagnostic; we avoid the confusion that a model might fit better by the estimate but look worse in the RMSE α diagnostic.

TABLE 2

FIRST-STAGE GMM ESTIMATES AND TESTS OF INVESTMENT RETURN FACTOR MODEL

A. NONSCALED MODEL

	PARAMETER ESTIMATES		
	b_0	b_{nr}	b_r
	Unconditional Estimates		
Coefficient	-9.5	99	-88
t-statistic	$-.11$	1.10	-3.27
	Conditional Estimates		
Coefficient	-293	408	-109
t-statistic	-1.70	2.23	-2.93

	TESTS		
	b_{nr}, b_r	J_T	Stock J_T
	Unconditional Estimates		
χ^2	1.2	8.4	
Degrees of freedom	2	8	
p-value (%)	27	40	
	Conditional Estimates		
χ^2	10.7	12.4	11.3
Degrees of freedom	2	14	12
p-value (%)	.47	57	51

B. SCALED FACTOR MODEL: CONDITIONAL ESTIMATES

	PARAMETER ESTIMATES						
	b_0	b_{nr}	b_r	$b_{nr \cdot tp}$	$b_{r \cdot tp}$	$b_{nr \cdot dp}$	$b_{r \cdot dp}$
Coefficient	-38	131	-90	50	-50	-44	44
t-statistic	$-.30$	.74	-1.04	2.03	-2.03	-1.07	1.06

	TESTS					
	Joint $b = 0$					
	No b_0	Unscaled	Scaled	All nr	All r	J_T
χ^2	17.4	1.1	9.3	5.3	5.4	12.3
Degrees of freedom	6	2	4	3	3	10
p-value (%)	.8	58	5.5	15	15	27

NOTE.—The same estimates and tests as given in table 1, except first-stage GMM (identity weighting matrix) rather than iterated or optimal GMM estimates and tests.

mates and tests pass the robustness check that they are not too different from first-stage estimates and tests.

D. Pricing Errors

Expected return pricing errors or α's are a useful characterization of a model's performance. Examining them helps to guard against accepting an uninteresting model: one that prices assets badly but produces large enough standard errors not to be rejected by the J_T statistic. It also helps to guard against the equally dangerous possibility of rejecting a good model: one that produces economically tiny pricing errors, but such small standard errors that the model is still statistically rejected.

Figure 2 presents the predicted versus actual mean excess returns for the nonscaled model (fig. 2a), the conditional estimates of the nonscaled model (fig. 2b), and the scaled model (fig. 2c). These values are calculated from equation (22). The straight line in each panel is the 45° line, along which all the assets should lie. Starting from the lower left of figure 2a, we have the Treasury-bill rate and two investment excess returns. The placement of the investment returns is not an essential feature of the model. It is easy to produce investment returns that lie farther apart or at different places along the line in figure 2, yet price about as well, by different choices of the fixed parameters η and δ. The group of assets up and to the right are the decile portfolios, with the smaller-size firm deciles farther out on the graph. In figure 2b and c, there are three triangles for each asset, corresponding to the asset and the asset scaled by each of the two instruments.

Figure 2 presents α's calculated from the *first*-stage estimates. The first-stage GMM estimate basically minimizes RMSE α's, so if we compare models by α plots or RMSE α's, we know that each model will fit as well as possible along this dimension. For comparison, figure 3 presents the *iterated* GMM predicted versus actual mean excess returns. The Treasury-bill pricing error is dramatic: its excess return is predicted at -4.6 percent, but the actual value is, of course, zero. This occurs because, as discussed above regarding figure 1, the Treasury-bill moment condition is very imprecisely measured; iterated GMM therefore pays little attention to the Treasury-bill return in order to better price the other assets. The iterated GMM estimates do a reasonably good job of pricing the remaining portfolios. Still, the spread is larger than in the first-stage estimates. The iterated GMM estimate would of course produce smaller pricing errors for the **S** eigenvalue portfolios such as shown in figure 1, whose pricing errors it minimizes.

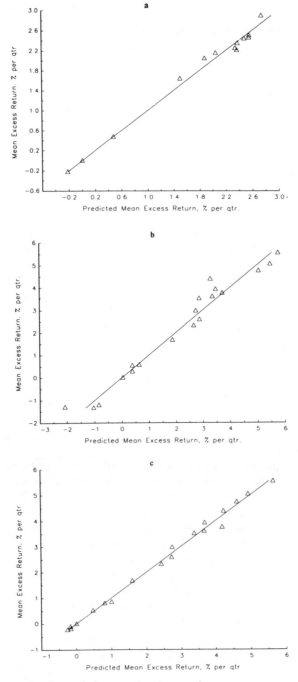

FIG. 2.—Predicted vs. actual mean excess returns, investment return model: *a*, non-scaled model; *b*, nonscaled model, conditional estimates; *c*, scaled model. First-stage GMM estimates.

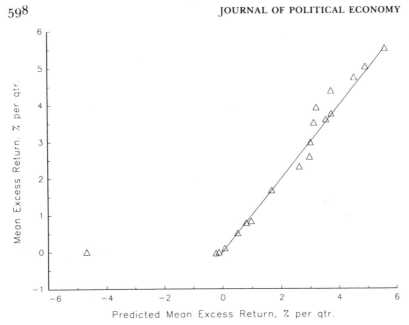

Fig. 3.—Predicted vs. actual mean excess returns, scaled investment return factor pricing model, iterated GMM estimate.

It is a good check that the iterated GMM pricing errors are not that different from the first-stage pricing errors, at least for the interesting assets. If the iterated GMM estimates produced wild pricing errors for the original assets in order to minimize the pricing errors of the S eigenvalue portfolios, we might suspect that the GMM estimates are not that reliable or that something is wrong with the model. Hence, the iterated GMM estimates pass another important robustness check.

The difference between figure 2 and figure 3 dramatizes a point made by Kandel and Stambaugh (1995): pricing error graphs are not robust to portfolio reformation. As long as the pricing errors are not zero, one can find a repackaging of portfolios to make graphs like figures 2 and 3 look arbitrarily good or bad. Therefore, it is important to examine a model's ability to explain the expected returns of economically interesting portfolios.

The main difference between first-stage estimates of table 2 and iterated estimates of table 1 is that the scaled factors seem only marginally statistically useful in the first-stage estimates. The conditional estimate of the nonscaled model fails to reject with p-values around 50 percent instead of the 4–7 percent p-values from the iterated estimate, and the scaled factors have only a 5.5 percent p-value in the scaled factor model.

However, the pricing errors or α's presented in figure 2 suggest that scaled factors are indeed important, since the pricing errors of the scaled factor model (fig. 2c) are decidedly smaller. Table 3 collects RMSE α's for a variety of models and tells the same story: the scaled model achieves an RMSE α of 0.15 percent, whereas the nonscaled model achieves only 0.42 percent, more than twice as much.

Part of the story for the decline in pricing errors with a scaled model is degrees of freedom: one always lowers the objective by adding more factors. The other part of the story is the danger of accepting models with large pricing errors but even larger standard errors. The sampling variance of the moments estimated in the nonscaled factor model is a good deal larger than for the scaled factor model. Thus larger pricing errors are less statistically significant. One way to see this point is in the fact that the nonscaled factor model is not rejected with a 57 percent p-value, yet we reject elimination of the scaled factors from the scaled factor model—using the *scaled* factor model variance-covariance matrix in the test—with a 5.5 percent p-value.

All the sample pricing errors are far from individually statistically significant (I use the diagonal elements of eq. [15] to calculate individual moment standard errors). The J_T test is based on a weighted sum of squares of the pricing errors plotted in figure 2. When it does not reject (tables 1 and 2), the pricing errors are jointly insignificant as well.

VI. Comparison with Other Models

The overidentifying restrictions (J_T) test the investment return model against no specific alternative. But *all* currently available nontrivial models can undoubtedly be statistically rejected if one uses a sufficiently rich set of assets and instruments and a long enough sample. Therefore, it may be more interesting to compare a given model to plausible competitors rather than simply reject or fail to reject it.

In this section, I compare the investment return model to the capital asset pricing model (CAPM), the Chen, Roll, and Ross (1986) factor model, the consumption-based model, and two ad hoc macro factor models. In each case, I estimate, test, and examine the competing model, in the style of tables 1 and 2 and figure 2. Then I estimate models that include *both* investment return and the other factors, to see which set of factors can be deleted in the presence of the other. The RMSE pricing errors and pricing error graphs like figure 2 provide an economic counterpart to the statistical comparison.

TABLE 3

EXPECTED RETURN PRICING ERRORS OR α'S

Assets	Model									
	r^i	CAPM	r^i + CAPM	CRR	r^i + CRR	$\Delta c^{-\gamma}$	$r^i + \Delta c^{-\gamma}$	Δc	$r^i + \Delta c$	ΔI
Nonscaled Models, Unconditional Estimates										
Stocks, r^i, r^{tb}	.099		.069		.028		.094		.098	
Stocks	.113	.094	.079	.037	.031	.054	.112	.301	.112	.096
Nonscaled Models, Conditional Estimates										
Stocks, r^i, r^{tb}	.42		.41		.21		.30		.32	
Stocks	.46	.94	.45	.33	.24	2.86	.30	1.81	.33	.51
Scaled Models (CRR and $\Delta c^{-\gamma}$), Conditional Estimates										
Stocks, r^i, r^{tb}	.15		.12		.11		.14		.14	
Stocks	.19	.49	.15	.33	.13	2.86	.16	.59	.17	.18

NOTE.—Entries are root mean square α's—mean return less predicted mean return—expressed in percentage per quarter. Entries are calculated as $\alpha_j = 100 \times E(m^r_j - p_j)/E(m)$. They are based on first-stage GMM estimates. Unconditional estimates use deciles 1–10 and investment returns and real Treasury-bill return where indicated. Conditional estimates use deciles 1, 2, 3, and 10 scaled by the constant, term premium, and dividend/price ratio, plus the Treasury-bill rate, investment returns, and scaled investment returns where indicated.

A. CAPM

Estimates and Tests of the CAPM

The CAPM is a single-factor model with the market return r^m as the factor, $m = b_0 + b_m r^m$.[11] Thus it trivially maps into the factor pricing–GMM framework outlined above.

Table 4 presents GMM estimates and tests of the CAPM. This estimation does not include any investment returns. The pattern of results is similar to that of the investment return factor model. In the unconditional estimates of the nonscaled model, the market return is a significant factor, with t-statistics of -3.2 (first-stage) and -3.5 (iterated). The J_T test does not reject with a 95 percent p-value. In the conditional estimates, the market return prices even more significantly, but the J_T test soundly rejects the model with a 0.7–1.6 percent p-value. However, in many derivations, the CAPM is a one-period or conditional model, so we should include scaled factors. When we do so (panel B), the b's are individually and jointly significant. In contrast to the investment model, however, the overidentifying restrictions of the scaled model are now rejected at a 2.6 percent p-value in the iterated GMM estimates, and nearly rejected at a 7.7 percent p-value even at the first stage. Overall, the first-stage and iterated estimates are similar in this table, with the iterated estimates giving slightly stronger statistical results.

Comparison Tests

Do the investment returns drive out the market return or vice versa? In a factor model that includes *both* the market and the investment returns, which factors are significant for pricing assets?

Table 5 collects such comparison tests. There are three tests: Wald tests for joint $b = 0$ conducted with the first- and second-stage estimates and χ^2 difference tests conducted by eliminating each set of factors in turn during the iterated GMM estimates. I compare scaled and nonscaled models separately. All the comparison tests are based on conditional estimates, including scaled returns.

The estimates in this table *do* include investment returns, for two reasons. First, including investment return moments is important for estimating the production function parameters mpk_{nr}, mpk_r. Second, we are interested in finding models that not only price financial assets but relate asset prices to events in the macroeconomy. To guard

---

[11] The CAPM can also be specified with the excess market return as the factor, $m = b_0 + b_1(r^m - r^f)$, or with the market return and risk-free rate or zero beta rate as two factors, $m = b_0 r^f + b_1 r^m$.

TABLE 4

GMM ESTIMATES AND TESTS OF CAPM

A. NONSCALED MODEL $m = b_0 + b_m r^m$

PARAMETER ESTIMATES

	Unconditional Estimates		Conditional Estimates	
	b_0	b_m	b_0	b_m
First-stage:				
Coefficient	6.5	-5.4	9.5	-8.4
t-statistic	3.74	-3.21	5.53	-5.05
Iterated:				
Coefficient	6.7	-5.6	9.8	-8.6
t-statistic	4.08	-3.53	5.94	-5.42

TESTS

	Unconditional Estimates	Conditional Estimates
	J_T	J_T
First-stage:		
χ^2	3.3	26
Degrees of freedom	9	11
p-value (%)	95	.71
Iterated:		
χ^2	3.3	23
Degrees of freedom	9	11
p-value (%)	95	1.55

B. SCALED MODEL $m = b_0 + b_m r^m + b_{tp}(r^m \times tp) + b_{dp}(r^m \times dp)$:
CONDITIONAL ESTIMATES

PARAMETER ESTIMATES

	b_0	b_m	b_{tp}	b_{dp}
First-stage:				
Coefficient	4.56	-2.66	$-.33$	$-.39$
t-statistic	1.48	$-.80$	-1.32	-2.05
Iterated:				
Coefficient	5.88	-4.62	.24	$-.36$
t-statistic	3.51	-2.70	2.26	-3.62

TESTS

	b_m, b_{tp}, b_{dp}	Scaled b	J_T
First-stage:			
χ^2	59	4.9	15.6
Degrees of freedom	3	2	9
p-value (%)	.00	8.6	7.7
Iterated:			
χ^2	67	15	18.9
Degrees of freedom	3	2	9
p-value (%)	.00	.06	2.6

NOTE.—r^m is the value-weighted NYSE return. No investment returns are included.

INVESTMENT-BASED ASSET PRICING

TABLE 5

MODEL COMPARISON TESTS

A. NONSCALED INVESTMENT RETURN MODEL

	ALTERNATIVE MODEL							
	Static CAPM		CRR		$\Delta c^{-\gamma}$		Δc	
Omitted factors	r^i	r^m	r^i	crr	r^i	c	r^i	c
Degrees of freedom	2	1	2	5	2	1	2	1
First-stage χ^2	5.0	.09	3.8	2.3	11	.01	8.3	2.5
p-value (%)	8.2	76	15	81	.4	91	1.6	12
Iterated χ^2	13.5	.68	2.0	5.4	26	.01	32	29
p-value (%)	.1	41	37	37	.00	94	.00	.00
$\Delta J_T \chi^2$	11.5	.68	1.7	5.4	27	.15	28	20
p-value (%)	.3	41	43	37	.00	70	.00	.00

B. SCALED INVESTMENT RETURN MODEL

	ALTERNATIVE MODEL							
	Scaled CAPM		CRR		$\Delta c^{-\gamma}$		Scaled Δc	
Omitted factors	r^i	r^m	r^i	crr	r^i	c	r^i	c
Degrees of freedom	6	3	6	5	6	1	6	3
First-stage χ^2	8.8	.96	6.4	1.9	24	.00	9.8	.44
p-value (%)	19	81	38	85	.05	95	13	93
Iterated χ^2	14.2	7.6	5.9	1.9	29	.06	13	2.4
p-value (%)	2.8	5.6	43	87	.01	80	4.4	50
$\Delta J_T \chi^2$	13	9.5	17	1.9	29	2.6	12	3.1
p-value (%)	4.5	.4	1.1	87	.01	11	5.3	37

NOTE.—Tests for joint $b_j = 0$ in models $m_0 = b_0 + b'_1 r^i + b'_2 f$, where r^i denotes investment returns and f denotes additional factors listed in each column. All tests are based on conditional moments: deciles 1, 2, 5, and 10, the Treasury-bill return, and investment returns, scaled by the constant, term premium, and dividend/price ratio. First-stage and iterated give Wald tests based on the indicated GMM estimate; ΔJ_T gives rise in the GMM objective when one set of factors is excluded.

against the danger that the comparison tests are driven by the investment returns, I include first-stage estimates and I compare stock return pricing errors.

The nonscaled model tests favor the investment return model. In the first stage, there is an 8.2 percent p-value for dropping the investment return factors, compared to 76 percent for dropping the market return. Iterated estimates and the ΔJ_T test raise this to 0.1–0.3 percent p-values for dropping the investment return factors, against 41 percent for dropping the market. Here and below, the similarity of Wald and ΔJ_T tests is comforting.

When we compare the scaled investment return model to the scaled CAPM, the table suggests that each set of factors is statistically important in the presence of the others. In the first stage, we cannot reject eliminating either set of factors, though the investment factors have somewhat stronger evidence (p-value 19 percent) than the market factors (p-value 81 percent). The iterated GMM Wald tests reject exclusion of the investment return factors (p-value 2.8 percent) but borderline reject exclusion of the scaled market factors (p-value 5.6 percent); but the ΔJ_T tests neatly reverse the pattern of these p-values, and small differences in p-values based on asymptotic distributions are a dangerous decision criterion.

Pricing Errors

Figure 4 plots the pricing errors or α's for the CAPM. In the unconditional estimates of the nonscaled model (fig. 4a), we see visually the nice fit suggested by the statistics in table 4. The outlier on the top right is the well-known small-firm effect. The point estimate gives a small-firm α of 0.23 percent per quarter, or about 1 percent per year.

The static CAPM has more difficulty with conditioning information, as seen in figure 4b. The four assets below the 45° line are the unscaled portfolios, with the scaled portfolios above the line. These pricing errors are much larger than the small-firm effect found in the unconditional estimates in figure 4a.

The scaled CAPM does a somewhat better job of handling conditioning information, as seen in figure 4c. However, the pricing errors are still fairly large, and this lies behind the statistical rejection shown in table 4. Even with scaled factors, the CAPM cannot price the scaled returns. This observation helps to give us some confidence that the investment model was not performing well only because of scaling.

Note also that the small-firm effect disappears once we include scaled market returns as factors. Thus the apparent small-firm effect may simply be due to inadequate treatment of conditioning information. Most derivations of the CAPM specify that the market is conditionally, but not unconditionally, mean-variance efficient, so this result is not too surprising. (It may also be due to a specific failure of the CAPM: none of the other models displays a small-firm effect.)

The pricing error in table 3 confirms the better visual fit of the investment return model in figure 2 versus the CAPM in figure 4. The unconditional estimate of the nonscaled CAPM produces a 0.09 percent RMSE α, about the same as the 0.11 percent value from the corresponding investment return model. However, the investment return model produces better than half the RMSE pricing errors in the conditional estimate: 0.46 percent versus 0.94 percent in the nonscaled model and 0.19 percent versus 0.49 percent in the scaled model.

Table 3 includes the RMSE pricing error for a model containing

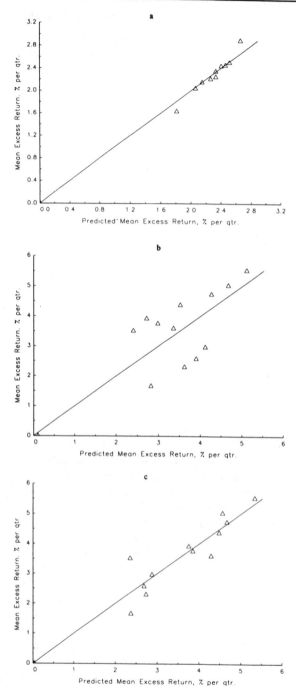

FIG. 4.—Predicted vs. actual mean excess returns, CAPM: *a*, static CAPM; *b*, static CAPM, conditional estimates; *c*, scaled CAPM, conditional estimates. All estimates first-stage GMM.

both investment return and market factors, so we can see the effect of dropping either set of factors in the style of the model comparison tests of table 5. The investment return *plus* market model does not do meaningfully better than the investment return model taken alone: reductions from 0.42 percent to 0.41 percent or 0.46 percent to 0.45 percent for the nonscaled model and 0.15 percent to 0.12 percent or 0.19 percent to 0.15 percent for the scaled model. However, the investment return plus market return model seems to do meaningfully better than the CAPM, reducing pricing errors by one-half.

In summary, the pricing errors confirm the statistical tests for the nonscaled models: the investment return model does better than the static CAPM and drives out the CAPM factors. For the scaled models, the statistical tests found both investment and market factors important. However, we find that the rise in pricing error when investment return factors are omitted is economically large, even if statistically small, and the rise in pricing error when market return factors are omitted is not economically meaningful, even if statistically significant.

B. Chen, Roll, and Ross Model

The Chen, Roll, and Ross (1986) (CRR) model was explicitly designed to link stock returns to economic fluctuations, and Chen, Roll, and Ross claim that their model drives out the market return. Thus it is an important alternative model to examine. Chen, Roll, and Ross advocate a five-factor model, in which the factors are MP (growth in industrial production), DEI (change in inflation forecast), UI (inflation forecast residual), UPR (return on corporate bonds minus return on 10-year government bonds), and UTS (return on 10-year government bonds minus return on bills). All but MP are based on bond returns (the inflation forecasts are based on Treasury-bill returns).

Table 6 presents GMM estimates and tests of the CRR model. The table presents only iterated estimates, since first-stage estimates were not different enough to warrant an extra set of numbers. Similarly, the ΔJ_T tests were almost identical to Wald tests, so I omitted them from the table.

In the unconditional estimates, only one of the CRR factors is individually significant, though they are jointly marginally significant with a 6.1 percent p-value. However, in the more efficient conditional estimate, two factors are individually significant, and the factors together are jointly significant with a 3.6 percent p-value. The model is comfortably not rejected by the J_T test, with 95 percent and 64 percent p-values.

It is not clear whether Chen, Roll, and Ross intend their model as

TABLE 6

CHEN, ROLL, AND ROSS MODEL

A. PARAMETER ESTIMATES

	b_0	b_{mp}	b_{dei}	b_{ui}	b_{upr}	b_{uts}
			Unconditional Estimates			
Coefficient	1.0	−1.4	−7.5	41	−54	−19
t-statistic	4.58	−.25	−.11	1.14	−1.88	−2.43
			Conditional Estimates			
Coefficient	1.8	−25	−68	−51	75	−.37
t-statistic	4.36	−2.30	−.51	−.82	2.39	−.03

B. TESTS

	$b_{mp-uts} = 0$	J_T
	Unconditional Estimates	
χ^2	10.6	1.15
Degrees of freedom	5	5
p-value (%)	6.1	95
	Conditional Estimates	
χ^2	11.9	5.13
Degrees of freedom	5	7
p-value (%)	3.6	64

NOTE.—Asset returns are deciles 1–10 in the unconditional estimates and deciles 1, 2, 5, and 10 scaled by the constant, term premium, and dividend price ratio in the conditional estimates. Assets do not include investment returns.

a conditional or unconditional factor model. Their test allows some variation in β's but imposes constant factor risk premia (λ's), and they only attempt to explain unconditional expected returns. Pragmatically, I do not include a scaled Chen, Roll, and Ross model since it would have $1 + (3 \times 5) = 16\ b$ parameters and I use only 13 asset return moments. One can use more moments, of course, but a comfortable moments/parameters ratio would leave us with an uncomfortable data points/moments ratio.

The column marked "CRR" in table 5 presents a comparison of the investment model with the CRR model. The ΔJ_T test of the scaled model strongly rejects dropping the investment return factors in the presence of the CRR factors. Otherwise, the table suggests that either set of factors can be dropped in the presence of the others. This is good news: it means that the investment return model can explain the relatively good fit of the CRR model.

Figure 5 plots the first-stage pricing errors and confirms the nice

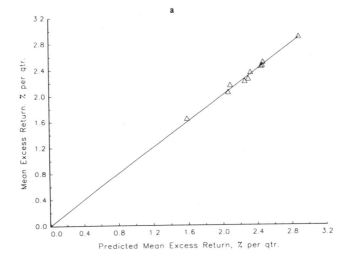

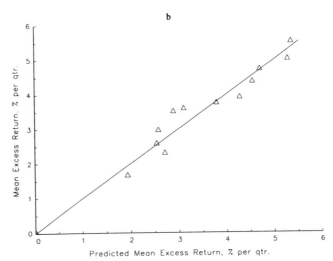

FIG. 5.—Predicted vs. actual mean excess returns, Chen et al. model, first-stage estimates: *a*, unconditional estimates; *b*, conditional estimates.

fit, at least for the unconditional estimates. Keep in mind, though, that the model has six factors to fit 11 moments in the unconditional estimates and 13 moments in the conditional estimates. The fit in these plots does not correct for degrees of freedom.

Comparing figure 5 with the investment return pricing errors in figure 2 and examining the pricing error in table 3, we see that the CRR model gives stock return pricing errors of 0.33 percent, about

INVESTMENT-BASED ASSET PRICING   609

halfway between the nonscaled (0.46 percent) and scaled (0.19 percent) investment return factor model. Thus the scaled investment return factor may provide an economically interesting improvement over the CRR model.

C. *Consumption-Based Model*

The consumption-based model is based on a measure of consumers' intertemporal marginal rate of *substitution*, where the investment model is based on a measure of firms' intertemporal marginal rate of *transformation*. It is perhaps the most appropriate comparison for the investment return factor model. Like the investment model, the consumption-based model relates asset returns strictly to macroeconomic data rather than other asset returns. It also provides an explicit link between asset return and macroeconomic events.

I limit my comparisons to the standard time-separable constant relative risk aversion formulation, which is about the same level of simplicity as this investment return model. It is possible that one of the many variations on the consumption-based model, such as habit persistence, durability, and so forth, may perform better than this simple model. (Campbell and Cochrane [1995] certainly hope so!) But it is also possible that one of the many possible variations on the investment model, such as production shocks, gestation lags, and so forth, performs better still.

Table 7 presents GMM estimates and tests of the basic consumption-based model. The model predicts that

$$m_t = \beta \left(\frac{c_t}{c_{t-1}} \right)^{-\gamma}$$

regardless of conditioning information, so I do not consider scaled consumption factors. The γ estimates are huge and the β's are often larger than one. This is the equity premium puzzle, a familiar pattern when this model tries to explain the cross section of asset returns.

The pricing errors for the unconditional estimates in figure 6a are huge. However, the imprecision of the estimate is so high that the unconditionally estimated model cannot be rejected by the J_T test—a graphic illustration of the dangers of looking only at J_T tests and not also the underlying pricing errors. Figure 6b shows that, like the CAPM, this consumption-based model has great trouble reconciling conditional and unconditional moments. In this case the pricing errors are so large that the model is resoundingly rejected by the J_T test with p-values of 0.3 percent in the first-stage estimate and 0.04 percent in the iterated estimate. Table 3 confirms the visual picture:

TABLE 7

CONSUMPTION-BASED MODEL

	PARAMETER ESTIMATES			
	Unconditional Estimates		Conditional Estimates	
	β	γ	β	γ
First-stage:				
Coefficient	.98	241	1.29	153
t-statistic	.49	.61	6.39	1.56
Iterated:				
Coefficient	1.27	71	1.29	116
t-statistic	10.9	2.17	13.9	3.36

	TESTS	
	Unconditional Estimates	Conditional Estimates
	J_T	J_T
First-stage:		
χ^2	6.17	28
Degrees of freedom	9	11
p-value (%)	72	.30
Iterated:		
χ^2	11.3	33.9
Degrees of freedom	9	11
p-value (%)	26	.04

NOTE.—GMM estimates and tests of consumption-based model: $m_{t+1} = \beta(c_{t+1}/c_t)^{-\gamma}$. Asset returns are deciles 1–10 in the unconditional estimates and deciles 1, 2, 5, and 10 scaled by the constant, term premium, and dividend/price ratio in the conditional estimates. Assets do not include investment returns.

the RMSE pricing error of the consumption-based model is 2.86 percent, 10 times higher than that of any of the other models.

The column marked $\Delta c^{-\gamma}$ in table 5 presents a comparison of the investment model against the consumption-based model. The unrestricted model here is $m = b_0 + \mathbf{b}'_1\mathbf{r}^I + \beta\Delta c^{-\gamma}$. Not surprisingly, all the tests decisively reject omitting the investment return factors, with *p*-values less than 1 percent and mostly less than 0.01 percent, while never rejecting dropping the $\Delta c^{-\gamma}$ factor.

D. Consumption Growth Factor Model

Perhaps *consumption* is not at fault, but the tight structure implied by the utility function and absence of free *b* parameters in the consumption-based model. Linearized versions of the consumption-based model such as Brown and Gibbons (1985) have been more successful. In this spirit, consider the model

$$m_{t+1} = b_0 + b_{\Delta c}\Delta c_{t+1},$$

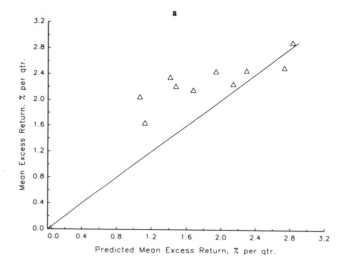

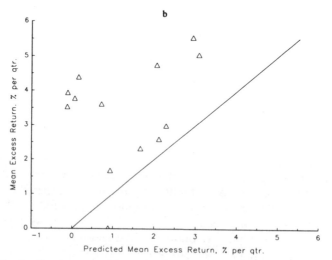

FIG. 6.—Predicted vs. actual mean excess returns, consumption-based model, first-stage estimates: *a*, unconditional estimates; *b*, conditional estimates.

where Δc_{t+1} denotes consumption growth, and a similar model with scaled factors.

Table 8 presents iterated GMM estimates of this model (the first stage was not different enough to warrant an extra set of numbers). A familiar pattern emerges: in the unconditional estimates, consumption growth significantly prices assets and the model is not rejected. In the conditional estimates, consumption growth prices more signifi-

TABLE 8

CONSUMPTION GROWTH FACTOR MODEL

A. NONSCALED FACTOR MODEL $m = b_0 + b_{\Delta c}\Delta c$

PARAMETER ESTIMATES

	Unconditional Estimates		Conditional Estimates	
	Constant	Δc	Constant	Δc
Coefficient	92	-90	108	-107
t-statistic	2.32	-2.30	2.84	-2.81

TESTS

	Unconditional Estimates	Conditional Estimates
	J_T	J_T
χ^2	9.88	34.8
Degrees of freedom	9	11
p-value (%)	36	.03

B. SCALED FACTOR MODEL $m = b_0 + b_{\Delta c}\Delta c + b_{tp}(\Delta c \times tp) + b_{dp}(\Delta c \times tp)$: CONDITIONAL ESTIMATES

PARAMETER ESTIMATES

	b_0	$b_{\Delta c}$	b_{tp}	b_{dp}
Coefficient	105	-102	$-.31$	$-.53$
t-statistic	2.73	-2.68	-1.76	-4.74

TESTS

	Scaled $b = 0$	J_T
χ^2	33	17
Degrees of freedom	2	9
p-value (%)	.00	4.6

NOTE.—Iterated GMM tests of consumption growth factor model. Asset returns are deciles 1–10 in the unconditional estimates and deciles 1, 2, 5, and 10 scaled by the constant, term premium, and dividend/price ratio in the conditional estimates. Assets do not include investment returns. Wald and ΔJ_T joint b tests give the same results, so they are not separately presented.

cantly, but the model is decisively rejected, with a 0.03 percent p-value that is much lower than corresponding rejections of the investment return factor model and the CAPM. Scaling helps: the scaled factors are mostly individually significant and jointly highly significant, and the model is now only borderline rejected with a 4.6 percent p-value.

The consumption-based factor model does not do all that well when compared to the investment return model in comparison tests in table 5, in pricing error comparisons in table 3, and by examination of the pricing errors in figure 7, however. In table 5, we reject exclusion of

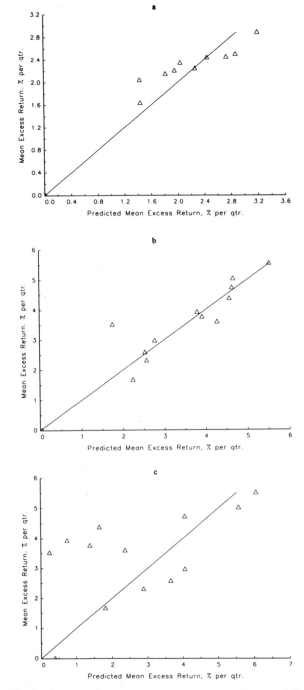

FIG. 7.—Predicted vs. actual mean excess returns, consumption growth factor model, first-stage estimates: *a*, unconditional estimates, nonscaled model; *b*, conditional estimates, nonscaled model; *c*, conditional estimates, scaled model.

the consumption growth factor only in the iterated estimate of non-scaled models; otherwise the evidence against dropping the investment return factors is much stronger than that against dropping the consumption growth factors. Figure 7 reveals pricing errors almost as large as those of the consumption-based model and dramatically worse than the fit of the other models. Table 3 shows that the RMSE pricing errors are three times greater than those of their investment return model and larger than the CAPM as well, whereas the investment return plus consumption growth model has pricing errors not much lower than those of the investment return model alone.

In summary, the problem does *not* seem to be the tight structure imposed by the consumption-based model, but that consumption data are less informative about stock returns than investment data.

E.   Investment Growth Model

How much of the success of the investment return factor model has to do with the precise functional forms used to infer investment returns from investment data? To investigate this question, I consider an ad hoc factor model based on investment *growth*,

$$m = b_0 + b_{nr}\Delta i_{nr} + b_r \Delta i_r,$$

and its scaled extension.

Table 9 presents the usual GMM estimates and tests of the investment growth factor model. Again, I present only second-stage estimates since the first stage was quite similar. The performance is overall a little *better* than the investment return factor model of table 1. However, this estimate uses fewer moments, since it tries to price only asset returns and not asset and investment returns simultaneously. As before, only the residential investment factor prices assets significantly in the unconditional estimates, but both factors significantly price assets in the conditional estimates. The unconditional estimate of the nonscaled model is not rejected (p-value 26 percent), but now the conditional estimate is not rejected as well, with a p-value of 65 percent. Given this fact, it is unsurprising that scaling seems not to be statistically necessary; the scaled investment growth factors are individually and jointly insignificant. Though the scaled model is not rejected either with a 32 percent p-value, the J_T declines only from 7.8 to 7.0 with a loss of four degrees of freedom.

Figure 8 presents pricing errors. The fit of the 10 deciles is quite good. The scaled returns are not priced quite as well. As with the investment return factor model, the *statistically* marginal or insignificant improvement from adding scaled factors masks a definite *economic* improvement in the sample pricing errors. The RMSE pricing errors in table 3 show that this model does about as well as the invest-

TABLE 9

Investment Growth (Not Return) Factor Model

A. Nonscaled Model

	Parameter Estimates					
	Unconditional Estimates			Conditional Estimates		
	b_0	b_{nr}	b_r	b_0	b_{nr}	b_r
Coefficient	−4.2	12.3	−7.1	−51	62	−9.8
t-statistic	−.55	1.56	−2.59	−2.35	2.86	−2.62

	Tests	
	Unconditional Estimates	Conditional Estimates
	J_T	J_T
χ^2	10	7.8
Degrees of freedom	8	10
p-value (%)	26	65

B. Scaled Factor Model: Conditional Estimates

	Parameter Estimates						
	Constant	b_{nr}	b_r	$b_{nr \cdot tp}$	$b_{n \cdot tp}$	$b_{nr \cdot dp}$	$b_{r \cdot dp}$
Coefficient	−41	50	−8.3	3.4	−3.2	.15	−.18
t-statistic	−1.18	1.38	−.78	.81	−.77	.02	−.03

	Tests		
	Unscaled b	Scaled b	J_T
χ^2	2.0	1.9	7.0
Degrees of freedom	2	4	6
p-value (%)	37	75	32

Note.—Iterated GMM tests of investment growth factor model, using residential (r) and nonresidential (nr) gross fixed investment. Asset returns are deciles 1–10 in the unconditional estimates and deciles 1, 2, 5, and 10 scaled by the constant, term premium, and dividend/price ratio in the conditional estimates. Assets do not include investment returns. Wald and ΔJ_T joint b tests give the same results, so they are not separately presented.

ment return factor model, producing 0.51 percent RMSE versus 0.46 percent for the investment return model with nonscaled factors and 0.18 percent versus 0.19 percent for the scaled factor model.

In summary, the good behavior of the investment return factor model does not depend on the specific functional form.

VII. Concluding Remarks

The simple investment return model performs surprisingly well. The investment return factors significantly price assets, the model is not rejected, and it is able to explain a wide spread in expected returns,

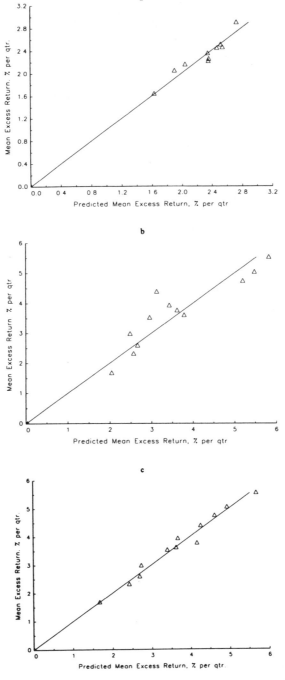

FIG. 8.—Predicted vs. actual mean excess returns, investment growth factor model, first-stage estimates: *a*, unconditional estimates, nonscaled model; *b*, conditional estimates, nonscaled model; *c*, conditional estimates, scaled model.

including managed portfolio returns formed by multiplying returns with instruments. The model performs about as well as two standard finance models, the CAPM and the Chen, Roll, and Ross factor model. The investment return model performs substantially better than the standard consumption-based model and an ad hoc consumption growth factor model. It is robust; an investment *growth* model performs about as well.

The fact that *any* model whose factors are related to economic theory and are based solely on quantity data is even in a position to challenge the empirical success of traditional finance models may be regarded as an encouraging initial success. Since any model can be expressed in terms of its mimicking portfolios and the latter are better measured, models based on quantity data or measures of real risk factors are always at a statistical disadvantage relative to models based on asset returns. And since one can always construct portfolios that perfectly price any set of assets ex post, the difficulty of obtaining a good fit depends entirely on the discipline one imposes in the search for factors.

The scaled factor models typically perform substantially better than the nonscaled factor models. This suggests that time variation in the parameters of asset pricing models, which can be handled by the simple expedient of including scaled factors, is an important ingredient for their empirical success.

A comparison of this paper and Cochrane (1991) with the empirical *q*-theory literature suggests that investment responds to changes in *risk premia* that the empirical finance literature has found to dominate changes in expected returns. Most *q*-theory models specify constant risk premia and try, without much success, to explain changes in investment from changes in risk-free rates. The relative success of the model presented here may help to rehabilitate the *q*-theory view of investment, amended to include substantial changes in risk premia over time.

More generally, macroeconomists are interested in the links between asset returns and fluctuations for the information they can provide about preferences, technologies, and market structures that will be useful in the construction of macroeconomic models. One lesson of these papers is that an adjustment cost (or some wedge between the price of installed and uninstalled capital), currently not included in most real business cycle models, is useful in order to reconcile investment and asset returns.

Appendix

A.   Derivation of Investment Returns from the Production Function

This section derives the investment return from the production technology and shows that the firm's first-order conditions direct the firm to remove

arbitrage opportunities between investment and asset returns. This derivation follows that of Braun (1991); Cochrane (1991) presents a derivation of
the investment return directly from its definition as the marginal extra sale
possible tomorrow from a marginal investment today.

The firm maximizes its present value,

$$\max_{\{i_t\}} E_t \sum_{j=0}^{\infty} m_{t,t+j}(y_{t+j} - i_{t+j} - w_{t+j}l_{t+j}), \qquad (A1)$$

subject to (1) and (2).

In a complete market, m are the contingent claims prices divided by probabilities, so this present value is the firm's time t contingent claim value. If
markets are less than complete, the firm still maximizes (A1), but m is now
an extension of the stochastic discount factor that prices asset returns rather
than *the* stochastic discount factor for the whole economy. The marginal
utility of a nonsatiated owner of the firm who can also trade assets is one
such m.

I derive the first-order condition by varying i_t. Note that $\partial k_{t+j}/\partial i_t = (1 - \delta)^j$. Hence,

$$\frac{\partial y_{t+j}}{\partial i_t} = \frac{\partial y_{t+j}}{\partial k_{t+j}} \frac{\partial k_{t+j}}{\partial i_t} = (1 - \delta)^j [f_k(t + j) - c_k(t + j)].$$

The notation $f_k(t)$ means partial derivative with respect to k, evaluated with
respect to the appropriate arguments at time t; $f_k(t) \equiv \partial f(k_t, l_t)/\partial k_t$. The
first-order condition is then

$$1 + c_i(t) = E_t \sum_{j=1}^{\infty} m_{t,t+j}(1 - \delta)^j [f_k(t + j) - c_k(t + j)]. \qquad (A2)$$

The left-hand side is the relative price of a unit of installed capital versus
output today; the right-hand side is the present value of its benefits.

We desire a model of returns, rather than price and present value. Using
$m_{t,t+j} = m_{t,t+1}m_{t+1,t+j}$, break the right-hand side of (A2) into two pieces:

$$1 + c_i(t) = E_t m_{t,t+1}(1 - \delta)[f_k(t + 1) - c_k(t + 1)]$$

$$+ E_t m_{t,t+1}(1 - \delta) \sum_{j=1}^{\infty} m_{t+1,t+1+j}(1 - \delta)^j$$

$$\times [f_k(t + 1 + j) - c_k(t + 1 + j)].$$

Substituting (A2) at time $t + 1$ for the sum in the right-hand side, we get

$$1 + c_i(t) = E_t[m_{t,t+1}(1 - \delta)[f_k(t + 1) - c_k(t + 1) + 1 + c_i(t + 1)]],$$

$$1 = E_t\left[m_{t,t+1}\frac{(1 - \delta)[1 + f_k(t + 1) + c_i(t + 1) - c_k(t + 1)]}{1 + c_i(t)c}\right]$$

or

$$1 = E_t[m_{t,t+1}r_{t+1}^i],$$

with

$$r_{t+1}^i = \frac{(1 - \delta)[1 + f_k(t + 1) + c_i(t + 1) - c_k(t + 1)]}{1 + c_i(t)c}.$$

For some production technologies it is not possible to summarize the price versus present value relation (A2) in a single-period investment return. For example, if the adjustment cost depends on p lags of investment, then a p-period investment strategy must be considered.

B. Data Description

All asset return data are taken from CRSP. National Income and Product Accounts data and yield data are taken from Citibase. The two investment returns are based on Citibase series GINQ and GIRQ. The stock return series are based on CRSP series EWRETD and VWRETD and the size decile return series DECRET1 . . . DECRET10. The default premium is based on Citibase series FYBAAC–FYAAAC. Quarterly data are obtained by using the last month of the quarter. The dividend/price ratio is based on CRSP EWRETD and EWRETX, the equally weighted portfolio returns with and without dividends. The returns are cumulated for a year to avoid the seasonal in dividends; then d/p = (annual EWRETD/annual EWRETX) − 1. Again, the last monthly observation in each quarter is the quarterly observation.

The investment data are quarterly averages, and the asset return data are point-to-point. As an ad hoc correction for this difference, I averaged monthly asset returns over the quarter to correspond with the investment returns (I thank Campbell Harvey for suggesting this transformation). Thus the second-quarter return is an average of returns from the last day in December to the last day in March, the last day in January to the last day in April, and the last day in February to the last day in May. Instruments for the second-quarter return are all observed at the end of December (i.e., all instruments are lagged twice).

I constructed Chen, Roll, and Ross factors as follows: MP is the growth rate of industrial production. Chen, Roll, and Ross lead this variable by one month to take account of the fact that industrial production (IP) is a monthly average and returns are end-of-month to end-of-month. To make the same adjustment for quarterly data, I average IP growth in a similar way to returns. For example, the second-quarter MP is

$$\text{MP} = \ln[\text{IP(Apr)}\,\text{IP(May)}\,\text{IP(Jun)}] - \ln[\text{IP(Jan)}\,\text{IP(Feb)}\,\text{IP(Mar)}].$$

UI is unexpected inflation and DEI is the change in expected inflation. These variables require an expected inflation series. Chen, Roll, and Ross take their values from Fama and Gibbons (1982). Therefore, I replicated the Fama and Gibbons procedure to extend the data set. Fama and Gibbons start with the Fisher equation

$$E_{t-1}(\pi_t) = TB_{t-1} - E_{t-1}(R_t),$$

where π is Consumer Price Index inflation, TB is the Treasury-Bill rate, r^{tb} is the ex post real rate, and $r_t^{tb} = TB_{t-1} - \pi_t$. They add a univariate time-series model for ex post real rates

$$r_t^{tb} - r_{t-1}^{tb} = u_t + \theta u_{t-1}.$$

Substituting, we get

$$E_{t-1}(\pi_t) = TB_{t-1} - r_{t-1}^{tb} - \theta u_t.$$

To construct this series, I take Fama and Gibbons's value of $\theta = 0.9223$. I start with $u_1 = 0$. Then I construct u_t by

$$r_2^{tb} - r_1^{tb} = u_2,$$

$$r_3^{tb} - r_2^{tb} = u_3 + \theta u_2,$$

and so forth. The expected real return on Treasury bills is then given by

$$E_{t-1} r_t^{tb} = E_{t-2} r_{t-1}^{tb} + (1 - 0.9223) u_{t-1}.$$

References

Braun, Phillip. "Asset Pricing and Capital Investment: Theory and Evidence." Manuscript. Evanston, Ill.: Northwestern Univ., 1991.

Brock, William A. "Asset Prices in a Production Economy." In *The Economics of Information and Uncertainty*, edited by John J. McCall. Chicago: Univ. Chicago Press (for NBER), 1982.

Brown, David P., and Gibbons, Michael R. "A Simple Econometric Approach for Utility-Based Asset Pricing Models." *J. Finance* 40 (June 1985): 359–81.

Campbell, John Y., and Cochrane, John H. "By Force of Habit: A Consumption-Based Explanation of Aggregate Stock Market Behavior." Working Paper no. 4995. Cambridge, Mass.: NBER, January 1995.

Chen, Nai Fu; Roll, Richard; and Ross, Stephen A. "Economic Forces and the Stock Market." *J. Bus.* 59 (July 1986): 383–403.

Cochrane, John H. "The Sensitivity of Tests of the Intertemporal Allocation of Consumption to Near-Rational Alternatives." *A.E.R.* 79 (June 1989): 319–37.

——. "Production-Based Asset Pricing and the Link between Stock Returns and Economic Fluctuations." *J. Finance* 46 (March 1991): 209–37.

Cochrane, John H., and Hansen, Lars Peter. "Asset Pricing Lessons for Macroeconomics." In *NBER Macroeconomics Annual 1992*, edited by Olivier J. Blanchard and Stanley Fischer. Cambridge, Mass.: MIT Press, 1992.

Cox, John C.; Ingersoll, Jonathan E., Jr.; and Ross, Stephen A. "An Intertemporal General Equilibrium Model of Asset Prices." *Econometrica* 53 (March 1985): 363–84.

De Santis, Giorgio. "Volatility Bounds for Stochastic Discount Factors: Tests and Implications from International Stock Returns." Manuscript. Los Angeles: Univ. Southern California, 1992.

Dybvig, Philip H., and Ingersoll, Jonathan E., Jr. "Mean-Variance Theory in Complete Markets." *J. Bus.* 55 (April 1982): 233–51.

Fama, Eugene F., and Gibbons, Michael R. "Inflation, Real Returns and Capital Investment." *J. Monetary Econ.* 9 (May 1982): 297–323.

Fama, Eugene F., and MacBeth, James D. "Risk, Return, and Equilibrium: Empirical Tests." *J.P.E.* 81 (May/June 1973): 607–36.

Ferson, Wayne E., and Foerster, Stephen R. "Finite Sample Properties of the Generalized Method of Moments Tests of Conditional Asset Pricing Models." *J. Financial Econ.* 36 (August 1994): 29–55.

Ferson, Wayne E.; Kandel, Shmuel; and Stambaugh, Robert F. "Tests of Asset Pricing with Time-Varying Expected Risk Premiums and Market Betas." *J. Finance* 42 (June 1987): 201–20.

Gibbons, Michael R.; Ross, Stephen A.; and Shanken, Jay. "A Test of the Efficiency of a Given Portfolio." *Econometrica* 57 (September 1989): 1121–52.

Hansen, Lars Peter. "Large Sample Properties of Generalized Method of Moments Estimators." *Econometrica* 50 (July 1982): 1029–54.

Hansen, Lars Peter; Heaton, John; and Luttmer, Erzo. "Econometric Evaluation of Asset Pricing Models." *Rev. Financial Studies* 8 (Summer 1995): 237–74.

Hansen, Lars Peter, and Jagannathan, Ravi. "Assessing Specification Errors in Stochastic Discount Factor Models." Manuscript. Chicago: Univ. Chicago; Minneapolis: Univ. Minnesota, 1991. (*a*)

———. "Implications of Security Market Data for Models of Dynamic Economies." *J.P.E.* 99 (April 1991): 225–62. (*b*)

Hansen, Lars Peter, and Richard, Scott F. "The Role of Conditioning Information in Deducing Testable Restrictions Implied by Dynamic Asset Pricing Models." *Econometrica* 55 (May 1987): 587–613.

Hansen, Lars Peter, and Singleton, Kenneth J. "Generalized Instrumental Variables Estimation of Nonlinear Rational Expectations Models." *Econometrica* 50 (September 1982): 1269–86.

Harvey, Campbell R. "Time-Varying Conditional Covariances in Tests of Asset Pricing Models." *J. Financial Econ.* 24 (October 1989): 289–317.

Kandel, Shmuel, and Stambaugh, Robert F. "Portfolio Inefficiency and the Cross-Section of Expected Returns." *J. Finance* 50 (March 1995): 157–84.

Knez, Peter J. "Pricing Money Market Securities with Stochastic Discount Factors." Manuscript. Madison: Univ. Wisconsin, 1991.

Luttmer, Erzo. "Implications of Asset Market Data for Economies with Transaction Costs." Manuscript. Evanston, Ill.: Northwestern Univ., 1992.

Newey, Whitney K., and West, Kenneth D. "Hypothesis Testing with Efficient Method of Moments Estimation." *Internat. Econ. Rev.* 28 (October 1987): 777–87. (*a*)

———. "A Simple, Positive Semi-definite, Heteroskedasticity and Autocorrelation Consistent Covariance Matrix." *Econometrica* 55 (May 1987): 703–8. (*b*)

Ross, Stephen A. "A Simple Approach to the Valuation of Risky Streams." *J. Bus.* 51 (July 1978): 453–75.

Shanken, Jay. "Intertemporal Asset Pricing: An Empirical Investigation." *J. Econometrics* 45 (July–August 1990): 99–120.

Sharathchandra, Gopalakrishnan. "Asset Pricing and Production: Theory and Empirical Tests." Manuscript. Dallas: Southern Methodist Univ., Cox School Bus., Finance Dept., 1991.

Snow, Karl N. "Diagnosing Asset Pricing Models Using the Distribution of Asset Returns." *J. Finance* 46 (July 1991): 955–83.

[18]

THE JOURNAL OF FINANCE • VOL. LIV, NO. 4 • AUGUST 1999

A Critique of the Stochastic Discount Factor Methodology

RAYMOND KAN and GUOFU ZHOU*

ABSTRACT

In this paper, we point out that the widely used stochastic discount factor (SDF) methodology ignores a fully specified model for asset returns. As a result, it suffers from two potential problems when asset returns follow a linear factor model. The first problem is that the risk premium estimate from the SDF methodology is unreliable. The second problem is that the specification test under the SDF methodology has very low power in detecting misspecified models. Traditional methodologies typically incorporate a fully specified model for asset returns, and they can perform substantially better than the SDF methodology.

ASSET PRICING THEORIES, such as those of Sharpe (1964), Lintner (1965), Black (1972), Merton (1973), Ross (1976), and Breeden (1979), show that the expected return on a financial asset is a linear function of its covariances (or betas) with some systematic risk factors. This implication has been tested extensively in the finance literature by the so-called "traditional methodologies." In the traditional methodologies, a data-generating process is first proposed for the returns, and then the restrictions imposed by an asset pricing model are tested as parametric constraints on the return-generating process. The approach taken by the traditional methodologies has a potential problem, which is that when the proposed return-generating process is misspecified the test results could be misleading. Therefore, in applying the traditional methodologies, researchers typically have to justify that the proposed data-generating process provides a good description of the returns. For example, when the proposed return-generating process is a factor model, one would like the model to have high R^2 in explaining the returns on the test assets, especially when the test assets are well-diversified portfolios.

As many of the earlier theories are special cases of the stochastic discount factor (SDF) model, recent empirical asset pricing studies have been focused on testing the pricing restrictions in terms of the SDF model, rather

*Kan is from the University of Toronto, Zhou is from Washington University in St. Louis. We thank Kerry Back, Philip Dybvig, Heber Farnsworth, Wayne Ferson, Campbell Harvey, Roger Huang, Ravi Jagannathan, Mark Loewenstein, Deborah Lucas, Akhtar Siddique, Hans Stoll, Zhenyu Wang, Chu Zhang, seminar participants at the National Central University of Taiwan, the University of Texas at Dallas, Washington University in St. Louis, and participants at the 1999 American Finance Association Meetings in New York for their helpful discussions and comments. Kan gratefully acknowledges financial support from the Social Sciences and Humanities Research Council of Canada.

than on the traditional risk measures such as the beta and the Sharpe ratio. One of the most prominent papers in this line of research is Cochrane (1996), where the SDF methodology is fully explained. The formulation typically estimates the parameters and tests the pricing implications *without a fully specified model* of how the asset returns are generated in the economy. On the one hand, this appears very general and requires fewer assumptions and parameters than the traditional methodologies. On the other hand, it seems counterintuitive that one can be sure the pricing restrictions are true even if one knows little about the dynamics of the returns—that is, without a fully specified model (either parametric or nonparametric) of the returns.

This paper shows that if asset returns are generated by a linear factor model, then by ignoring the full dynamics of asset returns, as is currently done in empirical studies using the SDF methodology, two potential problems arise. The first problem is that the accuracy of the parameter estimation can be poor: the standard error of the estimated risk premium is often more than 40 times greater than that of the traditional methodologies, which should make one extra cautious when applying the SDF methodology. The second problem with the SDF methodology is that its specification test has very low power against misspecified models. With the usual sample size that we encounter in empirical studies, our simulation evidence suggests that the SDF methodology is not very reliable in detecting even gross misspecifications in an asset pricing model, especially when the proposed factors are not highly correlated with the returns.

The rest of the paper is organized as follows. The next section presents the traditional beta pricing model and the SDF model, and the empirical methodologies that are typically used to estimate and test such models. Though these are standard in the literature, the purpose here is to introduce notations and to facilitate later discussions. We also provide the intuition why the SDF methodology may not perform well when there is a lack of a fully specified model for the asset returns. In Sections II and III, we use asymptotic theory and Monte Carlo simulations to compare the performance of the traditional and SDF methodologies. The conclusions are in the final section.

I. Traditional and SDF Methodologies

A. Tests of the Traditional Beta Pricing Model

In order to make the results more easily understood, we present them in the simplest form. Let r_t be the excess return (in excess of the risk-free rate) on N risky assets at time t. Traditional methodologies begin by proposing a return-generating process for the excess returns, typically one that provides good explanatory power on the excess returns. For example, one may propose that excess returns are generated by a one-factor model

$$r_t = \alpha + \beta f_t + \varepsilon_t, \tag{1}$$

A Critique of the Stochastic Discount Factor Methodology   1223

where f_t is the realized value of a systematic risk factor at time t, $\boldsymbol{\varepsilon}_t$ is the idiosyncratic risk of the assets with $E[\boldsymbol{\varepsilon}_t|f_t, \boldsymbol{\Phi}_{t-1}] = \mathbf{0}_N$ and $\text{Var}[\boldsymbol{\varepsilon}_t] = \boldsymbol{\Sigma}$, where $\mathbf{0}_N$ is an N-vector of zeros, $\boldsymbol{\Phi}_{t-1}$ is the information set at $t-1$, and $\boldsymbol{\beta} = \text{Cov}[\boldsymbol{r}_t, f_t|\boldsymbol{\Phi}_{t-1}]/\text{Var}[f_t|\boldsymbol{\Phi}_{t-1}]$ is the factor loadings of the returns with respect to the common factor. Since only unexpected shocks matter for unexpected returns, f_t can be modeled as a martingale difference sequence; that is, $E[f_t|\boldsymbol{\Phi}_{t-1}] = 0$. Under these assumptions, $\boldsymbol{\alpha} = E[\boldsymbol{r}_t|\boldsymbol{\Phi}_{t-1}]$ is the expected excess returns on the N assets. In the rest of the paper, the trivial case $\boldsymbol{\alpha} = \mathbf{0}_N$ is precluded. In general, $\boldsymbol{\alpha}$ and $\boldsymbol{\beta}$ can be functions of information variables at $t-1$, but for the purpose of simplifying technical details and focusing on the main point of this paper, we assume they are constants. Nevertheless, we do not assume $\text{Var}[\boldsymbol{\varepsilon}_t|\boldsymbol{\Phi}_{t-1}, f_t] = \boldsymbol{\Sigma}$, so conditional heteroskedasticity in $\boldsymbol{\varepsilon}_t$ is allowed in our setup.

A beta pricing model, in the exact form, suggests that the expected excess return of an asset is a linear function of its betas with respect to the systematic factors. In our one-factor case, the beta pricing model suggests

$$\boldsymbol{\alpha} = \boldsymbol{\beta}\lambda, \tag{2}$$

where λ is the risk premium. This clearly imposes a testable restriction on the parameters of the return-generating process in equation (1). Traditional tests of beta pricing model are basically done by carrying out various statistical tests of this restriction.

There are many alternatives to estimate the risk premium λ and test the beta pricing model. We describe two representative approaches here. If one is willing to make distributional assumptions on $\boldsymbol{\varepsilon}_t$, one can use the maximum likelihood approach. A popular choice is to assume conditional on f_t, $\boldsymbol{\varepsilon}_t \sim N(\mathbf{0}_N, \boldsymbol{\Sigma})$. Following Zhou (1991, 1995), we define $\boldsymbol{f} = [f_1, f_2, \ldots, f_T]'$, $\boldsymbol{X} = [\mathbf{1}_T, \boldsymbol{f}]$, $\boldsymbol{Y} = [\boldsymbol{r}_1, \boldsymbol{r}_2, \ldots, \boldsymbol{r}_T]'$, where T is the number of time series observations, and $\mathbf{1}_T$ is a T-vector of ones. Let $\xi_1 \geq \xi_2 > 0$ be the two eigenvalues of

$$\boldsymbol{A} = (\boldsymbol{X}'\boldsymbol{X})^{-1}(\boldsymbol{X}'\boldsymbol{Y})(\boldsymbol{Y}'\boldsymbol{Y})^{-1}(\boldsymbol{Y}'\boldsymbol{X}). \tag{3}$$

Under the normality assumption, the maximum likelihood estimator of λ is given by

$$\hat{\lambda}_{ML} = \frac{a_{12}}{\xi_1 - a_{11}}, \tag{4}$$

where a_{ij} are the (i,j)th elements of $\boldsymbol{A}$. The likelihood ratio test (with the Bartlett correction) of equation (2) is[1]

$$\text{LRT} = -\left(T - \frac{N+3}{2}\right)\log(1 - \xi_2) \overset{A}{\sim} \chi^2_{N-1}, \tag{5}$$

where $\overset{A}{\sim}$ means an asymptotic distribution.

---

[1] Based on simulation evidence, Zhou (1995) shows that the Bartlett correction can improve the small sample properties of the likelihood ratio test. The exact small sample distribution of the likelihood ratio test is also available from Zhou (1991, 1995).

If one does not wish to make any strong distributional assumptions on ε_t, then an alternative approach is to use the generalized method of moments (GMM) of Hansen (1982) to estimate the parameters and test the beta pricing model. Following, for example, MacKinlay and Richardson (1991) or Harvey and Zhou (1993), the GMM test of equation (2) uses the following moment conditions:

$$E[\boldsymbol{\varepsilon}_t] = E[\boldsymbol{r}_t - \boldsymbol{\alpha} - \boldsymbol{\beta}f_t] = E[\boldsymbol{r}_t - \boldsymbol{\beta}\lambda - \boldsymbol{\beta}f_t] = \boldsymbol{0}_N, \tag{6}$$

$$E[\boldsymbol{\varepsilon}_t f_t] = E[(\boldsymbol{r}_t - \boldsymbol{\alpha} - \boldsymbol{\beta}f_t) f_t] = E[(\boldsymbol{r}_t - \boldsymbol{\beta}\lambda - \boldsymbol{\beta}f_t)f_t] = \boldsymbol{0}_N. \tag{7}$$

To apply the GMM methodology, we define the sample moments as

$$\boldsymbol{g}_{1T}(\lambda,\boldsymbol{\beta}) = \frac{1}{T}\sum_{t=1}^{T}[\boldsymbol{z}_t \otimes (\boldsymbol{r}_t - \boldsymbol{\beta}\lambda - \boldsymbol{\beta}f_t)], \tag{8}$$

where $\boldsymbol{z}_t = [1, f_t]'$. We assume f_t and $\boldsymbol{\varepsilon}_t$ are jointly stationary and ergodic with finite fourth moments, and under the true parameters,

$$\sqrt{T}\boldsymbol{g}_{1T} \stackrel{A}{\sim} N(\boldsymbol{0}_{2N}, \boldsymbol{S}_1), \tag{9}$$

where $\boldsymbol{S}_1$ is a $2N \times 2N$ positive definite constant matrix. This condition is much weaker than those assumed in other methods of testing asset pricing models. It allows for a variety of forms of autocorrelation and heteroskedasticity in $\boldsymbol{z}_t \otimes \boldsymbol{\varepsilon}_t$. In the GMM methodology, the estimators of the true parameters λ and $\boldsymbol{\beta}$ of the one-factor model, $\hat{\lambda}^*$ and $\hat{\boldsymbol{\beta}}^*$, are given by the solution of the following minimization problem,

$$\min_{\lambda,\boldsymbol{\beta}} \boldsymbol{g}_{1T}(\lambda,\boldsymbol{\beta})'\boldsymbol{W}_{1T}\boldsymbol{g}_{1T}(\lambda,\boldsymbol{\beta}), \tag{10}$$

where $\boldsymbol{W}_{1T}$ is a (possibly stochastic) $2N \times 2N$ positive definite weighting matrix with a limit $\boldsymbol{W}$ that is positive definite and nonstochastic. The standard approach is to choose an optimal weighting matrix equal to a consistent estimate of $\boldsymbol{S}_1^{-1}$.[2] Although there are $N + 1$ parameters in the beta pricing model and the optimization problem is a nonlinear one, it does not present as a serious problem to the estimation because, conditional on a given value of λ, the objective function is linear in $\boldsymbol{\beta}$ and the minimization problem can

---

[2] When the optimal weighting matrix depends on parameters, an iterative method has to be used. In the first round, a positive definite matrix, say, the identity matrix, is used as the weighting matrix to estimate the parameters. In the second round, the model is reestimated using the optimal weighting matrix based on the estimated parameters from the first round.

A Critique of the Stochastic Discount Factor Methodology   1225

be solved analytically. As a result, the estimation problem can be written as a function of λ alone and a simple line search can be used to find the optimal $\hat{\lambda}^*$.[3]

A test of the traditional beta pricing model $\alpha = \beta\lambda$ can be carried out by using Hansen's (1982) overidentification test. Since we have $2N$ moment conditions and only $N + 1$ parameters, there are $N - 1$ overidentification conditions, and hence

$$J_1 \equiv Tg_{1T}(\hat{\lambda}^*,\hat{\beta}^*)'W_{1T}g_{1T}(\hat{\lambda}^*,\hat{\beta}^*) \overset{A}{\sim} \chi^2_{N-1}, \tag{11}$$

where W_{1T} is a consistent estimate of the optimal weighting matrix.[4] However, as Cochrane (1996) and Jagannathan and Wang (1996) suggest, it is sometimes desirable, for good economic reasons, to use a nonoptimal weighting matrix. In this case, J_1 will no longer have a simple chi-square distribution, but rather will be a weighted sum of chi-square distributions. Zhou (1994) provides a simple chi-square GMM test for an arbitrary weighting matrix, which can be used to bypass the difficulty of having to calculate a weighted sum of chi-square distributions. A numerically identical test is also proposed by Cochrane (1996). But an alternative optimal chi-square test can be obtained from the scoring algorithm, as presented by Newey (1985) and analyzed by Zhou (1994).

B. SDF Model

As discussed by Cochrane (1996), the beta pricing model is a special case of the SDF model. Under the SDF model, there exists a random variable m_t, the stochastic discount factor, such that

$$E[r_t m_t] = 0_N. \tag{12}$$

When the exact one-factor asset pricing model in equation (2) holds, the stochastic discount factor is given by

$$m_t = \delta_0 - \delta_1 f_t \tag{13}$$

for some constants δ_0 and δ_1. As an econometric model, the parameters in equation (13) are not uniquely defined. If (δ_0,δ_1) satisfies the equation, so does any multiplier of it. Therefore, it is common to normalize the parameters by writing

$$E[r_t(1 - f_t \lambda)] = 0_N, \tag{14}$$

---

[3] Details of the optimization are available upon request. For some special weighting matrices, Zhou (1994) even obtains an analytical solution to this optimization problem.

[4] Another way of testing $\alpha = \beta\lambda$ is to estimate α and β in equations (6) and (7) as a fully specified model and test the nonlinear restriction on the parameters using a Wald test.

where $\lambda = \delta_1/\delta_0$. If Var$[f_t] = 1$, then $\boldsymbol{\beta} = E[\boldsymbol{r}_t f_t]$ and the λ in equation (14) is exactly the same as the λ in equation (2). For ease of comparison, we assume Var$[f_t] = 1$ in the following discussion.[5]

Intuitively, equation (14) only relates m_t to the asset returns in terms of covariances, not how they impact on each other. In theory, equation (14) is well established; there are no problems with the asset pricing restrictions at all. It is the empirical studies of equation (14) that give rise to the potential problems pointed out earlier. Current empirical studies in testing the SDF model typically focus on testing equation (14) alone without specifying the data-generating process in equation (1) that $\boldsymbol{r}_t$ follows. We argue in this paper that such a practice leads to serious problems.

Before we move on to discuss the estimation and test methodology of the SDF model, we point out that although equation (14) holds when we have the true systematic factor f_t, there are other factors that also allow equation (14) to hold exactly. We consider two classes of factors that have this property.

1. *Noisy factor.* Suppose we define

$$g_t = \frac{f_t + n_t}{\sqrt{1 + \sigma_n^2}}, \tag{15}$$

where n_t is a pure measurement error with mean zero and finite variance σ_n^2 and it is uncorrelated with f_t and $\boldsymbol{\varepsilon}_t$.[6] By specifying g_t as the factor in the SDF model, then for

$$\lambda_g = \lambda\sqrt{1 + \sigma_n^2}, \tag{16}$$

we have

$$E[\boldsymbol{r}_t(1 - g_t \lambda_g)] = E\left[\boldsymbol{r}_t\left(1 - \frac{f_t}{\sqrt{1 + \sigma_n^2}}\lambda_g\right)\right] - \frac{E[\boldsymbol{r}_t n_t]\lambda_g}{\sqrt{1 + \sigma_n^2}}$$

$$= E[\boldsymbol{r}_t(1 - f_t \lambda)] = \boldsymbol{0}_N. \tag{17}$$

Therefore, the noisy factor g_t does the same job as the true factor f_t in pricing the assets. That pure measurement error does not affect the linear pricing relation is well known in the literature. It is discussed, for example, in Breeden, Gibbons, and Litzenberger (1989), and Co-

---

[5] In practice, standardizing macroeconomic factors is a nontrivial issue. The correct approach is to explicitly model their conditional distribution as in Cochrane (1996) and He et al. (1996), and include their estimation as part of the moment conditions. We ignore this issue here in order not to distract from the discussion of the main issue.

[6] The limiting case of $\sigma_n^2 \to \infty$ (i.e., $g_t = n_t/\sigma_n$) is the case that g_t is a useless factor, which is studied by Kan and Zhang (1999a, 1999b).

A Critique of the Stochastic Discount Factor Methodology   1227

chrane (1996). Although the linear pricing relation is retained, the risk premium for the noisy factor is higher than that for the true factor. In fact, from equation (16), we can see that the noisier the factor, the higher is its risk premium. One may like to think that when σ_n^2 is large, the SDF model that uses the noisy factor is more likely to be rejected in finite samples than the one with the true factor. We will show with simulation that this view cannot be justified.

2. *Unsystematic factor.* We define

$$h_t = \frac{\boldsymbol{\beta}'\boldsymbol{\Sigma}^{-1}\boldsymbol{\varepsilon}_t}{\sqrt{\boldsymbol{\beta}'\boldsymbol{\Sigma}^{-1}\boldsymbol{\beta}}}, \tag{18}$$

and h_t is a linear combination of $\boldsymbol{\varepsilon}_t$. Therefore, h_t has mean zero and it is uncorrelated with f_t. By specifying h_t as the factor in the SDF model, then for

$$\lambda_h = \lambda\sqrt{\boldsymbol{\beta}'\boldsymbol{\Sigma}^{-1}\boldsymbol{\beta}} \tag{19}$$

we have

$$E[r_t(1 - h_t\lambda_h)] = E[r_t] - \frac{E[\boldsymbol{\varepsilon}_t\boldsymbol{\varepsilon}_t']\boldsymbol{\Sigma}^{-1}\boldsymbol{\beta}}{\sqrt{\boldsymbol{\beta}'\boldsymbol{\Sigma}^{-1}\boldsymbol{\beta}}}\lambda_h$$

$$= \boldsymbol{\alpha} - \boldsymbol{\beta}\lambda = \mathbf{0}_N, \tag{20}$$

and h_t prices the N assets perfectly. Although h_t is an unsystematic factor by construction, we will still be tempted to conclude that it is "priced."

The fact that these two classes of "wrong" factors can satisfy equation (14) suggests the danger of attaching economic meaning to the test outcome of an SDF model. When one specifies a set of macroeconomic factors and finds that it satisfies equation (14), one really cannot tell whether it is the true factor f_t, the noisy factor g_t, or if it is just an unsystematic factor h_t. It should be pointed out that if g_t or h_t is proposed as the factor in the data-generating process, it is also difficult for the traditional methodologies to detect these "wrong" factors. However, because g_t and h_t typically do not possess good explanatory power on the returns of the test assets (especially when σ_n^2 is large and the test assets are well-diversified portfolios), they are less likely to be included as the systematic factors under the traditional methodologies. In contrast, the SDF methodology does not pay any attention to the return-generating process, hence g_t and h_t could easily be proposed and be mistaken as the "true" systematic factors.

Recognizing that there are countless SDFs that represent countless asset pricing models for a given set of asset returns, Hansen and Jagannathan (1991) solve explicitly the SDF that has the minimum variance among all the SDFs. Hansen and Jagannathan (1997) further show how to use SDFs to assess specification errors of asset pricing models. What we have shown here is that there are in fact many SDFs for a given linear factor model. Therefore, explicitly constructed "wrong" factors can potentially help to explain the failure of an asset pricing model. This highlights the danger of using factors in the SDF framework without a careful examination of the explanatory power of the factors.

C. GMM Estimation and Test of SDF Models

In estimating parameters and testing pricing restrictions of equation (14), the GMM is used almost exclusively. For illustrative purposes, we assume, as we did earlier for the traditional methodologies, that the model is estimated and tested without using the information/instrumental variables at $t-1$. The test of this simple form amounts to the so-called "unconditional test of the unconditional model" defined in Cochrane (1996). Let $\boldsymbol{u}_t = \boldsymbol{r}_t(1 - f_t\lambda)$ and $\boldsymbol{g}_{2T} = (1/T)\sum_{t=1}^{T}\boldsymbol{u}_t$. We assume under the true parameter that

$$\sqrt{T}\boldsymbol{g}_{2T} \overset{A}{\sim} N(\boldsymbol{0}_N, \boldsymbol{S}_2) \tag{21}$$

for some positive definite constant matrix $\boldsymbol{S}_2$. The true parameter λ is estimated by

$$\hat{\lambda} = \operatorname{argmin}_\lambda \boldsymbol{g}_{2T}(\lambda)'\boldsymbol{W}_{2T}\boldsymbol{g}_{2T}(\lambda), \tag{22}$$

where $\boldsymbol{W}_{2T}$ is typically a consistent estimate of $\boldsymbol{S}_2^{-1}$. The GMM estimation of the SDF model is very simple to implement because there is only one parameter, λ, to be estimated, and it can be analytically obtained as

$$\hat{\lambda} = (\boldsymbol{D}_{2T}'\boldsymbol{W}_{2T}\boldsymbol{D}_{2T})^{-1}(\boldsymbol{D}_{2T}'\boldsymbol{W}_{2T}\bar{\boldsymbol{r}}_T), \tag{23}$$

where $\boldsymbol{D}_{2T} = (1/T)\sum_{t=1}^{T}\boldsymbol{r}_t f_t$ and $\bar{\boldsymbol{r}}_T = (1/T)\sum_{t=1}^{T}\boldsymbol{r}_t$.

A test of the SDF model in equation (14) is usually carried out by using Hansen's (1982) overidentification test. Since we have N moment conditions and only one parameter, there are $N-1$ overidentification conditions; hence

$$J_2 \equiv T\boldsymbol{g}_{2T}(\hat{\lambda})'\boldsymbol{W}_{2T}\boldsymbol{g}_{2T}(\hat{\lambda}) \overset{A}{\sim} \chi_{N-1}^2, \tag{24}$$

when $\boldsymbol{W}_{2T}$ is a consistent estimate of the optimal weighting matrix $\boldsymbol{S}_2^{-1}$.

Therefore, if the beta pricing model is correct, both J_1 in equation (11) and J_2 have an asymptotic chi-square distribution and there are no strong reasons to prefer one test over the other. However, in finite samples, their per-

A Critique of the Stochastic Discount Factor Methodology   1229

formance could differ. More importantly, when the model is misspecified, J_1 and J_2 could have very different power. We study these issues by simulation in Section III.

Although the estimation problem of the SDF methodology is very simple, ignoring the full dynamics of asset returns introduces serious problems. Intuitively, equation (14) is a restriction on part of the first and second moments between the asset returns and the factor. Testing equation (14) alone without using a fully specified model amounts to ignoring many other first and second moments entirely. As a result, it is not surprising that the estimation error of λ can be substantially large. It is also not surprising that a tested factor can be important in equation (14), but in fact may have little to do with the returns. This is the fundamental reason that causes the problems emphasized by this paper. In the following sections, we provide a comparison of the traditional methodologies with the SDF methodology in terms of the estimation accuracy of risk premium, and in terms of the size and the power of their tests of the asset pricing model.

II. Estimation Accuracy of Risk Premium

In this section, we demonstrate in two ways that there can be substantial loss of efficiency in estimating λ by using the SDF methodology. First, we provide theoretical results to show that the asymptotic variance of the estimated λ in the SDF methodology is greater than the variances of the traditional methodologies. Second, we provide Monte Carlo simulations to further illustrate that the standard error of the estimated λ in the SDF methodology is indeed very large (in small samples), and may not be reliable in applications. In contrast, the estimated λ for the traditional methodologies is very accurate even in small samples, making it better suited for estimating risk premia.

The consistency of $\hat{\lambda}_{ML}$, $\hat{\lambda}^*$, and $\hat{\lambda}$ is well known; that is, as sample size T increases, they all approach the true parameter λ. At a given finite sample size T, however, there will be an estimation error. In assessing the accuracy of $\hat{\lambda}$ in the SDF methodology with that of $\hat{\lambda}_{ML}$ and $\hat{\lambda}^*$ in the traditional methodologies, we can compare their asymptotic variances. The following proposition shows that $\hat{\lambda}^*$ is asymptotically more accurate than $\hat{\lambda}$ and it has the same efficiency as $\hat{\lambda}_{ML}$ under the normality assumption.[7]

PROPOSITION 1: *Suppose f_t is the true factor and it has a continuous distribution. We have*

$$\text{Avar}[\hat{\lambda}^*] < \text{Avar}[\hat{\lambda}].\qquad(25)$$

---

[7] Proposition 1 can be extended to the multifactor case to show that the vector of estimated risk premium is more accurate under the traditional methodologies than the SDF methodology. Results are available upon request.

For the case that ε_t has a multivariate normal distribution conditional on f_t, we have

$$\text{Avar}[\hat{\lambda}_{ML}] = \text{Avar}[\hat{\lambda}^*] = \frac{1 + \lambda^2}{\beta' \Sigma^{-1} \beta}. \tag{26}$$

Proposition 1 suggests that regardless of the distribution that ε_t follows, with or without conditional heteroskedasticity, traditional methodologies that incorporate the return-generating process will always provide an estimated risk premium that is asymptotically more efficient than that from the SDF methodology. One may like to think that the reason we achieve higher accuracy in $\hat{\lambda}^*$ is that we use more moment conditions than the SDF methodology. However, this is not the main reason for the improvement because, although we do have more moment conditions in the traditional methodology, we also have more parameters to estimate.

There are two main reasons why the full GMM estimator $\hat{\lambda}^*$ in the traditional methodology is more efficient than the SDF estimator $\hat{\lambda}$. The first reason is that the full GMM uses $\hat{\beta}^*$ to explain average excess returns, whereas the SDF methodology uses $D_{2T} = (1/T)\sum_{t=1}^{T} r_t f_t$ to explain average excess returns. Both $\hat{\beta}^*$ and D_{2T} are consistent estimates of β when $\text{Var}[f_t] = 1$; however, in general, $\hat{\beta}^*$ is a more accurate estimator of β than D_{2T}. For example, under the multivariate normality assumption on f_t and ε_t, it can be shown that $\text{Avar}[D_{2T}] = \Sigma + \beta\beta'$, which is much larger than

$$\text{Avar}[\hat{\beta}^*] = \frac{1}{1 + \lambda^2}\left[\Sigma + \frac{\lambda^2 \beta\beta'}{\beta' \Sigma^{-1} \beta}\right] < \Sigma.^8$$

In the traditional methodology, the moment conditions in equation (7) and the restriction $\alpha = \beta\lambda$ allow us to obtain an estimate of β with high degree of accuracy. In contrast, the SDF methodology abandons the more accurate beta estimation and only relates the average returns to the average covariances.

The second reason the full GMM estimator $\hat{\lambda}^*$ in the traditional methodology is more efficient than the SDF estimator $\hat{\lambda}$ is that the realized return is a very noisy measure of expected return. The traditional methodology makes use of the factor structure of the return-generating process by taking away the systematic component βf_t from r_t in the moment conditions. When βf_t accounts for a significant portion of the variations of r_t, then $r_t - \beta f_t$ is

---

[8] The expression for $\text{Avar}[\hat{\beta}^*]$ can be obtained from the proof of Proposition 1. The inequality follows because

$$\frac{1}{1 + \lambda^2}\left[\Sigma + \frac{\lambda^2 \beta\beta'}{\beta' \Sigma^{-1} \beta}\right] = \Sigma - \frac{\lambda^2}{1 + \lambda^2}\Sigma^{1/2}[I_N - \Sigma^{-1/2}\beta(\beta'\Sigma^{-1}\beta)^{-1}\beta'\Sigma^{-1/2}]\Sigma^{1/2}$$

and the second term is a positive semidefinite matrix.

a much less noisy measure of expected return than r_t. The SDF methodology, however, does not incorporate the return-generating process in its moment conditions and only relates realized excess returns r_t to realized covariance $r_t f_t$. When both of these two measures are very noisy, it is not surprising that the SDF methodology does not deliver a very accurate estimate of the risk premium.

The above analysis shows that the traditional methodology, which utilizes the fully specified asset return model, helps to substantially improve the estimation accuracy of λ. As a result, it may be tempting to estimate λ by using all of the moment conditions, those of the traditional ones in equations (6) and (7), and those of the SDF ones in equation (14). It turns out that there is some overlap between these moment conditions. Out of the $3N$ moment conditions, $N - 1$ of them are redundant. For example, if we know ε_t, $\varepsilon_t f_t$, and $u_{1t} = r_{1t}(1 - f_t \lambda)$ where $\beta_1 \neq 0$, then we can obtain the other elements of u_t by using the relation

$$\varepsilon_{it} - \lambda(\varepsilon_{it} f_t) + \frac{\beta_i}{\beta_1}[u_{1t} - \varepsilon_{1t} + \lambda(\varepsilon_{1t} f_t)]$$

$$= [r_{it} - \beta_i(\lambda + f_t)](1 - f_t \lambda) + \frac{\beta_i}{\beta_1}\beta_1(\lambda + f_t)(1 - f_t \lambda)$$

$$= r_{it}(1 - f_t \lambda)$$

$$= u_{it}, \quad \text{for } i = 2, \ldots, N. \tag{27}$$

Therefore, one can use at most $2N + 1$ moment conditions to estimate λ. Denote λ^{**} and $\boldsymbol{\beta}^{**}$ as the estimator of λ and $\boldsymbol{\beta}$ using any $2N + 1$ of the combined $3N$ moment conditions. The following proposition suggests that once the moment conditions in the traditional methodology are used, the additional one from the SDF model does not help to improve the accuracy of the estimation.

PROPOSITION 2: *Suppose f_t is the true factor. We have*

$$\text{Avar}\begin{bmatrix} \hat{\lambda}^* \\ \hat{\boldsymbol{\beta}}^* \end{bmatrix} = \text{Avar}\begin{bmatrix} \hat{\lambda}^{**} \\ \hat{\boldsymbol{\beta}}^{**} \end{bmatrix}. \tag{28}$$

Note that Proposition 2 does not suggest that any $2N$ out of the combined $3N$ moment conditions will do the same job as the traditional methodology. For example, if we combine the N moment conditions in equation (6) (or the N moment conditions in equation (7)) with the N moment conditions in equation (14) of the SDF methodology to estimate λ, it can be shown that the asymptotic variance of the estimated λ using these $2N$ moment conditions is still the same as that of $\hat{\lambda}$ from the SDF methodology. Therefore, it is important to choose the proper set of moment conditions to obtain a good estimate of λ. Proposition 2 suggests the moment conditions used by the traditional methodology are the best and they are sufficient to learn almost everything about the parameters. Adding the SDF moment conditions into the traditional ones provides only redundant information.[9]

Although Proposition 1 suggests that the estimated risk premium in the traditional methodologies is asymptotically more accurate than that of the SDF methodology, it does not tell us the magnitude of improvement, nor does it tell us whether this result holds in finite samples. We address these issues by simulation. The setup of our simulation experiment is as follows. In our simulation, we generate excess returns on 10 assets using a one-factor model. The factor is generated independently from a standard normal distribution and it is designed to capture the behavior of the standardized excess return on the value-weighted market portfolio of the NYSE; that is,

$$f_t = \frac{r_{mt} - E[r_{mt}]}{\sigma_m} \sim N(0,1), \tag{29}$$

where r_{mt} is the excess return on the market portfolio and σ_m is its standard deviation. The betas of the 10 assets are set to equal the sample betas of the 10 size-ranked portfolios of the NYSE with respect to f_t, estimated using monthly returns from January 1926 to December 1997. The true risk premium is chosen to make the expected excess returns close to the average excess returns of the 10 size portfolios over the sample period; that is,

$$\lambda = \text{argmin}_\lambda (\bar{r} - \boldsymbol{\beta}\lambda)'(\bar{r} - \boldsymbol{\beta}\lambda), \tag{30}$$

where $\bar{r}$ and $\boldsymbol{\beta}$ are the average returns and sample betas of the 10 size-ranked portfolios. Finally, the model disturbances are independently generated from a multivariate normal distribution

$$\boldsymbol{\varepsilon}_t \sim N(\mathbf{0}_N, \boldsymbol{\Sigma}), \tag{31}$$

where $\boldsymbol{\Sigma}$ is chosen to be the sample covariance matrix of the market model residuals of the 10 size-ranked portfolios. In Table I, Panel A, we present the parameters $\boldsymbol{\alpha}$, $\boldsymbol{\beta}$, and λ of the 10 assets we use in our simulation. Note that the value we choose for λ (0.1373) is very close to the sample Sharpe ratio for the value-weighted market portfolio of the NYSE, which is equal to 0.1248 for the period January 1926 to December 1997.[10]

We generate returns from this one-factor model for different lengths of time series and apply the traditional and the SDF methodologies to estimate the risk premium λ. In Panel B of Table I, we present a summary of the

---

[9] Similar to Proposition 1, Proposition 2 continues to hold for the multifactor case. When there are k-factors, only k of the SDF moment conditions can be added to the traditional moment conditions, and they do not improve the estimation accuracy of the risk premium and the betas. Results are available upon request.

[10] Under our definition of f_t, λ is equal to the Sharpe ratio of the market portfolio if the CAPM holds.

A Critique of the Stochastic Discount Factor Methodology 1233

estimation results in 10,000 simulations. For the traditional methodologies, we report the average and standard deviation of the estimated risk premium using the maximum likelihood approach and the GMM approach.[11] Both the maximum likelihood approach and the GMM approach that uses the traditional moment conditions produce very reliable estimates of risk premium. Their estimated risk premia are almost unbiased and they are tightly distributed around the true λ. Although Proposition 1 suggests that under normality assumption on $\boldsymbol{\varepsilon}_t$, we have $\text{Avar}[\hat{\lambda}_{ML}] = \text{Avar}[\hat{\lambda}^*]$, the maximum likelihood estimator is better behaved than the full GMM estimator when the sample size T is small.

The last two columns of Panel B report the average and standard deviation of $\hat{\lambda}$, the estimated risk premium from the SDF methodology. The difference between the performance of the estimation risk premium in the SDF and the traditional methodologies is striking. The estimated risk premium using the SDF methodology is biased and volatile. For example, when $T = 120$, the average $\hat{\lambda}$ in our 10,000 simulations is 0.1497, quite far from the true value of $\lambda = 0.1373$. Furthermore, the standard deviation of $\hat{\lambda}$ is 0.1049, so the estimated risk premium from the SDF methodology could easily be negative. Although the bias and the standard deviation of $\hat{\lambda}$ reduce as T increases, $\hat{\lambda}$ is still volatile for T as large as 720. On average, the standard deviation of the estimated risk premium under the SDF methodology is more than 40 times larger than that of the traditional methodologies. Therefore, for the purpose of estimating risk premium, the traditional methodologies are much better suited for the job than the SDF methodology.

Before we move on to discuss the size and power of the tests in the traditional and the SDF methodologies, we should note that the excess returns in our simulation experiment for Panel B are generated in a way that is most favorable to the maximum likelihood approach. When $\boldsymbol{\varepsilon}_t$ is not normally distributed or its distribution is unknown, the maximum likelihood approach is difficult to apply. However, the results based on the GMM approach remain fairly robust to the distributional assumption on $\boldsymbol{\varepsilon}_t$. So the advantage of using the traditional moment conditions over the SDF moment conditions is still important, even when $\boldsymbol{\varepsilon}_t$ is not normally distributed. To illustrate this, we generate f_t and $\boldsymbol{\varepsilon}_t$ from a multivariate t-distribution with ν degrees of freedom and mean zero. The covariance matrix of f_t and $\boldsymbol{\varepsilon}_t$ stays the same as in the multivariate normal case (i.e., $\text{Var}[f_t] = 1$, $\text{Var}[\boldsymbol{\varepsilon}_t] = \boldsymbol{\Sigma}$), and they are uncorrelated with each other. The reason we choose the multivariate t-distribution is that it offers an opportunity for us to investigate the effect of conditional heteroskedasticity on our results. When f_t and $\boldsymbol{\varepsilon}_t$ have a multivariate t-distribution, the conditional variance of $\boldsymbol{\varepsilon}_t$ depends on f_t. More specifically, when $\nu > 2$, we have

$$\text{Var}[\boldsymbol{\varepsilon}_t | f_t] = \left(\frac{\nu - 2 + f_t^2}{\nu - 1} \right) \boldsymbol{\Sigma} \tag{32}$$

[11] The GMM estimation results are based on the second stage GMM with the identity matrix as the initial weighting matrix. Simulation results of the third and fourth stage GMM are mostly similar to the ones using the second stage GMM, therefore they are not separately reported.

Table I

Estimation Accuracy of Risk Premium under the Traditional Methodologies and the Stochastic Discount Factor Methodology

The table presents the performance of the estimated risk premium under traditional methodologies and the stochastic discount factor (SDF) methodology. Excess returns on 10 assets are simulated using a one-factor model

$$r_t = \alpha + \beta f_t + \varepsilon_t,$$

where the values of $\alpha = \beta \lambda$ (in percentage per month) and β are presented in Panel A. The parameters are chosen to mimic the returns on 10 size-ranked portfolios of the NYSE. The factor and the model disturbance are generated as $f_t \sim N(0,1)$ and $\varepsilon_t \sim N(\mathbf{0}_N, \mathbf{\Sigma})$, where $\mathbf{\Sigma}$ is set to equal the sample covariance matrix of the market model residuals of the 10 size-ranked portfolios of the NYSE, estimated using monthly returns over the period January 1926 to December 1997. The estimation results of 10,000 simulations are reported in Panel B. For each length of time-series observations, T, we present the average and standard deviation of the estimated risk premium from the maximum likelihood method and the (second stage) GMM method using the traditional moment conditions and the SDF moment conditions. Panel C reports the same results as in Panel B but for the cases that (f_t, ε_t) are generated from a multivariate t-distribution with 5 and 10 degrees of freedom.

Panel A: Parameters of the One-Factor Pricing Model

					Size-Ranked Portfolios					
	1	2	3	4	5	6	7	8	9	10
α	1.129	1.070	0.993	0.954	0.923	0.911	0.875	0.833	0.810	0.709
β	0.082	0.078	0.072	0.069	0.067	0.066	0.064	0.061	0.059	0.052

$$\lambda = 0.1373$$

Panel B: Distribution of Estimated Risk Premium under Multivariate Normality Assumption

	Traditional Methodologies				SDF Methodology (λ)	
	Maximum Likelihood (λ_{ML})		GMM (λ^*)			
T	Average	Standard Deviation	Average	Standard Deviation	Average	Standard Deviation
120	0.1374	0.0020	0.1375	0.0045	0.1497	0.1049
240	0.1373	0.0014	0.1374	0.0020	0.1438	0.0689
360	0.1373	0.0011	0.1373	0.0014	0.1417	0.0553
480	0.1373	0.0010	0.1373	0.0011	0.1404	0.0477
600	0.1373	0.0009	0.1373	0.0009	0.1399	0.0426
720	0.1373	0.0008	0.1373	0.0008	0.1396	0.0386

Panel C: Distribution of Estimated Risk Premium under Multivariate t-distribution Assumption

	Traditional Methodology (λ^*)		SDF Methodology (λ)	
T	Average	Standard Deviation	Average	Standard Deviation
5 degrees of freedom				
120	0.1374	0.0046	0.1611	0.1162
240	0.1374	0.0020	0.1513	0.0764
360	0.1374	0.0014	0.1480	0.0612
480	0.1374	0.0011	0.1456	0.0513
600	0.1374	0.0009	0.1440	0.0454
720	0.1373	0.0008	0.1432	0.0411

Table 1—*Continued*

	Traditional Methodology (λ^*)		SDF Methodology (λ)	
T	Average	Standard Deviation	Average	Standard Deviation
10 degrees of freedom				
120	0.1374	0.0045	0.1511	0.1088
240	0.1373	0.0020	0.1448	0.0713
360	0.1373	0.0014	0.1422	0.0567
480	0.1373	0.0011	0.1409	0.0486
600	0.1373	0.0009	0.1401	0.0431
720	0.1373	0.0008	0.1395	0.0394

and the conditional variance of ε_t is higher when the absolute value of f_t is large. In Panel C, we report the simulation results in 10,000 simulations for the case that f_t and ε_t are generated from a multivariate t-distribution with five degrees of freedom, and also for the case of 10 degrees of freedom. For the GMM estimated risk premium using the traditional moment conditions $\hat{\lambda}^*$, the results do not change much from those in Panel B; $\hat{\lambda}^*$ continues to be very accurate even in the presence of nonnormality and conditional heteroskedasticity. As for the GMM estimated risk premium using the SDF moment conditions, $\hat{\lambda}$ continues to be an unreliable estimator of λ. Therefore, the SDF methodology does not outperform the traditional methodology even when ε_t exhibits conditional heteroskedasticity. In fact, compared with the results in Panel B, we can see that both the bias and the standard deviation of $\hat{\lambda}$ are higher for the case of multivariate t-distribution, making the SDF methodology even less suitable for the purpose of estimating the risk premium in this case.

III. Size and Power of Overidentification Tests

Unlike the case of risk premium estimation where we can show that the traditional methodologies are superior, it is not entirely clear whether the traditional methodologies or the SDF methodology is better suited to test the asset pricing restriction $\boldsymbol{\alpha} = \boldsymbol{\beta}\lambda$. Both methodologies provide tests that have an asymptotic distribution of χ^2_{N-1} when the model is correct, and an asymptotic probability of 1 in rejecting the model when it is wrong. The real issue here is about their respective performance in finite samples. In this section, we rely on simulation evidence to assess whether these tests have the correct size in small samples and whether they have power in rejecting misspecified models.

To assess the size of the likelihood ratio test, LRT, and the two overidentification tests J_1 and J_2, we generate excess returns from a one-factor model as before.[12] We then compute LRT and J_1 of the traditional methodologies,

[12] Simulation results for the multivariate t-distribution are qualitatively similar to the case of multivariate normal distribution; therefore we do not separately report the results for the multivariate t-distribution case in this section.

and J_2 of the SDF methodology for three different models. In the first model, we use the true factor f_t to construct the sample moments and the test statistics. In the second model, we use a noisy factor $g_t = (f_t + n_t)/\sqrt{5}$ instead of f_t to compute the sample moment and the test statistics, where n_t is a measurement error that is generated from a normal distribution with mean 0 and variance 4. In the final model, we specify the unsystematic factor $h_t = \beta \Sigma^{-1} \varepsilon_t / \sqrt{\beta' \Sigma^{-1} \beta}$ as the true factor to perform the test. Although economically these three factors are very different, statistically they are all considered to be correctly specified models.[13] Therefore, asymptotically, all three tests should have an asymptotic distribution of χ^2_{N-1} for the three correctly specified models.

In Table II, we report the rejection rates of the LRT, J_1, and J_2 for the three models at the 10 percent, 5 percent, and 1 percent significance levels based on the χ^2_{N-1} distribution. For the case of the true factor, we observe in Table II that the probability of rejection in finite samples is very close to the size of the test for all three tests. This indicates that using the asymptotic distribution is a very good approximation when we have the true factor in the model. For the case of the noisy factor, the probability of rejection is typically less than the size of the test, especially when T is small. In this case, the performance of the three tests is roughly the same in small samples. For the case of unsystematic factors, the finite sample distribution of all three tests differs greatly from the asymptotic distribution of χ^2_{N-1} and all three tests underreject the null hypothesis. However, the problem of underrejection for J_2 is more serious than that of LRT and J_1. In summary, when the asymptotic distribution is used to make the acceptance and rejection decision, the traditional methodologies seem to do no worse than J_2 of the SDF methodology when we have the correctly specified model. However, when the proposed factor does not explain the returns well, we have to be more cautious in using the asymptotic distribution of the tests to make the acceptance and rejection decision.

Likelihood ratio tests and GMM overidentification tests are designed to detect misspecified models, so the major concern is on their power. Misspecification can take various forms; we focus here on the case in which there is a missing factor in the proposed model. In this case, the expected return of the assets is not a linear function of the beta of the proposed factor; that is, there does not exist a λ such that $\alpha = \beta\lambda$. To study the power of the tests, we simulate returns using a two-factor model. The two factors are independently generated from a bivariate normal distribution and are designed to capture the behavior of the standardized excess returns on the value-weighted market portfolio of the NYSE and the long-term Treasury bond; that is,

---

[13] This is because the moment conditions in equations (14), (6), and (7) can be satisfied with g_t or h_t, instead of f_t. Although the parameters β and λ are different for the three sets of factors, the exact linear pricing relation holds in all three cases.

A Critique of the Stochastic Discount Factor Methodology 1237

Table II
Size of the Likelihood Ratio Test and the GMM Overidentification Tests of Traditional and Stochastic Discount Factor Methodologies

The table presents the probability of rejecting three correctly specified models using the likelihood ratio test (LRT) and the (second stage) GMM overidentification tests using the traditional moment conditions and the SDF moment conditions. Excess returns on 10 assets are simulated using a one-factor model

$$r_t = \alpha + \beta f_t + \varepsilon_t,$$

where the values of $\alpha = \beta \lambda$ (in percentage per month) and β are presented in Table I. The factor and the model disturbance are generated as $f_t \sim N(0,1)$ and $\varepsilon_t \sim N(0_N, \Sigma)$, where Σ is set to equal the sample covariance matrix of the market model residuals of the 10 size-ranked portfolios of the NYSE, estimated using monthly returns over the period January 1926 to December 1997. For each length of time-series observations, T, we present the probability of rejecting three different models at various significance levels in 10,000 simulations. The three models differ in terms of the factor they use. The first model uses the true factor f_t. The second model uses a noisy factor $g_t = (f_t + n_t)/\sqrt{5}$, where n_t is measurement error, distributed as $N(0,4)$. The third model uses an unsystematic factor $h_t = \beta' \Sigma^{-1} \varepsilon_t / \sqrt{\beta' \Sigma^{-1} \beta}$.

	True			Noisy			Unsystematic		
	Significance Level			Significance Level			Significance Level		
T	10%	5%	1%	10%	5%	1%	10%	5%	1%
Panel A: Maximum Likelihood Method (LRT)									
120	0.099	0.048	0.010	0.082	0.037	0.007	0.013	0.003	0.001
240	0.098	0.047	0.008	0.090	0.042	0.007	0.026	0.008	0.001
360	0.098	0.048	0.010	0.093	0.043	0.008	0.035	0.012	0.001
480	0.098	0.048	0.009	0.090	0.046	0.007	0.040	0.015	0.002
600	0.099	0.049	0.011	0.092	0.047	0.009	0.052	0.022	0.002
720	0.101	0.050	0.012	0.098	0.048	0.011	0.059	0.024	0.004
Panel B: GMM Using Traditional Moment Conditions (J_1)									
120	0.093	0.043	0.007	0.076	0.032	0.006	0.017	0.004	0.000
240	0.097	0.046	0.009	0.088	0.042	0.008	0.025	0.007	0.000
360	0.099	0.049	0.010	0.095	0.045	0.008	0.031	0.010	0.000
480	0.099	0.049	0.010	0.095	0.048	0.009	0.041	0.016	0.001
600	0.097	0.046	0.010	0.096	0.046	0.008	0.048	0.017	0.002
720	0.102	0.048	0.010	0.098	0.047	0.009	0.053	0.020	0.002
Panel C: Stochastic Discount Factor Methodology (J_2)									
120	0.097	0.046	0.007	0.079	0.037	0.006	0.017	0.008	0.001
240	0.098	0.047	0.009	0.086	0.041	0.007	0.013	0.006	0.001
360	0.102	0.048	0.008	0.092	0.043	0.008	0.010	0.006	0.001
480	0.101	0.048	0.009	0.094	0.043	0.007	0.012	0.007	0.002
600	0.101	0.051	0.011	0.093	0.046	0.010	0.012	0.007	0.003
720	0.104	0.051	0.009	0.098	0.047	0.010	0.011	0.008	0.004

$$f_{1t} = \frac{r_{mt} - E[r_{mt}]}{\sigma_m} \sim N(0,1), \tag{33}$$

$$f_{2t} = \frac{r_{bt} - E[r_{bt}]}{\sigma_b} \sim N(0,1), \tag{34}$$

$$\mathrm{Cov}[\,f_{1t}, f_{2t}] = 0.2, \tag{35}$$

where r_{mt} and r_{bt} are the excess returns on the market portfolio and the long-term Treasury bond, and σ_m and σ_b are their standard deviations. The betas of the 10 assets are set to equal the sample betas of the 10 size-ranked portfolios of the NYSE with respect to f_{1t} and f_{2t}, estimated using monthly returns from January 1926 to December 1997. The true risk premia of the two factors are chosen so that the expected excess returns are close to the average excess returns on the 10 size portfolios over the sample period; that is,

$$(\lambda_1, \lambda_2) = \mathrm{argmin}_{\lambda_1, \lambda_2} (\bar{r} - \boldsymbol{\beta}_1 \lambda_1 - \boldsymbol{\beta}_2 \lambda_2)'(\bar{r} - \boldsymbol{\beta}_1 \lambda_1 - \boldsymbol{\beta}_2 \lambda_2), \tag{36}$$

where $\bar{r}$, $\boldsymbol{\beta}_1$ and $\boldsymbol{\beta}_2$ are the average returns and sample betas of the 10 size-ranked portfolios. Finally, the model disturbances are independently generated from a multivariate normal distribution

$$\boldsymbol{\varepsilon}_t \sim N(\mathbf{0}_N, \boldsymbol{\Sigma}), \tag{37}$$

where $\boldsymbol{\Sigma}$ is chosen to be the sample covariance matrix of the residuals of the 10 size-ranked portfolios in the two-factor model. In Table III, Panel A, we present the parameters $\boldsymbol{\alpha}$, $\boldsymbol{\beta}_1$, $\boldsymbol{\beta}_2$, λ_1, and λ_2 of the 10 assets that we use in our simulation. Under our simulation, the first factor is one that explains a lot of the time-series variations of the excess returns (with an average R^2 of 84.73 percent) and the second factor has a very low explanatory power on the excess returns (with an average R^2 of 2.51 percent). Nevertheless, neither $\boldsymbol{\beta}_1$ nor $\boldsymbol{\beta}_2$ alone can fully explain the expected excess return $\boldsymbol{\alpha}$.

In Table III, we report the rejection rates of LRT, J_1, and J_2 for two misspecified models at the 10 percent, 5 percent, and 1 percent significance levels based on the χ^2_{N-1} distribution. Panel B contains the results when only the first factor is included in the model, Panel C contains the results when only the second factor is included in the model. Since both models are misspecified models, we would like the test to reject them with high probability. For the case of the misspecified model that includes only the first factor, we can observe that all three tests have roughly the same power in rejecting the model. With T as large as 360, we can only reject the misspecified model at the 5 percent level roughly 12 percent of the time, but the power steadily increases as T goes up. This suggests that when the proposed factor has strong explanatory power on the returns and the model misspec-

A Critique of the Stochastic Discount Factor Methodology　　1239

ification is not serious, there is not much of a difference between the traditional methodologies and the SDF methodology.

Ironically, when the proposed factor in the model is a weak factor, the misspecified model becomes even more difficult to detect for the SDF methodology. This can be seen from our simulation results in Panel C of Table III. In this case, LRT and J_1 have reasonably good power in rejecting this misspecified model. When $T = 360$, these two tests reject the misspecified model at the 5 percent level for approximately 34 percent of the time. However, J_2 of the SDF methodology performs much worse than LRT and J_1. Even for $T = 360$, we still find that J_2 rejects the misspecified model less often than the size of the test, making it almost impossible to reject such a misspecified model. The poor performance of J_2 in finite samples is due to the fact that S_2 is unknown and has to be estimated. When the model is misspecified, the estimated S_2 will tend to be large because of the pricing error, and hence its inverse will be small. Since the inverse of estimated S_2 is used to compute J_2, the test statistic can be very small for grossly misspecified models, especially when the factor does not explain much of the return. Asymptotically, this is not a concern because eventually the pricing errors will dominate as T increases, but in finite samples, using an estimated S_2 makes the over-identification test J_2 very unreliable. Although the same problem also plagues LRT and J_1 of the traditional methodologies, we can see in Panel C that its impact on LRT and J_1 is much less severe. Therefore, if one has to pick a specification test to use, it appears that the ones from the traditional methodologies are superior to the one from the SDF methodology.

We should also note that J_2 of the SDF methodology seems to prefer models with a poor factor to the model with a good factor. This suggests, among other things, the danger of using the *p*-value of the likelihood ratio test or GMM overidentification test to choose models. In this regard, the traditional methodologies are superior because a poor factor is less likely to be proposed to be the only factor in the return-generating process. The SDF methodology does not specify a return-generating process and a poor factor could potentially be chosen as the only factor in the model. As our simulation experiment shows, such poor factors could make the model pass the GMM overidentification test of the SDF methodology easily, even though they do not explain much of the excess returns and their betas do not fully explain the expected excess returns.

As always, simulation evidence cannot be generalized to other scenarios, so our recommendation should be taken with caution. Nevertheless, from our simulation evidence, it does appear that there are compelling reasons to prefer the traditional methodologies to the SDF methodology. A more rigorous analysis of the size and power of these tests would go a long way in settling these issues.

Finally, we remark that even though nonstandard GMM overidentification tests, such as the one suggested by Jagannathan and Wang (1996), do not use the estimated covariance matrix of the sample moments to compute the test statistic, the estimated covariance matrix is still used in computing

Table III

Power of the Likelihood Ratio Test and the GMM Overidentification Tests of Traditional and Stochastic Discount Factor Methodologies

The table presents the probability of rejecting two misspecified models using the likelihood ratio test (LRT) and the (second stage) GMM overidentification tests using the traditional moment conditions and the SDF moment conditions. Excess returns on 10 assets are simulated using a two-factor model

$$r_t = \alpha + \beta_1 f_{1t} + \beta_2 f_{2t} + \varepsilon_t,$$

where the values of $\alpha = \lambda_1 \beta_1 + \lambda_2 \beta_2$ (in percentage per month), and β_1 and β_2 are presented in Panel A. The factors and the model disturbance are independently generated from a multivariate normal distribution with $f_{1t} \sim N(0,1)$, $f_{2t} \sim N(0,1)$, $\text{Cov}[f_{1t}, f_{2t}] = 0.2$, and $\varepsilon_t \sim N(0_N, \Sigma)$, where Σ is set to equal the sample covariance matrix of the residuals of the 10 size-ranked portfolios of the NYSE in a two-factor model. The two factors are the excess return on the value-weighted market portfolio of the NYSE and the excess return on the long-term Treasury bond. The model is estimated using monthly returns over the period January 1926 to December 1997. For each length of time-series observations, T, Panels B and C present the probability of rejecting the two misspecified models at various significance levels in 10,000 simulations. Panel B presents the results for the first misspecified model which includes only the first factor f_{1t} in the model. Panel C presents the results for the second misspecified model which includes only the second factor f_{2t} in the model.

Panel A: Parameters of the Two-factor Pricing Model

					Size-Ranked Portfolios					
	1	2	3	4	5	6	7	8	9	10
α	1.280	1.163	1.001	0.940	0.926	0.891	0.836	0.748	0.703	0.628
β_1	0.084	0.079	0.073	0.070	0.068	0.067	0.064	0.061	0.059	0.052
β_2	-0.0083	-0.0063	-0.0035	-0.0027	-0.0031	-0.0024	-0.0017	-0.0001	0.0006	0.0001

$$\lambda_1 = 0.1225, \lambda_2 = -0.3047$$

A Critique of the Stochastic Discount Factor Methodology   1241

Panel B: Misspecified Model with Only the First Factor

T	Likelihood Ratio Test			Traditional GMM (J_1)			SDF Methodology (J_2)		
	Significance Level			Significance Level			Significance Level		
	10%	5%	1%	10%	5%	1%	10%	5%	1%
120	0.129	0.068	0.017	0.119	0.057	0.012	0.131	0.066	0.012
240	0.166	0.096	0.023	0.166	0.088	0.021	0.162	0.088	0.022
360	0.212	0.123	0.037	0.206	0.122	0.032	0.207	0.120	0.032
480	0.245	0.153	0.051	0.244	0.147	0.044	0.244	0.150	0.042
600	0.290	0.188	0.066	0.289	0.185	0.058	0.288	0.180	0.057
720	0.334	0.222	0.083	0.332	0.222	0.078	0.329	0.213	0.078

Panel C: Misspecified Model with Only the Second Factor

T	Likelihood Ratio Test			Traditional GMM (J_1)			SDF Methodology (J_2)		
	Significance Level			Significance Level			Significance Level		
	10%	5%	1%	10%	5%	1%	10%	5%	1%
120	0.111	0.052	0.008	0.110	0.050	0.006	0.038	0.017	0.002
240	0.295	0.185	0.053	0.299	0.182	0.047	0.059	0.023	0.003
360	0.472	0.338	0.135	0.474	0.341	0.139	0.081	0.037	0.007
480	0.613	0.481	0.246	0.617	0.487	0.248	0.134	0.062	0.011
600	0.730	0.608	0.362	0.731	0.613	0.367	0.219	0.110	0.020
720	0.816	0.717	0.484	0.815	0.710	0.480	0.319	0.176	0.039

the eigenvalues to construct the weights of the linear combination of χ_1^2 distribution that the test statistic is compared with. Therefore, the nonstandard GMM overidentification test does not escape from the problem that plagues the standard GMM. Although not reported, simulation evidence suggests that the nonstandard GMM overidentification test that uses the identity matrix as the weighting matrix generally has lower power than that of the standard GMM overidentification test in detecting our misspecified models.

IV. Conclusions

This paper exploits the fact that current empirical studies of asset pricing models using the SDF methodology typically ignore a fully specified model for asset returns. When asset returns are generated by a linear factor model, there are two potential problems associated with the use of the SDF methodology: (1) the accuracy of the estimated risk premium can be very poor and (2) its overidentification test has very little power in detecting misspecified models. These problems arise because the moment conditions the SDF methodology uses are very volatile, making accurate estimation and testing difficult under this methodology.

By specifying the return-generating process of the asset returns as in the traditional methodologies, these two potential problems can be mitigated. We demonstrate that, under the assumption that assets returns are generated by a linear factor model, the standard error of the risk premium under the traditional methodologies is much lower than that of the SDF methodology. The reason for such improvement is that the traditional methodologies use moment conditions that are much less volatile than that of the SDF methodology, and as a result they provide far more reliable inferences on the parameters. Moreover, the specification tests in the traditional methodologies generally have higher power in rejecting misspecified models than the SDF methodology. Our analysis focuses exclusively on linear factor models. This is not only due to their tractability, but also their premier importance in asset pricing. However, to the extent that any nonlinear model can be well approximated by a linear one, our results should also have implications on the use of the SDF methodology in nonlinear models where one must be cautious about the explanatory power of the factors, the parameter estimation error, the size, and the power of the tests.

Despite the fact that the SDF methodology has an interesting perspective to offer and a parsimonious model to estimate, there are costs associated with these benefits. In any event, it appears safe to say that the traditional methodologies are here to stay. In particular, traditional tests of asset pricing models will continue to play important roles in understanding the risks associated with investing, and perhaps even more so than the stochastic discount factor methodology for portfolio choice and performance evaluation problems.

A Critique of the Stochastic Discount Factor Methodology   1243

Appendix

Proof of Proposition 1: We begin by deriving the asymptotic variance of $\hat{\lambda}^*$, which is given by the (1,1) element of $(D_1' S_1^{-1} D_1)^{-1}$, where

$$D_1 = E\left[\frac{\partial g_{1T}}{\partial \lambda}, \frac{\partial g_{1T}}{\partial \beta'}\right] \tag{A1}$$

and

$$S_1 = E[(z_t \otimes \varepsilon_t)(z_t \otimes \varepsilon_t)']. \tag{A2}$$

Define $a = [1,0]'$ and $b = [\lambda,1]'$; then we have

$$D_1 = -[a \otimes \beta, b \otimes I_N]. \tag{A3}$$

Therefore, using the identity $a \otimes \beta = (a \otimes I_N)(1 \otimes \beta) = (a \otimes I_N)\beta$, we have

$$D_1' S_1^{-1} D_1 = \begin{bmatrix} (a' \otimes \beta')S_1^{-1}(a \otimes \beta) & (a' \otimes \beta')S_1^{-1}(b \otimes I_N) \\ (b' \otimes I_N)S_1^{-1}(a \otimes \beta) & (b' \otimes \beta')S_1^{-1}(b \otimes I_N) \end{bmatrix}$$

$$= \begin{bmatrix} \beta'(a' \otimes I_N)S_1^{-1}(a \otimes I_N)\beta & \beta'(a' \otimes I_N)S_1^{-1}(b \otimes I_N) \\ (b' \otimes I_N)S_1^{-1}(a \otimes I_N)\beta & (b' \otimes I_N)S_1^{-1}(b \otimes I_N) \end{bmatrix}.$$

From the partitioned matrix inverse formula, the (1,1) element of $(D_1' S_1^{-1} D_1)^{-1}$ is

$$(\beta'[A'S_1^{-1}A - A'S_1^{-1}B(B'S_1^{-1}B)^{-1}B'S_1^{-1}A]\beta)^{-1}, \tag{A4}$$

by writing $A = a \otimes I_N$ and $B = b \otimes I_N$. Defining $d = [1,-\lambda]'$ and

$$U = (d' \otimes I_N)S_1(d \otimes I_N), \tag{A5}$$

we will show that the (1,1) element of $(D_1' S_1 D_1)^{-1}$ can be simplified to $(\beta' U^{-1} \beta)^{-1}$. To prove this identity, we define a matrix $C = [a,b]$ and consider the inverse of

$$(C' \otimes I_N)S_1^{-1}(C \otimes I_N) = \begin{bmatrix} A'S_1^{-1}A & A'S_1^{-1}B \\ B'S_1^{-1}A & B'S_1^{-1}B \end{bmatrix}. \tag{A6}$$

Defining $D = [d, e]$, where $e = [0, 1]'$, it is easy to verify that $C^{-1} = D'$ and $(C')^{-1} = D$. Therefore, we have

$$[(C' \otimes I_N)S_1^{-1}(C \otimes I_N)]^{-1}$$

$$= (D' \otimes I_N)S_1(D \otimes I_N)$$

$$= \begin{bmatrix} (d' \otimes I_N)S_1(d \otimes I_N) & (d' \otimes I_N)S_1(e \otimes I_N) \\ (e' \otimes I_N)S_1(d \otimes I_N) & (e' \otimes I_N)S_1(e \otimes I_N) \end{bmatrix}. \tag{A7}$$

Note that the upper left block of $[(C' \otimes I_N)S_1^{-1}(C \otimes I_N)]^{-1}$ is just U. Another way to obtain this submatrix is to apply the partitioned matrix inverse formula to $(C' \otimes I_N)S_1^{-1}(C \otimes I_N)$, which gives the identity

$$U = [(A'S_1^{-1}A) - (A'S_1^{-1}B)(B'S_1^{-1}B)^{-1}(B'S_1^{-1}A)]^{-1}. \tag{A8}$$

For the GMM estimation of the SDF model, we have $D_2 = E[\partial g_{2T}/\partial \lambda] = -\beta$, hence $\text{Avar}[\hat{\lambda}] = (D_2'S_2^{-1}D_2)^{-1} = (\beta'S_2^{-1}\beta)^{-1}$. Using $r_t = \beta(\lambda + f_t) + \varepsilon_t$ and

$$(1 - f_t \lambda)\varepsilon_t = (d'z_t)\varepsilon_t = (d' \otimes I_N)(z_t \otimes \varepsilon_t), \tag{A9}$$

we have

$$S_2 = E[r_t r_t'(1 - f_t \lambda)^2]$$

$$= E[\varepsilon_t \varepsilon_t'(1 - f_t \lambda)^2] + E[\beta\beta'(\lambda + f_t)^2(1 - f_t \lambda)^2]$$

$$= (d' \otimes I_N)E[(z_t \otimes \varepsilon_t)(z_t \otimes \varepsilon_t)'](d \otimes I_N) + c\beta\beta'$$

$$= U + c\beta\beta', \tag{A10}$$

where $c = E[(\lambda + f_t)^2(1 - f_t \lambda)^2]$. Note that $c > 0$ unless $P[f_t = -\lambda \text{ or } 1/\lambda] = 1$, which is impossible when f_t has a continuous distribution. Since

$$S_2^{-1} = U^{-1} - \frac{U^{-1}\beta\beta'U^{-1}}{\beta'U^{-1}\beta + \dfrac{1}{c}}, \tag{A11}$$

we have

$$\beta'S_2^{-1}\beta = \beta'U^{-1}\beta - \frac{(\beta'U^{-1}\beta)^2}{\beta'U^{-1}\beta + \dfrac{1}{c}}$$

$$\Rightarrow (\beta'S_2^{-1}\beta)^{-1} = \frac{1}{\beta'U^{-1}\beta} + c > \frac{1}{\beta'U^{-1}\beta}, \tag{A12}$$

A Critique of the Stochastic Discount Factor Methodology   1245

which proves the inequality.

For the case that $\boldsymbol{\varepsilon}_t \sim N(\mathbf{0}_N, \boldsymbol{\Sigma})$ conditional on f, the log-likelihood function under the null is

$$\mathcal{L} = -\frac{NT}{2}\log(2\,\pi) - \frac{T}{2}\log|\boldsymbol{\Sigma}| - \frac{1}{2}\sum_{t=1}^{T}(\boldsymbol{r}_t - \lambda\boldsymbol{\beta} - \boldsymbol{\beta}f_t)'\boldsymbol{\Sigma}^{-1}(\boldsymbol{r}_t - \lambda\,\boldsymbol{\beta} - \boldsymbol{\beta}f_t).$$

(A13)

Hence, we have

$$\frac{\partial\mathcal{L}}{\partial\lambda} = \boldsymbol{\beta}'\,\boldsymbol{\Sigma}^{-1}\sum_{t=1}^{T}(\boldsymbol{r}_t - \lambda\,\boldsymbol{\beta} - \boldsymbol{\beta}f_t),$$

(A14)

$$\frac{\partial\mathcal{L}}{\partial\boldsymbol{\beta}} = \boldsymbol{\Sigma}^{-1}\sum_{t=1}^{T}(\boldsymbol{r}_t - \lambda\,\boldsymbol{\beta} - \boldsymbol{\beta}f_t)\,(f_t + \lambda).$$

(A15)

Then,

$$-\frac{1}{T}\,E\,\frac{\partial^2\mathcal{L}}{\partial\lambda^2} = \boldsymbol{\beta}'\boldsymbol{\Sigma}^{-1}\boldsymbol{\beta},$$

(A16)

$$-\frac{1}{T}\,E\,\frac{\partial^2\mathcal{L}}{\partial\lambda\partial\boldsymbol{\beta}'} = \frac{1}{T}\,E\boldsymbol{\beta}'\boldsymbol{\Sigma}^{-1}\sum_{t=1}^{T}(\lambda + f_t) = \boldsymbol{\beta}'\boldsymbol{\Sigma}^{-1}\lambda,$$

(A17)

$$-\frac{1}{T}\,E\,\frac{\partial^2\mathcal{L}}{\partial\boldsymbol{\beta}^2} = \frac{1}{T}\,E\boldsymbol{\Sigma}^{-1}\sum_{t=1}^{T}(f_t + \lambda)^2 = (1 + \lambda^2)\,\boldsymbol{\Sigma}^{-1}.$$

(A18)

Now, it is known that the asymptotic variance matrix of the maximum likelihood estimator of $(\lambda, \boldsymbol{\beta})$ should be the inverse of the Hessian matrix $\boldsymbol{H}$, where $\boldsymbol{H}$ is given by

$$\boldsymbol{H} = -\lim\frac{1}{T}\,E\begin{bmatrix} \dfrac{\partial^2\mathcal{L}}{\partial\lambda^2} & \dfrac{\partial^2\mathcal{L}}{\partial\lambda\partial\boldsymbol{\beta}'} \\[2ex] \dfrac{\partial^2\mathcal{L}}{\partial\boldsymbol{\beta}\partial\lambda} & \dfrac{\partial^2\mathcal{L}}{\partial\boldsymbol{\beta}\partial\boldsymbol{\beta}'} \end{bmatrix}$$

$$= \begin{bmatrix} \boldsymbol{\beta}'\boldsymbol{\Sigma}^{-1}\boldsymbol{\beta} & \boldsymbol{\beta}'\boldsymbol{\Sigma}^{-1}\lambda \\[1ex] \lambda\boldsymbol{\Sigma}^{-1}\boldsymbol{\beta} & (1 + \lambda^2)\boldsymbol{\Sigma}^{-1} \end{bmatrix}.$$

(A19)

When $\boldsymbol{\varepsilon}_t \sim N(\mathbf{0}_N, \boldsymbol{\Sigma})$ conditional on f, we have $\boldsymbol{S}_1 = \boldsymbol{I}_2 \otimes \boldsymbol{\Sigma}$ and $\boldsymbol{H}$ has the same expression as $\boldsymbol{D}_1' \boldsymbol{S}_1^{-1} \boldsymbol{D}_1$. This completes the proof. Note that our proof only depends on r_t having a factor structure and the beta pricing model holding; it does not require the true factor f_t. Therefore, Proposition 1 continues to hold when g_t or h_t is used as the factor. ∎

Proof of Proposition 2: Without loss of generality, we assume the $2N + 1$ sample moment conditions used to estimate λ and $\boldsymbol{\beta}$ are

$$
\boldsymbol{g}_{3T} = \begin{bmatrix} \boldsymbol{g}_{1T} \\ \dfrac{1}{T}\sum_{t=1}^{T} r_{1t}(1 - f_t \lambda) \end{bmatrix}, \tag{A20}
$$

where $\beta_1 \neq 0$. Define $\boldsymbol{d} = [1, -\lambda]'$ and $\boldsymbol{e}_1 = [1, \mathbf{0}_{N-1}']'$. Since

$$
\begin{aligned}
u_{1t} &= \boldsymbol{e}_1' \boldsymbol{u}_t \\
&= \boldsymbol{e}_1'(\boldsymbol{d}' \otimes \boldsymbol{I}_N)(\boldsymbol{z}_t \otimes \boldsymbol{\varepsilon}_t) + \boldsymbol{e}_1' \boldsymbol{\beta}(\lambda + f_t)(1 - f_t \lambda) \\
&= (\boldsymbol{d}' \otimes \boldsymbol{e}_1')(\boldsymbol{z}_t \otimes \boldsymbol{\varepsilon}_t) + \beta_1(\lambda + f_t)(1 - f_t \lambda),
\end{aligned}
$$

the asymptotic variance of $(\hat{\lambda}^{**}, \hat{\boldsymbol{\beta}}^{**})$ is given by $(\boldsymbol{D}_3' \boldsymbol{S}_3^{-1} \boldsymbol{D}_3)^{-1}$ where

$$
\begin{aligned}
\boldsymbol{D}_3 &= E\left[\frac{\partial \boldsymbol{g}_{3T}}{\partial \lambda}, \frac{\partial \boldsymbol{g}_{3T}}{\partial \boldsymbol{\beta}'} \right] \\
&= \begin{bmatrix} \boldsymbol{D}_1 \\ (\boldsymbol{d}' \otimes \boldsymbol{e}_1')\boldsymbol{D}_1 \end{bmatrix}
\end{aligned} \tag{A21}
$$

and

$$
\begin{aligned}
\boldsymbol{S}_3 &= E\begin{bmatrix} (\boldsymbol{z}_t \otimes \boldsymbol{\varepsilon}_t)(\boldsymbol{z}_t \otimes \boldsymbol{\varepsilon}_t)' & (\boldsymbol{z}_t \otimes \boldsymbol{\varepsilon}_t)u_{1t}' \\ u_{1t}(\boldsymbol{z}_t \otimes \boldsymbol{\varepsilon}_t)' & u_{1t}^2 \end{bmatrix} \\
&= \begin{bmatrix} \boldsymbol{S}_1 & \boldsymbol{S}_1(\boldsymbol{d} \otimes \boldsymbol{e}_1) \\ (\boldsymbol{d}' \otimes \boldsymbol{e}_1')\boldsymbol{S}_1 & \boldsymbol{e}_1' \boldsymbol{S}_2 \boldsymbol{e}_1 \end{bmatrix}.
\end{aligned} \tag{A22}
$$

From the proof of Proposition 1, we know that $\boldsymbol{S}_2 = \boldsymbol{U} + c\boldsymbol{\beta}\boldsymbol{\beta}'$, where $c = E[(\lambda + f_t)^2(1 - f_t \lambda)^2]$. Using the partitioned matrix inverse formula, we have

$$
\boldsymbol{S}_3^{-1} = \begin{bmatrix} \boldsymbol{S}_1^{-1} + (c\beta_1^2)^{-1}(\boldsymbol{d} \otimes \boldsymbol{e}_1)(\boldsymbol{d}' \otimes \boldsymbol{e}_1') & -(c\beta_1^2)^{-1}(\boldsymbol{d} \otimes \boldsymbol{e}_1) \\ -(c\beta_1^2)^{-1}(\boldsymbol{d}' \otimes \boldsymbol{e}_1') & (c\beta_1^2)^{-1} \end{bmatrix}. \tag{A23}
$$

A Critique of the Stochastic Discount Factor Methodology   1247

Therefore,

$$D_3' S_3^{-1} D_3 = D_1' S_1^{-1} D_1 + (c\beta_1^2)^{-1} D_1'(d \otimes e_1)(d' \otimes e_1')D_1$$

$$- (c\beta_1^2)^{-1} D_1'(d \otimes e_1)(d' \otimes e_1')D_1$$

$$- (c\beta_1^2)^{-1} D_1'(d \otimes e_1)(d' \otimes e_1')D_1$$

$$+ (c\beta_1^2)^{-1} D_1'(d \otimes e_1)(d' \otimes e_1')D_1$$

$$= D_1' S_1^{-1} D_1,$$

and the asymptotic variance of $(\lambda^{**}, \beta^{**})$ and (λ^*, β^*) are identical. This completes the proof.　∎

REFERENCES

Black, Fischer, 1972, Capital market equilibrium with restricted borrowing, *Journal of Business* 45, 444–454.

Breeden, Douglas T., 1979, An intertemporal asset pricing model with stochastic consumption and investment opportunities, *Journal of Financial Economics* 7, 265–296.

Breeden, Douglas T., Michael R. Gibbons, and Robert Litzenberger, 1989, Empirical tests of the consumption-oriented CAPM, *Journal of Finance* 44, 231–262.

Cochrane, John H., 1996, A cross-sectional test of an investment-based asset pricing model, *Journal of Political Economy* 104, 572–621.

Hansen, Lars Peter, 1982, Large sample properties of the generalized method of moments estimators, *Econometrica* 50, 1029–1054.

Hansen, Lars Peter, and Ravi Jagannathan, 1991, Implications of security market data for models of dynamic economies, *Journal of Political Economy* 99, 225–262.

Hansen, Lars Peter, and Ravi Jagannathan, 1997, Assessing specification errors in stochastic discount factor model, *Journal of Finance* 52, 557–590.

Harvey, Campbell R., and Guofu Zhou, 1993, International asset pricing with alternative distributional specifications, *Journal of Empirical Finance* 48, 107–131.

He, Jia, Raymond Kan, Lilian Ng, and Chu Zhang, 1996, Tests of the relations among market-wide factors, firm-specific variables, and stock returns using a conditional asset pricing model, *Journal of Finance* 51, 1891–1908.

Jagannathan, Ravi, and Zhenyu Wang, 1996, The conditional CAPM and the cross-section of expected returns, *Journal of Finance* 51, 3–53.

Kan, Raymond, and Chu Zhang, 1999a, GMM tests of stochastic discount factor models with useless factors, *Journal of Financial Economics*, forthcoming.

Kan, Raymond, and Chu Zhang, 1999b, Two-pass tests of asset pricing models with useless factors, *Journal of Finance* 54, 203–235.

Lintner, John, 1965, The valuation of risky assets and the selection of risky investments in the portfolios and capital budgets, *Review of Economics and Statistics* 47, 13–37.

MacKinlay, A. Craig, and Matthew P. Richardson, 1991, Using generalized method of moments to test mean-variance efficiency, *Journal of Finance* 46, 511–527.

Merton, Robert C., 1973, An intertemporal capital asset pricing model, *Econometrica* 41, 867–887.

Newey, Whitney K., 1985, Generalized method of moments specification testing, *Journal of Econometrics* 29, 229–256.

Ross, Stephen A., 1976, The arbitrage theory of capital asset pricing, *Journal of Economic Theory* 13, 341–360.

Sharpe, William F., 1964, Capital asset prices: A theory of market equilibrium under conditions of risk, *Journal of Finance* 19, 425–442.

Zhou, Guofu, 1991, Small sample tests of portfolio efficiency, *Journal of Financial Economics* 30, 165–191.

Zhou, Guofu, 1994, Analytical GMM tests: Asset pricing with time-varying risk premiums, *Review of Financial Studies* 7, 687–709.

Zhou, Guofu, 1995, Small sample rank tests with applications to asset pricing, *Journal of Empirical Finance* 2, 71–93.

Name Index